# THE OXFORD HANDBOOK OF
# LATINO STUDIES

# THE OXFORD HANDBOOK OF

# LATINO STUDIES

*Edited by*
ILAN STAVANS

Oxford University Press is a department of the University of Oxford. It furthers
the University's objective of excellence in research, scholarship, and education
by publishing worldwide. Oxford is a registered trademark of Oxford University
Press in the UK and certain other countries.

Published in the United States of America by Oxford University Press
198 Madison Avenue, New York, NY 10016, United States of America.

© Oxford University Press 2020

All rights reserved. No part of this publication may be reproduced, stored in
a retrieval system, or transmitted, in any form or by any means, without the
prior permission in writing of Oxford University Press, or as expressly permitted
by law, by license, or under terms agreed with the appropriate reproduction
rights organization. Inquiries concerning reproduction outside the scope of the
above should be sent to the Rights Department, Oxford University Press, at the
address above.

You must not circulate this work in any other form
and you must impose this same condition on any acquirer.

Library of Congress Cataloging-in-Publication Data
Names: Stavans, Ilan, editor.
Title: The Oxford handbook of latino studies / edited by Ilan Stavans.
Description: New York, NY: Oxford University Press, 2020. | Includes
bibliographical references and index.
Identifiers: LCCN 2019041315 | ISBN 9780190691202 (hardcover) |
ISBN 9780190691233 (epub)
Subjects: LCSH: Hispanic Americans. | Latin Americans—United States.
Classification: LCC E184.S75 O975 2020 | DDC 973/.0468—dc23
LC record available at https://lccn.loc.gov/2019041315

1 3 5 7 9 8 6 4 2

Printed by Integrated Books International, United States of America

# Contents

| | |
|---|---|
| *Contributors* | ix |
| *Introduction* | xi |

## I. ROOTS, IDENTITIES, CONNECTIONS

1. North–South, East–West: Topographies of Latinidad … 3
   ILAN STAVANS

2. Latina/os and Race … 12
   SILVIO TORRES-SAILLANT

3. Latinx Midwest Folklore … 62
   STACEY M. ALEX AND FREDERICK LUIS ALDAMA

4. Bridges to Cuba and Latina/Latino Studies … 91
   RUTH BEHAR

5. Atlantic Continuities in Tomás Rivera and Rudolfo Anaya … 104
   SARAH M. QUESADA

## II. MELTING THE POT

6. The Chicano Movement in the New America … 127
   MARIO T. GARCÍA

7. Women, Gender, and Sexuality in Latina/o Culture … 148
   ALICIA ARRIZÓN

8. Latino Urbanism and the Gentrifying City … 175
   ERUALDO R. GONZÁLEZ

## III. BETWEEN FAITH AND REASON

9. Latino Philosophy — 199
   SUSANA NUCCETELLI

10. Latina/o Religious Studies Since the 1970s — 219
    FELIPE HINOJOSA

11. Barrio Music, Spirituality, and Social Justice in Latino Hip-Hop — 236
    ALEJANDRO NAVA

## IV. WHIRLING TONGUES

12. Notes on Latino Philology — 265
    ILAN STAVANS

13. The Bilingualisms of Latino/a Literatures — 282
    ROLANDO PÉREZ

14. Rhetoric and Affect in Bilingual Latinx Literature — 307
    MATYLDA FIGLEROWICZ AND DORIS SOMMER

15. Always in Translation: Ways of Writing in Spanish and English — 330
    REGINA GALASSO

16. Spanglish: Current Issues, Future Perspectives, and Linguistic Insights — 347
    SILVIA BETTI AND RENATA ENGHELS

## V. WAYS OF BEING

17. Latinx Pop Cultural Studies *Hoy!* — 383
    FREDERICK LUIS ALDAMA

18. Reflections on Latina/o Theater — 394
    DEBRA CASTILLO

19. Transcolonial Gothic and Decolonial Satire in Ramón Emeterio Betances — 412
    IVONNE M. GARCÍA

20. A Borderlands History of Latinx Cinema — 433
    PAUL A. SCHROEDER RODRÍGUEZ

21. Television and Its Impact on Latinx Communities  462
    MARI CASTAÑEDA

22. Latino/as and Sports  485
    JORGE IBER

*Appendix: Does Latino Literature Matter? A Conversation*  509
    ILAN STAVANS AND CHARLES HATFIELD

*Index*  521

# Contributors

**Frederick Luis Aldama**, Department of English, Ohio State University

**Stacey M. Alex**, Center for Latin American Studies, Ohio State University

**Alicia Arrizón**, Department of Women's Studies, University of California, Riverside

**Ruth Behar**, Department of Anthropology, University of Michigan

**Silvia Betti**, Department of Modern Languages, Literatures, and Cultures, University of Bologna and The North American Academy of the Spanish Language

**Mari Castañeda**, Department of Communication, University of Massachusetts Amherst

**Debra Castillo**, Latino/a Studies Program, Cornell University

**Renata Enghels**, Department of Linguistics, Ghent University

**Matylda Figlerowicz**, Department of Comparative Literature, Harvard University

**Regina Galasso**, Department of Spanish and Portuguese Studies, University of Massachusetts Amherst

**Ivonne M. García**, Diversity, Equity and Inclusion Office, College of Wooster

**Mario T. García**, Department of Chicana and Chicano Studies, University of California, Santa Barbara

**Erualdo R. González**, Department of Chicana and Chicano Studies, California State University, Fullerton

**Charles Hatfield**, Program in Literature, The University of Texas at Dallas

**Felipe Hinojosa**, Department of History, Texas A&M University

**Jorge Iber**, College of Arts & Sciences, Texas Tech University

**Alejandro Nava**, Department of Religious Studies and Classics, University of Arizona

**Susana Nuccetelli**, Department of Philosophy, St. Cloud State University

**Rolando Pérez**, Department of Romance Languages, Hunter College

**Sarah M. Quesada**, Department of English, University of Notre Dame

**Paul A. Schroeder Rodríguez**, Department of Spanish, Amherst College

**Doris Sommer**, Department of Romance Languages and Literatures and of African and African American Studies, Harvard University

**Ilan Stavans**, Department of Spanish, Amherst College

**Silvio Torres-Saillant**, Department of English, Syracuse University

# INTRODUCTION

## ILAN STAVANS

*No estudio para saber más, sino para ignorar menos.*
I don't study to know more, but to ignore less.
—Sor Juana Inés de la Cruz, *Respuesta a Sor Filotea* (1691)

The emergence of Latino studies is one of the most exciting phenomena in the humanities in the last several decades. The discipline is so diverse and multifaceted that it gives the impression of having been around for quite some time. Truth is, it came about in its current form just a few decades ago, in the 1980s. As statement of its vitality, this is the first Oxford handbook ever produced on the discipline.

Its consolidation is directly linked to the astronomical demographic growth of the Latino minority, approximately sixty million in 2020, which comprises around 18 percent of the total population of the United States. The history of this minority is understandably complex, the result of an assortment of factors that include conquest and colonialism as well as immigration and transculturation. Up until the last quarter of the twentieth century, various national groups (Mexicans, Puerto Ricans, Cubans, Dominicans) were approached as separate, self-sufficient scholarly themes. Combining all of them into a single whole was not a trend. Consequently, the Mexican–American War of 1846–1848, the Spanish–American War between Spain and the United States fifty years later; the Bracero Program; the periodic riots in California, Texas, and New York; and the surging and impact of the Chicano Movement; and the activities of the Young Puerto Rican Lords were invariably seen as disconnected events.

It was during the Nixon administration that the term "Hispanic" was first used in government documents, including census data, thus making these national subgroups converge in a centralized narrative. Before then, Latinos had been collectively described as Latins, Spanish people, and Spanish-language speakers. The new favored term was Hispanic. It immediately drew fire, being accused of highlighting the Iberian influence (Hispania was how Spain was known by the Romans) at the expense of the culture's aboriginal dimension. Other terms were suggested, including Latino and Mestizo. The former stuck, although not without its gender-specific quality, a legacy of the Romance languages, being contested.

Before Latino studies there were Chicano studies, Puerto Rican studies, Cuban studies, and so on. Although the consolidation of the discipline hence responded to a larger trend, it was also seen on campuses as a strategy to focus on larger geographic, historical, political, and cultural currents affecting Latin America in its entirety. In that sense, one of the true precursors is Latin American studies, at least in the way it brought together disparate countries. That discipline has its roots in the middle of the nineteenth century, as the United States was engaged in an expansionist drive. It became a staple of American universities in the 1930s, during the Franklin D. Roosevelt administration, in particular as a result of its Good Neighbor policy.

In terms of structure, Latino studies is considered an area studies field that benefits from an interdisciplinary perspective. As in the case of other area studies (black, Jewish, etc.), it is rooted in and cross-pollinates with a variety of disciplines: political science, sociology, anthropology, cultural studies, American studies, and linguistics. This means that in specific institutions, whether they be small liberal arts colleges or research universities, a Latino studies degree will be comprising an assortment of components offered by diverse specialists. The rationale is simple: Latinos need to be understood from myriad viewpoints. Consequently, scholars frequently have two or more appointments within the academic map, dividing their responsibilities accordingly. The drawback of this development is seen in the hyperspecialization of scholars. Rather than fostering a generation of generalists capable of looking at Latinos in toto, it compartmentalizes them according to topographical areas. That fragmentation might be counterproductive, failing to offer a unified view. Latino students frequently feel disoriented by this approach. They come from backgrounds they are eager to see validated at the level of curriculum. What they get instead is a diet of theories, ideologies, and area information that, while expanding their horizon as students, divides the pie in such a way that the parts are emphasized but not the sum of them.[1]

For better or worse, language—Spanish or the lack of it—has been a prism through which Latinos are approached. In that sense there is also a dislocation. It is a well-known fact that teaching *el español* on American campuses is a fraught endeavor. For one thing, unlike German, French, Italian, Portuguese, Arabic, and Chinese, which are the foreign languages most often taught to undergraduates in the United States, Spanish has never been truly foreign. From the Treaty of Guadalupe Hidalgo, signed in 1848, when Mexico, after losing a war, sold two-thirds of its territory to the American government, onward to 1902, when Puerto Rico began its path toward becoming a commonwealth (in Spanish, *un estado libre asociado*), to the present, with its plethora of Latinos from literally every Hispanic country, the presence of Cervantes's and Sor Juana's tongue has been an essential part of this nation's identity, even when that identity has been heavily contested. Heritage speakers, as fully or partially bilingual students as they are sometimes referred to, are not traditional language learners. Even when Spanish for them is described as "broken," they never arrive in the classroom with the same expectations—or for that matter, with the same objectivity—of other language learners.[2] Studying *el español* is not about starting from scratch but about regaining what has been lost.

It is fundamental to remember that, like black studies, Latino studies is a by-product of sit-ins, marches, and other forms of political activism whose origins are traceable to the fight for legitimacy of Chicano studies and Puerto Rican studies. In other words, the discipline is intricately connected with the ideological struggle by this minority against racism and other forms of diminishment. Unlike other fields that became part of the curriculum after donations from alums and outside sources, its development is not divorced from the day-to-day search for legitimacy on the street, the voting booth, the office, and other real-life spaces. The price tag for Latino studies scholars to achieve respect in academia is inseparable from the genuine desire for collective affirmation.[3]

In my own scholarly career, the study of the triumvirate—politics, culture, and language—has been a priority. I have resisted the temptation of simply looking at Latinos as another immigrant group. Instead, they are an extremity of Latin America in the United States and, as such, they need to be understood through the prism of north–south relations. Within the minority, there is also the bipolarity of east–west viewpoints, with the west leaning toward a Mexican and Central American perspective, whereas the east is more Caribbean in nature. My mission has been to foster a generalist trend in Latino studies, exhorting young scholars to embrace specialization only as a ticket for an ample, wide-ranging outlook. Indeed, I believe academia does a disservice when it persuades students to know as much as they can about as little as possible.[4]

The objective of the *Oxford Handbook of Latino Studies* is twofold. It is a statement reflecting current viewpoints on Latino studies but also looks at its future from myriad perspectives. It follows the multidisciplinary structure of the field in that it is built on constant accrual of new knowledge. I invited twenty-two emerging and established scholars from diverse national, geographic, gender, ideological positions, and academic interests in a variety of subfields of Latino studies to produce eight-thousand-word essays in which they offer a candid look at what has been accomplished in the discipline since its inception and the directions it might take in the near future. I also sought to give voice to academics from heterogeneous institutions. And I looked for ways to offer as all-inclusive a picture of Latino life as possible. Each of these scholars then decided on their own topic. Some preferred to concentrate on the forest (Latinos and sports, for instance, or Latinos and the American city), while others opted to focus on a single author (Puerto Rican activist Ramón Emeterio Betances). And while the outcome is characterized by specialized views, I have encouraged contributors to reach beyond their intellectual confines to offer a complex, even surprising picture of what Latino scholars are capable of.

The overall content is divided into five parts, each consisting of three to six essays. The first part is "Roots, Identities, Connections." It opens with my essay "North–South, East–West: Topographies of Latinidad," an invitation to understand not only perspectives but also knowledge as linked to geography. Divided into two halves, the first is a compendium of nineteen theses—in the spirit of José Ortega y Gasset's *Meditaciones del Quijote* (1914) and Walter Benjamin's *"Über den Begriff der Geschichte"* (1940)—on the importance of geography in the understanding of Latino culture and identity. In the book *What Is la Hispanidad?* (2011), coauthored with historian Iván Jaksić, I explored the contested term in the title with regard to Spain and Latin America: where it came from, how it has evolved, what are its contours. On this occasion and in an equally multidisciplinary approach, I focus on *Latinidad*, except that this time around I emphasize the geographical dimensions of the concept. My argument is that as a result of history, Latinos in the United States are defined by topographic dimensions, depending on where they originally come from as immigrants and what attachment they nurture with the place once called home. For the portion of the minority that never immigrated, topography is an equally valid reference.

Silvio Torres-Saillant offers a probing look at issues of race from outside as from within the community in "Latina/os and Race," arguing that the subjects of racism and race are crucial to Latino studies in that the historical conditions responsible for birthing gospels of phenotype and fundamentalisms of ancestry began in sites of Hispanic colonial domination in our hemisphere. Only later did racial literacies and pedagogies travel to other colonial domains within the hemisphere and across the globe. Torres-Saillant's chapter stresses the crisis of Christian piety that caused colonizing nations to produce discourses of disparagement meant to reduce or stigmatize the humanity of their subjects, the eminently historical nature of racial thought, and the role of cultivated intellects in defining, demeaning, and debasing conquered populations that differed from them in heritage, origin, and appearance. It posits that racist violence, including of the genocidal kind, is not an aberration but a vital factor of the civilization that European colonial ventures forged in the Americas. It offers an outline for a pan-hemispheric history of discourse from the Anglo and Iberian Americas to illustrate how feasibly one can claim that in the hemisphere one is racist by default. The exclusion of black, Indian, or Asian-descended people not only recurs as an ideal for the region's foremost thinkers, political theorists, and founding fathers, but it also creeps into the pages of schoolbooks and the media in general. This scenario leaves it up to the maligned groups in the citizenry to devise ways of surviving the animosity hurled at them from various levels of public discourse in their own country. Nothing, then, would seem more urgent to fuel visions of humane solidarity and peaceful coexistence across difference of phenotype and ancestry in the Americas than to rehabilitate social relations by disabling the app of racial acrimony installed in the social fabric of our nations by the founding discourses that created our civilization.

In "Latinx Midwest Folklore," coauthors Stacey M. Alex and Frederick Luis Aldama examine, through interviews, how Latinx artists engage with folklore in the Midwest as cultural capital for placemaking while combating discursive and social erasure including barriers to state arts funding, as well as social and geographic isolation from more widely recognized Latinx cultural centers. Historically, Latinx groups have moved to the Midwest to escape oppression. While often finding more socially benign spaces, they continue to confront racism. The corrido musical form offers nineteenth-century examples of folkloric storytelling as resistance to the racialized dispossession of South Texan Mexicans, while contemporary *corridos* recount the travails and perseverance of undocumented immigrants. Latinx folkloric music, dance, storytelling, visual arts, and festivals are investigated as vehicles to support social justice and solidarity.

"Bridges to Cuba and Latina/Latino Studies," by Ruth Behar, focuses on the complex relationship between Cuban studies and Latina/Latino studies. A full engagement between the two scholarly endeavors is often difficult because of the ongoing efforts at reconciliation among the Cuban people. While more fluidity now exists, there are continuing divisions between Cubans of the island and the diaspora. So long as Cuba continues to be a site of obsessive fascination both to Cuban Americans and to non-Cuban promoters of Cuban identity and culture in the United States, it is challenging for scholars in Cuban studies to address connections with the intersectional approaches at the heart of Latina/Latino studies. Drawing on a personal approach and the author's own experiences as a scholar, writer, and activist for cultural exchanges with Cuba, this article explores the generational changes that have taken place in the search for bridges to and from Cuba and how this search for identity and belonging contributes idiosyncratic but important nuances to the field of Latina/Latino studies.

And circling back in this part to the theme of topography, "Atlantic Continuities in Tomás Rivera and Rudolfo Anaya," by Sarah M. Quesada, draws from Tomás Rivera's poetry and Rudolfo Anaya's short story "The Man Who Could Fly" (2006) to read continuities of an Atlantic world formation within the Southwest. Specifically, this essay compares paradigms of a remembered "Congo" informed by dialectics of empire concerning both Central African exploration—in the case of Rivera—and plantational Latin American and American slavery—in the case of Anaya. While this article argues that in the case of Rivera, Henry Stanley's exploration haunts the spatialization of Rivera's poetry, in Anaya, by contrast, Atlantic continuities are chiefly embedded in a transnational comparison with Latin American Caribbean writers such as Gabriel García Márquez and Alejo Carpentier. Applying Caribbean thinker Edouard Glissant's theorization of "Relation" to these Chicano narratives, this chapter decodes the racial geographies of the Southwest to theorize how landscape and fiction work together to memorialize subaltern Atlantic memory.

The second part of the *Oxford Handbook of Latino Studies* is called "Melting the Pot." It starts with "The Chicano Movement in the New America," by Mario T. García, a reevaluation by an esteemed historian of the legacy of the Chicano Movement in the age of multicultural identities. The Chicano Movement was the largest and most widespread civil rights and empowerment movement by the people of Mexican descent in the United States. As part of the 1960s and 1970s social movements, the movement made Chicanos and other Latinos national political actors and laid the foundation for contemporary Latino political power in the twenty-first century. It assured that the old America would no longer survive. Chicanos and other minorities were the future and still are the future.

"Women, Gender, and Sexuality in Latina/o Culture," by Alicia Arrizón, begins delving into the intersectionality of the conceptual knowledge embedded in the terms women, gender, and sexuality. The evolution of these three concepts has been largely exemplified in and has transformed the field of Women, Gender and Sexuality studies. While drawing on feminist and interdisciplinary methods to center on women's issues, the field examines constructs of gender power relations, systems of oppression, and privilege.

Students and scholars in the field examine these concepts as they intersect with other identities and social sites such as race, sexual orientation, inequality, class, and disability. The article begins with a general examination of the epistemological inquiries considered in the title's terminology. It then traces the interdisciplinarity of women's studies and feminist theory while contextualizing Latina feminism within Third World feminisms as conceptualized in the twentieth century. The article also argues that in Latina/o culture, the epistemology of these terms is entrenched by the power of heterosexuality, patriarchy, and the ramifications of colonial history. In this framework, the article examines the dichotomy of *marianismo* and *machismo* as markers of the legacy of colonialism. In what contexts does this legacy influence Latina feminist discourses and views in the nineteenth and twentieth centuries? What type of genealogies have been fundamental in tracing the colonial history of Latina/American feminism across borders? What kinds of methodological considerations for studying sexuality, and non-conforming gendering processes in Latina/o/Latinix culture in the twenty-first century are currently relevant? Are Latinas becoming more visible and influential in the twenty-first century? These inquiries are considered relevant to engage with categories that are cutting-edge today.

And "Latino Urbanism and the Gentrifying City," by Erualdo R. González, argues that the nexus between Latina/o studies and urban planning scholarship is thin but slowly growing. There remains opportunity to add critical perspectives to this emerging body of work. This article examines key conditions and trends in urban planning and the political economy context in Latina/o communities in American cities. It also reviews the intentions of the urban planning field and discusses key themes and progress within the Latino urbanism scholarly movement. The article then examines the political economy dimensions and profound implications of gentrification on the Latina/o population, especially in major US cities, and emerging *gentefication* on racial and class debates. The article concludes with a forward-looking orientation by offering *gentefication* and gentrification research agendas.

The third part of the volume is called "Between Faith and Reason." It looks at currents of thought and belief in the Latino community. It opens with "Latino Philosophy," by Susana Nuccetelli, in which she posits that Latino philosophy and Latin American philosophy, in spite of their close relation, are taking different paths on foundational questions about their own significance, prospects, and even existence. Furthermore, Latino philosophy must continue to avoid two extreme positions that figure prominently in Latin American philosophy: radical skepticism and overconfident optimism. By resting on exceedingly narrow conceptions of the nature of this type of philosophy, neither of them can help to overcome the challenges facing these fields. But Latino philosophy may have a brighter future, provided it expands the use of reasoned argument beyond the issues discussed in this essay. Some concern the nature of Latino philosophy and its closest relatives. Others involve Latino philosophy's contribution to solving a recurrent puzzle about which ethnic-group term (if any) is best for talking about US residents who are from the officially Spanish-speaking nations of Latin America by birth or ancestry.

"Latina/o Religious Studies Since the 1970s," by Felipe Hinojosa, moves the discussion to the realm of faith, offering an overview of the study of personal and institutionalized religions in the Latino minority for over half a century. Motivated by the political tenor of the times, Latina/o religious studies begins as a political project committed to contextualizing theological studies by stressing racial identity, resistance to church hierarchy, and economic inequality. Rooted in a robust interdisciplinary approach, Latina/o religious studies pulls from multiple fields of study. This article, however, focuses on the field's engagements with ethnic studies in the last fifty years, from the 1970s to the contemporary period. It argues that while the field began as a way to tell the stories, faith practices, and theologies of religious insiders (i.e., clergy and religious leaders), recent scholarship has expanded the field to include the broader themes of community formation, labor, social movements, immigrant activism, and an intentional focus on the relationships with non-religious communities.

And "Barrio Music, Spirituality, and Social Justice in Latino Hip-Hop," by Alejandro Nava, connects religious fervor with the making of Latino music, specifically hip-hop. This essay explores the spiritual and social concerns of US Latino and Latin American hip-hop. Beginning with a description of hip-hop's influence on the author's educational journey, the essay considers some of the key influences of Latino music on US rap music, as well as the growing dominance of hip-hop among Latino youth throughout the Americas. Besides documenting the influences of US rap on Latino music, it charts the distinct idioms, styles, and philosophies of Latino hip-hop, emphasizing the unique contributions of this subgenre to the broader culture of hip-hop.

The fourth part of the *Oxford Handbook of Latino Studies* is "Whirling Tongues." It is about language being a portal leading to understanding the multilayered dimension of Latino lives. The section opens with my reflexive essay "Notes on Latino Philology." The essay is divided into two halves: the first is a personal reflection on the path I have taken to become a philologist; and the second is an attempt at understanding the history of the Spanish language from a Latino perspective, a position never offered before. This attempt is presented in the form of a non-existent book called *A Brief History of the Spanish Language in Five Sentences*. The second half offers a rationale for each of the five sentences in such a volume, placing them in historical context.

In his essay "The Bilingualisms of Latino/a Literatures," Rolando Pérez offers an incisive look at how bilingualism ought not be seen as a monochromatic dimension but as heterogeneous in its strategies depending on the author and cultural milieu. This essay deals with the multiple languages of Latino/a literature: English, English and Spanish (code-switching), Spanglish, and Spanish. It traces the linguistically and thematically diverse Latino/a literatures of today back to the Nuyorican literary movement of the late 1960s and 1970s. The argument here is that Latino/a writers like Sandra Cisneros, Judith Ortiz Cofer, and Cristina García, and even those who write exclusively in Spanish today, as for example, Tina Escaja, Marta López Luaces, and Miguel Ángel Zapata, are the literary heirs of Miguel Algarín, Sandra María Esteves, Pedro Pietri, Miguel Piñero, and Tato Laviera, the writers who bravely paved the way for them.

"Rhetoric and Affect in Bilingual Latinx Literature," coauthored by Matylda Figlerowicz and Doris Sommer, is another look at bilingualism, this time through the lens of emotions. Latinx writers cross boundaries between languages, renovating the experience both of language and of literature. This article takes up the invitations of several creative/disruptive artists: Víctor Hernández Cruz, Guillermo Cabrera Infante, Ana Lydia Vega, William Carlos Williams, Gloria Anzaldúa, and Tino Villanueva. The analysis shows how bilingualism transforms rhetorical figures and affective structures, arguing that metonymy—understood as contiguity and as desire—is a predominant figure of bilingualism: a figure of almost arbitrary coincidence, an unintended intimacy that writers exploit. Through rhetorical and affective gestures, bilingualism alters genre conventions and opens a new space for aesthetic pleasure and political discussion, which requires and forms an alert audience with new ways of reading. The essay traces the visions of future (and its fantasies) and of past (and its memories) from the perspective of bilingualism, showing how operating between languages allows for new ways of constructing knowledge.

"Always in Translation: Ways of Writing in Spanish and English," by Regina Galasso, argues that for outsiders, the languages of Latino literature are English, Spanish, and code-switching between the two languages. What is more, code-switching is considered a symptom of not knowing either language well. At the same time, Latinos themselves feel anxiety toward perceived deficiencies in both languages. This essay argues that Latino literature offers a complex use of language that can be appreciated through the lens of translation. This essay explores the forms of translation present in Latino literature suggesting that Spanish and English always exist in the presence and under the influence of each other. Discussions of Felipe Alfau, Junot Díaz, and Urayoán Noel highlight the centrality of translation issues in Latino writing ranging from creative output and expression to the making of subsequent versions of literary texts. Overall, considerations of translation in Latino studies can lead to a more complex understanding of the work of translators and multilingual writing in general.

And "Spanglish: Current Issues, Future Perspectives, and Linguistic Insights," coauthored by academics Silvia Betti and Renata Enghels, is an assessment of the rapid yet controversial development of Spanglish as a discipline of study. This article studies a series of important issues concerning Spanglish as a hybrid language. It discusses why Spanglish has constituted a growing topic of interest ever since it first attracted the attention of specialists, be it from a linguistic, literary, or sociocultural perspective. The study also discusses the main challenges Spanglish is expected to be confronted with in the (near) future given that, more than ever, the identity of its speakers is at stake. A final part argues in favor of the maintenance of Spanglish as a unique form of bilingualism. By adopting a cognitive and functional viewpoint on language, it is shown that the analysis of Spanglish grammar offers insights into the main characteristics of human language, including basic principles such as iconicity, economy, creativity, and productivity.

The fifth and final part of the volume is "Ways of Being." It gathers together pieces about art and aesthetic pursuits as well as sports and other forms of entertainment. It starts with "Latinx Pop Cultural Studies *Hoy!*," by Frederick Luis Aldama, an investigation into the enormous influence of pop culture (movies, graphic novels, comics, superheroes, etc.) in the shaping of the Latino community. Aldama's important thesis is that the highbrow is ultimately less influential than mass culture. Despite Latinxs being the largest growing demographic in the United States, their experiences and identities continue to be underrepresented and misrepresented in the mainstream pop cultural imaginary. However, for all the negative stereotypes and restrictive ways that the mainstream boxes in Latinxs, Latinx musicians, writers, artists, comic book creators, and performers actively metabolize all cultural phenomena to clear positive spaces of empowerment and to make new perception, thought, and feeling about Latinx identities and experiences. In film, one sees Latinx actors in mainstream and Latinx films, playing Latinx-identified characters. It is important to understand, though, that Latinxs today consume all variety of cultural phenomena. For corporate America, therefore, the Latinx demographic represents a huge buying demographic. Viewed with cynical and skeptical eyes, the increased representation of Latinxs in the entertainment industry is a result of this push to capture the Latinx consumer market. Within this schema, Latinx actors are rarely cast as the protagonists. As such, there is an active metabolizing and critical redeployment of these narratives as well as the fashioning of entirely new cultural phenomena. Latinx filmmakers are working in the realist, motion-photographic mode to push back and clear new spaces for Latinx subjectivities and experiences; they are also innovating in the pop cultural space of music videos. Some Latinx creators use the Internet to convey the richly layered aspects of being Latinx. Meanwhile, relative low production costs in areas such as music and comic books have led to a tremendous outpouring of Latinx pop cultural creation in these areas.

In "Reflections on Latina/o Theater," by scholar and practitioner Debra Castillo, the understanding of the term "theater," modified by the adjective "Latina/o," like any other genre of human expression, becomes extraordinarily rich. It includes the legacy, and continuing vitality of varied and often conflicting aesthetic projects. This article discusses the vexed definitional problem of what is theater by, about, and for Latinas and Latinos, both in terms of production of plays and the academic study of theater. It provides a historical timeline that focuses on the 1960s to the present, a commentary on play production, an overview of academic discussions, and conclusions drawn from a survey of course syllabi. It uses the examples of Lin Manuel Miranda's *Hamilton* and works by the Coatlicue Theater Company to challenge simplistic understandings of what Latina/o theater is and does.

"Transcolonial Gothic and Decolonial Satire in Ramón Emeterio Betances," by Ivonne M. García, uses the postcolonial tropes as well as the prism of nineteenth-century gothic views as transposed from Europe to the Caribbean to consider the work of influential Puerto Rican thinker and freedom fighter Ramón Emeterio Betances. This article examines Ramón Emeterio Betances's *The Virgin of Borinquen*, not previously translated into English, and *The Travels of Escaldado*, also not yet in a full English translation, to show how they exemplify the transcolonial gothic and decolonial satire, respectively. Situating Betances within the transamerican tradition in Latinx studies emerging from the nineteenth-century confrontation among empires, the chapter introduces Betances's works to an Anglophone audience unfamiliar with how the author engaged with US authors, such as Edgar Allan Poe and Benjamin Franklin, to provide a counternarrative of the colonial experience at a moment of competing and interconnected empires to critique imperialism across different geopolitical contexts.

"A Borderlands History of Latinx Cinema," by Paul A. Schroeder Rodríguez, focuses on cinematic representations of the Latinx experience of the B/borderlands over the course of five distinct periods: silent cinema (1900s–1920s), commercial sound cinema (1930s–1960s), social problem films (1930s–1950s), New Latinx cinema (1970s), mainstream televisual cinema (1980s–1990s), and cinema in the digital age (2000s–present). Throughout her book *Borderlands/La Frontera*, Anzaldúa associates lowercase borderlands with destructive confrontations, and uppercase Borderlands with productive transformations. By this double definition, cinematic representations of the Latinx borderlands with a lowercase b have always dominated the big screen via Latinx characters who are either negative stereotypes or simply absent. But even as early as the silent period there have been attempts to represent the complex and oftentimes contradictory perspectives of the Latinx experience of the Borderlands with a capital B, where the switching of cultural, cinematic, and linguistic codes creates a new language: the language of a Borderlands cinema.

"Television and Its Impact on Latinx Communities," by Mari Castañeda, investigates the intersections of television with Latinx communities, and the ways in which the evolving televisual context is mediating diasporic translatinidades. It focuses on five areas: (1) the role of Latinas in television set manufacturing, (2) the representation of Latinos in mainstream television, (3) the rise of Spanish-language television, (4) the importance of telenovelas in global television, and (5) the emergence of TV streaming as new venues for translatinidades. Taken together, these five topics construct an ample canvas for investigating television and how it reflects social, political, economic, and cultural lived experiences. Ultimately, the goal of this chapter is to investigate how television and its relationship with Latinx communities cannot be uniformly characterized as one static practice but must in fact be recognized as a multilayered and evolving formation that is culturally embedded as well as closely interconnected to market power.

Finally, "Latino/as and Sports," by Jorge Iber, takes readers into the realm of athletics as an entryway to American culture and its values. Spanish-surnamed athletes have been part of American sports for many decades, yet they have not been adequately recognized for their contributions, particularly at the collegiate and high school levels. As the nation's demographics continue to change, Latino/as in rural areas are even becoming prominent in athletics, as well as in states outside of the areas considered "traditional" for this population. How will such changes impact social relations both on and off the fields of athletic competition? It is important to focus on two critical issues with this burgeoning population: (1) Why do Latino/as continue to be underrepresented at all levels of collegiate sport?; and (2) What are some of the issues concerning the classification of Latino/a athletes who do not have Spanish surnames? Are they to be chastised if they do not choose to represent the nations of their ethnic background?

The volume concludes with an appendix in which Charles Hartfield of the University of Texas at Dallas and I engage in conversation on the value of Latino literature. The dialogue delves head-on into issues of literacy among Latinos and the durability of literature in the age of instant and ubiquitous entertainment. Have the classics lost their centrality as tools to appreciate Latino life? Are they being permanently replaced by other forms of aesthetic inquiry? Is the written word itself less important than before?

A note on style: as is clear even in this introduction, it has become customary in the discipline to take divergent approaches when referring to Latinos. Following the Romance languages pattern, some use the masculine, "Latino," to encompass the whole group; others prefer "Latina/o," or else "Latinx." There are a few who also dislike the term "Latino," using instead "Hispanic." Likewise, national currents such as "Chicano," "Chicana/o," "Chicanx," and so on are approached variously. Needless to say, the instability of the name points to larger issues of identity and power.

I myself have preferences, expressed, among other places, in a *New York Times* op-ed piece.[5] But it is not my prerogative as editor to force on others a particular approach. Therefore, in their respective articles each author employs the term most suitable to their tastes. That the volume showcases a plethora of approaches in and of itself is a statement of where the discipline stands on these issues: open-ended and deliberately unresolved.

I wish to thank Julia Kostova, the commissioning editor at Oxford, for coming up with the idea for this handbook, Elda Granata for expertly seeing it through the editorial process, and the wonderful Cecily Berberat for being my superb in-house partner all through the process.

A final note on the cover: *El hombre astral* is by the extraordinary Uruguayan artist José Gurvich (1927–1974). A potter and a musician as well, he was, most famously, one of the leading members of the Constructivist Movement in Latin American art. Gurvich moved to New York City with his wife and son in 1970 and died there. His paintings are a transcultural tour de force.

## Notes

1. The entrance of Latino students into higher education is a crucial step toward the ascendance of the minority into the middle class. See my essay "Betraying Latino Students," in *A Critic's Journey* (Ann Arbor: University of Michigan Press, 2009), 44–47.
2. The topic of teaching Spanish as a foreign language in the United States has generated much debate. See my essay "Teaching Spanish," in *A Critic's Journey*, 22–28.
3. I have explored the connection between these two disciplines in my essay "Black Studies vs. Latino Studies," in *A Critic's Journey*, 162–168. This and other pieces included in the volume, and referred to in these endnotes, were originally published in *The Chronicle of Higher Education*.
4. See my Q&A book *Latinos in the United States: What Everyone Needs to Know* (New York: Oxford University Press, 2018). See also my four-volume *Encyclopedia Latina* (Danbury, CT: Grolier/Scholastic, 2005); and the three-volume *Latin Music: Musicians, Genres, and Themes* (Boulder, CO: ABC-Clio, 2013).
5. See my op-ed "The Meaning of Latinx," *New York Times en Español*, November 14, 2017: https://www.nytimes.com/es/2017/11/14/el-significado-del-latinx.

# PART I

## ROOTS, IDENTITIES, CONNECTIONS

# CHAPTER 1

# NORTH–SOUTH, EAST–WEST

*Topographies of Latinidad*

ILAN STAVANS

## Nineteen Theses

GROUNDED in José Ortega y Gasset's *Meditaciones del Quijote* (1914) and Walter Benjamin's "*Über den Begriff der Geschichte*" (1940), these theses offer a critique of geography as the portal through which Latinidad, the Hispanic diaspora in the United States, is understood: individually as well as culturally. There are two coordinates defining everything its population does, even (and especially) when those coordinates are not consciously understood: north ⇆ south and east ⇆ west. But the configurations are more complex, building an unexpected web of connections.

I. There is no universal *tropos* (from Ancient Greek τρόπος, meaning a turn, a way, a manner, a location). Geographical knowledge is not a continuum. Instead, it is relative (e.g., biased and incapable of objective understanding). This means that an individual or group is always somewhere, turning that perspective into a specific vantage point.

II. Individuals and groups are endowed with cognitive maps, an internal mechanism allowing them to recognized the specific coordinates in which they find themselves. Only a small portion of people are incapable of accessing this device. The absence of such a map is known among scientists as developmental topographical disorientation. To compensate for it, markers that help identify a location—a hill, a pole, a crossroad, a natural or artificial sign—are frequently used.

III. There is no progress in topography. Although individuals and groups talk of arriving at a desired location, that arrival is relative, too. It satisfies specific individual and group needs in their self-standing existence, which in turn are replaced by new needs.

IV. As per Walter Benjamin's "*Über den Begriff der Geschichte*" (1940), history is also not a continuum, nor is the past. This means progress in time is an illusion. In other words, the past is not a universal past but rather what each individual and group makes of it.

V. Like individuals and groups, cultures also have cognitive maps, although they are often far less attuned to them. In part, this is because in general they are less mobile than individuals. (Rule breakers are the Roma and the Jews. For hundreds of years, their transient existence has depended on the sharpness of their cognitive maps.) Yet in order to mature, cultures (again, like individuals and groups) require those maps in order to measure themselves vis-à-vis their neighbors.

VI. In its relativity, topography is therefore a sine qua non for existence: to know oneself, it is crucial to understand where one comes from, where one is, and where one is going.

VII. Refugees, exiles, immigrants, and other transients have cognitive maps enabling them to regenerate their sense of place based on their move from one another place. While that move frequently involves suffering, it eventually allows them to become someone new. Newness as a category is understood as the magical capacity to refurbish reality.

VIII. The maxim "Geography is destiny" is fatalistic in that it reduces a person's character or an array of cultural traits to a specific response to nature, social forces, and other large forces. However, it is no secret that determinism is a feature of life. In his opposition to Descartes, José Ortega y Gasset put it succinctly: "*yo soy yo y mi circunstancia*"—I am myself and my circumstance (*Meditaciones del Quijote*, 1914).

IX. In academia, topography and geography in general are often ugly ducklings. Departments devoted to their study lack capital. This is in spite of the fact that map making was a respected, lucrative career. This is no longer the case, mainly because of the flashy digital gadgets available to place us in a specific location.

X. *Hispanidad* is an abstract concept encompassing a diverse assortment of people irrigated between two continents and across almost 7.5 million square miles, disjointed by a common language. (I reflected on this, with historian Iván Jaksić, in *What Is la Hispanidad?* [2011].) It is a civilization with a loose (e.g., conjectural) sense of geography. That sense projects itself relentlessly, shaping stereotypes defined by two coordinates that strive from the way people perceive their differences.

XI. The first coordinate is north ⇆ south. North denotes character, control, and organization emanating from a grounding in the past. In contrast, south represents newness, loss, disorientation, and chaos. It is unwieldly and dangerous. North claims not only to represent history but to guide it toward progress. South is sheepish. It is not surprising that major trends in tourism usually run from north to south while equally significant are immigration flows from south to north. Sightseeing is about taking a vacation without abandoning the centers of power. Relocation is about usurping those centers of power.

XII. The second coordinate is east ⇆ west. Since the general movement of human history is from east to west, these locations bring about a *tropos* connected with roots. East means origins, foundation, wisdom. It is old. West, in comparison, is new. It means superficiality, lightheartedness, and an easy-going approach to reality. East is logical, assertive, and punitive. West is impulsive, temperamental, and forgetful. A variety of couplings push these established polarities in new directions, especially northeast ⇆ southwest and southeast ⇆ northwest. Those new equations propose different paradigms of power.

XIII. The connection with other concepts intimately linked to Latino identity is an outcome of this geographic coordinates. *Mestizaje* is a racial cross-pollination that resulted from the Spanish colonial enterprise. It is the shaping of a double-consciousness, rooted in Mesoamérica, which points to Europe as the source of white, Catholic, forward-looking framing, in contrast with the indigenous world as dark, idolatrous, and anchored in the past. Likewise, in the Amazon (Brazil, especially) Tropicalism is a rhythmic (e.g., syncopated), polymorphous response to the binary-modeled Western setting.

XIV. The foundation of this topology dates back to even before 1492, with the arrival of Europeans to the Americas. It came about after the collapse of the Roman Empire and the establishment of the Age of Byzantium. Still, the transplantation of the Old Continent to the New Continent emphasized it.

XV. Just as Hispanidad is cut at its core by these coordinates, Latinidad exists in a state of schizophrenia. Scholarship carried out in the northeast commands attention, whereas its counterpart in the southwest is perceived as derivative: likewise, the condescending views of academic research done south of the Rio Grande. For a proud north, they are the product of unstable conditions.

XVI. Tourism and immigration, while refreshing views on location, do not have enough sway to reconfigure the way cultures in their essence employ their cognitive maps.

XVII. The unsettling of these coordinates in Hispanidad is unlikely to take place anytime soon and as long as the shape of cognitive maps remains grounded as they are in the early decades of the twenty-first century. Only an upheaval of epic proportions is capable of a new geographic configuration.

XVIII. The US–Mexico border, because of its fluidity, is an uber-national zone. Topography is turned upside down and inside out in it. That mishmash is perfectly tangible in the languages that converse in the region. Spanglish is only superficially its lingua franca. In truth, Spanglish is a Rubik's-Cube test.

XIX. All rules depend on, and are ratified by, exceptions.

## Topographies of Latinidad

What follows is a rumination.

José Ortega y Gasset was not a fatalist as much as he was a *fatelist*, meaning that he believed fate was one's path through life with little deviation. On his part, Walter Benjamin, inspired by the Paul Klee painting *Angelus Novus* (1920), used the concept of the Angel of History to offer a catastrophic view of the history.

In contrast, I am an optimist. I believe Hispanic civilization is an ever-evolving entity. I believe freedom is always negative: we cannot do what we want, only what we are capable of, given the constraints in which we exist. Likewise, I do not believe culture reduces us to marionettes; instead, it serves as a runway for us to take off in whatever direction is possible without the parameters of the time and space in which we perform.

A person living near a mountain or a river is always positioned according to where these natural sites are located. Without the mountain or the river, the person is disconnected, non-localized. In the age of satellite communication and GPS orientation, we often forget, or else disregard, the natural features.

Hispanidad is a generally accepted "glue" (culture as a system of shared commonalities) establishing a community of approximately half a million people worldwide, in Europe and the Americas. It is a concept rooted in the idea that Spain (Hispania was the name the Romans gave to the region in the Iberian Peninsula) is the fountain whose couture irrigates its colonies, from the US–Mexico border to Patagonia and portions of the Caribbean Basin.

To a large extent, this irrigation has used the Spanish language as its primary instrument. Language is never only words; it is the culture embedded in them. Starting in 1498, by means of conquest Spain transported its essence to other geographies. That essence was not absorbed in unfiltered fashion. Instead, it required adaptation (e.g., a mixing of elements with the aboriginal culture that created an assortment of cultural varieties).

The richness of Hispanidad is to be found precisely in those varieties. Argentina and Mexico, for instance, are different modalities. There is much that they share; but each of them has distinct local characteristics. In that sense, Hispanidad is a galaxy-like conglomeration of satellites all loosely connected with the mother source.

This approach is confessedly skewed, though. The indigenous culture of each of those regions is of at least some importance in the shaping of the collective identity. The gauchos in Argentina and the rancheros in Mexico have enormous influence. In those nations' collective imagination, these archetypes are positioned in specific locations. Proof of it is José Hernández's epic poem *The Gaucho Martín Fierro* (1872), considered to be Argentina's most important literary classic. Likewise, *Pedro Páramo* (1955), the novel about the Mexican countryside written by Juan Rulfo, is seen as a mirror through which Mexico's DNA might be understood.

As explored in my book of conversations *What Is la Hispanidad?* (2011, coauthored with Iván Jaksić), Hispanidad is shaped by geography. In each nation, there is a north and a south, as well as an east and a west. In Mexico, the north is connected with US views, whereas the south is linked to the rest of Latin America. In that sense, the 1994 Zapatista revolution, for instance, was a realignment of indigenous loyalties with other aboriginal groups. A similar pattern took shape in Argentina, Colombia, Venezuela, and other countries.

In the larger continental scheme, Mexico is seen as El Norte and Argentina as El Sur. East and west are likewise intricately connected: the former is identified with the mind, while the latter is connected with the body. José Enrique Rodó, a formidable essayist that belonged to the Modernista movement, explored these topics in his book *Ariel* (1900), in which he depicted two characters, Ariel and Caliban, in Shakespeare's last play *The Tempest* (1610–1611), as representing polar opposites in the north/south equation. Caliban is the implacable United States while Ariel is the ethereal Latin America.

At the core of Hispanidad there are still other important concepts. The first is *mestizaje*. Though the term was in vogue in colonial Mesoamérica (today's Mexico, the southwestern United States, Guatemala, El Salvador, Nicaragua, and Honduras), it became a theoretical concept at the beginning of the twentieth century in the pen of José Vasconcelos, a racist, anti-Semitic thinker, politician, educator, and presidential hopeful. In his book *The Cosmic Race* (1925), Vasconcelos formulated a half-baked vision of the future of the Americas as dominated by the "*raza de bronce*," a bronze civilization made of mestizos. His readings in eugenics ultimately led him to believe Europe, Asia, and Africa were historically doomed. It was Latin America, in particular the Mestizo population, who in Vasconcelos's opinion were called upon to dominate the globe.

He injected mestizaje with a political grip that propelled intellectuals and artists to believe their oeuvre was instrumental in an international transformation. That transformation was geographically based. It had Mesoamérica as its center of gravity, from which migrant waves would colonize other parts of the planet through miscegenation. In Vasconcelos's imagination, the topography of mestizaje as a prophetic race will come about after the collapse of other races, each located in a particular space on the map.

It is important to mention, as I do in my book *The Prophet of Race* (2011), the extent to which these same arguments gave place to Nazism and the concept of the superiority of the Aryan race in Germany in the 1930s. Rather than seeing Latin America as reactive, Vasconcelos turned it into an engine of racial, ideological, and cultural homogenization. The US Chicano Movement in the 1960s and subsequent Latino activists, including Gloria Anzaldúa, whose book *Borderland/La Frontera: The New Mestiza* (1987) defined a generation, have been inspired by this idea.

The second concept is Tropicalismo. It is southern and western in essence, seeking to respond to the rigor of US life with flexibility and joie de vivre. The source comes from French anthropologist Claude Lévi-Strauss's work in Brazil, developed in his book *Tristes tropiques* (1955). It looks at the tropics as a polytheistic, polymorphic civilization that resists a strict binary worldview.

One of the most foundational, aspiring manifestations of this aesthetic is Oswaldo de Andrade's "Cannibalist Manifesto" (1928), in which he and a group of Brazilian vanguardists—painter Tarsila do Amaral was among them—visualized a response to European colonialism by means of devouring the very ogre (e.g., the imperial forces) whose arrival to the Americas changed their fate forever. The manifesto itself is written in a fragmented prose that is closer to the language of dreams than to a reasoned, coherent argument.

Once again, Tropicalismo is a geographically positioned category. It looks at the tropics as a contesting force defying the homogenizing strategy of Western civilization. Its heart is in the jungle, where heat deliberately slows things down. Another crucial argument it makes is that originality as professed by Europe is a trap. To copy, to plagiarize, to create derivatives, and even to cannibalize (to eat one's progenitors) is a genuine survival mechanism that ought to be emulated, not condemned.

Tourism is essential to appreciating the contours of these aesthetic views. No civilization exists in isolation; they are in constant dialogue with neighbors near and far, a dialogue that shapes them at all times. Visitors, tourists, chroniclers, and others jump from one side of the divide to another, comparing essential elements and—directly and otherwise—teaching lessons. In other words, we are who we are because of our communication with those around us, as Ortega y Gasset argues: "*Yo soy yo y mi circunstancia.*"

Octavio Paz makes this point in his influential study of Mexicanidad, *The Labyrinth of Solitude* (1950). It is developed throughout the book but is particularly tangible in the controversial first chapter, "The Pachuco and Other Extremes," in which Paz explores the psychological traits of Mexicans and their descendants, called Pachucos (in several ways, forerunners of the Chicanos) living in California in the 1940s. He posits that Pachucos are inauthentic e.g., caricatures of what true Mexicans on the other side of the US–Mexico border are like.

In his portrait, Paz himself is trapped in his own Mexican condition. He sees immigration as a deterioration of the self, not as a refreshing reincarnation. In being critical of Pachucos as impostors, he fails to understand that cultures exist by interacting with others and that, as a result, the essence of a people is never static. In truth, Pachucos are as authentic as a Mexican with European traits.

One of the extremities (e.g., tributaries) of Hispanidad, and the topic of the nineteen theses, is Latinidad. How this term came to be is in itself a fascinating theme. It came about as a result of permutations of names (Latins, Spanish-speaking people, *hispanos*, Hispanics, and a number of national possibilities, such as Mexicans, Cubans, Puerto Ricans, Dominicans, Colombians, and so on). The term as such was fixed in the early years of the twenty-first century.

That culture is heterogeneous in nature. A person might be a recent immigrant or a US-born citizen. Their ancestry might be from Mexico, Central, and South America, or it might be from Cuba, Puerto Rico, and the Dominican Republic. Brazil, in part because of its language (Brazilian Portuguese), is at times included in this category. The same goes for countries like Jamaica, Trinidad and Tobago, and the Bahamas.

In and of itself, Latinidad is topographically framed. Historically, the eastern United States has been inhabited by Spanish-speaking Caribbeans. Their worldview is hence defined by that duality. The west is Mexican and Central American. Although these two varieties define Latinos all the same, topography shapes their Weltanshauung. The east is methodical, interested in the intellect; the west is free-flowing, unrooted, and fascinated by the body. To ignore the geographic coordinates of emigration is to simplify the nuances of Latino identity.

That bipolarity finds its counterpart in the north–south relationship between the United States and its southern neighbors. The Anglo vision of life is forward looking. It sees progress as determined by individual commitment. Alternatively, the Hispanic view is attached to the past and is collectivist in nature. The Hispanic view highlights the role of family kinship, friendship, and comradeship. As a result of having one foot in each geographic dimension, Latinidad is a struggle between these viewpoints: individualist and collectivist, futuristic and anchored in memory. In that sense, Latinidad is not exclusively an extension, a renewal of Hispanidad; it is perhaps also its refutation.

Likewise, the north obsesses with law and order; it is rigid in its conception of morality. The south plays loose in this regard; it sees ethics as malleable, elastic, and even accommodating. Again, there is a constant overstepping of these polarities, achieved through immigration, tourism, and other movements, real or imagined. The north ventures into the south while the south reconquers the north. The east antagonizes the west, yet they also idealize each other.

Successive waves of Hispanic immigration to the United States are a constant test to the geographical modes of Latinidad. Cubans living in Miami; Guatemalans, Nicaraguans, Hondurans, and Salvadorans in Los Angeles; Mexicans in Chicago; Puerto Ricans in New York; and a plethora of others just about everywhere suggest that north and south and east and west are never static coordinates.

Take the example of Hondurans in Los Angeles. Immigrants from a variety of urban and rural, rich and poor, black, mestizo, and white immigrants from that country, who felt compelled to leave as a result of a variety of circumstances, settle in various sections of the Southern Californian city. Their topographic traits are subsumed to an unending river of identities, not only within Latinidad but as part of the multicultural American city. As a result, their Honduran culture is reshaped, interacting with one another in ways that were unforeseen while they were still in Honduras.

Yet their geographic characteristics remain a feature of their character. An upper-class citizen of Tegucigalpa therefore might connect faster in Los Angeles with a similarly positioned Salvadoran than with a working-class Honduran. They will find in common certain tastes, ideas, and connections with America as a whole and with other immigrant groups (Filipinos, Italians, Blacks, Senegalese, Chinese, Jews, etc.). The neighborhoods in Los Angeles where they settle will likewise define their political persuasion, cultural tastes, education, and other aspects.

Finally, the US–Mexican border is a unique microcosm with which to grasp the dimensions of Latinidad. Nowhere else in the world do the misnamed First and Third Worlds coexist with such friction. For starters, it is a territory disputed in countless historical moments, having changed its position in the last several centuries. The current line dividing the two nations was the habitat of various aboriginal tribes at the time European explorers arrived, such as Álvar Nuñez Cabeza de Vaca, author of *Chronicle of the Narváez Expedition* (1527–1536). In successive periods, depending on spatial-related power struggles, it took the shape its dwellers gave it.

To understand the volatility of the area, it is enough to ponder the different ways in which the river that forms part of the border has various names depending on who is referring to it. Most notably, it is the Rio Grande from one perspective and Río Bravo from another.

This divide goes further. South of the border, Mexican border culture has a particular idiosyncrasy that is different from other types of national culture in say Yucatán, Oaxaca, central, or even northern Mexico. Likewise, American culture one finds in Laredo, Texas, is diametrically different from its counterpart in San Diego, California.

The north–south binary, hence, is more complex than what it seems. Depending on where one is pointing to, there is a type of Latinidad on the US side of the border that in character is unlike the Hispanidad on the Mexican side of the border, which again was subject to change depending on location. I have explored these nuances in poetic terms in my book *The Wall* (2018).

But the US–Mexico border is also an uber-national zone. It is not only militarized; it is also visited by a broad variety of people, from migrants to journalists, from militia members to activists, and from international observers to peacekeepers. In that sense, it is a non-place. Or else, an Aleph in the Borgesian sense of the term: a site where the entire universe is synthesized.

Linguistically, the US–Mexico border is a stunning symphony of accents, languages, and morpho-syntactic structures. The Spanish language one listens to in the region is a sum of provenances, mostly from Mexico, Central, and South America, always in contact with English, lending and borrowing words, sentences, and other elements. The English that is present is a bit less complex yet equally playful. Of course, the doings and undoings of these two tongues, and their infinite tributaries produce what has come to be known as Spanglish.

The Spanglish of the border is different the Spanglish anywhere else in the United States, Latin America, the Caribbean, and Europe; it is also different from cyber- and social-media Spanglish. It is less settled and more disorganized—in eternal flux. I have studied it over the past few decades. It changes depending on who is passing through, what historical factors are affecting the area, and how the region is being portrayed in the media, among other factors.

*Merriam-Webster* defines typography as "the art or practice of graphic delineation in detail usually on maps or charts of natural and man-made features of a place or region especially in a way to show their relative positions and elevations." The lexical definition implies that maps are intrinsically unstable, changing according to human will. Consequently, the impact of topography on culture is changeable, adapting to circumstance. Add to it the mutating nature of the environment. The identity that emerges is nothing if not fluid.

## Bibliography

Andrade, Oswald de. "Manifesto antropófago/Cannibalist Manifesto." Translated by Lesley Bary. *Latin American Literary Review* 19, no. 39 (July–December 1991): 38–47.

Anzaldúa, Gloria. *Borderland/La Frontera: The New Mestiza*. San Francisco: Aunt Lute Foundation, 1987.
Benjamin, Walter. "Über den Begriff der Geschichte." In *Gesammelte Werke*, edited by Hermann Schweppenhäuser and Rolf Tiedemann, 690–708. Vols. 1–2. Frankfurt am Main: Suhrkamp, 1991.
Borges, Jorge Luis. *El Aleph*. Buenos Aires: Editorial Emecé, 1976.
Cabeza de Vaca, Álvar Nuñez. *Chronicle of the Narváez Expedition*. Translated by Fanny Bandelier. Introduction by Ilan Stavans. New York: Penguin Classics, 1998.
Hernández, José. *El gaucho Martín Fierro*. Buenos Aires: Editorial Nacional, 1965.
Lévi-Strauss, Claude. *Tristes tropiques*. Paris: Librairie Plon, 1955.
Ortega y Gasset, José. *Meditaciones del Quijote*. Madrid: Espasa-Calpe, 1996.
Paz, Octavio. *El laberinto de la soledad*. Mexico City: Fondo de Cultura Económica, 1987.
Rodó, José Enrique. *Ariel*. Mexico City: Fondo de Cultura Económica, 1988.
Rulfo, Juan. *Pedro Páramo*. Mexico City: Fondo de Cultura Económica, 1971.
Stavans, Ilan. *Spanglish: The Making of a New American Language*. New York: Harper, 2003.
Stavans, Ilan. *José Vasconcelos: The Prophet of Race* (with a translation of the essay "The Cosmic Race"). New Brunswick, NJ: Rutgers University Press, 2009.
Stavans, Ilan, with Iván Jaksić. *What Is La Hispanidad?* Austin: University of Texas Press, 2011.
Stavans, Ilan. *The Wall*. Pittsburgh, PA: University of Pittsburgh Press, 2018.

# CHAPTER 2

# LATINA/OS AND RACE

### SILVIO TORRES-SAILLANT

## Preamble: History, Race, Slavery, and Intellectuals

A pan-ethnicity that in the 2010 Census stood out as the largest ethnic minority in the population of the United States, Latina/os trace their origins to the Iberian Peninsula, Latin America, the Hispanic Caribbean, the US Southwest, and the other territories formerly under the judicial domain of the Spanish Empire. That is, they may hail from anywhere in the large geography that fell under Iberian control in the course of the colonial transaction that followed the transoceanic voyage of the fortune-seeking mariner Christopher Columbus in 1492. Ethnologically, the US Hispanic population encompasses a culturally and linguistically manifold assortment of peoples of varied heritages, ancestries, and phenotypes whose variegated social formation stemmed from historical phenomena that took place across the western hemisphere. A Latina/o is almost by definition an heir to the historical crossings that cohered in the Americas in the wake of the competition, clashes, coexistence, tensions, and confluence of the Iberian and British colonial ventures out of which new civilizations emerged in the region. The study of race is crucial to an understanding of the Latino as well as the human experience in the entire hemisphere. It is hard to think of an element that looms more prominently than race among the constitutive factors that count as pillars of the civilization of the region from the moment that Christian nations of Europe laid claim to the lands, peoples, and destinies of this part of the world.

These pages offer an overview of race as a core factor of the civilizations created in the Americas by European colonial projects on the ruins of the indigenous civilizations they sought to destroy upon arrival in these parts. Understanding "race" as a phenomenon begotten by history, we contend that the events surrounding the conquest and colonization of the region lent a valence to what today we call "racism" that was unprecedented in the history of social relations across the globe. We regard "race" as epiphenomenal to acts of "racism." By the latter, we mean a behavior aiming to condemn, impair, dominate, or reduce other people because of their difference of ancestry and/or phenotype. Because discourses on race come to offer paradigms that seek to rationalize or justify behaviors of "racial" antipathy already in practice (racist actions), we take it that conceptually racism precedes race. Insofar as in the Americas discourses that aimed to naturalize practices of "racial" antipathy lingered as staples of everyday life that helped to sustain the status quo created by the conquest and colonization, long after the physical violence of the initial onslaught had subsided, it follows that the discourses we inherit from the past play a much larger role than the actual fact of former domination in fueling our present racial disquiet. Since it fell on the learned—teachers, clergymen, writers, statesmen, and political thinkers, among others—to protect by *the pen* the social order that the armies of the conquistadores had created by *the sword*, the subject of race and racism necessarily must occupy itself with a scholastic heritage bequeathed by the learned over four centuries. In that respect, race, the offspring of racism, became a core emphasis of the intellectual history of the Christian West, the dominant global civilization that emerged from the colonial transaction.

This article studies "race," therefore, by focusing only tangentially on the current social trauma that disturbs our psychological well-being when we turn on the news at night or find instances of it sporadically in school or the workplace. Our primary focus here is on outlining the prolegomena for tracing the history of social relations that brought race into being and highlighting the role played by the intellectuals in its articulation, spread, and normalization. We propose that racism remains vibrant as a mediator of social relations in our world today primarily because of the enduring legacy of the discourses of disparagement articulated by learned elites and their epigones from the mid-sixteenth century onward. The discursive legacy of the learned, the concerted intellectual effort of sundry generations of lettered voices from across the centuries intent on disparaging subject populations differing from them in appearance and origin, bears the lion's share of responsibility for the recurrence of racist utterances and deeds in our day. The resonance of the racially infused speech acts, pedagogies, and literacies propagated by the educated classes in their detractions of civilizational others matters more today than any influence one might wish to ascribe to lingering memories of past oppressions. In the United States, for instance, the facts of material domination or slavery proper—be it by the settler's gun or the lash of the overseer on plantation labor camps—cannot explain the racist tensions we experience today so many centuries after the conquest and so many generations since legally sanctioned racialized, coerced, labor formally ended.

For instance, the words "slavery is our original sin" said in August 2014 by former Secretary of State Hillary Clinton in Ferguson, Missouri, as she grappled with expressing her dismay at the killing in that city of Michael Brown, an unarmed eighteen-year-old African American male shot by a white police officer, may not quite point in the right direction. The remark suggests that we owe our racial troubles to the fact that until the 1863 Emancipation Proclamation *we had* slavery. However, that causal explanation would seem insufficient if we remembered that slavery has been around since time immemorial. The oldest written legal documents of highly advanced civilizations factored slavery as a normal feature of their social system. The famous *Code* of Mesopotamian law enacted during the reign of Babylonian King Hammurabi, *ca.* 1754, nearly three and a half millennia prior to the arrival of English settlers at Jamestown, recognizes enslaved people and their owners alike as subjects of the law, susceptible to punishment and dispensation. The *Code* mediated between the two to ensure that neither abused their relative entitlements, clearly indicating that captivity did not annul the humanity of the enslaved. Besides, enslavement in some countries within the large geography of the former Ottoman Empire even outlasted bondage in the western hemisphere. Yet we do not hear of other regions of the world where the aftermath of slavery has remained as constant, acrimonious, and powerful an issue complicating the daily lives of people tracing their roots to enslaved forbears, the descendants of slave masters, and the offspring of both as it has remained in the Americas, and especially the United States. Since other regions have had histories of servitude that did not yield the distressful lingering impact on present social relations as it did in this part of the world, it seems safe to conclude that captivity in and of itself will not suffice to account for our difficulty to behave humanely across difference. While sympathizing with Clinton's invocation of "our original sin," here we choose to look rather for the historical circumstances that made the ancient ordinary practice of slavery so "peculiar" that, even to this day, we seem unable to transcend it. We therefore focus on the distinct morality that the experience of dominating assumed when Christian nations of Europe had their successful crack at conquest and colonization in the Americas.

Our line of inquiry requires a privileged attention to the history of discourse production given that this time around arguments of justification gained a degree of significance that they did not seem to have had in earlier moments of domination. In these Christian times we find cultivated intellects playing an unprecedented role in the business of conquest and colonization, operating as self-appointed scribes of the subjugating nations and committed to the task of disparaging the humanity of the vanquished. The learned produced knowledge about the ontology of the defeated with the discernible intent to lend the swords of the plunderers a nobility of purpose that previous generations of conquerors had not needed to claim. The previous history of domination as far as we can tell shows no precedent for this arrangement whereby robust cohorts of thinkers, clergymen, scholars, scientists, men of letters, teachers, and statesmen step up to the plate and gradually create a discursive superstructure to go along the ventures of the conquering hordes. The learned contributed conceptual tools for understanding the conquered populations in ways that deprived them of virtues and thereby represented the violence and destruction inflicted upon them as stemming from a selfless and divinely condoned quest for the advancement of civilization and the good of humanity on the part of the victors. The knowledge produced by those scribes of the colonial transaction about the "races" was so widespread and so normalized in the course of several centuries that it came to inform common sense judgements among the descendants of the captors as well as the heirs of the vanquished. Over four hundred years after its production began, its teachings can still be detected even in the utterances of disempowered and unschooled racists who are under the impression that they are thinking for themselves when they divide the human species between *us*, the noble race, and *them*, the debased ones that threaten the stability of *our* world. Murderous brutes who commit unspeakable hate crimes against racial others may be deemed "brutish" because of their frontal acts of bloodshed, but the line of thought that orients their violence often matches to the letter the utterances of some of the loftiest intellects of the Christian West.

On June 17, 2015, in Charleston, South Carolina, twenty-one-year-old white supremacist Dylann Roof, consumed with the thought that blacks were "raping our women and taken over our country," walked into Mother Emmanuel AME Church during a Bible study session and opened fire, slaying nine African American parishioners. US Attorney General Loretta Lynch condemned the killings by calling them "a barbaric crime" that had "no place in our country...no place in a civilized society" (Official of the Attorney General). The Attorney General spoke as the situation demanded. People of goodwill in the citizenry needed to hear that their leaders do not regard racist violence of this magnitude as normal but as odd occurrences that will trigger immediate condemnation and hopefully intervention from the authorities. Considering the incident historically, however, one might wonder if "civilized society" passes the test for humane interaction that Ms. Lynch's pathos-filled indictment of the horror committed by Roof seems to assume. An awareness of the nature of social relations in our hemisphere over the past five centuries would necessarily cause an observer to differ. A retrospective look at the events that have transpired in the Americas since the start of the colonial transaction would lead to the realization that barbaric crimes and civilization need not be mutually exclusive. Walter Benjamin said quite compellingly that "there is no document of civilization which is not at the same time a document of barbarism" in that, as Maynard Solomon would gloss, "The cultural possessions of mankind, the highest achievements of the spirit, were born *intra feces et urinas* [among the feces and urine] of class oppression.[1] In the Americas, the civilization marshalled by the European Christian conquerors and their descendants ended up being built *intra sudore et caedes* [among the sweat and tears] of racial oppression, race attaining so overpowering a force in the imagination of the colonial administrators that class would become subsumed by it.

The lyrical piece "Mission Bell" by the great Dominican American poet Rhina P. Espaillat evokes the difficult trajectory of civilization in the Americas given that even the civilizing act of erecting a church to honor the greater glory of God can become tangled with savage cruelty against innocent children, thereby tainting the very notion of grace. The poem uses as epigraph the words of a Native American guide, in Acoma Pueblo, New Mexico, 1988, that provide background to the origin of the bell in the Mission: *The priest at that time traded ten of the village children to slavers in exchange for this bell.* The speaker in Espaillat's brief, free-verse, three-stanza poem addresses the man of God whose dark dealing secured the bell: "Did you transform their/cries in dry desert silence/into litanies// in praise of Jesus?/ Did you stop their mothers' ears /with hymns to Mary?// Priest, did you weigh them/ against this heavy brazen/tongue tolling God's love?"[2]

## Racist Violence as Civilization

This is not the place to recount the events surrounding the invasion, conquest, and colonization of the lands and peoples of the hemisphere by Christian nations of Europe, but, in sum, one can understand the process as disempowering and traumatic for the natives even as it represented a historic jackpot for the people who came from across the seas. The work of domination undertaken by the newcomers required an intense investment in the difficult task of keeping their captives down in a position of subservience. The wholesale deployment of ruthless violence played a key role in sustaining the control of vast territories with their large populations, but it did not suffice, especially as the accumulation of wealth required the importation of captive workers from other regions, especially tropical areas of Africa, as well as indentured laborers from China and other parts of Asia. The stability of the colonial regime came to depend on the strict segmentation of society by means of a racial accounting system that stipulated the phenotype of the conquerors, eventually acquiring the label "whites," as representing the epitome of human value, with all the other differentiated populations occupying ranks of worth in descending order. Colonial societies harbored diverse populations that were materially unequal in their differential degrees of access to resources, power, and prestige as would have been the case with the downtrodden in any previous chapter of the history of domination. But the social system established by the Christian conquerors construed their subject peoples as unequal also in the realms of the intangible, intrinsic, and spiritual makeup of their being.

The exultation of the complexion and other somatic features of the conquerors, along with the degradation of the other populations, eventually cohered into a pigmentocracy, a phenotypically stratified social order, which resulted in a racialized status quo that operated at the level of work, reward, opportunities, mobility, prestige, protection of the law, and the possibility of charting one's own future in a promissory way. The conquerors and settlers set the terms of unequal social relations across difference in the way of structuring colonial societies that counted on expendable, coerced, or cheap labor for their prosperity. As the leaders of the separatist movements that led to the declarations of independence and the creation of new sovereignties across the hemisphere were typically the progeny of the conquerors and the original colonists, they did not have much of a problem with retaining the social stratification that had prevailed during the colonial period. With the offspring of the former masters setting the terms of the social system, when sovereign nations came around the values of the colonists stood for the values of the whole. This meant in effect that the other populations of indigenous, African, or Asian ancestry did not figure conceptually in the national imaginary from the start of the republic in the modern societies of the region. The European-descended and mestizo elites who controlled the discourse of collective representation for the most part did not think highly of the other segments of the population. Often ideas of nation and projections of the country's future included harsh invectives against segments of the national population that traced their origins to regions outside of Europe.

Especially in the nineteenth century, with the new independent nations seeking to chart their future throughout the hemisphere, the effort to define national identity and each country's potential for modern advancement became a frequent subject of inquiry. The beginning of what one might call social theory dates from that period for most societies in Latin America and the Caribbean, no less than in the United States. The ruling elites typically expressed a yearning for progress and civilization. With disturbing frequency, they regarded themselves, the descendants of conquerors and settlers, as the agents of advancement, while defining the other populations as useful only for their labor. While they valued the labor of their racial others, the ruling elites tended to express concern about the extent to which the ethnological differences of the other groups could contaminate the whole to the point of impeding or retarding advancement. Often, they defined the nation in contradistinction to the non-European-descended portions of their own populations even in cases where the latter constituted the overwhelming majority. Social theory in the Americas, then, starts from a stance of antipathy toward differentiated segments of the national population, articulating adversarial views of Indians, blacks, and Asians, characterizing them as obstacles to civilization and sometimes espousing their extermination.

The Argentinian writer, social theorist, and lawyer Carlos Octavio Bunge (b. 1875–d. 1918) viewed the future of his country and of Spanish America in general through a feverishly racial lens. He regarded the progress of the capital city of Buenos Aires favorably, and he reasoned that it had resulted from its "cold climate" and "the poverty of the Pampean tribes," which had enabled it to "continue to receive a steady flow of European immigrants." No less important, the city "during the colonial era maintained a relative and growing distance from the indigenous population." Also, Bunge piously praises the Lord ("Thank God!") for "alcoholism, smallpox, and tuberculosis," three factors that he gratefully credits with having "decimated the indigenous and African populations of the province-capital, cleansing its ethnic element, Europeanizing them, Hispanicizing them."[3] Bunge regarded racial mixture as a source of the region's arrested development insofar as each "physical race is also a psychic race."[4] Explaining the extent to which ancestry determines civilization, he spoke with certainty about the elements that each population had contributed to the region. He contended that the Spanish gave Latin America their "loftiness, indulgence, theological uniformity, and honor; the Indians, their fatalism and ferocity; and Blacks, their servility and malleability; and when they commingle with whites, a certain hyper-excitement of the aspiring capacity that could very well be called hyperesthesia of aspirability."[5]

The extreme self-adulation of the dominant group led to their confection of tales of the national experience consisting primarily of the exploits of their forebears. The actions taken by European invaders and their descendants in the process of depriving indigenous peoples of their native lands, their social structure, their freedom, and their chance to aspire realistically to a humane future for their offspring outside the ill-disposed will of their captors came to fill the narrative of national history in each of the former colonies that became an independent republic in the region. The substance of the narrative invariably extolled the glory of the conquerors and sought to elicit the reader's empathy for the enormous sacrifice made by those Christians who first ventured across the Atlantic to come to these parts and the vicissitudes they underwent in their resolve to build the societies of the "new" world. The poem by Peruvian bard José Santos Chocano (b. 1875–d. 1934) "Los caballos de los conquistadores" [The horses of the conquerors], perhaps the best-known single text from the poet's 1906 collection *Alma América: Poemas indo-españoles* [Soul of America: Indo-American poems], is a case in point. Its first stanza reads:

> !Los caballos eran fuertes! /!Los caballos eran ágiles! / Sus pescuezos eran finos y sus ancas / relucientes y sus cascos musicales.?! / Los caballos eran fuertes! /!Los caballos eran ágiles!" [Oh! The battle-steeds were mighty! / Oh! The battle-steeds were nimble! / Their haughty necks were slender / And their broad breasts silken, shining! / Oh! The battle-steeds were mighty! / Oh! The battle-steeds were nimble!][6]

Written from a perspective of sympathetic identification with the "exciting spirit" that the Conquest must have infused in the hearts of Spanish adventurers about to acquire vast fertile lands and unimaginable wealth, the poem undertakes to create sonically the stirring quality of the enterprise. Reproducing an English version of the poem, translated by Edna W. Underwood under the title "The Arab Steeds of the Conquerors," Phyllis Rodríguez-Peralta's study of Chocano noted decades ago the formal features whereby the poem conveys the stridency of the "heroic" endeavor undertaken by the conquerors: "The surging, insistent rhythm marks the clatter and pawing of the horses' hoofs as they traverse mountains and valleys—manes flying and heads erect"[7] The poem achieves its dramatic tension by singing to the great deeds of the horses, reminding readers that "it wasn't just the warriors" who accomplished the great feat of the conquest "of the jungles and the Andes." Chocano recreates the equestrian quests of the "Andalucian horses" of "winged Arab breeds," trekking over and across the driest screes, wet marshes, Pampean silent snows, mountain ranges, and forests and valleys.[8] The last stanza tells us that in "the midst of the decisive/ splendor of combat/ the horses overwhelmed the Indians/ with their breasts and charged ahead."[9] The speaker's enthusiasm soars as he identifies with the glory of the quadrupeds that enabled the Christian conquerors to overpower the Incas whose lands they invaded and took over, clearly honoring the greatness of the imposing mammals, while the native population that endured the impact of the invasion appear in the poem merely as part of the challenging environment that the horses mastered in the exercise of their greatness. Given the prestige that Chocano enjoys in Peruvian literary history, one wonders about how teachers in the middle school literature class would approach the discussion of the glorification of the horses that played a key role in the defeat of the Incas, the ancestors of a fair share of the students in the classroom, as one can reasonably expect given Peru's ethnic composition. One wonders if the teachers will safeguard the youngsters under their care instead of instilling uncritical admiration for the poetic talent that honors the lives of the horses while disdaining those of the Indians.

Whether a teacher will side with Chocano's horses or with the indigenous students' Inca ancestors will depend on his or her individual level of awareness about the politics of knowledge. In a worst-case scenario, the teacher may be of indigenous heritage and still focus on training pupils to appreciate the achievement of the renowned Peruvian poet. Whether the lesson goes one way or the other, we would still need to contend with a prevailing perception in Latin America that views any non-white population as a "social implant," as described by an Afro-Argentinian social scientist who explains a process whereby the body of the nation accepts the Indian, the black, and the Asian as external to itself and not fully a part of the national community (see *Afroargentines* 2002). Fittingly, the collection of short fiction *La rebelión pocomía y otros relatos* (1976) by Afro-Costa Rican writer Quince Duncan appeared with a telling commentary on the back cover written by one of the readers who had vetted the manuscript for the publisher. Appearing as a blurb, the words of the unidentified reviewer assume the voice of a Costa Rican of European ancestry who marvels at what Duncan has done as "an intellectual of color." The blurb writer tells us that the Afro-Costa Rican author has conjured "this unheard of vision, the eye that looks at us from within from a narrow opening through which only black Costa Ricans can see us," which, among other things, "surprises us." The blurb praises Duncan's work for "making us feel that we are barely beginning to know...one another fully (A similar thing will happen some day when our aborigines become incorporated into our culture)" (blurb, back cover) While doubtlessly an earnest expression of solidarity and a progressive call to compatriots of all origins to recognize themselves as a national community with multiple ancestries, the framing of the reviewer's appeal remains trapped rhetorically in the duality of the unmarked Costa Rican "us" (which means "white") vs. the racialized African-descended "them" living on Puerto Limón or the indigenous population whose integration into "our culture" may occur "someday."

The difficulty to break free of the us/them binary aside, the blurb on the back cover of Duncan's book marks a radical delinking from the frenetic racism that had marked the positions of public figures in previous generations in Costa Rican and overall Latin American societies. In a document that sets out to outline the development of racist thought in modern history, Duncan highlights a telling racial detail that the Costa Rican government insisted on in relation to the 1891 contract signed with a US railway company to build the Pacific Railroad. The contract stipulated that the contractor would "not introduce people of Asian race to work on the railways, nor introduce either Asians or blacks to work on or colonize the lands herein being granted."[10] This desire to block the entry of people from devalued ancestries matched the sentiment of the political leadership throughout the hemisphere. From 1862 onward, Costa Rica, like Venezuela, had banned the entry of people of African and Asian descent while seeking to attract Europeans immigrants, and in 1896 the government would set up a fund to help finance the relocation of Europeans from their home countries.[11] The ruling elites' ambition of a pristinely white population uncontaminated by racial others succeeded only in part due to the imperatives of industries in need of cheap laborers plus the insufficient availability of the desired European immigrants.[12]

The local leaderships often needed to bend before the weight of economic expediency, hesitantly receive the unwanted but needed "colored" migrants, and continue anxiously to fret over their elusive demographic ideal. The less sustainable their material conditions to impede the presence of racial others in their midst, the greater their zeal to preach the dogma of racial purity and the dread of miscegenation. Still nearly a half century after the 1891 railroad contract, Costa Rica's most renowned scientist, the botanist and zoologist Clodomiro Picado (b. 1887–d. 1944), deemed it urgent to speak to the nation about the menace of the country's growing blackness. In a May 1939 open letter sent to the newspaper *Diario de Costa Rica*, the enfevered scientist warned as follows: "OUR BLOOD IS BLACKENING!, and if it continues thus, out of the pot will emerge not a gold nugget but a chunk of coal. It might not yet be too late to rescue the patrimony of our European blood which is what until now has possibly saved us from declining into African-like systems, be it in politics or in tendencies that liken the arts and refinement to sad and ridiculous forms."[13]

A rapid abridgement of racist interventions in the hemisphere should offer further data to dispel any impression of Clodomiro Picado's negrophobic frenzy as in any way exceptional nor particularly salient for his generation, the preceding ones, or those that followed his. The venerated General Simón Bolívar (b. 1783–d. 1830), one of the most enlightened of the Latin American leaders heading the nineteenth independence movement from imperial Spain, conceived an emancipation scheme that seemed motivated by the desire to ensure that only a small number of the enslaved blacks remained after the war no less than by the wish to secure military victory over the Spanish forces. In an April 20, 1820, memorandum to his comrade General Santander, he explained his order to free "all slaves available for bearing arms" and suitable for enlisting in the independence forces.[14] Understanding that for the slaves there is no "more fitting or proper means by which to win freedom than to fight for it" and thinking it unfair for "free men" to "die for the liberation of the slaves," Bolívar poses this chilling rhetorical question: "Is it not proper that the slaves should acquire their rights on the battlefield and that their dangerous numbers should be lessened by a process both just and effective?" Bolívar speaks of the free population dying and the unfree surviving, which he claims had been the case in Venezuela. Thus, he wished to forestall the chance that they might "outlive us again."[15] Though explicitly apprehensive about the possibility of ending up with an independent society with a numerically substantial black population, Bolívar does not figure among the truly ardent white supremacists among the intellectual and political leaderships of nineteenth-century Latin America.

The best-known and arguably most influential white supremacist thinkers in Latin America voiced their disparagement of peoples of non-European ancestry as part of an ideal of national development, progress, modernity, and civilization. Their antipathy against the black, indigenous, and Asian-descended populations acquired a patriotic texture insofar as they formulated it as advocacy for the national good. As a result, they retain a place of distinction in the intellectual and political history of their respective countries, whose populations value their contributions to the nation-building effort at a key juncture in the homeland's past. Therein lies, for instance, the continued appeal of the 1852 essay, *Bases y puntos de partida para la organización política de la República Argentina* by the political thinker, man of letters, and diplomat Juan Bautista Alberdi (b. 1810–d. 1884). A seminal text that strongly influenced the 1853 Argentinian constitution, the essay went through numerous editions in the nineteenth and twentieth centuries, remaining in circulation until our day. On the sesquicentenary of its publication in 2002, the National Academy of Law and Social Sciences in Córdoba Province honored the occasion by means of the compilation *Homenaje a Juan Bautista Alberdi: Sesquicentenario de las* Bases (1852–2002), a two-volume festschrift totaling nearly a thousand pages by philosophy, social science, and legal scholars paying tribute to the author's legacy.

These and numerous other honors notwithstanding, Alberdi's *Bases* minced no words when it came to identifying the ancestries that functioned as an asset and those that constituted an impediment to the advancement of Argentinian society. He advocated taking away any good land inhabited by "savage Indians" to make it available to "German, English, and Swizz settlers," secure as he was in the thought anyone "would one thousand times prefer to have his sister or daughter marry an English shoemaker than an Indian noble from the Arauca region."[16] Similarly, Alberdi overtly denied value to any ancestry other than the European, stating that all "in our country's civilization is European" and that "we are nothing but Europeans born in America," the old country providing all the constitutive elements: "Skull, blood, color."[17] Alberdi's compatriot and political kindred Domingo Faustino Sarmiento (b. 1811–d. 1888), a statesman and very prolific author of journalistic and travel books, most memorably of his 1845 creative nonfiction work *Facundo o civilización y barbarie*, served as president of Argentina for the 1868–1874 period. As president, Sarmiento promoted European immigration, invested in public education, and upheld the United States as the ultimate model of modernization for Latin America to follow. A devout believer, like Alberdi, in the inextricable link between advancement and ancestry, Sarmiento put great effort into organizing his white supremacist doctrine in the 1883 essay *Conflicto y armonía de las razas*, a volume containing some eerie passages of discernible gloating over the decimation of the indigenous population of the land. Similarly, as if heralding good tidings, Sarmiento saluted the dwindling number of blacks in the country by predicting that a person in "Buenos Aires, in twenty more years, will need to go to Brazil to see them in the purity of their race."[18]

Sarmiento's gleeful 1883 prediction seems striking given that at the beginning of the century, as indicated by population census figures for the period around the end of Spanish rule, "one out of every three settlers of the current Argentinian territory was black" (Gabino, 2007. "¿Hay negros en Argentina?" *bbcmundo.com*). Contemporary Argentina does not come quickest to mind as an important site of the African experience even though in the early nineteenth century the black presence there matched that of any other slave-based colonial territory in the Americas. José de San Martín (b. 1778–d. 1850), one of the key leaders of the war of independence from Spain, recruited blacks into the army of liberation in 1812, and the year after a constitutional assembly promulgated the freedom of wombs (*libertad de vientre*) law, which established the automatic freedom of children born of slave mothers. The Batallón de Pardos y Morenos, a regiment that grouped free mulattos and blacks, accrued a noteworthy military record in the independence war. With the birth of the republic, black soldiers appeared at the vanguard in the war with Brazil (b. 1825–d. 1828), the Batalla de Caseros (1852), and the war with Paraguay (1864–1870). Scholars have compellingly argued that the salient role of black soldiers in the wars reveals their use as cannon fodder. The Argentinian historian Felipe Pigna explains the decrease of the African-descended Argentinian population as a result of overrepresentation on the battlefield. During the independence struggles, he observes, "many of the patrician families" served the war effort while keeping their eligible sons out of harm's way by sending their slaves to the front instead. Argentinian blacks fought in the civil wars in large numbers as well. The war with Paraguay, which overlapped for two years with the rule of President Sarmiento, left "a heavy toll of blacks killed in combat."[19] If the negrophobia that informed political and military practice in Argentina, assisted by Sarmiento's characterization of blacks as a group bound to disappear shortly, did not quite extinguish the African presence in the country, it nonetheless succeeded in erasing them from the national imaginary. Cape Verdean–descended Argentinian civil rights activist Miriam Gomes illustrates the phenomenon of Afro-Argentine invisibility by recalling the 1996 visit of President Carlos Menem to Howard University in Washington, DC. During a conversation with students, the president answered a question about the condition of blacks in Argentina by saying: "There are no blacks in Argentina; it's Brazil that has that problem." [20]

The genocidal texture of Sarmiento's views about the African-descended and indigenous populations of Latin America did not tarnish the reputation he went on to enjoy as one of the founding fathers of civilization in the region, one of the builders of Hispanic American culture, and one of the intellectual and literary giants of the Iberian world. The Argentinian positivist philosopher, physician, and man of letters José Ingenieros (b. 1877–d. 1925) wrote a fervent panegyric to the sociological ideas expostulated by Sarmiento in *Conflicto y armonía*. Clearly sharing the author's white supremacist ideology, Ingenieros assigned to race a greater impact as a mover of history than Karl Marx and Friedrich Engels had attributed to class. He argued that the formation of Argentina, no less than of those other countries in the region, "initially inhabited by an inferior race," constitutes an episode in the struggle between the races and their adaptation to "physical nature's geographic conditions."[21] He envisions this national experience as one that in the future could figure in the chapter covering "the expansion of the white race and the growing preponderance of its civilization."[22] One might hasten to credit the racism exuded by the prose of Ingenieros to his sharing Sarmiento's outlook and ideology. But as we look more closely in the region, we find the vision of Sarmiento reflected in the writings of authors from across the ideological gamut.

The Uruguayan essayist José Enrique Rodó formed part of an intellectual elite associated with *modernismo*, a school of thought that advocated an aesthetic approach to life, aristocratic taste, and a shunning of material pursuits. While not sharing Sarmiento's admiration for the type of national development marshalled by the United States, Rodó did coincide with him in espousing a racial hierarchy that assigned greater value to those groups displaying "the skull size of the thinking races," as we read in his famous 1900 essay *Ariel*.[23] Unlike Sarmiento, the Mexican philosopher, politician, and man of letters José Vasconcelos (b. 1882–d. 1959) did not aspire to racial purity. Perhaps not wishing to delude himself with yearnings for unmitigated whiteness given the massive inter-racial breeding that had already taken place in the Americas, Vasconcelos opted for embracing amalgamation and positing it as a strength, one that made the region the birthplace of the best race, a "cosmic race" that consisted of a fusion of all races. Articulated in his 1925 essay *La raza cósmica*, his cosmic vision could not extricate itself from the stain of the region's pervasive racism in that his "new" composite breed emerged out of a coming together of elements that he regarded as unequal in value. Whiteness, the "superior race," provided the organizing principle that allowed the "inferior races" to subordinate themselves to it. The latter would derive benefit from the virtues therein acquired, undergoing a process of "voluntary extinction."[24]

The notion of "the cosmic race" starts out as a lofty ideal promising a de-racialization of the world with Latin America leading the way. But the racist logic that had educated Vasconcelos ended up cheapening the lofty potential of his notion, which declined conceptually to a mere regurgitation of the old vulgar equation that granted "white blood" the power to improve the genes of the lower races via carnal commingling. Vasconcelos wished for blacks, Indians, and Asians ("the inferior races") without having to kill them by having their difference dissolve within the purifying waters of the white gene pool. He thereby voiced what is arguably the genocidal ideation characteristic of the champions of civilization in the Americas.

# Killing Difference and Nation-Building in the Americas

The homicidal approach to difference has pervaded the minds of civilizers in the region from the outset of the nation. Professor Wolfgang Mieder of the University of Vermont in his study of anti-Indian sayings refers to the motto "Civilization or death to all American savages" recorded as an entry for 1779 in the journal of Major James Harris, who served in the Continental Army during the Revolutionary War.[25] Whatever precedents it may have had in the earlier colonial periods, its life during the republican period could be documented into the late 1950s.[26] Nor is there much reason for surprise here. Killing Indians and taking over their lands was often a way of getting ahead in the world in the United States. Andrew Jackson (b. 1767–d. 1845), a powerful slave owner who became the seventh president of the United States, first established his credentials as a foe of natives in the Creek War (1813–1814) and the First Seminole War (1817–1818), both of which culminated with the defeated Indians having to relinquish territories for occupancy by white settlers. As President, Jackson signed and advocated for the Indian Removal Act, which set the policy that thenceforward would remove native people from their ancestral homelands in the southeastern United States, the area that the government deemed most desirable for development by whites. Indians would then relocate to designated lands in a vaguely defined region west of the Mississippi called the central United States. President Jackson articulated his case to the US Congress on December 7, 1830, with an awareness of the compassion that envisioning tens of thousands of aborigines forced to march over a thousand miles dragging their belongings from the Appalachian Mountains to Oklahoma could trigger in many lawmakers. This human drama, especially the portion of it corresponding to the Cherokee, would become known emblematically as the "Trail of Tears." Self-assured that the removal policy would advance "the general interests of the human race," President Jackson shrugged off the occasion for regret:

> Philanthropy could not wish to see this continent restored to the condition in which it was found by our forefathers. What good man would prefer a country covered with forests, and ranged by a few thousand savages, to our extensive republic studded with cities, towns, and prosperous farms embellished with all the improvements which art can devise, or industry execute occupied by more than twelve millions of happy people, and filled with all the blessings of liberty, civilization and religion.[27]

The president, then, had no qualms about formulating a view of "liberty, civilization, and religion" based on a policy that would inflict wholesale excruciating pain on the population native to the land his ancestors had usurped. Structurally every person of European heritage, whether immigrant or US-born, who would advance their dream of prosperity through access to land made available to them by the policy of Indian removal, entered knowingly or otherwise into a racial compact which explicitly elevated the value of their bodies, minds, and lives over those of the expendable natives. Such a state of affairs, which makes the elevation of some inextricable from the diminishment of others, allows for racism to operate as a tool of advancement that becomes necessary. The prejudicial lens that a civilization built on and sustained by inequality across difference of phenotype and ancestry instills in the populations becomes hardened by virtue of its necessity. Once the logic of disparagement and devaluing the lives of people of other phenotypes and ancestries becomes solidified as a core organizing principle of the civilization, it functions as a frame of reference irrespective of the differential degrees of power and prestige separating one powerful white settler from another of modest means.

While Jackson was establishing his trustworthiness as a nation builder implementing policies inhumane to some but fortunate to others for the good of the country, his Uruguayan colleague Jose Fructuoso Rivera y Toscana (b. 1784–d. 1854) was doing likewise elsewhere in the hemisphere. As the first constitutional president of Uruguay, Fructuoso led the Salsipuedes massacre, named for the gulch where the event took place in July 1831, against the Charrúa Indians. Finding them incompatible with the vision that he and his peers had formed for the newly created sovereignty, he convened the Charrúa chiefs to a peace talk at the appointed site. Eduardo Galeano evokes the moment thus: "The chiefs came accompanied by their people. They were promised peace, jobs, respect. They ate, drank, and continued drinking until they passed out. Then, by sword and bayonet they were executed."[28] The president then called the production of some five hundred corpses "a civilizing mission to put an end to the raids of the savage hordes."[29] Mass killings of people deemed too different for absorption into the body politic has served as a staple in nation building at the hands of Hispanics or Anglos north and south of the hemisphere.

Spanish-dominated colonial societies spread in regions north of the Rio Grande when expeditions of conquest began to succeed following the Florida failure of Juan Ponce de León (b. 1460–d. 1521) first in 1513 and later in 1521 as well as that of Pánfilo de Narváez (b. 1479–d. 1528) in 1527. The Spanish reduced the indigenous populations they came into contact with, and their civilizing process created a social system that placed the diverse groups whose lot it was to inhabit those parts on different tiers of human value. The mission system in the regions of California, Texas, New Mexico, Colorado, Arizona, and Florida leaves little doubt of the unequal arrangement therein created, with the encomienda providing indigenous labor power for the benefit of the Catholic Church and individual beneficiaries of land grants issued by the Spanish Crown. We can get a glimpse of that history from the utterances of some of the most important precursors of Latino literature. The California literary artist María Amparo Ruiz de Burton (b. 1832–d. 1895) and the Tejana folklore specialist Jovita González (b. 1904–d. 1983) dedicated their interventions in fiction and scholarship respectively to evoking the cultural heritage and the social advancements that their forbears had brought to California and Texas. They felt compelled to the legacy of their ancestors as a way to respond to the attempt at obliteration that the memory of Hispanic civilization in the Southwest had endured since the advent of the Anglocentric cultural regime that predominated in the schools and history books following the 1848 Guadalupe Hidalgo Treaty whereby, as a war booty following the victorious invasion of Mexico in 1846, the United States acquired the formerly Mexican territories north of the Rio Grande.

Ruiz de Burton's novel *The Squatter and the Don* (1885, reprinted in 1992) is a text in which the author negotiates her reconciliation with US domination of California with intermarriage between upper-class Californios and their new rulers. In its mediating role the novel seeks to set the record straight regarding the greatness that was in California prior to arrival of the Anglos. Don Mariano, the land-owning patriarch of the Alamar family who figures centrally in the plot, speaks amply about the pedigree of people like him who had inherited vast land holdings. They had first acquired "huge tracts of land" as a grant made initially by the Spanish Crown and later by the Mexican government to those citizens who would develop "the wilderness" to turn it into villages and cities: "They also employed Indians, who thus began to be less wild. Then, in times of Indian outbreaks, the landowners with their servants would turn out, as in feudal times in Europe, to assist in the defense of the missions and the openly settled country threatened by the savages."[30] Similarly, coming generations after Ruiz de Burton, the educator Jovita González traces her genealogy back to the Olivares colonial settlers in a brief autobiography included in her posthumous collection of pre-Anglo Texas folklore

*Dew on the Thorn* (1997). She starts with Don Juan José, the "first of the Olivares, who came in 1748 as Surveyors of the Spanish Crown. At the time the Indian infested region north of Nuevo León had been created into the new province of Nuevo Santander" and "a military expedition came with a two-fold purpose, namely to subdue the warlike Indian tribes and to look for suitable locations for settlements in the region between Rio Grande and the Nueces River."[31] The adversarial interaction of the author's ancestors with the native peoples whose lands the former had invaded continued for several generations, as she makes clear in the reference to "Don José Alejandro, the oldest son and successor of Captain Olivares. José Alejandro flourished at the time of Mexico's independence struggle from Spain, but "whether as the subject of his Catholic Majesty or citizen of the newly created Republic," his chief interest "remained the same, to protect his family from the Indian invasions and to increase his holdings."[32] It seems that Gonzalez did not have a sense of irony keen enough to realize the oddity of using the term "invasions" to describe indigenous responses to the Hispanic settlers or to see those "invasions" as causally related to the resolve of the settlers to grow their "holdings" which necessarily involved clearing the "Indian infested" territories of their native occupants.

Neither Ruiz de Burton nor González appeared to have a problem with the representation of the aborigines of California or Texas as a historical nuisance that their Spanish forbears had had to deal with as they used the land grants they had received to find "suitable locations for settlements" or build "villages" or "increase [their] holdings." The idea that the aborigines may actually have felt it as an inconvenience to have among them the invasive presence of greedy Spaniards, violent, heavily armed with weapons of mass destruction, and carrying on their bodies germs that proved lethal and played a key note in the decimation of the Native population seemed unavailable to these worthy ancestors of Latino literature. Here among US Hispanics we see the recurring pattern discernible in sites of settler colonialism, namely the peculiar mental operation whereby the invading settlers quickly come to see themselves as natives to the sites they intrude upon and just as they quickly come to see the aborigines as external to those places, an outside unwanted presence that creates discomfort for the somehow autochthonous aliens. New Mexico, the land that received the 1598 expedition of conquest by Juan de Oñate (b. 1550–d. 1626), and of the resistance of the Acoma Pueblo, witnessed unspeakable levels of violence by the invaders. The Spanish butchered nearly a thousand men, women, and children, leaving only some five hundred survivors of whom, after a trial judged by Oñate himself, the conqueror sentenced most of the five hundred survivors to twenty years of forced personal servitude with a foot cut off to all men over the age of twenty-five.[33] A native of Zacatecas in New Spain (colonial Mexico), hence a proto-Latin American, Oñate did not come to New Mexico as a European invader. He was a Criollo fighting a local population, and that proximity to the "enemy" may have intensified the degree of his cruelty and his lack of regard for the lives of indigenous peoples of the region. The conquest of the Acoma Pueblo was memorialized in *Historia de la Nueva México* (1610), an 11,338-line epic poem in thirty-four cantos by Gaspar Pérez de Villagrá, also a Creole, having been born in Pueblas, New Spain. Literary scholars

Genaro Padilla and María Herrera-Sobek have evocatively stressed the extent to which the poet, though operating as a scribe of the colonizing enterprise, somehow managed to convey some of the humanity of the Acoma and of the atrocious cruelty of the fate that befell them at the hand of their ruthless Christian conquerors.[34]

By the end of the nineteenth century, nearly three hundred years since the arrival of Oñate, some elite Hispanic voices still seemed to adhere to the view that regarded Indians as an unwelcome presence in the land. Illustrative of such a case, José Escobar, a Mexican immigrant who arrived in New Mexico in the late 1880s and became immersed in cultural advocacy on behalf of the literary pursuits and overall print culture of Spanish-speaking Hispanos in the region, spoke scornfully of the indigenous people there. Escobar excelled as a newspaperman, and with support from Colorado lawmaker and cultural broker Casimiro Barela, he started the newspaper *Las Dos Repúblicas* in January 1896.[35] In the July 1896 issue of the paper, Escobar published an article entitled "Progreso Literario de Nuevo México" in which he outlined the advancement made in the state by Hispanos, especially their literary pursuits, their work as journalists, and in general, their enterprising thirst in areas related to print culture and intellectual activities. The article on the one hand stresses the inroads made by Hispanos in the decades since the arrival of the new political order that stemmed from the 1848 takeover by the Anglos and the emergence of a status quo that the columnist associated with "progress and civilization." On the other hand, the piece also wants to acknowledge the "natural inclination" of the Hispanos in the territories "to seek enlightenment," a disposition that he attributes to their repository of cultural values spawned by their own Hispanic heritage. Escobar reports that prior to the recent decade of auspicious development, people there had to contend with structural impediments that stunted their "magnificent natural talent," namely their isolation from the "great urban centers" in the immense desert lands from Missouri to the banks of the Rio Grande. Most important, they had to occupy themselves constantly with the task of saving their lives and their property from "the herds of savage barbarians who by fire and sword attacked the burgeoning colonies of the civilized Creoles."[36]

Like Ruiz de Burton in California and González in Texas, Escobar, writing about New Mexico from the pages of his Colorado-based newspaper, found it natural to speak of Native Americans, the original inhabitants of the land, as making trouble for the Hispano settlers, who by then had so acclimated their minds to the idea of the aborigines as intruders that they thought of themselves as the true natives: "nativos" being a term that Escobar uses to refer to New Mexican Hispanos (NP). This perception about the Indians seems to have cut across levels of privilege. Escobar, at the time, was by no means a major stakeholder economically or politically in New Mexico. In fact, he speaks as if from a social margin when defending Hispanos and their heritage from the inimical gaze of Anglos. His article more than once refers to the aspersions cast upon them in the English language and the Eastern press. Escobar's perception matches that of those Hispanos who operated as equal partners with Anglos as players in the existing status quo, as is the case of the first territorial governor of New Mexico Miguel Antonio Otero Jr.

In the first volume of his memoirs *My Life on the Frontier: 1864–1884* (1935, reprinted 2007), Otero represents Native Americans occasionally as a source of amusement, as when he tells of a spring night 1877 involving him and his friend Neil Newall, both teenagers, during a long journey on horseback. Having gotten tired, they picked a spot to camp and went to sleep, only to realize when they finally woke up that they had made their camp close to "a large band of Ute Indians who were on a deer hunt." To their pleasant surprise, they found that the Ute hunters "were not on the warpath," displayed "a most friendly mood," and several came over to their camp, bringing "a nice piece of venison" that "we added to the breakfast menu and ate with much relish."[37] But, for the most part, the Native population appears as a source of stress, as when the business of Buffalo hunting came to Hays City, and it turned out to be "dangerous" as a way to make a living "because of the Indians."[38] The "more venturesome" hunters took the risk anyway because "there was good money in hides."[39] The narrator recalls seeing "thousands of dead buffalo on the plains, killed solely for their hides."[40] As the son of a businessman whose warehouse stored buffalo hides and wolf skins for shipment to Eastern markets, with correspondingly hefty profits, Otero remembers "distinctly that at one time we had more than thirty thousand buffalo hides and five thousand grey-wolf skins.[41] But nowhere do Otero's recollections pause to consider why Indians would want to harass buffalo hunters and cause them to desist from the killing of an animal whose extermination more than one US military strategist had equated with the destruction of Native Americans.

One colonel in 1867 told a contrite wealthy hunter weighed with a heavy conscience after shooting thirty bulls in one trip, "Kill every buffalo you can! Every buffalo dead is and Indian gone."[42] General William Tecumseh Sherman (b. 1820–d. 1891) in a May 10, 1868, letter to General Sheridan, contended that Indians (the Sioux) would go to Nebraska for hunting, refusing to commit to a life with a plow under white control, as long as the buffalo roamed those parts, hence his sublime idea: "I think it would be wise to invite all the sportsmen of England and America there this fall for a Grand Buffalo hunt, and make one grand sweep of them all."[43] The buffalo had once numbered more than 30 million, but only a few hundred remained in the wild by the end of the nineteenth century. Exterminating the Indians from the central plains region between the Platte and Arkansas seemed to Sherman a prerequisite to the smooth operation of the railroads, stage lines, and telegraph there. That the large-scale, systematic killing of the buffalo, in addition to the profit it yielded, sought to advance Sherman's genocidal vision of civilization may be discerned from a September 23, 1868, letter he wrote to his brother John. There the general encapsulated his gory aspiration thus: "The more we kill this year, the less will have to be killed the next year, for the more I see of these Indians, the more convinced I am that they all have to be killed or maintained as a species of paupers. Their attempts at civilization are simply ridiculous."[44] William Cody, better known as Buffalo Bill, joined the US cavalry at age seventeen, and he earned his nickname for the 4,280 buffalo he claimed to have killed in one eighteen-month stretch. By contributing to the near extermination of the buffalo, thereby prompting the radical shrinking of the indigenous population of the territory now known as the United States,

Cody played a key role as builder of US civilization of the same kind as the Otero family with its warehouses replete with tens of thousands of bison skins was playing.

Otero's insensitivity to the humanity of Indians, whom many by the period evoked in his pages had already come to view as a "vanishing race," may be seen as a distinguishing feature of the racial location he occupied as a white Spanish-descended American devoid of the slightest hint of conflict with the prevailing white supremacist status quo. That his disdain for indigenous humanity extended to other non-European descended populations seems clear from a recollection Otero shares about a childhood moment in Leavenworth, eastern Kansas, where his family relocated in 1864 after his father partnered with C. R. Moorhead and Company, the firm founded by the Missouri-born businessman who would subsequently become an influential banker in El Paso, Texas. Otero recalls an incident around 1866, a time when Leavenworth housed a large number of infantry and cavalry Union soldiers, a needed military presence given that "the animosity between the anti-slavery and the pro-slavery factions" there "was still red hot."[45] Thinking back on those days of "hatred and bitter feeling," he reasons that much of the tension "might have been avoided had those in authority on the border between Kansas and Missouri used cooler judgment and more temperate means." He cites as an egregious example "a stupid policy on the part of the commander officer of Fort Leavenworth to place, as he sometimes did, negro officers with the rank of lieutenant, captain, or even major, in command over Southern sympathizers who might have been arrested for merely expressing an opinion."[46] He found such appointments "unfortunate and probably unnecessary," only serving "to inflame the pro-slavery people," and becoming "the direct cause of many of the killings that marked these years."[47] Ironically, the presence of Union soldiers in Leavenworth, as with all other Southern cities that the army occupied in the early years of Reconstruction, had sought precisely to elevate the social standing of blacks by enabling them to enjoy the civil rights of which slavery had deprived them, and that could not be done without disrupting the white supremacist expectation to see them only in positions of subservience. We find Otero here indicting as "stupid" and "unnecessary" a situation that put some blacks in positions of authority over some whites for the discomfort it caused those who viewed them as inherently inferior to them on account of their ancestry and phenotype. In short, Otero regarded the racial sensibility of negrophobic Southern whites as deserving of greater attention than the desire to affirm the equality of blacks before the law.

No less than President Jackson or General Sherman, Otero, like Ruiz de Burton, Escobar, and González—forerunners of Latina/o letters in the United States—partake of perhaps the most distinct sensibility spawned by the history that gave rise to the societies that emerged in the western hemisphere. When it came to the realm of social relations, that sensibility was first and foremost racial just as the ontological basis of selfhood became primordially racial. With racism in ascendancy as the dominant logic informing social relations among groups with disparate ancestries and phenotypes, the racial principle came to inform the imagination of the descendants of the conquerors as wells as the descendants of the vanquished. Those who had endured disparagement and abuse because of their heritage and appearance were not exempt from the formative influence that the ambient and pervasive racist literacy had on the societies involved. In many respects, the prejudicial lens that rendered a person inferior in the eyes of assessors who fancied themselves superior, worked as a powerful pedagogy that typically instilled in the person in question a way of seeing the world which he or she would subsequently utilize as a main prism through to look at humanity. Contrary to the often-repeated mantra that only those brandishing concrete power to diminish the humanity of others can be racist, one could reasonably argue that the opposite is true. The less empowered the person in a racist milieu, the greater the chance that the dominant prevailing ideology will operate as the sole system of value available to shape his or her worldview because the structures of racism will have precluded his or her access to alternative outlooks. It should raise no alarm to find members of groups that have historically endured abuse and disparagement subjecting other populations to the same treatment that they have received. The oppressed often becomes the oppressor, as specialists working with adults who maltreat their children or abuse their spouses too often verify.

Hispanic violence against the Chinese in mid-nineteenth-century California during the Gold Rush recurs as a leifmotif in the 1854 novel *The Life and Adventures of Joaquín Murieta* by the Anglo-Cherokee author John Rollin Ridge (Yellow Bird). While the narrative traces Joaquín's route as he seeks to vindicate the wrongs committed by Anglos against Mexicans, its pages sporadically point to a pervasive predisposition against the Chinese among the characters. At one point, Joaquin intervenes to save a "Chinaman" from the murderous hand of his fierce associate Three-Fingered Jack, who tries to explain his criminal impulse by saying he "can't help it" as he finds the Chinese "such easy work" apart from confessing to loving "to smell" the blood of a Chinaman.[48] Reis, one of Joaquín's lieutenants, boasts of having killed 150 "Chinamen," a record that the narrator explains by pointing to the convenient preference of Reis to kill "Chinamen" instead of "Americans [i.e., whites] for no one cared for so alien a class, and they were left to shift for themselves." Outside of literature, the historical record concerning the 1871 Chinese Massacre in Los Angeles shows at least three Hispanics—Esteban Alvarado, Refugio Botello, and Jesús Martínez—among the eight men convicted of manslaughter and sentenced to prison terms in San Quentin, but who on appeal had their penalty overturned due to a technicality.[49] A mob of some five hundred white or mestizo people filled with anti-Chinese sentiment barged into Chinatown on Calle de los Negros, beating, robbing, and killing the enclave's residents, leaving a toll of some twenty neighbors dead by hanging. Sinophobic state legislation eighteen years earlier had deprived Asians of the right to testify in court against white persons, thereby depriving them of an important portion of protection before the law.[50]

During the 1870s, the workingman's party of California, led by Irish immigrant Dennis Kearney—that is, a member of an ethnic group that had endured intense vilification from the Anglo press—declared war on Chinese railroad workers with the slogan "The Chinese Must Go!" as its rallying cry.[51] Such a climate of animosity helped to galvanize the adversarial racial sentiment that culminated in the passing of the Chinese Exclusion Act of 1882. Initially the act set out to bar immigrants from

China into the United States for a period of ten years, getting renewed for another ten years in 1892 and then declared permanent in 1902, remaining in effect during four more decades until 1943, when it was repealed. Ironically, the end of Chinese exclusion after six decades occurred at a moment when another Asian-descended population had become the focus of ethno-racial antipathy in the United States. On February 19, 1942, as dictated by President Franklin D. Roosevelt's Executive Order 9066, the internment of people of Japanese ancestry had begun in response to the December 7, 1941, attack on Pearl Harbor by the air force of the Japanese Empire. Anti-Japanese sentiment in the country precedes the Pearl Harbor event, dating back to the migration of Japanese people to the West Coast and their successful incursion in farming and other industries.

Witness the famous photograph of the front porch of a wooden house with a woman pointing with her left arm to a huge sign nailed to the upper part just below the roof with a message, warning, "Japs keep moving. This is a White Man's Neighborhood" (dated *ca.* 1920 by Getty Images). But with the military action by Japanese forces against the United States, animosity became normalized. This is so much the case that for its December 22, 1941, issue, the influential *Life* magazine published a public service piece that aimed to instruct readers on the differences between a "Jap" and a Chinese person. The magazine editors expressed concern over the violent attacks lately suffered by Chinese Americans whom angry "US citizens" had mistaken for Japanese. Since, on the international war scene, China had joined forces with the Allies against the Axis powers (Germany, Italy, Japan), the article sought to instruct *Life* readers to distinguish "friendly Chinese" from "enemy alien Japs."[52] Nothing in the article seems aimed at advising readers to refrain from public acts of violence such as those recently endured by Chinese Americans. Its implicit motivation was to provide readers with necessary mentorship about each group's appearance, overall demeanor, and body language so that they could identify their victims with greater accuracy. A photo of journalist Joe Chiang wearing a prominent sign on his chest announces the carrier's identity thus: "Chinese reporter. Not Japanese Please." The image shows a resourceful member of a minority community officially despised until quite recently making quick use of the relative privilege occasioned by the reduced Sinophobia brought about by the place of China as a member of the Allied forces. Chiang wore his sign to ensure safe admission to a White House Press Conference.[53] The ancestry of the Chinese had become temporarily better than that of the Japanese. Another subtitle in the *Life* article reads: "How to Tell Your Friends from the Japs."

Akin to this odd mutation in the identity of the current ethno-racial adversary, African Americans, it appears, could not afford to allow themselves an inkling of human solidarity regarding the pitiable destitution and disempowerment endured by Japanese Americans during the internment period. Maya Angelou meditates on the phenomenon in her autobiography *I Know Why the Caged Bird Sings* (1969; reprinted 2009), where she devotes a penetrating passage to the psychopathology of one disadvantaged group that finds itself gaining relative empowerment as a result of having been temporarily replaced by another minority group that had become the object of fiercer acrimony.

Angelou recalls that in 1942 African Americans from the rural South jumped at the chance to access housing, business ventures, and a new solvency that opened up for them in San Francisco by the removal of the West Coast Japanese to the internment camps. They built new homes and livelihoods there without even daring to name the disturbing connection between their relative upliftment and the coerced absence of the Japanese. They arrived in San Francisco after long years of laboring as sharecroppers, uncompensated mine workers, and the other indignities associated with the Jim Crow period. This arrival offered them the opportunity to have something of their own after their abject poverty and subsistence living. In a way, they could not afford the luxury of human solidarity. However, the narrator ventures to speculate that racial othering may have also played a role in enabling African Americans to cope with their morally difficult bind. In her view, despite their white skin hue, the evacuees had a language, set of customs, and facial features that made them profoundly alien to the black newcomers. As such, the narrator surmises, the interned Japanese "were not white folks," and "since they didn't have to be feared, neither did they have to be considered."[54] One can hardly avoid considering the disturbing implication of the alienness in question. Hypothetically, the humanity of negrophobic white supremacists who had long diminished black personhood, having attained familiarity by virtue of the hegemonic reach of their civilizing violence, would have had a better chance of triggering solidarity in those African Americans who were newcomers to San Francisco.

## NEGROPHOBIA AND CIVILIZATION

In the United States, African Americans suffered on their backs the devastating consequences of the racial passion harbored by the likes of South Carolina statesman John C. Calhoun (b. 1782–d. 1850), a resolute supporter of slave-owning interests in the US South who held the office of vice president of the United States under presidents John Quincy Adams and Andrew Jackson. Ardent in the credo that professed the unequal distribution of human worth among peoples of varying phenotypes and ancestries, Calhoun stood out for his vehement defense of black slavery by refuting its condemnation as "sinful and odious, in the sight of God and man" to define it, instead, as "a good—a positive good." Convinced that people of European descent were superior (i.e., belonged to a higher form of humanity) vis-à-vis the enslaved African-descended population, he preached that the captivity of the latter benefitted those in bondage no less than it profited their masters. He argued that if the slavers derived material well-being from the labor of their slaves, so did the captives derive improvement in their human caliber through contact with their superiors. "I appeal to facts," says Calhoun, and then, without the slightest gesture to engage in demonstration, he asserts that "Never before has the black race of Central Africa, from the dawn of history to the present day, attained a condition so civilized and so improved, not only physically, but morally and intellectually. [They came] among us in a low, degraded, and savage condition," and, in just a few generations, as result of "the fostering care of our institutions," they have risen to their "present comparative civilized condition."[55]

Calhoun spent much of his public life promoting his view of the inherent inferiority of blacks and the debt of gratitude they owed to their white masters for the relative racial upgrade they had undergone during their *benign bondage* under a superior people. In so doing, he contributed to creating in the US South a climate of rigid intolerance for the very idea that slavery could ever end, or that, should its end ever come, that free blacks could possibly partake of the condition of civil equality as citizens under the law. To forestall the likelihood of such an affront, the South seceded from the United States in 1861, prompting the Civil War, an armed conflict that lasted until 1865, leaving a toll of nearly a million Union and Confederate soldiers dead. With the defeat of the secessionists, the emancipation of the slaves by the administration of Abraham Lincoln, and the Reconstruction measures dictated by the US Congress to implement the newly granted citizenship rights of the freed population, the South experienced the new status quo as a humiliation and became further entrenched in the contempt for racial equality fomented by Calhoun and other obdurate ideologues of white supremacy going back to the negrophobic excesses of Thomas Jefferson's *Notes on the State of Virginia* (1785; reprinted 1984).

Putting to effective use the implements of violence, the South set out to resist and dismantle the policies of Reconstruction, with the freeman population as its incessant target. The engraving "The First Vote" by London-born American illustrator Alfred Rudolph Waud (b. 1828–d. 1891), which appeared in the November 16, 1867, issue of *Harper's Weekly*, records a memorable election held in Virginia on October 22, 1867. Reconstruction forces still empowered, a military order had granted African Americans the right to elect and appear as candidates for delegates to the convention that would set out to write a new state constitution. Nearly 106,000 blacks registered to vote, with over 93,000 actually voting to select the delegates, and the final 105-member roster of those who would represent the state in the 1868 Virginia Constitutional Convention included twenty-four African Americans. The slice of history captured by Waud's engraving speaks to the zeal with which freedmen set out to reclaim their besmirched humanity by asserting themselves as civic subjects on the political arena. With the assurance that their right as US citizens "to vote shall not be denied or abridged" by municipal, state, or federal authority "on account of race, color, or previous condition of servitude," as stipulated in the Fifteenth Amendment to the US Constitution, ratified on February 3, 1870, African Americans had sound reason to believe that they had a chance.

However, by the time of the ratification of the Fifteenth Amendment, paramilitary terrorist organizations staffed initially by former confederate soldiers, chiefly the Ku Klux Klan (KKK), the White Man's League, and the Red Shirts, founded in 1865, 1874, and 1875 respectively, had already shown how far they were willing to go to prevent black freedom, economic opportunity, suffrage, and citizenship from normalizing. They had already established a record of coercive, destructive, and ferocious actions aimed at repressing the voting and overall civil rights of freemen and their white supporters, numbering countless acts of homicide, vandalism, and chilling threats. On April 20,

1871, the US Congress passed the Third Force Act (a.k.a. Ku Klux Act) authorizing President Ulysses S. Grant to "declare martial law, impose heavy penalties against terrorist organizations, and use military force to suppress the Ku Klux Klan."[56] But the words of the president on December 7, 1874, during his sixth State of the Union address rang threnodic in their lamentation for the continued intransigence of the violent element:

> I regret to say that with preparation for the late election decided indications appeared in some localities in the Southern States of a determination, by acts of violence and intimidation, to deprive citizens of the freedom of the ballot.... [M]urders enough were committed to spread terror among those whose political action was to be suppressed, if possible, by these intolerant and criminal proceedings.[57]

The state of affairs evoked by President Grant continued unabated until the swearing-in as US President of Rutherford B. Hayes in 1877. Hayes came to the White House burdened with a "compromise" that required him to make concessions to the white supremacist leadership of the formerly Confederate states. Extending an olive branch to the steadfast champions for "state rights," the new administration agreed to desist from further attempts to enforce militarily the civil and voting rights of blacks in the South, proceeding to withdrew federal troops from those Southern states that still had them. The Reconstruction era thus came to an end, and from that moment onward African-descended citizens would have to fend for themselves in a staunchly white supremacist and rabidly negrophobic region. It did not take long for the short-lived civic enthusiasm of the freeman population to relent under the weight of a barrage of aggressive measures aimed at reducing them to a condition of near servitude. By 1904, in a state like North Carolina, where an African-descended middle class had once thrived, black voter turnout had plummeted to near zero.[58] The revolting actions of murderous hordes created what amounted to a culture of extra-judicial killings of African Americans by means of the well-known lynchings, gruesome spectacles that attracted large audiences of amused onlookers, including judges, police officers, and parents with their children.

Typically the bloodthirsty conveners would set their eyes on a black person either convicted, accused, or simply rumored to have done wrong, including offenses as trivial as whistling to a white woman or displaying a cocky demeanor in the presence of whites. They would identify the whereabouts of their targets, yank them from their dwelling, workplace, or even county jail, drag them to the spot designated for the public executions, and hang them usually from a tree. Members of the posse or the audience added their distinct flourishes, such as setting the hanging bodies afire, mutilating them or disfiguring them, while some would capture the gory scenes in photographs that they would later gleefully share with relatives, friends, and acquaintances. Just as law enforcement and court personnel frequently figured among the cheering crowd, the press covered these events quite neutrally, as one can gather from the compilation *100 Years of Lynching*, edited by the publisher and social critic Ralph Ginzburg (1962). Occasionally media venues conveyed a note of indignation, and in the South, as the daily newspaper *Montgomery Advertiser* illustrates, one could find them ostensibly decrying the illegal actions of the lynch mobs while making sure to editorialize their contempt for blacks by speaking against the posse's choice to take the law in their own hands while lending legitimacy to the indignation that had driven whites to resort to such measures against criminous blacks.[59]

Beside the lurking threat of violence and the strident awareness of having been forsaken by the law, African Americans in the South stood on juridically hostile ground. Supreme Court Judge Roger B. Taney (b. 1777–d. 1864) had declared that people of African descent had entered the law of the land "as beings of an inferior order, and altogether unfit to associate with the white race," and that on account of such inferiority, "they had no right that the white man was bound to respect"[60] The South seemed bent on fulfilling in every aspect of the daily lives of African Americans the vision of social relations made explicit by Justice Taney's baneful majority opinion. Thus, lawmakers and related authorities applied themselves assiduously to the task of crafting laws, statutes, and ordinances deliberately intended to curtail the mobility of freemen, diminish their economic options, block their chances of self-sufficiency, render them subservient to their former masters or whites in general, force them into an invariable attitude of meekness and self-effacement, drill in them a sense of their lesser human value, and make prohibitions against them so numerous that they would find it hard to avoid infraction. The law in the South, known as Jim Crow laws or the Black Code, made it illegal for blacks to be without a job, to assemble without the supervision of a white person, to carry a weapon, to pursue literacy, to engage in miscegenation, to gamble, to use obscene language, to spit while on the road, to sell alcoholic beverages, to violate a contract with a white employer, to raise their voice in the presence of a white woman, to practice illegal voting, and to incur in false pretense, among numerous other illicit acts.[61] Bound to the will of unscrupulous white landowners via sharecropping farming deals designed to keep them invariably in debt, freemen languished in pervasive vulnerability before the law. Contemporaneous with this dynamic sprouting of edicts, rules, and regulations that criminalized much of ordinary life for blacks in the region, bringing about a disproportionate rise in the frequency of their incarceration, an early version of the prison industrial complex developed that made incarcerated black bodies a lucrative source of wealth for private industries and state governments. Convict leasing, which provided a cheap source of labor to private enterprise, became a major source of income for state and local governments in the region, with Alabama figuring among the first states to realize the economic blessings of selling the labor of black inmates to mining, road gangs, lumber camps, farms, and other private enterprises.[62] The growing use of uncompensated black labor turned into a win-win proposition for the companies that tapped into the convict leasing pool of workers. The companies could maximize their capital gains by pushing workers beyond the limits of human endurance without having to answer to anyone since the state authorities supplying the labor force did not require contractors to account for the physical or mental well-being of the convicts. Should the inmates perish due to exhaustion, extreme corporal punishment, or illness contracted in the unsanitary and pestilential sites where they were forced to toil, the contractors would simply go back to the state to procure the needed replacements, which the latter would gladly replenish. Correlating the high volume of incarceration sustained by blacks with the desire of state and municipal authorities to have a ready supply of bodies to satisfy leasing demands, observers of this lugubrious chapter of American history have pointed to a disturbing pattern. Local records show a swift intensification of black arrests precisely around the time when private company scouts were expected in town to fill their seasonal convict leasing quotas. This convenient arrangement that made fortunes for private industry while sustaining the finances of state and local governments in the South went on for generations as Douglas Blackmon has carefully documented in *Slavery by Another Name* (2008), a historical expose that became the basis for a 2012 PBS documentary by the same title. Kept in place by legislators, clergymen, scholars, educators, public servants, and business leaders whose impetuous racism had driven them to regard their absolute power over the lives of blacks as their un-renounceable birthright, this malevolent deal extended black slavery in the South, with the rest of the country looking on and often reaping economic benefits, for over eighty years after the signing of the Emancipation Declaration. Members of the Northeastern intelligentsia—scholars, policymakers, journalists, and the like—even allowed themselves to be educated by Southern prison statistics about the criminal proclivities of the black race instead of recognizing the high rates of incarceration as resulting from a judicial scam devised by negrophobic whites in the effort to prolong their control of a people they valued only as capital gain.[63] Southern malfeasance prevailed in the application of the law to African Americans during the eight decades when Jim Crow policies reigned supreme, creating the stereotype of the black as proverbially criminal and dangerous. Today that biased perception still informs the instincts of law enforcement agents, which probably explains the frequency with which, when dealing with a black suspect, white cops will resort to lethal force to avert an imminent danger to their lives even if the suspect in question is unarmed and running away from rather than toward them.

## Racism as Knowledge

The foregoing background of inexorably racialized relations, with racial reason and racial personhood inscribed in the texture of the region's history over four centuries, can support the contention that in the western hemisphere one is racist by default. Recognition, acceptance, and valuing of other people's humanity across ancestral and phenotypical difference occurs in the region most often by experiencing a sort of de-education. No doubt the region has long harbored cases of nonracist persons from particularly enlightened homes or communities, "enlightened" in that they display the capacity to view their fellow human beings devoid of the prejudicial lens with which centuries of pervasive and naturalized ethno-racial inequality have equipped the various sectors of the population. However, for most others in the Americas, racism is where one starts from. Freeing oneself from the overwhelming power of the prejudicial lens would normally entail a moral transformation brought on by some humane political awakening allied with an epistemological break that tears asunder long-held assumptions about the structure of the world and the desirable kind of rapport among the peoples inhabiting it. Experiencing a sort of epiphany, one would free oneself from some of the core racial tenets that inform the worldview of the region's inhabitants, tenets that have largely determined their way of knowing the history of which they are a part and have shaped the logic orienting the way they treat one another and envision one another's future.

As a phenomenon that has mediated social relations in modern history, race stems from racism, namely, the act of condemning, impairing, or seeking to reduce other people due to their different ancestry or phenotype. It emerges from contexts in which people of varied origins and appearances have come together in situations marked by unequal relations of force, with the mightier dominating the weaker, especially if the former find it useful to condemn, impair, or reduce the latter in a manner that explicitly stresses the ancestral and phenotypical difference which they embody. In other words, if racism becomes a factor in circumstances of domination, the concept of race then comes to the fore as a taxonomic tool owing to the desire of the victors to classify the vanquished with an eye on placing them in ontological pigeonholes that become identities. Ethnocentrism results from the common tendency of humans to judge unfamiliar others by means of one's own ways as a normative model or frame of reference. Upon exposure to knowledge about the unfamiliar other, the ethnocentric gaze may give way to an understanding of the other's unfamiliarity as a recognition of the ample diversity of humanity. Racism differs from ethnocentrism in that, unlike the latter, it operates as self-sufficient knowledge and it comes equipped with its own intransigent system of self-validation. It is a way of knowing that organizes the facts of history and social reality in a manner that reinforces the precepts of a racial epistemology that elevates ancestry and phenotype to the rank of *primum mobile* of the human condition. It finds the dominion of the conquering races and the subjection of the vanquished ones inscribed irrevocably in the structure of the world, the order of nature, and the will of God.

Because it is rooted so firmly in so authoritative a scheme, racism, beginning as a dogma of those at the conquering end, does not require acquaintance with "the unfamiliar other" in order to know them. The doctrinaires of racism would invariably dispense with historical fact or other acquired pieces of knowledge about the populations condemned, impaired, and reduced. Part of their epistemological self-confidence lies in the assurance that they know those whom they would subject before ever learning the first detail about them given their preternaturally accessed preeminent knowledge that they can tap into, dispensing with cognitive engagement. As a system of knowledge, a way of knowing, and a design for assembling bodies of knowledge that has oriented the writings of an alarming number of major thinkers of the Christian West over the last four centuries, racism occupies a central role in intellectual history, a notion that in these pages differs significantly from what tends to be called "history of ideas." We do not in these pages go back through the chronology of learned discourse production in hopes of locating the instances when someone expressed in writing an "idea" that one could deem "racial," be it a disparagement of another with an explicit reference to their phenotype or ancestry or an essentialist claim about the lesser or greater quality of people sharing a distinct origin. Racism does not enter intellectual history the moment an individual philosopher in ancient Stagira considers whether nature may have made certain types of people suitable for enslavement, or when in 55 BCE Julius Caesar finds no greater signs of creativity among the British than their use of woad (*isatis tinctoria*) to paint their bodies blue or when in the *Travels* (*ca.* 1300) the Venetian adventurer Marco Polo refers to people of Siberia disapprovingly as having a "pallid complexion," living "in the manner of brute creation" without "laws and usages," and finds that their "intellects are also dull, and they have an air of stupidity."[64]

Racism enters intellectual history when meditating about people of other ancestries and phenotypes becomes a bread-and-butter operation for the learned and the regimes on behalf of which they speak. In that respect, it may creditably be said to have entered during the colonial transaction, those centuries when the Christian countries of Europe that figured among the naval powers resolved to pursue their wealth accumulation by means of an economy of maltreatment that flourished as a result of their overseas expeditions of conquest. These expeditions involved the invasion and violent takeover of large territories in the Americas, Africa, Asia, and Oceania; the conquest and enslavement of indigenous populations; destruction of long-established societies; and the creation of vast worldwide labor camps where the vanquished could often spend their entire lives for generations toiling in harrowing conditions for the exclusive benefit of their captors. At the very start of the new economy, Christendom's intellectual elites found themselves assieged by the morally unsettling, impious, and eminently un-Christian nature of the economic development to which they owed their material well-being. They had to contend with the difficult fact that the mode of accumulation to in which they had become immersed entailed a downright economy of deliberate economy of maltreatment. Nor did they seem to have the moral fortitude and herculean willpower that it would have taken for them to walk away from an enterprise that already in its first decade had revealed its potential for yielding profits of incalculable and unprecedented magnitude.

A crisis of Christian piety promptly ensued, triggered by the denunciations of morally unimpeachable Christian voices who likened the ethics of the new economy with the affairs of the Prince of Darkness. Since the new economy of maltreatment was simply too lucrative for its leaders to bend before the weight of spiritual condemnation, they simply opted to fight back, responding to their detractors, formulating counterarguments, and justifying the justice of the new economy by construing their manner of domination in the same way that, over three centuries later, US Southern advocate of black enslavement John C. Calhoun would address the moral condemnation of the "peculiar institution" launched by abolitionists. Calhoun, like his ideological forbears over three hundred years before, characterized the domination in question as "not a necessary evil," but as "a good, a positive good." But, to return to the pioneers of the colonial transation in the sixteenth century, their sinous self-defense, as they undertook to establish their own goodness in the face of the blatant contradiction of the economy of maltreatment to which they had committed themselves body and soul, led them to a conceptual resource that would prove most inffective in ennobling their colonial enterprise in the eyes of the denizens of Christiandom,

The line of moral self-defense from the flank of the first Christian champions of the benefits of the colonial transaction seemed rather simple: No, Christian conquerors had committed no infraction though they had made war against people who had not provoked them, invaded foreign lands, enslaved alien peoples, deprived others of their resources, plundered their cities, destroyed their societies, engaged in genocidal killings, and reduced the survivers to the most inhumane living conditions. They were doing God's work by bringing to justice unruly populations whose ways of life, belief systems, and social organization showed their defiance of the "true religion" and their animosity toward the Almighty. The founding voice of what would become the racist dogma, the Dominican philosopher and theologian Juan Ginés de Sepúlveda, would contend that the war of expoliation against the natives of the overseas territories conquered by Spain was "a just war." Sepúlveda characterized the conquered as lacking the moral sense, the intelligence, the learning, the physical aptitude, the humane disposition, and the respect for the lives of others necessary for making fair and salutary use of the abundant riches with which the Lord had blessed their lands. They, therefore, had squandered the goods and comforts that the Creator had entrusted in them, which amounts to an insult to God's generosity. To take their stuff, then, did not constitute theft but, instead, a reclamation whereby the accidental belongings of those wretched *homunculi* (little men) returned to legitimate hands, namely, those of Christians, who did have the physical, moral, intellectual, spiritual, social, and cultural virtues qualifying them to benefit from the selfless charity of our Lord. In other words, the disparagement of the conquered populations provided the way out of the crisis of Christian piety that the ungodly new economy of maltreatment had elicited at the start of the colonial transaction.

The catalog of indignities attributed to the conquered to render them deserving of their destruction while making the rapacity of the victors a beneficent mission toward the good of humanity and the greater glory of God resulted in the formation of the racist dogma. An inadvertent outcome of the effort to resolve the moral disquiet produced by the contradiction of pious Christian conquerors perpetrating horror against their fellow human beings—in plain violation of the ethics of goodness which presumably distinguished them from the adepts of the other religions of the earth—inaugurated a new prism through which from then onward Europeans would look at the other inhabitants of the planet, creating a formulaic approach to interacting with ancestral and phenotypical difference. As a dogma, a way of knowing, and a skewed manner of arranging the facts of history, racism became the cultural logic of the Western civilization that emerged in the wake of the colonial transaction.

Racism, to recapitulate, owes its birth to the plight of the learned who found themselves at a historical juncture in which they had to address the ardent denunciations of the greed, barbarity, and depraved savagery displayed by the naval powers of Christian

Europe in their overseas colonial enterprises. When the business of conquest and colonization in the Americas opened up, they took to it with utmost alacrity and in so doing forfeited their claim to piety, mercy, empathy, and compassion. The creation of a discourse of contempt for the conquered *Other* came to render "Christian" the reputedly un-Christian practice of wronging one's fellow human beings for the sake of economic gain. Now devout believers could engage in the appropriation of other people's belongings, perpetrating murderous violence against unprovoking foreigners, coveting their lands, destroying their households, and the like, while still fancying themselves pious Christians uncompromised by moral tresspass. The phenotypical and ancestral difference of the people they wronged and whose societies they disrupted freed the perpetrators from the weight of moral burden insofar as the alterity of their victims sufficed to exonerate European Christians from the mantle of protection, mercy, compassion, and empathy that their faith compelled them to extend to their brethren, namely, all of God's children.

The discourse of disparagement spawned by the need to justify the new economy of maltreatment produced a conceptual breakthrough in the history of social relations. It led to a radically novel epistemological scenario in which invaders of overseas territories whose people had done nothing to provoke the invasion could think of their uninvited incursion as the execution of a duty to promote the betterment of the human family overall. US President Andrew Jackson in 1830, as we saw earlier, found nothing unholy about committing large-scale cruelty of depriving Native Americans of their lands and social stability to send them on a forced march over a thousand miles carrying their belongings on foot from the Appalachian Mountains to Oklahoma. In fact, he could persuade himself that in so doing he was advancing "the blessings of liberty, civilization and religion." At times, aggressors would go as far as to represent their depredation and violence as selfless acts of sacrifice that duty beckoned them to perform even when the benighted natives of the lands they invaded met them with ingratitude.

In his 1899 poem "The White Man's Burden," the India-born English poet Rudyard Kipling characterizes uninvited Western imperial incursions into foreign lands as driven by the mere desire "By open speech and simple, / An hundred times made plain, / To seek another's profit, / And work another's gain."[65] To the colonizing nations, the speaker in Kipling's poem proposes a cathechism of sacrifice: "Send forth the best you breed- / Go bind your sons to exile / To serve your captives' need."[66] The poet refers to the captives in question as "Your new-caught, sullen peoples, / half devil and half child."[67] This enterprise, the speaker muses, the "White Man" ought to take on without a glimmer of optimism given that the captives in question are not easy to teach despite the conqueror's noble intentions: "And when your goal is nearest / the end for others sought, / Watch Sloth and heathen Folly / bring all your hope to nought."[68] In the end, the poet warns the "White Man," champion of civilization, of the obdurate resilience of "the sloth and heathen folly" of the conquered: "By all ye cry or whisper, /By all ye leave or do, / The silent, sullen peoples / Shall weigh your God sand you."[69] It little profits, therefore, to occupy oneself with the opinion of the natives. Therefore, the speaker eggs the

"White Man" on to focus on the only opinion that matters: "The judgement of your peers!", that is, that of other white men.

The juncture where the disparagement of the vanquished, defeated, or enslaved succeeded as the miracle strategy for addressing the problem of Christian piety vis-à-vis the otherwise ungodly economy of maltreatment that produced their spectacular wealth spawned the new logic that would inform the development of Western civilization from then onward. A priori contempt became a way of knowing other human beings across difference of phenotype and ancestry, an attitude that the ancients show no sign of having cultivated. Herodotus of Halicarnassus (circa 485-425 BCE?), for instance, could travel in India, Egypt, Persia, Lybia, and the parts of Africa that Hellenic Greek authors referred to generically as *Ethiopia*, without his encounter with difference of skin hue, hair texture, or facial features giving him any grounds for assuming anything concerning the human caliber of the people he saw. In the *Histories*, he is constantly looking to learn things about the peoples and places he visits, often differentiates the things he knows from empirical evidence, those he has heard from sources he has queried, those he has taken the liberty conjecture, and those that he admittedly does not know. Occasionally we read his comparative analysis of cultural practices, bodies of knowledge, and belief systems of his society and those of foreigners without ever boasting the superiority of his over theirs. At times he even grants greater credence to information emanating from other peoples than that from his own. Regarding the geography of Egypt and its relationship to the Nile River, for example, he says, "some Greeks, wishing to be notable for cleverness, put forward three opinions" of which two deserve no "mention, save to show only what they are," and the third, while "the most pausible by far, yet is of all the most in error."[70] He also ascribes to people in those foreign regions superlative qualities that he does not attribute to his own, such as when he finds in Ethiopia "the tallest and fairest and longest-lived of all men."[71]

Unlike the ancients, the Christian nations of Europe that spearheaded the conquest and colonization of the Americas developed the aforementioned miracle strategy, which in addition to assuaging the moral burden that would have ensued from the sinful economy in which they had fallen, gave them a ready-made tool-kit for knowing their foreign captives without undergoing the learning process that characterized Herodotus's acquaintance with people of other ancestries and phenotypes. Contempt for people about whom one knows nothing other than their distinct texture, skin hue, facial features, and ancestral origin became a central building block of the civilization created in the hemisphere by the colonizing nations, namely Spain, Holland, France, and England. Conceptually armed with the tool kit that would become the basis of the racist dogma, the colonizers charged forward with self-confidence, convinced that they knews all there was to know about other people strictly on the basis of what they could extrapolate from their phenotype or ancestry. They came to believe fervently in the veracity of their thaumaturgic knowledge, which gave them sufficient grounds for deciding whether or not to assign value to them as humans. They they had a priori knowledge of the peoples of the world outside of Europe and the Middle East, and confidently imputed to them a negative ontology that rendered them inept for advancement, civilization, economic progress, social organization, and intellectual elevation as well as devoid of spiritual values, morality, and beauty. Concomitanly, in obsessive self-adulation, the colonizers emphatically proclaimed their own superiority in every respect, while ardently preaching the lesser humanity of the peoples they had vanquished.

The process began formally in the 1540s with the founding work of Juan Ginés de Sepúlveda, mentioned earlier. A Dominican priest, trained in philosophy and theology, Sepúlveda took it upon himself, as a high-ranking staff member in the court of Charles V, at the time King of Spain and Emperor of the Holy Roman Empire, to demonstrate through erudite arguments, that the invasion, pillage, killings, and enslavement of the native peoples of the hemisphere in no way tarnished the piety of His Majesty Charles Caesar, Spain, or the "true religion." Sepúlveda's philosophical and theological dialogue *Democrates Secundus*, written in the 1540s, set out to exculpate Spain, the champion of the colonial transaction, and especially his boss, Charles Caesar, of any wrongdoing by turning the aggression suffered by indigenous Amerindian populations into a *just war*. In a passage that puts the author's elaborate and vehement line of argumentation in a nutshell, Sepúveda, who never set foot anywhere in the Americas, contends that it is "with supreme right...that the Spanish exercise their rule over inhabitants of the new world and adjacent islands (*noui orbis et insularum adiacentium*), those Barbarians who in prudence, talent (*ingenio*), and all manner of virtues and humane sentiments are so inferior to the Spanish as are children to grown-ups, women to men, the cruel and the brutish to the extremely gentle, the exceedingly intemperate to the moderate and restrained, {and finally I might say apes to men}."[72] To enrich the catalogue of indignities he ascribes to the indigenous populations of the conquered lands of the *orbe novo*, he asks his interlocutor (since he writes the in the dialogue form) to consider the outstanding virtues of the Spanish character, the leaning of the Spaniards toward greatness and goodness, and the proclivity of their hearts to embrace the teachings of the Christian faith even when they enter the battlefield. Following this prodigious fit of self-adulation, he then puts the question on his interlocutor's court thus: "Compare now these qualities of prudence, talent, magnanimity, humane sentiment, and religion with the character of those manikins (*homunculos*) in whom one can hardly discern vestiges of humanity, who lack not only instruction but do not even use or have knowledge of letters, nor conserve monuments of their history, except for some obscure and vague memory of particular events captured in certain pictures. They lack written laws and have only Barbaric institutions and customs. And, speaking of virtues, if you want to learn about their temperance and gentleness, what can one expect of people given to all sorts of passions and unspeakable lewdness with not a few among them involved in feeding on human flesh?"[73]

The discourse of disparagement of the populations of the western hemisphere codified in the 1540s by a well-remunerated scholar whose job it was to ennoble the violence and theft of the conquest and colonization of the region perpetrated by his employer and benefactor cohered into the dogma that we know today as racism. That dogma became the way of knowing others across difference of phenotype and ancestry and provided a genetic scheme that relied on a bloodstream archive for people in the colonizing societies to interpret their ascendancy in the modern world. Though triggered by the accidental contact of European Christians with populations they did not know had existed in a region of the world entirely unknown to them, the codification of the racist dogma became a primary instrument of domination even as their colonialist offensives enveloped regions of the planet which they had known about since time immemorial. The racist dogma, as an entirely new way of knowing, needed to reorganize the details of history and culture to suit the newly born conception of the planet as a racialized space. Thus, knowingly or not, the intellectual elites of the Christian West, under the spell of their fundamentalism of ancestry and gospel of phenotype, proceeded to resignify their knowledge of the ancient world.

As Africa and Asia became objects of colonial cupidity, which required inferiorization as a tool of domination, it seemed fitting not to recognize those regions as occupying a place of dignity in the narrative of the ancient world, which had validated them in the realms of knowledge, industry, commerce, and civilization. Self-induced amnesia thus needed to kick in as it related to the otherwise narratively inconvenient ancestral and phenotypical integration of the ancient world. The Mediterranen world, which for millennia had served as a crossroads of difference, had to be pnemomically domesticated so that the memory of its past could accord with the newly minted racial worldview that the Christian West had embraced as it came into being in connection with the colonial transaction. The ancient military, technological, navigational, architectural, and scholarly feats of China, for instance, had to move to the realm of oblivion. The place of China as a trade depot open to international commerce in antiquity, which the anonymous *Periplus of the Erythraean Sea* (circa second century CE) makes clear, would become obscured by planned forgetting.[74] That included the prowess of the Great Wall in addition to those amenities of the Christian West's modernity which the Chinese had developed hundreds and often thousands of years prior to their becoming available in European countries, as the late Eduardo Galeano, the venerable Uruguayan essayist, captured succinctly in his one-page vignette "What Did the Chinese Not Invent?"[75]

Similarly, Africa or Cush (an area encompassing several countries, including those in the Horn of Africa) could no longer hold the place it had held in Hebrew, Greek, or Roman antiquitity, where one finds it invoked with as much admiration as any other great site of creativity, beauty, and civilization. Witness the self-assertiveness of the African woman who speaks in the *Song of Songs*, calling herself "black *and* beautiful" (μέλαινά εἰμι ἐγὼ καὶ καλή, I.5), as rendered in a direct translation of the Hebrew original in the second century BCE Greek Old Testament or *Septuagint*.[76] Miriam and Aaron's rebuke of their brother Moses because "he had married a Cushite woman" so infuriates God that the Almighty resorts to afflicting Miriam with a severe case of leprosy and only relents after Moses pleads on behalf of his sister, who then has her punishment reduced to only seven days, during which she would remian "shut up outside the camp."[77] Prophet Zaphaniah identifies himself as "the son of Cushi," and his exultations, as he prophesies in the name of the Lord, encompasses the geography of Africa. He proclaims, "[f]rom beyond the rivers of Ethiopia / my suppliants, the daughter / of my dispersed ones/ shall bring my offering."[78] Homer's *Iliad* invoked "the blameless Ethiopians" as the inhabitants of a fortunate realm where Zeus and the rest of the gods went to feast for twelve days every year.[79] The Roman poet's Ovid's *Metamorphoses* tells of the astonishing beauty of Andromeda, the daughter of the Ethiopian rulers whom Perseus marries after rescuing her from the sea monster Cetus.[80] Ovid also recounts the heart-rending grief of the goddess Aurora at the death of his human son Memnon, the great warrior who came from Ethiopia at the head of an army in support of the Trojans who resisted the Achaean invasion. When he meets his death at the hands of the ferocious Achilles, Aurora grieves so inconsolably that Jupiter, her father, agrees to turn Memnon into a god.[81]

## Belief over Cognition in Thaumaturgic Reasoning

The cross-cultural, inter-lingual, and transnational exchanges of the ancient world, with commerce, exploration, and downright invasions—which often led to intermingling across difference of various sorts, including carnal—resulted in cultural promiscuity and hybrid interbreeding across regions of humanity, particularly in the Mediterranean. Ancient intermixture much disturbed the scions of the new world order of the Christian West that emerged from the colonial transaction. The history unleashed by the events of 1492 and their aftermath over the next centuries created conditions that induced an understanding of humanity as a species partitioned along levels of worth, with the conquerors and their descendants representing the pinnacle of value. Becoming most acerbic between the latter half of the seventeenth century and the first half of the twentieth century, racism, as a way of knowing and of arranging the facts of history, gained paramount prominence in the discourse of the learned. This was so much the case that in his essay *Le péché vraiment capital*, the French man of letters René Etiemble could in 1957 convincingly affirm that "all humanism is ridiculous which does not set as its main objective the elimination of racism" (Etiemble 1957: 21). No less significantly, an admirer of the sixteenth-century French essayist Michel de Montaigne, Etiemble could find no more encompassing quality with which to praise Montaigne's remarkable moral caliber vis-à-vis others in the modern intellectual history of France than to exonerate him of racism: "Just show me, in his context, a phrase, just one, that in any way favors racism."[82]

Becoming increasingly acerbic in its exclusionary compulsions, the dismissal of phenotypical and ancestral others stood out as the conceptual prism through which the colonial project spearheaded by Christian nations of Europe would interact with peoples from other regions of the world. This was the case whether they had known of those peoples from time immemorial or had only made their acquaintance through the eventful "discoveries" unleashed by the contact of 1492. Following the inaugural discursive work done by the enlightened protégé of Charles V, voices from the learned elites linked to each of the rival colonial projects engaged for the next 450 years in a large-scale production of disparaging discourse intended to impugn the ancestry of conquered and colonized peoples while glorifying their own virtues. The catalogue of indignities that Sepúlveda codified for reducing the humanity of the Amerindian populations subdued by Spain in the first decades of the colonial transaction would recur with hardly any alteration at every new site of domination, be it in Africa, Asia, or Oceania. Repeating incessantly and widely disseminating their catalogue of indignities to impugn non-European others became a central obsession and arguably the most salient distinguishing mark of the intellectual history of the Christian West as compared with learned discourse from antiquity through the fourteenth century CE.

The African person underwent a radical makeover in the discourse of the colonizers and their descendants. In a typical articulation of the intellectual inferiority that the prevalent racial discourse ascribed to those of African ancestry, Dr. Cameron, a salient character in the 1905 novel *The Clansman* by the North Carolinian Baptist minister and novelist Thomas Dixon, Jr., defines "the Negro" as "half-child, half-animal." Given the mental deficiency of such a being, the Doctor refutes the idea that education could in any way benefit them. "Education," he intunes, "is the development of that which *is*. Since the dawn of history the Negro has owned the continent of Africa—rich beyond a poet's fancy, crunching accres of diamond beneath his bare black feet. Yet he never picked up one from the dust until a white man showed to him its glittering light. His land swarmed with powerful and docile animals, yet he never dreamed a harness, cart, or sled. A hunter by necessity, he never made an axe, spear or arrow-head worth preserving beyond the moment of its use.... He lived as his fathers lived—stole his food, worked his wife, sold his children, ate his brother, content to drink, sing, dance, and sport as the ape."[83] Though a Christian clergyman, Dixon had managed not to remember Queen Candace, whose treasurer, referred to as the "Ethiopian Eunuch," makes a memorable appearance in the book of the New Testament's "Book of the Acts." Since Africa was the place he knew thaumaturgically, one cannot expect him to have heard of the prodigious wealth of Musa I, the tenth Mansa of the Mali Empire.

*The Clansman* is a virulently negrophobic work of fiction, conceived with the express purpose of vilifying African Americans and ennobling the great service that the Ku Klux Klan had rendered to the "white race" by reducing the black population to a subservient position in American society, restoring the US South to its former greatness by means of racial violence. Ironically, the racial antipathy of the author and the explicit anti-black agenda of the novel did not deter William P. Pickett, the author of a study purporting to demonstrate the benefits of Black emigration as a solution to the problem of racial conflict in the country, from quoting the aforementioned passage from *The Clansman* as an intellectually creditable source of knowledge. Pickett introduces the passage from the novel thus: "I quote from Thomas Dixon, Jr., the following expressive words, which without exaggeration adequately portray the record of this non-progressive race."[84] Here racism, as a way of knowing, reveals it manner of operation. Dixon utters his statement about the inferiority of blacks by invoking a *self-verying* truth claim about African history, that is, one in which the disparaging utterance serves as its own substantiation. Another author who shares the former's opinion substantiates his truth claim by citing the authority of the previous author's *self-verifying* formulation. Then sheer, incessant repletion makes the formulation so familiar, no natural that it becomes knowledge. It's a process that goes from Sepulveda through the twentieth century non-stop, amounting to a 450-year-long campaign of *trolling*.

Racial aggrandizement and extreme ethnic self-adulation came home to roost during the 1930s in the Christian West, with ascent to the German government of Adolf Hitler, whose political autobiography *Mein Kampf* (1925) had laid out his animosity toward particular ethnic groups in Europe. Nazi Germany would embrace racism as a central public policy with ruinous consequences for the Jewish-descended segment of the population, and Italy's Fascist regime under Benito Mussolini soon followed suit. Yet, at the time, it still seemed difficult for members of the European intelligentsia to delink from racial reasoning when assessing human societies, hence the case of Paul Hazard (1878–1944), a comparative literature scholar who taught at some of the most prestigious French universities, such as the Sorbonne and the Collège de France, and who enjoyed prestige as a humanist. His writings reached the Anglophone world first with his book *La crise de la conscience européenne: 1680-1715* (1935), translated into English as *The European Mind: The Critical Years—1680-1715* (1953). Hubris of ancestry marked the way Hazard valued the achievements of his own people, and he could not endeavor to articulate his self-adulation without diminishing the value of other branches of the human family. While he recognizes an appreciable share of "envy, hatred, and strife" internally among the various European nations, he contends that in the end Europeans come together united by their shared virtues. He echoes the words of Bernard de Fontenelle (1657–1757) who ascribed to Europe "a certain quality of mind or genius" to be found nowhere else on the planet, a disposition that, in addition to science and philosophy, encompasses "art, and taste, and beauty, in which spheres I doubt if there is any race in the world that equals us."[85] Europeans, Hazard says, pride themselves in their "tradition of heroic voyages, of new discoveries, of galleons laden with gold, of glorious banners floating proudly over the ruins of barbaric empires."[86] While "divided against herself," he affirms, she "always closes her ranks ... when she has to confront continents she has brought beneath her sway before," which she stands ready to "subdue again" if necessary Europe can "overawe East and West" because of the resolve of her men, who, if called upon by their rulers, would "fly to arms for the mere glory of it" more eagerly than the Asiatics or the Africans could get together by lavish bribes of gold and silver," he says, citing the seventeenth-century French travel writer Louis du May.[87] In spite of the aforementioned warlike spirit and creed of domination, Hazard nonetheless attributes to Europe the ceaseless pursuit of "two goals," namely "Happiness" and "Truth," especially the latter, which gives her a monopoly on thought. By contrast, elsewhere in the world, except when touched "by her civilizing graces, whole masses of the human race live on from day to day, never bestirring themselves to think, satisfied simply to be."[88]

Whether coming from the ruminations of a fervent advocate of racial segregation like Dixon in the United States during the Jim Crow Era or from the meditations of a French humanist three decades later, racist discourse remained linked to the brand of thaumaturgic reasoning that we found in the formulations of Sepulveda. Western psychologists and anthropologists have conventionally termed "magical thinking" the irrational thought patterns they often attribute to populations outside their world.[89] *Thaumaturgic* here refers to the irrational nature of racism, a peculiar way of knowing that convinces the person whose mind is possessed by it that she, he, or they need not learn anything about another and still know what the latter is capable of intellectually, morally, or otherwise. Whether it's Rivera ordering the killing of the Charrúa in Uruguay, lawmakers drafting legislation that enabled white mobs to lynch African Americans in the US South, or Hitler authorizing the "Final Solution" during Germany's Third Reich, the possession of thaumaturgic knowledge has embolded people to visit upon others the most devastating atrocities while fancying themselves free of wrongdoing.

Thaumaturgic reason endowed conquerors and their descendants with an attitude of a priori contempt that suspended their possibility of remorse for the destruction that they wrought in the lives of the peoples whose lives they dominated. As a result, once they had completed the work of domination, ensuring that their captives had resigned to their condition of subservience, the conquerors went on proudly to memorialize their exploits in a manner that exalted the glory of their victory, dispensing with the slightest compassion for the devastation they had occasioned in the populations whose societies they had destroyed. Their boastful narratives became naturalized and hardened throughout the region via the "crónicas de Indias," the tales of the contact and conquest inaugurated by the precarious prose of Christopher Columbus (b. 1451–d. 1506), the Genoese sailor and fortune seeker who, travelling under the Spanish flag, made the initial landing in the Caribbean, and formalized by Gonzalo Fernandez de Oviedo (b. 1478–d. 1557), a soldier and man of letters appointed by Emperor Charles V officially as the first historian of the Indies. The leaderships of the colonies established by the European conquerors across the hemisphere, followed by elites of the independent republics that emerged in the region when the Creoles south and north of the hemisphere came to sever their political binds that tied them to their forebears. The learned elites and statesmen of the republics of the Americas narrated the colonial beginnings glowingly, construing the traumatic arrival and takeover by the Christian adventurers into an admirable saga of pioneering vision, enterprising restlessness, and remarkable boldness whose exploits would become a beacon for leaders in industry, politics, and the academy to look up to and draw inspiration from.

One would not run the slightest risk of incurring in exaggeration by proposing the white supremacist dogma, pervasive ancestral othering, and radical racialization of populations of origins other than European as central pillars of the civilization born in the Americas as a result of the conquest and colonization. The conquerors and their heirs organized a civilization on the backs of indigenous peoples whose lands and labor they robbed as well as those of the coerced workforce whose enslavement they prompted and sustained for nearly four hundred years. Christian captivity had to diminish ontologically the humanity of those in bondage. No previous conquering nations in antiquity had occupied themselves with the ongoing task of rendering its vanquished peoples inferior nor theorizing the misfortune of the defeated as a direct outcome of the defective ontology that was connected to their ancestral origins. The racist doctrine emerged as a function of Christian piety. Catholic Spain encountered an unprecedented event in human history with its support of a Genoese sailor's expedition that had promised to find to a water route west from Europe to commerce in the East without having to pay expensive tolls to the Ottoman powers that controlled the existing sea routes. Much to their amazement, instead of merely saving on toll payment to the Ottomans in order to reach their commercial destinations in Asia, the Spanish stumbled upon prodigiously vast territories until then unknown to Europe, regions whose soil teemed with the most desirable natural resources that either in agricultural yield or in precious metals, minerals, ores, and gems translated into immediate wealth of until then unimaginable proportions.

To make their find even more astonishing, the arrivants from across the ocean *discovered themselves* capable of taking over all the wealth before their wide-open eyes by overpowering the region's innumerable native inhabitants who happened to lack weapons of mass destruction to match those of the invading Spaniards. In short, they hit a geopolitical jackpot that would quickly multiply their power, influence, and prestige in the world. The takeover, exploitation, and accumulation that ensued placed the Spanish settlers as leaders of industries and accumulation practices that involved unearned enslavement of so-called Indians whom they found at home not provoking them. They had to destroy the social and communal lives of the natives, the pervasive theft of the possession of their victims, the regular pillaging of every new village encroached upon, and periodic mass murder. In short, the colossal wealth, power, and influence they would derive from the lands and the peoples they *discovered themselves* capable of possessing and ardently willing to possess entailed the spiritually damning transgression of every facet of Christian piety. Unlike most other creeds, Christianiy commits the believer to an ethic of radical goodness that urges us to refrain from harming others even if they harm us. If someone slaps us on the face, we do not slap back. We are responsible for guarding the well-being not only of those linked to us by family, religion, country, or friendship but also of the entire species of which we are a part in that, having been created by the same holy father, all humans are brothers and sisters.

Happenstance had presented Spanish Christians with an opportunity for limitless riches and unequalled might that caused them to tread very thorny spiritual ground but which they lacked the moral will to walk away from. This was the case especially after several pious Christian voices, beginning with the famous sermon of the young Dominican priest Fray Antón de Montesinos, who openly condemned the perversion of the colonial transaction at the very moment of its inception on Advent Sunday in December 1511 in La Española or Santo Domingo, Spain's first colony in the "new world." Thus, trapped in an economy of thievery and injury, with maltreatment of their brethren functioning as an inexorable factor of economic development to amass their material fortune, the colonizers needed some sort of spiritual remedy to help assuage their state of transgression. The advocacy of father Montesinos and other Christians who took seriously the pious ethos of their own creed had an impact on the thinking of the metropolis. The administration of Ferdinand II of Aragon, hearing the case presented by the young priest and its rebuttal offered by the colonists of Santo Domingo, paid enough attention to the former as to issue the 1512 Laws of Burgos, which became the first juridical attempt of the monarchy to reduce the maltreatment that the "Indians" could legally sustain at the hands of their Christian masters. The Burgos reforms did not resolve the crisis of Christian piety that Montesinos had provoked by calling out what others had seen but found it convenient to look the other way because of the promise of wealth in the economy of maltreatment.

The New Laws of Burgos ensued in 1542, and shortly thereafter Charles V would convene Valladolid debates in 1550–1551, again with no satisfactory results. Since business as usual could not be stopped because of the wealth involved, *Democrates Secundus* penned by Sepúlveda (b. 1494–d. 1573) came to save the day by giving colonial administrators a magic tool that in painstaking argumentation made a powerful case to establish that the work being done by Spain in the overseas colonies was fueled by the noblest purpose and advanced the greater glory of God. Sepúlveda was a man of humble means who did well in school and managed to move up in the world, becoming the official historian of the Spanish Crown under Charles V. A philosopher and theologian whom the Emperor liked and funded lavishly, he reciprocated, producing a manual that removed the aura of sin that had surrounded the Crown's colonial exploits since the calling out by Montesinos and the continued moral militancy of Fray Bartolome de las Casas and others. The manual turned colonial exploitation into a salvific quest and a civilizing mission that enabled the monarch to be reassured in the stability of his piety. Whether having read him or even heard of him or not, the champions of racist discourse since the 1540s have simply regurgitated the ills, weaknesses, godlessness, vices, moral defects, savagery, ugliness, intellectual deficiency, and moral turpitude that Sepúlveda imputed to the indigenous population of the Americas. Those coming after him also had the job of ennobling the acts of invading, conquering, enslaving, and despoiling the conquered tantamount to a service to humanity, even to the vanquished themselves. Whatever the ancestry or phenotype of the people disparaged by a particular instance of racist discourse, the reader will not find meaningful variation nor expansion on what Sepúlveda said about the ontology of the Indians in *Democrates Secundus*.

## COERCED CULTURAL CONVERSION AS BLOODLESS GENOCIDE

US Army Colonel Henry Richard Pratt (b. 1840–d. 1924) developed a reputation as a "friend of the Indian" for challenging the white American attitudes that regarded the Native American population with contempt. He countered prevailing prejudice by proposing instead a program of education that would prepare them for integration into white American society. After taking charge of Indian prisoners and taking them to Fort Marion, Florida, where they underwent an intense process of acculturation that revealed positive results in the eyes of assessors, he secured permission to start an industrial school for Indians at Carlisle, Pennsylvania, which he ran as a superintendent from 1879 to 1904. Pratt recognized the long record of injustices perpetrated by whites against the indigenous population, including the massacres, the deceitful treaties to dispossess them of their lands, and the practice of forcible removals, whose beginnings, along with the system of reservations, he traced to the ill-advised Indian policies of Thomas Jefferson.[90] Colonel Pratt thus distanced himself from the tradition that had viewed the indigenous population as a negative presence that had best be exterminated, a sentiment encapsulated in the saying "The Only Good Indian is a dead Indian," a proverb whose parentage many attribute to General Philip Sheridan (b. 1831–d. 1888) but that Mieder, drawing on lexicology and paremiology, has established as enjoying a wide circulation before and after Sheridan.[91]

Pratt formed part of a cadre of charitable and often wealthy Northeasterners known as "Friends of the Indian," who convened the annual Lake Mohonk Conference in Ulster County, New York, to discuss ideas pertinent to the betterment of the Native American population with an eye on influencing policymakers. As stated earlier, Pratt did not espouse the murderous racism encapsulated in the statement he attributed to "a great general," namely that "the only good Indian is a dead one" But, though distancing himself from that "high sanction of destruction" which had promoted "Indian massacres," he admitted to this: "In a sense, I agree with the sentiment," meaning, that he desired to extirpate "the race" of the aborigines, that which makes them "Indian," for the sake of cultivating in them a sense of the "human," hence, his own dictum: "Kill the Indian in him, and save the man."[92] Addressing an audience in Denver, Colorado, in 1892, Pratt advocated for a plan that, contrary to the reservations and the missions, would create conditions that enabled Native Americans to interact with whites whom they could emulate so as to become civilized. He believed that acculturation had worked for African Americans, saying that for long "we greatly oppressed the black man, but the germ of human liberty remained among us and grew, and in time "there came from the lowest savagery into intelligent manhood and freedom among us more than seven millions... who are today an element of industrial value with which we could not well dispense." The elevation of the "Negro race," Pratt explains in terms of the inscrutability of "the ways of Providence. Horrible as were the experiences of its introduction, and of slavery itself, there was concealed in them the greatest blessing that ever came to the Negro race, seven millions of blacks from cannibalism in darkest Africa to citizenship in free and enlightened America; not full, not complete citizenship, but possible—probable—citizenship, and on the highway and near to it."[93] "Denied the right of schools," Pratt waxes, they "learned through the influences of association," meaning their proximity to whites, they learned from "the higher race," a feat that "no other influence or result" could have "so speedily accomplished." He proposes that left "in Africa, surrounded by their fellow savages, our seven millions of industrious black fellow-citizens would still be savages."[94] Possibly a good man, Pratt relied on the same way of knowing and the same thaumaturgic reasoning that informed his negrophobic campatriots Dixon and Pickett. Nor had his socialization prepared him to think abou the Indians in a manner that could reveal him truly as their "friend."

Pratt regretted that because of lack of political will, interest, or disdain for the Aborigines on the part of the US authorities, the "Indians under our care remained savage."[95] Allowing them to live only in the company of their own in reservations, tribal schools, or missions had discouraged them from becoming "civilized and incorporated into the nation," a problem that the Carlisle Institute had vowed to address.[96] During an address at the Lake Mohonk Conference in 1891 entitled "A Way Out," Colonel Pratt stressed the success he had at Carlisle in the practice of placing hundreds of Indian children with white families during the summer.[97] To make them palatable to enter the homes of white families, as we learn from the overview of the Carlisle School in the documentary *In the White Man's Image* (2007), the youngsters needed to suppress their native language and speak only English, change their ethnic attires in exchange for European-styled dress, and cut their hair in the style of Protestant school teachers, the girls, and US army recruits, the boys. Pratt's institution also focused on "individualizing them," that is, training the children in self-interest over solidarity by *helping* them to overcome their tendency to "cling to their communistic surroundings.[98] Pratt's own words to the effect that "Carlisle has always planted treason to the tribe and loyalty to the nation at large" translate into a deliberate attempt to blast any sense of community in the youngsters since the "nation" that late nineteenth-century US capitalist society envisioned was informed by the individualistic ethos suggested by the recurring motif of "the self-made man." Killing their sense of commitment to the collective and replacing it with an "each man for himself" or "dog-eat-dog" ethos was a key aspiration for kind-hearted reformists like Pratt, who dreamed about having Indians disappear from their midst without having to perpetrate the massive bloodshed that the likes of Andrew Jackson, Fructuoso Rivera, Philip Sheridan, and William Tecumseh Sherman had undertaken.

Today we often hear the term "cultural genocide" to refer to the demand that other people relinquish everything that makes them distinct, the overall trappings of their difference from those making the demand. The generation of Colonel Pratt, however, heard the term "civilization," which meant using all the means of destruction at our disposal to force other people to relinquish their ways of life, values, and understanding of the world for the sake of aping ours even as we remain secure in our conviction that in forcing them to become copies of ourselves we are extending to them a most invaluable kindness. That Pratt's mission of obligatory cultural conversion for Native Americans (and, by consequence, other non-white segments of the US population) has a long history may be derived from the August 1, 1743, letter by American missionary Reverend John Sergeant (b. 1710–d. 1749) to Dr. Benjamin Colman (b. 1673–d. 1747), both New England men of letters, regarding the idea of educating the aborigines. Reverend Sergeant used the occasion to submit to the perusal of his respected interlocutor a rough draft of a precis he had written on the "Education of Indian Children." There, the Reverend proposes to absorb Native American children in a form of instruction "as shall in the most effectual manner change their whole habit of thinking and acting; and raise them, as far as possible into the Condition of a civil, industrious and Polish'd People; while at the same Time, the Principle of Vertue and Piety shall be carefully instilled into their Minds in a Way, that will make the most lasting Impression and withal introduce the *English Language* among them instead of their own imperfect and barbarous Dialect."99

There is little difference conceptually between the racism that produced segregation in the US South along with the horrors of Jim Crow and that of a "friend of the Indians" like Col. Pratt. When he set out to kill the Indian in a Cheyenne child in order to bring out the human in the kid, he was trapped in the seriously racist paradigm that permitted him to recognize humanity only if it spoke, thought, dressed, behaved, and looked like a Caucasian. Basically, an Indian man would have nothing of value—in his heart, his culture, his thought, his art, his demeanor, his worldview, his looks—unless he had the good luck and the good sense to acquire it from a Caucasian. Pratt lacked what it takes to respect the lives of human beings across difference of ancestry and phenotypes, just as Reverend Sergeant lacked it several generations before him. The homogenizing aspiration of the ruling elites in the hemisphere created societies that devalued the lives of too many people across the region. Nor is it clear whether the situation has changed to the point of enabling us to start a process that could lead to rehabilitating and enhancing social relations across difference.

When the Nobel Prize–winning Peruvian novelist Mario Vargas Llosa had occasion to meditate about the future of Latin America a propos of the quincentennial of the arrival of Columbus in the Americas, he seized onto the need "to fight hunger and misery," which he thought could only be done by means of "modernization," but "modernization is possible," he affirmed, "only with the sacrifice of the Indian cultures."100 He found that the utopia of "preserv[ing] the primitive cultures of America" may be "incompatible with this other and more urgent goal—the establishment of societies in which social and economic inequalities between humans be reduced...and where everybody can enjoy at least a decent and free life."101 If having to "choose between the preservation of Indian cultures and their complete assimilation," he says, he would choose the latter.102 Thaumaturgically, Vargas Llosa arrives at this conclusion, in the same essay in which he has marveled at what the Incas had achieved in Peru prior to the trauma of the conquest: "This civilization had managed to eradicate hunger in that immense region. It was able to distribute all that was produced in such a way that all its subjects had enough to eat. Only a very small number of empires throughout the whole world have succeeded in achieving this feat."103 Now, one wonders, if hunger came to Peru with the social systems created by the conquerors who arrived from abroad and sustained by their descendants who—the likes of Vargas Llosa—remain deftly Europeanized, how can it be that the solution to the region's imported problems requires the elimination of all traces of pre-Columbian indigenous life? As far as we can tell, it is not indigenous peoples but foreign-aping European-descended elites that have steered the ship of state throughout the region generation after generation since the moment of independence from Spain. Peru and the rest of the societies in Latin America have invariably fashioned themselves in the likeness of the West. Why are the Indians the problem? What could be behind the dissonance between the details at hand and the conclusion that the novelist draws from them if not the difficult rapport between cognition and belief and the thaumaturgic throught patterns that racism puts in the minds of even the most erudite individuals?

It would seem that the novelist is trapped in the same paradigm that limited the capacity of Col. Pratt to see the human in the Indian. Despite his restraint, Vargas Llosa's insistence in representing indigenous difference as an impediment to Peruvian or Latin American progress partakes of moral kinship with the vision of Julio Maria Sanguinetti, the former president of Uruguay who as recently as 2009 justified the massacre of Salsipuedes led by Fructuoso in 1831. He dismissed the event as merely "a clash among so many others," adding that although the clash was "indeed terminal" for "the hut dwellers," theirs was "a way of life that was doomed from the first day when Spanish civilization set foot in our territory."[104] Ironically, the only realistic hope of a salutary future for the region could very well be predicated on a rehabilitation of social relations that would enable people to see one another's humanity across difference of phenotype and ancestry. We would need to transcend the prejudicial lens that racism installed in the region, interrupting empathy, mercy, and compassion across origin and appearance. Ironically, this would mean finding ways of overcoming the most enduring civilizing and modernizing interventions of the Christian West. People need to restore a way of life that will enable them to live in harmony with rather than in an adversarial relationship to the environment that they inhabit, which requires some of the sense of community that capitalist advancement discouraged in Indians as it gave preeminence to individualism.

The primary source of hope may lie in the possibility of recovering bodies of knowledge and worldviews capable of fomenting a humane coexistence. Part of it may involve securing a greater sense of familiarity with a view of wholeness such as is rooted in Abya Yala. It may also involve connecting with a vision of capacious intercultural identity such as Rodolfo Corky Gonzalez enacts in *I am Joaquín*, a poem dating from a time when the cultural wing of the Chicano Movement encouraged the search for clues to existence beyond the sources inherited from the colonizing nations. Enhancing social relations across difference in our region may ultimately requiere a pan-hemispheric effort of rehabilitation fueled by a "truth and reconciliation" aspiration. I imagine this as an honest disposition to ask prodding questions about our history of the past five centuries, beginning with one that I regard as the most urgent. Can serious thinkers who claim to care for humanity in all honesty continue to invoke the notion of civilization, or its offspring *modernization*, given the iniquitous ways that the thing assumed among us, namely, plunder, theft, murder, disparagement, enslavement, abuse, rape, insult, and the cruelest effort to reduce the human dignity of entire populations?

Montesinos knew that the invaders of the Americas whom he saw at work in 1511 had not come to the region to save or elevate anything other than their bank accounts, and he spoke truth to power in his Advent Sunday sermon much to the chagrin of the Santo Domingo colony's Governor, military leaders, church authorities, and entrepreneurs in the burgeoning economy of maltreatment. The poem "On Savages" by the Venezuelan bard Gustavo Pereira begins with a prose description of the imagery used by various indigenous peoples of Venezuela to describe the environment, the humans in it, and their sentiments. The Pemon Indians say *spit from the stars* to refer to dawn, *eye sap* to denote tears, and *gut's seed* to call the heart. The Warao people on the Orinoco river say *bosom's sun* to mean the soul, *my other heart* to refer to a friend, and *forgive* to mean to mean forget. The rest of the poem, written in verse, consists of two stanzas which read as follows: "The foolish ones do not know what they say / They call the land "mother" / To mean mother they say "tenderness" / To refer to tenderness they use the word "surrender."

They have such emotional confusion / that it's little wonder that we / fine people that we rare / call them *savages*."[105] Pereira's evocative poem invites us to consider what civilization has meant for us and, if history's record of heartless atrocities matters to characterize savagery, who has been the savage over these five centuries.

## Notes

1. Walter Benjamin, "Three Theses on the Philosophy of History," in *Marxism and Art*, ed. Maynard Solomon (Detroit: Wayne State University Press, 1979), 560; and Maynard Solomon, "Walter Benjamin," in *Marxism and Art*, ed. Maynard Solomon (Detroit: Wayne State University Press, 1979), 547.
2. Rhina P. Espaillat, *Playing at Stillness*, New Odyssey series (Knoxville: Truman State University Press, 2005), 62.
3. Carlos Octavio Bunge, *Nuestra América (Ensayo de Psicología Social)* (Buenos Aires: Valerio Abeledo, Editor-Librería Jurídica, 1905), 156.
4. Bunge, *Nuestra América*, 102.
5. Bunge, *Nuestra América*, 103.
6. José Santos Chocano, *Alma América: poemas indo-españoles*, ed. Francisco de Bendezú (Lima: Serie Escritores de Lima. Editorial Nuevos Rumbos, 1958), 41; and Phyllis W. Rodriguez-Peralta, *José Santos Chocano* (New York: Twayne Publishers, 1970), 68–69.
7. Rodríguez-Peralta, *José Santos Chocano*, 67–69.
8. Chocano, *Alma América*, 41.
9. Chocano, *Alma América*, 43.
10. Quince Duncan, "Documento I: Génesis y evolución del racismo real-doctrinario" (Instituto Interamericano de Derechos Humanos, typescript, n.d.), 17.
11. Tanya Katerí Hernández, *Racial Subordination in Latin America: The Role of the State, Customary Law, and the New Civil Rights Response* (Cambridge, UK: Cambridge University Press, 2013), 26–31.
12. Hernández, *Racial Subordination in Latin America*, 32–33.
13. Duncan, "Documento I," 18.
14. Simón Bolívar, *Selected Writings of Bolívar*, ed. Harold A. Bierck Jr., Vol. 1 (New York: Colonial Press/Banco de Venezuela, 1951), 222.
15. Bolívar, *Selected Writings of Bolívar*, 223.
16. Juan Bautista Alberdi, *Las Bases*, Biblioteca Argentina (Buenos Aires: Libreria La Facultad, 1915), 77.
17. Alberdi, *Las Bases*, 75–76.
18. Domingo Faustino Sarmiento, *Conflicto y armonía de las razas*, introduction by José Ingenieros (Buenos Aires: La Cultura Argentina, 1915), 118.

19. Rosario Gabino, "¿Hay negros en Argentina?" news.bbc.co.uk/hi/Spanish/specials/2007/esclavitud/newsid. March 16, 2007.
20. Gabino, "¿ Hay negros en Argentina?"
21. José Ingenieros, "Las ideas sociológicas de Sarmiento," introduction to Domingo Faustino Sarmiento (*Conflicto y armonía de las razas*) (Buenos Aires: La Cultura Argentina, 1915), 11.
22. Ingenieros, "Las ideas sociológicas de Sarmiento," 11.
23. José Enrique Rodo, *Ariel* (Colección Austral, 1971), 140.
24. José Vasconcelos, *The Cosmic Race/La raza cósmica*, ed. and trans. Didier T. Jaén. (Baltimore, MD: Johns Hopkins University Press, 1997), 32.
25. Wolfgang Mieder, "'The Only Good Indian Is a Dead Indian': History and Meaning of a Proverbial Stereotype," *The Journal of American Folklore* 106, no. 419 (Winter 1993): 38–60, 39, http://www.jstor.org/stable/541345.
26. Mieder, "'The Only Good Indian Is a Dead Indian,'" 49–50.
27. Andrew Jackson, Message of the President of the United States to both Houses of Congress at the Commencement of the Second Session of the Twenty-first Congress, December 7, 1830, x. Appendix to the Register of Debate in Congress.
28. Eduardo Galeano, *Mirrors: Stories of Almost Everyone* (New York: Nation Books, 2009), 248.
29. Galeano, *Mirrors*, 248.
30. Maria Amparo Ruiz de Burton, *The Squatter and the Don*, ed. Rosaura Sánchez and Beatrice Pita (Houston, TX: Arte Público Press, 1992), 176.
31. Jovita González, *Dew on the Thorn* (Houston, TX: Arte Público Press, 1997), 3.
32. González, *Dew on the Thorn*, 6.
33. Michael L. Trujillo, "Remembering and Dismembering in Northern New Mexico," *Atzlan: A Journal of Chicano Studies* 33, no. 2 (2008): 91–99.
34. Genaro Padilla, "Historia de la Nueva Mexico Published, 1610," Newmexicohistory.org. Accessed July 15, 2018; and María Herrera-Sobek, "New Approaches to Old Chroniclers: Contemporary Critical Theories and the Pérez de Villagrá Epic," in *Recovering the US Hispanic Literary Heritage*, ed. Maria Herrera-Sobek and Virginia Sánchez-Korrol, vol. 3 (Houston, TX: Arte Publico Press, 2000).
35. A. Gabriel Meléndez, *Spanish Language Newspapers in New Mexico, 1834–1958* (Tucson: University of Arizona Press, 2005), 93.
36. José Escobar, "Progreso literario de Nuevo México: Sus periódicos—Historiadores, Sus Poetasy Novelistas," *Las Dos Repúblicas* 1, no. 27 (1896).
37. Miguel Antonio Otero, *My Life on the Frontier, 1864–1882* (Santa Fe, NM: Sunstone Press, 2007), 116.
38. Otero, *My Life on the Frontier*, 12.
39. Otero, *My Life on the Frontier*, 12.
40. Otero, *My Life on the Frontier*, 12.
41. Otero, *My Life on the Frontier*, 28–29.
42. J. Weston Phippen, "Kill Every Buffalo You Can! Every Buffalo Dead Is an Indian Gone," *The Atlantic*, May 13, 2016, http://www.theatlantic.com/national/archive/2016/05/the-buffalo.
43. Phippen, "Kill Every Buffalo You Can!
44. Russell Frank Weigley, *The American Way of War: A History of United States Military Stretegy and Policy* (New York: Macmillan, 1973), 160.
45. Otero, *My Life on the Frontier*, 4.

46. Otero, *My Life on the Frontier*, 4.
47. Otero, *My Life on the Frontier*, 4.
48. John Rollin Ridge [Yellow Bird], *The Life and Adventures of Joaquín Murieta the Celebrated California Bandit* (Norman: University of Oklahoma Press, 1977), 64.
49. Paul R. Spitzzeri, "Judge Lynch in Session: Popular Justice in Los Angeles 1850–1875," *Historical Society of Southern California Quarterly* 87, no. 2 (Summer 2005): 408.
50. Paul M. De Falla, "Lantern in the Western Sky," in *The Historical Society of Southern California Quarterly* (March 1960a): 57–58; Paul M. De Falla, "Lantern in the Western Sky," *The Historical Society of Southern California Quarterly* (June 1960b), 42.
51. Nancy Kang and Silvio Torres-Saillant, "'Somos Asiáticos': Asian Americans, Latinos, and Hispanics of Asian Ancestry." *Latino Studies* 14, no. 4 (2016): 550.
52. "How to Tell Your Friends from the Japs," *Time* December 22, 1941, 81.
53. "How to Tell Japs from the Chinese," 81.
54. Maya Angelou, *I Know Why the Caged Bird Sings* (New York: Random House, 2009), 207; and Kang and Torres-Saillant, "'Somos Asiáticos,'" 549.
55. John C. Calhoun, "Remarks on Receiving Abolition Petitions (Revised Report)." [In the Senate, February 6, 1837]. *The Papers of John C. Calhoun*, edited by Clyde N. Wilson, vol. XIII, 1835–1837 (Columbia: University of South Carolina Press for the South Carolina Department of Archives and History and the South Carolina Society, 1990), 391–398.
56. "The Ku Klux Klan of 1871," *History, Art and Archives: House of Representatives*. history.house.gov/HistoricalHighlight. Accessed August 22, 2019.
57. Ulysses S. Grant, "Sixth Annual Message," To the Senate and House of Representatives. December 7, 1874. *The American Presidency Project*. http://www.presidency.ucsb.edu/ws/?pid=29515.
58. Richard H. Pildes, "Democracy, Anti-Democracy, and the Canon," *Constitutional Commentary* 17, no. 295 (2000), 12–13.
59. Brian Lyman, "'There Will Be Lynchings': How *The Advertiser* Failed Victims of Racial Terror," http://www.montgomeryadvertiser.com. 2018.
60. Paul Finkelman and Melvin I. Urofsky, eds., "Dred Scott v. Sanford." 60 U.S. 393 (19 How. 393) (1857), in *Landmark Decisions of the United States Supreme Court*, 2d. ed. (Washington, D.C.: CQ Press, a Division of Congressional Quarterly, 2008), 86–87.
61. Douglas A. Blackmon, *Slavery by Another Name: The Re-enslavement of Black Americans from the Civil War to World War II* (New York: Doubleday, 2008), 99.
62. Blackmon, *Slavery by Another Name*, 100.
63. Khalil Gibran Muhammad, *The Condemnation of Blackness: Race, Crime, and the Making of Modern Urban America* (Cambridge, MA: Harvard University Press, 2010).
64. Julius Caesar, *Gallic War*, vol. 14 (Cambridge, MA: Harvard University Press, 1966); and Marco Polo, *The Travels of Marco Polo [The Venetian]*, ed. Manuel Komroff (New York: Garden City Publishing, 1930), 347.
65. Rudyard Kipling, *The Collected Poems of Rudyard Kipling*, introduction by R. T. Jones, Wordsworth Poetry Library (Hertfordshire, UK: Wordsworth Editions Limited, 2001), 334.
66. Kipling, *The Collected Poems*, 334.
67. Kipling, *The Collected Poems*, 334.
68. Kipling, *The Collected Poems*, 334.
69. Kipling, *The Collected Poems*, 335.
70. Herodotus, *The Histories*, The Loeb Classical Library, vol. 1 (Cambridge, MA: Harvard University Press, 1946), 299.

71. Herodotus, *The Histories*, The Loeb Classical Library, vol. 2 (London: William Heineman, 1928), 141.
72. Juan Ginés Sepúlveda, *Demócrates Segundo o de las justas causas de la guerra contra los Indios* (Madrid: Consejo Superior de Investigaciones Científicas Instituto Francisco de Vitoria, 1951), 33.
73. Sepúlveda, *Demócrates Segundo,* 35.
74. Anonymous, *The Periplus of the Erythreaen Sea* (London: The Hakluyt Society/ The British Library, 1980), 56, 124–125, 156.
75. Galeano, *Mirrors,* 96.
76. "Songs of Songs." *The Septuagint Version of the Old Testament,* with an English translation by Sir Lancelot Lee Brenton. (London: Samuel Bagster and Sons, 1972), 830.
77. "Numbers," *The Oxford Annotated Bible,* revised standard version, edited by Herbert G. May and Bruce M. Metzger (New York: Oxford University Press, 1962), 160–213.
78. "The Book of Zephaniah," *The Oxford Annotated Bible,* revised standard version, edited by Herbert G. May and Bruce M. Metzger (New York: Oxford University Press, 1962), 1140–1144.
79. Homer, 1961: 70.
80. Ovid [Publius Ovidius Naso], *Metamorphoses,* ed. Charles Martin (New York: W. W. Norton, 2010), 112–115.
81. Ovid, *Metamorphoses,* 362–364.
82. René Etiemble, *Le péché vraiment capital. Les Essais LXXXV* (Paris: Gallimard, 1957), 47.
83. Thomas Dixon Jr., *The Clansman: A Historical Romance of the Ku Klux Klan* (Lexington: University of Kentucky Press, 1970), 292.
84. William P. Pickett, *The Negro Problem: Abraham Lincoln's Solution* (New York: G. P. Putnam's Sons, 1909), 30.
85. Paul Hazard, *The European Mind: The Critical Years, 1680–1715,* trans. J. Lewis May, 2nd ed. (New York: Forham University Press, 1990), 439–440.
86. Hazard, *The European Mind,* 440.
87. Hazard, *The European Mind,* 440.
88. Hazard, *The European Mind,* 440–441.
89. Andrew M. Colman, *A Dictionary of Psychology,* 3rd. ed. (Oxford: Oxford University Press, 2012).
90. Richard H. Pratt, "The Advantages of Mingling Indians with Whites," in *Americanizing the American Indians: Writings by the "Friends of the Indian" 1880–1900,* ed. Francis Paul Prucha (Cambridge, MA: Harvard University Press, 1973), 261–262.
91. Mieder, "The Only Good Indian Is a Dead Indian"; and Dee Brown, *Bury My Heart at Wounded Knee: An Indian History of the American West* (New York: Reader/Henry Holt, 2009), 170.
92. Mieder, "The Only Good Indian Is a Dead Indian," 261.
93. Mieder, "The Only Good Indian Is a Dead Indian," 263.
94. Mieder, "The Only Good Indian Is a Dead Indian," 263.
95. Mieder, "The Only Good Indian Is a Dead Indian," 263.
96. Mieder, "The Only Good Indian Is a Dead Indian," 269.
97. Richard H. Pratt, "A Way Out, " in *Americanizing the American Indians: Writings by the "Friends of the Indian" 1880–1900,* ed. Francis Paul Prucha (Cambridge, MA: Harvard University Press, 1973), 272–276.
98. Pratt, "A Way Out," 269.

99. John Sergeant, "Letter to Dr. Colman, 1 August 1743." Samuel Hopkins, *Historical Memoirs Relating to the Housannuk Indians: Or an Account of the Methods Used and the Pains Taken for the Propagation of the Gospel Among that Heathenish Tribe* (Boston: Printed and sold by S. Kneeland, 1753. Rpt. Whitefish, MT: Kessinger Legacy Reprints, 2010), 97–101.
100. Mario Vargas Llosa, "Questions of Conquest: What Columbus Wrought and What He Did Not," *Harper's*, December 1990, 53.
101. Vargas Llosa, "Questions of Conquest," 52.
102. Vargas Llosa, "Questions of Conquest," 52–53.
103. Vargas Llosa, "Questions of Conquest," 48.
104. José María Sanguinetti, "El Charruismo," *El País* (Montevideo), April, 19, 2009.
105. Gustavo Pereira, *Sobre salvajes: Antología poética*, Selección y prólogo de Norberto Codina (Havana, Cuba: Fondo Editorial Casa de las Américas, 2007), 200.

## Bibliography

Alberdi, Juan Bautista. *Las Bases*. Biblioteca Argentina. Buenos Aires: Libreria La Facultad, 1915.
Angelou, Maya. *I Know Why the Caged Bird Sings*. New York: Random House, 2009.
Anonymous. *The Periplus of the Erythreaen Sea*. Second Series No. 151. London: The Hakluyt Society/The British Library, 1980.
Benjamin, Walter. "Three Theses on the Philosophy of History." In *Marxism and Art*, edited by Maynard Solomon, 559–561. Detroit: Wayne State University Press, 1979.
Blackmon, Douglas A. *Slavery by Another Name: The Re-enslavement of Black Americans from the Civil War to World War II*. New York: Doubleday, 2008.
Bolívar, Simón. *Selected Writings of Bolívar*. Compiled by Vicente Lecuona, edited by Harold A. Bierck, Jr., and translated by Lewis Bertrand. Vol. 1. New York: Colonial Press/Banco de Venezuela, 1951.
Brown, Dee. *Bury My Heart at Wounded Knee: An Indian History of the American West*. New York: Reader/Henry Holt, 2009.
Bunge, Carlos Octavio. *Nuestra América (Ensayo de Psicología Social)*. Buenos Aires: Valerio Abeledo, Editor-Librería Jurídica, 1905.
Caesar, Julius. *Gallic War* V.14. Cambridge, MA: Harvard University Press, 1966.
Chocano, José Santos. *Alma América: poemas indo-españoles*. Edited by Francisco de Bendezú. Lima: Serie Escritores de Lima. Editorial Nuevos Rumbos, 1958.
Colman, Andrew M. *A Dictionary of Psychology*. 3rd. ed. Oxford: Oxford University Press, 2012.
Dixon, Thomas, Jr. 1905. *The Clansman: A Historical Romance of the Ku Klux Klan*. Lexington: University of Kentucky Press, 1970.
"Dred Scott v. Sanford." 60 U.S. 393 (19 How. 393) (1857). *Landmark Decisions of the United States Supreme Court*. 2nd. ed. Edited by Paul Finkelman and Melvin I. Urofsky, 86–87. Washington, DC: CQ Press, a Division of Congressional Quarterly, 2008.
Duncan, Quince. "Documento I: Génesis y evolución del racismo real-doctrinario." Instituto Interamericano de Derechos Humanos, typescript, n.d., 17.
Duncan, Quince. *La rebelión pocomía y otros relatos*. San José: Editorial Costa Rica, Ellis, 1976.
Escobar, José. "Progreso literario de Nuevo México: Sus periódicos—Historiadores, Sus Poetas y Novelistas." *Las Dos Repúblicas* 1, no. 27 (1896).

Espaillat, Rhina P. *Playing at Stillness*. New Odyssey Series. Knoxville: Truman State University Press, 2005.

Etiemble, René. *Le péché vraiment capital. Les Essais LXXXV*. Paris: Gallimard, 1957.

Falla, Paul M. De. "Lantern in the Western Sky." *The Historical Society of Southern California Quarterly* vol. 42, no. 1 (March 1960a): 57–58.

Falla, Paul M. De. "Lantern in the Western Sky." *The Historical Society of Southern California Quarterly* 42 (June 1960b): 161–185.

Fortes, Jorge, and Diego Ceballos, dirs. *Afroargentines*. The African Diaspora in the Americas Collection, 2002.

Gabino, Rosario. "¿Hay negros en Argentina?" news.bbc.co.uk/hi/Spanish/specials/2007/esclavitud/newsid. March 16, 2007.

Galeano, Eduardo. *Mirrors: Stories of Almost Everyone*. New York: Nation Books, 2009.

González, Jovita. *Dew on the Thorn*. Houston, TX: Arte Público Press, 1997.

Grant, Ulysses S. "Sixth Annual Message." To the Senate and House of Representatives. December 7, 1874. *The American Presidency Project*. http://www.presidency.ucsb.edu/ws/?pid=29515.

Hammurabi. *Code of Hammurabi King of Babylon about 2250 BC*. Translated, transliterated, and edited by Robert Francis Harper. Chicago: University of Chicago Press/Callaghan & Company/Luzac & Company, 1904.

Hazard, Paul. *The European Mind: The Critical Years, 1680–1715*. Translated by J. Lewis May, 2nd. ed. New York: Forham University Press, 1990.

Hernández, Tanya Katerí. *Racial Subordination in Latin America: The Role of the State, Customary Law, and the New Civil Rights Response*. Cambridge, UK: Cambridge University Press, 2013.

Herodotus. *The Histories*. Vol. 1 (Books I and II), The Loeb Classical Library. Cambridge, MA: Harvard University Press, 1946.

Herodotus. *The Histories*. In four volumes with an English translation by A. D. Godley, vol. 2 (Books III and IV), The Loeb Classical Library. London: William Heineman, 1928.

Homer. *The Iliad*. Translated by Richard Lattimore. Chicago: University of Chicago Press, 1961.

Herrera-Sobek, María. "New Approaches to Old Chroniclers: Contemporary Critical Theories and the Pérez de Villagrá Epic." In *Recovering the US Hispanic Literary Heritage*, vol. 3, edited by Maria Herrera-Sobek and Virginia Sánchez-Korrol, 154–162. Houston, TX: Arte Publico Press, 2000.

Ingenieros, José. "Las ideas sociológicas de Sarmiento." Introduction to Domingo Faustino Sarmiento. *Conflicto y armonía de las razas*, 7–40. Buenos Aires: La Cultura Argentina, 1915.

Jackson, Andrew. Message of the President of the United States to both Houses of Congress at the Commencement of the Second Session of the Twenty-first Congress, December 7, 1830, pp. ii–xiii. Appendix to the Register of Debate in Congress.

Jefferson, Thomas. *Notes on the State of Virginia*, 1785. In *Works by Thomas Jefferson*. Literary Classics of the United States. New York: The Library of America, 1984.

Kang, Nancy, and Silvio Torres-Saillant. "'Somos Asiáticos': Asian Americans, Latinos, and Hispanics of Asian Ancestry." *Latino Studies* 14, no. 4 (2016): 545–564.

Kipling, Rudyard. *The Collected Poems of Rudyard Kipling*, 334. Introduction and notes by R. T. Jones. Wordsworth Poetry Library. Ware, Hertfordshire (UK): Wordsworth Editions Limited, 2001.

Lesiak, Christine. *In the White Man's Image*. Co-produced by Matthew L. Jones. Boston: WGBH Boston Video, 2007.

Lyman, Brian. "'There Will Be Lynchings': How *The Advertiser* Failed Victims of Racial Terror." http://www.montgomeryadvertiser.com. 2018.

Meléndez, A. Gabriel. *Spanish Language Newspapers in New Mexico, 1834–1958*. Tucson: University of Arizona Press, 2005.

Mieder, Wolfgang. The Only Good Indian Is a Dead Indian': History and Meaning of a Proverbial Stereotype." *The Journal of American Folklore* 106, no. 419 (Winter 1993): 38–60. http://www.jstor.org/stable/541345.

Muhammad, Khalil Gibran. *The Condemnation of Blackness : Race, Crime, and the Making of Modern Urban America*. Cambridge, MA: Harvard University Press, 2010.

Otero, Miguel Antonio. *My Life on the Frontier, 1864–1882*. Santa Fe, NM: Sunstone Press, 2007.

Ovid [Publius Ovidius Naso]. *Metamorphoses*. Translated and edited by Charles Martin. A Norton Critical Edition. New York: W.W. Norton, 2010.

Padilla, Genaro. "Historia de la Nueva Mexico Published, 1610." Newmexicohistory.org. Accessed 15 July 2018.

Pereira, Gustavo. *Sobre salvajes: Antología poética*. Selección y prólogo de Norberto Codina. La Honda, La Habana: Fondo Editorial Casa de las Américas, 2007.

Phippen, J. Weston. "Kill Every Buffalo You Can! Every Buffalo Dead Is an Indian Gone." *The Atlantic*, May 13, 2016. http://www.theatlantic.com/national/archive/2016/05/the-buffalo.

Pickett, William P. *The Negro Problem: Abraham Lincoln's Solution*. New York: G. P. Putnam's Sons/The Knickerbocker Press, 1909.

Pildes, Richard H. "Democracy, Anti-Democracy, and the Canon." *Constitutional Commentary* 17, no. 295 (2000): 295–319.

Polo, Marco. *The Travels of Marco Polo [The Venetian]*. Edited by Manuel Komroff. New York: Garden City Publishing, 1930.

Pratt, Richard H. "The Advantages of Mingling Indians with Whites." In *Americanizing the American Indians: Writings by the "Friends of the Indian" 1880–1900*, edited by Francis Paul Prucha, 260–280. Cambridge, MA: Harvard University Press, 1973.

Pratt, Richard H. "A Way Out." In *Americanizing the American Indians: Writings by the "Friends of the Indian" 1880–1900*, edited by Francis Paul Prucha, 273–276. Cambridge, MA: Harvard University Press, 1973.

Ridge, John Rollin [Yellow Bird]. 1854. *The Life and Adventures of Joaquín Murieta the Celebrated California Bandit*. Norman: University of Oklahoma Press, 1977.

Rodo, José Enrique. *Ariel*. 4th ed. Colección Austral. Madrid: Espasa-Calpe, S.A., 1971.

Rodriguez-Peralta, Phyllis W. *José Santos Chocano*. New York: Twayne Publishers, 1970.

Ruiz de Burton, Maria Amparo. 1885. *The Squatter and the Don*. Edited by Rosaura Sánchez and Beatrice Pita. Houston, TX: Arte Público Press, 1992.

Sanguinetti, José María. "El Charruismo." *El País* (Montevideo), April, 19, 2009.

Sarmiento, Domingo Faustino. *Conflicto y armonía de las razas*. Introduction by José Ingenieros. Buenos Aires: La Cultura Argentina, 1915.

Sepúlveda, Juan Ginés. *Demócrates Segundo o de las justas causas de la guerra contra los Indios*. Bilingual edition. Latin original with Spanish translation and introduction by Angel Losada. Madrid: Consejo Superior de Investigaciones Científicas Instituto Francisco de Vitoria, 1951.

Solomon, Maynard. "Walter Benjamin." In *Marxism and Art*, edited by Maynard Solomon, 541–547. Detroit: Wayne State University Press, 1979.

Spitzzeri, Paul R. "Judge Lynch in Session: Popular Justice in Los Angeles 1850–1875." *Historical Society of Southern California Quarterly* 87, no. 2 (Summer 2005): 83–122.

Trujillo, Michael L. "Remembering and Dismembering in Northern New Mexico." *Atzlan: A Journal of Chicano Studies* 33, no. 2 (2008): 91–99.

Vargas Llosa, Mario. "Questions of Conquest: What Columbus Wrought and What He Did Not." *Harper's*, December 1990, 45–53.

Vasconcelos, José. *The Cosmic Race/La raza cósmica*. Edited and translated by Didier T. Jaén. Afterword by Josefa Gabilondo. Baltimore, MD: Johns Hopkins University Press, 1997.

Weigley, Russell Frank. *The American Way of War: A History of United States Military Stretegy and Policy*. New York: Macmillan, 1973.

CHAPTER 3

## LATINX MIDWEST FOLKLORE

STACEY M. ALEX AND FREDERICK LUIS ALDAMA

> For seven years she worked in a black community in Illinois, but she felt the need to get in touch with her own culture and people. Also, she knew that before she could help the Mexican Americans, she would have to learn more about her Hispanic heritage. Although her parents were Mexican Americans, she had never lived in a Mexican American community and had limited exposure to the Hispanic way of life: "Finding my Mexican identity," Sister Marilyn says, "was like having a blood transfusion." Her experiences with the migrants have helped define her place in the Mexican American community.[1]
>
> —Vicky McNamara
>
> When we played for the Fiesta on stage and one guy said, "I already told the people that were in charge, how come they have to bring a group from Texas, the group from Topeka is better than they are." The people from Texas know more songs. But I thought it was good for him to say that. It felt real good.[2]
>
> —Teresa Cuevas

AFTER learning about her culture for three years in Mexico, Sister Marilyn Reyes decided she was better prepared to support migrant workers and began the next chapter of her work in Topeka, Kansas.[3] Teresa Cuevas was born in Topeka in 1920 after her father found work on the Santa Fe Railway and her parents emigrated from Leon, Guanajuato, where the Mexican Revolution made life difficult. Teresa's only exposure to mariachi music growing up was through records until a Catholic priest from Guatemala introduced the form to the Topeka parish choir. Founded in 1977, her all-female band took workshops throughout the western United States to overcome feelings of isolation in Kansas and strengthen their traditional base. After apprenticing in California and Texas, Teresa took on her own apprentices.[4] For well over a century, Latinx culture has thrived in Midwestern communities. Now, these communities are often larger and stronger, and many new cultural sites have emerged. However, long after Reyes's and Cuevas's journeys in the 1970s and 1980s, some Latinx Midwesterners continue to seek ways to connect culturally, despite growing Latinx networks and the support of new technologies.

This article examines how Latinx artists in the Midwest use folklore as cultural capital to forge a sense of belonging while creatively responding to a variety of personal and social issues. By providing profiles and interviews with artist-educators, it traces Latinx storytelling, visual arts, festivals, folk music, and folk dance to demonstrate how Latinxs in the Midwest creatively engage with folklore as place-making while combating erasure and hostility as well as social and geographic isolation from more widely recognized Latinx cultural centers. The profiles provided here are not intended to represent all Midwestern Latinx folk artists but rather capture the diversity of their experiences as well as common triumphs and struggles. Across their differences, the physical and emotional distance from more dominant Latinx cultural centers often fuels a strong sense of responsibility to represent, preserve, and educate others about Latinx culture, as well as forge strong intra-cultural ties between Latinx groups in the Midwest.

The American Folklore Society (AFS) maintains that no one definition of folklore is sufficient because it reaches an immense dimension of culture and identity. By sharing a variety of definitions, AFS shows that folklore does not mean "old-fashioned," "exotic," or "uneducated": "Though folklore connects people to their past, it is a central part of life in the present, and is at the heart of all cultures—including our own—throughout the world."[5] Folklore will be defined here as "artistic communication between two people" and qualified with examples including folktales, jokes, rhymes, greetings, folk costume, folk art, folksongs, names, games, festivals, customs, and so on.[6] Herrera-Sobek also explains that "folklore" is often difficult to untangle from conceptions of "popular culture"; while the former relates to oral traditions, the latter is found in mass media, although folk elements often appear in mass media as well.[7] Folklore, therefore, belongs to and is practiced by everyone. However, because of the vastness of the topic, this article focuses on Latinx individuals who choose to practice folklore as artists and educators.

María Eugenia Cotera asserts that, as it has developed in contexts of colonization, genocide, slavery, and the US empire, Latinx folklore is always already blended and diasporic; Latin American and Latinx cultural forms are shaped by Creolization, mestizaje, dislocations, and migrations.[8] She also warns against the assumption that all Latinx folklore is counter-hegemonic because, although it has been used to recover and express historically marginalized ways of knowing, its production of "common sense" often "reinforces relations of domination and subordination *within* minoritized communities."[9] While this is important to keep in mind, this article investigates the way that Latinx artist-educators use folklore as resistive cultural consciousness. This is especially the case for Latinx folk artists who struggle to maintain visibility and claim authority outside of prescribed notions of where Latinx folklore is thought to live.

The Latinx folklore artist-educators profiled here often face the double duty of both promoting Latinx self-knowledge, acceptance, and belonging, as well as raising awareness among non-Latinxs. An anonymous Latinx artist in Ohio explains that volunteerism is often expected of Latinx artists because "everyone wants to bring diversity, often it is what is required by grant funders, but they do not want to budget for it and pay Latino artists what they are worth."[10] Several contributors to *This Bridge Called My Back*, including Judit Moschkovich and Audre Lorde, insist that "it is not the duty of the oppressed to educate the oppressor"[11] because, especially in racist white women's organizations, "This is a diversion of energies and a tragic repetition of racist patriarchal thought."[12] While the Latinx artists presented here endeavor to educate non-Latinx groups about Latinx heritage, they perform this work on their own terms that demand self-determination.

Education, Institutions, and Cultural Values are three of the organizational goals established in El Plan Espiritual de Atzlán (The Spiritual Plan of Atzlán) to move La Raza toward liberation. These were declared at the First National Chicano Liberation Youth Conference in 1969. Nearly fifty years later, many Anglo-dominated institutions now use the term "inclusivity" in their mission statements, but Latinx access to these institutions, and to state arts funding in particular, is limited and must be investigated further. In Midwestern K-12 schools, it is difficult to find bilingual education or Latinx history and culture that confront the continuation of social injustices today. Folklore, as the transmission of culture, can be a vehicle for self-determined Latinx resistance to disenfranchisement. It may also open new possibilities for education that affirms complex Latinx identities. The models provided here may inform the development of education that moves beyond "inclusivity" of Latinx worldviews to treat them as foundational to the constitution of educational and cultural institutions. There is a great potential for Latinx folklore to advance social justice issues for Latinx communities, but continued structural racism limits resources available to Latinx folk artists. This includes erasure in scholarship and barriers to state-funded support, including a lack of Latinx representation at various levels of decision-making.

## A Brief History of Latinxs in the Midwest

Maintaining traditions in the Midwest has presented challenges to Latinxs in areas that are more socially isolated from other Latinxs and geographically separated from their families' origins in the Southwest United States or other countries of origin. Yet there is a long history of Latinx migration and community building in the Midwest due to a number of factors. Beginning primarily with Mexican immigrants, many fled the violence of the Mexican Revolution from 1910 to 1917; others met an increasing demand for labor as European immigrants experienced upward mobility and new European immigration was limited by the Immigration Act of 1917. Recruitment of Mexican laborers was common for agricultural and manufacturing jobs, as well the construction of railroads that in 1914 connected Mexico and its natural resources with Kansas City, St. Louis, and Chicago. Increased industrialization during World War I and labor shortages during World War II, and the Bracero Program again brought more Mexicans and Mexican Americans to the Midwest.[13] Many other Latinx groups migrate to and expand in the Midwest due to employment opportunities, a low cost of living, and established social networks.

Despite an increase in deportations, tough working conditions, and anti-Latinx feelings in areas where non-Latinx residents have little personal experience with Latinxs, a variety of state and federal regulations have made the Midwest, by comparison with other regions, seem less hostile to Latinxs.[14] However, the integral contributions of Latinx communities in the Midwest have been left out of many official histories. In the case of Kansas City, Steven Driever writes that the archival Latinx invisibility in the area before the 1950s is the result of discrimination connected to housing segregation and the general assumption that Latinx people are not really Americans.[15] Latinx scholars such as Theresa Delgadillo and Elena Foulis counter this archival erasure of Latinxs in the Midwest by collecting oral histories. Delgadillo recounts how she was moved to do this work for her book, *Latina Lives in Milwaukee*, after discovering the limited number of documents related to Mexican Americans at the Milwaukee County Historical Society. She wonders, "What could we know about ourselves, and what could others know about us, if so little was in the archive? What other parts of city life were absent from the historical record?"[16] Delgadillo asserts that, in addition to Latina/os of Mexican heritage, we must document the heterogeneity of multi-ethnic Latina/o life and the stories of "other Latinas/os," especially since they make up 44 percent of communities such as Milwaukee.[17]

In the face of these exclusions, Latinx Midwestern communities created their own publications to advance community consciousness and belonging. Many of them were organized by state-sponsored Midwestern Hispanic advocacy groups. Roger P. Davis explains that the catalyst for the formation of these groups throughout the 1970s and 1980s was national rather than regional demographic growth and a change in attitude driven by veterans of both World War II and Vietnam who returned home to demand social, economic, and political equality. A new attitude in federal government with the Johnston/Kennedy war on poverty also contributed to this movement with the civic philosophy of community empowerment. In addition to assessing needs of their Hispanic communities and making recommendations in key areas such as health and education, these agencies were also "charged with securing appropriate recognition of the accomplishments and contributions of their communities and leaders"[18] Newsletters from this period are a rich source of information and deserve further study.

Descriptions of cultural traditions often stand side by side with more explicitly political items in these publications. Davis describes how the *Epoca* newsletter from the Ohio Commission detailed festivals as well as rallies and pending legislation while newsletters from Kansas and Nebraska feature Hispanic leaders and events.[19] The promotion of cultural events, including food, dance, and music, is particularly evident in *Herencia, Fiestas, Horizontes*, published by the State of Kansas Advisory Committee on Mexican

American Affairs in 1978–1979. The word "fiestas" is aptly placed in the middle of the title to show how present-day cultural practices draw on the past (herencia) to imagine possibilities for the future (horizontes). Meeting minutes from MECHA (Movimiento Estudiantil Chicanx de Aztlán/Chicanx Student Movement of Aztlán), League of United Latin American Citizens (LULAC) students of the month, government appointments, and career opportunities are featured alongside descriptions of local dances and festivals. Now, as the Kansas Hispanic and Latino American Affairs Commission, the group continues to publicize cultural events in newsletters, although often with only the basic details in calendar format.

## Changing Approaches to Folklore: Working Against a History of Exclusion

The inclusion of Latinx folk artists in the popular radio show *A Prairie Home Companion* and a Folksongs of Illinois CD series may give the impression of multicultural harmony. Yet US folklore collections have and continue to exclude Latinx contributions to the nation's sociocultural fabric, along with the reservation of "American" identity for Anglos. This is especially true for US regions with typically smaller Latinx populations such as the Midwest. When acknowledged, Latinx folklore is carefully limited. For example, a section on folksong in *Kansas Folklore* claims to exclude national groups, including German, Swedish, Welsh, and Mexican, because their songs are only preserved in their native languages.[20] Yet Swedish and German terms are used later to discuss national customs while Mexican customs do not appear at all.[21] With the rise of multiculturalism through area studies after the Cold War and the efforts of bilingual and bicultural scholars to open up new lines of research, more academic fields turned their attention to non-European cultural issues. Folklorists expanded their field to consider not only rural but urban populations and, in addition to oral traditions and celebrations, to explore dynamic, everyday customs. Folklorist Richard Dorson's work exemplifies this trend by conducting fieldwork in the urban Midwest.

In *Land of the Millrats*, Dorson categorizes ethnic traditions from the Calumet region of Indiana into four categories: presentational-public, such as festivals; historical-civic, such as political coalitions; communal-social, such as weddings and baptisms; and esoteric-private, such as daily folk belief, medicine, and religion. While they have different functions, all "help to reaffirm ethnic self-confidence and vitality in the midst of mainstream culture." Dorson recognizes that these categories often overlap, such as the blending of public and civic functions through social protest theater in Teatro del Desengaño del Pueblo (People's Enlightenment Theater) in Gary, Indiana. Its director, Nicolás Kanellos, is of Greek and Puerto Rican heritage and was involved with Chicano theater developed by Luis Valdez. Dorson documents the group's informal dramatic sketches and song as a Hispanic folk forms to demonstrate how they both entertain and stir a Latin-American constituency to take social action to protect Hispanic language and culture through initiatives such as bilingual education.[22]

Because Latinx folk dance and folk music performances often take place in public arenas and advance social justice issues, Dorson's criteria will be used to examine further examples here that combine public, civic, and social functions of folklore. A crucial example of this combination is LULAC's use of folklore in its political efforts to increase Latinx representation in higher education by fundraising for scholarships. There are fifty-seven LULAC councils in the Midwest: thirteen in Illinois (five of which are in Chicago), eleven in Wisconsin (eight of which are in Milwaukee), twelve in Iowa, ten in Ohio (four of which are in Cincinnati), five in Kansas, two in Indiana, one in Missouri, and one in Michigan. LULAC Council #10 in Davenport, for example, has awarded 750 students with scholarships amounting to over $475,000.[23] One of their fundraising events is an annual Fiesta. The 2014 Fiesta, for example, included performances from Mariachi Campirano and the Quad Cities Ballet Folklórico, as well as the crowning of the LULAC Queen.[24]

While Dorson's work provides a valuable framework for understanding Latinx folklore in the Midwest, more recent folklore collections continue to exclude the Midwest or treat Latinx folklore in the Midwest as additive. For example, *American Folktales: From the Collections of the Library of Congress* only includes Latinx oral traditions from Texas, Colorado, and Florida. Moreover, they are limited to only two sections: jokes and stories for children.[25] Scholarship on folklore in the Midwest tends to reinforce the misconception that Latinx culture is a new development in the region and often frames it as peripheral. An entry on folk art and crafts in *The American Midwest: An Interpretive Encyclopedia*, for example, generalizes that Hispanics from Mexico, the Caribbean, and the American Southwest "added" to and "enrich" diverse Midwestern culture.[26] This ignores other Latinx groups in the Midwest and erases a long history of Latinx communities in the region. Other entries in this collection, however, offer valuable information about the significance of Midwestern Mexican-American low-rider culture (419–421) as well as the production of corridos in Chicago by performers such as Silvano Ramos and Daniel Ramirez that recount migration routes to the Midwest.[27]

Another troubling example of "inclusivity" is *The Greenwood Encyclopedia of American Regional Cultures: The Midwest*. Although the introduction quotes Gloria Anzaldúa to discuss the Midwest as a crossroads and borderland of socioeconomic ambiguities, Latinx Midwestern folklore is often overlooked. Latinx influences are mentioned in relation to food and immigration but often absent in its description of folk and ethnic music. In an entry on "Ethnic, Recreational, and Occupational Identity in the Midwest," Latinx presence is limited to a subsection about the Dutch, which claims that "Across the Midwest, such ethnic festivals flourish, sometimes in spite of changes in town demographics. Holland's Tulip Time Festival, for example, has come to include a Fiesta celebration, which reflects the growth of the Hispanic population in the town."[28] While it is valuable to investigate cultural contact, scholars must break away from the tradition of celebrating white tolerance of racialized others.

Latinx studies offers important investigative inroads but often avoids identifying objects of study as "folklore," perhaps because of the popular perception that the term relegates culture as belonging to a static past and may reinforce stigmatization and racialization of Latinx people. However, recent scholarship takes up the term proudly, such as *Celebrating Latino Folklore: An Encyclopedia of Cultural Traditions*, edited by María Herrera-Sobek. This collection provides an excellent history of folklore scholarship and traces a shift from Hispanicists, who attribute roots to Spain, to Mexicanists, who recognize roots in Mexico. Herrera-Sobek identifies five generations of Latinx folklore scholars and highlights the foundational importance of Américo Paredes's attention to race, class, and politics to develop theoretical paradigms for folklore analysis.[29] The Midwest is mentioned in relation to the saint status of Pedrito Jaramillo, family altars,[30] boogie woogie,[31] corn,[32] folk health beliefs,[33] and *descansos*, handmade memorials on roadsides.[34]

A growing interest in Latinx Midwest scholarship has spurred a number of publications, including an upcoming special issue of *Missouri Folklore Society Journal*—" Latinx and Chicanx Traditional Culture in the Midwest," edited by Norma Cantú. Another upcoming special edition is "Latinas/os and the Midwest" of *The Journal of Latino/Latin American Studies*, edited by Aidé Acosta and Sylvia Martinez. It features the work of Rachel V. González-Martin on Midwestern *quinceañeras* as visual, testimonial/autobiographical narratives. She argues that they render Latinas visible through the claiming of public spaces and social control to author their own stories, especially in small towns with less extensive Latinx networks. José E. Limón's chapter in *The Latina/o Midwest Reader* concerns the translocal cultural connections between Texas and the Midwest that include corridos, conjunto and Tejano music, and folk healing through the pilgrimage site of Don Pedrito Jaramillo in Corpus Christi. Limón argues that studies of Latinx culture in the Midwest must account for the diversity of experiences and affiliations built between various US regions as well as with other Latin American nationalisms.[35] With these important contributions and others, there still remains an urgent need for research on folklore in this field.

## Folklore as Cultural Capital: A Latinx Youth Summit in Iowa

To begin with both the past and future, my first spotlight on Midwest Latinx folklore combines storytelling, one of the most commonly identified types of "folklore," and its potential impact on Latinx youth. The annual Iowa Latinx Conference, now in its nineteenth year, is hosted by the University of Iowa and includes a Latinx Youth Summit for high schools students across the state.[36] Its "Latinx Community Cultural Wealth" workshop contests the ways Latinx students are viewed by majority Anglo institutions as culturally and linguistically deficient. Students tell stories about barriers they faced while others identify assets from the stories using Yosso's Cultural Wealth Model.[37] This six-part cultural capital framework allows students of color and educators to perceive their backgrounds as strengths in order to negotiate obstacles and be successful in higher education.[38]

The Omeyocan Dance Company often presents at the Iowa Latinx Youth Summit. It was co-founded by two brothers, Roberto and Alejandro Franco, who moved to Wisconsin from Mexico in 1999 and 2000.[39] Their performances are not simply entertaining but empower Latinx youth because they engage folklore as a self-affirming and political act. Dance and storytelling fall into Yosso's description of linguistic capital as cultural wealth because they involve intellectual and social skills through communication in multiple languages and/or styles that "may include memorization, attention to detail, dramatic pauses, comedic timing, facial affect, vocal tone, volume, rhythm and rhyme. Linguistic capital also refers to the ability to communicate via visual art, music or poetry."[40] Yosso acknowledges graffiti and hip-hop poetry as examples, but it is also necessary to include traditional arts since they connect expressive forms with their transmission through familial and social networks.

Tissue paper flower centerpieces at the event, along with dance and storytelling, also constitute familial and social capitals, defined by Yosso as "cultural knowledges nurtured among familia (kin) that carry a sense of community history, memory and cultural intuition" and "networks of people and community resources," respectively[41] As a cultural art form, the flowers mark a long history of working together and pooling resources in order to organize events that bring Latinx communities together. All three folkloric elements contribute to the mission of this "cherished gathering to emphasize strengths of Latinx culture and to provide networking opportunities for students and leaders in Iowa."[42]

## Storytelling in Ohio

Elena Foulis also engages with storytelling to reveal the ways Latinxs have shaped the state of Ohio over the last hundred years. While confronting historical amnesia and the myth that Latinxs are an economic burden, she argues that demographics do not tell the whole story. For this reason, the oral histories she shares in *Latin@ Stories Across Ohio* establish a communal past to better understand the conditions, culture, language, and overall impact of Latinx presence in the region.[43] Foulis is invested in portraying Latinx individuals not only as laborers but as fully engaged community members in leadership positions and involved in cultural place making.

For Foulis, adaptation and preservation of culture, rather than assimilation, are goals shared across a number of oral histories from her collection. Many share their experiences with culture shock and the difficulties they faced not having the same kind of Latinx support networks as they did in other regions of the United States or home countries. Grace (Altagracia) Ramos, however, was used to a predominantly Anglo community since she was raised in Fort Madison, Iowa. She developed a Mexican atmosphere in her home in Dayton, Ohio, but her daughter refused to speak Spanish after she was teased at school. Grace resisted this stigma by educating the community about Mexican and Hispanic culture through slideshows and tortilla-making demonstrations at school. This decolonial work required her to do some learning herself since her childhood in Iowa provided little access to some Mexican cultural experiences. She spent time in Texas, where both she and her husband were born, learning about traditional food, mariachi music, and folkloric dance. Armed with these new tools, Grace organized a folkloric dance group that helped to normalize Mexican culture in Dayton through performances that included Anglo children. By making these cultural elements visible, Grace bolstered her daughter's pride in her heritage and resisted racialization.

Grace's daughter also lamented that she had no famous ancestors like her classmates, who were related to the pilgrims. In response, Grace sent an article about Hispanics in the United States to her teacher and told her that "Sabrina's ancestors met the people on the Mayflower...and not only did they meet them, they spoke in Spanish to them (Laughs)" and reminded Sabrina that "the Pilgrims came to your land."[44] While indigenous groups in the Northeast most likely did not speak Spanish, Grace creatively rewrites history to assert their belonging and insists on the legitimacy of their linguistic heritage as well. Midwestern Latinx communities may not rely as readily on the mythology of Aztlán as Chicanxs in the Southwest, but they can count on a shared history with First Peoples of the Americas. This claim to place and belonging is a powerful intervention in Dayton public schools because it educates non-Latinx audiences and Latinx audiences who may share common experiences with stigmatization.

The final storyteller presented here is Alicia Pagan, a school teacher and president of the League of United Latin American Citizens (LULAC) Council #39000 in Dayton, Ohio. Along with her partner, Raymond Two Crows Wallen Ga-li, Pagan offers music and storytelling workshops that connect Latinx, Native American, and other American experiences. In a personal interview, she shared how her retelling of the "The Woman Who Outshone the Sun: The Legend of Lucía Zenteno" impacted both Anglo and Latinx audiences in Ohio. As part of Zapotec oral tradition from the state of Oaxaca, Mexico, the tale recounts how a community shuns a girl with mystical powers and consequently loses their river and fish that leave with her. Hearing Pagan's version of the story prompted three Anglo women to recognize the exclusion of Latinx members in Perry, Ohio. They decided to organize a festival to help the community better understand and provide resources for their emerging Latinx community. Although the event experienced growing pains, one attendee was the superintendent of schools. He had just recently lost his mother, who suffered from Alzheimer's disease. Pagan remembers how he thanked her for reminding him of his new Latinx relatives; he had forgotten them, just as his mother often forgot who he was, but never that she loved him. The experience motivated him to build personal connections with Latinx parents by inviting them to share their culture and engage with the schools.

Another person impacted by Pagan's retelling of the Lucía Zenteno story was a student in her fourth-grade class, Jazaline Gomez; it made her feel that her culture was valued even though she feared her parents were going to be deported. Now she is a student at Sinclair Community College in Dayton and served as a panelist at the LULAC state conference. Pagan feels that "LULAC gave her the opportunity to find her voice. As a storyteller and teacher, I was part of someone else finding their way." Her work exemplifies the dual objectives shared by many Midwestern Latinx folk artists: raise consciousness among non-Latinxs and empower Latinx youth.

## Wearing Folklore: Charrería Culture and Papel Picado

According to the 2014 population estimates, about 9.3 percent of the US Hispanic population lives in the Midwest.[45] Francisco Galvez, owner of a booming online *charrería* (Jalisco and Zacatecas cowboy culture) apparel store, Charro Azteca, says that 18 percent of his sales of come from the Midwest. Some of this may be accounted for by population growth since 2014; however, Illinois is his third largest source of clients after California and Texas. A good deal of these sales may also come from customers with little access to local vendors or those who want higher quality materials. Galvez was raised with mythical stories of *charreadas* (rodeos) because his father grew up as a charro in Mexico. Growing up in LA, it was difficult to have horses due to limited space and a high cost of living, but Galvez decided to continue the tradition through his business.[46] Inspired by his frustrations to find a charro outfit for his son's baptism, people from across the United States now send him orders to mark special events such as weddings and proms.[47] Charro items are available for sale in the Midwest, at places such as the Westland Flea Market in Columbus, Ohio. Yet, as made evident by Galvez's success, technology continues to improve access to popular traditions that celebrate folkloric roots, regardless of location.

Beatriz Vasquez designs costumes as well but uses paper instead of fabric. She moved with her family from Brownsville, Texas, to Indiana in 1990 where she faced culture shock and isolation from other Latinxs. In 2007, after realizing that her studies at the School of Art and Design in Indianapolis had not helped her to identify as a Mexican American artist, Vasquez traveled to her mother's birthplace, San Luis Potosí, Mexico, to work with craftsmen in a variety of mediums. This was a return since Mexico is a second home to her after having spent much time with her mother's family in Matamoros. In San Luis Potosí, she discovered the art of papel picado. Her work honors the tradition of decorative tissue paper banners, but involves individually cut pieces. While some are wall sized and others are wearable art such as dresses, many explore issues of feminism and social justice.[48]

Although Vasquez does not identify as a Midwestern artist and recently moved to San Francisco for a residency, she feels "grateful to have been deprived of my Mexican culture in the Midwest. This deprivation only strengthened my love for my culture."[49] For Vasquez, the problem is not a lack of diversity, but rather a lack of appreciation for diversity. She worked against this trend while working in the Indianapolis Public Schools (IPS) for eight years, first as an ESL associate and later as an administrator and the first artist resident for IPS. One example of her art-activism at IPS is a papel picado, bilingual poster she designed for The Connection Fair, which put Spanish-speaking families in contact with community resources.[50]

Even now that Vasquez is a full-time artist, she continues to educate others by accompanying her exhibitions with lectures about the importance of preserving papel picado as an indigenous craft and honoring those who still create it in its traditional form. Her art "derives from my desire to bring indigenous crafts accepted and recognized in the world of fine art."[51] In 2015, she created "La Negrita PAN" for the annual Venezuelan Ball in Indianapolis. This piece honors traditional foodways by recreating the iconic face of a mestiza woman from the corn flour food label Harina PAN.[52]

## Fairs and Festivals

Fairs take place all over the United States, but they are often larger and longer in the Midwest because of the region's agricultural roots. Political presence at Midwestern state fairs is also important to secure support for candidates at both the state and national level. According to the White House Rural Council, during Obama's first term, six of eight Cabinet Secretaries and administration officials that visited state fairs traveled to the Midwest.[53] The US national imaginary also maintains that the Midwest is a geographically insulated and culturally primed site to preserve culture in the "simple" heartland. This popular perception is both reflected and perpetuated in the Rodgers and Hammerstein hit stage musical and 1945 film *State Fair* based on Philip Strong's 1932 novel about the Iowa State Fair. Through the love stories of a farmer's children, it mediates growing pressures for rural Midwesterners to leave home for bigger cities. With changing socioeconomic landscapes and declining Anglo birth rates, both rural and metro Midwestern populations have depended on Latin American immigrants and long-established Latinx populations as economic lifelines.[54]

There are a wide variety of state-wide and local Latinx festivals across the Midwest. One of the oldest is "Fiesta Mexicana," established in 1933 in Topeka, Kansas, to raise funds for the parish school at Our Lady of Guadalupe Church, which continues today.[55] "Fiesta del Sol" was founded in the Pilsen neighborhood of Chicago in 1972. Nationally publicized as the "largest Latino festival in the Midwest," it is part of the Pilsen Neighbors Community Council's (PNCC) year-round community organizing. The PNCC is a nonprofit organization dedicated to addressing social justice issues including "immigration reform, education reform, work force development and healthcare. We work to develop new local leaders, facilitating coalitions and assisting in the development of campaigns."[56] "Fiesta del Sol" now includes a Recorrido del Sol 5K run to support scholarships for undocumented students through the Illinois Dream Fund, a college fair, and an expungement workshop. Similar to LULAC's efforts, this festival combines presentational-public and historical-civic functions in order to promote cultural vitality and improve Latinx life chances.

In a conversation with the authors, Elena Foulis said that "Festival Latino" in Columbus, Ohio, is an opportunity to recognize Latinx communities' long-standing impact on the region while also opening spaces to learn about the diversity within one's own Latinx communities. Sharing her own observation that there is something "muy Midwest" about festivals, Foulis finds they provide a unique opportunity for people to come together and connect over common interests, celebrating everything from produce to ethnic and immigrant groups. She explains that people mark "Festival Latino" on their calendars and travel from other cities and states, even if they have their own local Latinx festivals: "I was there when it started, in 1996 when it began and I remember even then people coming from different parts of Ohio craving for music, flavors, anything that reminded them of home. And it continues to be that way."[57] Folklore is an integral part of these place-making events, including traditional foods, music, dance, and artesanías such as Mexican tissue paper flowers.

It is also important to note Latinx participation in multiethnic folk festivals across the Midwest. The National Folk Festival, developed by the National Council of Folk Arts in 1934 in St. Louis, claims to be the first to present a Tex-Mex conjunto at an event of national stature. Although an itinerant event, it was hosted twenty-three times in the Midwest and provided infrastructure for the continuation of locally run festivals such as the Great Lakes Folk Festival in East Lansing established by the Michigan State University Museum after a three-year partnership with the National Folk Festival from 1999 to 2001.[58] Over time, the Great Lakes Folk Festival has presented a wide variety of Latinx musical forms, including Tejano, Mariachi, Dominican merengue, Puerto Rican Bomba and Plena, and Andean music.[59]

## Musical Traditions: Corridos, Cumbia, and Confronting Isolation

José Limón traces the historic links built between the Midwest and Texas, including the work of Américo Paredes and his analysis of power dynamics, in "El corrido de Kiansis." This work foregrounds the superior skill and strength of Mexican cowboys to their Anglo counterparts and how Anglo domination treats Mexican lives as disposable. The lyrics highlight the contributions of Mexicans and Mexican Americans in the cattle drives of the 1860s that made the emerging industrialization of the Midwest possible, even before the construction of railroads to the region. Limón demonstrates both how Midwestern Anglos brought racist labor hierarchies with them after purchasing land in Texas and how Mexicans inherited some Tejano Mexican resistance when passing through on their way to the Midwest, including the corrido form.[60] Today, Latinx individuals born in the Southwest and elsewhere continue to be transplanted to the

Midwest because of family, work, or studies. Along with a growing Latinx population, corridos and other Latinx folk music styles remind audiences how Latinx people shape sociocultural landscapes in the Midwest.

Two contemporary Midwestern corrido artists are Jesus "Chuy" Negrete and Juan Díes. Both were born in San Luis Potosí, Mexico. Negrete grew up in Texas and then South Chicago, where he became involved with the farm workers movement and Chicano theater.[61] As an ethnomusicologist and son of a Bracero, Negrete led a Smithsonian traveling exhibit on the migration of Braceros in the 1940s through the 1960s, during the labor shortage of World War II.[62] In addition to using folk music to teach about the history of Mexican labor in the United States, Negrete uses corridos to resist current socioeconomic oppression, such as the stripping away of workers' rights in Wisconsin and violence affecting Latinx communities.[63] With the family of Delfino Mora, a sixty-two-year old Mexican immigrant killed in a Chicago alley, Negrete performed a corrido about Mora's life and death.[64] At the end of the corrido, Negrete calls, "Delfino Mora?" four times and the group answers, "Presente!" This custom is used in manifestations to mark participants' presence as social actors as well as witnesses. Not only do they demand that Mora be remembered, but they join together in social struggle.

Juan Díes immigrated to the United States at eighteen to attend Indiana University. Like Negrete, he studied folklore/ethnomusicology and later moved to Chicago. There, he co-founded Sones de México Ensemble, a nonprofit funded in part by the Illinois Arts Council. In 2015, Díes and Sones de México represented the Latinx Midwest nationally by hosting the first workshop to be led entirely in Spanish at the Library of Congress's American Folklife Center. Together with students, they developed a corrido about Sandra Bland along with Poet Laureate Consultant in Poetry, Juan Felipe Herrera, who translated the song into English. Forming part of a national debate on police brutality and racism, the lyrics cast suspicion on her death in 2015, which was officially ruled a suicide. The song warns others: "Tengan esto muy presente: / la violencia seguirá / Aunque se grabe en video / eso no te salvará" (Violence is going to continue. (Think about it.) / Even though you have a video / It may not save you). The only line written originally in English is a call to action: "This isn't our last stand."[65] Their collaboration follows corrido narrative tradition by portraying Sandra as a hero who stood up for her rights.

Quinto Imperio, a first-generation Mexican immigrant band, confronts social injustice in Chicago through lyrics about their own experiences as undocumented immigrants.[66] They lead fundraising efforts for The Dreamers and Allies Run Scholarship for undocumented youth from the Barrio de las Empacadoras (Back of the Yards) neighborhood. Band member Quintiliano "Kin-T" Rios explains that because cumbia adapts to different local socioeconomic climates, it is "a gateway that gave us an opportunity to express our feelings, frustrations, and experiences as immigrants. As we explored our hybrid of sounds, we remained true to folk elements from our background."[67] These include playing and teaching folk styles such as Marimba (from Veracruz, Mexico), which inspires much of the melodic arrangements on their album *Crónica Inmigrante*. Mariachi corridos, particularly from Jalisco, Mexico, inform storytelling techniques throughout their lyrics. Rios describes how "much like the corridos, our songs honor the virtues and challenges immigrants face, particularly in times where our community is under attack through policies aiming to instill fear and disenfranchise us. At the end of the day, we hope to let them know that we have to keep on going and not lose hope through our music." For Rios, the song "Cumbe" especially exemplifies the importance of folklore to their music as it recounts how African and indigenous grit made it possible to survive and pass down their culture to their present generation.[68]

Like Quinto Imperio, the Kansas City rock band Making Movies confronts anti-immigrant hostilities with music informed by folk traditions. Band member Enrique Chi explains that there are no easy divisions in American music because, as a compilation of Spanish, African, indigenous American, and Middle Eastern cultures, it is a living testament to migration history that cannot be denied by contemporary political borders: "Politicians lie, but music doesn't."[69] They drive this message home with the words "We are all immigrants" printed on T-shirts and a flag waved during performances. While Enrique and his brother Diego Chi are Panamanian Americans, bandmates and brothers Juan Carlos and Andres Chaurand are Mexican American. Enrique first met their mother, Maria Chaurand, after seeing her Westside Kansas City folk dance troupe, El Grupo Folklorico Atotonilco. She encouraged him to meet her sons due to their shared interest in music. Making Movies' percussion sometimes features the Chaurand brothers tapping, a folk element they learned from their mother. The band created a yearly summer camp for underprivileged youth at Mattie Rhodes, a nonprofit health, arts, and social service center.[70]

The Chi family moved to the Kansas City area when Enrique was six because of his father's studies and to their particular suburb because of a highly recommended public school English as a Second Language teacher. Although isolated from other Latinos, Enrique says this teacher allowed him to survive the immigrant experience with a positive outlook. Shielding him from closemindedness, he would later discover, she inspired him to become an educator and activist himself. His mother also taught him to connect with Spanish speakers in the community by inviting them into their home and sometimes requesting a cooking lesson on a dish from their culture to help them feel needed and valued. As he discovered groups of other Latin American backgrounds in the Kansas City community, Enrique also took up instruments from their cultures. He became an "honorary Puerto Rican for the night" during Christmas parrandas thanks to his willingness to learn to play the Puerto Rican cuatro. He explains, "If I could play something that would make them remember and make them feel connected to their past lives, it would light up the room. Even in little bar shows, or just jamming with my dad, I realized maybe that's the role that I was meant to play, music that connects with heritage or past."[71]

While Chi is invested in preserving the particularities of Latinx folk cultures, he also strives to help others recognize shared ethos across musical traditions. Both the title of Making Movies' last album, *I Am Another You*, based on a Mayan phrase, and lyrics about Chi's family history draw attention to shared experiences of humanity. Chi plans to ask audiences to record family stories on their phones and send them to the band so they can be used to create future work. This kind of documentation is important to Chi because "our elders won't be here forever."[72] Like Delgadillo and Foulis, Chi is working against the archival erasure of Latinx lives.

Ed East is an Afro-Latinx musician who made in home in Iowa after receiving a scholarship to attend the University of Northern Iowa. He has taught instrumental music in Clinton and Waterloo, Iowa. East confided during an interview that living in the Midwest can be isolating because of the cold weather and the lack of Latinxs needed to create a sense of community. However, performing Latin American music affords him the opportunity to help break that feeling of isolation by bringing Latinxs together who otherwise would have not known each other. When asked to compare his experiences playing with other Latinx members in bands including Calle Sur, Los Llaneros, Mariachi de Colores, and The Afro-Latin Project, with his experience as the only Latinx member of Orquesta Alto Maíz (OAM) for twenty-six years, he feels that with OAM:

> it was an honor to be in the company of the best musicians in the state who shared a love for the kind of music I grew up listening to and who would turn to me as the "authenticity police" whenever they wanted to sound authentic. The difference between OAM and other bands who have Latino/a members is that background vocals are easier with the latter! :) With Latino members, we share a common body of music which can be accessed without a musical score. Also, the rapport with the Spanish speakers in the audience becomes more dynamic.[73]

While OAM performs some contemporary arrangements of folk tunes or arrangements in a folkloric style, the other bands endeavor to preserve folk traditions or "re-create music the way it's always been performed (as far as we know)." East once traveled with other OAM members to Cuba to "witness the roots of salsa music and dance, and I was able to learn about this genre directly from some of the most respected authorities on Afro-Cuban folk music and dance." He said it was a transformative experience and led him to develop the Afro-Latin Project, a series of educational programs that teach about African cultural influences throughout Latin America. When asked about how he deals with the distance from Latinx cultural centers, he explained that although most musicians strive for innovation, many reach back to folkloric styles, often through audio and video recordings. Once considered rare recordings, many are now available online, which East is grateful for, but he and fellow musicians also attend live lessons and performances when possible.[74]

During workshops, East often challenges the misconception that all Latinx people share a single racial identity because he is often mistaken as African American while his light-skinned and Colombian Calle Sur colleague, Karin Stein, is assumed to be Anglo. Similarly, Daniel Martinez, a Peruvian musician and director of the band Jarana in Nebraska, counters the assumption that all Midwestern Latinxs are of Mexican heritage. He emphasizes the beauty and value of Latinx diversity, especially because many do not have opportunities to travel outside of their own communities. For Martinez, the Spanish language and its colonial history are like a clothesline from which Latin American national heritages hang; they have things in common, such as the guitar, but the individual articles of "clothing" look quite different because of particular traditions and beliefs. He describes the power of the Spanish language to make connections with Latinx students:

> It is a very interesting and wonderful feeling to be related to the kids in a way that nobody else will understand...if I play music from Mexico, I see a smile on their face, it's like they are proud to have a Latino guy performing in front of them. Like, "this is a guy from my race, he is one of us," this is the pride I feel from them. For me it's a big responsibility because I want to make sure that whatever I do, they will keep feeling proud of me, even though we have never met before.[75]

Martinez feels that his teaching opens up possibilities for acceptance and equality in the face of everyday realities of racism and discrimination. He also instills this pride in his own children by maintaining musical traditions at home such as Christmas tunes called *villancicos*.

## Folkloric Dance as Cultural Capital in Ohio

Like Latinx folk music, Latinx folk dance is practiced across the Midwest through a variety of settings, styles, and national backgrounds. While this diversity cannot be fully examined here, this article compares the experiences of two Mexican American folk dance directors in Ohio. One common thread between their work and that of other artist-educators mentioned here is that they engage a pedagogy of love that Marjorie Faulstich Orellana describes as confronting dominant social processes such as deportation and the shaming of translanguaging, meaning the use of two or more languages or registers to mediate understanding. Orellana argues that rather than view bilingual and bicultural children as deficient, educators must value students' linguistic and cultural resources and recognize how they allow students to accomplish meaningful tasks.[76] Yosso and Orellana's work provides valuable frameworks for understanding Latinx folklore as a vehicle to combat the silencing of Latinx youth in educational institutions.

In Cleveland, Lilly Corona Moreno's Ballet Folklorico Tepehuani Nelli (True Conqueror in Nahuatl) embodies a pedagogy of love by creating a safe place to use Spanish and connect with others: "We are a family, we become very close. Some of the people I danced with as a teen, I still keep in touch. We have gatherings at each other's homes, cookouts, parties at houses, for Christmas."[77] Her parents, Amalia and Jorge, immigrated to Cleveland from Mexico in the 1960s and founded Grupo Cultural Azteca in the mid-1970s. She recounts how her parents went to great lengths to keep their culture alive, such as traveling to Mexico to bring back knowledge and materials for the group. Although Moreno Corona acknowledges there is greater access today through tutorials on YouTube and the social media of other folkloric groups, she continues to struggle with distance and isolation:

> Because we are so far it's very easy to lose our culture, our language, our history and I know it has helped me through our group to learn about our culture and now I'm teaching our children. We are not always surrounded by Mexicans or Latinos and I think it's easy to lose and the dance group has been a tremendous treasure; it goes beyond the stage, the costumes. They really nurtured us in that way.[78]

Corona Moreno renamed the group after taking over from her mother in 1999. She teaches dances from a variety of Mexican states, making sure that both dancers and workshop participants understand the regional histories and symbolic meanings behind particular costumes and movements. The group also presents pre-Hispanic dances but as folkloric performance rather than ritual (as they did not grow up in indigenous communities). However, Corona Moreno takes care to explain the significance of ritual elements and belief systems involved in these dances, such as saluting the cardinal directions, the use of copal incense to drive away negative energies, and asking mother earth for permission to dance. Giving workshops in schools helped her decide she wanted to be a Spanish teacher, and both roles offer opportunities to replace "lazy Mexican" stereotypes with appreciation for indigenous knowledge. While reactions to the group are overwhelmingly positive, one case of racist behavior led to student suspensions, which she says also served as a learning experience.[79]

Elaina Hernández founded the folkloric dance group El Corazon de Mexico in Toledo, Ohio, in 1996. Hernández's paternal grandfather emigrated from Michoacán, Mexico, to work on the railroad in Toledo. His wife, Pauline Soto, was as Mexican folk dancer who passed on the tradition to Hernández's aunt. In an interview, Hernández shared that she makes sure that people of all linguistic and cultural backgrounds are welcome to join: "Many dancers don't speak Spanish. I teach in English, and even if someone doesn't speak it, you don't have to worry to explain everything. When we have workshops, they only teach in Spanish, it's not really a problem, you can understand counts and that…Luckily I have a lot of people around me to help, I can understand half, they understand half, together we can make it connect."[80] Hernández invites translanguaging as a natural part of their learning process. Although her father is Mexican, he does not speak Spanish because he was told, along with many of his generation, that he would be ignorant. Her mother, who is Italian and German, is a Spanish speaker because she wanted to help migrant workers in Toledo as a social worker. Hernadez's mother also makes all of their costumes according to her instructions and free of charge. In the rasquache way, they clip coupons for fabric, make sure not to waste any scraps, fundraise through local businesses, and enjoy free publicity for performances from their local newspaper, *La prensa*.

Hernández studied to be a public school teacher but did not want to teach to a test. She finds she can be "more involved with students, you know their parents, can ask them about school, talking to them about boyfriends, making sure they are making good choices; you can't talk to your students that way in a school setting, or even give your student a hug."[81] Hernández says that some of her students, who are said to have behavior problems in school, are respectful and helpful during dance practice. This may be because Hernández creates an environment in which students find their experiences affirming and purposeful, key ingredients to a pedagogy of love as described by Orellana.[82] This may be true for other extra-curricular activities, but members often join because "their grandmother and mother danced, or mom wanted to dance. It's tradition or family connection that brings people into the group. People not from Toledo, they'll remember learning dances for Mother's Day, memories from where they were little."[83] Because Hernández is a role model and an important part of her students' lives and later in their children's lives, she wants them to be politically conscious of what is going on in the world. She takes them to the Farm Labor Organizing Committee social justice parade and elections, encourages dancers that are eligible to vote, and lets them know they can turn to her for help. When an undocumented young boy in the group was detained by Immigration and Customs Enforcement, she was the one he called for support.[84]

Corona Moreno and Hernández's work exhibits how folk dance draws on familial, social, and linguistic capital. Both directors inherited an interest in folk dance from their families and teach these traditions to their children. Their groups embody Yosso's description of familia, or kinship ties, that extend beyond blood relatives to build a healthy network of community and resources.[85] For her leadership, Hernández won the Ohio Heritage Fellowship, a $5,000 award and recognition event. However, neither Hernández nor Corona Moreno runs a nonprofit organization. Hernández prefers to maintain the group's independence from government funding while Corona Moreno has considered it but is hesitant because she has heard it is a difficult process. While Latinx folklore does not depend on grant funding, it is important to examine both the opportunities and limitations of government support.

## Latinx Representation and Access to Arts Resources

Some Latinx folklore artists have benefited from state funding, especially from traditional arts apprenticeship programs that allow artists to pass down their knowledge to younger generations. In addition to Teresa Cuevas's Kansas Folk Arts apprenticeship mentioned in the introduction, other examples include a Missouri Arts Council apprenticeship led by Carmen Dence, director of a Carribbean dance troupe called Grupo Atlantico, and Wisconsin Arts Board apprenticeships led by J. Alberto Campos in Mariachi music and Roberto Franco in Mexica dance.[86] Among the artists interviewed here, Daniel Martinez feels fortunate to be part of the Nebraska Arts Council's teaching and touring artist rosters. Ed East says that the Iowa Arts Council provides fair opportunities but should offer more assistance with grant applications. Beatriz Vasquez received the

Creative Renewal Grant from the Indianapolis Arts Council in 2015 but asserts that the council must do more because "there are many talented and gifted Latino artists on the Midwest, but it seems that without the proper nationality, residency or education they continue to be unrecognized, uncelebrated and ignored. I believe art related administration positions should start with diverse staff members to encourage knowledge of diverse artists and their work."[87]

State arts agencies across the United States distribute funding from their legislatures and the National Endowment of the Arts (NEA). Even when their budgets are not under attack, there is concern about the accessibility of these funds to Latinx artists. Juan Díes, the Chicago-based ethnomusicologist-folklorist discussed previously, was hired by the Ohio Arts Council (OAC) to address this issue through a twenty-five-day fieldwork project in 2009. By documenting 187 artists, he created an Ohio Latino Artist Directory with a focus on folk and traditional arts. Through interviews, Díes found that Latinx artists in Ohio are often isolated from one another and from resources due to cultural and linguistic barriers, including unfamiliarity with grant culture and difficulties stemming from a shift to an online grant submission system.

Díes also learned that Latinx artists felt mistrust toward the OAC because of a failed Latinx artist organization formed in 1993 through OAC technical and financial support. Members of that organization, OLAA (perhaps Ohio Latino Arts Alliance), traveled around the state offering help with grant submissions, which resulted in thirty applications. The group met throughout the 1990s but dissolved due to lack of leadership. Those involved with OLAA said that they received the same amount of funding in 2003 as in 1993. Furthermore, they felt it "was a ploy of tokenism to meet the short-term political interests of the OAC" and were skeptical about Díes's new work to increase Latinx involvement. This sentiment is expressed by poet Joe Carrillo in *This Bridge Called My Back*:

> In leftist feminist circles we are dealt with as a political issue, rather than as flesh and blood human beings. We represent the party line, but the truth is, "We're not as happy as we look/on their/wall." We have had it with the word "outreach" referring to our joining racist white women's organizations. The question keeps coming up—where exactly then, is in? It smells like white to us. We have had it.[88]

In response to artists' frustrations, Díes encouraged the OAC to act as a catalyst for emerging Latinx artistic leadership by publicizing successful collaborations and suggested three Latina candidates to serve as grant panelists of Latinx artists with OAC.

Despite these recommendations, only 23 of 7,866 grants (about 0.3%) from 2006 and 2017 were awarded to organizations that identify as Hispanic/Latinx. Many of the non-Latinx identifying organizations may showcase Latinx artists and serve Latinx audiences, and yet, it is alarming that during the same period only 10 of 6,275 individual excellence grants were awarded to individuals who self-identify as Hispanic/Latinx (about 0.16% of the total), although three additional annual awards were won by Latinxs.[89] Moreover, there is no significant change of Latinx OAC grant awardees after Díes's study, although it is unclear whether this reflects of a lack of follow-through with his proposals or a need for new strategies.

Even with a lack of improvement in Latinx representation, the OAC is the only Midwestern state arts agency to compile a Latinx Artist Directory, although Latinx artists are often included in general folk artist directories. The Wisconsin Arts Board, for example, includes Cuban and Mexican artists on its website (wisconsinfolks.org) and plans to continue fieldwork in Latinx and immigrant communities begun in 2003.[90] The OAC has had two Latinx board members in its history, but the current Latinx board member is not directly involved in the arts in any other capacity. While tokenism may still be a concern, some Midwestern states such as Nebraska have never had Latinx board members while others claim they are unable to provide this information. Several states report that they do not collect data on the ethnicity of their panelists, boards, nor awardees, perhaps as a result of a culture of colorblindness or because the NEA only requires data about the ethnicities of benefiting audiences. Collecting more data on ethnicity and creating Latinx artist directories may be important first steps to increase Latinx access and visibility in the arts, but they are not the only interventions needed.

# FUTURE DIRECTIONS OF MIDWEST LATINX STUDIES

As we have endeavored to model here, Midwest Latinx studies must continue to cross disciplinary boundaries in ways that bring together methodologies and insights from across the humanities. Coauthorship is, unfortunately, less common in several of these fields. Valuable frameworks may emerge from approaching research questions from a variety of perspectives not only across anthologies but within individual studies. Moreover, this interdisciplinary work can only be productive by remaining rooted to the material and social realities of the Midwest as they shape Latinx communities in ways that are both similar to and unique from other Latinx populations throughout the United States. For this reason, we cannot envision the future of Latinx Midwest studies without addressing the need to make Midwestern Latinx voices foundational to its development. Just as we have shown how Latinx artists continue to struggle with issues of access, both to grant funding for their own work and to open access to higher education for Latinx youth, we must consider the impact of these racialized limitations to our own field.

Latinx students, who may arrive to university campuses already equipped with both the bicultural and bilingual skills needed to investigate a wide variety of Latinx studies issues, including Latinx folklore, are often poorly represented across Midwestern universities. For example, 4 percent of undergraduates and 3 percent of graduate students enrolled in the university system of Ohio in 2016 were Hispanic, which appears proportionate considering 3.6 percent of Ohio's population was Hispanic that year.[91] However, the Hispanic population is younger than the white population: 25.7 is the median age for Hispanics in Ohio, versus 39.3 for all Ohioans, meaning a greater proportion are college-aged.[92] In 2016, 5 percent of students enrolled in Ohio K-12 public schools were Hispanic, 3.7 percent of incoming freshman at Ohio State University were Hispanic, but only 2.3 percent were Latinx and residents of Ohio.[93] For this reason, even at universities where Latinx students are represented proportionately in comparison with their Midwest Latinx state population, Midwestern Latinx youth are still underrepresented. Of course, being Latinx and growing up in the Midwest are hardly prerequisites for contributing to this field. However, Midwest Latinx perspectives and participatory research should inform future trajectories. Higher numbers of Latinx students and faculty in Midwestern universities can contribute to further legitimizing Midwest Latinx studies as an emerging field of study and help convince administrations of the urgent need to continue building Latinx Studies programs in general. For example, The University of Iowa first began to offer a Latina/o studies minor in the spring of 2015 after several attempts in the early 2000s to garner support.[94]

The struggle for people of color and nondominant ethnicities to become leaders of their fields continues across the nation. In 2016, only 7 percent of doctorate recipients across the United States were Hispanic or Latino,[95] compared to 17.6 percent Latinx of the total US population.[96] Only 4.7 percent were Hispanic or Latino who were also US citizens or residents, meaning they were more likely to have grown up in the United States. Furthermore, Latinxs who successfully enter academic positions as faculty continue to be racialized in their efforts to obtain tenure. Because Latinx faculty are more likely than white faculty to have additional service responsibilities and administrative duties, Ponjuan argues that work roles should be clarified and that excessive workloads should be reduced or delegated to other faculty members.[97] Structural changes must be made to address the continuation of inequalities so that all of the fields that inform Midwest Latinx studies can be driven by a more racially, ethnically, and socioeconomically diverse group of scholars, including Latinx scholars from the Midwest.

One example of efforts to repair the broken educational pipeline for Latinx students in the Midwest is the Latinx Space for Enrichment & Research (LASER) founded by Frederick Aldama. This mentoring program not only prepares high school Latinx students in Columbus, Ohio, to navigate college admissions but also provides a network of support to retain Latinx undergraduate and graduate students at Ohio State University. From tenured faculty to high school students, scholars from each level of education reach back to encourage and guide those who are striving to break into the next level of study and research, bringing with them unique cultural and linguistic knowledge that has historically been excluded. Mentoring programs and department/university policies should be carefully designed and revised to these ends. More can be accomplished if Midwestern institutions work together by sharing their successes and struggles with each another to determine best practices.

## CONCLUSION

The fields of education, literary and cultural studies, and folklore studies may use different terminology to discuss the transmission of cultural values, practices, and knowledge, but they can inform one another by sharing insights across fieldwork and analysis. This article placed these perspectives in dialogue with one another in order to demonstrate how many Latinxs in the Midwest envision folklore as central and not peripheral to claiming public spaces and calling attention to the diversity of Latinx experiences. While this may also be true in other regions of the United States, there is an increased sense of urgency in areas that are not typically perceived as sites of Latinx folklore production. From Latinx folk artists to Latinx Studies scholars working in folklore, there is a strong commitment among Latinx Midwesterners to both forge a sense of belonging through shared history and build bridges between Latinx and non-Latinx understandings. Yosso's Cultural Wealth Model and Orellana's pedagogy of love can be used to conceptualize folklore as self-affirming and self-determined Latinx education as resistance to erasure and marginalization. Further scholarly and artistic connections must be made across folkloric art forms, states, and regions to further investigate Latinx access to resources.

## NOTES

1. Vicky McNamara, "Sister Marilyn Reyes Applies Experience to Assisting Migrant," *Herencia, Fiestas, Horizontes,* The State of Kansas Advisory Committee on Mexican American Affairs, 18–20, 1979. http://cdm16884.contentdm.oclc.org/cdm/singleitem/collection/p16884coll49/id/45/rec/5.
2. Kansas Historical Society, "Teresa Cuevas: Kansas Folk Art," 2001. https://www.kshs.org/kansapedia/teresa-cuevas-kansas-folk-art/16546.
3. McNamara, "Sister Marilyn Reyes Applies Experience to Assisting Migrant," 1979.
4. Kansas Historical Society, "Teresa Cuevas: Kansas Folk Art," 2011.
5. American Folklore Society, "What Is Folklore?" *Asknet.org*, Retrieved from https://www.afsnet.org/page/WhatIsFolklore?
6. Maria Herrera-Sobek, *Celebrating Latino Folklore: An Encyclopedia of Cultural Traditions* (Santa Barbara, CA: ABC-CLIO, 2012), xxiv–xxv. http://public.eblib.com/choice/publicfullrecord.aspx?p=995935.
7. Herrera-Sobek, *Celebrating Latino Folklore,* xxv.
8. María Eugenia Cotera, "Latino/a Literature and the Uses of Folklore," in *The Routledge Companion to Latina/o Literature*, ed. Suzanne Bost and Frances R. Aparicio (London: Routledge, 2013), 216–228.
9. Eugenia Cotera, "Latino/a Literature and the Uses of Folklore," 217.
10. Juan Díes, "Ohio Latino Arts Directory Final Report," *Ohio Folk and Traditional Arts: Fieldwork Projects,* 2009. http://www.ohiofolkarts.org/ohio-latino-arts-directory/.

11. Judit Moschkovich, "But I Know You American Woman," in *This Bridge Called My Back: Writings by Radical Women of Color*, ed. Cherríe Moraga and Gloria Anzaldúa (Albany: State University of New York Press, 2015), 73–77.
12. Audre Lorde, "The Master's Tools Will Never Dismantle the Master's House," in *This Bridge Called My Back: Writings by Radical Women of Color*, ed. Cherríe Moraga and Gloria Anzaldúa (Albany: State University of New York Press, 2015), 94–102.
13. Eileen Diaz McConnell, "Latinos in the Rural Midwest: The Twentieth-Century Historical Context Leading to Contemporary Challenges," in *Apple Pie and Enchiladas: Latino Newcomers in the Rural Midwest*, ed. Ann V. Millard and Jorge Chapa (Austin: University of Texas Press, 2004), 26–40.
14. Diaz McConnell, "Latinos in the Rural Midwest."
15. Steven L. Driever, "Latinos in Polynucleated Kansas City," in *Hispanic Spaces, Latino Places: Community and Cultural Diversity in Contemporary America*, ed. Daniel D. Arreola (Austin: University of Texas Press, 2004), 207–233.
16. Theresa Delgadillo, *Latina Lives in Milwaukee* (Urbana: University of Illinois Press, 2015), 11.
17. Delgadillo, *Latina Lives in Milwaukee*, 7–8.
18. Roger P. Davis, "The Heard Voice: The Emergence of the Hispanic Across the Mid-West: 1971–1985." *Journal of Latino-Latin American Studies* 3, no. 1 (Spring 2008): 4–15.
19. Davis, "The Heard Voice," 11.
20. Henry H. Malone, "Folksongs and Ballads: Part I," in *Kansas Folklore*, ed. S. J. Sackett and William E. Koch (Lincoln: University of Nebraska Press, 1961), 139, 138–160.
21. S. J. Sackett, "Customs," in *Kansas Folklore*, ed. S. J. Sackett and William E. Koch (Lincoln: University of Nebraska Press, 1961), 196–205.
22. Richard M. Dorson, *Land of the Millrats* (Cambridge, MA: Harvard University Press, 1981), 138–147.
23. LULAC Council 10. "We Want Students to Succeed in College!" 2013. http://www.lulac10.org/scholarship.html; LULAC Councils. 2017. http://lulac.org/about/find_lulac_councils/.
24. Hola America News, "Celebrating 55 Years of LULAC Davenport," September 4, 2014. http://holaamericanews.com/es/celebrating-55-years-of-lulac-davenport/.
25. Carl Lindahl, *American Folktales: From the Collections of the Library of Congress* (Armonk, NY: M.E. Sharpe, 2004).
26. Robert T. Teske, "Folk Arts and Crafts," in *The American Midwest: Folklore*, ed. Andrew R. L. Cayton, Richard Sisson, and Chris Zacher, 363-365 (Bloomington: Indiana University Press, 2007), 354.
27. William Lockwood, "Car Customizing," in *The American Midwest: Folklore*, ed. James P. Leary, Andrew R. L. Cayton, Richard Sisson, and Chris Zacher, 419–421 (Bloomington: Indiana University Press, 2007); W. K. McNeil and James P. Leary, "Folk Song," in *The American Midwest: Folklore*, ed. Andrew R. L. Cayton, Richard Sisson, and Chris Zacher (Bloomington: Indiana University Press, 2007), 390–393.
28. Ruth Olson, "Folklore," in *The Greenwood Encyclopedia of American Regional Cultures: The Midwest*, ed. Joseph W. Slade, and Judith Yaross Lee (ABC-CLIO, 2004).
29. Herrera-Sobek, *Celebrating Latino Folklore*, xxv–xxviii.
30. Herrera-Sobek, *Celebrating Latino Folklore*, xxv–xxviii.
31. Herrera-Sobek, *Celebrating Latino Folklore*, 135.
32. Herrera-Sobek, *Celebrating Latino Folklore*, 748.
33. Herrera-Sobek, *Celebrating Latino Folklore*, 190.

34. Herrera-Sobek, *Celebrating Latino Folklore*, 400.
35. Jose E. Limón, "Al Norte toward Home: Texas, the Midwest, and Mexican American Critical Regionalism," in *The Latina/o Midwest Reader*, ed. Omar Valerio-Jimenez, Santiago Vaquera-Vasquez, and Claire Fox (Urbana: University of Illinois Press, 2017).
36. The University of Iowa, "The 19th Annual Latinx Conference," *Diversity at Iowa: Building Community*, 2017. https://diversity.uiowa.edu/event/19th-annual-iowa-latinx-conference.
37. T. J. Yosso, "Whose Culture Has Capital?" *Race, Ethnicity and Education* 8, no. 1 (2005): 69–91.
38. The University of Iowa, "Workshop Descriptions," n.d. https://uiowa.edu/iowalatinoconference/workshop-descriptions.
39. Omeyocan Dance Company, "About Us: Our Mission." http://www.aztecfiredance.com/index_files/Page1677.htm.
40. T. J. Yosso, "Whose Culture Has Capital?" *Race, Ethnicity and Education* 8, no. 1 (2005): 69–91, 78–79.
41. Yosso, "Whose Culture Has Capital?," 79.
42. University of Iowa, "The 19th Annual Latinx Conference," 2017.
43. Elena Foulis, *Latin@ Stories Across Ohio. iBooks* (Columbus: Ohio State University, 2015).
44. Foulis, *Latin@ Stories Across Ohio*.
45. Pew Research Center, "Demographic and Economic Profiles of Hispanics by State and County, 2014: Latinos as Percent of Population, by State, 2014." 2017. http://www.pewhispanic.org/states/.
46. Francisco Galvez, e-mail message to author, June 9, 2017.
47. Jessica Garcia, "After the Problem He Ran into with His Son's Baptism, This Latino Dad Decided to Create His Own Charro Apparel Store," *We are Mitú: Identities*, May 23, 2017. https://wearemitu.com/identities/this-latino-entrepreneur-is-delivering-authentic-charro-apparel-to-people-all-around-the-u-s-and-the-outfits-are-stunning/.
48. Jennifer Delgadillo, "Carving Out Her Name: Papel Picado with a Modern Twist," NoMeanCity.com. June 8, 2016. http://nomeancity.com/carving-out-her-story.
49. Beatriz Vasquez, e-mail message to author, September 7, 2017.
50. Indianapolis Public Schools, "ESL Connections Resource Fair," 2015. https://www.myips.org/site/Default.aspx?PageID=124&PageType=17&DomainID=65&ModuleInstanceID=65&EventDateID=18230.
51. Vasquez, e-mail message.
52. Vasquez, e-mail message.
53. Kori Shulman, "Obama Administration Officials Continue to Visit State Fairs," *White House Rural Council*, 2010. https://obamawhitehouse.archives.gov/realitycheck/blog/2010/08/16/obama-administration-officials-continue-visit-state-fairs.
54. Rob Paral, "Immigration a Demographic Lifeline in Midwestern Metros," The Chicago Council on Global Affairs, March 23, 2017.
55. Our Lady of Guadalupe Church, "History of Our Lady of Guadalupe Fiesta Mexicana," 2017. http://www.olgfiestamexicana.org/olg-fiesta-history.html.
56. Pilsen Neighborhood Community Council, "Our Work Year-Round," *Fiesta del sol*, 2017. http://fiestadelsol.org/about-us/our-work-year-round/.
57. Elena Foulis, interview with author, March 3, 2017.
58. National Council for the Traditional Arts, "The National Folk Festival: Request for Proposal, 2018–2020" (Silver Spring, MD: NCTA, 2016). http://ncta-usa.org/wp/wp-content/uploads/2016/08/NCTA_NFF_RFP_2018_20_Final.pdf.

59. Michigan State University, "History of the Festival," in *University Outreach and Engagement: Great Lakes Folk Festival*, 2017. http://greatlakesfolkfest.net/2017/about/history-of-the-festival/.
60. Limón, "Al Norte Toward Home," 46–47.
61. Linda Fregoso, "Chuy Negrete: Historian, Musician, Composer, Playwright, Organizer, Activist," *Onda Latina*. University of Texas at Austin: The Benson Latin American Collection. June 25, 1981. http://www.laits.utexas.edu/onda_latina/program?sernum=000510979&term.
62. Refugio Gonzalez, "San Juanita Project: Jesus Chuy Negrete," *YouTube*, September 2, 2015. https://www.youtube.com/watch?v=tb5UPdnvLhs&t=3s.
63. Julia Burke, Jesus "Chuy" Negrete Shares Mexican Labor Songs with Wisconsin Workers," *Isthmus*, November 14, 2013. http://isthmus.com/music/jesus-chuy-negrete-shares-mexican-labor-songs-with-wisconsin-workers/.
64. Liam Ford, "Man Gets 33 Years in Fatal Beating, Robbery Posted on Facebook," *The Chicago Tribune*, February 1, 2017. http://www.chicagotribune.com/news/local/breaking/ct-33-years-for-facebook-killing-20170130-story.html; jreyestrib, "Jesus Chuy Negrete Corrido a Delfino Mora," *YouTube*, July 22, 2002. https://www.youtube.com/watch?v=VsjVyo_7RFc.
65. Stephen Winick, "The Poet Laureate Joins an AFC Workshop on Corridos," *Folklife Today*, Library of Congress, American Folklife Center and Veterans History Project, October 28. https://blogs.loc.gov/folklife/2015/10/the-poet-laureate-joins-an-afc-workshop-on-corridos/.
66. Agencia Efe, "Quinto Imperio, un grupo de inmigrantes mexicanos de Chicago que da voz a los indocumentados," *Univision.com*, May 19, 2017. http://www.univision.com/chicago/wgbo/quinto-imperio-un-grupo-de-inmigrantes-mexicanos-de-chicago-que-da-voz-a-los-indocumentados.
67. Quintiliano Rios, "Kin-T." Facebook message to author, August 27, 2017.
68. Ibid.
69. Chi Enrique, phone interview with author, August 10, 2017.
70. Ibid.
71. Ibid.
72. Ibid.
73. Ed East, 2017. Facebook message to the author, August 29, 2017.
74. Ibid.
75. Daniel Martinez, phone interview by author, August 22, 2017.
76. F. M. Orellana, *Immigrant Children in Transcultural Spaces: Language, Learning, and Love* (New York: Routledge, 2016).
77. Lilly Moreno Corona, phone interview by the author, May 23, 2017.
78. Moreno Corona, phone interview by the author, May 23, 2017.
79. Ibid.
80. Elaina Hernández, phone interview by author, May 23, 2017.
81. Ibid.
82. Orellana, *Immigrant Children*.
83. Hernandez, phone interview.
84. Ibid.
85. Yosso, "Whose Culture Has Capital?" 79.
86. B. MacRobie, "Masters and Apprentices Strengthen Missouri's Folk Arts Web," *The Missouri Arts Council*, 2015. https://www.missouriartscouncil.org/graphics/assets/

documents/73a24f6cfb6f.pdf; Wisconsin Arts Board, "Wisconsin Arts Board Folk and Traditional Arts Apprenticeship Program," 2017. https://artsboard.wisconsin.gov/Documents/AwardsRecord_FY17.pdf.

87. Vasquez, e-mail message to author, September 7, 2017.
88. Jo Carrillo, "And When You Leave, Take Your Pictures with You: Racism in the Women's Movement," in *This Bridge Called My Back: Writings by Radical Women of Color*, ed. Cherríe Moraga and Gloria Anzaldúa, 57–61 (Albany: State University of New York Press, 2015), 57–58.
89. Kathy Signorino, e-mail message to author, July 31, 2017.
90. Kaitlin Berle, e-mail message to author, August 24, 2017.
91. Ohio Department of Higher Education, "Undergraduate and Graduate Student Diversity Fall 2016: University System of Ohio Institutions," *Reports: Research*, 2017. https://www.ohiohighered.org/sites/ohiohighered.org/files/uploads/data/statistical-profiles/enrollment/diversity_2016.pdf.
92. Ohio Department of Education, "Fall Enrollment (Headcount) October 2016 Public Districts and Buildings." Retrieved from http://education.ohio.gov/Topics/Data/Frequently-Requested-Data/Enrollment-Data.
93. Victor Mora, e-mail message to author. The Ohio State University Office of Enrollment Services: Analysis and Reporting, February 23, 2018.
94. Chris Higgens, "New Latino Studies Minor in Effect," *The Daily Iowan*, December 2, 2014. http://www.dailyiowan.com/2014/12/02/Metro/40214.html.
95. National Science Foundation, *Doctorate Recipients from U.S. Universities*, National Center for Science and Engineering Statistics Directorate for Social, Behavioral and Economic Sciences, March 2018, 2. https://www.nsf.gov/statistics/2018/nsf18304/static/report/nsf18304-report.pdf.
96. United States Census Bureau, "Hispanic Heritage Month 2017," in *Facts for Features*, August 31, 2017. https://www.census.gov/newsroom/facts-for-features/2017/hispanic-heritage.html.
97. L. Ponjuan, "Recruiting and Retaining Latino Faculty Members: The Missing Piece to Latino Student Success," *Hispanic Outlook in Higher Education* 22, no. 19 (2012): 17–19.

## Bibliography

Agencia Efe. "Quinto Imperio, un grupo de inmigrantes mexicanos de Chicago que da voz a los indocumentados." *Univision.com*. May 19, 2017. http://www.univision.com/chicago/wgbo/quinto-imperio-un-grupo-de-inmigrantes-mexicanos-de-chicago-que-da-voz-a-los-indocumentados.

American Folklore Society. "What Is Folklore?" *Asknet.org*. Retrieved from https://www.afsnet.org/page/WhatIsFolklore?

Burke, Julia. Jesus "Chuy" Negrete Shares Mexican Labor Songs with Wisconsin Workers." *Isthmus*, November 14, 2013. http://isthmus.com/music/jesus-chuy-negrete-shares-mexican-labor-songs-with-wisconsin-workers/.

Carrillo, Jo. "And When You Leave, Take Your Pictures with You: Racism in the Women's Movement." In *This Bridge Called My Back: Writings by Radical Women of Color*, ed. Cherríe Moraga and Gloria Anzaldúa, 57–61. Albany: State University of New York Press, 2015.

Cotera, María Eugenia. "Latino/a Literature and the Uses of Folklore." In *The Routledge Companion to Latina/o Literature*, edited by Suzanne Bost and Frances R. Aparicio, 216–228. London: Routledge, 2013.

Davis, Roger P. "The Heard Voice: The Emergence of the Hispanic Across the Mid-West: 1971–1985." *Journal of Latino-Latin American Studies* 3, no. 1 (Spring 2008): 4–15.

Diaz McConnell, Eileen. "Latinos in the Rural Midwest: The Twentieth-century Historical Context Leading to Contemporary Challenges." In *Apple Pie and Enchiladas: Latino Newcomers in the Rural Midwest*, edited by Ann V. Millard and Jorge Chapa, 26–40. Austin: University of Texas Press, 2004.

Díes, Juan. "Ohio Latino Arts Directory Final Report." *Ohio Folk and Traditional Arts: Fieldwork Projects*. 2009. http://www.ohiofolkarts.org/ohio-latino-arts-directory/.

Delgadillo, Jennifer. "Carving Out Her Name: Papel Picado with a Modern Twist." *NoMeanCity.com*. June 8, 2016. http://nomeancity.com/carving-out-her-story.

Delgadillo, Theresa. *Latina Lives in Milwaukee*. Urbana: University of Illinois Press, 2015.

Dorson, Richard M. *Land of the Millrats*. Cambridge, MA: Harvard University Press, 1981.

Driever, Steven L. "Latinos in Polynucleated Kansas City." In *Hispanic Spaces, Latino Places: Community and Cultural Diversity in Contemporary America*, edited by Daniel D. Arreola, 207–233. Austin: University of Texas Press, 2004.

Foulis, Elena. *Latin@ Stories Across Ohio*. iBooks, Columbus: The Ohio State University, 2015.

Fregoso, Linda. "Chuy Negrete: Historian, Musician, Composer, Playwright, Organizer, Activist. *Onda Latina*. The University of Texas at Austin: The Benson Latin American Collection. June 25, 1981. http://www.laits.utexas.edu/onda_latina/program?sernum=000510979&term.

Ford, Liam. "Man Gets 33 Years in Fatal Beating, Robbery Posted on Facebook." *The Chicago Tribune*, February 1, 2017. http://www.chicagotribune.com/news/local/breaking/ct-33-years-for-facebook-killing-20170130-story.html.

Garcia, Jessica. "After the Problem He Ran into with His Son's Baptism, This Latino Dad Decided to Create His Own Charro Apparel Store." *We are Mitú: Identities*, May 23, 2017. https://wearemitu.com/identities/this-latino-entrepreneur-is-delivering-authentic-charro-apparel-to-people-all-around-the-u-s-and-the-outfits-are-stunning/.

Gonzalez, Refugio. "San Juanita Project: Jesus Chuy Negrete." *YouTube*, September 2, 2015. https://www.youtube.com/watch?v=tb5UPdnvLhs&t=3s.

González-Martín, Rachel. Forthcoming. "Quinceañeras as Ephemeral Autobiography: Narrating Latina Lived Experiences in America's Heartland." Special Issue of *The Journal of Latino/Latin American Studies*, "Latinas/os and the Midwest," edited by Aidé Acosta and Sylvi Martinez.

Herrera-Sobek, María. *Celebrating Latino Folklore: An Encyclopedia of Cultural Traditions*. 2012. http://public.eblib.com/choice/publicfullrecord.aspx?p=995935.

Higgens, Chris. "New Latino Studies Minor in Effect." *The Daily Iowan*. December 2, 2014. http://www.dailyiowan.com/2014/12/02/Metro/40214.html.

Hola America News. "Celebrating 55 Years of LULAC Davenport." September 4, 2014. http://holaamericanews.com/es/celebrating-55-years-of-lulac-davenport/.

Indianapolis Public Schools. "ESL Connections Resource Fair." 2015. https://www.myips.org/site/Default.aspx?PageID=124&PageType=17&DomainID=65&ModuleInstanceID=65&EventDateID=18230.

jreyestrib. "Jesus Chuy Negrete Corrido a Delfino Mora." *YouTube*, July 22, 2015. https://www.youtube.com/watch?v=VsjVyo_7RFc.

Limón, José E. "Al Norte toward Home: Texas, the Midwest, and Mexican American Critical Regionalism." In *The Latina/o Midwest Reader*, ed. Omar Valerio-Jimenez, Santiago Vaquera-Vasquez, and Claire Fox. Urbana: University of Illinois Press, 2017.

Lindahl, Carl. *American Folktales: From the Collections of the Library of Congress*. Armonk, NY: M.E. Sharpe, 2004.

Lockwood, William. "Car Customizing." In *The American Midwest: Folklore*, ed. James P. Leary, Andrew R. L. Cayton, Richard Sisson, Chris Zacher, 419–421. Bloomington: Indiana University Press, 2007.

Lorde, Audre. "The Master's Tools Will Never Dismantle the Master's House." In *This Bridge Called My Back: Writings by Radical Women of Color*, ed. Cherrie Moraga and Gloria Anzaldúa, 94–102. Albany: State University of New York Press, 2015.

LULAC Council 10. 2013. "We Want Students to Succeed in College!" Retrieved from: http://www.lulac10.org/scholarship.html.

McNamara, Vicky. "Sister Marilyn Reyes Applies Experience to Assisting Migrant." *Herencia, Fiestas, Horizontes*. The State of Kansas Advisory Committee on Mexican American Affairs, 18–20, 1979. http://cdm16884.contentdm.oclc.org/cdm/singleitem/collection/p16884coll49/id/45/rec/5.

MacRobie, Barbara. "Masters and Apprentices Strengthen Missouri's Folk Arts Web." *The Missouri Arts Council*. 2015. https://www.missouriartscouncil.org/graphics/assets/documents/73a24f6cfb6f.pdf.

Malone, Henry H. "Folksongs and Ballads: Part I." In *Kansas Folklore*, edited by S. J. Sackett and William E. Koch, 138–160. Lincoln: University of Nebraska Press, 1961.

McNeil, W. K., and James P. Leary. "Folk Song." In *The American Midwest: Folklore*, edited by Andrew R. L. Cayton, Richard Sisson, and Chris Zacher, 390–393. Bloomington: Indiana University Press, 2007.

Michigan State University. "History of the Festival." *University Outreach and Engagement: Great Lakes Folk Festival*. 2017. http://greatlakesfolkfest.net/2017/about/history-of-the-festival/.

Moschkovich, Judit. "—But I Know You American Woman." In *This Bridge Called My Back: Writings by Radical Women of Color*, ed. Cherrie Moraga and Gloria Anzaldúa, 73–77. Albany: State University of New York Press, 2015.

National Science Foundation. *Doctorate Recipients from U.S. Universities*. National Center for Science and Engineering Statistics Directorate for Social, Behavioral and Economic Sciences, March 2018. https://www.nsf.gov/statistics/2018/nsf18304/static/report/nsf18304-report.pdf.

NCTA National Council for the Traditional Arts. "*The National Folk Festival: Request for Proposal, 2018-2020*." Silver Spring, MD: NCTA. 2016. http://ncta-usa.org/wp/wp-content/uploads/2016/08/NCTA_NFF_RFP_2018_20_Final.pdf.

Ohio Arts Council. "Lilly Corona Moreno." *Ohio Folk and Traditional Arts*. 2017. http://www.ohiofolkarts.org/lilly-corona-moreno/.

Ohio Development Services Agency. n.d. "Ohio Hispanic Americans." https://www.development.ohio.gov/files/research/P7002.pdf.

Olson, Ruth. "Folklore." In *The Greenwood Encyclopedia of American Regional Cultures: The Midwest*, edited by Joseph W. Slade and Judith Yaross Lee. ABC-CLIO, 2004.

The Omeyocan Dance Company. n.d. "About Us: Our Mission." Retrieved from http://www.aztecfiredance.com/index_files/Page1677.htm.

Orellana, M. F. *Immigrant Children in Transcultural Spaces: Language, Learning, and Love*. New York: Routledge, 2016.

Paral, Rob. "Immigration a Demographic Lifeline in Midwestern Metros." *The Chicago Council on Global Affairs*. March 23, 2017.

Ponjuan, L. "Recruiting and Retaining Latino Faculty Members: The Missing Piece to Latino Student Success." *Hispanic Outlook in Higher Education* 22, no. 19 (2012): 17–19.

Sackett, S. J. "Customs." In *Kansas Folklore*, edited by S. J. Sackett and William E. Koch, 182–208. Lincoln: University of Nebraska Press, 1961.

Shulman, Kori. "Obama Administration Officials Continue to Visit State Fairs." *White House Rural Council*. 2010. https://obamawhitehouse.archives.gov/realitycheck/blog/2010/08/16/obama-administration-officials-continue-visit-state-fairs.

Teske, Robert T. "Folk Arts and Crafts." In *Folklore: The American Midwest*, edited by Andrew R. L. Cayton, Richard Sisson, and Chris Zacher, 363–365. Bloomington: Indiana University Press, 2007.

El Universal. "Chuy" *Negrete, el trovador inmigrante*. January 27, 2009. http://archivo.eluniversal.com.mx/espectaculos/88063.html.

The University of Iowa. n. d. "Workshop Descriptions." https://uiowa.edu/iowalatinoconference/workshop-descriptions.

Wisconsin Arts Board. "Wisconsin Arts Board Folk and Traditional Arts Apprenticeship Program." 2017. https://artsboard.wisconsin.gov/Documents/AwardsRecord_FY17.pdf.

Winick, Stephen. "The Poet Laureate Joins an AFC Workshop on Corridos." *Folklife Today*. Library of Congress, American Folklife Center and Veterans History Project. October 28, 2015. https://blogs.loc.gov/folklife/2015/10/the-poet-laureate-joins-an-afc-workshop-on-corridos/.

Yosso, Tara J. "Whose Culture Has Capital?" *Race, Ethnicity and Education* 8, no. 1 (2005): 69–91.

CHAPTER 4

# BRIDGES TO CUBA AND LATINA/LATINO STUDIES

RUTH BEHAR

ALMOST every fall at the University of Michigan I teach a course called "Cuba and Its Diaspora" that is cross-listed in anthropology and Latina/Latino studies. I started teaching this course over twenty years ago, in the mid-1990s. It was unusual to teach a course that examined a Latin American or Caribbean country as well as that country's population living abroad. Courses tended to focus on one or the other, but not on both together, and this largely continues to be true today. The concept of "diaspora" was not widely used in the 1990s when referring to the Cubans who had left the island. It was more typical to speak of the exile community. To call those who had left "immigrants" was an insult to many in the community who stubbornly referred to themselves as "exiles," even as the decades passed and Communism remained intact on the island. Departing their beloved homeland out of an ardent belief in the political ideals of democracy, they felt certain they were in the United States only temporarily and would one day return to a "free Cuba." The ideology stemmed from the upper- and middle-class position of these "historic exiles." Many were educated professionals in fields ranging from medicine to engineering or owners of confiscated businesses and refused to see themselves as helpless immigrants. Nevertheless, they accepted aid from the Cuban Refugee Program on arrival and committed themselves to regaining the wealth lost in Cuba, becoming "golden exiles" and setting themselves apart from Latino farmworkers.[1]

Long before it became commonplace, I chose the term "diaspora" to speak of the Cubans who had left because it could encompass both exiles and immigrants and refer to the "greater Cuba" that existed outside of the island. With the growing awareness of displacement and globalization, the scholarly term "diaspora" had gained popularity in the 1990s. *Diaspora: A Journal of Transnational Studies* was launched in 1991, Boyarin and Boyarin's essay on "Diaspora: Generation and the Ground of Jewish Identity" appeared in 1993, and Clifford's essay on "Diasporas" in 1994.[2] My vision of a Cuban diaspora came from the influence that critical Jewish theory and anthropology had on my thinking as well as my own background as a Cuban Jew.

My course would start with "Cuba and Its Diaspora" with a discussion of the Cuban revolution of 1959 and the role that Fidel Castro's charismatic leadership played in its success. And every year I would say, "If Fidel Castro dies this semester, we'll throw away the syllabus and just read the obituaries." I'd add, "But that's not going to happen. He's been in power for so long, he's come to seem eternal." The students always laughed. And my prediction came true year after year. And then in the fall of 2016, during the Thanksgiving break, Fidel Castro died. It was Friday, November 25, and when we came back to class for our last two weeks, we finished up the semester reading the obituaries and contrasting the different narratives about Fidel Castro as a person and a politician and his reign's effect on Cubans and on people around the world. It was a fitting end to the course. All the students agreed that Castro had died at a most convenient time.

In the fall of 2017, for the first time in the history of the course, we actually began by reading about the revolution *and* about Castro's death.[3] The years had passed, and this new crop of students had not yet been born when I started teaching the course. For them, Castro was an intriguing dinosaur from the previous century. But they were fascinated to learn about the ideal of revolution and the various ways Castro had been turned into a myth while alive and was being turned into a myth in his death. Teaching about Castro's death felt as if we had crossed an invisible line, as if at last Cuban studies could legitimately be part of Latina/Latino studies, as if the long wait of the exiles was finally over, and we could now speak of Cubans in the United States as true immigrants—or even more dramatically, as Latinos—because no one was going back to the lost homeland to jumpstart a life left behind. We could finally quiet down and dissolve into the fastest-growing minority in the United States and simply become one more Spanish-speaking group.

We were in the United States to stay, for better or for worse, and there was nothing exceptional about us. In fact, earlier in the year, in his last week in office in January 2017, President Obama ended the special immigration policy for Cubans, which had granted automatic residency to Cubans who set foot on US soil, an incredible privilege not given to other Latinas/Latinos. A policy dating from the era of the Cold War, it had been crafted at a time when Cubans were seen as oppressed by Communism. Each Cuban who was welcomed into the United States served as living proof that the revolution was a failure. But after the 1990s, it became clear that most Cubans were leaving the island for economic betterment. That change, coupled with the fact that the Obama administration had restored ties with Cuba in December 2014, and huge numbers of Americans were traveling to the island, made it seem hypocritical to maintain a policy that only satisfied the most hardline Cubans in Miami who refused to negotiate with the government of Cuba. As Obama said in a statement quoted in *Reuters*, "With this change we will continue to welcome Cubans as we welcome immigrants from other nations, consistent with our laws" (January 12, 2017).[4] If the death of Castro was the first step toward making Cuban studies a more integral part of Latina/Latino studies, the official end of Cuban immigration privileges reinforced the idea that Cubans were to be viewed as ordinary immigrants, no longer as exceptional immigrants to be coddled.

And yet, curiously, everything has changed and nothing has changed: for the relationship between Cuban studies and Latina/Latino studies remains vexed and frequently ambivalent. The island is still a site of obsessive fascination and the reconciliation among the Cuban people continues to be a work in progress. Various forms of Cuban exceptionalism are alive and well, carefully curated by Cuban Americans as well as non-Cuban promoters of Cuban identity and culture in the United States, who have found their way into ever more prestigious universities and institutions. Even Cuban Americans of the third or fourth generation are unable to let go of the island's hold on their imagination, though their bond is different than that of the exile generation or the bridge-making generation.

The centrality of the island in discussions of the Cuban diaspora ultimately stands in the way of a deep engagement with Latina/Latino studies, setting Cubans apart from others of Latin American and Caribbean heritage with whom they converge in the United States. These lingering exceptionalist tendencies influence the trends in scholarship. It is rare, for example, to find work in Cuban studies that engages with concerns in Chicana/Chicano studies or that takes a hemispheric approach. On the other hand, Cuban studies is not unique in being self-centered. The distinctions that exist within Latina/Latino studies, including Chicana/Chicano studies and Boricua studies, suggest that the mosaic approach to scholarship seems to be what most of us prefer.

Part of the problem, at least within Cuban studies, is that there is more scholarly prestige to be gained from carrying out work on Cuba than on Cuban Americans, especially in fields such as anthropology that continue to value fieldwork in exotic locations, the "exotic" now being defined in terms of political complexity and the challenges of obtaining permission to do the research. The subjects most frequently studied have been Afro-Cuban religiosity, especially Santería, and Afro-Cuban music, the impact of tourism, gay sexuality, and race issues, and typically scholars focusing on the African diaspora have a more fluid border sensibility.[5] But while scholarship remains focused on Cuba, there are interesting trends taking place in Miami, which is now a hub not simply for Cubans but for people from all over the Américas. Miami has become a crossroads for intercultural connections in the arts, as seen in the project on "Havana, Haiti: Two Cultures, One Community," and this work offers a model for other kinds of dialogues that need to happen on a broader scale between Cuban studies and Latina/Latino studies.[6]

In recognizing that Cuban exceptionalism is difficult to undo, I need to acknowledge how I am implicated in the patterns I am describing here. My own work, since I began traveling regularly to Cuba in the early 1990s, has been concerned with establishing scholarly, cultural, and artistic bridges to and from the island. The anthology I edited in 1995, *Bridges to Cuba/Puentes a Cuba,* was one of the first books to bring together the essays, stories, art, and scholarship of Cubans on the island and in the diaspora.[7] The distinction between the "island" and the "diaspora" was clearly demarcated then, as Cuba rose out of the ashes of its defunct relationship with the former Soviet Union and contemplated how to reconnect with the global capitalist world, including the United States and sympathetic Cuban Americans seeking to find their roots on the island. At the time, when the Cuban exile community viewed any travel to Cuba as a betrayal, the very act of going to Cuba as a Cuban American was a political statement. I was both publicly and privately maligned and ridiculed for my desire to create "bridges."

But I discovered that I was not alone in my quest to define a relationship to the island I had left as a child (or rather had "been taken from" as Cubans on the island preferred to say). The project of *Bridges to Cuba* put me in touch with numerous other Cuban Americans who had quietly returned to Cuba, searching for family, old homes, their schools, the ancestors in the cemetery, and the places they remembered or had heard about all their lives but had never been able to see with their own eyes. At my insistence, several of the scholars that participated agreed to write personally for the first time. María de los Angeles Torres wrote about her experience as a Peter Pan child sent out as an unaccompanied minor in 1961, and she has since become an important proponent for linking Cuban studies with critical race studies and Latina/Latino studies.[8] On the island, in a period before the Internet, and before contemporary writers on the island were being translated and published in the United States, many participants gave me the only printed copy they had of a poem or essay, trusting me to carry their work safely across the border and bring it to the attention of the English-speaking world.

The anthology came together in 1994 as two special issues of the *Michigan Quarterly Review* and then as a book in 1995. The twentieth-anniversary edition was published in 2015 with a new introduction. In that time span, several of the Cuban Americans who wrote for the book went on to create semester-abroad programs in Havana that gave them the opportunity to spend more time in Cuba and introduce students directly to the history and culture of the island. In contrast, a couple of the participants from the island left Cuba and became part of the diaspora, among them the poet Jorge Luis Arcos and the historian Raquel (Kaki) Mendieta. One of the highlights of the *Bridges to Cuba* anthology was a personal chronicle Kaki Mendieta wrote about her cousin, Ana Mendieta, the famed Cuban American artist, who was sent out of Cuba with her sister through the Peter Pan Operation in 1961, and grew up in orphanages in Iowa, eventually becoming a feminist artist in New York.[9] Known for imprinting silhouettes of her own body in her earth works, Ana Mendieta visited Cuba in the late 1970s and early 1980s, producing rupestrian-style works in the caves of Jaruco in Matanzas. Then in 1985 she fell mysteriously to her death in New York. The moving chronicle Kaki Mendieta produced had sat forgotten for years in a desk drawer. I begged Kaki Mendieta to let me publish it, never imagining it represented a tragic premonition.

Kaki Mendieta, who seemed like the last person who would ever leave Cuba, surprised everyone by choosing to immigrate to the United States. She seemed to be making a new life for herself as a Cuban American, studying for a second doctorate at Stanford University so she could one day become a professor again as she had been in Cuba. Then the news broke that she had committed suicide in a park in San Francisco. The sudden, traumatic loss of Kaki Mendieta led me to question my hopes for a bridge to Cuba and to reflect on the dark side of wanting such a bridge. In my essay entitled "The Woman Who Wanted Bridges," I wrote:

> Kaki had died because she wasn't supposed to stay in the United States. She was supposed to return to Cuba, so that I could keep extending my bridge to her. But she had wanted to be part of "us" here. And "we" had welcomed her. She wasn't supposed to die... She was supposed to... become a "golden exile" like all the rest of us Cubans who shine with the luster of our success and fortune... Kaki burned the bridge.[10]

Writing about this tragic individual moment in Cuban American history led me to reflect on how Cubans have become a deterritorialized people since the revolution, with close to 20 percent of the island's population living abroad, not only in the United States but in Spain, France, Italy, Germany, Russia, Chile, Mexico, Venezuela, Argentina, Israel, Angola, Australia, and other places. Working with Lucía Suárez, we edited a kind of sequel to *Bridges to Cuba*, which we entitled *The Portable Island: Cubans at Home in the World*. This volume, published in 2008, brought together several participants from the earlier anthology to offer an update on their thinking as well as renowned Cuban American poets Richard Blanco and José Kozer and Cuban poet and book artist Rolando Estévez. The question of what and where is home was our central theme. We sought to offer a transnational approach to the relationship between Cuban studies and Latina/Latino studies. To this end, we downplayed the island's all-important role in defining Cubanness and gave diaspora locations greater weight in the forging of identity and a sense of belonging. Our argument was that the island is "portable" and there is a certain freedom in detaching from it and at the same time a painful uncertainty. As Richard Blanco puts it at the end of his personal essay for the volume, "*I am a citizen of the world, I don't have to belong anywhere, this is my legacy as a child of exile*, I tell myself as we land and I am returned to a place that doesn't feel like home, still hoping it would."[11]

The fluidity between the island and the diaspora has grown markedly in the last twenty years. Several factors helped to ease the flow of people, ideas, and goods between the island and the diaspora. The aging of the "historic exiles" opened a space for a more tolerant generation to arise, concerned with family reunification and intellectual and cultural ties. The rise of the Internet and its expansion in Cuba gave people access to email and social media, allowing for communication to take place rapidly and inexpensively, and for alternative information, beyond the official *Granma* and government news sources, to find its way to the island, including through the offline project of the *paquete semanal*, which offers everything from foreign magazines to TV serials and movies at a reasonable price to anyone with a memory stick.[12] After Raul Castro took power in 2006, the Cuban government softened travel restrictions, allowing Cubans to be out of the country for up to two years without losing their citizenship or property on the island, a stark contrast to the stripping of citizenship and the expropriations that took place in the early era of the revolution. Another fascinating development has been the possibility of repatriation for Cubans living abroad, allowing those who lost their citizenship to regain it, to buy property on the island, to start a small business, and receive free health services, a prospect that has appealed to some in the Cuban diaspora, and a clear acknowledgment by the Cuban government of how much it depends on remittances.[13] In turn, the restoration of ties between the United States and Cuba in 2014 opened the door to commercial travel options on Delta Airlines, American Airlines, and other airlines, making it easier for travelers to move back and forth between Cuba and the United States, without being subject to the random and exploitative regulations of charter companies.

The Obama moment of friendly relations with Cuba began at the end of 2014, reaching its climax in March 2016 with Obama's visit to Cuba, and ending at the start of 2017 when Obama left office. Relations with Cuba were restored on a symbolic day: December 17, 2014, the day of San Lázaro, or Babalu-Ayé, a powerful deity in Cuban spiritual life who represents healing.[14] The restoration of ties set off a Cuba boom in the United States that yet again put the spotlight on the island, though Obama made efforts to be consciously inclusive of the Cuban diaspora. His historic visit to Cuba was a moment of Obama magic, when it seemed as if the years of animosity between the governments of Cuba and the United States would melt away and both governments would turn a new page.

Together with an old neighbor who still lives in the building where I lived as a small child, I watched on Cuban television as Obama delivered his speech to the Cuban people on March 22, 2016, at the Gran Teatro de La Habana.[15] It was a thrilling and surreal experience. Beginning by quoting José Martí's most famous poem, in which he offers a white rose to both his friend and his enemy, Obama not only acknowledged Martí's profound role in the struggle for Cuban independence but affirmed his importance as a Cuban exile who lived in New York for fifteen years. Indeed, Martí wrote his *Versos sencillos* in the Catskills and formed part of a community of Cuban New Yorkers.[16] Obama then went on to delineate the differences between the governments of Cuba and the United States but quickly shifted the discussion to what the two countries shared. "The United States and Cuba are like two brothers that have been estranged for many years, even as we share the same blood," Obama declared. Both, he said, have a heritage of slaves and slave owners and have welcomed immigrants to their shores. He noted that "Cuba has emphasized the role and rights of the state, and the United States is founded upon the rights of the individual." Despite these differences, Obama forthrightly stated that the embargo needed to be lifted, while at the same time celebrating the American freedoms of protest and open debate that had made it possible for him "to stand here today as an African American and as president of the United States."

But Obama's most daring statements were offered in support of the movement toward reconciliation among the Cuban people. He presented a positive narrative of Cuban Americans and their struggle. In Obama's words, "I know that for some Cubans on the island, there may be a sense that those who left somehow supported the old order in Cuba. I am sure there's a narrative that lingers here, which suggests that Cuban exiles ignored the problems of pre-revolutionary Cuba and rejected the struggle to build a new future." Obama went on to speak with emotional depth about the Cuban exiles and how they "carry a memory of painful and sometimes violent separation. They love Cuba. A part of them still considers this their true home. That's why their passion is so strong, and that's why their heartache is so great." Perhaps Obama had read some of the wrenching personal stories in *Bridges to Cuba*, because he invoked the image of the bridge: "And I've come here, I've traveled this distance on a bridge that was built by Cubans on both sides of the Florida straits." Ultimately Obama called for what my generation of bridge builders had dreamed of for decades: "the recognition of a community humanity... Understanding, listening and forgiveness."

Long before he spoke in Cuba, Obama was setting the stage for Americans to revise their image of Cuban Americans. It was no accident that he chose Richard Blanco, a Cuban American gay poet raised in Miami, to write and present a poem at his second inauguration ceremony in January 2013. Richard Blanco shared his inaugural poem, "One Today," with an audience of millions. He later vividly described the experience in his book, *For All of Us, One Today*. Finding himself with his mother at the ceremony, he turned to her before going up to the stage and said, "'*Mamá*, I think we're finally *americanos*.' She gives me a tender look as if saying, *I know, I know*."[17] This was a telling confession; the journey had been a long one before he and his mother crossed the line from being Cuban to becoming American. Becoming Latino was not an option in Blanco's cartography of identity at that moment, as is the case for other Cuban-American writers and critics for whom the hyphen between "Cuban" and "American" remains central.[18]

Subsequently, Richard Blanco was invited to write and present a poem to commemorate the historic reopening of the United States Embassy in Havana on August 14, 2015. "Matters of the Sea/Cosas del Mar," which Blanco asked me to translate into Spanish, raised new questions, and his author's note spoke of his concerns as he looked to the future: "Was I Cuban enough for a new Cuba? Would I be too Cuban for America? Would the stories of my exile family and community be discounted? Could I be faithful to the people of two countries and cultures I adored?" Revising his previous thinking about his identity, he noted, "I've started to think of myself not as a choice between American or Cuban, nor as a hyphenated Cuban-American, but as an *Americuban*. I've realized that, indeed, my heart is big enough to embrace the people of two countries, two cultures, two histories, two homes."[19]

On June 6, 2015, just before I accompanied Richard Blanco to Havana to participate in the reopening of the US Embassy, the two of us launched the blog Bridges to/from Cuba: Lifting the Emotional Embargo. Building on my Bridges to Cuba project and on Richard Blanco's concern that we reflect on "emotional embargos," the blog was a fusion of our efforts to connect Cubans and Cuban Americans. In describing our blog, we spoke of how our aim is "to build bridges that connect Cubans everywhere and lift the emotional embargo among us all, as we moved forward together with our apprehensions and hopes, questions and convictions, doubts and dreams, into a new era of US-Cuban relations and the Cuba of tomorrow."[20] In this way, the project of building bridges not only *to* Cuba but *from* Cuba entered the digital age, making it possible for us to publish work on a regular basis that could be easily and quickly circulated to readers. We have since posted thirty-two pieces on our blog, ranging from poems to essays to interviews to photographic accounts, maintaining a policy of always posting the work in English and Spanish.

As writers, Richard Blanco and I both place emphasis on the written word as our preferred form of communication, but the next generation has found another way of creating bridges to and from Cuba. The CubaOne Foundation, modeled on Birthright

Israel, sponsors free heritage trips to Cuba for young Cuban Americans (ages twenty-two to thirty-five) who have never been to the island.[21] CubaOne seeks to gracefully navigate the complex relationship between culture and politics in Cuba, promoting the first and keeping a careful distance from the second. In my generation, there were Cuban Americans who supported the revolution and traveled to Cuba in the late 1970s as part of the Antonio Maceo brigade, led by Lourdes Casal, an Afro-Cuban scholar and poet who taught at Rutgers and returned to live in Havana and died there.[22] But the majority of Cuban Americans who left Cuba with their families in the early decades of the revolution, as I did, did not publicize their trips to Cuba in the 1980s and 1990s, fearing they might be maligned or harassed, or even assaulted, for doing so. They wanted to respect parents and grandparents of the exile generation who opposed their desire to set foot on the island and felt betrayed by their need to go back to a place left behind (in their minds) for good reason. The self-torment felt by many who went on these return journeys has led scholar Iraida López to describe them as "impossible returns."[23]

The younger generation is certainly less vexed. The CubaOne Foundation asks participants to describe how stories of Cuba inspire them and to share ideas for how they envision a relationship with Cuban colleagues to support emerging entrepreneurs or collaborate on artistic endeavors, so they can "give back to Cuba." The themed trips, focusing on such topics as agriculture and urban farming, religion, literature and the arts, or gender and sexuality, foster bonds between the Cuban American participants as well as with the Cubans they interact with on the island. Many participants meet up with family members they are getting to know for the first time. Founded by four young Cuban Americans in Miami as a nonprofit organization, CubaOne uses social media to promote their platform. They avidly post images and stories on Instagram and Facebook about their trips to Cuba and support entrepreneurs on the island, such as Clandestina, a graphic design company that makes hipsterish T-shirts with amusing slogans such as "Actually I'm in Havana" and "99% diseño cubano" which are now available online in the United States.[24]

Relations between the United States and Cuba have been on a perennial seesaw since 1959, depending on the American president in power. The Obama moment has passed, and President Trump has brought back an intense level of antagonism not seen for decades in relations between the United States and Cuba. A travel advisory is now issued to anyone traveling to the island from the United States, making many apprehensive about going to Cuba. The US Embassy in Cuba has been reduced to a skeletal staff, so Cubans seeking visas to travel to the United States must obtain them from the US Embassy in Mexico, Colombia, or Ecuador. Travel to the United States is now prohibitively expensive for most Cubans on the island, unless they obtain invitations from institutions that can cover additional costs. These restrictions are closing down the bridge established by Obama, who was beloved by many in Cuba, to such an extent that people on the street wore homemade T-shirts with his face emblazoned on them.

Even in the midst of this return to Cold War–era relations, the Kennedy Center of the Performing Arts organized an ambitious festival, "Artes de Cuba: From the Island to the

World," in May 2018, bringing over two hundred artists and performers to Washington, DC, for "a festival celebrating the artistic richness that has emerged from this island archipelago in the sun." As the organizers proudly stated, "This unprecedented gathering of Cuban and Cuban-American artists represents some of the world's greatest from the island and the Diaspora."[25] It is clear that the artistic richness of Cuba and its diaspora is so deeply desired as a cultural commodity that, whatever the obstacles, the most prestigious American institutions will pay the price to celebrate it and consume it.

Cuba has become one of those rare places that everyone seems to want to claim. It no longer belongs only to those for whom it is a native land or a heritage. Indeed, as the title of the festival suggests, Cuba, having had the audacity to carry out and maintain a Communist revolution in the backyard of the United States, now belongs to the world. And so the quandary of how to connect Cuban studies to Latina/Latino studies remains. As long as the bond to the island is asserted, the forging of an identity as Latinas and Latinos will remain on hold for Cubans in the United States. Navigating the border between "Cuban" and "American" and between "Cuban" and the "world" will be the main focus of efforts to define identity and the primary concern of scholars. And yet in reality Cubans have come to resemble other Latinas/Latinos, shifting from being exiles to rafters to ordinary immigrants. Cuban Americans, who now include a substantial community of Afro-Cuban Americans, face similar forms of race and class discrimination as African Americans and Latina/Latinos.[26]

In conclusion, let me share a story.[27] On March 22, 2016, the day after Obama strolled through La Habana Vieja in the pouring rain, I took a stroll with an old friend through the same streets. The sun was out. At the Plaza de Armas, we stopped at El Templete to pay homage to a ceiba tree, which had replaced the old ceiba that had become sick and termite ridden. The ceiba has a spiritual meaning for African-based religions in Cuba. Offerings are left at the foot of this tree, requesting luck and prosperity. The ceiba at El Templete has always had special significance for habaneros, and for Cubanos generally. It is located at the site of the founding of the city of Havana. Every year, on November 16, the day when Havana was founded in its current site, people line up and wait hours to make a circle around the tree and offer their prayers. Over the centuries, different ceibas have been planted there. And as if destiny decreed it, the last ceiba in that location had been planted in the year 1959, when the new revolutionary social order began. Its decline, the foliage withered, the trunk deteriorated, had made many people sad.

A week before Obama arrived in 2016, the government rushed to beautify as much of Havana as possible. The new ceiba was planted: a new era, a new ceiba. But that ceiba was short lived, just like the Obama magic. In the past, a ceiba could easily last a hundred years. By March 2017 it had died. And again, another ceiba was planted in April 2017.

Who can say how long this ceiba will last? Perhaps, with so many Cubans living in the diaspora, the roots no longer cling to the soil of the island as deeply as they did in the past. But the island, it seems, will continue planting ceibas and calling those who left with its unceasing faith and hope.

## Notes

1. Guillermo J. Grenier and Lisandro Pérez, *The Legacy of Exile: Cubans in the United States* (Boston: Pearson Education, 2003).
2. *Diaspora: A Journal of Transnational Studies*, launched in 1991; Daniel Boyarin and Jonathan Boyarin, "Diaspora: Generation and the Ground of Jewish Identity" *Critical Inquiry* 19, no. 4 (Summer 1993): 693–725; and James Clifford, "Diasporas," *Cultural Anthropology* 9, no. 3 (August 1994): 302–338.
3. Ann Louise Bardach, "Obama's Favorite Castro," *Politico*, August 13, 2015, 1–17; Achy Obejas, "The Little Fidel in All of Us," *New York Times*, November 27, 2016; Yoani Sánchez, "Cuba Survives Fidel Castro," *14ymedio*, November 27, 2016: (originally in *El País*); Andrea Rodriguez and Michael Weissenstein, "From Milk to Lightbulbs, Fidel Castro Reshaped Life in Cuba," Associated Press, November 28, 2016; Jon Lee Anderson, "The Audacious Funeral and Quiet Afterlife of Fidel Castro," *New Yorker*, December 4, 2016; Ana Dopico, "On Mourning and Fidel," *Cuba Cargo/Cult Blog*, December 4, 2016. https://cubacargocult.blog/author/anadopico/.
4. *Reuters*, January 12, 2017.
5. Aisha M. Beliso-De Jesús, *Electric Santería: Racial and Sexual Assemblages of Transnational Religion* (New York: Columbia University Press, 2015); L. Kaifa Roland, *Cuban Color in Tourism and La Lucha: An Ethnography of Racial Meanings* (Oxford: Oxford University Press, 2011); Amelia Rosenberg Weinreb, *Cuba in the Shadow of Change: Daily Life in the Twilight of the Revolution* (Gainesville: University Press of Florida, 2009); Noelle Stout, "When a Yuma Meets Mama: Commodified Kin and the Affective Economies of Queer Tourism in Cuba," *Anthropological Quarterly* 88, no. 3 (2015): 665–692; Umi Vaughan and Carlos Aldama, *Carlos Aldama's Life in Batá: Cuba, Diaspora, and the Drum* (Bloomington: Indiana University Press, 2012); Antonio López, *Unbecoming Blackness: The Diaspora Cultures of Afro-Cuban America* (New York: New York University Press, 2012).
6. http://havana-haiti.com/theproject/.
7. Ruth Behar, ed., *Bridges to Cuba/Puentes a Cuba* (Ann Arbor: University of Michigan Press, 1995; twentieth anniversary edition, 2015).
8. María de los Angeles Torres, "Beyond the Rupture: Reconciling with Our Enemies, Reconciling with Ourselves," in *Bridges to Cuba/Puentes a Cuba* (University of Michigan Press, 1995, ed. Ruth Behar; twentieth anniversary edition, 2015), 25–42.
9. Raquel (Kaki) Mendieta Costa, "Silhouette," in *Bridges to Cuba/Puentes a Cuba*, ed. Ruth Behar (Ann Arbor: University of Michigan Press, 1995; twentieth anniversary edition, 2015), 72–75; José Quiroga, "Still Searching for Ana Mendieta," in *Cuban Palimpsests* (Minneapolis: University of Minnesota Press, 2005), 173–195.
10. Ruth Behar, "The Woman Who Wanted Bridges," in *The Portable Island: Cubans at Home in the World*, ed. R. Behar and L. M. Suárez (New York: Palgrave Macmillan, 2008), 129–138.
11. Richard Blanco, "Wherever That May Be," in Ruth Behar and Lucía M. Suárez, eds., *The Portable Island: Cubans at Home in the World* (New York: Palgrave Macmillan, 2008), 19–24.
12. Antonio García Martínez, "Inside Cuba's D.I.Y. Internet Revolution," *Wired*, July 26, 2017.
13. Sarah Moreno, "Thousands of Cuban Exiles Are Exploring an Unusual Option: Returning to Cuba to Live," *Miami Herald*, March 12, 2018; Susan Eva Eckstein, *The Immigrant Divide: How Cuban Americans Changed the U.S. and Their Homeland* (New York: Routledge, 2009): 178–228.

14. Ruth Behar, "My Parents Are Cuban Exiles. Here's What Obama's Decision Means to Us," *Washington Post*, December 18, 2014.
15. Remarks by President Obama to the People of Cuba, Gran Teatro de La Habana, Havana, Cuba, March 22, 2016: https://www.whitehouse.gov/the-press-office/2016/03/22/remarks-president-obama-people-cuba.
16. Alfred J. López, *José Martí: A Revolutionary Life* (Austin: University of Texas Press, 2014); Lisandro Pérez, *Sugar, Cigars, and Revolution: The Making of Cuban New York* (New York: New York University Press, 2018).
17. Richard Blanco, *For All of Us, One Today: An Inaugural Poet's Journey* (Boston: Beacon Press, 2013), 83.
18. Gustavo Pérez-Firmat, *Life on the Hyphen: The Cuban-American Way* (Austin: University of Texas Press, 1994); Ana Menéndez, *In Cuba I Was a German Shepherd* (New York: Grove Press, 2001); Jennine Capó Crucet, *How to Leave Hialeah* (Iowa City: University of Iowa Press, 2009); Alberto Sergio Laguna, *Diversión: Play and Popular Culture in Cuban America* (New York: New York University Press, 2017).
19. Richard Blanco, *Matters of the Sea: A Poem Commemorating a New Era in US-Cuba Relations*, August 14, 2015, United States Embassy, Havana, Cuba (Pittsburgh: University of Pittsburgh Press, 2015): vii, ix.
20. https://bridgestocuba.com/, blog co-created by Ruth Behar and Richard Blanco to provide a cultural and artistic platform for sharing the real lives and complex emotional histories of thousands of Cubans across the globe.
21. http://cubaone.org/.
22. Ruth Behar, "Introduction: Looking Back and Forward," and essays by Laura Lomas, Jenna Leving Jacobson, Yolanda Prieto, and Iraida H. López, in "Dossier: Rereading the Work of Lourdes Casal," *Cuban Studies* 46 (2018): 3–84.
23. Iraida H. López, *Impossible Returns: Narratives of the Cuban Diaspora* (Gainesville: University Press of Florida, 2015).
24. https://clandestina.co/.
25. https://cms.kennedy-center.org/festivals/cuba#support.
26. Silvia Pedraza and Rubén Rumbaut, eds., *Origins and Destinies: Immigration, Race, and Ethnicity in America* (Belmont, CA: Wadsworth Publishing, 1996); Antonio López, *Unbecoming Blackness: The Diaspora Cultures of Afro-Cuban America* (New York: New York University Press, 2012).
27. An earlier version of this story appeared in Ruth Behar, "The Sea and the Ceiba," *Cuba Counterpoints*, September 1, 2016. http://cubacounterpoints.com/archives/3712.

## Bibliography

Anderson, Jon Lee. "The Audacious Funeral and Quiet Afterlife of Fidel Castro." *New Yorker*, December 4, 2016.
Bardach, Ann Louise. "Obama's Favorite Castro." *Politico*, August 13, 2015, 1–17.
Behar, Ruth. "Introduction: Looking Back and Forward." *Cuban Studies* 46 (2018): 3–9.
Behar, Ruth, ed. *Bridges to Cuba/Puentes a Cuba* (1995). Ann Arbor: University of Michigan Press, twentieth anniversary edition, 2015.
Behar, Ruth. "My Parents Are Cuban Exiles. Here's What Obama's Decision Means to Us." *Washington Post*, December 18, 2014.

Behar, Ruth. "The Woman Who Wanted Bridges." In *The Portable Island: Cubans at Home in the World*, edited by Ruth Behar and Lucía Suárez, 129–138. New York: Palgrave Macmillan, 2008.

Beliso-De Jesús, Aisha M. *Electric Santería: Racial and Sexual Assemblages of Transnational Religion*. New York: Columbia University Press, 2015.

Blanco, Richard. *Matters of the Sea: A Poem Commemorating a New Era in US-Cuba Relations*. Pittsburgh: University of Pittsburgh Press, 2015.

Blanco, Richard. *For All of Us, One Today: An Inaugural Poet's Journey*. Boston: Beacon Press, 2013.

Blanco, Richard. "Wherever That May Be." In *The Portable Island: Cubans at Home in the World*, edited by Ruth Behar and Lucía Suárez, 19–24. New York: Palgrave Macmillan, 2008.

Boyarin, Daniel, and Jonathan Boyarin. "Diaspora: Generation and the Ground of Jewish Identity." *Critical Inquiry* 19, no. 4 (Summer 1993): 693–725.

Capó Crucet, Jennine. *How to Leave Hialeah*. Iowa City: University of Iowa Press, 2009.

Clifford, James. "Diasporas." *Cultural Anthropology* 9, no. 3 (August 1994): 302–338.

Dopico, Ana. "On Mourning and Fidel." *Cuba Cargo/Cult Blog*, December 4, 2016. https://cubacargocult.blog/author/anadopico/.

Eckstein, Susan Eva. *The Immigrant Divide: How Cuban Americans Changed the U.S. and Their Homeland*. New York: Routledge, 2009.

García Martínez, Antonio. "Inside Cuba's D.I.Y. Internet Revolution." *Wired*, July 26, 2017.

Grenier, Guillermo J., and Lisandro Pérez. *The Legacy of Exile: Cubans in the United States*. Boston: Pearson Education, 2003.

Laguna, Alberto Sergio. *Diversión: Play and Popular Culture in Cuban America*. New York: New York University Press, 2017.

Leving Jacobson, Jenna. "Race and Reconciliation in the Work of Lourdes Casal." *Cuban Studies* 46 (2018): 39–50.

Lomas, Laura. "On the 'Shock' of Diaspora: Lourdes Casal's Critical Interdisciplinarity and Intersectional Feminism." *Cuban Studies* 46 (2018): 10–38.

López, Alfred J. *José Martí: A Revolutionary Life*. Austin: University of Texas Press, 2014.

López, Antonio. *Unbecoming Blackness: The Diaspora Cultures of Afro-Cuban America*. New York: New York University Press, 2012.

López, Iraida H. "Entre el ideal de la nación mestiza y la discordia racial: 'Memories of a Black Cuban Childhood' y otros textos de Lourdes Casal." *Cuban Studies* 46 (2018): 63–84.

López, Iraida H. *Impossible Returns: Narratives of the Cuban Diaspora*. Gainesville: University Press of Florida, 2015.

Mendieta Costa, Raquel (Kaki). "Silhouette." In *Bridges to Cuba/Puentes a Cuba (1995)*, edited by Ruth Behar, 72–75. Ann Arbor: University of Michigan Press, 2015.

Menéndez, Ana. *In Cuba I Was a German Shepherd*. New York: Grove Press, 2001.

Moreno, Sarah. "Thousands of Cuban Exiles are Exploring an Unusual Option: Returning to Cuba to Live." *Miami Herald*, March 12, 2018.

Obama, Barack. "Remarks by President Obama to the People of Cuba." Delivered at Gran Teatro de La Habana, Havana, Cuba, March 22, 2016. https://www.whitehouse.gov/the-press-office/2016/03/22/remarks-president-obama-people-cuba.

Obejas, Achy. "The Little Fidel in All of Us." *New York Times*, November 27, 2016.

Pedraza, Silvia, and Rubén Rumbaut, eds. *Origins and Destinies: Immigration, Race, and Ethnicity in America*. Belmont, CA: Wadsworth Publishing, 1996.

Pérez, Lisandro. *Sugar, Cigars, and Revolution: The Making of Cuban New York.* New York: New York University Press, 2018.

Pérez-Firmat, Gustavo. *Life on the Hyphen: The Cuban-American Way.* Austin: University of Texas Press, 1994.

Prieto, Yolanda. "Lourdes Casal and Black Cubans in the United States: The 1970s and Beyond." *Cuban Studies* 46 (2018): 51–62.

Quiroga, José. "Still Searching for Ana Mendieta." In *Cuban Palimpsests*, 173–195. Minneapolis: University of Minnesota Press, 2005.

Rodriguez, Andrea, and Michael Weissenstein. "From Milk to Lightbulbs, Fidel Castro Reshaped Life in Cuba." Associated Press, November 28, 2016.

Roland, L. Kaifa. *Cuban Color in Tourism and La Lucha: An Ethnography of Racial Meanings.* Oxford: Oxford University Press, 2011.

Sánchez, Yoani. "Cuba Survives Fidel Castro." *14ymedio*, November 27, 2016.

Stout, Noelle. "When a Yuma Meets Mama: Commodified Kin and the Affective Economies of Queer Tourism in Cuba." *Anthropological Quarterly* 88, no. 3 (2015): 665–692.

Torres, María de los Angeles. "Beyond the Rupture: Reconciling with Our Enemies, Reconciling with Ourselves." In *Bridges to Cuba/Puentes a Cuba* (1995), edited by Ruth Behar, 25–42. Ann Arbor: University of Michigan Press, 2015.

Vaughan, Umi, and Carlos Aldama. *Carlos Aldama's Life in Batá: Cuba, Diaspora, and the Drum.* Bloomington: Indiana University Press, 2012.

Weinreb, Amelia Rosenberg. *Cuba in the Shadow of Change: Daily Life in the Twilight of the Revolution.* Gainesville: University Press of Florida, 2009.

Zengerle, Patricia. "Obama Administration Ends Special Immigration Policy for Cubans." Reuters, January 12, 2017. https://www.reuters.com/article/us-usa-cuba-immigration/obama-administration-ends-special-immigration-policy-for-cubans-idUSKBN14W2ZO.

CHAPTER 5

# ATLANTIC CONTINUITIES IN TOMÁS RIVERA AND RUDOLFO ANAYA

SARAH M. QUESADA

> To relate this entity with that entity, and that entity with still another, and finally relating everything with everything else...he became even happier.
> —Tomás Rivera
>
> "What is totality...if not the relation of each matter to all others?
> —Édouard Glissant

As a comparatist, I initiated my literary education in French before I ever came close to Latino studies.[1] After working for a French National Education program in Cayenne, French Guiana, it became clear that, far from a romantic paradisiacal *département d'outre mer*, the French Caribbean's Atlantic history translated into deep economic and social disparity. The French Guianese were French by law but de facto second-class citizens, a neocolonial condition more aptly described by Aimé Césaire's *Cahier d'un retour au pays natal/ Notebook of a Return to my Native Land* (1939) or Alejo Carpentier's *El siglo de las luces/ Explosion in a Cathedral* (1962) than by any of the French eighteenth-century revolutionaries I had studied and greatly admired. In graduate school at Stanford University, under the tutelage of some of the best comparatists in the field, I drew closer to the transatlantic history of Caribbean literature. My years living in Francophonie—both physically and textually—even facilitated my research in former African colonies. But walking the paths of the Slave Trade Route and interviewing guides, historians, writers, and everyday citizens, offered a counterdiscourse to the many archives of Francophone, Lusophone, and Spanish missionaries I had read over the years.[2] I became mindful of the myriad ways in which the Slave Trade is remembered by way of heritage trails, oral histories, *and* fiction on *both* sides of the ocean.

Ironically, it was upon my return from this fieldwork that I came back to my roots and approached Latino studies unequivocally. Perhaps the blasting of Selena on radio airwaves in Benin or the Spanglish writing on Senegalese walls brought me into a conscious inquiry regarding the possibilities of the Atlantic nature of Latinos, including Mexican Americans like myself. How might West and Central African memory, extracted from a variety of sources, inform notions of psychic trauma left unassessed in Latinidad? How might diasporic memory along with Latino and Chicano literature work together to bridge the misunderstanding of each other? How did we remember West and Central Africa in ways that these African regions could not remember us? And why did this matter? I view the field of Latino literary studies as *relational*. Martinican thinker Édouard Glissant terms "Relation" the bridge "in which each and every identity is extended through a relationship with the Other."[3] A Caribbeanist position such as this one crystallizes a multifaceted Latinidad but also Chicano identity. Indeed, it is a relational quality through the prism of memory that makes prominent Chicano writer Tomás Rivera identify with the Congo. If Mexican American Rivera once stated that the book that remained ingrained in his memory was Anglo-American Henry M. Stanley's *In Darkest Africa* (1890), memorialization of transatlantic historiography must have played a crucial role in Rivera's literary imagination. In this chapter, I examine what it means to remember the Atlantic world—both colonial and imperial—through the works of two prominent Chicano authors: Tomás Rivera and Rudolfo Anaya. Specifically, I look at how two different modes of African historiography operate—whether consciously or unconsciously—in the myriad ways Mexicanity remembers (or actively forgets) the discursive continuities of an Atlantic region. What the example of these two authors illustrates is that in the process of recovering African historiography, the texts are constantly grappling with an active erasure embedded in centuries of colonial conquest.

While never having visited the Congo themselves, this chapter addresses how Rivera and Anaya map out a discursive terrain in which the entanglement of capitalist-based society is subversively grafted onto the tenuous delimitations of Atlantic continuities. In borrowing the spatiality from empire, these authors relocate their coordinates and create a *relational* bridge with an African memory that we have neglected for far too long.

## Rivera's Memory of an Imperial Congo

During an interview with Juan Bruce-Novoa in 1980, Rivera, who was then Chancellor of the University of California at Riverside, admitted that Stanley's *In Darkest Africa* had made a significant impression on him as he came of age in the US Southwest. Stating that the adventures and maps traced by Stanley had "stuck in his memory," by 1981 Rivera had made a name for himself.[4] A working-class farmworker who had pursued higher education, he earned a PhD in Romance Languages at the University of Oklahoma in 1969, became a writer that had inspired the Chicano Movement, and was now serving on various national boards and committees in higher education.[5] Reflecting on how far he had come, Rivera memorialized Stanley's Tarzan-like adventures. Whether he summoned Stanley's Imperialist text for its raciology or for the projection of a self-made man remains unclear. What is to be certain is that Stanley's Congo indeed haunted Rivera from youth to adulthood. Nevertheless, and unbeknownst to Rivera during the period of his professional rise, Stanley's statue was toppled in Kinshasa. Reviled and scorned as a relic of Imperialism, it was leveled long before Stanley's birthplace in Wales erected its own statue honoring Stanley's legacy. By the time Wales's statue made headlines, however, Rivera was not alive to offer an opinion on the ironic developing dichotomy.

While the politics of memory enveloping memorialization are telling of the myth of Stanley, what I want to emphasize is the spatiality that Rivera adopted but *readapted* from Stanley. In his interview with Bruce-Novoa, he states once again the "fascination" he had with the "maps of the terrain which Stanley had to travel," which in turn inspired Rivera's racial geography. In his own words, Rivera admitted that he "started making maps of the terrain [his family] traveled" and that he and his brothers "would explore and draw maps."[6] Amy Kaplan once noted that the Congo represented the "frontier tale" over which "American studies is conceived."[7] That Rivera's transnational spatiality—that of his journeying within the Southwest but also Latin America—has its origins in his reading of an Imperialist Congo both complicates and entangles continuities of Imperialism over a transatlantic continuum.

Commonly serving as a rubric to the studies of Caribbean origins, the Atlantic world system is infrequently applied to Southwestern historiography. But the Atlantic world formation (i.e., the transcontinental and European-led long-distance transfer of African captives to the American hemisphere) enables what Glissant terms "Relation." This theoretical apparatus as a contact zone serves as a bridge that binds the historiography of diverse regions. I therefore find the Glissantian apparatus useful as a hermeneutical and historiographical site similar to that of Aztlán, which, as Theresa Delgadillo has stated, stages "conflict and meeting between nations, peoples, races, and religions."[8] For Glissant, this relation of points of contact emerges like the site of Aztlán, where "domination and resistance"[9] converge and said contact zones serve as a racial geography where "by taking up the problems of the Other, it is possible to find oneself."[10] I thus have come to view the formation of Latino and/or Chicano identity through this relational lens where points of contact amplify a sense of origin and/or identity in a more holistic manner against a backdrop of ethnic disciplinary fragmentation.

Juan Poblete has stated that our Ethnic studies post-boom era has witnessed a schism by virtue of "cultural and nationalistic autonomy."[11] Most recently, however, Ylce Irizarry has elucidated that the disciplines of comparative studies in the Chicano, Latino, and Latin American studies in terms of "ideological solidarity" certainly "invites additional thinking" as Irizarry's recent work confirms.[12] Thus reading Rivera's work transhemispherically enables Mexican American studies specifically and Latino studies in general to, as Claudia Milian points out, "rethink the interpretive possibilities of global Latino literary modes and the sculpting of transnational discursive opportunities."[13]

Tomás Rivera's statement in his final vignette of the canonical novel *Y no se lo tragó la tierra/ And Earth Did Not Devour Him* ("*Tierra*," 1971), which I share in the epigraph, argues for such a vision: "Relacionar esto con esto, eso con aquello, todo con todo" ("finally relating everything with everything else...") humanity, he seems to imply, can be rendered "happier."[14] I offer that Rivera's insistence on relation here is not accidental. Rather, from prose to essay to poetry, his artistic output has always reflected "a conviction that we're all interconnected."[15] Perhaps unpremeditatedly, Rivera's textuality optimistically promotes Chicanos as a comparatist vector to revitalize "Third World" alliances. Thus, a Glissantian reading of relation binds together Empire's impact on the Chicano and the African as imperialist subjects that mirror the effects of Manifest Destiny. We can then conceive of Central and West Africa as what Gloria Anzaldúa famously termed an "open wound borderland," hermeneutically tracing continuities from the Atlantic to the Southwest.

Rivera noticeably (dis)places features of Stanley's spatiality in his poetry. Not only does his collection *The Searchers* seem to be inspired by Stanley's exploration, but in Rivera's posthumously published poem "Searching at Leal Middle School," the poetic voice literally embodies patterns of Stanley's praxis.[16] Parodying Stanley's journal, Rivera's presumably young child narrator announces that on a "foggy," "rainy" morning, the weather is "a good day for searching."[17] Despite the proper conditions, the poetic voice asserts that it is "lost in my past" visualizing the "long/roads,/dusty roads" that were "beyond [him]self" and "went on forever."[18] At the same time that the poetic insistence on "roads" emphasizes a search for the past, it also signals the quest for an identity. As the narration settles into the school, a transformation is announced: "I became Henry L. in the forest."[19]

The inhabiting of Stanley's Congo-occupying body over the space of Leal Middle School is preceded by a remarkable array of Stanley-inspired visions. The recurring motifs of a "dump yard," amid "smoke," "long sticks," and "half-rotten fruit"[20]—all objects common in Stanley's memoir—dot the schoolyard. But when the poetic voice comes across a book in the "dump yard"—notably, Stanley's memoir—Rivera's alter-ego now more obviously materializes onto the poetic voice. Upon this turn of events, Stanley's memoir contains accounts of "Livingston's exploration of Africa" complete with the juxtaposition "the maps/the blacks."[21]

Drawing from Rivera's childhood experience, the book's contents then inscribe an emphatic racialization. Suddenly, the enunciation of the charged "blacks" registers an echo of the earlier descriptions of the schoolchildren's hair. The earlier bilingual anaphora of "negro" (or black) and "pelo" (or hair) point to the blackness of bodies occupying the school space in "black hair heads/ Cabezas de pelo negro, negro era/ Cabezas de pelo negro."[22] Not only is this image of black heads formally echoed in his poetic summa—"Searchers"—in the lines "heads/at the back of heads," the imagery of blackness becomes entangled with a transatlanticism projected in Stanley's Congo.[23]

What becomes apparent as the poem unfolds is that Rivera's poetics of identity politics ambiguously mirror the Eurocentric perception—via Stanley—of blackness. If as Achille Mbembe has stated "[a]cross early capitalism, the term 'Black' referred only to the condition imposed on peoples of African origin,"²⁴ in the twentieth century the term becomes "generalized" and "expanded."²⁵ Thus, Rivera triangulates a complicated relationship with the past, or looking "backwards" during a search for identity, but one that has to overcome the perception of race mediated by the Western gaze in his present. While Julián Olivares argues that the "search" in this poem is equal to "the act of discovering, the creative act,"²⁶ I argue that said lyrical praxis is also inspired by a transatlantic spatial reading of Stanley's discoveries.

The lines "I became Henry L. in the forest" not only reappropriate a Eurocentric body, the poetics of space visibly retrace a relatable spatial dimension of adventure. Indeed, Stanley exhibited himself as a mythical warrior, no different from the exciting adventures Rivera admittedly admired in Américo Paredes's *With his Pistol in His Hand* (1958).²⁷ But more specifically, the spatiality within the expedition itself is what must have first lured and shocked Rivera. After all, Stanley's imperialistic descriptions of blackness are anticipatedly problematic.

On June 8, 1888, at the Fort Bodo banana plantation, Stanley relates the difficulties of mounting a civilizing mission in the Congo. Anchored in his construction of a racial dichotomy is his perception that his fellow Belgian explorers are "consoled" with "knowing that heaven is above" while he doubts the "black men, the 'brutes,' 'niggers,' 'black devils,' feel" the same way.²⁸ The fact that Stanley uses quotation marks is telling of his impulse to quote the status quo of his time. That is, the positivist Jim Crow that he was acquainted with while in New Orleans, that views the African body under said labels. Nevertheless, the racial implications of the terminology he indulges remain problematic as do his references to unknown black men as "mobs" or as nothing more than an "elevation black with masses of men."²⁹ As is implied by Stanley, the descriptions of their very subject-hood as mere bodies, "masses" or "mobs," seem to imply that their presence prevents the establishment of a western civilization by virtue of their race.

By contrast, Rivera's familiarization with blackness in his poem—that of "the backs of black hair heads/negro era" to "maps/the blacks"—takes a subversive turn. Far from distancing itself from blackness, Rivera conjures its presence within Stanley's forced absence. In other words, Rivera seems to use the spaces in which Stanley pitted Congolese against white civilization to then summon a parallelism between that blackness and the spaces of Leal Middle School. After the poetic voice impersonates Stanley, it then looks up at its guardian, Doña Cuquita. The poetic voice takes in Cuquita's "long apron rolled up/heavy with sweet-smoked fruit" but most significantly her "cobwebbed eyelashes" that "could not hide her dark eyes/ojos oscuros que fascinan."³⁰ While the positive imagery of dark eyes resurfaces in "Searchers" with "into their eyes/and searched for perfection,"³¹ the insistence on blackness in the original poem—by using Spanish and English—create a repetition of blackness that is at once endearing and "fascinating." Yet the desire for relation here turns to subtle regret, as that connection linked to raciology seems tenuous: the poetic voice wonders, "Did she know about Livingston?/ Through smoke."³²

Rivera's repetition of blackness at the beginning of the poem (referring to children's hair), midway through the poem (referring to "the exploration of Africa"), and now through the diaphora of "Livingstone" as Doña Cuquita's cognizance of the missionary is questioned memorializes Africa through a veil of smoke. Indeed, it is Stanley's Eurocentric lens that must first be deconstructed to then remap the "long" "road" of racial recovery. Africa might have been written about and described through Stanley's pen, but more important the "exploration of Africa" is now actively recovered in the "dump" of history.[33] This necessary exploration of Africa in the backyard of Leal Middle School implies a return to the source punctuated by loss. Not only has Rivera implied a return to the source in poems such as "En la hora de las semillas" (with "volvemos a las primas semillas," "we return to the seeds,")[34] or in "Las voces del olvido" (where the poetic voice seeks "los siglos durmientes," "the sleeping centuries,"), his poems "Me lo enterraron," "the Overalls," and "the Searchers" also magnify the sense of forgotten memory.[35] In his Leal poem, this search for identity is also "lost in my past," where again, roads are "long" and "dusty," but nonetheless include African historiography "discarded by the rich" as the poetic voice doggedly seeks to recover an uncorrupted version of blackness.[36]

Turning away from this meditation on racialized bodies, the poetic voice refocuses on "bultos" and "discovered bundles of / manos en la bolsa." Channeling Stanley's logs, another journal entry is noted: "Monday 11" and then another, "Thursday, foggy day / a good day for finding at / Leal Middle School."[37] But different from Stanley, Rivera has entangled the Leal schoolchildren's black hair and eyes with a transatlantic exploration. In the final lines, the poetic voice settles back to its original imagery: "cabezas de pelo negro/ de ojos oscuros."[38] The enjambment of dark eyes and heads as well as the anaphora of smiling eyes ("cabezas de pelo negro/de ojos oscuros" and "ojos oscuros / ojos sonrientes) reposition Stanley's described blackness. Intead, Rivera inscribes a sense of "limitlessness" ("limitless" as it is described in the poem) in the diacope of "ojos sin límites/ojos oscuros / ojos sonrientes,/juguetones" ("eyes without limits/ dark eyes/ smiling eyes/ playful"), where marginality occupies center stage.[39] As Rivera's final repetition echoes the beginning lines of his poem, blackness is recentered around the emphasized smiling ("sonrientes") and playful ("juguetones") faces, no longer shackled to the racialized and marginalized spaces in which Stanley's descriptors had blackness confined.

Meaningful to this comparative frame is the fact that hyphenated men share the localization of blackness but differ drastically in their implementation of black bodies occupying borderland space. If for Stanley, the otherness of blackness signifies an opposition to European delimitation of African borders, for Rivera, the school occupies a blackness that is relational to space. Even though Rivera inhabits Stanley's body to project himself as an avid explorer, the borderland he projects creates a contradictory space vis-à-vis Stanley. Henri Lefebvre terms "contradictory spaces" as those emerging from a Cartesian-based logic fused with "the social *res*, of the commodity, of capital."[40] This capital-based logic conceives of space as one that solves "practical problems of bureaucracy and power, rent and profit, and so on, so creating the illusion of a less chaotic reality" where a delimited logocentric space is imposed.

The main issue with this ideology is that space becomes occupied as a means to exploit capital gain and implement stability under the guise of progress. This social order,

Lefebvre explains, renders "social space" as "indistinguishable" from spaces of power (defined by Lefebvre as "planners, politicians and administrators," architects, and sectors of "social constructed character").[41] Regardless if Westernized others are indigenous to land, their inability to "integrate" into the social order of what Aníbal Quijano terms the "coloniality of power"[42] renders them expendable, threatening, and ultimately outcasts from the demarcations of profiteering logic.

For Stanley's imperialistic gaze, the Congolese challenge the spatial delimitations of civilization, especially as blackness is equated often with savagery. Stanley repeatedly references people's savagery throughout his memoir as this signifier bleeds into the land in "[a]ll things are savage."[43] As a result, Stanley's racialized bodies highlight an unwillingness of landscape to adhere to Empire. By contrast, in Rivera's work, as José David Saldívar has cogently argued, a "utopian unity of a collectivity" is expressed in "responding to a white supremacist view of Chicano farmworkers who were treated 'worse than *slaves*'"(emphasis added) as Rivera himself asserted.[44] This comparative dialectic referencing exploited labor conjures the United States' historical plantocracy, admitting not only the reemerging traumas of slavery in the Southwest, but a planetary capital-based coloniality affecting multiple populations of people of color along the US-Mexican divide. More specifically, and expanding from Saldívar, I argue that this "utopian unity of collectivity" extends transatlantically, precisely because Rivera invokes a "postmemory"[45] of the Atlantic world's effects. Rivera thus entwines Stanley's Congolese slaves with the capitalistic model over which the United States' historiographical foundation is built.

In tracing routes of temporal subalternity, the aesthetics of Stanley's searching for Dr. Livingstone in a seemingly foreign space are not merely coincidental. The epistemology of "Search" in Rivera's poetics is punctuated by what Héctor Calderón has termed an individualized "locus of hope"[46] referring to Rivera's canonical *Tierra* (1971). As the poetic voice registers patterns of anthropological praxis in the search for self, I argue that Rivera's poetics operate on the level of the personal—seeking the individual American Dream—but also attempt to appropriate identity politics, of race, along delimited but not necessarily national borders.

Rivera's poems "Odio" (1972), "Perfection of Perfections" (1973), and "This Solitude" inscribe this racialization against a backdrop of loss, highlighted by the words "whiteness," "night," and "dark, blackness/through powers of the body" respectively. Particularly it is in his poem "Odio" ("Hate" in Spanish) where the lines "Weeds rupture the marble/and I laugh at the whiteness" reiterate the weight of racialized landscape. Contrasted with his posthumously published "Noon-Night" where alienation with whiteness articulates scorn (in "To hate him, anyone/a white face"), in "Odio" the racialized resentment conveys assuaged anger and hope. Whereas "Noon-Night" ends with the gloomily tensioned lines "I am not free./ I am discovering evil.", "Odio" operates on a hopeful platform of oppositional defiance. In the poem, the "weeds" signify resistance not only in their laughing at (white) hegemony but also in their coming through a solid expanse of "marble."[47]

Yet in "Odio," the backdrop of sordid violence resurfaces in the cacophony of "daggers,/knifing,/ soundless,/ unloved through death." While the caesura in this metric line forces a careful recognition of conflict, the punctuated trochaic trimeter in "daggers,/knifing,/soundless" isolate the *form* of violence, tracing it back to dichotomies of a savage landscape opposite white civilization.[48] Even though Stanley's attributing death to the native land is liberally expressed in moments such as this one, "150 men were lost in the *remorseless woods, surrounded by savages*" (emphasis added), the expression manufactures otherness vis-à-vis the Congolese while Rivera's atmosphere of death results from coloniality.[49] In Rivera's juxtaposition in "Odio," a dislocated racialized spatiality underscores instead the violent legacy of Manifest Destiny as brown bodies are "torn from the earth" and "left to dry,/to die,"[50] as his assonant rhyme indicates.

From a decolonialist vantage point, the poem seeks to disarticulate the exhaustive and violent productive capacity of Empire. Rivera formally isolates hope in the poem, as visualized here in the fragmented stanzas:

> Future in the seed
> Stone upon stone
> of despair.
> Stone from which
> come the weeds
> who blade each other
> without love
> to be torn from the earth
> and thrown to the earth.
> The seed is here
> on the stone
> on my forehead.

Not only does the poem accentuate the search for self in years to come by isolating "Future in the seed" aesthetically, the expression of futurity here both repeats and structurally aligns with the last stanza "The seed is here/on the stone/on my forehead." From "Weeds rupture the marble" to "The seed is here/on the stone," the poem also disarticulates Stanley's white geocultural space "unloved through death."

Yet these poetics seem to contrast with his earlier and highly acclaimed *Tierra*, where brown bodies are figuratively tied to the earth—"Por qué es que nosotros estamos aquí como enterrados en la tierra?" (Why should we always be tied to the dirt?").[51] Inversely, in "Odio," while Rivera never releases these subjected bodies, he does produce a space in which labor and exploitation can be "torn from the earth." If the expressions above infer what John Cutler Alba explains is a "piecing together [of] the economic and social processes subordinating Mexican American farmworkers to the demands of U.S. capital" (71), in his poetry specifically, Rivera reproduces the same frames of reference through the mention of "whiteness."[52] Racial dichotomy leads to a collective and productive space in "Stone upon stone." This new fertile ground now invites Rivera to graft onto the resistant brown body an oppositional consciousness. Rivera's racial body and the signified location it occupies produce this resisting spatial practice, indeed a counterhegemonic discourse that literally "laughs" back "at whiteness." As the laughing marker dehistoricizes hegemony, jettisoning oppressive signifiers, the poetic figure clears a path for the communal to consolidate, as Glissant affirms, "a fundamental relationship with the Other."[53]

Returning to the spatial analysis of the poem, it is clear that for Rivera's output described here, the Congo serves as a *relatable* common denominator for both the historiographic African slaves Rivera *imagined* (and referred to) and the *actual* farmworkers he knew. Disrupting Stanley's logocentrism, the Quinto Sol poet triangulates the processes of capitalistic exploitation under the guise of social progress. Rather than syntactical, the discursive register of Rivera's relational model reconstructs an ethnic origin on both sides of the Atlantic. For Chicanos, Rivera seems to convey that progress is not limited to tracing history back to an ethnopoiesis source as he expertly textualizes in "The Searchers": "in our solitude/ we found our very being/We moved into each other's/ almost carefully, deliberately."[54] Rather, Rivera's decolonial spatial production admits that Atlantic continuities might remain—after all, we "had been finding [coloniality's pieces] for centuries," the searcher admits.[55]

As if recreating an aubade for a new dawn, Rivera's hopeful poetic voice asserts that "We are not alone" and "we will continue to/ to search."[56] This encouraging ending in the enjambment that concludes his book of poems, like that of "Searching at Leal Middle School," seeks to *remember* not a dialectic binary system, but a "thirding-as-Othering" beyond simple dichotomies.[57] The complicated road to recovery redeems colorism while underlying the myriad trajectories it had to overcome. But indeed, if Rivera's *Tierra* once "functioned aesthetically and ideologically as a memorial to and partial reconstitution of the forgotten history of a peoples oppression,"[58] as Ramón Saldívar has persuasively argued, Rivera's poetry memorializes an expanded "search" that goes "beyond" the self.[59] As the Chicano explorer ruminates on Stanley's *textual* memory (whose *physical* memorialization erupted onto the stage of twentieth-century memory politics), Rivera's poems—particularly "Searching at Leal Middle School" and "Odio"— complicate and reconfigure the spatial dimensions of an expansive borderland.

## The Colonial Atlantic and Anaya's Gift of Flight

While the Congo proved distinct in the imaginary of a Chicano writer, another instance of African historiography embedded in foundational Chicano literature references a period stretching further back in time. I am referring to the era of the Slave Trade that plagued the Southwest, even as this era is commonly dismissed as affecting mainly the Caribbean. Historically, former African slaves from the seventeenth century in what is today the US-Mexican borderland "found themselves being swept into an indigenous world...and assimilated fully into native communities."[60] But significantly, following

Texas's independence, admitting to African ancestry meant losing land entitlements that had been previously ceded to afromestizos by the Mexican government.[61]

What ensued was a racialized effect, as Saldívar has pointed out: "By the end of the nineteenth century, the ideological rhetoric of white supremacy dominated Southern and Southwestern politics and eventually became institutionalized in state discourses, laws, and narratives," to the point that Chicano authors such as Anaya have lamented the repression of literary Afrolatinidad.[62] So even if afromestizos retained deep structures in the Southwest, identity along with *spatial* repression was commonplace. Nevertheless, it is important to remember, as historian Martha Menchaca has long pointed out, that the history of slavery along the Rio Grande included "the migration of people of African descent to the Southwest" beginning "in 1598, when the first colony was established in New Mexico."[63] This historical précis is significant considering New Mexican native Anaya and his short story, "A Man That Could Fly" (2006), the subject of analysis in this second part. While Luis Leal states that canonical Anaya was "greatly influenced by the legendary cuentos" from Mexico—notably that of Congolese El Negrito Poeta influencing New Mexican folklore directly—and that Anaya assumed the role of cuentero to keep alive "the craft of the santero,"[64] I argue here that Anaya's decolonial meditation on witches, slavery, and entrapment is also derived from a colonial (and perhaps even unconscious) Atlantic location.

Best know for his coming-of-age novel *Bless Me, Ultima* (1972), Anaya's short story published decades later in his collection *The Man Who Could Fly and Other Stories* (2006) features the farmworkers of Agua Bendita gathering for storytelling after a long day of work. As the aircraft above them remind us that we are in the midst of the Vietnam War, their upward gaze arguably points to the wishful detachment of their selfless bodies from labor. Don Sarco, one of the elder farmworkers then comments, "What about those people who can fly without the aid of machines," as doña Catalina dismisses him with the utterance "Witches."[65] But Don Sarco then insists: "I heard of a man over in Llano Seco who could fly... Yes, they claimed the old man could fly."[66] Jokes ensue until Don Volo, the most impoverished among them, recounts a startling tale. Anaya's frame story gives way to Don Volo's ambiguous account of a landowner who made a losing bet against a mysterious older cook.

With a dance party taking place ten miles away in a village significantly called "las Animas" ("the souls"), a surprised landowner asks the cook if he was not joining the the partygoers who were leaving the rancho. When the cook confidently responds that he will arrive to the dance before everyone else, despite not leaving with them, the amused ranch owner bets his cattle in exchange for the cook's slavery: "If we are there before you, then you must work for me without pay for the rest of your life."[67] But the cook raises the bet: "My life of work for your herd is not an even bet... why not add all the land you own."[68] Upon arriving to las Animas, the astonished landowner finds the old cook waiting for him just as the cook had foretold. When the villagers refuse to believe Don Volo's story, the former reveals that *he* was the ranch owner.

In the end, the emphasis of the story is not placed on Don Volo's understandable loss of land, but rather on "the moment of magic": that "man can fly."[69] The final statement of the story is ambiguous, as expected, mostly because we are left to speculate whether don Volo is referring to flight literally, that is, the magical possibility of men flying, or metaphorically. That metaphor can be interpreted in two ways: colonially, that greed can render man a slave, or postcolonially, that man can escape slavery through the artifact of flight.

Whereas in Rivera, Imperialism is precise in its location of the Congo, in Anaya, coloniality has erased a precise geographical location. Rather, it is a specific narrative element in Anaya's short story that functions as a signpost that demarcates the confines of an Atlantic world. Perplexingly, this textual object uncannily dialogues with Latin American fiction, while flight's transnational comparison makes evident the elements of the slave trade that rise to the textual surface. I am referring mainly to traced continuities between Anaya's artifact of flight and Colombian Gabriel García Márquez's two narratives: "El señor muy viejo con alas enormes"/ "A Very Old Man with Enormous Wings" (1955) and *Crónica de una muerte anunciada/ Chronicle of a Death Foretold* (1981).

The use of wings as a marginalized marker is descriptive of slavery in a hemispheric America. Don Necio's comment that "flight is for the birds. Or for angels" uncannily relates to García Márquez's short story.[70] Warning against the "tricks" the "devil" plays in "A Very Old Man," the town priest "argued that if wings were not the essential element in determining the difference between a hawk and an airplane, they were even less so in the recognition of angels."[71] García Márquez's short story appearing from Gregory Rabassa's translation in *Leaf Storm* features a tired, winged old man who becomes the town's principal attraction. Denied an angelical ontology by virtue of his otherness, the Church allows his exploitation for capital gain. Confined to a chicken coop, the townspeople pay to gaze upon his distinctive body until his "demonic" feathers resprout and empower his flight toward freedom.

Vera Kutzinski has read this story together with Alejo Carpentier's *El reino de este mundo/ The Kingdom of This World* and the *Book of Negro Folklore* through the Derridaean lens of *pharmakos* (healer, wizard, magician, sorcerer). In her analysis, she points out how in all three cases, the winged bodies ruminate on the impossibility of shackling an enslaved body. This oxymoron defies Eurocentric logic, while all three narratives also resignify flight. In Carpentier's narration, set in late eighteenth-century pre-revolutionary Haiti, as masters prepare the public corporal punishment of rebel Macandal—a runaway slave—his body metamorphoses:

> At that moment, Macandal moved the stump of his arm, which they had been unable to tie up, in a threatening gesture which was none the less terrible for being partial, howling unknown spells and violently thrusting his torso forward. The bonds fell off and the body of the Negro rose in the air, flying overhead, until it plunged into the black waves of the sea of slaves. A single cry filled the squares: "Macandal saved."
>
> En ese momento, Mackandal agitó su muñón que no habían podido atar, en un gesto conminatorio que no por menguado era menos terrible, aullando conjuros desconocidos y echando violentamente el torso hacia adelante. Sus ataduras cayeron, y el

cuerpo del negro se espigó en el aire, volando por sobre las cabezas, antes de hundirse en las ondas negras de la masa de esclavos. Un solo grito llenó la plaza: "*Mackandal sauvé.*"[72]

Mocking the powerlessness of brute force, Macandal's gift of flight is one of resistance to Empire inasmuch physical as metaphysical. His marooned flight in turn ideologically liberates another slave, Ti Noel, who watches the entire spectacle.[73]

Carpentier attributes a metaphor for escaping the captivity to the gift of flight, and shares with Anaya the symbolism of freedom originally triggered by *The Book of Negro Folklore*. Here, another old man exhorts a beaten slave to flee: "The old man cried out to him, and stretched out his arms as he had done for the other two; and he, like them, leaped up, and was gone through the air, flying like a bird over field and wood."[74] Once the masters witness the old man's rebellion, they beat him mercilessly. As cruelty is exerted over his tired body, the old man also leaps away, empowering others to follow suit:

> And as he spoke to them, they all remembered what they had forgotten, and recalled the power which once had been theirs. Then all the Negroes, old and new, stood up together; the old man raised his hands; and they all leaped into the air with a great shout, and in a moment were gone, flying, like a flock of cows, over the field, over the fence, and over the top of the wood.[75]

Whether an allegorical or imaginary tale, flight operates as an escape. Thus, if for Mbembe, Western thinking "locked" the "Black Man [in] the prototype of a prehuman figure incapable of emancipating itself,"[76] the oral tale recounted in all these American narratives,[77] including Anaya's, unlocks this confining imperialist impulse. Rather than a display of transnational tautology, I argue that the artifact of flight in all of these stories triangulates an expression of Atlantic continuities.

If the artifact of flight conveys affinities to liberty in Chicano, African American, and Latin American tradition, another common denominator these narratives share is that "flight" has universally been scorned as demonic. In both Anaya's and García Márquez's stories, the wings not only prevent the marginalized object's acceptance as an angel or bird (or even artifact), they relegate said subject to the position of the fiend. The insistence on flight as witchcraft both locates the bizarre as the literal signifier of difference but also of *spatiality's* confining nature, echoing Rivera's farmworkers "why do we always have to be tied to the land?" In Anaya, the otherness of the cook is punctuated by the delimitation of his reality to the rural landscape. As Don Volo admits, the man "lived in a world of magic we do not understand," a world that exiles this othered being behind the walls of normalcy while others can gaze out with both admiration and fear.[78] It is fair to say that this boarded-off space invests its inhabitant with special powers, as Don Volo points out. He explains that when he shook the cook's hand, he felt a sudden "surge of energy he had never felt before," justifying in analepsis Doña Catalina's speculation that flying men are "Witches."[79]

A term used interchangeably such as "savagery" or "barbarian" for describing all that is outside of our understanding, I would like to suggest that Doña Catalina's "Witches" comments on the indistinguishable marker of an Atlantic world order. Specifically, this utterance links the images of witchcraft in the nineteenth-century US-Mexico borderland with those of the sixteenth-century Congo. As signifiers of otherness, *feiticeiros, curanderos*, healers, and witches were the epitomic site of difference when it came to ethnicity in the Southwest. Ethnologist and captain John Gregory Bourke in the nineteenth-century depicted the Mexican "herb doctors" or "professional 'bruja' or witch" along the Mexican-American border as "nefarious"[80] in his 1894 spatial account "The American Congo." The Eurocentric filtering of spirituality in which Mexicans are signified as "degraded, turbulent, ignorant, and *superstitious*" parallels their ethnicity to that of the Congolese. While Bourke locates an imagined African axis along the Río Grande, that systematic undermining of subaltern spirituality in Bourke's term "superstitious" is found in the site of subaltern health care much earlier, in Central Africa.

During the era of the slave trade, Italian missionary Antonio Cavazzi, traveling to the Congo for the Spanish Crown, praised the natural remedies of feiticeiros. Yet he found them to be "abominable" and the population that worshiped them "superstitious" and "evil," echoing—anachronistically—Bourke's terminology for the Southwest.[81] The Congo's native spirituality thus functioned indirectly as the threat to civil society as Western ethnocentrism used the marker of witchcraft to justify colonial domination. The logic of coloniality mandated that to sustain evangelization and civil society, the practitioners of said traditions either had to be destroyed or traded in for labor, thus justifying their slavery.

Anaya and García Márquez elaborate on slavery precisely over the space where flight occurs. If, in Anaya's story, the fictional town of Las Animas is the space where the "magic" of flight is revealed, it is telling that "Animas" is also the port of Cartagena's slavery in García Márquez's *Crónica* (1981). Before his proleptic murder, Santiago Nasar, a wealthy townsperson presumed to have deflowered the soon-to-be-married Angela Vicario, is depicted "flying through the almond trees" ("que volaba sin tropezar por entre los almendrones," García Márquez, 4, 7) in his dream. When he wakes, Santiago joins his friends at the pier. Over this signified site, he points to a light in the horizon over Cartagena's Bay of Souls (Bahía de las Animas). There, he announces that the lights symbolize the "the soul in torment of a slave ship that had sunk with a cargo of blacks from Senegal" ("ánimas en pena de un barco negrero que se había hundido con un cargamento de esclavos del Senegal" 67, 77). Telling of a historical space that recalls subaltern memory is the pier, named after the very souls that lost their lives there and whose spirits are still hauntingly manifested by the horizon's shining. Santiago's almost imperceptible invocation of their spirits in the novel remains the only notable memorialization of Cartagena's slavery and is admittedly a troubling one.

Santiago is, significantly, the only member of the community that has drawn out this memory publicly, and this only moments prior to his also public assassination. Although his notable remembrance of slavery marks him as a custodian of Atlantic history, our suspicion of his moral character comments on the tragedy and irony of an unreliable narrator as the archivist of slavery's memory. Don Volo's Flying Man that practices witchcraft is as unreliable to Doña Catalina as flying Santiago is to any Cartagena townsfolk. Recalling Rivera, the roads that lead to remembering an African heritage are "dusty," barely perceptible behind clouds of "smoke." If tracing these continuities back to the archive, its illegibility was precisely the point. As Atlantic historian James Sweet notes, healing practices by indigenous communities of the Congolese region were not only "condemned and marginalized as 'sin' and 'idolatry,' they also were misinterpreted as the work of the Devil," precluding any real understanding of the healing procedures of these Atlantic indigenous regions.[82]

Thus, the tragedy in *Crónica*, like that of Anaya, is complicity in the erasure of Atlantic history. In *Crónica*, not only are the townspeople guilty of the murder of a man—unable as they are to prevent his death—they are also guilty of disassociating themselves from the very Atlantic fabric from whence they came. This is because the moment Santiago dies, so too does the barely perceptible memory of Cartagena's slavery. In Anaya, this disassociation is reflected upon through the object of flight, scorned as witchcraft or the work of the devil. But like Rivera's recovery of blackness, Anaya's story read against a frame of internationalism reveals Atlantic continuities. Flight indeed exists, Anaya claims, because according to Don Volo, the cook could indeed fly, and fly he does towards freedom similar to the Latin American and African American tradition. In the process, however, the flying man teaches Don Volo a heartening lesson against arrogance but significantly never enslaves Don Volo as, indeed, he would have done to the cook. Flight becomes synonymous with what Saldívar terms "discontinuities" of coloniality, manifested over a space that conflates "borderland" and "diaspora."[83] Anaya's symbolic flight embraces a "diasporic" Southwest that seems to argue that "many structural and ethno-racial similarities about identity formations" are bound to a "colonizing past."[84] But identity can also evolve from this past. It is significant then that Anaya's confined spaces of Agua Bendita and elocution of upward flight—and upward mobility—find iterations of a Cavazi-like or Slave Trade era witchcraft speculation but insist on "discontinuing" its logic.

By offering various examples of how narratives employ the "Flying Man" or the "Flying African," I am not attempting to merely draw comparisons to form exclusively but also proposing we read these stories comparatively through an interdisciplinary and transatlantic framework. This spatial position grants us the vantage point of visualizing how the era of the Slave Trade situates a parallel structuralization of ethno-race. In other words, this comparatist project is not for the sake of a renewal of transnational dimensions. Rather, it seeks an exploration of the multiple and relational ways that transnational literature manifests the legacies of an expansive colonialism and imperialism originating in West Africa as mutually constitutive of and implicated in the multifaceted diasporas of the Americas.

# Final Words

The movement of peoples into the national US space has always involved a meditation on the ways in which empire affects arrival, while at times overlooking points of departure. The Atlantic world created ports of departure that, as sites of memory, continue to capture the imagination of writers meditating on Chicano's placement within this arrival-departure continuum. Some of the most relevant works in the Chicanx literary tradition are Ana Castillo's *So Far From God* (1993) and *My Father was a Toltec and Selected Poems* (1995), Emma Pérez's *Forgetting the Alamo or Blood Memory* (2009), and, most significantly, Alicia Gaspar de Alba's *Calligraphy of the Witch* (2007) about Sor Juana Inés de la Cruz's afromestiza scribe sold into slavery in New England. Atlantic continuities affect the borderland imagination but also place Chicano authors in a position of both literally and metaphorically *relating* experiences of displacement, subjection, and racialization.

Similar to the transatlantic departure this chapter has focused on, the recent wave of 86,000 Syrian refugees in the continental United States significantly informs US Americanity. Since 2014, this group becomes one of the newest scapegoats in nativist rhetoric—one built on a persistent short-term memory that ignores the US Imperialist hand in yet another transatlantic displacement of 11 million.[85] Understanding the transpacific injustices of the US Philippine occupation as well as the internment of Japanese Americans as relatable to empire's practices in the transatlantic world are just as crucial when integrating points of departure as sites of memory that inform Americanity. This is because the realities of the US borderlands are much more fluid than meets the eye, not only because immigration and diaspora are ever-evolving between lateral US borders if we consider back-and-forth Latin American immigration. But also because distant borders—such as those in the Congo, or Syria, or the Philippines—continue to be etched into the historiographical imaginary of our national identity.

Rivera and Anaya must have instinctively understood the implications of this brand of transhemispheric traffic. As Imperial subjects from the vantage point of the post- and decolonial worlds, they could recognize a post-imperialist Africa being reproduced in their own backyard. As a consequence, their narratives related the oppressive Third World struggles across the globe. In Glissantian terms it is a relation that "makes the understanding of every culture limitless."[86] Decolonizing the filtered gaze of Empire—a gaze that affirms space delimitation and commodification of oppressed subjects—Rivera and Anaya expand the unadulterated deep structures of Atlantic traditions that color the Chicano experience. As a result, reading relationally and transatlantically, these Chicano narratives offer an exploration of the cross-cultural union of multiculturalism affecting Chicano's sense of otherness while extending the reach of Americanity into new hemispheres, as far as those in Central Africa.

## Notes

1. At times, I choose to use the term "Latino" to encompass all ethnic and racial categories of Latinidad, such as "AfroLatino," "Chicanx," and "Caribbean," when generalizing is useful and strictly as a means of coherence. Further, I borrow from Paula Moya's logic that the term "Latino" articulates "a kind of 'imaginary community' that is based partly on the common experience of being interpellated as a particular kind of 'minority' person in the United States," "Why I Am Not Hispanic," 17.

2. Ever since 1992, the Republic of Benin (in partnership with Haiti) developed a circuit of memorialization that other West African nations have emulated. This Route consists of renovated memorials honoring the memory and history of slaves who would embarked on ships bound for American plantations during the era of the Transatlantic Slave Trade. See "UNESCO" Slave Route," http://www.unesco.org/culture/pdf/slave/the-slave-route-the-road-travelled-1994-2014-en.pdf.
3. Édouard Glissant, *Poetics of Relation* (Ann Arbor: University of Michigan Press, 2009), 11, 172-174.
4. Juan Bruce-Novoa, *Chicano Authors: Inquiry by Interview* (Austin: University of Texas Press, 1980), 143. In his interview, Rivera states: "There is one which especially impressed me: *In Darkest Africa* by Henry M. Stanley. I found it myself in the dump, you see; a two-volume collection of Stanley's expedition into Africa in search for Dr. Livingstone. Of course, I didn't know anything about history at the time, or the exploration of Africa.... I haven't read them for a long time, but that title *stuck in my memory* because of the exploratory aspect. Later, when I ran into other similar things, I was able to understand the exploration of America and Latin America because I could understand this one man's exploration of the Dark Continent" (emphasis added).
5. Luis Leal and Ilan Stavans, eds., *A Luis Leal Reader* (Chicago: Northwestern University Press, 2007).
6. Bruce-Novoa, 143.
7. Amy Kaplan and Donald E. Pease, *Cultures of United States Imperialism* (Durham, NC: Duke University Press, 1999), 3, 9.
8. Theresa Delgadillo, *Spiritual Mestizaje: Religion, Gender, Race, and Nation in Contemporary Chicana Narrative* (Durham, NC: Duke University Press, 2011), 159.
9. Glissant, 173.
10. Glissant, 18.
11. Juan Poblete, *Critical Latin American and Latinx Studies* (Minneapolis: University of Minnesota Press, 2003), xiv. The same can be said about the integration of African American and African studies. Most recently in the historical discipline, Atlantic historical research has attempted to bridge the epistemic divide between both fields. Consider the works of John Thornton's *A Cultural History of the Atlantic World, 1250–1820* (2012), Peter Mark and José da Silva's *The Forgotten Diaspora* (2011), and James Sweet's *Domingos Álvares, African Healing, and the Intellectual History of the Atlantic World* (2011), to name a few of the most recent examples.
12. Ylce Irizarry, *Chicana/o and Latina/o Fiction: The New Memory of Latinidad* (Urbana: University of Illinois Press, 2016), 34.
13. Tomás Rivera and Julián Olivares, *The Complete Works* (Houston, TX: Arte Público Press, 1992), 175.
14. Tomás Rivera, *Y no se lo tragó la tierra: And the Earth Did Not Part* (Berkeley, CA: Editorial Quinto Sol Publications, 1971), 169, 177.
15. John David Maguire, "Searching: When Old Dreams Find Their Youth Again," *Bilingual Review/La Revista Bilingüe* 13, nos. 1/2 (1986): 106–112.
16. Rivera and Olivares, 231-233. In this poem, the first stanza states: "December 11,/ Thursday,/ foggy day,/morning,/a good day for searching./I discovered children through the fog/ bundles, bultos,/manos en la bolsa turning/bultos in serenity/*Leal*." The figures of Livingstone and Stanley emerge in the third stanza: "It was a good day for searching/Yet I became lost in my past/I saw myself and became/each one for an instant/and grasped for a second/ the curious blink./In split instances I became/the student, silent, staring/

beyond myself, backwards/to joys so long forgotten of long/roads,/dusty roads/that went forever,/and friends running towards me/from far away./Away in the dump yards / where smoke curled and/with long sticks we turned and turned and/found half-rotten fruit/to be washed and eaten/and books—/Livingston's exploration of Africa,/the maps,/the blacks,/I became Henry L. in the forest.—" In the fourth stanza, Livinsgtone resurfaces: "And her apron/long apron rolled up/heavy with sweet-smoked fruit/sitting down to eat and listen/cobwebbed eyelashes could not/hide her dark eyes/ojos oscuros que fascinan/Did she know about Livingston?/Through the smoke."

17. Rivera and Olivares, 231.
18. Rivera and Olivares, 232.
19. Rivera and Olivares, 233.
20. See Tomás Rivera and Julián Olivares, *The Complete Works* (Houston: Arte Público Press, 1992). According to Olivares, the "dump" serves simultaneously as a "symbol of search" as well as a metaphor illustrating "the mountain of refuse into which *la raza* had and has been thrown" (xl).
21. Rivera and Olivares, 232-233.
22. Rivera and Olivares, 231.
23. Rivera and Olivares, 224.
24. Achille Mbembe, *Critique of Black Reason* (Durham, NC: Duke University Press, 2017), 5.
25. Mbembe, 6.
26. Olivares, xxxviii.
27. See Ramón Saldívar, *Chicano Narrative* (Madison: University of Wisconsin Press, 1990), 26, 79, where Saldívar explains the "exploratory" dimension of *With His Pistol* that particularly inspired Rivera's novel. See also *A Literary History of the American West*, 512, and Frederick Aldama, *The Routledge Concise History of Latinx/a Literature* (2013), 59.
28. Henry M. Stanley, *In Darkest Africa* (London: S. Low, Marston, Searle and Rivingston, 1890), 456.
29. Stanley, 323.
30. Rivera and Olivares, 233.
31. Rivera and Olivares, 226.
32. Rivera and Olivares, 233.
33. Rivera and Olivares, 233.
34. Rivera and Olivares, 234.
35. Rivera and Olivares, 236.
36. Rivera and Olivares, 232.
37. Rivera and Olivares, 233.
38. Rivera and Olivares, 233.
39. Rivera and Olivares, 231.
40. Henri Lefebvre, *The Production of Space* (Oxford: Blackwell Press, 2007), 300.
41. Lefebvre, *The Production of Space*, 300.
42. In "Coloniality of Power, Eurocentrism, and Latin America" (2000), Aníbal Quijano defines "coloniality of power" as a "codification of the differences between conquerors… and the conquered in the idea of race." For Quijano, this Eurocentric idea of race supposes innate differences justifying a natural "inferiority" based on racial hierarchy.
43. Stanley, 169.
44. José David Saldívar, *The Dialectics of Our America: Genealogy, Cultural Critique, and Literary History* (Durham, NC: Duke University Press, 1991), 57, 58.

45. Marianne Hirsch, *The Generation of Postmemory: Writing and Visual Culture After the Holocaust* (New York: Columbia University Press, 2012), 22. Hirsch acknowledges that "postmemory" narratives emerge in the 1980s, accounting for traumas of the Holocaust. These are stories that are "mediated not through recollection but through an imaginative investment and creation" from ancestors.
46. Rivera and Olivares, 112.
47. Rivera and Olivares, 235.
48. Rivera and Olivares, 235.
49. Rivera, 4.
50. Rivera and Olivares, 200.
51. Rivera, 1971, 68, 76.
52. John Alba Cutler, *Ends of Assimilation: The Formation of Chicano Literature* (New York: Oxford University Press, 2014).
53. Glissant, 14.
54. Rivera and Olivares, 223.
55. Rivera and Olivares, 224.
56. Rivera and Olivares, 227.
57. Edward Soja, *Thirdspace: Journeys to Los Angeles and Other Real-and-Imagined Places* (Cambridge, UK: Blackwell, 1996), 31.
58. Saldívar, *Chicano Narrative*, 77.
59. Rivera and Olivares, 232.
60. Ben Vinson and Matthew Restall, *Black Mexico: Race and Society from Colonial to Modern Times* (Albuquerque: University of New Mexico Press, 2009), 10.
61. Martha Menchaca, *Recovering History, Constructing Race: The Indian, Black and White Roots of Mexican Americans* (Austin: University of Texas Press, 2006), 21.
62. Saldívar, *Dialectics of Our America*, 77; Bruce-Novoa, *Chicano Authors: Inquiry by Interview* (Austin: University of Texas Press, 1980), 194. Specifically, Anaya reflects on his disappointment that few people—especially Chicanos—have read or recognize Nuyorican poet Víctor Hernández Cruz, author of the widely anthologized poem "African Things."
63. Menchaca, 22.
64. Leal, 252, 330.
65. Anaya, 190.
66. Anaya, 191.
67. Anaya, 193.
68. Ibid.
69. Anaya, 194.
70. Anaya, 191.
71. García Márquez, *Leaf Storm and Other Stories*, 107. From its original, "que el demonio tenía la mala costumbre de recurrir a artificios de carnaveral" and "[a]rgumentó que si las alas no eran elemento escencial para determiner las diferencias entre un gavilán y un aeroplano, mucho menos podían serlo para reconocer ángeles," 10.
72. Alejo Carpentier, *El reino de este mundo* (Havana, Cuba: Editorial Letras Cubanas, 1949, 1989), 35–45; *The Kingdom of this World* (New York: Farrar, Straus and Giroux, 1957, 2006), 45–46.
73. This strength, we learn later in the novel, comes from a cognizant sense of African-centered legacy: "He once again saw the heroes that had revealed to him the strength and abundance of his faraway ancestors in Africa" ("volvió a ver a los héroes que le habían revelado la fuerza y la abundancia de sus lejanos antepasados del África,"), 178, 149.

74. Arna W. Bontemps and Langston Hughes, *The Book of Negro Folklore* (New York: Dodd, Mead, 1958). 64.
75. Bontemps and Hughes, 64.
76. Mbembe, 17.
77. The gift of flight notably left an indelible mark in the cultural imagination, spreading as a trend in Latin America during the age of plantocracy. Found in *Biografía de un cimarrón/ Biography of a Runaway Slave* (1966), it is most perceptible in films such as Tomás Guitierrez Aléa's *La última cena* (1976), Sergio Giral's *El otro Francisco* (1976), and Gloria Rolando's *Raíces de mi corazón* (2001).
78. Rivera and Olivares, 192.
79. Rivera and Olivares, 193.
80. John Gregory Bourke, "The American Congo," *Scribners' Magazine* 15 (1894): 590–610, 606.
81. Giovanni Antonio Cavazzi, and Graciano Maria de (tr) Leguzzano, *Descrição histórica dos três reinos do Congo, Matamba e Angola* (Lisbon: Junta de Investigações do Ultramar, 1965), 83.
82. James Sweet, *Domingos Álvares, African Healing, and the Intellectual History of the Atlantic World* (Chapel Hill: University of North Carolina Press, 2011), 106.
83. José David Saldívar, *Trans-Americanity: Subaltern Modernities, Global Coloniality, and the Cultures of Greater Mexico* (Durham, NC: Duke University Press, 2012), 10.
84. Ibid.
85. See "Profile of Syrian Immigrants in the United States" and "Syrian Refugees in the United States" from the *Migration Policy Institute*. http://www.migrationpolicy.org/research/profile-syrian-immigrants-united-states.
86. Glissant, 172.

## Bibliography

Alba Cutler, John. *Ends of Assimilation: The Formation of Chicano Literature*. New York: Oxford University Press, 2014.

Aldama, Frederick Luis. *The Routledge Concise History of Latino/a Literature*. New York: Routledge, 2013.

Anaya, Rudolfo. *Bless Me, Ultima*. Berkeley, CA: Quinto Sol Publications, 1972.

Anaya, Rudolfo. *The Man Who Could Fly and Other Stories*. Norman: University of Oklahoma Press, 2006.

Bontemps, Arna W., and Langston Hughes. *The Book of Negro Folklore*. New York: Dodd, Mead, 1958.

Bourke, John Gregory. "The American Congo." *Scribners' Magazine* 15: 590–610, 1894.

Bruce-Novoa. *Chicano Authors: Inquiry by Interview*. Austin: University of Texas Press, 1980.

Calderón, Héctor, Saldívar, José. *Criticism in the Borderlands: Studies in Chicano Literature, Culture, and Ideology*. Durham, NC: Duke University Press, 1991.

Carpentier, Alejo. *El reino de este mundo*. La Habana, Cuba: Editorial Letras Cubanas, 1949, 1989.

Carpentier, Alejo. *The Kingdom of This World*. New York: Farrar, Straus and Giroux, 1957, 2006.

Carpentier, Alejo. *El siglo de las luces*. La Habana: Editorial Letras Cubanas, 2001.

Carpentier, Alejo. *Explosion in a Cathedral*. Translated by John Srturrock. Minneapolis: University of Minnesota Press, 2001.

Castillo, Ana. *My Father Was a Toltec and Selected Poems, 1973–1988*. New York: Norton, 1995.

Castillo, Ana. *So Far from God: A Novel*. New York: Plume, 1994.
Cavazzi, Giovanni Antonio de, and Graciano Maria de (tr) Leguzzano. *Descrição histórica dos três reinos do Congo, Matamba e Angola*. Lisbon: Junta de Investigações do Ultramar, 1965.
Césaire, Aimé. *Cahier d'un retour au pays natal*. Paris: L'Harmattan, 1939, 2008.
Césaire, Aimé. *Notebook of a Return to my Native Land*. Translated by Mireille Rosello and Annie Pritchard. Newcastle: Bloodaxe Books, 1995.
Delgadillo, Theresa. *Spiritual Mestizaje: Religion, Gender, Race, and Nation in Contemporary Chicana Narrative*. Durham, NC: Duke University Press, 2011.
García Márquez, Gabriel. *La increíble y triste historia de la cándida Eréndira y de su abuela desalmada*. Buenos Aires: Del Bolsillo, 1972, 2003.
García Márquez, Gabriel. *Leaf Storms and Other Stories*. Translated by Gregory Rabassa. New York: Harper and Row, 1972.
García Márquez, Gabriel. *Crónica de una muerte anunciada*. Barcelona: Bruguera, 1981.
García Márquez, Gabriel. *Chronicle of a Death Foretold*. Translated by Gregory Rabassa. New York: Vintage, 2003.
Gaspar de Alba, Alicia. *Calligraphy of the Witch*. Houston, TX: Arte Público, 2007.
Glissant, Édouard. *Poetics of Relation*. Translated by Betsy Wing. Ann Arbor: University of Michigan Press, 2009.
Hirsch, Marianne. *The Generation of Postmemory: Writing and Visual Culture After the Holocaust*. New York: Columbia University Press, 2012.
Irizarry, Ylce. 2016. *Chicana/o and Latina/o Fiction: The New Memory of Latinidad*. Urbana: University of Illinois Press, 2016.
Jeal, Tim. *The Impossible Life of Africa's Greatest Explorer*. London: Faber and Faber, 2007.
Kaplan, Amy, and Donald E. Pease. *Cultures of United States imperialism*. Durham, NC: Duke University Press, 1999.
Kutzinski, Vera M. "The Logic of Wings: Gabriel Garcia Marquez and Afro-American Literature." *Latin American Literary Review*, 13, no. 25 (1985): 133–146.
Leal, Luis, and Ilan Stavans, eds. *A Luis Leal Reader*. Chicago: Northwestern University Press, 2007.
Lefebvre, Henri. *The Production of Space*. Oxford: Blackwell Press, 2007.
Maguire, John David. "Searching: When Old Dreams Find Their Youth Again." *Bilingual Review/La Revista Bilingüe* 13, no. 1/2 (1986): 106–112.
Mbembe, Achille, and Laurent Dubois. *Critique of Black Reason*. Durham, NC: Duke University Press, 2017.
Menchaca, Martha. *Recovering History, Constructing Race: The Indian, Black and White Roots of Mexican Americans*. Austin: University of Texas Press, 2006.
Milian, Claudia. "Latinx/a Deracination and the New Latin American Novel." In *Junot Díaz and the Decolonial Imagination*, edited by Jennifer Harford Vargas, Monica Hana, and José David Saldívar, 173–200. Durham, NC: Duke University Press, 2016.
Moya, Paula. "Why I Am Not Hispanic: An Argument with Jorge Gracia." *APA Newsletter* 0.2 (2001): 100–105.
Perez, Emma. *Forgetting the Alamo or Blood Memory: A Novel*. Austin: University of Texas Press, 2009.
Poblete, Juan. *Critical Latin American and Latinx Studies*. Minneapolis: University of Minnesota Press, 2003.
Quijano, Aníbal. "Coloniality of Power, Eurocentrism, and Latin America." *Nepantla: Views from the South* 1, no. 3(2000): 533.

Rivera, Tomás. *Y no se lo tragó la tierra: And the Earth Did Not Part*. Berkeley, CA: Editorial Quinto Sol Publications, 1971.

Rivera, Tomás, and Julián Olivares. *The Complete Works*. Houston, TX: Arte Público Press, 1992.

Saldívar, José David. *The Dialectics of Our America: Genealogy, Cultural Critique, and Literary History*. Durham, NC: Duke University Press, 1991.

Saldívar, José David. *Trans-Americanity: Subaltern Modernities, Global Coloniality, and the Cultures of Greater Mexico*. Durham, NC: Duke University Press, 2012.

Saldívar, Ramón. *Chicano Narrative: The Dialectics of Difference*. Madison: University of Wisconsin Press, 1990.

Soja, Edward. *Thirdspace: Journeys to Los Angeles and Other Real-and-Imagined Places*. Cambridge, UK: Blackwell, 1996.

Stanley, Henry M. *In Darkest Africa*. London: S. Low, Marston, Searle and Rivington, 1890.

Sweet, James. *Domingos Álvares, African Healing, and the Intellectual History of the Atlantic World*. Chapel Hill: University of North Carolina Press, 2011.

Thereoux, Paul. "Stanley, I Presume" Sunday Book Review, *The New York Times*, 2009.

Thornton, John. *A Cultural History of the Atlantic World, 1250–1820*. Cambridge, UK: Cambridge University Press, 2012.

Vinson, Ben, and Matthew Restall. *Black Mexico: Race and Society from Colonial to Modern Times*. Albuquerque: University of New Mexico Press, 2009.

Western Literature Association. *A Literary History of the American West*. Fort Worth: Texas Christian University Press, 1987.

# PART II
# MELTING THE POT

CHAPTER 6

# THE CHICANO MOVEMENT IN THE NEW AMERICA

## MARIO T. GARCÍA

THE Chicano Movement impacted many lives. It inspired a whole new generation of Mexican Americans to believe that they could bring about change not only in their personal lives but more importantly in the lives of others and those in their community. This was the heady 1960s, where a new American generation as a whole also believed in political and social change. It was the Age of Aquarius. It was Black Power, "black is beautiful," Dr. Martin Luther King, and Malcolm X. But it was also Chicano Power: Aztlán, César Chávez, Dolores Huerta, Corky Gonzales, and the blowouts, and more. Many were born of the Mexican Americans who were part of the so-called Greatest Generation but excluded from the media representation of it by Tom Brokaw and Ken Burns. These were Chicanos who in droves went to fight against Hitler, Mussolini, and the Imperial Japanese. Many never returned, and those who did had lost limbs, had nightmares, and could not speak to their sweethearts and children about the war they fought.[1] They gave birth to a new generation who would not remain silent. They also went to war in the jungles of Vietnam, but their war continued in the *barrios* (*La lucha esta aquí!* [The war is here in the barrios]). The war spilled over in the fight for civil rights and community empowerment, as this generation tried to change the world. They sought to change America, especially. This was the Chicano generation of the Chicano Movement; beginning in the mid-1960s to the late 1970s (and for some, beyond) these Chicanos engaged in the most widespread Mexican American movement for full American rights and for respect as Chicanos. But the movement did not occur in a vacuum. It reflected and shaped what was becoming the new America. It was an America becoming colorized in the age of color television. It would no longer be a white America but a mixed-race Melting Pot

America. A brown America that like the color brown would reflect the mingling of different ethnic groups. The Chicano Movement foretold what has now become (and is still becoming) the new America.[2]

## Chicano Identity

Chicanos began to revert back to their baptismal names. They had changed their names to Mary, Joey, Frankie, and Letti. But now as part of the Chicano Generation, they became María or la Mary, José, and Leticia. Only poor Mario who could not readily Americanize his name (nor have the nuns do it for him) was proudly now Mario. Chicanismo replaced Americanization, or so this new generation thought. They were mostly second or third generation and so were more Americanized than their parents and spoke mostly English with some smattering of Spanish or *caló*, the language or tongue of the *pachucos* and zoot-suited youngsters of the 1940s.[3]

"Hey man, let's go to the borlo [dance]." The movement saw itself as looking backward to Mexico and a more "authentic" culture, but in fact it was the product of acculturation or transculturation: the blending of cultures to create a new ethnic and cultural synthesis that would become the future brown America. Still, the Chicano Generation was in search of the "authentic Chicano" not realizing that they were already "authentic" Chicanos. Cultural revival in fact was a symptom of a new culture that had less to do with Mexico than with the United States.

Identity, or often a new identity, was central to the movement. Who are we? What are we? Are we Americans? Mexican? What the hell is a Mexican American? These were all ethnic markers that revolved in the new generation's collective consciousness. They knew that by birth most of them were Americans, but they had a sense that they were not really accepted as Americans. Americans were whites, not Mexicans. Americans were the *gaupachos*, gringos, or *bollios*, the *pachuco* term for "whites." Americans spoke English, and so did the new generation. But then why, as in many cases, did they speak Spanish at home both to their parents and certainly to their grandparents? Why did they sometimes have to go with Spanish-speaking aunts downtown to pay the bills and translate or interpret for them? All of this affected identity issues. Mexican for them meant immigrants—such as either their parents or their grandparents. They knew the term "Mexican American" perhaps from earlier community groups such as LULAC or the American GI Forum that used the term. But why did you have to be both Mexican and American? It's not that everyone had a psychological problem, but there was still this ambivalence about identity and even insecurity. Of course, many also knew the term "Chicano," especially in the urban areas, whether one lived in the barrios or mixed neighborhoods. But "Chicano" was a term for kids from the hardcore barrio and linked to the *pachucos* and gangbangers. It had an attraction as a countercultural term: but did it apply to you?

*Chicano Power!* This was one of the cries or *gritos* of the movement. But where did the term "Chicano" come from? Although the term was popularized during the movement, the origins of the word "Chicano" go further back. By the 1920s, some early Mexican immigrant workers were already using the term. Some believe it is a version of *mexicano* with an indigenous pronunciation and so pronounced as *Chicano*. But the term itself has had an interesting evolution. By the 1940s young Mexican Americans in the cities, especially the *pachucos* and zoot-suitors rediscovered the term and adopted it as part of their counterculture. "*Somos Chicanos!*" the *pachucos* brazenly proclaimed ("We are Chicanos!") The term caught on and continued into the 1960s. The new generation rediscovered it and appropriated it, only with a clear difference. The term was politicized. To be a Chicano during the movement was to be an activist or supporter of the movement itself. Hence the term evolved from its use by Mexican immigrant workers to *pachucos* and zoot-suitors to the Chicano Generation. Chicano during the movement expressed not only ethnic pride but political commitment. Chicano meant both male and female, although the term Chicana was also used to specifically note the role of women in the movement.

Seeing themselves as more acculturated Mexican Americans, the new Chicano generation sought to achieve a distinct cultural presence. They were not just of Mexican descent; they were *indios* or native Americans. Many always knew this but found it hard to articulate. They could see that many were brown rather than white (although some were white in skin tone). But the movement shunned whiteness and embraced *indigenismo* or a preferential option for indigeneity. Some growing up were called Indio or *la India*. Their parents at each new year collected calendars at the *panaderias* or bakeries that displayed Aztec warriors with beautiful Indian women draped over them in subordinate positions. They knew that they were in part *indios*, but now the movement prioritized this and validated it. The young Chicano poet Alurista studied the pre-Columbian cultures of Mexico and discovered Aztlán, the ancient homeland of the Aztecs. He found that this land lay north of present-day Mexico City or Tenochtitlán, the capital of the Aztec Empire. But how far north? Northern Mexico? No, Alurista proclaimed in 1969 at the National Chicano Youth Liberation Conference in Denver, "We are standing on Aztán." The Southwest is Aztlán. We live in our ancestral lands. We are Aztlán. We're not immigrants; we live in our historical homeland. The Plan Espiritual de Aztlán written by Alurista proclaimed this and called for the independence of Aztlán. But Aztlán was also the new America, and so the plan in effect was calling for a new independence movement for a new American nation.[4]

# Chicano History

The concept of the historical homeland—Aztlán—also led to the Chicano generation learning a new kind of American history. One of the features of this generation was that it was also in search of an "authentic history." For years, young Chicanos had learned the history of the United States; however, as they now became more politically conscious, these young Chicanos realized that they had been excluded from this history. There were no Chicanos (and no one like them) in American history. As one young Chicano poet wrote: "If George Washington was my father why wasn't he Chicano?" This only added to insecurities that somehow Chicanos were not really Americans. So what was their true history? For one, the movement's rediscovery of Aztlán and of indigeneity focused attention on the pre-Columbian history of Chicanos in Mexico: the Aztecs, Mayans, and other indigenous civilizations prior to the Spanish Conquest. But if Aztlán was the historical homeland, it was also the lost homeland. Aztlán was the Southwest or so the movement proposed, but this region of the United States was controlled by Anglos or whites and not Chicanos. How was Aztlán lost? In addressing this question further, Chicanos discovered the Mexican-American War (1846–1848): it was war of conquest, annexation, and of choice. The United States declared war on Mexico in order to take Mexico's northern half—El Norte. As a war of conquest, the Mexican-American War also led to the lost homeland. Aztlán was now occupied—occupied by America. Chicanos were a colonized people. Their lands were taken from them—from Texas to California and much in between (New Mexico, Arizona, Nevada, Colorado, and Utah). Chicanos were not immigrants; they were a conquered people. Learning about how the first generation of Mexicans in the United States became Americans added to the counter-history and oppositional consciousness of the Chicano Generation. It was a history that had been denied to them and a history rarely discussed in their high school texts and in college. It was a history that a professor would likely set aside in order to get to the Civil War, despite the fact that half of his class was Mexican American. But for Chicanos, this history became a starting point.[5]

Chicano history became fundamental to the Chicano Movement. Chicanos wanted to know what their real history was. Did Chicanos make history? Did they write history? Were they American history? Although some earlier historians had written about Mexicans in the United States prior to the movement, very little was know about this history. The only important text about this history that existed was Carey McWilliams's seminal *North From Mexico* published in 1948.[6] Although it was not heavily researched, this was the first book that provided an overview and chronology on Mexican American history. McWilliams started his history not with the indigenous past as many later Chicano historians would but with the Spanish colonial borderlands, or what would become the American Southwest. By so doing, McWilliams suggested that what would be called "Chicano history" had deep roots in what would become a part of the United States. This, in a way, complemented the later concept of the historical and lost homeland. McWilliams also paid attention to early and mass Mexican immigration to the United States starting in the early twentieth century; early labor struggles by Mexican immigrant workers; the mass deportation of Mexicans during the Great Depression; the large numbers of Mexican Americans in World War II; and the rise of the *pachucos* and zoot-suitors. All of these topics would fascinate the Chicano Generation and especially a new generation of professional historians that the movement spawned. Unfortunately, McWilliams only covered up to the immediate post–World War II period. It would up to be Chicanos to fill in the rest up to and through the movement. That more immediate history would represent the key manifestations of the Chicano Movement. But these new historians were also rewriting American history—a history that would now be inclusive of all Americans and create a new American narrative.

## César Chávez and the Farmworkers Struggle

There is no question that the most recognized Latino figure in American history is César Chávez. But who was Chávez? He can be considered the godfather of the Chicano Movement. Even though chronologically he belonged more to the previous Mexican American generation, his historical impact begins during the period of the movement. Chávez's position in American history was attained through accomplishing what had never been done before: he successfully organized farmworkers. And thus, American labor history was transformed. Chávez knew what it meant to be a farmworker, having worked as a young boy alongside his parents and other siblings in the California fields. His effort to organize farmworkers out of his base in Delano, California, in the state's central valley, not only reverberated with farmworkers but also with the young Chicanos in the cities. His courage along with that of his supporters such as Dolores Huerta influenced the developing Chicano Generation. This next generation was inspired to exhibit similar courage in taking on the issues that Chicanos faced in the urban areas where most Mexicans lived and worked. Moreover, Chávez was a brilliant organizer who employed Mexican ethnic symbols to reach out to his mostly Mexican-origin members in what came to be the United Farm Workers (UFW). These included the image of Our Lady of Guadalupe, patron saint of Mexico; the eagle image in the union's banner that his Mexican American supporters interpreted as the eagle on the Mexican flag; his use of terms such as *huelga*, the Spanish term for "strike" as well as various other Mexican symbols that gave the workers a sense that this was *their* union. Chávez and other UFW organizers spoke using the workers' cultural terms. These Mexican ethnic symbols, in turn, influenced the Chicanos in the cities to reexamine their own ethnic identity and to have a sense of pride in their Mexican background. If Chávez, Huerta, and the farmworkers displayed pride in their Mexican ethnic identity, so should the new generation. For these and other reasons, César Chávez and the farmworker struggle helped spawn the Chicano Movement and to empower the Chicano Generation. Chávez's mantra of *sí se puede* [yes we can] gave Chicanos a sense that they could also do it—that is, empower themselves as a social movement to correct injustices in their own communities. For this, they looked to César Chávez for inspiration. César Chávez is part of a new pantheon of American heroes that reflect a changing of the guard and the meaning of who makes American history.[7]

## Blowout! The Chicano Struggle for Educational Justice

"Blowout! blowout!" This was the cry of thousands of Chicano high school students who walked out of their classes in the East Los Angeles public schools during the first week of March 1968. It is estimated that perhaps as many as twenty thousand students engaged in this action not only in East Los Angeles but in other parts of the city in solidarity with the striking students. This historic action came to be known as the "blowouts." This represented the largest high school strike in American history. The students inspired by charismatic Chicano teacher Sal Castro protested against years of segregated, discriminatory, and inferior education in the public schools. These conditions went as far back as the early twentieth century when the first mass influx of immigrants from Mexico commenced. In the growing urban barrios or Mexican neighborhoods in the Southwest where most Mexican immigrants settled, the public schools quickly appeared. These early schools were referred to as "Mexican schools." They were only for the children of Mexican immigrants. Many of these children were born in the United States; thus, they were Mexican Americans. The schools were segregated not by state laws as was the case for blacks in the South, and for Asians and Native Americans along with blacks in California, for example. In the case of the Mexican schools they were segregated by decisions made by local schoolboards that did not want Mexican children (whom they deemed inferior, mentally and culturally, as well as representing a non-white race) to attend school with white American children. This was a form of de jure segregation. The schools were inferior because they provided only limited education—no more than a sixth-grade education in most areas. They were also inferior and discriminatory because they were overcrowded, lacked school supplies such as books and desks, had no cafeterias, no playgrounds, and no restrooms for students. These schools also had no sensitivity to students' cultural backgrounds and often punished them (including corporal punishment) for speaking Spanish in class. But the worst social sin committed by these schools was the teachers' low expectations of their students. There is no worse crime a teacher can commit than to believe that his/her students are not capable of a rigorous and demanding academic curriculum. Yet such low expectations of Mexican American students characterized the Mexican schools. These racist views were reinforced by biased IQ tests that began to be administered throughout the country in the early part of that century. Given the language and cultural differences of Mexican American students, many (if not most) scored very low on these tests, which made the teachers and administrators consider them idiots and mentally handicapped. These conditions continued to characterize public education and Mexican Americans well into the twentieth century.[8]

However, by 1968 and beginning in Los Angeles, a new generation of Chicano students made it clear that enough was enough. *Basta!* They said. *Enough!* The blowouts in East Los Angeles and similar incidents throughout the Southwest challenged the legacy of the Mexican schools. With the help of teachers such as Sal Castro, students began to realize that they were not responsible for the failures of these schools (e.g., the high dropout rates and few students going on to attend college). They began to realize that the educational system was the problem not them, their parents, or their culture as they had been told. They demanded a more academic curriculum and less reliance on vocational education that had characterized the Mexican schools for many years. And they wanted more college counselors and college preparatory measures in the curriculum. As they came under the influence of the Chicano Movement and began to assert themselves as Chicanos, the students also demanded that their history and culture as Mexican Americans be respected and that the curriculum begin to integrate Chicano studies and bilingual education. With their actions and demands, the students in East Los Angeles forced the schoolboard to consider their grievances and to negotiate these changes with their parents and community leaders. Some of these reforms were not implemented quickly, but what was important was that the students realized that they had the power—student power—to force the system to acknowledge them and to change its discriminatory practices. The blowouts empowered not only students in Los Angeles but students across the country as well. One of the student leaders of the blowouts, Paula Crisostomo, was asked by a reporter why many of the student demands had not been met after the walkouts. She responded by saying: "Well perhaps not much in the schools have changed yet, but I've changed!" That brief but powerful statement said it all. This was the baptism of the Chicano student movement not only in the high schools but in the colleges; it would have a profound impact on the movement and on American education. The student movement by no means accounted for the Chicano Movement in total, but it was a major factor and catalyst.[9]

But in addition to Chicano high school students, Chicano students in the colleges and universities likewise organized and protested. By the late 1960s, as a result of the pressures by the Chicano Movement in actions such as the blowouts, California and southwestern colleges began through affirmative action to recruit Chicano/Latino students for the first time. UCLA, for example, went from two hundred Chicano students before the walkouts to two thousand Chicano students after the walkouts. Chicano college students began to identify one another and came together collectively. Some of the initial Chicano college organizations began as early as 1966. In California, the most significant early group was UMAS (United Mexican American Students). Even though these students were becoming Chicanos, they initially retained organizationally the term Mexican American. In Texas, the first significant college student group was MAYO (Mexican American Youth Organization). Other names were also used in different locations. These early organizations focused on developing a new Chicano identity but also worked on various social projects such as support for the farmworkers, recruiting more Chicano students to their campuses, educational support programs such as EOP (Educational Opportunity Programs), and efforts to establish Chicano studies programs. But Chicano students also wanted unity among all the campuses. California led the way in this effort. In the spring of 1969, representatives of student groups at all levels including the UC system, the Cal-State system, and the community colleges met at the University of California at Santa Barbara to establish a new unified Chicano student movement.

They drafted what came to be known as "El Plan de Santa Barbara," which aimed to do two things. First, it called on all student groups to unify under the new name of the Movimiento Estudiantil Chicano de Aztlán (MEChA). Secondly, it called for the establishment of Chicano studies courses on all campuses that did not already have such programs. The result was that (at least in California) all student groups adopted the new name MEChA, and on many campuses students successfully pressured their administrations to form Chicano studies departments or programs including research components and library units. The implementation of these programs also led to the first sizeable hiring of Chicano faculty, administrators, and staff. Chicano students in other states, even out of the Southwest, followed suit. And Chicano student organizations, many of them under the MEChA moniker, sprang up all over the country as did Chicano studies programs.[10]

Chicano students from these organizations in turn not only supported changes on their campuses but also in the community. Besides assisting the farmworkers—especially with the grape boycott that began in 1968—students also involved themselves in community struggles such as protesting police repression and profiling, joining the Chicano anti-Vietnam War movement, working for the efforts of independent Chicano political party La Raza Unida, and other community struggles. Although Chicano students saw themselves as the vanguard of the Chicano Movement, in fact there were many other vanguards, especially in the community. Nevertheless, many of the Chicano Generation first became politicized and developed a Chicano oppositional consciousness in the student movement. Chicano students engaged in changing the meaning of American colleges and universities has led to the new "Brown University" in America—a university where knowledge is more universal and inclusive to reflect the new America of diversity and the mixtures of cultures.

## Chicano Studies

Chicano studies—a different kind of studies; this is what the Plan de Santa Barbara envisioned. Chicano studies was to be an extension of the Chicano Movement. It would not be like any other traditional department. It would be a liberating and empowering experience. It would not be business as usual or an ivory tower. Professors of Chicano studies would reflect this and be scholars/activists—and perhaps even more activist than scholars. "What have you done in the community?" This question was the litmus test for hiring professors and administrators. The question was not "what are your research and academic interests?" Students had created Chicano studies through their protests, and therefore students would be the major decision makers in a Chicano studies department—not professors. All Chicano studies courses needed to be "relevant" to students in that they had to consider the relationship of these classes to the community and to the Chicano Movement itself. "We don't need your stinking PhDs." Chicano studies professors could be hired without a PhD. A master's degree would be sufficient, and in some cases just a bachelor's degree would be fine. These were just some of the guiding tenets of early Chicano studies departments and programs. Were they successful as oppositional bodies on campus? Yes and no. Chicano studies became a galvanizing force on campuses, and many Chicano (and non-Chicano) students took Chicano studies classes. Administrations usually looked the other way with respect to academic standards in Chicano studies classes and reacted to these programs purely from a political perspective. Chicano studies became a political animal on campuses.

There was something certainly refreshing and exciting about these early programs. But over time they could not be sustained in this way. Many political and ideological divisions as well as cults of personality affected Chicano studies. The movement sowed the seeds of these divisions by promoting Chicano studies as a political entity. These seeds unfortunately are still sprouting many years later. At the same time, greater professionalization in the discipline of Chicano studies eventually took place. But this professionalization (PhDs, research, writing, etc.) had to be reconciled with preserving the legacy of the movement and to the community. Such pressures have created psychological dilemmas for many faculty and even students. As a discipline, Chicano studies has been a mixed bag: with some programs achieving a semblance of order while others still brimmed with tensions and divisions.[11]

While Chicano studies has had its share of problems, its success is ironically in its scholarship. Although the origins of Chicano studies did not always stress scholarship, the fact is that many Chicano and Chicana students inspired by the Chicano Movement and its legacy not only acquired undergraduate degrees but also entered graduate programs (including doctoral programs). By the mid-1970s, for example, the first generation of professional Chicano historians emerged—the Generation of '75. The same was true in other social science and humanities fields and to a lesser extent in the sciences. For the first time, thanks to the Chicano Movement that forced open the doors to these opportunities, Chicanos, both men and women, had access not only to higher education but to graduate education. Many of these newly minted PhDs not only began to fill positions in Chicano studies programs but also obtained faculty positions in more traditional departments. Moreover, they chose to do dissertations in Chicano studies. Young Chicano historians began to explore the neglected past of Mexican Americans. Taking a cue from Carey McWilliams, these new historians began to explore the histories of their own communities so that many of these dissertation topics in all fields possessed an autobiographical connection. Inspired by the movement, these historical and other studies represented oppositional and alternative studies: critical studies of race, class, gender, and sexuality. They are not mainstream or conventional studies but ones intended to empower Chicanos to know their history and their true position in American society. Equipped with this new and empowering knowledge, they can change society and achieve a more democratic society. These studies also have attempted to change the contours of American history and American studies by stressing inclusiveness so that we come to understand the full dimensions of this history and culture. With this perspective, the Chicano Movement produced a renaissance of scholarship unprecedented in Chicano history. This has only continued to grow. Every month, new scholarly texts appear that can only be described as amazing. We now know more about Chicanos and Latinos, both men and women, than we have ever known, and this is one of the accomplishments of the Chicano Movement. But because we know more about Chicanos and Latinos, we also know more about American history—the new and inclusive American history.

# Chicanismo

The Chicano Movement had no set ideology in that it could point to a specific document that spelled out what the movement was all about. Contributing to the collective composition of what came to be called "Chicanismo" were documents such as "El Plan de Santa Barbara" (1969), "El Plan Espiritual de Aztlán" (1969), "I Am Joaquin" (1967), and other movement proclamations including the myriad of movement newspapers such as *El Gallo* (Denver), *La Raza* (Los Angeles), *El Grito del Norte* (New Mexico), and many others. As an ideology, Chicanismo borrowed from the influences of the Mexican Revolution of 1910, the Black Power movement, the Cuban Revolution of 1959, other Third World movements for national liberation, Marxism, and even the Declaration of Independence (the poet Alurista has stated that his "El Plan Espritual de Aztlán" was patterned after the Declaration of Independence). Chicanismo at its core expressed what also came to be known as cultural nationalism. Chicanos acquired and invented a new positive image of themselves through realizing that they represented a subjugated group and were racialized as an inferior one. Through developing a critical consciousness they rejected such subjectivity and instead forged a new subjectivity that made Chicanos feel good about themselves. How? They sought out what they considered to be their true undisclosed past by discovering their indigenous roots—especially the majestic Mayan and Aztec cultures. It was good to be indio. *Brown is beautiful!* They discovered that they had been colonized through Yankee encroachment of their native lands. An internal colonialism had been imposed on them. But they also possessed a history of resistance and revolution to secure their rights. As Corky Gonzales said, they were Pancho Villa and Emiliano Zapata of the Mexican Revolution. They were all of this and more. They were a people. They were Aztlán. They were a nation, and they had a national culture: cultural nationalism. This is who they were, and their unity and movement would be forged by recognition of their authentic culture. This is what they had in common. This was their essence. This was their politics of identity. They came to understand that a movement—a Chicano Movement—could not succeed with an ambiguous identity. Who are we? A Chicano Movement had to have a secure identity. You are Chicano: be proud of it and move on. This was Chicano nationalism.

Chicanismo propelled the Chicano Movement. *Viva La Raza! Chicano Power!* Chicanismo was powerful and seductive. It revived memories of growing up Mexican. It made people feel good about their families and their family culture. They were no longer ashamed of their Spanish-speaking grandmothers. It was okay to speak Spanish or to be bilingual or to speak caló, the countercultural language of the *pachucos* and zoot suitors.

Chicanismo was an ideology of nostalgia and of memories and of fantasies. But it worked because it was more porous than imagined. It was not fixed. It had apertures. For what? For other visions and other beliefs. Some Chicanos asked, what about class? Okay, Chicanismo can accept a Marxist class analysis, since the authentic culture being revived was a working-class and barrio culture. Yes, a class analysis could fit. You could wear a "Chicano Power" button on one lapel and a Che Guevara one on the other. Race and class together. What about gender? That's okay, too. Cultural nationalism made room for Aztec female warriors: Las Adelitas, Luisa Moreno, Josefina Fierro, Emma Tenayuca, Dolores Huerta—all of whom were figures in Mexican and Chicana history. Yes, gender critiques could fit into Chicanismo—but not without tensions. No ideology comes without tension, as people evolve, think, and debate. Yet, all came to agree that the core of the Chicano Movement was the *mexicanidad* or Mexican experience on both sides of the border (or no border at all: *Sin Fronteras*). This was the big tent of the cultural and ethnic revival that ignited the Chicano Movement and sent thousands of converts into the streets to protest and thus into history. It was a conversion, and no one is more militant about their faith than converts. Chicanismo was powerful and transforming, but it had implications beyond Chicanos. Chicanismo was the new Americanization composed of brown people. This meant that minorities, through their particular struggles and their intersectional ties, began transforming the meaning of America and Americanization.[12]

## Chicano Politics

Inspired by Chicanismo, the Chicano Generation and Chicano Movement manifested in a variety of ways throughout California, the Southwest, and other parts of the country. One such area of protest was electoral politics. For years people had referred to the "Sleeping Giant" that Mexican Americans allegedly represented. The "Sleeping Giant" term alluded to the fact that Mexican Americans had significant potential politically if they just voted and got involved. But they did not get involved, or so proponents of this theory suggested. It was thought that something within Mexican Americans—perhaps their culture and maybe even their genes—made them apolitical. All of this, of course, was nonsense and even racist. If Mexican Americans did not vote as much as they could have it was because they had never been encouraged to do so and, in fact, obstacles were placed in their way. The most notorious of these was the poll tax that Texas and other Southern states adopted under the Jim Crow (or some in Texas might say "Juan" Crow) system. Poll taxes in these states were primarily aimed at discouraging the black vote; however, in Texas it also affected poor Mexican Americans. Moreover, the Democratic Party—the only real party in Texas—rarely if ever promoted Mexican American candidates or addressed Mexican American issues; as a result, there were even fewer incentives for Mexican Americans to get involved politically. But this did not mean that Mexican Americans were apolitical. Prior to the Chicano Movement, and especially in the Mexican American Generation (1930–1960), some Mexican Americans organized around civil rights issues to confront segregation and discrimination in education, jobs, wages, and access to public facilities. These involved community grassroots efforts as well as legal ones. Organizations such as LULAC and the American GI Forum spearheaded many of these drives. In the post–World War II period, returning veterans who had put their lives on the line for American democracy were no longer willing to be deprived of the fruits of this democracy. They encouraged voting, and many ran for local offices. Some succeeded. The two most notable electoral victories were the election of Edward Roybal to the Los Angeles City Council in 1948 and the election of Raymond Telles as mayor of El Paso in 1957.[13] Moreover, in 1960, Mexican Americans for the first time participated as a group in a national presidential election by organizing "Viva Kennedy" clubs in support of Senator John F. Kennedy, the Democratic nominee for president.[14] No, Mexican Americans were not politically asleep during this period. Many were active and laid the groundwork for the political struggles of the Chicano Movement.

While the Chicano Generation was obviously political, where it differed from the Mexican American Generation was its distrust and rejection of the two-party system and especially the historic ties between Mexican Americans and the Democratic Party that had its origins in the New Deal under President Franklin Roosevelt. Mexican Americans believed that it was FDR who felt the pain of the poor and minorities. Chicanos had a much different take on this relationship. The Chicano Generation saw the Democrats as a party that used the Mexican American vote and then failed to deliver on its promises either to advance the economic interests of Chicanos or their political ambitions. As for Republicans, who cared about them? They had never appealed to Mexican Americans, anyway. "The two-party system," Corky Gonzales proclaimed, was a "two-headed monster." Both were harmful to Chicanos. With this bold assertion, the Chicano Movement chose a third way—an independent political party. They called it La Raza Unida Party (RUP) and explained that it meant "united people's party." Although third parties are not strangers to American political history, what was different here was that this was one built around a specific ethnic group—Chicanos. Black Power advocates similarly organized the Black Panther Party, which in some areas (such as in Oakland) ran electoral campaigns. La Raza Unida Party was intended to provide an alternative to the two-party system and especially an alternative to the Democrats. It was also a way not only to elect RUP candidates to promote the agenda of the Chicano Movement but also a vehicle to publicize the movement and its key issues: support for the farmworkers, for the land grant movement in New Mexico, for Chicano control of public schools in the barrios, for Chicano studies; for economic opportunities and effective job training programs, for Chicano community control of its resources, and for immigrant rights.

In Denver, Colorado, at the first National Chicano Youth Liberation Conference (1969), part of the discussion concerned organizing a third-party movement. In 1967, there were protests against President Lyndon Johnson's meeting on Mexican American issues in El Paso: many objected to it as exclusive and irrelevant and left the meeting to march to the south-side barrio and proclaim a Raza Unida movement for Chicano self-determination. Chicanos could only empower themselves. They did not need LBJ to do this or his blessing (which he would not bestow anyway). Those who did not follow a new Chicano way were *vendidos* or "sellouts." These were harsh condemnations and unfair, but in the heat of the moment younger Chicanos indeed questioned anyone over thirty as did the general youth uprising in the country. But who would actually organize this third party—the La Raza Unida Party? "We will!" came the response from Chicanos in San Antonio and in South Texas. Led by a charismatic, articulate, bilingual young man by the name of José Ángel Gutiérrez, the birth of the RUP was conceived in small South Texas towns such as Crystal City and others where Mexican Americans formed the majority. They first ran candidates who took over schoolboards and then city and county governments. These successes emboldened them to take on the entire state of Texas. They ran candidates in 1972 for state offices including for the governorship. They did not win, but they gained many votes and brought much attention to the Chicano Movement. They also scared the dominant Democratic Party, who feared that a strong RUP movement would drain votes from them and allow Republicans into office for the first time since the period of Reconstruction.

The RUP movement in Texas, in turn, inspired Chicanos throughout the Southwest to also form chapters and run candidates. This included Denver, Los Angeles, Tucson, and many other locations. Of course they wanted to win; but even just running for office was seen as a success. They used their campaigns to bring attention to movement issues and to challenge the validity of the two-party system. All of these activists felt empowered politically, and they confidently organized a national convention of the RUP. (Think of this as the Democratic and Republican nominating conventions.) It was a way of telling the rest of America that the Chicanos' time had come. Chicanos would no longer be ignored or taken for granted. They would become a force in American politics. No sleeping giant here. They selected El Paso as a central point to hold the convention along the shores of the Rio Grande and the US-Mexico borderlands. It was a way of saying, "This is our land; this is our homeland; this is Aztlán!" The convention hall was filled with delegates from all over the Southwest and other parts of the country. They met in caucuses and debated a platform. And they put up candidates as the future leaders of El Partido (or "the party"). Their platform was a litany of all of the movement issues. Should they also debate on whether the party should endorse any of the presidential candidates of the mainstream parties? Should they endorse Senator George McGovern, the Democratic candidate who was against the war in Vietnam? Or should they endorse—a real longshot—President Richard Nixon, who widened the war in Vietnam? Neither was appealing, and so neither candidate was endorsed (perhaps an unfair condemnation of McGovern). Nevertheless, the mood was not one of conciliation with the establishment but of confrontation with it.

With several thousand delegates and much local and national media covering the conference, this historic assembly concluded with delegates selecting a national chairperson to guide the RUP until the next convention. There was high drama and tension involved. The two main candidates, Corky Gonzales and José Ángel Gutiérrez, were already icons of the movement. Corky as head of the Crusade for Justice in Denver had hosted the National Chicano Youth Liberation Conference in 1969 that drafted El Plan Espritual de Aztán and the accompanying El Plan de Aztlán, which were key documents for the movement. José Ángel had been the only RUP leader who had successfully won elections. Both were cocky and had huge egos, but both had demonstrated leadership. Corky was the sentimental choice, since many delegates had gone to the (by then) four youth conferences and many knew Corky's epic poem "I Am Joaquin" that Luis Valdez and the Teatro Campesino of the UFW had adapted into a short but powerful documentary film. Their hearts were with Corky, but many realistically believed that José Ángel was the better organizer and natural leader of the RUP. They chose him over Corky, and the conference came to a resounding close, although some (including Gonzales) were left bitter over his defeat. Still, they made a good show of it, and both were joined at the stage by the legendary Reies López Tijerina, who had just been released from the penitentiary for his actions on the land grant movement in New Mexico.

The RUP convention was considered a success. It helped publicize the RUP and the Chicano Movement nationally. It was a high point of the movement, but unfortunately it did not go much beyond this. Ego and personal politics got in the way as the tensions between Gonzales and Gutiérrez over the leadership of the party continued to fester; this prevented any subsequent national meetings of the RUP. The party at the state and local levels continued into the 1970s in different locations; however, as a national party it never achieved that dream. Still, the RUP, which had fizzled out by the late 1970s, had succeeded politically by pushing the Democrats and even the Republicans to an awareness of Chicano issues and of Chicano voters. Increasingly, both parties (but in particular the Democrats) began to advocate for Chicano causes and to select Chicano candidates. La Raza Unida Party did not survive, but along with other movement manifestations it was a step forward in setting the foundation for the twenty-first century's recognition of Latino political power and the new American politics.[15]

## THE CHICANO ANTIWAR MOVEMENT

*Raza Si! Guerra No! La Batalla Esta Aquí.* (Yes to the People, No to War! The War is Here!) With these *gritos*, or cries, Chicanos opposed the US war in Vietnam and Southeast Asia. Like their fathers and even grandfathers before them, Chicanos in the 1960s went off to war: this time in the jungles of South Vietnam. But this was not "the Good War" of World War II; it was not even the Korean War. This was a war that made no sense. Politicians said it was a Communist invasion of South Vietnam, but in fact there was a civil war in South Vietnam and an effort at national reunification with North Vietnam. Politicians said it was a war to protect democracy in South Vietnam, but there was no democracy in South Vietnam. What there were were natural resources and imperialist goals to be gained, but the politicians conveniently failed to mention this. So thousands of young men again were drafted to fight a war of choice and not of necessity. It was a war that our politicians knew was unwinnable, but yet they still sent young American men to be killed and maimed. This included Chicanos. In fact, it was mainly minorities and poor whites that fought this war: many of these soldiers had not gone to college, which was the only way to avoid the draft without facing jailtime. One Chicano professor did his homework and discovered that Chicanos were being disproportionately drafted. Chicanos comprised 10 percent of the Southwest's population, and yet 20 percent of the casualties in Vietnam were Chicanos from this region. One early Chicano antiwar activist called this "genocide." Chicanos also began to realize that federal funds from President Johnson's "War Against Poverty" were being cut in order to pay for the war in Vietnam. For these and other reasons, the Chicano Generation concluded that this was not their war; in their view, if they were going to fight a war it should be in the barrios against racism and discrimination and for educational and economic justice. And so they did.

Beginning with resistance to the draft, Chicano activists soon realized that the best way to end the draft was to end the war. They organized a National Chicano Moratorium Committee and called for a moratorium on the war. They organized antiwar marches and rallies throughout the Southwest and California and participated in the national moratoriums staged by white antiwar protestors. At no other point in US history had so many Americans protested an American war. By the millions, Americans (especially young Americans) marched against the war and against Democratic and Republican administrations. Chicanos marched in step with them but also organized themselves. The Chicano antiwar movement climaxed on August 29, 1970, when some twenty thousand people, mostly Chicanos, marched against the war in the streets of East Los Angeles. It was the largest protest of the Chicano Movement. Protestors came from far and wide. Protestors included men and women. Vietnam veteranos or veterans marched with their army jackets on to protest a war they should have never been sent to and one in which they lost other Chicano buddies. *Basta!*, they shouted as they marched down Whittier Boulevard toward Laguna Park, which was the site of the rally.

At Laguna Park, others had arrived early to find shade for the rally. It included families with young children as well as *viejitos* and *viejitas* (the seniors). As the marchers entered the park after a long and hot march, Mexican folkloric dancers accompanied by Chicano musicians entertained the crowd. The key leader of the moratorium committee, Rosalio Muñoz, gave the first speech. But as he concluded he noticed some stirrings in the back of the park. Soon the park became a war zone. What seemed like hundreds of county sheriffs descended on the park, firing tear gas projectiles and moving on the crowd with their striking batons. They later claimed that some Chicanos had stolen a six pack of beer from a nearby store and went to the park. The sheriffs called for backup, and within minutes an army of sheriffs showed up. No evidence was ever presented of a theft occurring. And even if the theft had taken place, did it take an army of sheriffs to deal with this? Instead, the sheriffs declared the rally to be an unlawful assembly and moved in. Chicanos fought back, but they were no match for the sheriffs, who were supported by Los Angeles police. They drove everyone out of the park. As payback, some Chicanos burned storefronts on Whittier Boulevard and police cars, too. East Los Angeles became a war zone as a result of what one Chicano called a "police riot."

Three people were killed, many were wounded, and scores were arrested. What had been a peaceful nonviolent protest had been violated by the police. They could not allow Chicanos to rule the streets of East Los Angeles for even one day. This was the sheriff's turf. Of the three Chicanos killed the most well known was Rúben Salazar, who was the premier Mexican American journalist in the country. Throughout the 1960s, Salazar was a reporter and columnist for the *Los Angeles Times*. He was the only Latino journalist on a major English-language newspaper in the country. He covered the Chicano community and the Chicano Movement. He became a voice for Chicanos. He also had become the news director of KMEX, which was the only Spanish-language television station in Los Angeles at that time. As news director, Salazar covered the Mexican American community and had done critical reporting on police violence in the barrios. The police hated Salazar. They killed him at the moratorium whether deliberately or not. After the breakup of the rally, Salazar and his TV crew went back on Whittier Boulevard and entered a bar called the Silver Dollar Café to get a beer and discuss what they had just witnessed and recorded. Shortly thereafter, a sheriff squad car arrived and the deputies positioned themselves outside the bar. When some people came out, one of the deputies, Thomas Wilson, forced them to return inside. Within a minute or so, Wilson shot at least two tear-gas projectiles into the bar violating the sheriff's code of not firing such a weapon into closed quarters. One of those missiles struck Salazar in the head, instantly killing him. His body was discovered a couple of hours later after the tear gas dissipated. The sheriffs later claimed that they had received a call from the bar that an armed person was inside. This was never proven. The news of Salazar's killing soon went viral and added one additional tragedy to an already tragic day. Nothing was ever done to Wilson or to the other sheriffs involved at the Silver Dollar Café. Salazar left behind three young children who still ask why their father was killed.

The destruction of the national moratorium, however, did not deter the Chicano antiwar movement, and many Chicanos continued to protest the war until the US military left Vietnam in defeat in 1975. The attack on the war moratorium gathering, moreover, only added one more grievance to the Chicano Movement: that of police abuse. And many demonstrated against it as well. What Chicanos had shown in their opposition to the Vietnam War was that they now better understood the nature of American imperialism and how it only benefitted the ruling elites and not American people such as Chicanos. They displayed in their opposition to the war that patriotism does not have to mean blindly supporting unjust wars; it can mean opposing them, too.[16]

## Chicana Feminism

Later Chicana feminists have criticized the Chicano Movement for excluding women or relegating them to marginal roles in the movement. This is not entirely wrong, but what is wrong is to suggest that somehow Chicanas—women—were not engaged in the movement. The cry of *Chicana Power!* went along with *Chicano Power!* Many women participated in the movement. This was their movement as well. Yes, they faced sexism from some of the men, and yet they fought back. They did not buy into the stereotype that Chicano men were inherently sexist or *machos*. It was not in their genes. They understood that they had been socialized to be *machos,* and if they had been socialized they could be resocialized to accept women as equals. Women participated in all of the manifestations of the movement: from the farmworkers' struggle, to the student movement, to La Raza Unida and the Chicano antiwar movement—and many more actions. In some cases, such as in the student movements on college campuses, they were elected as chairs and vice chairs. Of course, the figure of Dolores Huerta looms over all this as the key figure along with César Chávez in the farmworkers' movement. Then there is Alicia Escalante, head of the Chicana welfare rights movement in Los Angeles. Elizabeth "Betita" Martínez published *El Grito del Norte* in New Mexico. They held conferences to discuss Chicana issues and published their own newspapers. They marched along with the men on August 29, 1970, to protest the Vietnam War. They called attention to the triple oppression of Chicanas and other minority women, who experienced race, class, and gender discrimination. In their documents and writings, they founded and developed contemporary Chicana feminism. Some erroneously believe that Chicana feminism is a postmovement expression beginning in the 1980s, but this is wrong and shortchanges the feminists of the movement. Chicanas, like other women, always had to struggle to assert their leadership and rights, but they did. And it represents a major feature of the Chicano Movement. The new Chicana was also the new American woman then and now.[17]

## THE CHICANO RENAISSANCE

Poets, artists, theater groups, and novelists also marched in step with the Chicano Movement. The movement inspired a flowering of artistic and literary production never before seen in the barrios. This was the Chicano Renaissance. These artists and writers and performers did not believe in art for art's sake. They challenged the false notion that politics polluted art. They advocated that all art is political—even the most abstract art—since it takes place in a historical context. The artist reacts consciously and unconsciously to their historical moment. Chicano artists deliberately linked their art to politics. It was political art and literature, and some of its prominent contributors were Alurista, Rodolfo Anaya, Tómas Rivera, Estella Portillo Trampley, Oscar Zeta Acosta, Judy Baca, Ester Hernández, the Royal Chicano Air Force, Los Four, Harry Gamboa, Barbara Carrasco, and many more artists and writers. Artists inspired by the Mexican Revolution and the great revolutionary muralists such as Diego Rivera, Siqueiros, and Frida Kahlo applied public art as they painted murals throughout the Southwest depicting movement struggles and Chicano history. The Chicano Renaissance painted the movement and inspired an entire generation of poets, artists, and writers. The Chicano Renaissance was also the new American Renaissance of what American culture now meant not only in the latter part of the twentieth century but into the new millennium. Chicano art was the new American art, and Chicano literature was the new American literature.[18]

## CHICANOS AND THE NEW AMERICA

The Chicano Movement was part, but it was also whole. It was a movement to change Chicanos, but it also changed America. It sought to bring a new awareness to Chicanos, but it also brought a new awareness to the rest of society. It imagined a new future for Chicanos, and it also inaugurated a new future for America. The Chicano Movement *was* the new America. It was a new America composed of brown people: in this case, a synthesis of peoples such as Chicanos, which was an identity made up of many ethnic and cultural influences. It was *mestizaje* (mixing) but at a higher level. The movement provided the basis for contemporary Latino political power, which is real and becoming more of a reality each day. But it also brought forth a new American politics as exemplified by the election of President Barack Obama. The promised land has been reached, and it is only a matter of time before the full occupation takes place. The Chicano Movement cannot or should not be seen in isolation; despite its flaws the movement needs to be seen in the larger cultural shifts that characterize the new America. We relive the past in order to live in the present and future.

## NOTES

1. This generation is the Mexican-American Generation of the 1930s through the 1950s. See Mario T. García, *Mexican Americans: Leadership, Ideology & Identity, 1930–1960* (New Haven, CT: Yale University Press, 1989).
2. On the Chicano Movement, see Mario T. García, *The Chicano Generation: Testimonios of the Movement* (Oakland: University of California Press, 2015). Also see Carlos Muñoz, Jr., *Youth, Identity, Power: The Chicano Movement* (New York: Verso Press, 1989); Ernesto Chávez, *Mi Raza Primero! Nationalism, Identity, and Insurgency in the Chicano Movement in Los Angeles, 1966–1978* (Berkeley: University of California Press, 2002); Juan Gómez-Quiñones and Irene Vásquez, *Making Aztlán: Ideology and Culture of the Chicana and Chicano Movement, 1966–1977* (Albuquerque: University of New Mexico Press, 2014); Mario T. García, ed., *The Chicano Movement: Perspectives From the Twenty-First Century* (New York: Routledge, 2014).
3. On the pachucos and zoot-suitors, see Luis Alvarez, *The Power of the Zoot: Youth Culture and Resistance during World War II* (Berkeley: University of California Press, 2008); Edward Obregón Pagán, *Murder at the Sleepy Lagoon: Zoot Suits, Race, and Riot in Wartime L.A.* (Chapel Hill: University of North Carolina Press, 2003); Edward Escobar, *Race, Police, and the Making of a Political Identity: Mexican Americans and the Los Angeles Police Department, 1900–1945* (Berkeley: University of California Press, 2003).
4. On the Plan de Aztlán, see Tony Castro, *Chicano Power: The Emergence of Mexican America* (New York: Saturday Review Press, 1974).
5. See Rodolfo Acuña, *Occupied America: The Chicano's Struggle Toward Liberation* (San Francisco: Canfield, 1972); Robert Blauner, *Racial Oppression in America* (New York: Harper & Row, 1972); John Chávez, *The Lost Land: The Chicano Image of the Southwest* (Albuquerque: University of New Mexico Press, 1984); David Weber, *Foreigners in Their Native Land* (Albuquerque: University of New Mexico Press, 1973).

6. Carey McWilliams, *North From Mexico: The Spanish-Speaking People of the United States* (first published 1948; see New York: Greenwood, 1968); also see latest edition, Alma A. García, ed., *North From Mexico* (Santa Barbara, CA: Praeger, 2016).
7. See Jacques Levy, *Cesar Chavez: Autobiography of La Causa* (New York: Norton, 1975); Richard Griswold del Castillo and Richard A. García, *César Chávez: Triumph of Spirit* (Norman: University of Oklahoma Press, 1995); Randy Shaw, *Beyond the Fields: Cesar Chavez, the UFW, and the Struggle for Justice in the Twenty-First Century* (Berkeley: University of California Press, 2008); Miriam Powell, *The Crusades of Cesar Chavez: A Biography* (New York: Bloomsbury, 2014); Matt García, *From the Jaws of Victory: The Triumph and Tragedy of César Chávez and the Farm Workers Movement* (Berkeley: University of California Press, 2012); Ilan Stavans, ed., *Cesar Chavez: An Organizer's Tale—Speeches* (New York: Penguin Books, 2008); Mario T. García, *The Gospel of César Chávez: My Faith in Action* (Sheed & Ward, 2007).
8. See Gilbert G. González, *Chicano Education in the Era of Segregation* (Philadelphia: Balch Institute, 1990); Guadalupe San Miguel, Jr., *"Let All of Them Take Heed": Mexican Americans and the Campaign for Educational Equality in Texas, 1910–1981* (Austin: University of Texas Press, 1987); Mario T. García, *Desert Immigrants: The Mexicans of El Paso, 1880–1920* (New Haven, CT: Yale University Press, 1981).
9. See Mario T. García and Sal Castro, *Blowout! Sal Castro and the Chicano Struggle for Educational Justice* (Chapel Hill: University of North Carolina Press, 2011).
10. Chicano Coordinating Council on Higher Education, *El Plan de Santa Barbara: A Chicano Plan for Higher Education* (Oakland, CA: La Causa, 1969); Armando Navarro, *Mexican American Youth Organization: Avant-Garde of the Chicano Movement in Texas* (Austin: University of Texas Press, 1995); Juan Gómez-Quiñones, *Mexican Students Por La Raza: The Chicano Student Movement in Southern California, 1967–1977* (Santa Barbara, CA: Editorial La Causa, 1978).
11. See Michael Soldatenko, *Chicano Studies: The Genesis of a Discipline* (Tucson: University of Arizona Press, 2011); Rodolfo F. Acuña, *The Making of Chicana/o Studies: In the Trenches of Academe* (New Brunswick, NJ: Rutgers University Press, 2011).
12. See Ignacio M. García, *Chicanismo: The Forging of a Militant Ethos Among Mexican Americans* (Tucson: University of Arizona Press, 1997); Jorge Mariscal, *Brown-Eyed Children of the Sun: Lessons from the Chicano Movement* (Albuquerque: University of New Mexico Press, 2005).
13. On the Telles election, see Mario T. García, *The Making of a Mexican American Mayor: Raymond L. Telles of El Paso* (Texas Western Press, 1998). For a revised edition of this book, see Mario T. García, *The Making of a Mexican American Mayor: Raymond L. Telles of El Paso and the Origins of Latino Political Power* (Tucson: University of Arizona Press, 2018).
14. Ignacio M. García, *Viva Kennedy: Mexican Americans in Search of Camelot* (College Station: Texas A&M University Press, 2002).
15. See Ignacio M. García, *United We Win: The Rise and Fall of La Raza Unida Party* (Tucson: Mexican American Studies and Research Center, University of Arizona, 1989); Armando Navarro, *La Raza Unida Party: A Chicano Challenge to the U.S. Two-Party Dictatorship* (Philadelphia: Temple University Press, 2000); Mario T. García, *The Chicano Generation: Testimonios of the Movement* (Oakland: University of California Press, 2015).
16. Lorena Oropeza, *Raza Si, Guerra No!: Chicano Protest and Patriotism during the Vietnam War Era* (Berkeley: University of California Press, 2005); García, *The Chicano Generation*; Mario T. García, ed., *Ruben Salazar, Border Correspondent: Selected Writings, 1955–1970* (Berkeley: University of California Press, 1995).

17. Alma A. García, ed., *Chicana Feminist Thought: The Basic Historical Writings* (New York: Routledge, 1997); Maylei Blackwell, *Chicana Power! Contested Histories of Feminism in the Chicano Movement* (Austin: University of Texas Press, 2011); Mario T. García, ed., *A Dolores Huerta Reader* (Albuquerque: University of New Mexico Press, 2008).
18. See Richard Griswold del Castillo, Teresa McKenna, and Yvonne Yarbro-Bejarano, eds., *Chicano Art: Resistance and Affirmation, 1965–1985* (Los Angeles: Wright Art Gallery, UCLA, 1991); Jorge A. Huerta, *Chicano Theater: Themes and Forms* (Ypsilanti, MI: Bilingual, 1982).

## Bibliography

Acuña, Rodolfo. *Occupied America: The Chicano's Struggle Toward Liberation*. San Francisco: Canfield, 1972.
Acuña, Rodolfo. *The Making of Chicana/o Studies: In the Trenches of Academe*. New Brunswick, NJ: Rutgers University Press, 2011.
Alvarez, Luis. *The Power of the Zoot: Youth Culture and Resistance during World War II*. Berkeley: University of California Press, 2008.
Blackwell, Maylei. *Chicana Power! Contested Histories of Feminism in the Chicano Movement*. Austin: University of Texas Press, 2011.
Blauner, Robert. *Racial Oppression in America*. New York: Harper & Row, 1972.
Castro, Tony. *Chicano Power: The Emergence of Mexican America*. New York: Saturday Review Press, 1974.
Chávez, Ernesto. *Mi Raza Primero! Nationalism, Identity, and Insurgency in the Chicano Movement in Los Angeles, 1966–1978*. Berkeley: University of California Press, 2002.
Chávez, John. *The Lost Land: The Chicano Image of the Southwest*. Albuquerque: University of New Mexico Press, 1984.
Escobar, Edward. *Race, Police, and the Making of a Political Identity: Mexican Americans and the Los Angeles Police Department, 1900–1945*. Berkeley: University of California Press, 2003.
Garcia, Alma A., ed. *Chicana Feminst Thought: The Basic Historical Writings*. New York: Routledge, 1997.
García, Ignacio M. *Chicanismo: The Forging of a Militant Ethos Among Mexican Americans*. Tucson: University of Arizona Press, 1997.
García, Ignacio M. *United We Win: The Rise and Fall of La Raza Unida Party*. Tucson: Mexican American Studies and Research Center, University of Arizona, 1989.
García, Ignacio M. *Viva Kennedy: Mexican Americans in Search of Camelot*. College Station: Texas A&M University Press, 2002.
García, Mario T. *Desert Immigrants: The Mexicans of El Paso, 1880–1920*. New Haven, CT: Yale University Press, 1981.
García, Mario T. *Mexican Americans: Leadership, Ideology & Identity, 1930–1960*. New Haven, CT: Yale University Press, 1989.
García, Mario T. *The Making of a Mexican American Mayor: Raymond L. Telles of El Paso*. El Paso: Texas Western Press, 1998.
García, Mario T., ed. *The Gospel of César Chávez: My Faith in Action*. Lanham, MD: Sheed & Ward, 2007.
García, Mario T., ed. *A Dolores Huerta Reader*. Albuquerque: University of New Mexico Press, 2008.

García, Mario T., ed. *The Chicano Movement: Perspectives From the Twenty-First Century*. New York: Routledge, 2014.

García, Mario T. *The Chicano Generation: Testimonios of the Movement*. Oakland: University of California Press, 2015.

García, Mario T., and Sal Castro. *Blowout! Sal Castro and the Chicano Struggle for Educational Justice*. Chapel Hill: University of North Carolina Press, 2011.

García, Mario T., and Ruben Salazar, ed. *Border Correspondent: Selected Writings, 1955–1970*. Berkeley: University of California Press, 1995.

Garcia, Matt. *From the Jaws of Victory: The Triumph and Tragedy of César Chávez and the Farm Workers Movement*. Berkeley: University of California Press, 2012.

Gómez-Quiñones, Juan and Irene Vásquez. *Making Aztlán: Ideology and Culture of the Chicana and Chicano Movement*. Albuquerque: University of New Mexico Press, 2014.

González, Gilbert G. *Chicano Education in the Era of Segregation*. Philadelphia: Balch Institute Press, 1990.

Griswold del Castillo and Richard A. García, *César Chávez: Triumph of Spirit*. Norman: University of Oklahoma Press, 1995.

Griswold del Castillo, Teresa McKenna, and Yvonne Yarbro-Bejarano, eds. *Chicano Art: Resistance and Affirmation, 1965–1985*. Los Angeles: Wright Art Gallery, UCLA.

Huerta, Jorge A. *Chicano Theater: Themes and Forms*. Ypsilanti, MI: Bilingual Press, 1982.

Levy, Jacques. *Cesar Chavez: Autobiography of La Causa*. New York: Norton, 1975.

Mariscal, Jorge. *Brown-Eyed Children of the Sun: Lesson from the Chicano Movement*. Albuquerque: University of New Mexico Press, 2005.

McWilliams, Carey. *North from Mexico: The Spanish-Speaking People of the United States*. New York: Greenwood, 1948.

Muñoz, Carlos, Jr., *Youth, Identity, Power: The Chicano Movement*. New York: Verso, 1989.

Navarro, Armando. *La Raza Unida Party: A Chicano Challenge to the U.S. Two-Party Dictatorship*. Philadelphia: Temple University Press, 2000.

Navarro, Armando. *Mexican American Youth Organization: Avant-Garde of the Chicano Movement in Texas*. Austin: University of Texas Press, 1995.

Oropeza, Lorena. *Raza Si, Guerra No! Chicano Protest and Patriotism during the Vietnam War Era*. Berkeley: University of California Press, 2005.

Pagán, Edward Obregón. *Murder at the Sleepy Lagoon: Zoot Suits, Race, and Riot in Wartime L.A.* Chapel Hill: University of North Carolina Press, 2003.

Powell, Miriam. *The Crusades of Cesar Chavez: A Biography*. New York: Bloomsbury, 2014.

San Miguel, Guadalupe. Jr., *"Let All of Them Take Heed": Mexican Americans and the Campaign for Educational Equality in Texas, 1910–1981*. Austin: University of Texas Press, 1987.

Shaw, Randy. *Beyond the Fields: Cesar Chavez, the UFW, and the Struggle for Justice in the Twenty-First Century*. Berkeley: University of California Press, 2008.

Soldatenko, Michael. *Chicano Studies: The Genesis of a Discipline*. Tucson: University of Arizona Press, 2011.

Stavans, Ilan, ed. *Cesar Chavez: An Organizer's Tale—Speeches*. New York: Penguin, 2008.

Weber, David. *Foreigners in Their Native Land*. Albuquerque: University of New Mexico Press, 1973.

# CHAPTER 7

# WOMEN, GENDER, AND SEXUALITY IN LATINA/O CULTURE

## ALICIA ARRIZÓN

WHILE the terms "gender" and "sexuality" can be used to express our identities and desires, more specifically, the notion of "woman" can be understood as a social construction about the operation of the female gender role. Whereas sexuality can be simply explained as the corporality of erotic desires or sexual orientation, gender can be understood as a category emphasizing the distinction between males and females and the fluidity of masculinity and femininity. While the gender binary system discourages people from crossing or mixing gender roles (or from creating multiple forms of gender expression altogether), it may result in some of the prejudices that stigmatize people who transgress this system. As a culturally defined code, the binary gender system supports "acceptable" behaviors fostering compulsory thoughts insisting that there are strictly men and women who are masculine and feminine. The binary system in turn reinforces the belief that men and women exist only in a complementary relationship, exclusive to one another. In an influential book, *Gender Trouble* (1990), Judith Butler argues that gender, along with heterosexuality, is a performative category.[1] Since its publication, Butler's book has become one of the most significant works of contemporary feminist theory and an essential work in gender studies. This view recognizes that neither gender nor heterosexuality is an innate, biological feature but rather socially and culturally constructed: individuals or groups participate in the construction of their perceived (and performed) social or cultural reality.

Women's studies and feminist theory generally focus on gender itself, analyzing gendered social and power relations, as well as the ways in which socially imposed and regulated norms impact women's sexualities and self-determination. Since the end of the 1970s, this analytical approach to gender became widely used, in particular by feminist scholars who challenge the hierarchies implied in binary oppositions. In this context, one must understand gender not limited to the binary man/woman but rather a set of different meanings that the sexes assume in particular societies. Gender is a sociocultural construction that includes a set of characteristics of men's and women's behaviors, lifestyles, ways of thinking, preferences, and life orientations. Therefore, the implications of femininity and masculinity should be understood not necessarily as biological categories of human existence but as the product of socialization and creative processes. Femininity and masculinity are structures of feelings that make people believe they belong to a gender. In the 1970s, Shulamith Firestone transformed contemporary thinking about gender in her book *The Dialectic of Sex*, which argues that gender distinctions structure every aspect of our lives. While claiming that gender difference is an elaborate system of male domination, power, and authority, she condemned the biological sexual dichotomy, particularly the biological division of labor in reproduction, as the root cause of male domination, economic class exploitation, racism, imperialism, and ecological irresponsibility.[2] As a hierarchical pair, women comprise the main group that is subjugated in a hegemonic system, in which the male is coded "superior," and female "inferior." A hegemonic system can be understood as an order, state, or ideas that dominate and subordinate others. Most recently, the notion of hegemonic masculinity in gender/women studies has been used to represent the gendered power relations, emphasizing the belief in the existence of a male behavior ideal. In general, it can be pointed out that society strongly encourages men to embody this kind of masculinity. The knowledge that power relations dominate and regulate the gendered behaviors and practices across many societies is applicable to explain the traditional value system embedded in US Latina/o culture and its embedded colonial legacy Although the term "Latino," as it is used in this handbook, makes relevant references to the heterogeneity embedded in its broad signification, the split gendered Latina/o used in this chapter provides agency to the feminine/feminist subject across time and space. While the feminist subject in the term Latina/o is attached to the gendered body, queer theorists have detached it through the new adaptation of the adjective Latinx—an alternative to Latino, Latina, or Latina/o.

## Gender Power Relations: *Marianismo* and *Machismo*

Although the gains made by Latinas in recent years are substantial, gender relations continue to be reinforced by patriarchal and Christian values in Latina/o culture. Even though patriarchy is common to a number of cultures, Latina/o culture has traditionally used religious figures to force women into silent submission. As contradictory value in Latina/o culture, the dichotomy of *marianismo* and *machismo* has perpetuated the subordination of women across national boundaries. Gender relations are a fundamental feature of all societies and cultures. Similar to that of Latin America, gender relations in the US Latino/a culture are reinforced by the power of heterosexuality, patriarchy, and religion. These institutions represent a system of cultural values that not only define the ways in which men and women should "act" but also have perpetuated the devaluation of women and femininity. Deeply rooted in the gender relations of the Americas' colonial histories is the duality of *marianismo* and *machismo*, which represents a gender role phenomenon based on traditional cultural norms and the impact of Catholicism. Modeled after the Virgin Mary, *marianismo* creates a feminine ideal of purity and passivity by which women are expected to live. Derived from Catholic beliefs of the Virgin Mary (La Virgen María), who, after giving birth to Jesús, became the Mother of God and a role model for women, *marianismo* perpetuates the gender roles, in which women should be self-sacrificing while following the ideal of the Virgin Mary. And like her, women should be eternally immaculate and giving. They were expected to be pure, and if they have sexual relations, it should only be with their husband and for the sole purpose of procreation.

On the other hand, *marianismo*'s counterpart, *machismo*, can be understood as a prominently exhibited or excessive form of masculinity. While some scholars believe that the term *machismo* has historical roots common in all "Latin" cultures since Roman times, others would argue that it is an ideology that originated in Spain, being implemented in the Americas during the Spanish Conquest. Scholars often associate *machismo* with *donjuanismo*, the cultural context that gave rise to the figure of Don Juan archetype: while men behave as the active force in sexual romantic encounters, having lavish and uncontrollable sexual appetites, women must be the passive keepers of the family honor. The women Don Juan hunts for seduction are those who present the most challenge: innocent young virgins, nuns, and married women, among others. *Donjuanismo* originated in Spain after the story of Don Juan was produced in a dramatic setting on stage in the 1630 play *El Burlador de Sevilla y convidado de piedra* (The prankster of Seville and his stone guest) written by a Spanish monk who published under the pseudonym Tirso de Molina (1571–1641). In the nineteenth century, *Don Juan Tenorio: Drama religioso-fantástico en dos partes* (Don Juan Tenorio: Religious-fantasy drama in two parts, 1844) by José Zorrilla was acclaimed as the most romantic literary interpretations of the legend of Don Juan in Spain.[3] Don Juan's essential attribute is to seduce and control women he sees as his inferior and submissive. This inferiority, Mexican philosopher and poet Octavio Paz believed, stems from women's sexuality (specifically, the vagina), which he defined as an open "wound" incapable of healing. The *macho*'s essential attribute is manifested by his capacity for penetrating that "wound." Paz wrote in his *Labyrinth of Solitude and Other Writings* (1985): "The macho represents the masculine pole of life," and he feels superior because he cannot be made to "open." The "real meaning" of macho, Paz wrote, "is no different from that of the verb *chingar* and its derivatives. The macho is the *gran chingón*."[4] In considering the resemblance between the figure of the macho and that of the Spanish conquistador, Paz reflected on the macho as "the model— more mythical than real—that determines the images the Mexican people form of men in power: caciques, feudal lords, hacienda owners, politicians, generals, captains of industry. They are all *machos, chingones*."[5]

In the United States, *machismo* has been more broadly used than in Latin America or in other Spanish-speaking countries. Folklorist Américo Paredes characterized the macho as "the superman of the multitude," a "national type" by which Mexico, as a nation, is often classified. In his study of *machismo*, Paredes discusses its folkloric origins and its stereotypical aspects. In his examination, Paredes asserts that if *machismo* sprung from the rape of some Indian women by some Spaniards during the Spanish conquest, then it is an ancient term.[6] Hernán Cortés's conduct in this area can be a model of the *machismo* alluded to by Paredes. As the conquistador of Mexico, he took as his interpreter and lover the young Indian woman named Malintzín Tenépal, whom he called Doña Marina and was popularly referred to as "la Malinche." Cortés, already married to a Spanish woman, recognized the son he had with Malinche but forced her to marry a soldier from his ranks. La Malinche has been characterized as the violated mother of the Mexican people; for Paz, she is the victim of colonization and a traitor to the nation. As the the *Chingada*, she represents all the Indigenous women who were violated or seduced by the conquistadores. In Paz's terms, the Mexican people become the sons of Malinche who "have not forgiven La Malinche for her betrayal. She embodies the open, the *Chingado*, to our closed, stoic, impassive Indians."[7] Although many Indigenous women were sexually abused by the conquistadores during the colonization in the Americas, many colonizers married those who contributed native nobility and significant dowries. As opposed to black women and mulatas, Indigenous women were not only free like the Spaniards, but in some cases, they were already allied with the colonialists who had made the women submissive to their power. That was precisely the case of Malintzín, who served as Hernán Cortés's interpreter and mistress and became the mother of his mestizo son. Additionally, she became the intermediary between the two cultures.

In the twenty-first century, conflicting emotions related to *machismo* and *marianismo* exist. Although young Latinas and Latinos acknowledge the existence of cultural norms embedded in the power relations of this gender phenomenon, the question regarding how both *marianismo* and *machismo* influence men and women remains complex. One must be careful not to generalize, as not all Latinas accept the traditional role of *marianismo*, and not all Latinos accept *machismo*. However, for some, *machismo* is acceptable and even expected. Undoubtedly, *machismo* epitomizes the colonial legacy of the Spanish conquistadores, manifested mainly in the rape of Indigenous women and in their power to socially and religiously control and dominate the Indigenous populations in the Americas.

# Iconic Transcendence: From *Malinchismo* to Feminist Indigeneity

> La gente Chicana tiene tres madres. All three are mediators: Guadalupe, the virgin mother who has not abandoned us, la Chingada (Malinche), the raped mother whom we have abandoned, and La Llorona, the mother who seeks her lost children and is a combination of the other two.[8]

La Malinche, as she was branded by the Indians, has become a symbol of the cultural tyranny embedded in the process of colonization.[9] If one joins her legacy with the narrative of the Virgin of Guadalupe, the virgin/Madonna/whore dichotomy can be captured in the context of conquest, colonization and Christianity. For Anzaldúa, these three iconic figures represent the symbolic "mothers" of the Mexican/Chicano people who have been used to propagate subjugation. She further elaborates, "the true identity of all three has been subverted—Guadalupe to make us docile and enduring, la Chingada to make us ashamed of our Indian side, and la Llorona to make us long-suffering people. This obscuring has encouraged the virgen/puta(whore) dichotomy."[10] This dichotomy denotes polarized perception of women as either "good," chaste, and pure or as immoral, promiscuous, and seductive whores. While both La Malinche and La Guadalupe represent powerful symbols of femininity across national borders, one is the epitome of purity and is venerated for her grace and devotion to God; and the second is despised for her defiance and for "provoking" lustful desires in men. In one of the most acclaimed essays written about La Malinche, "Traddutora, Traditora: A Paradigmatic Figure of Chicana Feminism" (1989), Norma Alarcón has considered both figures as oppositional mediating forces, in which "Guadalupe has come to symbolize transformative powers and sublime transcendence" and La Malinche the embodiment of "feminine subversion and treacherous victimization" after becoming Cortes's translator.[11] In Alarcón's view, both are intrinsically connected and "have become a function of each other. Be that as it may, quite often one or the other figure is recalled the 'origins' of the Mexican community, thereby emphasizing its divine and sacred constitution or, alternately, its damned and secular fall."[12]

In-between La Malinche and La Guadalupe, the legend of La Llorona (the wailing woman) subsists with various manifestations. The most common narrative presents a woman who was betrayed by her husband. When her husband left her to be with another woman, she drowned their two children in a nearby river out of anguish and vengefulness. The legend is that she roams rivers and lakes in Mexico, California, and the American Southwest, searching and wailing for her lost children. Images of her often resemble a banshee type: an apparition of a woman dressed in white.[13] The conflation of La Malinche and La Llorona is remarkably inherent. Like La Malinche, La Llorona represents motherhood in negative terms. While La Malinche's betrayal of her people ("children") was the result of her relationship with their oppressive "father" (Cortés), La Llorona's treacherous motherhood is irrevocably deviant. For this sin, she is condemned with her continual wailing as a reminder to all of her wrongdoing and its after-effects. From the historical legacy of Malinche, to the mythical Llorona, the sense that women are inherently sinful and must be controlled has long survived and has contributed to reinforce the negative views that most Mexicans/Latinos hold of their symbolic mothers.

In Aztec mythology, Tlazoltéotl is associated with the moon and earth. She is the goddess of sex. In her incarnation as Teteoinnan, Mother of the Gods, she is protector of the midwives, *curanderas* (doctor women), and fortune tellers. Tlazoltéotl is one of the most endearing and complex goddesses of the Mesoamericans and is usually depicted wearing the skin of a human sacrificial victim and squatting over something. She can also be seen carrying a grass broom as a symbol of cleaning or wearing a spindle of raw cotton on her headdress (Figure 7.1).

In her discussion of Indigenous deities, Anzaldúa suggests that the process of decolonization must occur by entering the "Coatlicue state." She uses the notion of "the Coatlicue state" in her *Borderlands* book to mark the conflicting powers of Coatlicue, Cihuácoatl, Tlazoltéotl, Tonantzín, Caotlalopeuh, and Guadalupe. Anzaldúa explains how Coatlicue's legacy represents all the different parts of the philosophy of the Aztecs. She writes that "Coatlicue is a symbol of the fusion of opposites: the eagle and the serpent, heaven and the underworld, life and death, mobility and immobility, beauty and horror."[14] A deity born of Coatlicue was Cihuácoatl, the serpent goddess who is also identified with Tonantzín, a goddess similar to the Christian Virgin Mother, and is referred to as "Our Lady." As deities, Cihuácoatl and Tlazoltéotl were disempowered and given evil attributes during the transformation of Coatlicue's good spirit, Tonantzín, into La Guadalupe. Tonantzín (Figure 7.2) became embodied as the chaste, protective mother of the mestizo nation, La Virgen de Guadalupe.

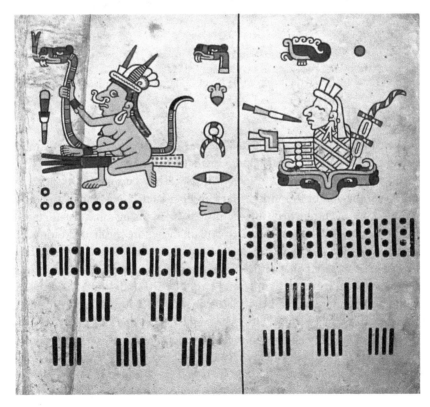

FIGURE 7.1. Tlazoltéotl, Codex Fejérváry-Mayer. World Museum in Liverpool, M12014. Gift of Joseph Mayer, 1867. Image in public domain.

**FIGURE 7.2.** Precolonial figurine believed to be of Tonantzín. Courtesy of National Museum of Anthropology, Mexico City.

After the conquest, Tonantzín/Guadalupe was established as the "good" mother of the mestizo nation. On the other hand, Coatlicue and her female deities Cihuácoatl and Tlazoltéotl were rendered into defiant beasts. They became the transgressors of *marianismo* (of the cult of the Virgin Mary and her subject position as the mother of God), imposed by an entrenched Christianity. As an opposing force, Coatlicue and her deities, Tlazoltéotl and Cihuácoatl, help to explain the whore-virgin dichotomy that has shaped gender relations and sexuality in post-Spanish colonial sites. Thus, the desirable qualities of a woman based on Coatlicue/Tonantzín/La Virgen de Guadalupe are goodness, humbleness, dedication to family, and virginity. The undesirable traits, as embodied in Cihuácoatl and Tlazoltéotl (La Malinche and La Llorona), are treachery, lying, deceitfulness, and sexual promiscuity. Although this distinction simply described as "virgin-whore" dichotomy has been universally identified as a psychological complex that develops in men who see women as either saintly Madonnas or debased prostitutes, in Mexican/Chicano culture, the dichotomy is tied specifically to Coatlicue's Christian transformation and beliefs about paganism, the devil, and female transgression as symbolized by Eve. The merging of these beliefs produces new depictions of Tonantzín and related goddesses. Colonial and Christian imposition negatively associated the

Christian serpent, devil, Eve, evil, and sin with these Aztec sacred energies. In "Goddess of the Américas in the Decolonial Imaginary: Beyond the Virtuous Virgen/Pagan Puta Dichotomy," Irene Lara argues that through connective epistemologies, "Tonantzín-Guadalupe becomes a decolonial figure capable of healing the virtuous virgen/pagan puta split perpetuated by Western patriarchal thought."[15]

While Chicana feminism has undertaken to recover La Malinche as more than a traitor, it reclaims her power as a strong female figure. Feminist theorists have shown that not only did La Malinche mediate her own success as an important figure in the new Spanish Empire but that she also negotiated for the interests of the Indigenous people. In the introduction of *Feminism, Nation and Myth: La Malinche* (2005), Amanda Nolacea Harris suggests that her legacy has compelled us to critically study intersections of race, class, and gender. According to her, La Malinche's narrative "demands that we decolonize all facets of her legacy, and disassemble and reconstruct concepts of nation, community, agency, subjectivity, and social activism."[16]

Carmen Tafolla's poetic subject responds clearly to these feminist demands when occupying the voice of La Malinche. While Tafolla rejects the only accepted notion of Malinche as a passive victim who was "used" or "raped" by Cortés, her Malinche does not accept her assigned nickname, asserting that "Chingada I was not":

And history would call *me*
Chingada.
But Chingada I Was not.
Not tricked, not screwed, not traitor.
For I was not traitor to myself–
I Saw a dream
and I reached it.
Another world
... la raza.
La raaaaaaa-zaaaaa...[17]

Artists, critics, and historians have repeatedly noted the historical and mythical representation of La Malinche as a paradigm of the legacy of betrayal, in some cases, proposing new readings as an attempt to rescue her from her condemnation. In Tafolla's poetic articulations, La Malinche becomes the mother of the new race in a "new world." The first victim of the Spanish colonization, La Malinche was known for her ability to speak and understand many different languages. By becoming Cortés's "tongue," she "betrayed" her people, but her legacy of "betrayal" has been considered to be crucial to understand the conflictive gender power relations ingrained in the social and cultural fabric of a colonized people. Chicanas and other feminists are continually revisiting her significance as a woman who endured a violent conquest and its recurring deployment embodying the unresolved upheaval and cataclysm of colonization. Her legacy is a crucial testimony that Indigenous women and their "encounter" with Spanish men were predestined by the conquest and by the conquistadores' insatiable sexual desire for

FIGURE 7.3. La Malinche and Cortés. Mural by José Clemente Orozco. Colegio de San Ildefonso, Mexico City. Painted in 1926.

them. As a paradigm of a colonial/sexual encounter and as a cultural construct, her presence traverses further than the geopolitical sites of colonization. La Malinche (Figure 7.3) is a critical force that has shaped both the feminine and feminist consciousness of contemporary Latinas in general, and more specifically of Chicanas/Mexicans.

## REVOLUTIONARY PRECURSORS: BORDERLESS *LATINOAMERICANAS*

The history of Latina/American feminism can be linked to the social movements beginning in the 1960s and 1970s that centered on women's liberation. From north to south of the US–Mexico border, women of Latin American descent joined a collective struggle for equality and against oppression and male supremacy. Although the women's liberation movements significantly transformed gender power relations, Latina feminist epistemologies have antecedents as early as the seventeenth century. One of the greatest feminist precursors emerged 130 years after the Spanish colonization: "Sor" Juana Inéz de Cruz (birth name Juana Inéz de Asbaje y Ramírez de Santillana) was born near Mexico City in 1648 as the illegitimate daughter of a Spanish captain and a *criolla* (Creole woman)—of Spanish descent but born in Mexico.[18] As a child, she was inquisitive and eager to learn: by the age of three, she could read. During her childhood, she had started asking permission to cut her hair short and disguise herself as a boy so she could attend the university. She was writing poetry and learning Latin as a pre-teenager, transforming into a young female prodigy and entirely self-taught. Her family sent her to stay with her aunt and uncle in Mexico City, where she continued to study Greek logic and Náhuatl (Indigenous language). Her aunt and uncle presented her to the court of the Viceroy Marquis de Mancera, which admitted her into the service of his wife, Vicereine Leonor Carreto. After being tested by a panel of scholars who were intrigued by her brilliance, she became disillusioned with the courtly lifestyle, entering the convent in 1667, which was the only alternative against the expectation of marriage (Figure 7.4).

FIGURE 7.4. Portrait of sor Juana Ines de la Cruz in her library, by Miguel Cabrera. Wikimedia commons.

The convent life offered Sor Juana the freedom to study and write, and the opportunity to teach music and drama. In the convent, Sor Juana possessed one of the largest private libraries in the New World, together with a collection of musical and scientific instruments. As a respectable nun and intellectual, she was able to continue her contact with other scholars and powerful members of the court. As a feminist writer, she became deeply disillusioned with men. Her famous poem, commonly known by its first two words, "Hombres necios" ("Foolish Men"), accuses men of the same illogical behavior that they accuse women of. The poem starts with a direct accusation against men: "Silly, you man—so very adept. At wrongly faulting womankind, not seeing you're alone to blame for faults you plant in woman's name."[19] This condemns men for being good at blaming women for faults that men themselves have displayed. Although Sor Juana's poetic subject never refers to women as "we," she is obviously speaking for women in general. While her short verses are easy enough to follow, Sor Juana repeats her view of men in various rephrased forms throughout the poem. Men win over women's resistance and then, becoming self-righteous, blame them for feminine frivolity. But by portraying men as illogical and deceitful, Sor Juana challenges the hegemonic masculinist world she inhabits. This poem, together with her "Respuesta a Sor Filotea" (known as the "reply" to Sister Filotea), where she defended women's rights to education, has positioned her as the first published feminist of the New World and as the most outstanding writer of the Spanish American colonial period.[20]

The colonial Latin America Sor Juana lived in was a patriarchal society: a world in which men occupied positions of authority and power, and education was a masculinist privilege. During the period of independence, in the nineteenth century, the problems of women under the effects of patriarchy remained. Unlike the patriarchy under colonialism, the patriarchy that emerged as result of the independence wars was proven by the empowerment of formally masculine emasculation. According to Melanie Byam, during the colonial rule, "The ultimate patriarchy was that of elite whites over the poor Indigenous peoples, whereas in the nineteenth century we see a reformation of patriarchy centered in the home, simply with men over women and children."[21] Thus the education of women during the nineteenth century was deemed as a tool of resistance to patriarchy in many Latin American regions. As a feminist project, the education of women became a fundamental issue for Rita Cetina Gutierréz, who is recognized in Mexico as the founder of the first secular school for poor girls in 1871. Named as *La Siempreviva* ("everlasting"), the school functioned also as an art college for young women. The foundations of a scientific and literary society and a newspaper with the same name were created simultaneously during that time. The publication of Piedad Peniche Rivero, *Rita Cetina, La Siempreviva y el Instituto Literario de Niñas: Una cuna del feminismo mexicano 1846–1908*, documents extensively the outstanding contributions of Cetina Gutierréz.[22] Another feminist precursor to the integral education of women in the nineteenth century was the writer Teresa González de Fanning in Perú, where she founded La Escuela de Señoritas o Liceo Fanning in 1881.[23] In their limited position as women confronting the hegemonic masculinities of the postindependence years, feminists like Cetina Gutiérrez and González de Fanning promoted education of women while fighting for their self-determination.

An outstanding case before the abolition of slavery in Puerto Rico was that of one of the first Afro-Puerto Ricans, Celestina Cordero, who joined the forces of her brother Rafael Cordero to establish in their own home, the first school for children in 1810. Despite the fact that they were subject to racial discrimination for being "black and free," they have been recognized as key players in the development of Puerto Rico's education system. In 1820, Celestina Cordero would open the first school for girls in San Juan. While she had to struggle to be recognized as a female educator, her brother was revered as the "father of Puerto Rican education system." Whereas three schools in Puerto Rico have been named after him, Celestina Cordero is largely unknown in today's Puerto Rican society. The confinement of women to the home in colonial Puerto Rico during the nineteenth century explains in part her underrepresentation.[24] The fact that women had limited opportunities for education or for participation in the public domain and were mostly relegated to the domestic sphere had a negative impact in the advancement of feminist causes. Nonetheless, revolutionary figures such as Celestina and, later, poet and activist Lola Rodríguez de Tío have made a difference in the colonial history of Puerto Rico. As *independentista* (independent rebel), Lola Rodríguez and her husband were forced to exile from Puerto Rico by the Spanish government. First they went to Venezuela, and on their second deportation they first moved to New York, where she worked with José Martí and other Cuban revolutionaries, and later she and her husband moved to Cuba, where the couple resided until their respective deaths. Inspired by Ramón Emeterio Betances's quest for Puerto Rico's independence and by the attempted revolution called the Grito de Lares, Rodríguez de Tío wrote the patriotic lyrics to La Borinqueña in 1868.[25] After the cession of the island to the United States, the revolutionary lyrics of Rodríguez de Tío were considered too subversive for official adoption. In 1903, Manuel Fernández Juncos wrote a nonconfrontational set of lyrics that were officially adopted as the Commonwealth's anthem in 1952.

During the nineteenth century in the United States, women of Latin American heritage have also made notable contributions in the development of a literary tradition. As it has been established by the Recovering the U.S. Hispanic Literary Heritage Project, under the direction of Nicolás Kanellos (founder of Arte Público Press), women writers of Latin American heritage have been writing since the nineteenth century.[26] An important author of this period, "recovered" by the Literary Heritage Project in the early 1990s, is Maria Amparo Ruiz de Burton (1832–1895), who has been considered the first published Mexican American writer after the war with Mexico (1846–1848), as well as the first Mexican American writer after this time to write in English. The relationship complexities between the Anglo expansionists and the Mexicans in the nineteenth century were uniquely represented in María Ruiz de Burton's novels *Who Would Have Thought It?* (1872, rep. 1995) and *The Squatter and the Don* (1885, rep. 1997). Although *Who Would* is considered the first novel written in English by a Mexican living in the United States, both works were unknown until rediscovered and reprinted in the late twentieth century.[27]

Later years, in the early twentieth century, Leonor Villegas de Magnón (b. 1876–d. 1955) writes in response to the Mexican Revolution (1910–1924). She was a political activist, teacher, and journalist who started a brigade of the international Mexican American relief service, La Cruz Blanca, during the Mexican Revolution.[28] Villegas de Magnón was born in the border city of Nuevo Laredo, Mexico. She was educated in the United States and married an American citizen, Adolpho Magnon, in 1901. During the Mexican Revolution, together with her friend Jovita Idar, they became sympathetic to the revolution while writing for *La Crónica*, a Laredo newspaper published by Nicasio Idar. As result of her writings, Villegas de Magnón was nicknamed La Rebelde. When Nuevo Laredo was attacked in March 1913, the two friends and other Laredo women crossed the Rio Grande to nurse the wounded. *The Rebel* (1994) becomes the autobiographical account of Villegas de Magnón's involvement in the Mexican Revolution. As explained in the preface by Clara Lomas, two versions of the book were discovered: one in Spanish titled "La Rebelde," written during the revolution, and a second, written in English during the late 1940s.[29] While the first one was targeting the postrevolutionary Mexican readership, the second was envisioning a reader in the United States. Called "novelized memoirs," Magnón wrote these manuscripts in the third person, writing about important figures in the revolution, including women who volunteered for Cruz Blanca's operations.

The contributions of Adelina "Nina" Otero-Warren (b. 1881–d. 1965) as woman's suffragist, educator, and politician in the United States are outstanding. Otero-Warren created a legacy of civil service through her work in education, politics, and public health, becoming one of New Mexico's first female government officials when she served as Santa Fe Superintendent of Instruction from 1917 to 1929. Otero-Warren has been recognized as the first Latina to run for Congress. She ran for a seat in the US House of Representatives as the Republican candidate for New Mexico in 1922. While she was running a progressive campaign, advocating for improved education, health care, and welfare services, news of her divorce came out, as well as concerns about her position on Spanish-language instruction in schools and employment, and she was defeated by Democrat John Morrow. Otero-Warren's contributions were beyond the political realm. She was involved in preservation of historic structures in both Santa Fe and Taos, and she worked closely with the arts community. She was instrumental in renewing interest in and respect for Hispanic and Indian culture. Her life on the family hacienda was documented in her book, *Old Spain in Our Southwest* (1936). Otero-Warren and her other two New Mexican contemporaries, Fabiola Cabeza de Baca Gilbert (b. 1894–d. 1991) and Cleofas M. Jaramillo (b. 1878–d. 1956), have distinguished themselves in the preservation of important attributes of Spanish American culture.[30]

## THIRD WORLD LATINA FEMINISM

During the early wave of feminisms, women's studies was dominated by the experiences of white middle-class women, thus leaving Latinas and other women of color feeling invisible or not fully part of the movement. In the 1980s, US feminist scholars started to engage with the questions of gender difference or distinctions: the question about difference from one culture to another, or how definitions of male and female, masculinity and femininity, have evolved; and how diverse constructions of gender and its power relations intersect with constructions of sexuality, social class, racial ethnicity, age, nation, religion, and other differences. Drawing on the feminist scholarship of US and Third World women of color, women's studies has adopted the conceptual method and theory of intersectionality, which examines how categories of identity (e.g., sexuality, race, class, gender, etc.) and structures of inequality are mutually constituted and must continually be understood in relationship to one another. For Latinas and other women of color, Third World feminisms provided a crucial politics of identification in order to create new spaces while transforming the dominant white feminist movement. Whether their skin is dark, black, or white, Latinas in the United States speak of the racialization of culture as a counter-hegemonic project. After the groundbreaking publication of *This Bridge Called My Back: Writing by Radical Women of Color* (1981, 1983, 2002, 2015), edited by Cherríe Moraga and Gloria Anzaldúa, the concepts of Third World women and women of color had developed as an oppositional reclaiming agency, not only to challenge mainstream feminism but to implement intersectional-related issues into the movement. While intersectionality became mainly linked to Kimberly Crenshaw after 1989 when she used the term as a way to understand multiple oppressions and or discriminations and how they affect marginal subjects, Moraga and Anzaldúa evidently embraced "the interlocking systems of oppression," commonly known as a precursor to intersectionality.[31] As Moraga and Anzaldúa noted in their introduction, *Bridge* was originally conceived as a project to consolidate the Third World feminist movement in the United States. The editors state that in order to consider the formation of a broad-based political movement, we must contemplate the following:

> (1) how visibility/invisibility as women of color forms our radicalism; (2) the ways in which Third World women derive a feminist political theory specifically from our radical/cultural background and experience; (3) the destructive and demoralizing effects of racism in the women's movement; (4) the cultural, class, and sexuality differences that divide women of color; (5) Third World women's writing as a tool of self-preservation and revolution; and (6) the ways and means of a Third World feminist future.[32]

The writers in *Bridge*—Latinas, African Americans, Asian Americans, and Native Americans—discuss their perceived invisibility and exclusion from the dominant white culture and from mainstream feminism. They invoke a collective process of identification for women of color, aiming to span the multiple differences of a silent community. The many writers in *Bridge* are invested in deconstructing the space of the dominant feminist subject by emphasizing their own narratives through what they described as "theory in the flesh." This theory refers to how "the physical realities of [their] lives—[their] skin color, the land or concrete [they] grew up on, [their] sexual longings—all fuse to create a politic born out of necessity."[33] As illustrated in *Bridge*, "theory in the flesh" is a tool that engages with the conceptual knowledge embedded in the slogan "The personal is political," which was adopted during the women's movement, expressing a common belief among feminists that the personal experiences of women are entrenched in their gender inequality. Although the origin of the phrase is uncertain, it became popular in 1970 following the publication of an essay of the same name by American feminist Carol Hanisch, arguing that many personal experiences of women are shackled within a system of power relationships.[34] For Cuban American Mirtha Quintanales, "the personal" is not only political but a response to "systemic" oppression. In her contribution in *Bridge*, "I paid very hard for my immigrant ignorance," she addresses her letter to Barbara Smith:

> As a Third World, Caribbean woman I understand what it means to have grown up "colonized" in a society built on slavery and the oppression of imperialist forces. As an immigrant and a cultural minority woman who happens to be white-skinned, I empathize with the pain of ethnic invisibility and the perils of passing (always a very tenuous situation—since acknowledgment of ethnic ties is inevitably accompanied by stereotyping, prejudice and various kind of discrimination—the problem is not just personal, but "systemic", "political"—one more reality of American "life").[35]

Quintanilla's letter to Barbara Smith is a reflection that connects her experience as a Caribbean immigrant in the United States with other women of color. Her letter is a testimony that aims to engage with other feminists trying to find common ground. From the publication of *Bridge* to the publication of *Telling to Live: Latina Feminist Testimonios* (2001), the narratives "theorizing in the flesh" or the practice of testimonial voices have been used in US Latino culture as a tool for understanding the complexities of Latina subjectivity or experience.[36] According to Aurora Levins Morales, Latina feminists "found a way to gather and talk, we threw away the agendas and began making theory out of the stuff in our pockets, out of the stories, incidents, dreams, frustrations that were never acceptable anywhere else."[37] Even though not all Latinas are black or brown, and some speak only English, some only Spanish and some Spanglish, the complexity embedded in national cultural markers of identity formation must be related to that which identifies women of Latin American descent in general, and Cuban American, Dominican, Chicanas, Nuyorican/Puerto Rican, and so on in particular. In Morales's testimonio, references to her identity as a Puerto Rican and as a feminist are symbolically marked:

> It has been in the critiques of feminist women of color of their own cultures that I have found the space as a Puerto Rican woman to speak most truthfully about my real experiences, not the ones I was supposed to be having as a U.S. Puerto Rican. That it was here that I could freely name the ambivalences and contradictions,

had a space to fiercely defend Puerto Rico from colonialism and still claim what I love about the United States, while still critiquing what I find unbearable about Puerto Rico.[38]

Morales's testimony attests to her identity as Puerto Rican, but it is through her feminist allegiances that she finds agency. While feminism is implicitly traced in the personal narratives of Latinas—from self-representation to theorizing "in the flesh"—definitions of Latina feminism are not absolute. Although many Latinas took leadership roles in the civil rights movements, their contributions for the most part have been ignored. For example, Dolores Huerta was one of the activists during the Chicano Movement whose contributions were tucked behind those of her male colleagues.[39] The emergence of Chicana feminism itself was a reaction to the male-dominated Chicano Movement, which relied on cultural nationalism to unify Mexican Americans around one identity: Chicanismo. However, cultural nationalism was limited due to its patriarchal ideologies and practices that subordinated Chicanas within the movement. Chicana feminism, also known as Xicanisma, was established as an ideology based on the rejection of the traditional "household" role of women of Mexican descent.[40] While challenging gender relations of power, Chicana feminism evolved as a middle ground between the Chicano Movement and the Women's Liberation Movement. Saturated with sexism, homophobia, and internal oppression, the Chicano Movement affected women's roles negatively. Moraga recounts that "women at the most, were allowed to serve as modern-day 'Adelitas'" and were expected to perform the "three fs": to feed, fight, and fuck their men.[41]

Like Chicanas' response to the Chicano Movement, the women in the Young Lords had to confront their male counterpart to directly address the impact of sexism in their struggles. The Young Lords were mostly a Puerto Rican organization (some African Americans and other Latino groups were members) that was organized by José Cha Cha Jiménez in Chicago (1968). The organization then networked to nearly thirty other cities including three branches in New York City. In general, this group contributes to redefine Puerto Rican identity in the United States: openly reclaiming their pride in being Boricuas, not "Spanish," but Afro-Taino; they were fighting for basic human rights such as clothing, shelter, food, and access to health care. Women in the group openly challenged machismo, sexism, and patriarchy; organized to build a people's movement; and fought the "revolution within the revolution," believing that their equality was inseparable from the society's progress as a whole. In *Through the Eyes of Rebel Women: The Young Lords, 1969–1976* (2016), a member of the group, Iris Morales, chronicles the revolutionary rise of the Young Lords, the contributions of women, and the group's decline. In the book's introduction, feminist scholar Edna Acosta-Belén writes: "These women activists are the Young Amazons of their time—the brave feminist warriors who battled for equality in intersecting (not isolated or separated) arenas of class, race, gender, ethnicity, and sexuality; part of that noble league of defenders of *universal human rights*."[42]

# From Latina/o Queerness to Nonconforming Identity Markers

Since the late 1970s, Chicana and Latina feminists have developed significant theories in order to re-conceptualize gender relations and gendered bodies outside the boundaries of binary thinking and heteronormativity. While heteronormativity can be considered a biased knowledge, it implies that human beings fall into two distinct and complementary categories, male and female, and that sexual relations are "normal" only between two people of different genders. Therefore, the effects of heteronormativity and homophobia have been contested for stigmatizing alternative concepts of both sexuality and gender and for making certain types of self-expression more difficult. By considering the social structures that preclude gendered/sexualized identities—such as gay and lesbian—and the sexual politics that separate men and women, the emergence of self-identified "queer" identities in translation has contributed to transform understanding of new Latina/o bodies and spaces. While the term "queer" is problematic and its own history must be considered elsewhere, when thinking of Latina/o gendered relations and gender theory, the commonly used Spanish-language queer words such as *joto* (male homosexual) or *jotería* (queer community) and others such as *maricón* (gay man), *loca* (literal for crazy female but also referring to gay man female attributes), or *marimacha* and *tortillera* (leabian), to mention a few, have expanded and transformed the Latina/o theories of gender. *Tortillera* is one of the most commonly used slang words in Spain and Latin America for lesbians: it symbolically alludes to women making love as analogous to the act of making tortillas. The representation of lesbian desire is imagined in the "clapping" of the hands that traditionally occurs when making corn tortillas. Moreover, this queer world in translation elucidates the sites of Anzaldúa's identification of El Mundo Zurdo, "the left-handed world" where women of color, the queer, the poor, and the physically challenged find a safe contact zone.

If language is one of the most powerful means through which the queer Latina/o body can be imagined, sexism and gender discrimination are perpetrated and reproduced also through linguistic transgressions. For example, the use of Latina/o is itself a feminist practice upholding discursive notions of identity while surpassing masculinist linguistic forms. Understandably, the split a/o in Latina/o identity differentiates the feminine from the masculine while subverting forms commonly and awkwardly used (Latino/a; Latino women; Latino/as); however, the binary relation is itself implicitly marked. Most recently, the gender neutral "Latinx" has rapidly made its way, not only in academic discourse but in mainstream media platforms. Similar to Latina/o, Latinx is a pan-ethnic label typically used to describe people of Latin American and Caribbean descent. While "Latinx" seeks to end the gendered designations in the Spanish language, replacing "Latino" and "Latina" with a term that theoretically includes both genders, it pertains to represent nonconforming and non-binary people, including transgender people. Thus the understanding of Latinx brings attention to how heteronormative linguistic practices can be oppressive and exclusionary to nonconforming people whose gender identity and expression does not fit traditional binary representations.

The argument against the use of the term "Latinx" has considered it as a "blatant form of linguistic imperialism." In "The Argument against the Use of the Term 'Latinx,'" Gilbert Guerra and Gilbert Orbea insist that they do not have any prejudice toward nonconforming or non-binary people but that this term is a "misguided desire to forcibly change the language we and millions of people around the world speak, to the detriment of all."[43] Under this transformative language system, according to them, other words will have a negative impact: "Words such as latinos, hermanos, and niños would be converted into latinxs, hermanxs, and niñxs respectively."[44] Although the authors' argument does not consider US Latinos and Latinas who only speak English, their critique is an attack on the linguistic resistance implicit in "Latinx," which deconstructs the "standard" Spanish. According to them, the term serves "as an American way to erase the Spanish language" and that the action of erasing gender in Spanish would erase the Spanish language itself because essentially it is a gendered language.[45] The authors fail to recognize that identity markers, like culture (and language), gender, and sexuality, are not fixed categories. Latina/o gender roles and sexual identities, like US Latino/a culture in general, are far more fluid and heterogeneous than generally assumed. These categories are never static; like people, they are in constant process.

Conversely, in response to Guerra and Orbea's oppositional views, in "The Case FOR 'Latinx': Why Intersectionality Is Not a Choice," María R. Scharrón-del Río and Alan A. Aja respond to their argument. While considering that their disagreement is extremely problematic, they believe that their position is a "symptom of unexamined privilege and internalized colonization," implying "that our Latinx identity is so frail that without protecting the integrity of the language of our colonizers, we risk losing the main instrument of colonization that still binds many of us."[46] As clearly explained in their counter-position, the use of the signifier "Latinx" aims to move beyond the masculine-centric "Latino" and the gender inclusive but binary embedded "Latina." Latinx provides a way to avoid choosing a gender for a group or an unknown individual, much like using singular "they" avoids the choice between "he" or "she" in English. Both are gaining steam in a time when America is rethinking gender and whatever boundaries might come with it. The transformative knowledge embedded in Latinx can be identified as a form of transculturation. If mestizaje is itself understood as a form of transculturation, Latinx can be used as method to demystify certain kinds of normative practices and to recognize the continuing influence of cultural difference and hybrid identities.[47]

# CONCLUSION

If we are not born, but rather we can become, to echo Simone de Beauvoir's formulations made in her *Second Sex* (1949), the difference between sex and gender is essential.[48] This must distinguish gender as an aspect of identity gradually developed and never fixed. This distinction has been crucial in feminist thinking that has centralized the debate between biological determinism and social constructionism. Essentialists usually rely on biological determinism, believing that a group's biological or genetic makeup shapes its social experience. In this instance, "sex" is typically associated with biology, where bodies are classified into two categories, male and female. Alternatively, social constructionism tells us that gender (and other categories such as race, sexuality, class) is the result of subject interpretation shaped by our environments. In this context, categories like "woman," "man," "black," "white," and "Latina/o" or "Latinx" are concepts that have changed and reproduced through historical processes within institutions and cultures. For women of Latina American heritage, "becoming" a Latina in the United States is to invoke not only the contradictions caused by conquest, annexation, and migration but also the complexity of heterogeneity that continues to construe identity formations as a result of fluid processes that are never static nor absolute. For associate justice of the US Supreme Court Sonia Sotomayor, becoming a Latina has been an experience connected to her ethnic pride as a US Puerto Rican:

> I became a Latina by the way I love and live my life. My family showed me by their example how wonderful and vibrant life is and how wonderful and magical it is to have a Latina soul. They taught me to love being a Puertorriqueña and to love America and value its lesson that great things could be achieved if one works for it.[49]

As the first Latina (and third woman) to hold her position as an associate justice of the Supreme Court, Sotomayor identifies as a Nuyorican, "born and bred New Yorker of Puerto Rican-born parents who came to the states during World War II."[50] The above passage is part of the text from the Judge Mario G. Olmos Memorial Lecture in 2001, delivered at the University of California at Berkeley School of Law. During her 2009 confirmation hearings, she was challenged for having speculated in this lecture that a "wise Latina" could see issues through a special and useful lens: "I would hope that a wise Latina woman with the richness of her experiences would more often than not reach a better conclusion than a white male who hasn't lived that life."[51] In her view, gender and ethnicity should matter for the progress of other women and other Latinas who need someone of high authority to be a visible role model who can inspire others. In particular, her view is badly needed as the twenty-first century unfolds and the effects of Trumpism continue to dehumanize women, Latinx, and immigrants. Women like Sotomayor join the ranks of Antonia Novello, Ellen Ochoa, and Maria Teresa Kumar, among others, whose success stories and public records have contributed to the visibility of Latinas in US society. While in 1990 Antonia Novello became the first Latina appointed as US Surgeon General, Ellen Ochoa is the first Latina to go into space and to serve as director of NASA's Johnson Space Center. In addition, as the founding president and CEO of *Voto Latino*, Maria Teresa Kumar was named one of the ten most powerful women in Washington, DC, by *Elle Magazine* in 2013. She has also been credited as a driving force in the national elections.

Conversely, Latina visibility, as it has been slowly evolving after the cinematic portrayal of Selena by Jennifer Lopez, Frida Kahlo by Salma Hayek, and Ana by America Ferrera (in *Real Women Have Curves*), represents feminine/feminist genealogies invested in the proliferation of cultural difference. In some ways, they have been able to transgress the "othering" practices of Hollywood's hegemonic culture and offer positive models for negotiating Latina identity as the product of cultural awareness. First, Lopez's and Hayek's presence in mainstream pop culture has undoubtedly broken some barriers for Latinas in mainstream popular culture. Their brown, curvaceous bodies deconstruct Hollywood's standards of beauty as well. Due to media hype, Lopez is especially known for her curvaceous backside, and she has used this "othering" practice of Hollywood to her advantage—using her sexuality to gain publicity and to sell her movies, music videos, and albums. In fact, Lopez has become the first Latina actress to have a lead role in a major Hollywood film since Rita Hayworth, and the highest-paid Latina actress in Hollywood's history. As a US Latina, Lopez appeals to a crossover audience. She has parlayed her success in the movies into an equally flourishing music career as well as lucrative business enterprises that include a fashion line, jewelry, perfumes, and scents.

In contrast, as a recent emigrant, Hayek often speaks of the hardships in "conquering" the film industry in the United States. Born in Coatzacoalcos, Veracruz, Mexico, Hayek came to the United States to seek fame and fortune in 1991 after a successful career in Mexico as a soap opera actress in the 1980s. However, Hayek consistently faces the dilemma of finding apt roles in Hollywood. She spoke about this candidly: "To begin with, I am foreign... Next I'm Mexican, and the Mexicans are probably the least welcome people in this country. On top of that, I'm a woman. And then, on top of it all, someone handed me the sex-symbol situation."[52] Hayek's quest to "conquer" Hollywood and her cultural specificity as a Mexican immigrant made her even more determined to make a film about Frida Kahlo's life and to play the title role. This movie is very personal to Hayek: "I want to tell this story about my country and my people. For a couple of decades, Mexico was an important center where great people from the arts and politics gravitated. I want to remind the world of that."[53] While Lopez and Hayek embody genealogies of representation that posit the Latina subjectivity as product of diverse processes, one as a US Latina of Puerto Rican descent and the other as a Mexican immigrant, dramatist Josefina López, who is a self-described all-around *chingona* (a tough independent woman), offers yet another distinctive way of negotiating Latina identity. Her play, *Real Women Have Curves* (1988), adapted into a film directed by Patricia Cardoso (HBO, 2002), is a symbol of hope for young Latinas. While the movie explores with humor the lives of hard-working immigrants in East Los Angeles, it is the story of the main protagonist Ana (played by America Ferrera) that is most relevant here.[54]

US Latina contemporary contributions in the formation of a literary canon are deeply rooted within cultural values and traditions, while critiquing the repressive, patriarchal elements of that tradition. Like Gloria Anzaldúa's new mestiza, Latina writers take inventory of their history, attempting to break with oppressive traditions of their experience as border subjects. Attempts to understand Latina literature have continually interrogated the politics of language, subject, and identity constructions. Do Latinas write in English, Spanish, or Spanglish or a combination of all three? Do you need to be a writer of Latin American heritage to be considered a Latina writer? Since many Latina authors are bilingual and write in English or Spanish (or they use both languages), there are no simple answers to these questions. As a result of diversity and multilingualism, the incorporation of the literature of Latinas into US college curriculums has a problematic history. While English departments were inclined to shy away from writers using Spanish words, Spanish departments were reluctant to teach texts written partially or totally in English. Its bilingualism was the pretext for both departments to dismiss it. Thus Latina literature in the United States was unheard of in the American literary canon until the late 1980s when authors such as Sandra Cisneros, Cherríe Moraga, Julia Álvarez, Gloria Anzaldúa, Cristina García, Ana Castillo, Helena María Viramontes, and Esmeralda Santiago, to mention a few, started publishing their works with small presses. The book *The House on Mango Street* (1984) by Sandra Cisneros, for example, had sold twenty thousand copies when it was only available from Arte Público in Houston. After the book was reprinted by Vintage Contemporaries (1991), it would sell well over a half million copies.

For many decades, Latina writers/theorists have underscored the significance of women's multiple subjectivities, paying attention to the intersections of race, class, sexuality, and gender. The intersectional method has contributed to generate theoretical spaces to critique sexism, homophobia, racism, and economic marginalization. In this context, the tools of intersectionality have been vital in demonstrating how theory can inform practice, exposing the complexities of women's experiences who are subjugated to more than one axis of oppression. Latinas sought the need for self-affirmation, insisting that their experiences have to be understood in particular contexts and histories. Their exclusion from both, ethnic nationalists and white-dominated women's movements, has inspired Latinas to create spaces that articulate a feminist consciousness in solidarity with third world women in the United States. This act of solidarity is crucial in the Trump era, and it should be about more than ending sexism. Especially as it becomes apparent that for every two steps forward this country takes three back, Latinas—writers, activists, working-class intellectuals, dreamers, and undocumented migrants—must work in solidarity with other women, queers, and Latinxs, to dismantle the interrelated systems of oppression that affect every one of us differently. How will solidarity help us further develop the practice and theory of intersectionality? How can the repercussions of Trump's election strengthen the potential for cross-movement coalition building? These questions can be used as markers to further imagine where the interdisciplinarity of women, gender, and sexuality—in relation to Latina/o studies—should be headed.

## NOTES

1. Judith Butler, *Gender Trouble and the Subversion of Identity* (New York: Routledge, 1990), 24–25.
2. Shulamith Firestone, *The Dialectic of Sex: The Case for Feminist Revolution* (New York: Farrar, Straus and Giroux, 2003), 8–10. Written by Canadian radical feminist over a few

months when Firestone was twenty-five, the book has been described as a classic of feminist thought. In this edition, the author notes that the book remains unrevised since its original publication in 1970.
3. The Don Juan story was rewritten in many languages. The French dramatist Molière wrote his own version of the Don Juan story in a play *Dom Juan, ou Le Festin de Pierre* (Don Juan, or the Feast of Statue, 1665). The Italian version, Don Giovanni, an opera in two acts by Wolfgang Amadeus Mozart (libretto by Lorenzo da Ponte, 1787), has been recognized as one of the greatest operas.
4. Octavio Paz, *The Labyrinth of Solitude and the Other Mexico*, trans. Lysander Kemp et al. (New York: Grove Weidenfeld), 81. The verb "chingar" literally translates as "fuck." As a Mexican cultural signifier, however, the word is used in many different contexts. Paz used this term in his book as a marker of a colonized people.
5. Paz, *The Labyrinth of Solitude*, 82.
6. Américo Paredes, *Folklore and Culture on the Texas-Mexico Border* (Austin: University of Texas Press), 215.
7. Paz, *The Labyrinth of Solitude*, 86.
8. Gloria Anzaldúa, *Borderlands/La Frontera: The New Mestiza* (San Francisco: Spinsters/Aunt Lute, 1987), 30.
9. In Mexico and in other countries the notion of *malinchismo* applies to all those who feel an attraction to foreign cultures and disregard for their own culture. To be a traitor is to be a *malinchista*.
10. Anzaldúa, *Borderlands/La Frontera*, 31.
11. Norma Alarcón, "Traddutora, Traditora: A Paradigmatic Figure of Chicana Feminism," *Cultural Critique*, no. 13 (1989): 61.
12. Alarcón, "Traddutora, Traditora," 62.
13. The legend of La Llorona has a universal dimension: she has been linked to the "White Woman" of the Germanic and Slavic tradition, the Lorelei, and, of course, the banshee. The trope of the woman who kills her children after being betrayed by her lover and discarded for a woman of higher status has also roots in the Greek tradition in the legend of Medea and Jason.
14. Anzaldúa, *Borderlands/La Frontera*, 47.
15. Irene Lara, "Goddess of the Américas in the Decolonial Imaginary: Beyond the Virtuous Virgen/Pagan Puta Dichotomy," *Feminist Studies* 34, no. 1–2 (2008): 103.
16. Amanda Nolacea Harris and Rolando Romero, eds., *Feminism, Nation and Myth: La Malinche* (Houston, TX: Arte Público Press, 2005), ix.
17. Carmen Tafolla, "La Malinche," in *Infinite Divisions: An Anthology of Chicana Literature*, Tey Diana Rebolledo and Eliana S. Riverso, eds. (Tucson: The University of Arizona Press, 1993), 199.
18. Most of her biographers, based on the assertions of the author herself, have erroneously dated her birth as 1651. As pointed out correctly in Wikipedia, she was baptized in 1651 (December 2) and described on the baptismal certificates as "a daughter of the Church."
19. Alan S. Trueblood, *A Sor Juana Anthology* (Cambridge, MA: Harvard University Press, 1988), 111.
20. The *Respuesta a Sor Filotea*, was written in 1691 as a response to a critique of the Bishop of Puebla included along with the publication of Sor Juana's "Carta Atenagórica" ("Letter Worthy of Athena"). In the "Respuesta" Sor Juana defends her right to devote to secular and artistic endeavors, such as the production of love poems and dramatic pieces, as well

as her right to study and develop intellectual pursuits as a woman in New Spain during the second half of the seventeenth century. Consult a critical edition and bilingual edition of the "Respuesta" in *Sor Juana Inés de la Cruz: The Answer/La Respuesta, Including a Selection of Poems* by Electa Arenal and Amanda Powell (Feminist Press, 1994).

21. Melanie Byam, "The Modernization of Resistance: Latin American Women Since 1500," *Undergraduate Review* 4 (2008), 147, http://vc.bridgew.edu/undergrad_rev/vol4/iss1/26.

22. Consult the book written in Spanish about the contributions of Rita Cetina by Piedad Peniche-Rivero: *La Siempreviva y el Instituto Literario de Niñas: Una cuna del feminismo mexicano 1846–1908* (México: Instituto Nacional de estudios históricos de las revoluciones de México, 2015).

23. For more information about the ideas of González de Fanning, consult the essay "Concerning the Education of Women," in *Women in Latin American History* (Los Angeles: UCLA Latin American Center Publication, 1980) and "Teresa González del Real de Fanning" in *Escritoras latinoamericanas del diecinueve* (colección virtual, 2015), http://eladd.org/autoras-ilustres/teresa-gonzalez-del-real-de-fanning/. Her most outstanding literary works consists of four romantic literary works: The novels *Ambición y abnegación* (1886) and *Regina* (1886), the novella *Indómita* (1904), and the historical novel *Roque Moreno* (1904). She also published *Lucecitas* (1893) in which she gathered a series of narrations, stories, and essays that she had published in various newspapers in Lima.

24. In "Celestina Cordero: A Black Puerto Rican Educator During the Era of Slavery," the trajectory of Celestina with regard to the difficulties she experienced in receiving the recognition she deserved as a formal educator is briefly traced. Unlike her brother, she had to confront the colonial administration and request both formal recognition as a schoolteacher and funding for her school. According to this document, she made numerous trips to the colonial administration and did not give up until she was given her title. Written by Rosario Méndez Panedas, this document was published in *Centro Voices* (Hunter College), February 21, 2019, https://centropr.hunter.cuny.edu/centrovoices/chronicles/celestina-cordero-black-puerto-rican-educator-during-era-slavery.

25. For more information about Lola Rodríguez and "La Borinqueña," consult Ilan Stavans, *The Norton Anthology of Latino Literature* (New York: W. W. Norton, 2011), 257–259.

26. In its mission statement, the US Hispanic Literary Heritage is described as "an international program to locate, preserve and disseminate Hispanic culture of the US in its written form since colonial times until 1960." Consult the project's website for more information, https://artepublicopress.com/recovery-program/.

27. Since the recent reprinting of her novels, María Amparo Ruiz de Burton (b. 1832–d. 1895) has become a key figure in the recovery of nineteenth-century Mexican American literature. Both novels, *Who Would Have Thought It?* and *The Squatter and the Don*, were reprinted as part of the series Recovering the U.S. Hispanic Literary Heritage program by Arte Público Press. Both novels were edited by Rousaura Sánchez and Beatriz Pita, who provided a well-researched historical and critical framework in their introduction and notes to the novel. Rosaura Sánchez and Beatriz Pita, *Who Would Have Thought It?* (Houston, TX: Arte Público Press, 1872, rep. 1995); Rosaura Sánchez and Beatriz Pita, *The Squatter and the Don* (Houston, TX: Arte Público Press, 1885, rep. 1997).

28. *Handbook of Texas Online*, Nancy Baker Jones, "Villegas de Magnon, Leonor," accessed March 11, 2019, http://www.tshaonline.org/handbook/online/articles/fvi19.

29. *The Rebel* is introduced and annotated by Clara Lomas, who is also the discoverer of the text and other works by Leonor Villegas de Magnon. This book was also published by Arte Público Press in 1994.
30. A biographical reference and fragment of *Old Spain in Our Southwest* (1936) can be found in *The Norton Anthology of Latino Lierature* cited previously (New York: W. W. Norton, 2011), 405–418.
31. The interlocking system of oppressions was introduced in a social movement context by the Combahee River Collective (CRC) in pamphlet form in 1977. The CRC was mainly a black feminist lesbian organization active in Boston from 1974 to 1980. The group was instrumental in denouncing that the white feminist movement was not addressing their particular needs. They are perhaps best known for developing the CRC Statement, a significant document in the history of contemporary black feminism. This document is also included in the pages of *This Bridge Called My Back*. They conclude their CRC statement with the following: "As Black feminists and Lesbians we know that we have a very definite revolutionary task to perform and we are ready for the lifetime of work and struggle before us" (218). Cherríe Moraga and Gloria Anzaldúa, eds., *This Bridge Called My Back: Writings by Radical Women of Color* (New York: Kitchen Table, 1981).
32. Moraga and Anzaldúa, *This Bridge Called My Back*, xxiv.
33. Moraga and Anzaldúa, *This Bridge Called My Back*, 23.
34. Hanisch's essay focused on men's power and women's oppression. The slogan appeared in the anthology *Notes From the Second Year: Women's Liberation in 1970*. Therefore, she is often credited with coining the phrase. Later, she wrote in an introduction to the 2006 reprinting of the essay that she did not come up with the title. She believed "The Personal Is Political" was selected by the editors of the anthology, Shulamith Firestone and Anne Koedt, who were both feminists involved with the group New York Radical Feminists. Consult this site for more information regarding Hanisch's disclaimer: http://www.carol-hanisch.org/CHwritings/PIP.html.
35. Moraga and Anzaldúa, *This Bridge Called My Back*, 151.
36. The book *Telling to Live* introduces a multigenerational group of Latinas who negotiate their place and identity in US society at the beginning of the twenty-first century. The book includes a diverse group of women, representing the heterogeneity of US Latinas: Puerto Rican, Chicana, Native American, Mexican, Cuban, Dominican, Sephardic, mixed heritage, and Central American. Calling themselves the Latina Feminist Group, the book includes writings by Luz del Alba Acevedo, Norma Alarcón, Celia Alvarez, Ruth Behar, Rina Benmayor, Norma E. Cantú, Daisy Cocco De Filippis, Gloria Holguín Cuádraz, Liza Fiol-Matta, Yvette Flores-Ortiz, Inés Hernández-Avila, Aurora Levins Morales, Clara Lomas, Iris Ofelia López, Mirtha N. Quintanales, Eliana Rivero, Caridad Souza, and Patricia Zavella.
37. Aurora Levins Morales, "Certified Organic Intellectual," in *Telling to Live: Latina feminist Testimonios*, ed. The Latina Feminist Group (Durham, NC: Duke University Press, 2001), 32.
38. Aurora Levins Morales, "My Name Is This Story," in *Telling to Live*, 103.
39. As the co-founder of the United Farm Workers in 1962, Huerta contributed with César Chávez to transform the US labor movement, making impressive gains for its members, including salary increases, medical insurance, and paid vacations. Most people associate those gains and the first national farmworkers' union mainly with the late Chávez. While Huerta was only twenty-five years old when she became the first woman to sit on the

UFW executive board, her contributions were only recognized in the 1990s by Chicana and Latina feminists.

40. In May 1971, over six hundred Chicanas gathered together in Houston, Texas, for The First National Chicana Conference. Chicanas gathered successfully in support of several resolutions, including calls for legalization of abortion; equal access to education; the establishment of child-care centers; and the abolition of traditional marriages. Despite their efforts, women did not find their voices and participation welcome within the Chicano National Movement.

41. Cherríe Moraga, *The Last Generation: Prose and Poetry* (Boston: South End Press, 1993), 157. The Adelitas, also known as soldaderas, or female soldiers, describe women who contributed to many aspects of the Mexican Revolution (1910–1924). These women worked as nurses, food providers, lovers, spies, messengers, and fighters. Consult my pieces: "Soldaderas and the Staging of the Mexican Revolution," *The Drama Review* 42, no. 1, (1998): 105–107; and "My Love Affairs with Soldaderas" (2015), https://www.kcet.org/shows/artbound/my-love-affairs-with-soldaderas.

42. Edna Acosta Belén, "Unveiling and Preserving a Puerto Rican Historical Memory," in *Through the Eyes of Rebel Women: The Young Lords, 1969–1976*, ed. Iris Morales (New York: Red Sugarcane Press, 2016), 6.

43. Gilbert Guerra and Gilbert Orbea, "The Argument Against the Use of the Term 'Latinx,'" *The Phoenix: An Independent Campus Newspaper of Swarthmore Since 1881*, November 19, 2015, 1, https://swarthmorephoenix.com/2015/11/19/the-argument-against-the-use-of-the-term-latinx/.

44. Guerra and Orbea, "The Argument Against the Use of the Term 'Latinx,'" 1.

45. Guerra and Orbea, "The Argument Against the Use of the Term 'Latinx,'" 1.

46. María R. Scharrón-del Río, and Alan A. Aja, "The Case FOR 'Latinx': Why Intersectionality is not a Choice," *Latino Rebels* (December 2015), http://www.latinorebels.com/2015/12/05/the-case-for-latinx-why-intersectionality-is-not-a-choice/.

47. The mestizaje/Latinx analogy has been recently construed in *The Latinx Revolution in US Culture, Society, and Politics* (Verso, 2018) by Ed Morales. I support his argument about the epistemology of Latinx identities and cultures, which are tied to the history of mestizaje and cultural hybridization.

48. *The Second Sex* was originally published and written in French (*Le Deuxième Sexe*, 1949) by the French existentialist Simone de Beauvoir. The book is considered as a major work of feminist philosophy and the starting point of second-wave feminism.

49. Sonia Sotomayor, "A Latina Judge's Voice," *New York Times*, May 14, 2009, https://www.nytimes.com/2009/05/15/us/politics/15judge.text.html. This is a reprinted version of Sotomayor's lecture, which was originally published in the Spring 2002 issue of *Berkeley La Raza Law Journal*, a symposium issue entitled "Raising the Bar: Latino and Latina Presence in the Judiciary and the Struggle for Representation." When she gave this lecture (2001), she was an appeals court judge.

50. Sotomayor, "A Latina Judge's Voice."

51. Sotomayor, "A Latina Judge's Voice."

52. Laura Winters, "She's Got to Have It" (interview with Salma Hayek), *Elle*, 124.

53. Stephen Farber, "Frida," in *The Book of Los Angeles: A Mind of its Own* (Los Angeles: Real Communications, 2000), 28.

54. Josefina López, *Real Women Have Curves* (Woodstock: Dramatic Publishing, 1996). While the play had been produced numerous times since the late 1980s with great success, the

movie also received astounding accolades. It was honored at the 2002 Sundance Film Festival with the Audience Award and with the Youth Prize at the 2002 San Sebastian International Film Festival. George LaVoo and Josefina López wrote the screenplay adaptation: *Real Women Have Curves*, dir. Patricia Cardoso (Los Angeles: HBO, 2002).

## Bibliography

Acosta, Katie L. *Amigas y Amantes: Sexually Nonconforming Latinas Negotiate Family*. New Brunswick, NJ: Rutgers University Press, 2013.

Alarcón, Norma, Ana Castillo, and Cherríe Moraga, eds. *The Sexuality of Latinas*. Berkeley: Third Woman Press, 1989.

Arce, Julissa. *Someone Like Me: How One Undocumented Girl Fought for Her American Dream 2018*. New York: Hachette Book Group, 2018.

Asencio, Marysol, ed. *Latina/o Sexualities: Probing Powers, Passions, Practices, and Policies*. Brunswick, NJ: Rutgers University Press, 2009.

Blackwell, Maylei. *¡Chicana Power! Contested Histories of Feminism in the Chicano Movement*. Austin: University of Texas Press, 2011.

Blake, Debra. *Chicana Sexuality and Gender: Cultural Refiguring in Literature, Oral History, and Art*. Durham, NC: Duke University Press, 2008.

Corrales, Javier, and Mario Pecheny, eds. *The Politics of Sexuality in Latin America: A Reader on Lesbian, Gay, Bisexual, and Transgender Rights*. Pittsburgh: University of Pittsburgh Press, 2010.

Cuevas, T. Jackie, Larissa M. Mercado-López, and Sonia Saldívar-Hull, eds. *El Mundo Zurdo 4: Selected Works from the 2013 Meeting of the Society for the Study of Gloria Anzaldúa*. San Francisco: Aunt Lute Books, 2015.

Fitch, Melissa. *Side Dishes: Latina American Women, Sex, and Cultural Production*. New Brunswick, NJ: Rutgers University Press, 2009.

Gaspar de Alba, Alicia. *Velvet Barrios: Popular Culture & Chicana/o Sexualities*. New York: Palgrave Macmillan, 2003.

Keating, AnaLouise, and Gloria González-López, eds. *Bridging: How Gloria Anzaldúa's Life and Work Transformed Our Own*. Austin: University of Texas Press, 2011.

Kellogg, Susan. *Weaving the Past: A History of Latin America's Indigenous Women from the Prehispanic Period to the Present*. New York: Oxford University Press, 2005.

Kroger, Joseph, and Patrizia Granziera, eds. *Aztec Goddesses and Christian Madonnas: Images of the Divine Feminine in Mexico*. New York: Routledge, 2012.

Mariano, Katherine M. *Feminism for the Americas: The Making of an International Human Rights Movement*. Chapel Hill: University of North Carolina Press, 2019.

Martínez, Elizabeth. *De Colores Means All of Us: Latina Views for a Multi-Colored Century*. New York: Verso Books, 2017.

Merrin, Stephanie, ed. *Feminist Perspectives on Sor Juana Inés de la Cruz*. Detroit: Wayne State University Press, 1991.

Morales, Iris, ed. *Latinas: Struggles & Protests in 21st Century*. New York: Red Sugarcane Press, 2018.

Pastrana, Antonio Jr., Juan Battle, and Angelique Harris, eds. *An Examination of Latinx LGBT Populations Across the United States: Intersections of Race and Sexuality*. New York: Palgrave Macmillan, 2017.

Perpetusa-Seva, Inmaculada, and Lourdes Torres, eds. *Tortilleras: Hispanic & U.S. Latina Lesbian Expression*. Philadelphia: Temple University Press, 2003.

Pitts, Andrea J., Mariana Ortega, and José Medina, eds. *Theories of the Flesh: Latinx and Latin American Feminisms, Transformation, and Resistance*. New York: Oxford University Press, 2019.

Rohrleitner, Marion, and Sarah E. Ryan, eds. *Dialogues Across Diasporas: Women Writers, Scholars, and Activists of Africana and Latina Descent in Conversation*. Lanham, MD: Lexington Books, 2013.

Rueda Esquibel, Catrióna. *With Her Machete in Her Hand: Reading Chicana Lesbians*. Austin: University of Texas Press, 2006.

Sampaio, Anna. *Terrorizing Latina/o Immigrants: Race, Gender, and Immigration Policy Post-9/11*. Philadelphia: Temple University Press, 2015.

Santos, Cristina. *Unbecoming Female Monsters: Witches, Vampires, and Virgins*. Lanham, MD: Lexington Books, 2017.

Schwindt-Bayer, Leslie A., ed. *Gender and Representation in Latin America*. New York: Oxford University Press, 2018.

Sigal, Pete. *The Flower and the Scorpion: Sexuality and Ritual in Early Nahua Culture*. Durham, NC: Duke University Press, 2011.

Sotomayor, Sonia. *My Beloved World*. New York: Vintage Books, 2013.

Trujillo, Carla, ed. *Chicana Lesbians: The Girls Our Mothers Warned Us About*. Berkeley, CA: Third Woman Press, 1991.

Valdés, Vanessa K. *Oshun's Daughters: The Search for Womanhood in the Americas*. Albany: State University of New York Press, 2015.

Villalon, Roberta. *Violence Against Latina Immigrants: Citizenship, Inequality, and Community*. New York: New York University Press, 2010.

CHAPTER 8

# LATINO URBANISM AND THE GENTRIFYING CITY

ERUALDO R. GONZÁLEZ

## Latina/o Population Growth

The Latina/o population in the twenty-first century continues to be highly visible in regions and states with a long history of immigration. The Southwestern states, such as California, Arizona, and Texas, continue to be home to the largest block of Latina/os and those of Mexican origin, and Puerto Ricans remain most visible in New York, Florida, and Illinois. Florida remains home to the largest Latina/o community of Cuban ancestry. But in the 2000s and 2010s, the Latina/o population has ballooned in regions and cities that historically did not have a significant Latina/o presence, many of them in the South.[1]

A severe shortage of affordable housing and low-paying jobs in cities with a history of Latina/o enclaves has driven the emergence of new ones in cities and towns with little history of Latina/o communities. For example, Census data show that between 1980 and 2000, the Latina/o population in Raleigh-Durham, North Carolina, grew 1,180 percent while Atlanta's Latina/o population grew 995 percent and Orlando's 859 percent. New England states have also seen an uptick in Latina/o residents, such as Puerto Ricans and Dominicans.[2] Research encapsulates these trends in observing that 75 percent of Latina/o growth in 1990–2000 occurred in neighborhoods where Latina/os were a minority in 1990.[3] These demographic growth patterns help tell the story of why over half of America's large cities in the largest metropolitan areas are now non-white.[4]

# Income Disparities and Latina/o Communities

The United States has experienced a widening gap in income and wealth since at least the 1980s made worse by the 2007–2009 Great Recession. The living standards of working-class and working-poor people have declined as a result, and populations living in major US cities and surrounding metropolitan areas have been hit the hardest by this class polarization.[5]

The restructuring economy, from heavy industry to professional and personal services, offers jobs that do not pay a living wage but are creating socioeconomic change and economic inequality in major metro and major city areas. Often, those who have access to high-paying jobs are those who tend to be of the "creative class," a class that includes highly educated and highly skilled people whose main tasks are to create ideas and technology, such as those in science and engineering, information technology, architecture and design, arts and entertainment, health care, and finance.[6] But service jobs, most of which do not pay enough to support individuals or families, let alone afford adequate housing, are heavily immigrant dependent.[7] Almost two-thirds of workers earning minimum wage or less in 2015 were employed in service occupations.[8] Some of the most common service jobs are food-service/restaurant, hotel hospitality, domestic work, janitorial, retail, gardening, construction, and factory and warehouse work, many of which are tied to global manufacturing enterprises.[9] Major cities, then, increasingly have mainly two economies: one for highly paid people and one for poorly paid people.

Latina/o families are a growing sector of the US working class.[10] Recent 2017 data on US Latina/os tell this story. For instance, the Pew Research Center shows the median annual household income in 2015 dollars for Latina/o adults sixteen and older was $44,800. This contrasts with $61,000 among non-Hispanic white households. The same report shows even more alarming economic hardships. For example, 21.9 percent of Latina/os lived in poverty compared to 9.8 percent of non-Hispanic whites. At the same time, Latina/o immigrants as a whole are poorer than US-born Latina/os generally. The Latina/o immigrant median annual household income was $41,000. Poverty is also a major issue in the general Latina/o population. Just over 20 percent of Latina/o immigrants and 22.5 percent of US-born Latina/os live in poverty.[11] Cumulatively, this reveals a significant working-class and working-poor portrait among Latina/os.

Latina/os as a whole have low levels of homeownership and represent a major portion of renters. In 2015, the national homeownership average in the United States was 63.1 percent, and Latina/o homeownership was about 20 percent lower, at 45.3 percent.[12] As with income, Latina/o immigrants have lower rates of homeownership than US-born Latina/os, 43.5 percent and 47.2 percent respectively. These numbers would indicate that the majority of Latina/os are part of the large and growing "renter nation" across the country that saw an uptick after the 2007–2009 recession in which 8.7 million more people in the United States were renting in 2016 (about 43 million) than in 2006, representing an increasing share of 5.4 percent.[13] Given the income trends noted earlier and these housing trends, we could expect tremendous disparities between Latina/o and white homeownership. Indeed, Latina/os are almost twice as likely as whites to rent their dwelling.[14] In fact, in 2016, for example, 54 percent of Latino/a households were renting compared with 28 percent of whites.

Extrapolating from Latina/os' class position, it is clear that homeowners and renters alike face more extreme housing burdens than white people. A higher percentage of their income goes toward housing expenses than an already high national average, which effectively reduces discretionary income. The Pew Charitable Trust reports that 38 percent of all renter households in the United States were "rent burden" in 2018, which means they spent more than 30 percent of pretax income on rent, thereby significantly reducing their discretionary income on basic needs, such as food and transportation. Such rent burden is a threat to housing stability and general quality of life for families and individuals. The Trust goes on to say that "Rent-burdened households have higher eviction rates, increased financial fragility, and wider use of social safety net programs, compared with other renters and homeowners."[15]

The potential negative implications of income and housing hardships run deeper for Latina/os in large cities and metro areas that are gentrifying.[16] For example, the four metro areas with the highest Latina/o population are Los Angeles–Long Beach–Anaheim (California), at 45 percent of the population; New York–Newark–Jersey City (NY-NU-PA), where Latina/os comprise 23.9 percent; Miami–Fort Lauderdale–West Palm Beach (Florida), where Latina/os comprise 43.3 percent; and Houston–The Woodlands–Sugar Land (Texas), where they are 36.4 percent of the population.[17] The Pew Research Center "class calculator" shows that on average 32 percent (range 22 percent to 38 percent) of adult households of four in these metro areas are working class.[18]

Taken together, it is becoming clear that cities and their industrial economies that once served as gateways for lesser-skilled immigrants moving toward upward mobility now have become what political scientists Orr and Morel call "large repositories for workers with lessened economic prospects."[19] One implication of the restructuring economy and large and growing number, as well as the class status of Latina/os in the United States, is that these families will likely struggle to live comfortably and securely and to avoid displacement if they are living within gentrifying areas.

# DEVELOPMENT MODELS AND GENTRIFICATION

There are three prevailing development models of choice for revitalization in the United States that are common in large cities and metro areas, and their use has been shown to leave people of low socioeconomic positioning vulnerable to gentrification. The models are New Urbanism (NU), Transit Oriented Development (TOD), and Creative Class (CC).[20]

Formed in 1993, the Congress for the New Urbanism (CNU) coined "New Urbanism" in the early 1990s, a movement that emphasizes market-rate housing and urban design to create dense, mixed-use, and pedestrian-friendly housing for people so they can conveniently walk to stores, restaurants, and other amenities, with work-live lofts often the prime example of housing.[21] CNU began with a strong desire to refashion in cities traditional ways of planning that are believed are not workable. We see this in the CNU Charter, which proclaims: "We dedicate ourselves to reclaiming our homes, blocks, streets, parks, neighborhoods, districts, towns, cities, regions, and environment."[22] New Urbanists promote design that is intended to foster security for residents and community interactions in public spaces, and the approach is built on an alleged premise that such redevelopment respects the local history, culture, and regional character.[23] The CNU includes a group of developers, urban designers, architects, bankers, historic preservationists, and government officials, all of whom came together to form the New Urbanism movement. From the start, the CNU explicitly made statements committing to market rate development and reinventing neighborhoods to look and function like "traditional" American master-planned neighborhoods, mainly citing economically prosperous and white neighborhoods, such as Princeton, New Jersey.[24]

Transit Oriented Development (TOD) models intend to reduce the number of people driving and increase the use of public transit within compact, pedestrian, and transit-friendly areas in specific neighborhoods.[25] It is intended to both serve residents who live in such spaces and regional consumers and employees looking to travel to the downtown nearby. The TOD connection to NU development is clear from the point of view that NU also calls for redevelopment that leverages a network of trains and related transit that connect transit-oriented neighborhoods to commercial and downtown districts.

The Creative Class (CC), or Creative City, approach to redevelopment emphasizes economic development and cultural programming that targets "the creative class," an economic class type that also tends to have social prestige. Charles Landry coined the idea "creative city" to encourage city authorities to direct redevelopment resources toward activities that support creativity, culture, and design by the start of the twenty-first century.[26] Richard Florida built on Landry with his "creative class" concept.[27] Through his consulting work with city leaders and economic developers, he argued that cities required a new economic identity in the postindustrial era focused on creative economies and people. This involved local government in creating and supporting public policies designed to attract the creative class, a broad group of people with skills in the arts, design, technology, music, engineering, software development, business, and education fields. He added that cities, especially central cities, could attract the creative class by rehabilitating older buildings and developing mixed-use projects and relatively affordable housing for this group. He further argued that the creative class has a preference for living and spending time in places that have cultural programming, art districts, technological development, and are accepting of ethnic, cultural, and sexual orientation diversity. By 2014, Florida and Mellander estimated that 35 percent of the workforce the United States was in the creative class.[28]

In summary, these development models gained traction in the United States in the 1990s and early 2000s and emphasized revitalization for middle-class and privileged groups. As the next section will describe, scholarship tied to Latino studies is only beginning to scrutinize the role of these models on Latina/o working-class lives and the spaces that are familiar to many within this community.

## A Brief Overview of Latino Studies–Urban Planning Scholarship

Latino studies is a field of study that has evolved especially since the 1980s and 1990s. Generally, the first two decades, the late 1960s and early 1980s, relied heavily on historical and political analysis of capitalism, colonialism, and empire in and with Chicanas/o and Puerto Rican communities in the United States.[29] Males produced the majority of the scholarship.[30] Feminists and subsequently queer scholars especially broadened the field in the 1980s and 1990s. Scholarship explored gender and sexual orientation with additional identity formation counter-hegemonic discourses and practices.[31] By the 2000s, the field grew further to include life histories, socioeconomic and political conditions, needs, and action, cultural expressions of affirmation, the border, identities and racial formation, education, language, and cultural citizenship.[32] Progress now also meant producing scholarship with a broader range of research populations, namely Cuban, Dominican, Salvadoran, and Guatemalan, as well as additional Central and South American national-origin populations.

We are approaching 2020, and the Latino studies field continues to mature. We see reflections of this growth in the recent Latino studies readers, authoritative sources of Latino studies scholarship. *The 2011 Latino Condition: A Critical Reader* (2nd ed.) (Delgado and Stefancic, eds.), the 2016 *The New Latino Studies Reader: A Twenty-First Century Perspective* (Gutiérrez and Almaguer, eds.), and the 2017 *Keywords for Latina/o Studies* (Vargas, La Fountain-Stokes, and Mirabal, eds.) generally and collectively focus on racial and ethnic identifications, demography, education, work and quality of life, immigration, and gender and sexuality. These sources largely include essays from scholars trained in sociology, literature, history, and political science.

Latino studies, however, has saliently underexplored urban planning topics and theoretical perspectives. The most recent Latino studies readers noted earlier collectively reflect this gap; together, they include 185 entries, only two of which explicitly treat as their primary topic "barrio" and "housing," core concepts in urban planning scholarship.[33] This is not to say that some Latino studies scholarship does not entertain questions about urban affairs. Latino studies work that includes analysis of urban conditions examining immigrant rights, identities, inclusion, gender, and community activism typically borrows heavily from sociology and cultural studies traditions (e.g., see *Beyond El Barrio* by Pérez, Guridy, and Burgos Jr.). As a result, theoretical and topical specificity to mainstream urban planning has been largely absent in this interdisciplinary field.

One reason for this low urban planning scholarly production is the dismal number of Latina/o urban planning scholars who conduct Latino studies–oriented research. According to the US Department of Education's National Center for Education Statistics, sixteen Latina/os earned Research Doctorate in Urban, Community, and Regional Planning from 2012 to 2016.[34] This is low, especially when we consider that 130 whites earned this type of doctorate in the same time frame.[35] Further, while we could expect Latina/o tenure-track urban planning faculty to lead the Latino studies–urban planning scholarly output, as of 2014, Latina/os made up only 6 percent of full-time faculty in Planning Accreditation Board-accredited programs.[36] In summary, there is low Latino studies–urban planning scholarly production and few Latina/os with urban planning research doctorates.

There is some optimism ahead for Latino studies scholarship that includes urban planning frameworks, however. Around 2010, scholars of color from the Association of Collegiate Schools of Planning, the flagship academic association for planners, began initiating activities designed to increase publications on urban planning and communities of color, including Latina/os.[37] We could expect some of this scholarship to be published in Latino studies journals and edited books, or inform Latino studies scholarship generally. The next section briefly reviews the urban planning profession and state of urban planning scholarship in Latina/o communities. My hope is that it helps scholars to craft Latino studies–urban planning research agendas into 2020 and beyond.

## What Is Urban Planning?

According to the American Planning Association, the goal of urban planning

> is to maximize the health, safety, and economic well-being for all residents. This involves thinking about how we can move around our community, the businesses and attractions in our community, where we want to live, and opportunities for recreation. Most of all, planning helps create communities of lasting value.[38]

Yin describes what the professional field does and why:

> Urban planning looks at what's good and bad about a community in the present and plans ahead for how the community can maintain and improve itself in the future. A good understanding of how the community works and how it's likely to change helps make plans for the future.[39]

Urban planning, according to these sources, is, in short, about people and places, health, safety, economics, the present and the future, and written plans that take these topics into consideration to chart paths toward sustaining happiness and community benefits in neighborhoods, commercial areas, open spaces, cities, and regions.

## Latino Urbanism

Pioneering scholars from the early 2000s who examine urban planning in Latina/o communities in the United States, like David Diaz, Mike Davis, Arlene Dávila, Raul Homero Villa, Victor Valle, and Rodolfo Torres, published research that informally and collectively formed the Latino urbanism movement. Their seminal books explicitly combined critical urbanism and ethnic studies theoretical orientations. Generally, these scholars emphasized theoretical views that critique mainstream urban knowledge and ideologies and power, inequality, injustice, exclusion, racialization, and exploitation that underpin capitalist social formations within and among cities and ideas that could emancipate or lead to more equitable and just urban futures.[40] Collectively, these sources scrutinize segregation, poverty, institutional discrimination, racism, and neoliberal redevelopment in the Southwest and East Coast and with Mexican or Puerto Rican communities. As a whole, this scholarship suggests that common Latina/o community experiences with urban planning have not lived up to urban planners'and the planning profession's avowed good intentions toward the communities they interact and serve.

Diaz focuses Chicana/o, Tejana/o, and Mexicana/o social production in urban spaces in the Southwest and lambastes much of mainstream urban planning history dating to 1880.[41] He also interrogates the planning profession and dominant planning practices of the 1980s and 1990s that helped contribute to housing, economic development, open space, and environmental inequalities in the Los Angeles metropolitan area. Another of Diaz's critiques is the so-called new urbanism movement. He writes that movement leaders ignore everyday practices in the barrio and colonias that lead to normative outcomes that new urbanism promotes, such as urban sustainability and social interaction; he argues that there is nothing new about "new urbanism." *Magical Urbanism: Latinos Reinvent the U.S. Big City* (2000) by Davis gives a sweeping and affirming account of the Latinization of America. This includes providing sociodemographic data on urban, work, labor, education, and general quality of life conditions, focusing on Los Angeles and the border cities of Tijuana and El Paso. Davis provides an abundance of Latina/o demographics and gives a rather oversimplified view of Latina/o popular culture's legendary (e.g., music) influence on everyday American urbanism. Dávila's *Barrio Dreams: Puerto Ricans, Latinos, and the Neoliberal City* (2004) offers a case study of East Harlem, New York, and neoliberal gentrification (referring to the US Housing and Urban Development's 1990s Federal Empowerment Zone initiative), an economic development model for distressed urban areas, and an overview of Latina/o marketing and art as appropriation of commercial areas.

*Latino Metropolis* (2000) by Valle and Torres examines 1990s Los Angeles through a political economy framework to analyze a host of topics, including assessing demographic shifts and capitalism on class relations, labor, working conditions, policing, and media representation. The authors devote an essay to downtown community development, focusing on labor's internal fissures, struggles, and successes in obtaining a living wage ordinance for jobs stemming from the development of the Staples Center. *Barrio-Logos: Space and Place in Urban Chicano Literature and Culture* (2000) by Raúl Homero Villa focuses on Southern California during the 1950s through the 1970s and discusses place-making, policing, and displacement through urban renewal and how the grassroots, artists, and journalists have used expressive culture to oppose planning policies. He provides ideas about what building blocks produce the form and meaning of the *barrio*, which is "barrioization"—the physical regulation of space, the effect of law, and the media effect, and "barriological"—culturally affirming spatial practices within the barrio to respond to internal and external barrio forces.[42]

The Latino urbanism movement broadened within a decade. Newer topics included urban design, community participation, and transit-oriented development. Some of this work offered case studies of nontraditional living regions for Latina/os in the United States, such as the South and Midwest. For example, *Dialogos: Placemaking in Latino Communities* and *Latino Placemaking: Cultural Resilience and Strategies for Reurbanization, Immigrants and the Revitalization of Los Angeles Development and Change in MacArthur Park*, and *Latino Urbanism: Placemaking in 21st Century American Cities*, a special issue in the *Journal of Urbanism*, collectively offer case studies focused on placemaking in select traditional and newer destination Latina/o ethnic spaces, both rural and urban, emphasizing appropriation, conversion, and revitalization of the built environment, such as parks, and "Latinization" of commercial centers and older commercial corridors, claiming of rights via grassroots action and networks, and a sense of belonging through civic involvement.[43]

This literature also grew in terms of urban and community development policy. *Latino Urbanism: The Politics of Planning, Policy, and Redevelopment* (2012) by Diaz and Torres is, as noted by the editors, the first edited book to bring together writings of this growing movement with a first-of-its-kind national perspective on current urban policy in Latina/o communities. It provides a mix of contemporary and historical case studies and essays about community development and housing policy in *colonias* and *barrios*, the politics of redesigning predominantly Latinized commercial spaces into new urbanist design aesthetics, the appropriation of space by transnational border culture, and a critique of new urbanism and gentrification for their role in reducing housing affordability, cultural and social economic diversity, and primarily serving the interests of developers. My work *Latino City: Urban Planning, Politics, and the Grassroots* is a case study and critical analysis of downtown community development models that many gentrification projects in major central cities across the United States have used—new urbanism, creative class, and transit-oriented development—and of grassroots resistance to these in the Southern California large city of Santa Ana, one of the most Mexican cities in the United States and the first major city to have an all-Latina/o city council.[44]

# The Gentrifying City and Latina/os (the 1980s to 2020s)

The political economy and urban planning landscape of American cities in the last two decades of the twentieth century and first two decades of the twenty-first century has had a profound impact on Latina/o quality of life.[45] The US economy is now mainly a service economy concerned primarily with providing services based more on knowledge, information, and technology than producing goods, and this economy generally is split into two sectors: one that affords economic privilege and one that provides what Marcuse calls "economic deprivation."[46] Income and wealth continue to widen among racial and ethnic groups. As noted earlier in this chapter, a significant portion of the Latino community forms part of the economic deprivation.

We are also witnessing a type of urban deprivation that significantly impacts those already deprived economically.[47] I focus on urban deprivation that stems from gentrification and specific development models that help the gentrification process. There is a body of research examining how new urbanism, creative class, and transit-oriented models of development play a major role in the production process of gentrification in barrios and commercial centers where historically the majority of the residents and consumers are economically deprived. Not surprisingly, some of this literature includes discussing how residents and activists come together to resist gentrification and wage anti-gentrification campaigns and community organizing tactics in hopes of saving or securing affordable housing, commercial spaces, and transit options.[48] These studies as a whole take issue with economic, political, and urban planning scenarios that are overwhelmingly creating opportunities for a few and excluding the most materially deprived, underpaid, materially exploited, and insecure members of the working class.[49]

We thus can reasonably expect future Latino studies–urban planning scholarship focusing on gentrification to grow. Gentrification forces are operating most clearly across the nation in older cities of major metropolitan areas where Latina/os make up a significant proportion of the families while urban elites work to "reclaim" downtown cores and surrounding areas. In turn, I outline key urban planning, economic, and urban political trends that brought us to what I refer to as the "contemporary gentrifying city" era. I fit this era within the more traditional postindustrial period. The intention is to help frame future Latin o studies–urban planning research agendas concerned with gentrification.

The contemporary gentrifying city generally consists of the 1980s to the present 2019 (and ongoing). I build on classic gentrification definitions, defining gentrification as the unnatural transformation of a working-class area, mainly housing, commercial, and vacant, into a middle-class one via a combination of additional processes, namely displacement and remodeling or new development and infrastructure improvements; a cumulative impact is that the social character of the area changes significantly as well.[50] I add "unnatural" to the gentrification definition because my premise is that large-scale gentrification is not an inevitable phenomenon; gentrification is human-made and a matter of public policy.[51] Hartman et al. argue that working-class and poor households are displaced due to macroeconomic and urban elite forces' ability to make living, operating, or claiming rights in the area "impossible, hazardous, or unaffordable."[52] I borrow from these perspectives that mostly focus on housing to stress that gentrification also engulfs commercial areas, especially those in and around downtown cores of central cities. In these commercial situations, we can borrow from Hartman et al. to suggest that macroeconomic and urban elite forces outside of the control of businesses marketing to the working class and working poor may be making for a business operating or claiming rights or staying open in the area impossible.[53]

Before I continue discussing the contemporary gentrifying city era, I discuss briefly how it stems from prior eras and is nestled within the more commonly referred and current postindustrial era of the 1990s to present.[54] The gentrifying city era is different from its preceding era, what Orr and Morel call the "redevelopment city" of the 1940s to the 1980s.[55] After World War II, US cities were adapting to the automobile and ongoing deindustrialization. Public officials were preoccupied with defining blight, with demolishing, rehabilitating, and rebuilding downtown housing, with encouraging commercial activity, and with attempting to curtail white flight to the suburbs. Central cities were increasingly becoming service-sector oriented. As Orr and Morel write, central cities "became impoverished relative both to their prior condition and to their suburban municipalities. Cities became poorer and blacker. Soon, many cities were losing population, a significant reversal from the days of the industrial city."[56] The federal government recognized these national trends and allotted urban renewal funding and programs to mayors and city officials. Orr and Morel further point out that mayors and city officials were charged with coming up with redevelopment activities and forming coalitions to chart cities forward.[57] They did this primarily with downtown corporate interests in efforts to revitalize downtowns by restoring historic buildings, expanding transit systems, and seeking to (re)attract local and chain downtown businesses and entice more white professional middle-class residents and consumers. Mayors sought to deconcentrate growing poverty and racial and ethnic others, but with limited success; poorer and non-white residents increasingly lived in older housing stock, remaking and sustaining downtown commercial zones and forming working-class urban ethnic enclaves.[58]

While the later years of the redevelopment city era, the 1970s, are not part of the gentrifying city era, seeds were starting to grow for the political economy of urban planning that opened the door for it. While the private sector partnered with government in the redevelopment city era, we began to see "hyper-involvement" from it during the 1970s.[59] Smith (1979) argues that this private sector involvement led to massive capital investment in central cities, a phenomenon he referred to as the "return of capital to the city movement." For Marcuse (2016) the physical remodeling that comes from large-scale private investments differs from urban renewal or urban redevelopment in their traditional United States forms in that, although all are fundamentally market-driven and involve combinations of public and private actions, this physical upgrading connected with gentrification is predominantly privately undertaken, while traditional redevelopment and urban renewal are predominantly public actions (1264). He adds such physical remodeling projects are, nevertheless, typically done in combination with public actions and therefore it is crucial to emphasize that redevelopment remains a matter of public policy, and elite urban actors and the general public should not confuse such actions as a strict private "free-market" process. In other words, such projects should, at the very least, have meaningful public involvement and governance and project accountability triggers. Activists and urban equity and social justice focused stakeholders have a democratic right to question and challenge urban elites who promote a neoliberal philosophy of free market privilege and freedom ideology in the pursuit of happiness, meaning profit. Indeed, such redevelopment is a public policy question and public policy questions are inherently a matter of public accountability.[60]

By the 1980s, we begin to see patterns of gentrification cropping up, especially in major metro areas. Redevelopment actors continued leveraging the market even more and having a significant influence on public urban policy economic activities responsible for large-scale gentrification.[61] Private corporations began increasing their involvement in state planning activities, accumulating capital gains in specific spaces, and (re) investing in the built environment and real estate.[62] The most visible of these private actors at the metropolitan and cities levels in contemporary times, who vary in economic power and influence, are developers, real estate investors, corporate property owners, urban planning, design, and architectural firms. These capital investment processes as a whole create "conditions ripe for re-making urban space to attract economically well-off groups, including creating a demand for such spaces through speculative activities."[63]

I described earlier that NU, TOD, and CC models are classic examples of capital investments and physical upgrading and remaking and gentrifying urban space. In practice, these models help to collectively reshape the physical, social, and cultural character of neighborhoods and downtown cores. Indeed, one can observe any number of gentrifying spaces in central cities and expect to see some combination of revitalization projects and cultural policies subsumed under these models, generally, such as lofts, new rail or trolley systems, and property-based improvement districts that oversee cultural and arts districts mainly targeting creative and middle classes.

A growing body of literature questions the New Urbanism (NU), Creative Class (CC), and Transit Oriented Development (TOD) models in terms of their effects on economically deprived groups and historically disinvested areas, especially in central cities. For instance, some criticisms toward many of TOD projects are that they could lead to reductions in bus service among the working class and aid gentrification. Detractors of NU argue that projects based on the model heavily privilege market-rate housing and fail to provide an equitable mix of affordable housing.[64] Diaz and Harvey point out that private sector and city official support of NU housing projects is a deliberate commitment to profit over economically deprived groups who cannot afford new market-rate housing.[65] We can understand these critiques when we consider that states vary in their requirements for setting aside a percentage of affordable housing for new projects like these; typically, states that do have a requirement generally put this around 20 percent.[66] Londoño and González note that a common critique of the CC model is that it is elitist for dismissing nonprofessionals and question its premise as a public-private solution to economic growth and improving alleged blight in the postindustrial era.[67] In more broad terms, I argue that Smith's "back to the city by capital movement" has spilled over exponentially to the gentrifying city era and now the capital movement's redevelopment model choices are NU, CC, and TOD.[68]

# Downtown Central Cities and *Gentefication*

We could expect working-class families living in and near downtown areas and businesses catering to them to be experiencing some gentrification, or at least to encounter some in the near future. For instance, a 2010 *Special Report* by the US Census Bureau shows dramatic population growth and racial population changes in the downtown core of major metropolitan areas from 2000 to 2010.[69] In 2011, for example, the populations of the major central cities of the country's largest metropolitan areas grew faster than their combined suburbs.[70] The largest population growth was in the most inner zone of the downtown core of these central cities. For instance, between 2000 and 2010, the area within a two-mile radius of city hall in the nine US cities with metropolitan areas with at least five million people, which collectively represent one quarter of the US population, experienced double-digit population growth, more than double the rate of these areas as a whole.[71] This population explosion included racial-spatial reconfigurations that are typical in US gentrification literature. Whites had the highest population growth in the two-mile radius of the central cities, Latina/o population growth was mainly concentrated in pockets at the edges or just outside the edges of these central cities, and African Americans increased mostly just outside of central cities.[72] Indeed, we are witnessing in many downtowns of the central city a parallel process of patterns of gentrification and racial-spatial reconfigurations.

## Gentefication

*Gentefication* refers to middle-class Latina/os operating a business in a gentrifying area that caters to peers who generally fit its intersecting economic and ethno- and popular cultural profile.[73] *Gentefication* has traditionally focused on businesses owners who tend to have some level of history living in the specific gentrifying zone or its broader city. The popular digital and news radio media has covered *gentefication* debates in Los Angeles and Santa Ana.[74] To my knowledge, the Latino studies field and mainstream gentrification literature have not kept pace. For example, I found no peer-reviewed research articles on *gentefication* while searching the Web of Science and One Search.

Next, I offer a brief critical discussion of the term and provide suggestions for scholars who wish to examine this concept.

The term *gentefication* is a portmanteau combining "gentrification" with "gente," which means "people" in Spanish. The origin of the definition replaces the "gentry"— which in its traditional sense literally means landowners in well-off economic positions but here refers to middle-class people of Mexican American backgrounds. In other words, businesses owned by middle-class Mexican Americans are part of broader commercial gentrification. The term has been covered in the media mainly by describing these individual-level commercial *gentefiers* and the positive contributions that their *gentefying* businesses are making among locals generally. The *gentefication* term has been attributed to Guillermo Uribe, a bar owner and denizen of a Los Angeles neighborhood contiguous to Downtown Los Angeles, Boyle Heights, that began gentrifying faster with TOD, NU, and CC redevelopment since the early 2000s. Uribe coined the term in 2007 and explained to a reporter in 2014:

> I started to see [in 2007] the potential of improving the community from the inside out. If gentrification is happening, it might as well be from people who care about the existing culture. In the case of Boyle Heights, it would be best if the gente decide to invest in improvements because they are more likely to preserve its integrity.[75]

Seen in isolation, *gentefication* and *gentefier* business owners, like those in Boyle Heights, are examples of elements of traditional gentrification definitions and individual upward mobility by business owners who have some history living in areas with a history of disinvestment. The businesses primarily target (and, presumably could or often also, to some extent, target the working-class consumer with some relatively affordable options) middle classes and seek to maintain "integrity," which we can assume partly means sustaining the area's "social character." The term, as originally conceived, largely represents well-intentioned and normative ideals of middle-class Mexican American individuals "giving back" to the specific barrios or historically disinvested areas where they grew up, an aspiration generally described in Vallejo's *From Barrio to Burbs*.[76] This contrasts Smith's description of "revanchist" gentrifiers seeking to reclaim their neighborhoods and cities.[77]

Nevertheless, I believe that scholars should strive to show, in concept and practice, what it is about *gentefication* that may or may not be well suited for commercial areas undergoing gentrification. I outline some conceptual issues here. Uribe's *gentefication* does not take into account the likely scenario that patterns of small businesses primarily or exclusively marketing to the working-class consumer, likely immigrant, Mexican, or Chicana/o, will be displaced and macro-economic factors and elite players' hand in scheming such large-scale commercial gentrification. *Gentefication* would suggest that such businesses can avoid displacement during gentrification. It fails to consider that upwardly mobile "gente" (and this is not to suggest that businesses owners marketing to the working-class are not or do not include a share of upwardly mobile people) and their businesses catering mainly to middle classes may contribute to the displacement, directly or indirectly, of business types catering to their poorer co-ethnics. Uribe's *gentefication* is buttressed by a lackadaisical attitude saying that gentrification is inevitable. These likely scenarios and views require that we scrutinize the term further.

Uribe's *gentefication* description indicates that businesses like his are meant to be well intended by aiming to reverse cultural character loss in an area. His fixation on culture sidesteps considering what it may mean for *gentefying* businesses to operate within and contribute to larger changes in the class character of an area. Marcuse, speaking of general homeowner gentrifiers, argues that "gentrifiers don't displace others with lower income due to moral wickedness, but because they lack affordable alternatives of equivalent quality and accessible location."[78] This logic, applied to business owner *gentefiers* would read as follows: "they don't open their businesses to displace businesses marketing primarily or exclusively to working-class consumers due to revanchist type sentiment." Whether such businesses owners lack affordable alternatives or not, popular media coverage of this phenomena indicates that a common motivation for these business owners is to "uplift" the area or "give back" to one's community while (potentially) profiting. Assuming that this premise is as a whole accurate, there are questions to address.

Based on the aforementioned premise, questions to ask should concern the extent by which such businesses contribute to, prevent, or take concern with *indirect displacement*.[79] Marcuse coined *indirect displacement* to bring attention to the temporal aspect of gentrification that can occur slowly across time and space.[80] *Indirect displacement*, applied to rental housing units, is when units vacated by low-income people are no longer affordable to other prospective low-income households; future low-income residents are excluded from moving into the neighborhood because they cannot afford to lease such unit types; they are priced out.[81] The specific individual or family displaced is not the unit of analysis. The unit of analysis is population, as in class population change; the grave concern is the erosion over time of individuals and families who fit the population class profile that was similar to that family or individual who was displaced initially. Through gentrification and over time, we would expect to see fewer working-class residents living in the area and this, more or less, also accumulates, either directly or indirectly, to fostering changes in the broader class character of an area. The likelihood is that the working-class resident base in an area, such as of a Census tract or specific section within it, reduces in size where it is no longer a majority or simply has lessened in size that could be discernable to the common person. Another more precise manner to suggest that an area is gentrifying or gentrified looks at changes in a collection of indicators, such as bachelor's degree or higher, median household income, percent non-Latina/o white, and median gross rent compared to county averages.[82]

Let us now examine the idea of *indirect displacement* with commercial gentrification and *gentefication*. I reintroduce Marcuse to define commercial indirect displacement as commercial properties vacated by business owners who were marketing to working-class consumers are no longer affordable to future or prospective business owners who also target primarily or exclusively working-class consumers.[83] They are excluded from opening up a business in a said commercial zone because they are priced out. As time passes, we could expect fewer businesses marketing to low-income consumer families or individuals. The reduction of these type of businesses is significant whereby it is no longer a noteworthy or staple sector in the area. As time progresses, the once visible pattern of such businesses and their target consumers diminishes, accumulating to reduce the general working-class character of the commercial zone. While the commercial gentrification literature is slower to develop business gentrification indicators, few researchers have begun mapping and conducting visual surveys of gentrifying commercial zones, examining changes to the type of businesses catering to working-class consumers to those that typically market to middle and creative classes, such as trendy cafes, bars, restaurants, art galleries, yoga studios, and upscale gyms.[84]

# CONCLUSION: RESEARCH AGENDAS LOOKING FORWARD

The Latino studies literature is thin with urban planning perspectives and could use a major boost with critical lenses. I offer four main and interrelated research agendas to help move the needle in this direction.

The first concerns adding nuance to questions about race and ethnicity. For example, some scholars within the Latino urbanism movement have reflected on the "Latino Question" in the context of urban planning and social sciences, generally.[85] Irazábal, for example, makes the case that the most useful scholarship would focus on specific ethnic-based practices and class and urban dynamics within and among Latina/o ethnic groups.[86] She coins the term *ethnurbanisms* to capture her sentiment, which she defines as "multiple, evolving and intermixing practices of placemaking that spring from and resonate with people's cultural traits."[87]

The second recommendation is to examine the intersection of multiple social ecological levels of analysis. This can include scrutinizing structural local urban planning policies and practices and how these may help determine specific neighborhood, commercial, and group-level outcomes.[88] This urban planning level scrutiny could involve examining the nature and extent of racialization, elitism, and discrimination, including but not limited that which is tied to gender, age, sexual orientation, national origin, and other identity markers.[89] In more practical terms, one could examine the successes, challenges, and contradictions of local groups who are challenging or modifying existing land-use policies or proposing new ones. This may involve looking at local activists and residents who participate both traditional state-supported and public-private planning activities as well as more progressive grassroots actions and how different activist groups within specific spaces negotiate or not their strategies and tactics in the name of collaboration or alliance, and equity and social justice. Another possibility is to offer a "thick description" of these models in action and analyze the extent by which they "fit" more traditional activist models of engagement or represent in some way a type of activist engagement innovation.[90]

Another research agenda is based on Valle and Torres and Ibarra, Carlos, and Torres, who collectively recommend that research examine macro-level political and economic forces that may be producing inequitable material conditions within the spaces that specific ethnic groups and people live and navigate and how these groups and people experience inequality.[91] This could include connecting macro-level concerns with practical and more local ordinances, resolutions, and public policies, proposed or implemented. Part of this public policy focus could include immersing in community and examining how existing groups are grappling with policy ideas for protections against commercial gentrification. In Boston, city economic development officials admit that commercial tenants lack the type of anti-displacement protections that renters are afforded.[92] This scenario compels us to examine the complexity of real-world experiences and research the multiplex nature of *gentefication* in action. Future research could examine community-wide views about debates and needs for protections for businesses marketing to working-class and working-poor immigrants and their families in gentrifying downtowns. These views could come from elected and appointed city officials and business owners, including those who may directly or indirectly benefit and not benefit from such protections. Moreover, a similar and more direct agenda is to examine the extent by which these actors are motivated to contribute to the localized common good and pursuit of a socially just distribution of businesses marketing to multigenerational working-class communities. If our premise is that too few commercial districts in the central city undergoing gentrification are remaining affordable and welcoming, then questions could examine the meanings and practices of the "common good" and "socially just distribution of businesses." Some possible questions here are: To what extent may *gentefication* represent spatial equity? Conversely, to what extent may *gentefication* represent spatial inequity? What are some contradictions of *gentefication*? There is also ample room to examine the Latina/o political representation. To what extent does racial and ethnic political representation facilitate or mitigate spatial equity in the gentrifying city?

Fourth, Latino urbanism–gentrification research could use a boost with policy evaluation and policy analysis and assess the effectiveness of resolutions, ordinances, and public policies designed to curtail or prevent gentrification.[93] The Urban Displacement Project has compiled a rather comprehensive list of policy ideas that local communities seem to be favoring in their neighborhood planning and activism that mainly focus on housing, such as just cause evictions, rent control/stabilization, density bonus ordinance, commercial linkage fee, and community land trusts. Researchers could examine the effectiveness of such public policies, including using mixed methods and multiple case studies.

Finally, I began this essay by making the case that the nexus between Latino studies and urban planning scholarship is thin but making progress. My assessment of the relevant literature is intended to help future Latino studies–urban planning scholars examine their work in the context of growing urban inequalities in the United States. Such an approach resonates with a fundamental interest in Latino studies, which is more equitable and just societies.[94]

## Notes

1. Marion Orr and Domingo Morel, "Latino Mayors and the Evolution of Urban Politics," in *Latino Mayors: Political Change in the Postindustrial City*, edited by Marion Orr and Domingo Morel (Philadelphia: Temple University Press, 2017), 71–97; Clara Irazábal and Ramzi Farhat, "Latino Communities in the United States: Place-Making in the Pre-World War II, Postwar, and Contemporary City," *Journal of Planning Literature* 22, no. 3 (2008): 207–228.
2. Llana Barber, *Latino City: Immigration and Urban Crisis in Lawrence, Massachusetts, 1945–2000* (Chapel Hill: University of North Carolina Press, 2017); Orr and Morel, "Latino Mayors and the Evolution of Urban Politics," 71–97.
3. Arun Peter Lobo, Ronaldo J. O. Flores, and Joseph J. Salvo, "The Impact of Hispanic Growth on the Racial/Ethnic Growth Composition of New York City Neighborhoods," *Urban Affairs Review* 37, no. 5 (2000): 703–27; Irazábal and Farhat, "Latino Communities in the United States: Place-Making in the Pre-World War II, Postwar, and Contemporary City," *Journal of Planning Literature* 22, no. 3 (2008): 207–228.
4. William Frey, *Melting Pot Cities and Suburbs: Racial and Ethnic Change in Metro America in the 2000s* (Washington, DC: Brookings, 2011).
5. David R. Diaz and Rodolfo D. Torres, "Introduction," in *Latino Urbanism: The Politics of Planning, Policy and Redevelopment*, edited by David R. Diaz and Rodolfo D. Torres (New York: New York University Press, 2012), 1–20.
6. Richard L. Florida, *The Rise of the Creative Class: And How it's Transforming Work, Leisure, Community and Everyday Life* (New York: Basic Books, 2002); Orr and Morel, "Latino Mayors and the Evolution of Urban Politics," 71–97.
7. US Department of Labor, "Foreign-Born Workers: Labor Force Characteristics-2018." US Department of Labor, 2018. https://www.bls.gov/news.release/pdf/forbrn.pdf. Accessed December 1, 2018.
8. Bureau of Labor Statistics, *Characteristics of Minimum Wage Workers, 2015*.
9. Armando Ibarra, Alfredo Carlos, and Rodolfo Torres, *The Latino Question: Politics, Laboring Classes, and the Next Left* (London: Pluto Press, 2018); Orr and Morel, "Latino Mayors and the Evolution of Urban Politics," 71–97; US Department of Labor, "Foreign-Born Workers: Labor Force Characteristics-2018."
10. Ibarra et al., *The Latino Question*, 71–97.
11. Pew Research Center, "Facts on U.S. Latinos: Statistical Portrait of Hispanics in the U.S." Pew Research Center, 2017. http://www.pewhispanic.org/2017/09/18/facts-on-u-s-latinos-current-data/. Accessed December 1, 2018.
12. Pew Research Center, "Facts on U.S. Latinos: Statistical Portrait of Hispanics in the U.S."
13. Anthony Cilluffo, Abigail Geiger, and Richard Fry, "More U.S. Households are Renting Than at Any Point in 50 Years." http://www.pewresearch.org/fact-tank/2017/07/19/more-u-s-households-are-renting-than-at-any-point-in-50-years/. Accessed December 1, 2018; Congress for the New Urbanism, 2001. *Charter of the New Urbanism*, 2017; The Pew Charitable Trust, *American Families Face a Growing Rent Burden: High Housing Costs Threaten Financial Security and Put Homeownership Out of Reach for Many* (Philadelphia: Pew Charitable Trust, 2018).
14. Cilluffo et al., "More U.S. Households are Renting Than at Any Point in 50 Years."

15. Cilluffo et al., "More U.S. Households are Renting Than at Any Point in 50 Years."
16. Diaz and Torres, "Introduction," 1–20.
17. Pew Research Center, "Facts on U.S. Latinos: Statistical Portrait of Hispanics in the U.S." Pew Research Center, 2017. http://www.pewhispanic.org/2017/09/18/facts-on-u-s-latinos-current-data/. Accessed December 1, 2018.
18. Richard Fry and Rakesh Kochhar, "Are You in the American Middle Class? Find Out With Our Income Calculator," Pew Research Center, 2018. https://www.pewresearch.org/fact-tank/2018/09/06/are-you-in-the-american-middle-class/. Accessed January 12, 2019.
19. Orr and Morel, "Latino Mayors and the Evolution of Urban Politics," 15.
20. Erualdo R. González and Raul P. Lejano, "New Urbanism and the Barrio," *Environmental and Planning A* 41, no. 12 (2009): 2946–2963; Erualdo R. González, *Latino City: Urban Planning, Politics, and the Grassroots* (London: Routledge, 2017); David R. Diaz, *Barrio Urbanism: Chicanos, Planning, and American Cities* (New York: Routledge, 2005); Mike Davis, *Magical Urbanism: Latinos Reinvent the US City* (New York: Verso, 2000); Michael Vanderbeek and Clara Irazábal, "New Urbanism as a New Modernist Movement: A Comparative Look at Modernism and New Urbanism," *Traditional Dwellings and Settlements Review* 19, no. 1 (2007): 41–57; Michael Pyatok, "Comment on Charles C. Bohl's 'New Urbanism and the City: Potential Applications and Implications for Distressed Inner-City Neighborhoods,' *Politics of Design: The New Urbanists vs. the Grassroots, Housing Policy Debate* 11, no. 4 (2000): 803–814; Dan Trudeau and Jeffrey Kaplan, "Is There Diversity in the New Urbanism? Analyzing the Demographic Characteristics of New Urbanist Neighborhoods in the United States," *Urban Geography* 37, no. 3 (2016): 458–482; and Emily Talen, *New Urbanism and American Planning: The Conflict of Cultures* (New York: Routledge, 2005).
21. Talen, *New Urbanism and American Planning*.
22. Congress for the New Urbanism, 2001; https://www.cnu.org/who-we-are/charter-new-urbanism
23. Susan S. Fainstein, "New Directions in Planning Theory," *Urban Affairs Review* 35 (2000): 451–478.
24. Joan A. Saab, "Historical Amnesia: New Urbanism and The City of Tomorrow," *Journal of Planning History* 6, no. 3 (2001): 191–213; Andres Duany, Elizabeth Plater-Zyberk, and Jeff Speck, *Suburban Nation: The Rise of Sprawl and the Decline of the American Dream*, 1st ed. (New York: North Point Press, 2000); Congress for the New Urbanism 2001; https://www.cnu.org/who-we-are/charter-new-urbanism; Stephen Filmanowic, 2010. "Smart Growth and New Urbanism: It Just Performs Better," Congress for the New Urbanism, 2010. http://www.slideshare.net/CongressfortheNewUrbanism/new-urbanism-just-performsbetter. Accessed February 4, 2016.
25. R. Cervero et al., *Transit-Oriented Development in the United States: Experiences, Challenges, and Prospects* (Washington, DC: Transportation Research Board, 2004).
26. Charles Landry, *The Creative City: A Toolkit for Urban Innovators*. London: Earthscan Publications, 2000.
27. Florida, *The Rise of the Creative Class*; Richard Florida, *Cities and the Creative Class* (New York: Routledge, 2005a); Richard Florida, *The Flight of the Creative Class: The New Global Competition for Talent*, 1st ed. (New York: HarperBusiness, 2005b).
28. Richard Florida and Charlotta Mellander, "The Creative Class Goes Global," in *The Creative Class Goes Global*, ed. Charlotta Mellander, Richard Florida, T. Bjorn Asheim, and Meric Gertler (New York: Routledge, 2014), 1–7.

29. Pedro A. Cabán, "Moving from the Margins to Where? Three Decades of Latina/o Studies." *Latino Studies* 1 (2003): 5–35.
30. Cabán, "Moving from the Margins to Where?; I. I. Blea, *Toward A Chicano Social Science* (New York: Praeger, 1988).
31. Cabán, "Moving from the Margins to Where?" K. M. Davalos, "Chicana/o Studies and Anthropology: The Dialogue that Never Was," in *The Chicano Studies Reader: An Anthology of Aztlán*, ed. Chon Noriega (Los Angeles: Regents of the University of California, 2001), 585–617; Suzanne Oboler, "Editorial." *Latino Studies* 1 (2003): 1–4.
32. Ramon Gutiérrez and Tomás Almaguer, eds., *The New Latino Studies Reader: A Twenty-First-Century Perspective* (Berkeley: University of California Press, 2016).
33. Gina M. Pérez, "Barrio," in *Keywords for Latina/o Studies*, ed. Deborah R. Vargas, Nancy Raquel Mirabal, and Lawrence La Fountain-Stokes (New York: New York University Press, 2017; Zaire Z. Dinzey-Flores, "Housing," in *Keywords for Latino Studies*, ed. Vargas, Mirabal, and Fountain-Stokes, 86–89.
34. http://www.datausa.io.
35. http://www.datausa.io.
36. Michael Hibbard, Clara Irazábal, June Manning Thomas, Karen Umemoto, Mulatu Wubne. ACSP Diversity Task Force, *Recruitment and Retention of Underrepresented Faculty of Color in ACSP Member Programs: Status and Recommendations*, 2011; Diversity Task Force Report, Submitted to the Governing Board of the Association of Collegiate Schools of Planning, 1–32.
37. Erualdo R. González and Clara Irazábal, "Emerging Issues in Planning: Ethno-Racial Intersections," *Local Environment* 20, no. 6 (2015): 600–610; Planners of Color Interest Group, *2011–2016 Strategic Plan* (Tallahassee, FL: Association of Collegiate Schools of Planning, 2011).
38. American Planning Association, "What Is Planning?" https://www.planning.org/aboutplanning/. Accessed November 12, 2018.
39. Jordan Yin, *Urban Planning for Dummies* (Canada: John Wiley & Sons, 2012), 10.
40. Neil Brenner, "What Is Critical Urban Theory?," in *Cities for People, Not for Profit: Critical Urban Theory and the Right to the City*, ed. Neil Brenner, Peter Marcuse, and Margit Mayer (London: Routledge), 11–23. 2012.
41. Diaz, *Barrio Urbanism*.
42. Raúl Homero Villa, *Barrio Logos: Space and Place in Urban Chicano Literature and Culture* (Austin: University of Texas Press), 8.
43. Michael Rios, Leonardo Vazquez, and Lucrezia Miranda, eds., *Diálogos: Placemaking in Latino Communities* (Milton Park: Routledge, 2012); Jesus L. Lara, "Latino Urbanism: Placemaking in 21st-Century American Cities," *Journal of Urbanism* 5, nos. 2–3 (2012): 95–100; Gerardo Francisco Sandoval, *Immigrants and the Revitalization of Los Angeles Development and Change in MacArthur Park* (Amherst, NY: Cambria Press, 2009).
44. Erualdo R. González, *Latino City: Urban Planning, Politics, and the Grassroots* (New York: Routledge).
45. Diaz and Torres, "Introduction," 1–20; Ibarra et al., *The Latino Question*.
46. Peter Marcuse, "Whose Right (s) to What City?," in *Cities for People, Not for Profit: Critical Urban Theory and the Right to the City*, ed. Neil Brenner, Peter Marcuse, and Margit Mayer (London: Routledge, 2012), 24–41.
47. Peter Marcuse, "From Critical Urban Theory to the Right to the City." *City* 13, nos. 2–3(2009): 185–196.

48. Diaz, *Barrio Urbanism*; Kristen Day, "New Urbanism and the Challenges of Designing for Diversity." *Journal of Planning Education and Research* 23, no. 1 (2003): 83–95; González, *Latino City*; González and Lejano, "New Urbanism and the Barrio," 2946–2963; Alfredo Huante and Kimberly Miranda, "What's at Stake in Contemporary Gentrification Movements?," *Society and Space, Latinx Geographies*, 2019. http://societyandspace.org/2019/02/06/whats-at-stake-in-contemporary-anti-gentrification/. Accessed February 10, 2019; Johana Londoño, "Aesthetic Belonging: The Latinization and Renewal of Union City, New Jersey," in *Latino Urbanism: The Politics of Planning, Policy, and Redevelopment*, ed. David R. Diaz and Rodolfo D. Torres (New York: New York University Press, 2012), 47–64; Gerardo Francisco Sandoval, "Planning the Barrio: Ethnic Identity and Struggles Over Transit-Oriented, Development-Induced Gentrification," *Journal of Planning Education and Research*, 2018. doi:10.1177/0739456X18793714.
49. Marcuse, "From Critical Urban Theory to the Right to the City," 185–196, 191.
50. Ruth Glass, "Introduction: Aspects of Change," in *Aspects of Change*, ed. Center for Urban Studies (London: McGibbon and Kee, 1964), xiii–xlii; Tom Slater, "'A Literal Necessity to be Re-Placed': A Rejoinder to the Gentrification Debate," *Internal Journal of Urban and Regional Research* 32, no. 1 (2008): 212–223; Marcuse, "Whose Right (s) to What City?," 24–41.
51. Slater, "'A Literal Necessity to be Re-Placed,'" 212–223.
52. C. Hartman, D. Keating, R. LeGates, and S. Turner, *Displacement: How to Fight It* (Berkeley: National Housing Law Project, 1982); Marcuse, "Whose Right (s) to What City?"
53. Marcuse, "Whose Right (s) to What City?"
54. Orr and Morel, "Latino Mayors and the Evolution of Urban Politics."
55. Orr and Morel, "Latino Mayors and the Evolution of Urban Politics."
56. Orr and Morel, "Latino Mayors and the Evolution of Urban Politics," 10.
57. Orr and Morel, "Latino Mayors and the Evolution of Urban Politics."
58. Diaz, *Barrio Urbanism*; Orr and Morel, "Latino Mayors and the Evolution of Urban Politics"; Irazábal and Farhat, "Latino Communities in the United States."
59. David Madden and Peter Marcuse, *In Defense of Housing: The Politics of Crisis* (New York: Verso, 2016).
60. Raul Lejano, *Frameworks for Policy Analysis: Merging Text and Context* (New York: Routledge, 2006).
61. Loretta Lees, Tom Slater, and Elvin Wyly, eds., *The Gentrification Reader* (New York: Routledge); Peter Marcuse, "Gentrification, Social Justice and Personal Ethics," *International Journal of Urban and Regional Research* 36, no. 6 (2010): 1263–1269.
62. Paul Kantor, *The Dependent City Revisited: The Political Economy of Urban Development and Social Policy* (Boulder, CO: Westview Press, 1995); Saskia Sassen, *The Global City: New York, London, Tokyo* (Princeton, NJ: Princeton University Press, 2001); Slater, "'A Literal Necessity to Be Re-Placed,'" 212–223; Marcuse, "Gentrification, Social Justice and Personal Ethics"; Loretta Lees, Hyun Bang Shin, and Ernesto López-Morales, eds., *Planetary Gentrification* (Cambridge, UK: Polity Press, 2016).
63. Kantor, *The Dependent City Revisited*; Sassen, *The Global City*; Slater, "'A Literal Necessity to be Re-Placed'"; Marcuse, "Gentrification, Social Justice and Personal Ethics"; Lees, Shin, and López-Morales, *Planetary Gentrification*.
64. Vanderbeek and Irazábal, "New Urbanism as a New Modernist Movement."
65. David Diaz, "Barrios and Planning Ideology: The Failure of Suburbia and the Dialects of New Urbanism," in *Latino Urbanism: The Politics of Planning, Policy, and Redevelopment*, ed.

David R. Diaz and Rodolfo D. Torres (New York: New York University Press, 2012), 21–46; and David Harvey, "The New Urbanism and the Communitarian Trap," *Harvard Design Magazine* (Winter/Spring), 1, 1997.

66. Teresa Wiltz, "In Sift, States Step In On Affordable Housing," The Pew Charitable Trust, 2018. https://www.pewtrusts.org/en/research-and-analysis/blogs/stateline/2018/10/15/in-shift-states-step-in-on-affordable-housing. Accessed December 4, 2018; Angela Hart, "Jerry Brown Signs New California Affordable Housing Laws," *The Sacramento Bee*, 2017. https://www.sacbee.com/news/politics-government/capitol-alert/article176152771.html. Accessed December 10, 2018.
67. J. Londoño and E. R. González. 2015. "The Changing Politics of Latino Consumption: Debates Related to Downtown Santa Ana's New Urbanist and Creative City Redevelopment." In *Race and Retail: Consumption Across the Color Line*, edited by Fabian, A. and M. E. Bay, 176–199. Rutgers University Press.
68. Neil Smith, "Toward a Theory of Gentrification: A Back to the City Movement by Capital, Not People," *Journal of the American Planning Association* 45, no. 4 (1979): 538–548.
69. US Census Bureau, "2010 Census Special Reports, Patterns of Metropolitan and Micropolitan Population Change, 2000–2010." C2010SR-01 (Washington, DC: US Government Printing Office, 2012).
70. William Frey, *Demographic Reversal: Cities Thrive, Suburbs Sputter* (Washington, DC: Brookings, 2012). https://www.brookings.edu/opinions/demographic-reversal-cities-thrive-suburbs-sputter/. Accessed November 19, 2018.
71. Steven G. Wilson, David A. Plane, Paul J. Mackun, Thomas R. Fischetti, And Justyna Goworowska (With Darryl T. Cohen, Marc J. Perry, And Geoffrey W. Hatchard). 2012. Patterns of Metropolitan and Micropolitan Population Change: 2000 to 2010. Report Number C2010SR-01.U.S. Department of Commerce, Economics and Statistics Department, U.S. Census Bureau.
72. US Census Bureau, "2010 Census Special Reports."
73. Julia Herbst, "Guillermo Uribe on the 'Gentefication' of East L.A." *Los Angeles Magazine*, 2014. https://www.lamag.com/citythinkblog/guillermo-uribe-on-the-gentrification-of-east-l-a/. Accessed October 13, 2018.
74. See Delgadillo 2016. Defining 'Gentefication' in Latino Neighborhoods. *CityLab*, 2016. https://www.citylab.com/equity/2016/08/defining-gentefication-in-latino-neighborhoods/495923/; Herbst, "Guillermo Uribe on the 'Gentefication' of East L.A."; Natalie Rivera, "How Gentefication is Putting Small Businesses at Risk." *Popsugar*, 2018. https://www.popsugar.com/news/What-Gentefication-44787362. Accessed September 15, 2018; Air Talk, "'Gentefication' vs. Gentrification in Boyle Heights, Long Beach and Other SoCal Hip Spots." AirTalk. 89.3 KPCC, Aug. 20, 2013. https://www.scpr.org/programs/airtalk/2013/08/20/33346/gentefication-vs-gentrification-in-boyle-heights-l; Gabriel San Roman, "Mexicans versus Mexicans in Downtown Santa Ana Gentrification Shout-off–Then Someone Yelled 'Wetback'" (*OC Weekly*, August 17, 2014). http://www.ocweekly.com/news/mexicans-vs-mexicans-in-downtown-santa-ana-gentrification-shout-off-then-someone-yelled-wetback-6448703.
75. Herbst, "Guillermo Uribe on the 'Gentefication' of East L.A."
76. Agius Jody Vallejo, *Barrios to Burbs: The Making of the Mexican American Middle Class* (Stanford, CA: Stanford University Press, 2012).
77. Neil Smith, *The New Urban Frontier: Gentrification and the Revanchist City* (London: Routledge, 1996).

78. Marcuse, "Gentrification, Social Justice and Personal Ethics."
79. Marcuse, "Gentrification, Abandonment and Displacement."
80. Marcuse, "Gentrification, Abandonment and Displacement."
81. Marcuse, "Gentrification, Abandonment and Displacement."
82. K. Chapple, *Mapping Susceptibility to Gentrification: The Early Warning Toolkit* (Berkeley, CA: Center for Innovation, 2009); K. Chapple et al., "Developing a New Methodology for Analyzing Potential Displacement," California Air Resources Board, Agreement No. 13–310; Loukaitou-Sideris, Gonzalez, and Ong, "Triangulating Neighborhood Knowledge to Understand Neighborhood Change: Methods to Study Gentrification," *Journal of Planning Education and Research*, 39, no.2 (2019): 227–242. doi:10.1177/0739456X17730890.
83. Marcuse, "Gentrification, Abandonment and Displacement."
84. E. R. González and L. Guadiana, "Culture Oriented Downtown Revitalization or Creative Gentrification?" In *The Routledge Companion to Urban Regeneration*, edited by Leary M.E and J. McCarthy, 536–547 (Oxon, UK: Routledge, Taylor & Francis Group, 2013); Loukaitou-Sideris, Gonzalez, and Ong, "Triangulating Neighborhood Knowledge to Understand Neighborhood Change."
85. Ibarra et al., *The Latino Question*.
86. González and Irazábal, "Emerging Issues in Planning."
87. González and Irazábal, "Emerging Issues in Planning," 263.
88. González and Irazábal, "Emerging Issues in Planning"; Erualdo R. González, Carolina S. Sarmiento, Ana Siria Urzúa, and Susan C. Luévano, "The Grassroots and New Urbanism: A Case from a Southern California Latino Community," *Journal of Urbanism: International Research on Placemaking and Urban Sustainability* 5, nos. 2–3 (2012): 219–239.
89. González and Irazábal, "Emerging Issues in Planning"; Raul P. Lejano and Erualdo R. González, "Sorting Through Differences: The Problem of Planning as Reimagination," *Journal of Planning Education and Research* 37, no. 1 (2016): 5–17.
90. C. Geertz, *The Interpretation of Cultures* (New York: Basic Books, 1973).
91. Victor M. Valle and Rodolfo D. Torres, *Latino Metropolis, Globalization and Community* (Minneapolis: University of Minnesota Press, 2000); Ibarra et al., *The Latino Question*.
92. Kathlene Conti, "Small Business Owners, City Frustrated by Development-led Displacement," *Boston Globe*, January 21, 2018. https://www.bostonglobe.com/business/2018/01/21/small-business-owners-city-frustrated-development-led-displacements/MN8W5rDNtlIlOWlMuhAQCN/story.html.
93. Loukaitou-Sideris, Gonzalez, and Ong, "Triangulating Neighborhood Knowledge to Understand Neighborhood Change."
94. Thank you Ilan Stavans, Rodolfo Torres, Michelle Zuñiga, and Alfredo Huante for providing very helpful comments and suggestions. Any misrepresentations are mine.

# PART III
# BETWEEN FAITH AND REASON

CHAPTER 9

# LATINO PHILOSOPHY

SUSANA NUCCETELLI

LATINO philosophy is a relatively new field of inquiry that has Hispanic and Latin American philosophy as its closest relatives. Like these kinfolk, it devotes considerable attention to self-regarding foundational debates concerning its nature, quality, and relations with other areas of philosophy. Yet Latino philosophy is a newcomer to foundational debates of this sort. Of the three fields, Latin American philosophy is the one that can claim the longest history of engagement in them, going back at least to the mid-twentieth century. Not surprisingly, then, Latino philosophy turns to this history in search of paradigms for its own reflection.

This essay argues, however, that the prospect of Latino philosophy's finding adequate paradigms in the works of most academic Latin American philosophers is quite bleak. For in Latin America, it is the so-called *pensadores* or *ensayistas* (thinkers or essayists) who have advanced the most interesting philosophical issues and arguments. Like *philosophes* Michel de Montaigne and Miguel de Unamuno, non-academic thinkers Bartolomé de las Casas and Juana de la Cruz during the colonial period, or José Martí and Octavio Paz during the twentieth century (to name but a few), have produced works with philosophical import that are original, insightful, and illustrative of the intellectual history of the region. They have produced them while reflecting on mostly literary, political, and social topics of the region. But underestimating these thinkers' issues and arguments, the academic philosophers instead focus on more universal questions of philosophy, which they pursue vigorously though, by their own assessment, not very successfully in terms of originality or internal and external visibility. As far they can see, this situation leaves them two options: either adopt some form of radical skepticism about Latin American philosophy's nature, significance, and even existence, or have an overconfident optimism about its achievements and prospects. Neither of these extremes can be of help in meeting the originality and invisibility challenges that, most agree, face Latin American philosophy.

Luckily, however, in its short history Latino philosophy has given a few signs that it might be able to avoid such extreme positions while continuing to develop its own areas of interest and gain professional recognition. The brief exploration offered here suggests that Latino philosophy counts on an active philosophical community in the United States, comprising philosophers of different theoretical frameworks who engage in reasoned argument, not only among themselves but also with their Latin American peers. In this essay, I look closely at two areas where their work supports the view that Latino philosophy has a bright future. One area concerns some recent debates about the foundations of Latino philosophy and its closest relatives. The other area involves Latino philosophy's contribution to the "Latino"-versus-"Hispanic" controversy.

## The Nature of Latino Philosophy and Its Closest Relatives

What counts, or should count, as Latino philosophy, if anything at all? Practitioners of this field of inquiry commonly take it to be a continuum with Hispanic and Latin American philosophy. They even hesitate about which of these types of philosophy best identifies their own work. Illustrating this overlap is the fact that, up to now, no major philosophical society or periodical publication in the United States bears the sole qualifier, *Latino*. The American Philosophical Association, for example, has a Committee on Hispanics that offers an annual prize for an essay in Latin American philosophy and publishes a by-annual *Newsletter on Hispanic/Latino Issues in Philosophy*. So in order to answer the earlier question, I need to start with a broader quest: determining the nature of Latino, Hispanic, and Latin American philosophy.

Practitioners of Latino philosophy, probably following the lead of Jorge Gracia, often think of this task as one that concerns this philosophy's "identity." But not all of those who reflect on this foundational issue agree with using the concept of identity in that way. Critics such as Jorge Garcia advocate the replacement of that locution with "instantiation" or "membership" of a type of philosophy. Yet since instantiation *is* partial identity (e.g., being a terrier in part identifies Maria's dog), it does not seem incorrect to regard our task as one of determining philosophical identity. In any event, I can avoid the underlying metaphysical discussion by simply taking our task to be that of determining the *nature* of Latino, Hispanic, or Latin American philosophy. A common approach to this task is to identify whatever properties works must have to fall under a certain kind of philosophy. In the case of Latino philosophy, it seems natural that, if Maria's and Jose's works are both instances of philosophy of that kind, then their works must share one or more properties that are necessary and sufficient for being included within it. Now we will consider some candidates for such properties.

# Latino, Hispanic, and Latin American Philosophy's Nature

A good starting place for identifying the defining properties for the fields of concern here is Gracia's view of Hispanic philosophy as "the philosophy developed in the Iberian peninsula, the Iberian colonies in the New World, and the countries that those colonies eventually came to form."[1] There seems to be consensus that a hybrid historico-geopolitical criterion along these lines determines what counts as Hispanic philosophy. For example, echoing Gracia, Jaime Nubiola maintains that Hispanic philosophy comprises "all the philosophical thinking that has been developed over the last few hundred years in Spain and Portugal, the Spanish colonies of the New World, and the countries which grew from them."[2] Nubiola traces this criterion to Eduardo Nicol's *The Problem of Hispanic Philosophy* (*El problema de la filosofía hispánica*, 1961), published during his exile in Mexico. Note that since Nubiola includes Portugal in the list, it seems natural to include Brazil as well (more on this later). Thus amended, the Nicol/Nubiola criterion for inclusion in Hispanic philosophy coincides with Gracia's.

But literally construed, this criterion locates within Hispanic philosophy the philosophy developed in the US states of Texas or California, each of which was once under Spanish rule. To avoid such a result, something along these lines is needed:

1. Hispanic philosophy is the philosophy developed in Spain, Portugal, and what today are the officially Spanish- and Portuguese-speaking nations of the Americas, from the time they were under Iberian rule to the present.

Now we have a definition that takes some linguistic, historical, and geopolitical properties to be necessary and sufficient for inclusion in Hispanic philosophy. And we may use analogous sets of properties to identify the nearby fields of Spanish American and Latin American philosophy in this way:

2. Spanish American philosophy is the philosophy developed in Spain and what today are the officially Spanish-speaking nations of the Americas, from the time they were under Spanish rule to the present.
3. Latin American philosophy is the philosophy developed in what today are the officially Spanish- or Portuguese-speaking nations of the Americas, from the time they were under Iberian rule to the present.

Corresponding to 1 through 3 are some existing fields of academic philosophy in the Spanish-speaking world, respectively known as (1) *filosofía hispana* or *hispánica*, (2) *filosofía hispanoamericana*, and (3) *filosofía latinoamericana* or *iberoamericana*.[3] Besides their currency, these categories seem flexible enough to allow for the inclusion of subsets such as Spanish philosophy, Brazilian philosophy, Puerto Rican philosophy, and so on. For example, Spanish philosophy comes out as a subset of Hispanic philosophy, and Brazilian philosophy as a subset of both Hispanic and Latin American philosophy. Of course, we might have second thoughts about a criterion that would include Brazilian philosophy as a type of Hispanic philosophy. But no criterion is likely to be free of borderline cases due to vagueness, so some degree of it must be tolerated. With this in mind, let us put a similar criterion at the service of identifying Latino philosophy. It yields something like this:

4. Latino philosophy is the philosophy developed by people from the Iberian Peninsula and Latin America who are living in the United States.

Here there is no linguistic property at work because some practitioners of Latino philosophy are speakers of neither Spanish nor Portuguese, though (4) adds an ethnic factor ("people from..."). But do we really wish to count as *Latino* the philosophy developed by US residents from Spain, Portugal, or Brazil? And do we really wish to exclude the philosophy developed by Latinos who have relocated to Canada or the United Kingdom just because they no longer live in the United States? Such borderline cases can be bracketed in this way:

5. Latino philosophy is the philosophy developed by anyone to whom the term "Latino" *definitely* applies.

Although Latino philosophers disagree about what to make of the borderline cases, they are likely to accept that

> "Latino" as an ethnic-group term *definitely* applies to people who reside in the US and are from the mainly Spanish-speaking nations of Latin America by birth or ancestry.[4]

Thus construed, our criterion invokes a complex set of properties concerning language, geopolitics, ethnicity, culture, and genetics (depending on how "ancestry" is construed). Yet in spite of its complexity, this set fails to provide any interesting sense of Latino philosophy—or so it is argued next.

## Latino Philosophy in an Interesting Sense

In fact, neither of the aforementioned hybrid criteria succeeds in capturing what is characteristic or distinctive (and therefore interesting) about Latino philosophy and its closest relatives. Given criterion 5, for example, Latino philosophy includes works ordinarily excluded, while excluding works ordinarily included. Thus, the criterion is both too broad and too narrow, as becomes clear in the cases of Ofelia Schutte and Ernesto Sosa, Cuban born philosophers living in the United States to whom the terms "Latina" and "Latino" definitely apply. By criterion 5, the philosophical work of either Schutte or Sosa falls into Latino philosophy. Yet it is only Schutte's work that clearly falls into that category, since Sosa's is entirely devoted to epistemology and other main branches of Western philosophy.

At the same time, philosophers to whom the term "Latino" definitely *does not* apply may produce works in Latino philosophy, provided those works bear on philosophical matters that are content-related to Latinos. Thus construed, Latino philosophy has a wide scope extending from the foundational issues of concern here to issues of feminist theory, applied ethics, political philosophy, and many more (e.g., affirmative action, Latino identity, human rights, immigration rights, and linguistic rights). For example, Lawrence Blum's 2009 analysis of some philosophical theories on Latino racial and ethnic identity, as well as James Sterba's 1996 moral reflection on Amerindians and the Spanish Conquest, are eligible for inclusion in Latino philosophy, even though (as far as I know) neither Blum nor Sterba is Latino.

Criterion 3 similarly fails to capture the nature of Latin American philosophy. After all, being produced in the officially Spanish- or Portuguese-speaking nations of the Americas is demonstrably neither necessary nor sufficient for instantiating that type of philosophy. In fact, most of the works by academic philosophers in Latin America count as Latin American philosophy only in a weak, quite un-interesting sense that fuels the radical skepticism and overconfident optimism mentioned earlier. By contrast, some works by non-academic thinkers would fit within that philosophy in a content-related sense analogous to the criterion I have proposed for the interesting sense of Latino philosophy.

That a content-related criterion of inclusion is more adequate follows from a more general principle according to which, to qualify as philosophy type X, a philosophical work (theory, argument, problem) must be *content-related* to X. Such a principle goes without saying. After all, to qualify as normative ethics, a philosophical work must be about, say, moral rules, values, or character traits. A philosophical work bearing on none of these simply falls under another branch of philosophy. Similarly, to qualify as Latino philosophy, a philosophical work must address issues that bear on some aspect of the experiences and theoretical concerns of Latinos. And to qualify as Latin American philosophy, a philosophical work must have some content relation to Latin America. Since many of the non-academic thinkers' works do bear that type of relation, we must count them as Latin American philosophy. Any alternative is likely to lead us to skepticism about the field's quality, whether the old skepticism of Risieri Frondizi and Augusto Salazar Bondy, or new skepticism of Guillermo Hurtado and Carlos Pereda, among others.

# The "Ethnic-Philosophy" Standard of Inclusion

Latin American academic philosophers sometimes do consider the non-academic thinkers' traditions. Circumstantialist Leopoldo Zea does examine positivism in

Mexico, and liberationist Arturo Roig does study the political thought of nineteenth-century nation builders. But these are isolated instances. Frondizi and Pereda illustrate the prevailing norm, which is to praise those thinkers' essays and then assign them no place in the philosophical history of the region. By contrast, in Latino philosophy they figure prominently, not only in the few courses for undergraduates and graduates now offered in the United States, but also in some training programs for instructors and publications aimed at teaching or research.[5] Textual evidence from these sources suggests that, in Latino philosophy, practitioners of different philosophical persuasions construe the field broadly, in ways that can accommodate the non-academic philosophical traditions.

But not all of them agree on how this is to be justified. After all, the non-academic philosophical traditions plainly flout widely accepted standards for what counts as philosophy in major centers of the West. Gracia attempts to justify their inclusion by offering a dual standard.[6] In his view, Latino philosophy comprises both the non-academic and the academic philosophical traditions of Latin America because it is an "ethnic" philosophy. Unlike non-ethnic philosophies, the ethnic can focus on non-academic philosophical traditions since whatever a relevant ethnos decides to include, it would fall within its philosophy. At the same time, whatever meets the universal criteria of Western philosophy would seem to count, too. After all, Gracia does include within the scope of Latino/Latin American philosophy the universalist philosophers mentioned earlier. In addition, he takes the ethnic-philosophy approach to best capture his view that no single property is necessary and sufficient for inclusion in Latino philosophy.

But Gracia's view does rely on a cluster of such properties after all, something that becomes evident when spelled out as follows:

*The Ethnic-Philosophy's Dual Standard of Inclusion*
   Any tradition/theory/argument counts as Latino philosophy just in case it has either
   a) the property of being counted as such by the Latino ethnos, or
   b) the properties of meeting Western philosophy's universal standards of inclusion and having been produced by a Latino/Latin American philosopher.

Given the relativistic property in (a), Latino philosophy comprises the works with philosophical import of non-academic thinkers, provided Latinos say so. Given the conjunction of properties in (b), Latino philosophy also comprises the works of Latino/Latin American philosophers that satisfy some objective criteria of inclusion. It follows that the ethnic-philosophy approach must satisfy either (a) or (b) to be sufficient for inclusion.

In any event, the ethnic-philosophy approach conflicts with the intuitions that (b) is not sufficient to qualify for Latino or Latin American philosophy, as suggested by the Schutte/Sosa case. That approach explicitly includes, for example, Risieri Frondizi's universalist work in axiology, on the grounds that it meets something like (b). And since it excludes similar work by the European philosopher who most influenced Frondizi, the rationale for including one while excluding the other must be that, of the two, only Frondizi was Latin American.[7] But most of Frondizi's work fails to qualify as Latin American philosophy in the interesting sense outlined earlier.

At the same time, it seems that the aforementioned properties in (a) and (b) pull in opposite directions. For as Renzo Llorente points out, given a universalist standard of inclusion in Latino philosophy, "We should either reject Gracia's view that the ethnos enjoys a privileged position in determining what artifacts count as ethnic philosophy or else opt for a word other than philosophy to designate the corpus of works that are judged by the ethnos as forming a part of its philosophy."[8] Furthermore, does the ethnic-philosophy theorist really avoid the academic philosophers' extreme positions mentioned at the outset? Consider radical skepticism, a view that generally questions the quality, not the existence, of Latin American philosophy. The ethnic-philosophy approach is consistent with radical skepticism. And since it offers no clear way to decide what to include in this field, it might contribute to perpetuating some biases that undermine Latino philosophy's standing in the United States, a problem we will have more to say about later.

In spite of these shortcomings, some Latino philosophers find merit in the ethnic-philosophy approach. For instance, José Antonio Orosco explicitly embraces it for Mexican American and Latin American philosophy on the grounds that, thus conceived, these types of philosophy can have great prospects in the United States. In his view, their main task is developing "the perspective of the Latin American ethnos...," which includes the perspective of the Latino ethnos. To do that, Latino philosophy should devote itself to reflection on "questions about [Latino] identity, power, and citizenship in the United States."[9] So its potential for making the expected contributions resides in its ability to deal with certain issues of applied ethics and political philosophy that can have an impact on "U.S. American political and social life." Here charity requires to avoid reading Orosco as suggesting some sort of reductionism according to which these are the *only* issues that matter, or should matter, to Latino philosophy. After all, such a reductionism would be self-defeating since Orosco himself engages foundational issues of Latino philosophy. Not only is reductionism an obstacle for making progress on such issues, it also has some unwelcome theoretical and practical consequences.

But before considering these, let us summarize the challenges facing the ethnic-philosophy approach to Latino philosophy. First, to avoid the thorough-going relativism implicit in its dual standard of inclusion, it must find a standard more objective than (a), the *mere* acceptance by the Latino ethnos. Second, it needs to meet counterarguments for thinking that *content-relation* to Latinos or Latin Americans is what matters most for inclusion in Latino and Latin American philosophy.[10] After all, as we have seen, there is no strong reason for including philosophers such as Sosa in those fields when construed in the interesting sense suggested earlier.

# Reductionism about Latino Philosophy and the Insularity Problem

Reductionism about Latino philosophy demonstrably has bad theoretical consequences. For one thing, it is incompatible with the view proposed here, according to which any philosophical work content related to Latinos qualifies as Latino philosophy. This view welcomes *any* philosophical subjects satisfying that condition, whether it be about foundational issues or issues of general and applied philosophy.

Given reductionism about Latino philosophy, no such openness is possible since Latino philosophy would be a mere instrument for remedying afflictions affecting Latinos, such as economic oppression and social injustice. Although proponents of reductionism of various sorts often leave implicit their instrumentalist conception of Latino philosophy, not all do. For example, Silva (2015) is quite explicit in assigning to it the single role of contributing to the struggle of Latinos and Latin Americans against colonialism. Now, are Latinos today still in need of liberation from that historical evil? The answer depends on very complex historical, political, and socioeconomic matters that cannot be settled from the philosopher's armchair. As a result, the burden of argument is on the reductionists, who are in need of supporting empirical data from history and the social sciences that they tend to ignore. Without such support, their arguments are simply unsound.

Moreover, reductionism also has some bad practical consequences. By resting on unsupported assumptions, it helps to perpetuate the bias that anything goes in Latino philosophy (i.e., that in this field, unsupported empirical claims go unchecked). There is evidence that such a bias undermines Latino philosophy's current standing in the philosophical community of the United States. Susanna Siegel, for instance, points to this bias while commenting on the "insularity" problem facing that field. She thinks that the problem is partly "due to the fact that philosophical questions are genuinely distinct from many questions in neighboring fields in both the social sciences and the humanities."[11] Latino philosophy should avoid conflating these because it simply lacks the resources for settling questions in neighboring fields.

Since reductionism has unwelcome theoretical and practical consequences, it should be rejected swiftly. It provides no good reason for limiting the scope of Latino philosophy to some sociopolitical matters. Moreover, since it conflates philosophical with nonphilosophical questions, it ends up making claims that are better investigated elsewhere. In addition, it stands in the way of an unbiased appraisal of Latino and Latin American philosophy, which in turn undermines the standing of Latino philosophers in the profession. Gracia, Mendieta, Sánchez, and Vargas are among those lamenting the fact that practitioners of either field lack the standing they deserve.[12]

# A Success Story: The "Latino" Versus "Hispanic" Puzzle

Qualifiers such as "Latino" and "Hispanic" have semantic and pragmatic features so puzzling that they have prompted one of Latino philosophy's most fruitful developments. For consider the following claims:

(i) Either "Latino" or "Hispanic" should be preferred as a term that definitely applies to US residents who are from the officially Spanish-speaking nations of Latin America by birth or ancestry.
(ii) No such ethnic-group term is devoid of some harmful connotations.
(iii) Terms with harmful connotations should never be used.

Claims (i) through (iii) create a puzzle because each of them seems true, yet they are inconsistent. Solving this puzzle requires abandoning at least one of them. Nihilism, a position rarely held in philosophy but not unknown in Latino studies, argues that since (ii) and (iii) are true, (i) must be rejected as false: there is no justification for using any such ethnic-group terms.[13] By contrast, Latino philosophers generally converge in holding that (iii) must be recast since it is false as stated. But before they can make an affirmative case for the choice of either "Latino" or "Hispanic," they should first consider the reasons underwriting nihilism.

# Nihilism about "Latino" and "Hispanic"

Nihilism offers moral and prudential reasons against the use of any ethnic-group term for the US residents who are from the Spanish-speaking world by birth or ancestry. They all point to the fact that their usage distorts our understanding of these diverse people and promotes harmful stereotypes and biases about them. Although practical reasons may justify using nationality terms (e.g., "Cuban," "Guatemalan," etc.) and even regional terms ("Latin American," "Mesoamerican," etc.), there is no justification for using "Latinos," "Hispanics," and the like. Neither of them refers to a sociologically interesting category, one that can capture an actual group of people. Rather, they appear to pick out a group made up for the purpose of social control, economic exploitation, or other forms of domination.

But more is needed to get nihilism off the ground since some seemingly plausible reasons recommend the adoption of "Latino," "Hispanic," or both. For example, Gracia contends that the widespread adoption of "Hispanic" may promote empowerment, pride, and liberation from relations of dependence.[14] He argues that "Latino" plays an analogous role.[15] In the course of objecting to Gracia's earlier preference of "Hispanic," Linda Alcoff offers similar arguments for the adoption of "Latino."[16] Both Alcoff and Gracia have reasons for thinking that the liberating role of "Latino" far outweighs any harmful connotations associated with that term. To avoid begging the question, nihilism must defeat those reasons. Even if they were defeated, it does not follow that there is no strong reason supporting the adoption of an ethnic-group term for the intended group.

Moreover, negative connotations associated with "Latino" or "Hispanic" operate at the pragmatic level and therefore need be neither stable nor permanent. To illustrate this, consider "Latin American." As the story goes, the French introduced this term in the nineteenth century to advance their colonialist, anti-Hispanic agenda in the region.[17] But, unaffected by the later defeat of that agenda, "Latin American" caught on in the speech community and became a term of pride, as is evident in the writings of many non-academic thinkers. Today the term has none of its colonialist initial connotations.

In reply, nihilism might invoke the morally objectionable role of some ethnic-group labels in human history. Think of "Marrano" and "Moor" in early Renaissance Spain, or "Jew" and "Gipsy" in Nazi Germany. Yet there is no evidence that either "Latino" or "Hispanic" has widespread associations that play a comparable evil role. In consequence, Latino philosophy's consensus against nihilism prevails. Nihilism falls short of supporting its rejection of (i) earlier, the thesis that either "Latino" or "Hispanic" should be preferred as a term that definitely applies to US residents who, by birth or ancestry, are from the officially Spanish-speaking nations of Latin America. We'll now consider Latino philosophy's attempt to solve the puzzle by recasting (iii), the thesis that no term with some harmful connotations should ever be used.

## The Semantics and Pragmatics of Ethnic-Group Terms

Latino philosophy's solution to the "Latino" versus "Hispanic" puzzle consists in first distinguishing the semantic from the pragmatic features of ethnic-group terms and then arguing that any harmful connotations associated with "Latino" or "Hispanic" are merely pragmatic. Furthermore, some positive results of adopting one of those terms far outweigh their negative pragmatic connotations. Given these claims, a preference for "Latino" or "Hispanic" ultimately depends on the evidence about these terms' connotations, together with an assessment of what term is best for the intended group of people prudentially and morally. Now we will have a closer look at the steps in Latino philosophy's solution to the puzzle.

In response to nihilism, Latino philosophy distinguishes the semantic features of ethnic-group terms (i.e., their meaning and reference) from their pragmatic connotations (i.e., the associations made by some users of the terms). Regarding their semantic features, Latino philosophy has produced two different accounts. Alcoff's and Gracia's works (chapters 1 and 3) have views about "Latino" and "Hispanic" more compatible with a descriptivist account, while Nuccetelli explicitly embraces a referentialist account.[18] The difference between these two hinges on whether they assign a central role to those terms' meanings in determining their reference. Descriptivism does, referentialism does not. True, Gracia holds that *no single description* or meaning can determine the reference of "Hispanic," because the term applies to an exceedingly diverse group of people who do not share a single essential property, such as having a certain language, religion, race, culture, or political conviction. But it is also true that he assigns the following *cluster of descriptions* to the group:

> Hispanics are the group of people comprised by *the inhabitants of the countries of the Iberian peninsula after 1492 and what were to become the colonies of those countries after the encounter between Iberia and America took place*, and *by descendants of these people who live in other countries (e.g., the United States) but preserve some link to those people*. It excludes the population of other countries in the world and the inhabitants of Iberia and Latin America before 1942 because, beginning in the year of the encounter, the Iberian countries and their colonies in America developed a web of historical connections which continues to this day and which separates these people from others.[19]

That is, on this account, "Hispanic" refers to anyone who satisfies one of these descriptions:

1. Being an inhabitant of Spain or Portugal after the Encounter of 1492; or
2. Being an inhabitant of Spain's or Portugal's colonies after 1492; or
3. Being a descendant of people with property 1 or 2, together with living somewhere else and having some link to those people.

Numbers 1 to 3 combine certain geopolitical-historical descriptions, while 1 adds a complex description that may involve biology ("being a descendant of") and possibly culture, language, or religion ("having some link").

When these descriptions are taken to determine the reference of "Hispanic," the view is vulnerable to counterexamples. For one thing, since it selects the Encounter of 1492 as crucial identity-conferring historical property, it faces challenges based on the arbitrariness of the selection. Robert Gooding Williams, for instance, asks why not choose 1441, the year Portugal launched its West African slave trade, an event that arguably enabled the ulterior Iberian expansion?[20] And Alcoff counters, why not 1898?[21] After all, 1492 is too remote to capture some historical events that have determined membership of the group and continue to do so. Here Alcoff has in mind sociopolitical, military, and economic developments pointing to US colonial policies toward Latin America (e.g., US interference in Puerto Rico, Cuba, Panama, Honduras, and so on). In her view, 1898 is the crucial identity-conferring date because it was then that the United States gave loud signals of its colonialist aspirations in the region and Spain lost its last foothold in it. To Alcoff, Latinos are still afflicted by American colonialism. Notice, however, that Alcoff is not only in the business of merely offering an arbitrariness objection to Gracia. She is also arguing for preferring "Latino" over "Hispanic," a choice likely motivated by political belief combined with consequentialist concerns regarding what is in the best interest of Latinos and Latin Americans. But in the course of raising her objection, she ascribes certain semantic features to her preferred term, thereby making her account a form of descriptivism as vulnerable to the arbitrariness objection as Gracia's. For why not choose 1848, when the Treaty of Guadalupe Hidalgo sealed the results of a colonialist war that, according to Carlos Fuentes, left a scar in the Latin American mind?[22] And if 1898 is the identity-conferring date for Latinos, which for Alcoff include residents of Latin America, it follows that Juana de la Cruz (b. 1651–d. 1695), Simón Bolívar (b. 1783–d. 1830), and Juan Bautista Alberdi (b. 1810–d. 1884) were not Latin American at all. To avoid such preposterous results, Alcoff might, like Gracia, propose a disjunctive cluster of descriptions that determine the reference of "Latino." But it would be difficult to come up with a cluster immune to counterexamples. The lack of consensus about which descriptions are best would imply that we do not know what we are talking about when we use the term.

Given referentialism, however, we *do* know it even if there is no consensus about the exact meaning of the term. On this alternative account, descriptivism runs into trouble because it assigns too large a semantic role to descriptive meanings, none of which is essential for determining the reference of "Latino," "Hispanic," and the like. What is essential instead is that these terms be used in ways that defer to the speakers who first introduced them with those references. It is not uncommon that speakers introduce a term to refer to an ethnic group and later see that term catch on in a speech community in spite of any initial misconceptions they associate with the term's reference. Such mistaken descriptions may not be shared by all users, or they may eventually disappear or change.[23] This suggests that they are inessential for an ethnic-group term in picking out its reference, though they may matter pragmatically.

Both descriptivists and referentialists can agree that when some ethnic-group terms have negative pragmatic connotations that outweigh any positive ones, they should not be used on moral and prudential grounds. But when that is not the case, the choice of a term depends on other pragmatic factors, such as context and purpose of utterance. Factors of these sorts in part explain the difficulty of settling the controversy of "Latino" versus "Hispanic," which depends also on the fact that the exact reference of these terms is still under negotiation (as is, for instance, the reference of "right action"—since ethicists are still debating whether it denotes any action that promotes overall happiness, one that respects persons as ends in themselves, one that leads to a good life, or one that does something else).[24]

# Solving the "Latino" Versus "Hispanic" Puzzle

Recall that on Gracia's view, "Hispanic" applies to all the post-Encounter peoples of Spain, Portugal, and Latin America, as well as to anyone living elsewhere who has some link to these peoples. "Latino" denotes a subset of Hispanics: roughly, Latin Americans living in the United States. Alcoff seems to agree. Given the Gracia/Alcoff view, then, it does not make sense to dispute which of these terms is best: the selection criterion for usage should be communicational need. After all, as Llorente points out, in this view, "What we have... is one ethnic group nested within another, larger group. Latino would be to Hispanic as, say, Guarani is to Latino or Ashkenazi is to Jew."[25] Thus, "We may sometimes wish to stress a person's status as a Latino rather than as a Hispanic." Note that Llorente also regards Latin Americans (represented by the Guarani in his argument) as a subset of Latinos, which adds to the present confusion about the reference of the relevant terms, since many would reject that classification altogether.

In philosophy, however, the usual antidote to conceptual confusion is stipulative definition, a strategy apparently adopted by Ilan Stavans when, after examining the history and connotations of the terms under controversy, he suggests:

- Use "Latino" for "those citizens from the Spanish-speaking world living in the United States."
- Use "Hispanic" for those citizens from the Spanish-speaking world "living elsewhere."[26]

But these stipulations are almost certain to face objection from philosophical quarters. Some might want an explicit broad construal of "being from..." inclusive of birth and ancestry. Others might object to the exclusion of borderline cases. For example, Gracia takes "Hispanic" to refer also to post-Encounter Portuguese and Brazilian people.[27] Tammelleo takes "Latino" to include Brazilians in its reference.[28] Angelo Corlett explicitly defers to Gracia's use of "Hispanic" as a source for his own use of "Latino," which he takes to refer to "those of us with Iberian ancestry."[29] But since Stavans and many others disagree with the inclusion of people from the Portuguese-speaking world in the reference of "Hispanic" and "Latino," their disagreement suggests that neither of these terms *definitely* applies to those peoples. At the same time, contra Stavans, some would deny that "Latino" also refers to the Spaniards who reside in the United States: in that case, those US residents might have grounds for affirmative-action claims. And it is not clear that they should have grounds for such claims on any adequate principle of compensatory justice. To avoid these unsettled discussions, Stavans's stipulations can be recast this way:

- Use "Latino" as a term that *definitely* refers to anyone who (a) is from Spanish-speaking Latin America, either by birth or descent, and (b) resides in the United States.
- Use "Hispanic" as a term that *definitely* refers to anyone else who (a) is from the Spanish-speaking world, either by birth or descent, and (b) resides outside the United States.

Since here the reference of "Latino" is not included in that of "Hispanic," the controversy about which term is best becomes otiose.

# The Upshot

Anyone exploring Latino philosophy will soon discover an incipient but active field of inquiry engaging practitioners of many philosophical persuasions. In spite of their differences, they nonetheless manage to establish a dialogue among themselves and with other peers on questions that, as this essay illustrates, range from Latino philosophy's foundations to some issues of philosophy of language and moral and social philosophy related to the experiences of Latinos in the United States. Although in exploring its own nature Latino philosophy faces challenges analogous to those that have stalled its closest relatives, on the basis of some promising signs Latino philosophy might be able to overcome those challenges.

One such challenge comes from the temptation to take the easy path of reductionism, a dogmatist outlook assigning Latino philosophy the sole task of advancing some sociopolitical agenda such as contributing to the liberation of Latinos from colonialist oppression. This essay has argued against reductionism on the grounds that not only does it make empirical claims without solid supporting evidence, but it also has the prudentially bad consequence of undermining Latino philosophy's status in the profession. Since these reasons appear to be stronger than any argument reductionism can field, Latino philosophy should reject reductionism summarily.

Another challenge for Latino philosophy is falling into either radical skepticism or overconfident optimism, two extreme positions that are familiar from the failure of Latin American philosophy to come up with a compelling account of its own nature. The best antidote against these afflictions is a proper understanding of the foundations of these fields. On my view, if Latino philosophy can move beyond a merely historical/geopolitical understanding of what distinguishes it from other types of philosophy, its prospect of avoiding those afflictions would be brighter. This article has suggested that it should conceive of itself as a philosophy that is *content-related to Latinos* rather than as a philosophy *produced by Latinos*. That should widen its already noticeable friendliness toward traditions that are content-related to Latinos, especially those of the non-academic philosophical thinkers of Latin America. By contrast, the universalist conception most favored by Latin American philosophers encourages their tendency to ignore the *pensadores.* They confine the pensadores' work to *pensamiento latinoamericano* ("Latin American thought"), a subfield in the margins of philosophy. But, given Latino philosophy's developments outlined here, there is great hope that it would not make that mistake, at least any time soon.

# Epilogue

While in graduate school in the United States, my classmates asked me on more than one occasion: "Why hasn't there been anyone working in Latino or Latin American philosophy who has achieved the international recognition of, say, American philosopher Willard van Orman Quine?" Questions along this line have also appeared in print—for example, in Euryalo Cannabrava's 1949 article in the prestigious *Journal of Philosophy*. Socioeconomic and cultural differences can account at least in part for this and other disparities in the philosophical development of the Americas. The answer to my classmates should have been a "So what?" For nothing of substance follows about the quality of these types of philosophy from the fact that they have no Quine. The study of this issue belongs not to philosophy but to the history and sociology of knowledge.

But such anecdotal evidence is suggestive of the negative attitude that those considering work in Latino philosophy may face from the academic philosophical establishment in North America. On my experience, that's no reason to be deterred. Philosophers willing to delve into issues of Latino philosophy at some length should be encouraged instead by the fact that, in spite of the skepticism of the establishment, a rising interest in Latino philosophy suggests that its issues are worth pursuing for their own sake—something this chapter has attempted to show. Furthermore, the practice of Latino philosophy can carry some positive practical consequences. For one thing, it can help overcome a bias that is partly responsible for the intellectual isolation of scholars working in Latino philosophy. These tend to be perceived as outsiders working on "nonphilosophical" topics. But the process of changing that perception is already underway, and new scholars can help to accelerate it. In addition, scholars in Latino philosophy have the opportunity to reflect on novel topics widely neglected in standard areas of philosophy, from ethics and social and political philosophy to philosophy of language and feminist philosophy. Serious work on those topics will contribute to shifting the burden of argument to establishment philosophers. In this way new scholars could make an important contribution not only to the understanding of issues that concern Latinos but also to the widening of the scope of North America's mainstream in the academic discipline of philosophy.

## Notes

1. Jorge J. Gracia, E. "Hispanic Philosophy: Its Beginning and Golden Age," *Review of Metaphysics* 46 (1993): 475.

2. Jaime Nubiola, "C. S. Peirce and the Hispanic Philosophy of the Twentieth Century," *Transactions of the Charles S. Peirce Society* 34, no. 1 (1998): 32.
3. See, for instance, Manuel Garrido, Nelson R. Orringer, Luis M. Valdés, and Margarita M. Valdés, eds., *El legado filosófico español e hispanoamericano del siglo XX* (Madrid: Cátedra, 2009) and José Luis Gómez-Martínez, ed., *Projecto Ensayo Hispánico: Antología del Ensayo Hispánico*, 1997–2015, http://www.ensayistas.org/.
4. Note that the exact reference of "Latino" is still under negotiation. While there is agreement that people who live in the United States and are from the mostly Spanish-speaking nations of Latin America definitely count as Latinos (see J. Angelo Corlett, "Race, Ethnicity, and Public Policy," in *Race or Ethnicity? On Black and Latino Identity*, ed. Jorge J. E Gracia [Ithaca, NY: Cornell University Press, 2007], 225–247) and Tammello counts also those from Brazil (see Steve Tammelleo, "Continuity and Change in Hispanic Identity," *Ethnicities* 11, no. 4 [2011]: 536–554). Alcoff includes them too—together with the non-US residents of Latin America, which she considers Latinos. See Linda Alcoff, "Latino vs. Hispanic: The Politics of Ethnic Names," *Philosophy and Social Criticism* 31 (2005): 395–408. Gracia is unclear about whether Latinos on his view include US residents who are from Portugal and Spain (by birth or ancestry) (see Jorge J. E. Gracia, *Latinos in America: Philosophy and Social Identity* [Oxford: Blackwell, 2008]). See Ilan Stavans, "Life in the Hyphen," in *The Essential Ilan Stavans* (New York: Routledge, 2000), 3–26. Stavans includes only US residents who are from the Spanish-speaking world; but this means that he classifies within the group the Spaniards who live in the United States—something that, as discussed later, some may dispute on justice grounds concerning eligibility for affirmative action.
5. Illustrating this tendency of Latino philosophy are two NEH-sponsored programs focused on the Latin American, non-academic philosophical traditions: a 2005 Summer Institute at the University of Buffalo co-directed by Jorge Gracia and Susana Nuccetelli, and a 2006 series of workshops at the University of Texas/Pan American co-directed by Susana Nuccetelli and Gary Seay. Collections of primary and secondary sources on them include Jorge J. E. Gracia and Elizabeth Millán-Zaibert, eds., *Latin American Philosophy for the 21st Century: The Human Condition, Values, and the Search for Identity* (Buffalo, NY: Prometheus, 2003); see also Susana Nuccetelli, Ofelia Schutte, and Otavio Bueno, eds., *Blackwell Companion to Latin American Philosophy* (Oxford: Wiley-Blackwell, 2009); Susana Nuccetelli and Gary Seay, eds., *Latin American Philosophy: An Introduction with Readings* (Upper Saddle Brook, NJ: Prentice Hall, 2004); and Jorge J. E. Gracia, ed., *Forging People: Race, Ethnicity, and Nationality in Hispanic American and Latino/a Thought* (Notre Dame, IN: University of Notre Dame Press, 2011). For a sample of current syllabi, see http://www.apaonline.org/members/group_content_view.asp?group=110430&id=380970#latin.
6. Jorge J. E. Gracia, *Latinos in America: Philosophy and Social Identity* (Oxford: Blackwell, 2008), 142–144.
7. Gracia, Jorge J. E. "Identity and Latin American Philosophy," in *Blackwell Companion to Latin American Philosophy*, ed. Nuccetelli, Schutte, and Bueno (Oxford: Wiley-Blackwell, 2009), 256.
8. Renzo Llorente, "Gracia on Hispanic and Latino Identity," *Journal of Speculative Philosophy* 27, no. 1 (2013): 75.
9. José Antonio Orosco, "The Philosophical Gift of Brown Folks: Mexican American Philosophy in the United States," *APA Newsletter on Hispanic/Latino Issues in Philosophy* 15 (Spring 2016): 23–28.

10. Susana Nuccetelli, "Is 'Latin American Thought' Philosophy?," *Metaphilosophy* 4 (2003): 524–537; and Ilan Stavans, "The Language Prism," in *Debating Race, Ethnicity, and Latino Identity*, ed. Iván Jaksić (New York: Columbia University Press, 2015), 131–137.
11. Susanna Siegel, "Reflections on the Use of English and Spanish in Analytic Philosophy," *Informes del Observatorio/Observatorio Reports*, Instituto Cervantes, Harvard University, 2014, http://cervantesobservatorio.fas.harvard.edu/sites/default/files/006_informes_ss_analytic_philosophy.pdf.
12. Jorge J. E. Gracia, *Hispanic-Latino Identity: A Philosophical Perspective* (Oxford: Blackwell, 2000); Eduardo Mendieta, "Is There Latin American Philosophy?," *Philosophy Today* 43 (1999): 50–61; Carlos Alberto Sánchez, "Philosophy and the Post-Immigrant Fear," *Philosophy in the Contemporary World* 18, no. 1 (2011): 31–42; Manuel Vargas, "Real Philosophy, Metaphilosophy, and Metametaphilosophy: On the Plight of Latin American Philosophy," *CR: The New Centennial Review* 7, no. 3 (2007): 51–78; and Manuel Vargas, "On the Value of Philosophy: The Latin American Case," *Comparative Philosophy* 1, no. 1 (2010): 33–52.
13. See, e.g., Martha Gimenez, "'Latino? Hispanic?' Who Needs a Name? The Case Against a Standardized Terminology," *International Journal of Health Services* 19 (1989): 557–571; and Suzanne Oboler, "The Politics of Ethnic Construction: Hispanic, Chicano, Latino…?," *Latin American Perspectives* 19 (1992): 18–36.
14. Gracia, *Hispanic-Latino Identity*, 21–26.
15. Gracia, *Latinos in America*.
16. Alcoff, "Latino vs. Hispanic."
17. Gracia, *Hispanic-Latino Identity*; Guillermo Hurtado, "El diálogo filosófico interamericano como un diálogo para la democracia," *Inter-American Journal of Philosophy* 1 (2010): 1–17.
18. Alcoff, "Latino vs. Hispanic"; Gracia, *Hispanic-Latino Identity* (chapters 1 and 3); Susana Nuccetelli, "'Hispanics,' 'Latinos,' and 'Iberoamericans': Naming or Describing?" *Philosophical Forum* 32 (2001): 175–188; Susana Nuccetelli, *Latin American Thought: Philosophical Problems and Arguments* (Boulder, CO: Westview, 2002); and Susana Nuccetelli, "Reference and Ethnic-Group Terms." *Inquiry* 6 (2004): 528–544.
19. Gracia, *Hispanic-Latino Identity*, 48–49, emphasis mine. See also Gracia, *Hispanic-Latino Identity*, 52.
20. Robert Gooding-Williams, "Comment on J. J. E. Gracia's *Hispanic/Latino Identity*," *Philosophy and Social Criticism* 27, no. 2 (2002): 3–10.
21. Alcoff, "Latino vs. Hispanic."
22. Carlos Fuentes, *The Buried Mirror: Reflections on Spain and the New World* (New York: Houghton Mifflin, 1992).
23. See Susana Nuccetelli, "'Hispanics,' 'Latinos,' and 'Iberoamericans': Naming or Describing?" *Philosophical Forum* 32 (2001): 175–188. This work illustrates this feature of ethnic-group terms with the case of "Patagones" (literally, "big patas or feet"), from which the name of a Southern Argentinian region derives. The term was introduced to refer to the native Tehuelche: some Spanish explorers in the sixteenth century first described them as "giant people." Taking hold in the imaginative narratives of other explores, "Patagones" eventually caught on in the speech community in spite of later evidence that the Tehuelche were not giants. Referentialism can explain this, and also why "Hispanic," "Latino," and "Latin American"—all of which seem to have some initial associated misdescriptions—like "Patagones," successfully refer to certain groups of people.

24. See, e.g., Philip B. Corbett, "Hispanic? Latino? Or What?" *New York Times*, June 9, 2009; Luis Fajardo, "Should Hispanics Instead Be Called Latinos?" *BBC Mundo*, November 11, 2016; and Paul Taylor, Hugo Lopez, Jessica Martínez, and Gabriel Velasco, "When Labels Don't Fit: Hispanics and Their Views of Identity," *Pew Research Center*, April 4, 2012.
25. Llorente, "Gracia on Hispanic and Latino Identity," 69.
26. Ilan Stavans, "Life in the Hyphen," in *The Essential Ilan Stavans* (New York: Routledge, 2000).
27. Jorge J. E. Gracia, *Hispanic-Latino Identity: A Philosophical Perspective* (Oxford: Blackwell, 2000).
28. Tammelleo, "Continuity and Change in Hispanic Identity."
29. J. Angelo Corlett, "Race, Ethnicity, and Public Policy," in *Race or Ethnicity? On Black and Latino Identity*, ed. Jorge J. E. Gracia (Ithaca, NY: Cornell University Press, 2007), 232.

# Bibliography

Alcoff, Linda. "Latino vs. Hispanic: The Politics of Ethnic Names." *Philosophy and Social Criticism* 31 (2005): 395–408.

Blum, Lawrence. "Latinos on Race and Ethnicity: Alcoff, Corlett, and Gracia." In *Blackwell Companion to Latin American Philosophy*, edited by Nuccetelli, Schutte, and Bueno, 269–281. Oxford: Wiley-Blackwell, 2009.

Cannabrava, Euryalo. "Present Tendencies in Latin American Philosophy." *Journal of Philosophy* 5 (1949): 113–119.

Corlett, J. Angelo. "Race, Ethnicity, and Public Policy." In *Race or Ethnicity? On Black and Latino Identity*, edited by Jorge J. E Gracia, 225–247. Ithaca, NY: Cornell University Press, 2007.

Frondizi, Risieri. "Is There an Ibero-American Philosophy?" *Philosophy and Phenomenological Research* 9 (1949): 345–355.

Fuentes, Carlos. *The Buried Mirror: Reflections on Spain and the New World*. New York: Houghton Mifflin, 1992.

Garcia, Jorge L. A. "Is Being Hispanic an Identity? Reflections on J. J. E. Gracia's Account." *Philosophy and Social Criticism* 27, no. 2 (2001): 29–43.

Garrido, Manuel, Nelson R. Orringer, Luis M. Valdés, and Margarita M. Valdés, eds. *El legado filosófico español e hispanoamericano del siglo XX*. Madrid: Cátedra, 2009.

Gimenez, Martha. "'Latino? Hispanic?' Who Needs a Name? The Case Against a Standardized Terminology." *International Journal of Health Services* 19 (1989): 557–571.

Gómez-Martínez, José Luis, ed. *Projecto Ensayo Hispánico: Antología del Ensayo Hispánico, 1997–2015*. http://www.ensayistas.org/.

Gooding-Williams, Robert. "Comment on J. J. E. Gracia's *Hispanic/Latino Identity*." *Philosophy and Social Criticism* 27, no. 2 (2002): 3–10.

Gracia, Jorge J. E. "Hispanic Philosophy: Its Beginning and Golden Age." *Review of Metaphysics* 46 (1993): 475–502.

Gracia, Jorge J. E. *Hispanic-Latino Identity: A Philosophical Perspective*. Oxford: Blackwell, 2000.

Gracia, Jorge J. E. *Latinos in America: Philosophy and Social Identity*. Oxford: Blackwell, 2008.

Gracia, Jorge J. E. "Identity and Latin American Philosophy." In *Blackwell Companion to Latin American Philosophy*, edited by Nuccetelli, Schutte, and Bueno, 253–268. Oxford: Wiley-Blackwell, 2009.

Gracia, Jorge J. E., ed. *Forging People: Race, Ethnicity, and Nationality in Hispanic American and Latino/a Thought*. Notre Dame, IN: University of Notre Dame Press, 2011.
Gracia, Jorge J. E., and Elizabeth Millán-Zaibert, eds. *Latin American Philosophy for the 21st Century: The Human Condition, Values, and the Search for Identity*. Buffalo, NY: Prometheus, 2003.
Hurtado, Guillermo. "Two Models of Latin American Philosophy." *Journal of Speculative Philosophy* 3 (2006): 204–213.
Hurtado, Guillermo. "El diálogo filosófico interamericano como un diálogo para la democracia." *Inter-American Journal of Philosophy* 1 (2010): 1–17.
Llorente, Renzo. "Gracia on Hispanic and Latino Identity." *Journal of Speculative Philosophy* 27, no. 1 (2013): 67–78.
Mendieta, Eduardo. "Is There Latin American Philosophy?" *Philosophy Today* 43 (1999): 50–61.
Nicol, Eduardo. *El problema de la filosofía hispánica*. Madrid: Technos, 1961.
Nubiola, Jaime. "C. S. Peirce and the Hispanic Philosophy of the Twentieth Century." *Transactions of the Charles S. Peirce Society* 34, no. 1 (1998): 31–49.
Nuccetelli, Susana. "'Hispanics,' 'Latinos,' and 'Iberoamericans': Naming or Describing?" *Philosophical Forum* 32 (2001): 175–188.
Nuccetelli, Susana. "Is 'Latin American Thought' Philosophy?" *Metaphilosophy*, 4 (2003): 524–537.
Nuccetelli, Susana. *Latin American Thought: Philosophical Problems and Arguments*. Boulder, CO: Westview, 2002.
Nuccetelli, Susana. "Reference and Ethnic-Group Terms." *Inquiry* 6 (2004): 528–544.
Nuccetelli, Susana, and Gary Seay, eds. *Latin American Philosophy: An Introduction with Readings*. Upper Saddle Brook, NJ: Prentice Hall, 2004.
Nuccetelli, Susana, Ofelia Schutte, and Otavio Bueno, eds. *Blackwell Companion to Latin American Philosophy*. Oxford: Wiley-Blackwell, 2009.
Oboler, Suzanne. "The Politics of Ethnic Construction: Hispanic, Chicano, Latino…?" *Latin American Perspectives* 19 (1992): 18–36.
Orosco, José Antonio. "The Philosophical Gift of Brown Folks: Mexican American Philosophy in the United States." *APA Newsletter on Hispanic/Latino Issues in Philosophy* 15 (Spring 2016): 23–28.
Pereda, Carlos. "Latin American Philosophy: Some Vices." *Journal of Speculative Philosophy* 3 (2006): 192–203.
Salazar Bondy, Augusto. *Existe una filosofía de nuestra America?* Mexico City: Siglo XXI, 1968.
Sánchez, Carlos Alberto. "Philosophy and the Post-Immigrant Fear." *Philosophy in the Contemporary World* 18, no. 1 (2011): 31–42.
Siegel, Susanna. "Reflections on the Use of English and Spanish in Analytic Philosophy." *Informes del Observatorio/Observatorio Reports*, Instituto Cervantes, Harvard University, 2014. http://cervantesobservatorio.fas.harvard.edu/sites/default/files/006_informes_ss_analytic_philosophy.pdf.
Stavans, Ilan. "Life in the Hyphen." In *The Essential Ilan Stavans*, 3–26. New York: Routledge, 2000.
Stavans, Ilan. "The Language Prism." In *Debating Race, Ethnicity, and Latino Identity*, edited by Iván Jaksić, 131–137. New York: Columbia University Press, 2015.
Sterba, James P. "Understanding Evil: American Slavery, the Holocaust, and the Conquest of the American Indians." *Ethics* 106, no. 2 (1996): 424–448.

Tammelleo, Steve. "Continuity and Change in Hispanic Identity." *Ethnicities* 11, no. 4 (2011): 536–554.

Vargas, Manuel. "*Real* Philosophy, Metaphilosophy, and Metametaphilosophy: On the Plight of Latin American Philosophy." *CR: The New Centennial Review* 7, no. 3 (2007): 51–78.

Vargas, Manuel. "On the Value of Philosophy: The Latin American Case." *Comparative Philosophy* 1, no. 1 (2010): 33–52.

CHAPTER 10

# LATINA/O RELIGIOUS STUDIES SINCE THE 1970S

## FELIPE HINOJOSA

IN 1976, the historian Juan Gómez-Quiñones posed three significant challenges to the field of Chicano history: move beyond parochialisms, improve theoretical approaches, and train future Chicano historians as broadly as possible incorporating Chicano, Latin American, and US history. These challenges reflected an honest assessment of the field in the 1970s even as they embodied the stream of thought prevalent in American history toward social and urban history at the time.[1] Following what Michael Kammen called the "historiographical whirlwind" of the 1970s, US historians turned away from political and social institutions as central categories of analysis and increasingly examined social and urban cultural life.[2]

The emergence of Chicana/o and Puerto Rican studies reflected part of these trends, especially in the areas of social and urban history. These fields challenged essentialist notions of the Latino origin population in the United States inherent in Southwestern, Borderlands, and US history.[3] They did so by adopting interdisciplinary approaches that provided a more complete view of the Latina/o community in the United States. As a result, our understanding of the intersections of race, gender, class, identity, rural/urban society, and labor in colonial and modern America has flourished since the 1970s. Chicana/o and Puerto Rican studies formed part of this emergent trend in the 1960s and 1970s as it drafted a counter-narrative that better resembled the complex and sometimes fractured identities of Latinos and Latinas in the United States. These fields garnered intense critique from some US historians who saw them as "soapboxes for political and academic opportunists" and without a "beginning, middle, or end."[4] These critiques, however, missed the ways Chicana/o and Puerto Rican studies resembled a process of becoming whose currents flowed both forward and backward.

Often left out of this conversation is the evolution of Latina/o religious studies, which also came of age in the 1970s. Motivated by the political tenor of the times, and focused almost exclusively on Christianity, Latina/o religious studies took seriously the call to contextualize theological studies by stressing racial identity, resistance to church hierarchy, and economic inequality. The writings of liberation theologians in Latin America, especially the Peruvian theologian Gustavo Gutierrez, served as a foundational resource for an entire generation of Latina/o theologians and religious studies scholars in the United States in the 1970s.[5] Theologians such as Virgilio Elizondo, Justo Gonzalez, Orlando Costas, Otto Maduro, and Ada María Isasí-Diaz each offered rich theological reflections that both contextualized the Latina/o experience and challenged Eurocentric assumptions about faith and God.[6] These scholars noted the dialectics of religion as encompassing the power to sustain the status quo even as it created "oppositional cultures" that resisted the religious imperatives of colonialism and racism. That legacy of "affirmation and resistance," as historian Mario T. García asserts, is critical to understanding the evolution of Latina/o religious studies.[7]

The following essay traces the development of Latina/o religious studies and its engagements with ethnic studies generally and Latina/o studies specifically. The religious historian Gastón Espinosa identifies at least six different interpretive frameworks used to asses Latina/o religious life and politics in the United States. They include traditional church history, liberation theological studies, popular theology, social scientific and phenomenological approaches, and ethnic studies.[8] While each approach is steeped in its own methodologies and literature, it is ethnic studies that have seen a significant crossover in terms of publications in recent years. For these reasons, this article focuses on the convergence of ethnic studies and religious studies in the last fifty years—from the 1970s to the present—to show the symbolic power of religion and how a motley crew of Latina/o religious outsiders and civil rights activists laid the groundwork for the rise of Latina/o faith politics.[9]

## History from the Margins

Today it has become fashionable for scholars to pose questions about the relevance of religious life and politics in Latina/o studies, especially with the growing religious pluralism reflected in every state across the country. Even as a majority of Latina/os in the United States are Catholic (nearly 55 percent), 22 percent adhere to an eclectic mix of mainline Protestantism and Pentecostalism while the remaining 18 percent are religiously unaffiliated, a number that has grown rapidly in the last few years.[10] This growing religious diversity offers new clues into the ways Latino/as have forged transnational networks, participated in electoral politics and immigrant rights' movements, and the ways they have transformed public space via storefront churches or sidewalk shrines. Rather than viewing religion as a roadblock to social change, Latina/o studies scholars have recognized religion as an area of study that helps us better understand transnational cultures, migrant streams, activist politics, and diverse forms of "spiritual mestizaje" that make up the visibilities of Latina/o life.[11]

The roots of Latina/o religion run deep and draw from rich cultural traditions across the Americas. The key to understanding Latina/o religion, as religious historian Luis D. León argued, is in recognizing its "in-betweeness" and in the ways in which its symbols, prayers, and festivals are expressions rooted in its Indigenous, Iberian, and African past. The cultural theorist Gloria Anzaldúa argued that "the religion of the Mexicans—Catholicism—is just a veneer... people only go to church, believe in Christ, and eat the host because that was happening in Aztec religion."[12] Latina/o religion, in other words, has a long and storied tradition rooted in the experiences, miracles, cultures, and worldviews of Indigenous groups across the Americas. Consider, for example, that Latino Catholicism originated in the sixteenth century with the first diocese established in 1511 in San Juan, Puerto Rico. Its evolution from there followed complex patterns of violence and cultural exchange, land theft, and religious innovation. As a result, Latina/o religion is a faith tradition steeped in the resistance and dignity of peoples across the Americas whose religious innovations—whose blending of European, Indigenous, and African spiritualities—were critical to their survival. Colonialism, in other words, was not an all-encompassing project.

One clear example of this is the Santuario Chimayó, the most popular site of Catholic pilgrimage in the United States, which links a sacred Native American site with Christian tradition. As historian Brett Hendrickson has shown, this historic place is an example of the ways persons of mixed ancestry drew on multiple healing traditions: from the Iberian Peninsula to the healing remedies of the indigenous populations.[13] This mix of remedies—and in some cases miracles—not only furthered the blending of Christian and Indigenous traditions, but also played a direct role in the spread of *Guadalupan* devotion across Mexico during the eighteenth and nineteenth centuries.

Recognizing the diverse legacy of Latina/o religion and the violence that sparked it forms part of the recovery project that scholars such as David Carrasco, Theresa Delgadillo, and Luis D. León have engaged as Ethnic and Religious studies scholars. The work of these scholars serves as a corrective to the long history of institutional church histories in the late nineteenth century and early twentieth centuries that long neglected the colonial roots of Latina/o religion. Sponsored by specific Christian denominations and intended for white Christian audiences, these works celebrated the nation-building aspirations of the ones doing the missionary work.[14] They erased the cultural and religious blending so central to Latina/o religion and instead drenched their writings with paternalism and one-dimensional views of the community. One of the first to push back against this trend was the anthropologist Manuel Gamio who in the 1930s made key observations about the religious lives of Mexican immigrants in his classic works, *Immigration to the United States* (1930) and *The Mexican Immigrant: His Life Story* (1931). His careful examinations of popular Catholic practices, church attendance, Protestantism, and anti-clericalism provided an up-close look at how religion eased the transition into American society for Mexican immigrants.[15] Gamio's humanistic take on religious life in the 1920s and 1930s remains an important source for religious historians, providing key insights that outside observers and church historians of the time for the most part ignored.

In the years after World War II, with the nation in the midst of a religious revival, the works of Samuel Ortegón (Mexican Protestants), Juan Lugo (Puerto Rican Pentecostals), and Carlos Castañeda (Spanish/Mexican Catholicism) emerged as important insider accounts of religion in the Latina/o community.[16] Even as they presented a romanticized view of Christianity and stressed the connections between religion and social uplift, these works reflected the emergence of scholars set on challenging simplistic notions of Mexican American and Puerto Rican culture while challenging racial discrimination. In this way, the works of Castañeda, Ortegón, and Lugo belong in conversation with scholars such as George I. Sánchez, Américo Paredes, and the muckraker journalist Carey McWilliams, all of whom published important works between the 1930s and the 1950s.[17] Together they represented diverse topical and interpretive approaches as each author dealt with accommodation, resistance, adaptation, and victimization within the rubrics of race, class, religion, and gender. The manner in which most academic studies at midcentury homogenized and essentialized the Mexican origin population required a nuanced view of culture and identity. This generation of scholars provided just that.

The mid-twentieth century witnessed the globalization of American religion as white Christians took on a more public role both in the United States and across the globe. More money was funneled to global and urban mission projects, church attendance was at a high, and construction on new churches took off. This was also a moment in American history when nearly 65 percent of Americans identified as members of a church or synagogue and where 96 percent claimed allegiance to a particular religious group.[18] Latina/o religious communities, on the other hand, remained absent from public consciousness; if they were visible, they remained marginal and as a population to be served and in need of salvation. The Baptist church historian Adam Morales noted that as Mexicans and Puerto Ricans migrated to the urban north at midcentury, Protestant missionaries followed closely to organize "trackside churches" along the Santa Fe and Union Pacific rail lines to share the Gospel message with railroad workers.[19] That's not to say that Latina/os were only the recipients of missions—they had their own cadre of missionaries—only that Latina/o religious life for much of this period was seen as an oddity, an aberration to traditional white Christianity in the United States. Social scientific studies that emerged in the 1950s, for example, tended to focus almost exclusively on the supposed superstitious beliefs of Latina/o Catholics and on their criminal tendencies.[20] In my own research on Mennonite missionaries in South Texas, accusations of Mexicans being "religiously confused" because of their shifting religious loyalties and blended religious traditions were common.[21]

These misrepresentations, or in some cases outright exclusions, continued well into the 1970s. Social scientific studies done by white scholars generally ignored Latina/o religious communities well into the 1970s. The sociologist Andrew Greeley excluded Latina/os from his 1977 book, *The American Catholic*, so as to avoid the "cross-cutting influence of race" on the mobility of religious groups.[22] That massive exclusion, as sociologist Anthony M. Stevens-Arroyo noted, led to two pioneering surveys: *Our Sunday Visitor* and *The Hispanic Catholic in the United States* (1985).[23] Both studies affirmed the relevance and importance of Latina/o religious life. But more important, they formed part of a larger movement that began in the early 1970s to document the history, culture, and theological orientations of Latina/os. As a result of the monumental decisions made during the Second Vatican Council (1962–1965), the church moved away from its fortress-like presence to one that vowed to engage the world and initiate a dialogue across faith traditions and practices—this revolution spoke of a more holistic view of God's people.

## Revolution from the Top

The Second Vatican Council differed significantly from the twenty previous ecclesiastical assemblies in the history of the Catholic Church. The theologian Han Kung put it this way, "We are in exodus from the Catholic ghetto in all directions, first toward other Christians, then toward the Jews, then toward all other religions of the world and finally toward the modern world in general. The church has initiated a new epoch in Christianity."[24] From Vatican II came new positions on education, divine revelation, and on the language used during Mass. This change, along with the Bishop's meeting on liberation theology in Medellin in 1968, confirmed the idea that all Catholics—not just the leadership—could be a force for change within the church. Liberation Theology, most notably with the writings of Peruvian Priest Gustavo Gutierrez, provided a striking critique of capitalism and insisted that the church work for structural change to eradicate poverty. Poverty, economic injustice, was no longer simply an economic condition, but now labeled as "sin" by liberation theologians. The shift proved monumental. The realignment of the Catholic Church across the Americas, together with the thorough realignment of politics in the United States, ushered in by the civil rights movement, put Latina/o religious communities on the map, and forced the church to deal with its racial exclusions in ways it had not done previously.[25]

But as monumental as Vatican II and liberation theology were to the life of the Catholic Church, the strongest push for religious involvement in Latina/o civil rights came not from clergy but from religious outsiders, labor leaders, and youth who had left the church years before. One of the most important examples of this is the labor leader Cesar Chavez. In 1968 Chavez penned an essay entitled "The Mexican American and the Church," where he called out the Catholic Church for failing to support striking farmworkers. Always the strategist, Chavez learned early on the power of the church, both Catholic and Protestant, during his days as an organizer with the Community Service Organization. It is why he forged alliances with clergy as a way to broaden the appeal of the movement beyond California and beyond the Mexican American community. His strategic use of the church, religious symbols—including *la virgin de Guadalupe*—caught the attention of activists in other sectors of the Latina/o civil rights movement.

Chavez wrote the essay during his twenty-five-day fast and later presented it at the Annual Mexican Conference in Sacramento, California, in 1968.[26] The hesitancy from church leaders to back striking farmworkers, Chavez argued, countered a history of advocacy and service, especially in California. The Protestant-led California Migrant

Ministry and the "Spanish Mission Band" of four "priests of the poor" had ministered and worked alongside farmworkers and Mexican braceros in the 1940s and 1950s.[27] The politics of the 1960s, however, had tempered the church's enthusiasm. Clergy in particular paid a price for their support of the farmworker strike. For their political commitments, clergy were silenced, transferred, or forced to leave the ministry because of their political commitments.[28] Religious leaders also feared that backing striking farmworkers could alienate wealthy constituents, many of whom were growers in central California. Thirty-one months after the National Farm Worker Association joined Filipino farmworkers to strike grape growers in Delano, California, religious leaders had to a large degree remained silent.

Chavez's essay helped turn the tide by calling the church into account. But Chavez's essay is also important for another reason. Not only did he demand that church leaders support farmworkers, Chavez also called on Mexican American activists to recognize the political power of the church, a point often overlooked by scholars. "I am calling for Mexican-American groups to stop ignoring this source of power," Chavez argued, "It is not just our right to appeal to the Church to use its power effectively for the poor, it is our duty to do so."[29] Whether Chavez was responsible for increased attention on the church, or activists already had their eye on it, the fact is that the late 1960s witnessed the greatest political engagement from Chicana/o and Puerto Rican activists with religious institutions.

Unfortunately, the historical scholarship on Latina/o religious politics has not yet caught up to this important point. Much of the work on Latina/o religious activism in the 1960s and 1970s, for example, focuses almost exclusively on the farmworker struggle and the relationship between Cesar Chavez and the church. The widely read primary source reader, *The Columbia Documentary History of Religion in America Since 1945*, is a prime example. A quick glance at the section on Latina/o civil rights and religion starts and stops with Cesar Chavez and the farmworker struggle.[30] To be fair, the abundance of primary documents and the fact that religion was central to the farmworker movement have made it a favorite topic for religious scholars. Areas in Latina/o religious studies that remain understudied include urban social movements, the religious left, and immigration, all themes first laid out by the Catholic journalist Moises Sandoval in the early 1980s. In his 1983 book *Fronteras*, Sandoval correctly argued that the Latina/o faith was not solely an inspiration for struggling farmworkers but also played a prominent role in urban movements, especially those that targeted urban renewal in places such as New York, Chicago, Houston, and Los Angeles.[31]

## Revolution from the Bottom

The urban rebellions of the late 1960s, and the activism that emerged from it, are a much more fruitful place to start thinking about the rise of Latina/o religious politics. In Chicago, for example, the Puerto Rican Young Lords, together with a coalition of community groups, occupied the McCormick Theological Seminary (Presbyterian) in May 1969.[32] Located in the heart of Chicago's Lincoln Park neighborhood, the McCormick occupation was a strategic move to hold the seminary at least partially responsible for its role in the city's urban renewal push in Lincoln Park. The Young Lords assembled a "rainbow coalition" of black, brown, and white activists that occupied the seminary for five days and pushed the Presbyterian Church USA to actively work against urban renewal in Chicago.

Part of what made this occupation big news was that it took place only days after James Forman had presented the "Black Manifesto," which in 1969 demanded $500 million as reparations for slavery from white Christians. Drafted by Forman, the former SNCC activist and civil rights leader, the Black Manifesto captured the attention of religious leaders across the country. And while Forman never came close to receiving the $500 million, the manifesto did spark an intense conversation between Catholic and Protestant leadership about how best to engage and support the calls for reform within religious institutions that for too long had stood on the sidelines of the civil rights movement. The Black Manifesto also helped pave the way for Latina/o activists to make their own appeals.

When James Forman stood in front of a room full of white Presbyterians at their 181st General Assembly in San Antonio in 1969 to speak on the Black Manifesto, he was joined by a quiet, all-male, and largely unknown Latino cadre that included the Rev. Roger Granados, Tomas Chavez Jr. (Spanish-American Outreach, Detroit), Eliezar Risco (editor and co-founder of La Raza newsletter, Los Angeles), and Obed López (director of the Latin American Defense Organization, Chicago).[33] A mix of religious insiders and outsiders, the group was there to speak about the occupation of McCormick Seminary in Chicago and to propose their own manifesto, the Brown Manifesto, which called for $500,000 for church programs in Latino communities, disinvestment in Latin America, and included a statement of solidarity and support for people of the Third World and the Black Manifesto.[34] Designed as an equivalent to the Black Manifesto, the Brown Manifesto sought to forge solidarity between black and brown activists and clergy.[35] While Forman garnered the most attention that day, making a speech that both inspired and troubled white Presbyterians, it was the largely forgotten words of the Rev. Granados, a Mexican American Presbyterian pastor from California, that shined a light on the emergence of Latina/o religious politics during the late 1960s.

> Church programs humiliated and bound us...we were objects of someone else's mission...The greatest majority of our people not interested in church...Many people trying to define Raza. For me it's an assertion: A new race neither Spanish nor Indian. Detroit Milwaukee, Puertorriqueno, Hispano, Mexicano, Español...among us no common denominator of details. No consensus on anything. Common cause is to be free.[36]

Granados's words speak volumes to the combined sense of loss and hope that many Latina/o religious leaders felt at the end of the 1960s. A belief that the institutional church—mainline Protestant in this case—had done more harm than good thrived alongside a hope for a new Latina/o identity emerging across the country. No consensus, no essentialisms, only a movement whose "common cause is to be free."[37]

The occupation of McCormick Seminary by the Young Lords caused a ripple effect. Later that year in Los Angeles a group called *Católicos Por La Raza* disrupted Christmas Eve Mass in December 1969 as a way to protest the newly constructed St Basil's Catholic Church and its $3 million price tag. Three days after that demonstration outside St. Basil's Catholic Church, the Puerto Rican Young Lords in New York took over the First Spanish Methodist Church (FSMC) in East Harlem on a cold Sunday morning. The takeover in East Harlem was followed up by another church takeover in Houston, Texas. On February 15, 1970, members of the Mexican American Youth Organization (MAYO) took over the Juan Marcos Presbyterian Church located in Houston's northside. MAYO activists occupied the church for three weeks, and in that time they started a free breakfast program, cultural education classes, and presented workshops on social services that were available in the area. After the third week, Brazos Presbytery leadership stepped in and cut the gas and electricity in the building and filed a district court injunction designed to evict MAYO out of the church.[38] MAYO leaders evacuated the building, but the demonstrations against Presbyterian churches across the city continued into April. Jose Gutierrez, state leader of MAYO, put churches across Texas on notice saying that MAYO will use occupation as a tactic to achieve social change."[39]

Each of these occupations offers a glimpse into the new religious and political consciousness of the late 1960s and early 1970s. The results, and the overall benefit of these occupations, is how they opened a path for Latina/o religious leaders. Latina/o religious leaders had already started advocating for more inclusion within both Catholic and Protestant groups. A number of church councils, leadership institutes, and conferences on race and the "Spanish-Speaking" had made the rounds in US churches. The occupations, however, were a different force, led by a group of religious outsiders, that put fear into the hearts of the mostly white religious leadership in both Catholic and Protestant churches. That was enough for religious leadership to finally take seriously the calls and demands being made by Latina/o religious insiders, especially clergy.[40] The occupations, and the disruption they caused for churches and religious leaders, gave rise to a new and more powerful Latina/o religious leadership.

## THEOLOGICAL REVOLUTION

In the 1970s Latina/o leaders, representing multiple religious traditions, demanded religious materials in Spanish, better representation in decision-making church structures, and greater opportunities for theological education. New programs in Latina/o theological studies, such as the Mexican American Cultural Center (San Antonio 1972) and the Mexican American Program at the Perkins School of Theology (Dallas 1974), led the way in making the 1970s a decade that saw the formative development of

Latina/o theology. Part of the educational developments that also saw the rise of many other programs in black, Chicano, and Puerto Rican studies, Latina/o theological studies moved away from a Eurocentric focus that excluded much of Latin America and Latina/os in the United States. Latina and Latino theologians such as Virgilio Elizondo, Justo Gonzalez, Marina Herrera, Ada Maria Isasi Diaz, and Allen Figueroa Deck all provided a rubric to better contextualize theology in Latina/o religious communities.[41] Latina/o theologians also introduced new frameworks to theological studies. Theologian Michelle Gonzalez identifies at least five distinct themes that are central to Latina/o theological studies. They include, socio-cultural context, mestizaje/mulatez, popular religion, *lo cotidiano* (everyday life), and praxis. Latina/o theologians took culture seriously and developed a frame of study that argued for theology's cultural specificity, rooted in a particular communities' history and social location. This was a critical moment because it situated, as Michelle Gonzalez correctly argues, that "racial and cultural mixture, the sense of people living between two worlds, reflects the context from which Hispanic theology emerges."[42]

Central to this racial and cultural mixing is the development of a Latina feminist theology. Scholars such as Ada Maria Isasí Díaz, Maria Pilar Aquino, and Loida Martell Otero look at women's lives and experiences as central in the development of theological studies. Over the years, contextualizing Latina feminist theology has taken multiple forms. From the rejection of the term "feminist" to an embrace of the identity "mujerista" to an identification with the experiences of "evangélicas," Latina theologians have been central to identifying the complexities and diversities inherent within both cultural and political streams of thought alive in Latina/o United States and in Latin America. That tension, and diversity, has strengthened the viability of Latina/o theology as a critical intervention in theological and religious studies.[43] Yet those very tensions are also rooted in questions over Latina/o theologies' political claims and whether they exist outside of the academy. For example, Maria Pilar Aquino questioned the use of the term "mujerista" because "there are no *mujerista* sociopolitical and ecclesiastical subjects or movements in the United States or Latin America." In response, Michelle Gonzalez adds that it is also fair to ask whether Latina feminist theological movements exist outside of the academy. Both are fair questions and critiques that are rooted in what is considered a central weakness of the Latina/o theology that emerged in the 1970s and 1980s: its lack of historical research. This is a point that Gonzalez addressed in another essay where she argued that "historical research needs to be an active component of Latino/a theological elaborations."[44] That active component emerged most forcefully in the 1980s by two important scholars, Moises Sandoval and Antonio M. Stevens-Arroyo.

Like Manuel Gamio's work in the 1930s, these scholars provided a historical context for colonialism, liberationist praxis, and *lo cotidiano*, all themes central to Latina/o theology. They mapped out a research agenda of important religious figures, events, and churches that scholars continue to pull from. Sandoval edited the classic text *Fronteras: A History of the Latin American Church in the USA Since 1513* and in 1990 wrote *On the Move: A History of the Hispanic Church in the United States* (it was reissued in 2006). In 1980 Stevens-Arroyo published his classic text, *Prophets Denied Honor: An Anthology on the Hispano Church in the United States*. In it, Stevens-Arroyo pulls together biography, theology, and history to tell the dynamic story of Latina/o religion in the United States, from Catholicism to storefront Pentecostal churches. He would go on to author and edit a dozen books and write more than a hundred scholarly articles on Latina/o religious politics. The works of Sandoval and Stevens-Arroyo recognized the agency of religious leaders and enacted a political tradition of affirmation and resistance to institutional church practices: themes that remain central to the study of Latina/o religious studies. They set the standard and paved the way for a new cadre of historians in the 1990s and early 2000s that expanded the field and moved it beyond its theological roots. The following section provides a brief overview of the major works in history and ethnic studies that have breathed life into some of the theological concepts first developed by Sandoval and Stevens-Arroyo in the 1970s and 1980s, especially those having to do with sociopolitical context and praxis. Since at least the mid-1990s, scholars have stepped up to provide a historical context for the social movements, festivals, and political engagements of Latina/o religious life in the United States.

## Historical Revolution

If the 1970s constituted the formative period for Latina/o theology in the United States, the late 1990s and first decade of the twenty-first century—the 2000s—produced some of the most important works in the field of Latina/o religious history. Scholars such as Rudy Busto, Lara Medina, Timothy Matovina, Arlene M. Sánchez Walsh, Gastón Espinosa, Roberto Treviño, and Mario T. García all published important books during this period.[45] These works shaped my own early academic career and confirmed my desire to become a Latino historian. I entered graduate school at the University of Houston eager to write about how Latina/o activists understood justice and power. Did religion, or the biblical text itself, have anything to say? Was there a spirituality that carried and strengthened the Chicana/o movement? Unfortunately, most of the books published by religious historians rarely made it into my Chicana/o and Latina/o history graduate reading lists. That meant that I had to create my own reading lists, piecing together the works on Latina Catholic activism (Lara Medina) and Chicana/o Pentecostals in Southern California (Arlene M. Sánchez Walsh).

In the 1990s no scholar helped further the study of Latina/o religious studies more than Timothy Matovina. In the years since, no one has been better at bridging the historiographical divide between theological studies and historical studies than Matovina. Both a theologian and a historian, Matovina is one of the few scholars whose work is cited and referenced in both theological studies specifically and in Latina/o studies more broadly. Back in 2006, when Rudy Busto called for a more concerted effort to bridge discussions between religious and ethnic studies, Matovina was already one of the few scholars who was actually already engaged in such disciplinary crossings.[46] His first book, *Tejano Religion and Ethnicity*, investigated religious cultures and festivals in a rapidly transforming Mexican, and later, American, frontier. Set in nineteenth-century San Antonio, Matovina argued that Tejano identity formed in relation to both a sense of connection to the Mexican homeland and relationships with Anglo immigrants.[47] As the politics of colonization changed the lives of many Tejanos, Matovina contends that adaptation to new political structures was tempered by cultural maintenance. This maintenance exhibited itself through religious practices and festivals. In comparison to European ethnics who often viewed their national cathedrals as way stations to American assimilation, Matovina contends that for Tejanos, the San Fernando Cathedral served as a hub for religious culture and maintenance. Far from unilateral assimilation, Tejanos used Catholicism as a means to practice their festivals, meet with each other, and as a safe space of community interaction. The notion that religion was instrumental in maintaining culture, rather than stripping it bare, affirmed much of the scholarship on mestizaje and praxis that was published by Latina/o theologians in the 1970s and 1980s.

Context also matters here. Matovina published his first book at a transformative moment in American history. In the 1990s, immigration from Latin America was at its highest rate in decades. That wave of immigration gave witness to the increasing religious plurality of the Latina/o immigrant population. While Catholicism still remained the most practiced faith in Latin America, movements such as Pentecostalism had seen a steady rise. Latin American scholars in Latin America had already been documenting the changes in the religious marketplace since the 1980s.[48] In the late 1990s, Latina/o scholars began to pay close attention to the growing numbers of Latina/o Pentecostals in the United States. In 2003, Arlene M. Sánchez Walsh's work, *Latino Pentecostal Identity*, opened up new possibilities for the future of Chicana/o and ethnic studies by examining the intersections between religious and ethnic identity and the manner in which Latina/os culturally coalesced multiple identities. The blending of the sacred with popular culture, Sánchez-Walsh asserts, opened the cultural doors to Latina/os as they redefined the meanings of Pentecostalism. Identifying "Victory Outreach" church in Southern California as a "Chicano church," Sánchez-Walsh showed how the church reached out to Latinos with programs such as "Barrios for Christ," rap/hip hop, street dramas, and various other forms of pop culture, especially in the post-movement era. In this way, religion, and specifically Pentecostalism, has served as an alternative cultural expression.[49]

While Sánchez-Walsh took a "cultural coalescence" approach to Chicano Pentecostals in Southern California, the work of Richard Martinez, Lara Medina, and Roberto Treviño focused instead on the social movements birthed within traditional Roman Catholicism and the relationship between religion and ethnicity. Rooted in social history, these works showed how Catholicism played an important role in the everyday lives of Mexican Americans from across the Southwest. At a moment when Latina/os comprise more than one third of the Catholic church—and soon they will make up roughly half of all US Catholics—these works explored how Catholicism shaped Mexican American and Latina/o identity and vice versa. With a focus on civil rights and community formation, Medina, Martinez, and Trevino moved away from framing the religious experience as a binary: institutional versus popular. Instead, they argued for a much more interactive experience that moved away from such neat binaries that fail to convey the complexities of Latina/o religious identities. Moreover, these works repositioned movement politics along cultural, spatial, and political lines and broadened our collective understanding of the spaces and varying political cultures active during the Chicana/o movement.

For Latina/o religious leaders in particular, this era matters because it is the moment when, according to historian Paul Barton, "Ethnic affiliation became as important to them as denominational affiliation."[50] In a very real way these works dismantled the notion that religion is simply a force for assimilation or political apathy. By building on social movement, feminist, and social histories, these works showed how Latina/o civil rights and religious activism are more integrated than previously thought. And perhaps the Chicana/o and Puerto Rican civil rights movements are not as secular as we believed them to be.

## New Contexts, New Directions

In the last ten years scholars have further interrogated the intersections of social movements and religion. Influenced at least in part by Latina/o immigrant communities that in 2006 took to the streets in the thousands to push back against the federal government's linking of anti-terrorism and immigration policing, scholars have focused their research on trying to historicize the church's critical role in movements for social change. Latina/o "faith politics," as Mario Garcia has called it, are anything but monolithic and have ranged from Latina/o activists occupying churches to Mexican Catholics in Chicago and Milwaukee to the role of Pentecostals in immigration and presidential politics. Scholars such as Sergio Gonzalez, Maggie Elmore, and Daisy Vargas represent a new wave of scholars exploring the religious implications on topics such as police violence, Latinx social movements, community formation in the Midwest, and immigration history.[51] This scholarship points toward a new direction in Latina/o religious studies. Rather than a church history focused on religious actors, Chicano priests or religious women for example, these scholars are posing new questions about the symbolic power of religion and the ways in which secular forces have shaped religious institutions and politics. It is a Latina/o religious studies from the outside in rather than simply from the inside out; a focus on non-religious forces that have shaped religious institutions.

At the heart of this new scholarship lies the question of spirituality. The cultural critic Michelle Tellez reminds us that our spirituality is closely tied to our evolving political beliefs, and that "spirituality, in the end, is how we relate to each other as human beings, independent of theology."[52] How else are we to understand the Sanctuary movement in the 1980s when churches across the country took in asylum seekers, or make sense of

Chicano activist groups such as the Brown Berets that essentially existed because of the support of a progressive Episcopal church in Los Angeles? Without a firm grasp of religion as a political force in history, how else are we to make sense of Latina/o immigrant settlement in the urban north in cities like Chicago and Milwaukee? An ethnic studies approach to religious studies, where rituals and festivals, protest movements, community formation, and immigrant rights take center stage, is critical if we are to tease out the spiritual roots of Latina/o activism in the United States. Doing so requires moving beyond parochialisms, crossing disciplinary borders, and taking Latina/o and ethnic studies in new and innovative directions. It means starting from the outside and considering how youth, religious outsiders, and Chicana/o and Puerto Rican activists all broke down barriers that since the 1970s have made it easier for clergy and laypeople to advocate for social change within their religious groups. This necessarily means expanding what we mean by Latina/o religious politics. It cannot remain solely fixated on religious figures: clergy or religious leaders. Scholars must dig deep to examine how secular and religious communities mix things up, how they collaborate, and where they converge and diverge. And finally, it means taking seriously our responsibilities as community leaders, activists, teachers, and scholars to present as diverse a field as possible. Seeing religion from its many sides, from the perspective of its detractors and its adherents, while exploring its political importance, offers us that possibility.

## Notes

1. Juan Gómez-Quiñones and Luis Leobardo Arroyo, "On the State of Chicano History: Observations on Its Development, Interpretations, and Theory, 1970–1974," *Western Historical Quarterly* 7, no. 2 (April 1976), 155–185.
2. For a good analysis on the way social history impacted the field of US history in the postwar era, see Michael Kammen, ed., *The Past Before Us: Contemporary Historical Writing in the United States* (Ithaca, NY: Cornell University Press, 1980).
3. Historian David Weber argued that the works of Albert Camarillo (1979), Richard Griswold del Castillo (1979), and Mario T. García used methods (oral histories, census data, draft registration cards) that helped provide a "collective portrait of a people." Roger Lotchin argued that three methodological themes dominated urban history in the 1960s: "topical diversification, a sensitivity to social science thought and methodology, and quantification."; see David Weber and Roger W. Lotchin, "The New Chicano Urban History: Two Perspectives," *The History Teacher* 16, no. 2 (February 1983), 226.
4. Weber and Lotchin, "The New Chicano Urban History," 228.
5. Gustavo Gutierrez, *A Theology of Liberation*. On the Gospel politics of mestizaje and Jesus Christ as mestizo, see Virgilio Elizondo, *Galilean Journey: The Mexican-American Promise* (Maryknoll, NY: Orbis Books, 1983).
6. Gilbert R. Cadena, "Chicano Clergy and the Emergence of Liberation Theology," *Hispanic Journal of Behavioral Sciences* 11, no. 2 (May 1989): 107–121. The dominant theme that materialized early out of this work had to do with the mixed racial and ethnic heritage of Latino/as (mestizaje), the relationship between colonialism and religion, and the meanings behind doing theological reflection from a Latina/o perspective.

7. Dwight B. Billings, "Religion as Opposition: A Gramscian Analysis," *The American Journal of Sociology* 96, no. 1 (July 1990): 27; Mario T. García, *Católicos: Resistance and Affirmation in Chicano Catholic History* (Austin: University of Texas Press, 2010).
8. Gastón Espinosa, "Methodological Reflections on Social Science Research in Latino Religions," in *Rethinking Latino/a Religion and Identity*, ed. Gastón Espinosa and Miguel De La Torre (Cleveland, OH: Pilgrim Press, 2006).
9. This essay is focused exclusively on the literature on the multiple forms of Christianity as practiced by the majority of the Latina/o population in the United States.
10. "The Shifting Religious Identity of Latinos in the United States," Pew Research Center, May 7, 2014. http://www.pewhispanic.org.
11. Recent scholarship is pointing us in this direction. See, for example, Roberto Treviño, *The Church in the Barrio: Mexican American Ethno-Catholicism in Houston* (Chapel Hill, NC: University of North Carolina Press, 2006); Paul Barton, *Hispanic Methodists, Presbyterians, and Baptists in Texas* (Austin, TX: University of Texas Press, 2006); Lara Medina, *Las Hermanas: Chicana/Latina Religious-Political Activism in the U. S. Catholic Church* (Philadelphia, PA: Temple University Press, 2005); Mario T. García, *Católicos: Resistance and Affirmation in Chicano Catholic History* (Austin, TX: University of Texas Press, 2010); Arlene M. Sanchez-Walsh, *Latino Pentecostal Identity: Evangelical Faith, Self, and Society* (New York: Columbia University Press, 2003); Theresa Delgadillo, *Spiritual Mestizaje: Religion, Gender, Race, and Nation in Contemporary Chicana Narrative* (Durham, NC: Duke University Press, 2011); Elaine Padilla, *Performing Piety: Making Space Sacred with the Virgin of Guadalupe* (Berkley: University of California Press, 2011).
12. Gloria Anzaldua, interview with Louis Keating, ed., *Interviews/Entrevistas* (New York: Routledge, 2000), 96.
13. Brett Hendrickson, *The Healing Power of the Santuario de Chimayó: America's Miraculous Church* (New York: New York University Press, 2017), 24.
14. Some of these works included Jean Baptiste Salpointe, *Soldiers of the Cross: Notes on the Ecclesiastical History of New Mexico, Arizona, and Colorado* (1898); Thomas Harwood, *History of Spanish and English Missions of the New Mexico Methodist Episcopal Church from 1850–1910*, 2 vols., (1908, 1910); Jay S. Stowell, *A Study of Mexicans and Spanish Americans in the United States* (1920); Theodore Abel, *Protestant Home Missions to Catholic Immigrants* (1933). For a thorough review of all of these works and the trajectory of Mexican American religious history, see Gastón Espinosa and Miguel De La Torre, *Rethinking Latino(a) Religions and Identity* (Cleveland, OH: Pilgrim Press, 2006).
15. Manuel Gamio, *Immigration to the United States* (Chicago: University of Chicago Press, 1930); Manuel Gamio, *The Mexican Immigrant: His Life Story* (Chicago: University of Chicago Press, 1931).
16. Samuel M. Ortegón, "The Religious Thought and Practice Among Mexican Baptists of the United States, 1900–1947," (1950); Juan Lugo, *Pentecostes en Puerto Rico: La Vida de un Misionero* (San Juan, PR: Puerto Rico Gospel Press, 1951); Carlos Castañeda, *Our Catholic Heritage in Texas, 1519–1936* (Austin, TX: Von-Boeckmann-Jones Co., 1976). In this way these works stressed an adaptation approach to the study of Mexicans and Puerto Ricans.
17. Carey McWilliams, *North From Mexico: The Spanish Speaking People of the United States* (New York: Greenwood Press, 1949); George I. Sánchez, *Forgotten People* (Albuquerque: University of New Mexico Press, 1940); Américo Paredes, *With a Pistol in His Hands* (Austin: University of Texas Press, 1957).

18. Paul Harvey and Philip Goff, eds., *The Columbia Documentary History of Religion in America Since 1945* (New York: Columbia University Press, 2005), 4.
19. Adam Morales, *American Baptists with a Spanish Accent* (King of Prussia, PA: The Judson Press, 1964), 41.
20. For more on mid-twentieth century Latino itinerant preachers, see Gastón Espinosa, "El Azteca: Francisco Olazábal and Latino Charisma, Power, and Faith Healing in the Borderlands," *Journal of the American Academy of Religion* 67, no. 3 (1999), 597–616; Anthony M. Stevens-Arroyo and Ana María Díaz-Stevens, *Recognizing the Latino Resurgence in U.S. Religion* (Boulder, CO: Westview Press, 1998), 2.
21. Felipe Hinojosa, *Latino Mennonites: Civil Rights, Faith, and Evangelical Culture* (Baltimore: Johns Hopkins University Press, 2014).
22. Hinojosa, *Latino Mennonites*, 3.
23. Hinojosa, *Latino Mennonites*, 4.
24. *Newsweek*, December 20, 1965, F094, File: Vatican II. Hispanic American Institute Collection, Austin Presbyterian Seminary, Austin, Texas.
25. John T. McGreevey, *Parish Boundaries: The Catholic Encounter with Race in the Twentieth Century* (Chicago: University of Chicago Press, 1996), 162.
26. Cesar Chavez, "The Mexican American and the Church," *El Grito* 4 (Summer 1968).
27. Chavez, "The Mexican American and the Church," 380. For more on the Farmworker movement in Texas, see Alan Watt, *Farm Workers and the Churches: The Movement in California and Texas* (College Station: Texas A & M University Press, 2010).
28. Moises Sandoval, *Fronteras: A History of the Latin American Church in the USA Since 1513* (San Antonio, TX: Mexican American Cultural Center, 1983), 381.
29. Chavez, "The Mexican American and the Church."
30. Harvey and Goff, *The Columbia Documentary History of Religion in America Since 1945*, 186–190. I should add that Harvey's exclusions here say as much about the lack of studies on Latina/o religious activism as they do about the broader ignorance of the field at large. In other words, much work remains to be done.
31. Sandoval, *Fronteras*, 380.
32. I am currently working on a book project on church occupations by Latina/o activists in the 1960s and 1970s. Part of that work has already been published: Felipe Hinojosa, "Sacred Spaces: Race, Resistance, and the Politics of Chicana/o and Latina/o Religious History" in *A Promising Problem: The New Chicana/o History*, ed. Carlos K. Blanton (Austin: University of Texas Press, 2016), 111–134; For more on church occupations, see Elias Ortega-Aponte, "Raised Fist in the Church! Afro-Latino/a Practice among the Young Lords Party: A Humanistic Spirituality Model for Radical Latino/a Religious Ethics." Phd diss., Princeton Theological Seminary, Princeton, NJ, 2011; Lilia Fernandez, *Brown in the Windy City* (Chicago: University of Chicago Press, 2012). For a treatment of the church as "sacred space" that developed across major metropolitan areas throughout twentieth-century America, see David Badillo, *Latinos and the New Immigrant Church: A Comparative History of Urban Religion* (Baltimore, MD: Johns Hopkins University Press, 2006), 206–207.
33. Roger Granados, "Notes from the UPUSA General Assembly," May 15, 1969, p. 3, Box F093, File: UPUSA General Assembly 1969. Hispanic American Institute Collection, Austin Presbyterian Seminary, Austin, Texas.
34. "Brown Revolution Manifesto," presented to the 181st General Assembly of the United Presbyterian Church USA at San Antonio, TX, May 15, 1969. Box F093, File: UPUSA

General Assembly 1969. Hispanic American Institute Collection, Austin Presbyterian Seminary, Austin, Texas.
35. Granados, "Notes from the UPUSA General Assembly," 7.
36. Roger Granados, "Notes from the UPUSA General Assembly," May 15, 1969, 1 and 2, Box F093, File: UPUSA General Assembly 1969. Hispanic American Institute, Austin Presbyterian Seminary, Austin, Texas.
37. Granados, "Notes from the UPUSA General Assembly," 1 and 2.
38. "Church Suit Asks Eviction of MAYO" March 5, 1970. Box 1, Folder 1. Salazar Collection, HMRC.
39. J. D. Arnold, "Chicanos Eye More Church Takeovers" *Houston Chronicle*, March 1970. Box 1, Folder 1. Gregory Salazar Collection, Houston Metropolitan Research Center, Houston, Texas.
40. Felipe Hinojosa, "Sacred Spaces: Race, Resistance, and the Politics of Chicana/o and Latina/o Religious History," in *A Promising Problem: The New Chicana/o History*, ed. Carlos K. Blanton (Austin: University of Texas Press, 2016), 111–134.
41. Eduardo Fernandez, *La Cosecha: Harvesting Contemporary United States Hispanic Theology, 1972–1998* (Collegeville, MN: The Liturgical Press, 2000). Virgilio Elizondo, *Galilean Journey: The Mexican-American Promise* (Maryknoll, NY: Orbis Books, 1983); Orlando Costas, *Christ Outside the Gate: Mission beyond Christendom* (Maryknoll, NY: Orbis Books, 1982); Ada María Isai-Díaz, *Mujerista Theology: A Theology for the Twenty-First Century* (Maryknoll, NY: Orbis Books, 1996); Yolanda Tarango and Ada María Isasi-Díaz, *Hispanic Women: Prophetic Voice in the Church* (New York: Harper & Row, 1988).
42. Michelle Gonzalez, "Latino/a Theology: Doing Theology Latinamente," *Dialog: A Journal of Theology* 41, no. 1 (Spring 2002), 65.
43. Michelle Gonzalez, "Latina Feminist Theology: The Past, Present, and Future," *Journal of Feminist Studies in Religion* 25, no. 1 (Spring 2009), 152.
44. Gonzalez, "Latino/a Theology: Doing Theology Latinamente," 69.
45. Mario García, whose work is best known in the field of Chicano history, came to this field quite late. But in the last ten years, no one has been more prolific in their writing on Latina/o religious history. His most recent work is a biography on Fr. Luis Olivares; see Mario T. García, *Father Luis Olivares, a Biography: Faith Politics and the Origins of the Sanctuary Movement in Los Angeles* (Chapel Hill: University of North Carolina Press, 2018).
46. Rudy V. Busto, *King Tiger: The Religious Vision of Reies Lopez Tijerina* (Albuquerque: University of New Mexico Press, 2005), 6.
47. Timothy Matovina, *Tejano Religion and Ethnicity in San Antonio, 1821–1860* (Austin: University of Texas Press, 1995).
48. See, for example, David Martin, *Tongues of Fire: The Explosion of Protestantism in Latin America* (Oxford: Blackwell Publishers, 1990).
49. Arlene M. Sánchez-Walsh, *Latino Pentecostal Identity: Evangelical Faith, Self, and Society* (New York: Columbia University Press, 2003).
50. Paul Barton, "*Ya Basta!*: Latino/a Protestant Activism in the Chicano/a and Farm Workers Movements," in *Latino Religions and Civic Activism in the United States*, edited by Gastón Espinosa, Virgilio Elizondo, and Jesse Miranda (Oxford University Press, 2005), 128. See also Paul Barton, *Hispanic Methodists, Presbyterians, and Baptists in Texas* (University of Texas Press, 2006); Arlene M. Sánchez-Walsh, *Latino Pentecostal Identity: Evangelical Faith, Self, and Society* (Columbia University Press, 2003). Both contend that Latino Protestant identity is formed along the tense dialectic of Anglo Protestantism and Latino Catholicism.

51. Sergio Gonzalez, "Interethnic Catholicism and Transnational Religious Connections: Milwaukee's Mexican Mission Chapel of Our Lady of Guadalupe, 1924–1929," *Journal of American Ethnic History*, 36, no. 1 (Fall 2016): 5–30; Maggie Elmore, "*Wielding the Cross: How Mexican Americans and the Catholic Church Made Immigration Reform a Civil Rights Issue, 1975–1986*," paper presented at the Western Historical Association, October 2018, San Antonio, Texas; Daisy Vargas, "Mexican Catholics at the Borders of the Nation-State: Critical Race Studies in American Catholic History," paper presented at the American Catholic History Association, January 2019, Chicago, IL.
52. Michelle Tellez, "Pero tu no crees en Dios": Negotiating Spirituality, Family, and Community," in *Fleshing the Spirit: Spirituality in Chicana, Latina, and Indigenous Women's Lives*, edited by Elisa Facio and Irene Lara (Tucson: University of Arizona Press, 2014), 156; Delgadillo, *Spiritual Mestizaje*, 3.

# CHAPTER 11

# BARRIO MUSIC, SPIRITUALITY, AND SOCIAL JUSTICE IN LATINO HIP-HOP

ALEJANDRO NAVA

I was raised on the raw, visceral stuff of soul music, hip-hop, and Spanish music. In my childhood hometown of Tucson, Arizona, I got bits and pieces of each: mariachi, cumbia, salsa, George Clinton and Parliament, the Gap Band, Earth Wind and Fire, Afrika Bambaataa, Grandmaster Flash, Rakim, Tupac, Nas, and so on. My taste in music wandered freely across various boundaries and genres, but I increasingly became hooked by the new styles and sounds emerging out of the ghettos and barrios of the United States. As odd as it may sound, I was under the assumption—a prevailing notion in my middle school of the early 1980s—that blacks and Mexicans were supposed to identify with the underground music of rap; rock 'n' roll was for white kids. Though my own wanton taste in music betrayed this decree, it was a compelling belief to many kids in my neighborhood. Many of the most fervent and pious disciples of hip-hop that I knew were black and Mexican. My brother was a b-boy, and his group, the Royal Rockers, was a breakdancing and rapping crew of blacks and Latinos. I never joined the group, but I identified with the flavors of the music, dance, clothing, and above all, the delicious rhymes and stories that gushed off the tongues of the most inspired rappers. Though it was largely unspoken, there was an interesting assumption lurking in these segregated patterns of musical affiliation: namely, that hip-hop was the new voice of black and brown experiences, the particular frequency or channel for disenfranchised cultures, the throbbing, booty-shaking, bass-rumbling sound of struggles, complaints, and triumphs in ghetto and barrio life.

Since I was the first in my family to graduate from college, rap music filled in some of the gaps and omissions in my education, schooling me at an early age in the sciences of language, culture, dance, music, and social justice. Even when restricted to the rhetoric of bombast and boast (the most common trait of early rap), the practice of black and brown kids screaming their name and announcing themselves had social and political significance in my mind. We now take it for granted that urban dialects and styles can have artistic value, but it was the culture of hip-hop that first brought the street flavors of black and brown cultures to the mainstream. For communities largely silenced in American life, these acts of self-expression were exercises in dissent, and they played a role in raising my consciousness to the blatant and subtle ways in which underrepresented communities have been excluded and consigned to invisibility.

With my curiosity awakened by the banging beats and rhymes of rap, I also began to develop a fascination with the mysteries of religion during my undergraduate years in college. Instead of a conservative force, however, my sympathy with the narratives of hip-hop and the histories of Latin America steered me toward the radical streams of Christianity, especially to the genre of liberation theology in the Americas. Though I began college at the University of Arizona as a pre-med major, I quickly became engrossed in the harrowing circumstances of the Sanctuary Movement, based in my hometown of Tucson. Fleeing desperate and violent conditions in Central America, many refugees found themselves at the doorsteps of our churches in Tucson seeking protection and asylum. Though my family has lived in the regions of Arizona for generations—long before Arizona became a US state in 1912—I was haunted by the numerous texts of the Bible on the subject of strangers: "Love the stranger, for you, too, were once strangers in the land of Egypt (*Deuteronomy* 10:19)." With this ringing in my ear, synchronized to the rebellious beats and lyrics of Public Enemy (*It Takes a Nation of Millions to Hold Us Back* was released around this time in 1988), I increasingly began to turn my attention to the subjects of religion, human rights, and hip-hop.

Not long afterward, I began graduate school at the University of Chicago in religious studies (the 1990s). By some nice happenstance, the years of my graduate education coincided with the emergence of some of hip-hop's most brilliant rappers, many of whom had a strong interest in religion and human rights. Tupac busted on the stage of hip-hop wearing multiple masks—villain and saint, pimp and preacher, street hustler and prophet—and many others would follow suit. Even when playing the part of these former characters, Tupac remained hounded by God, and would frequently interrupt his raps with prayers, supplications, wails, and Job-like protests unto God. "Shed So Many Tears," for instance, combines a description of raw anguish with a desperate longing for God's presence: "Lord, I suffered through the years, and shed so many tears/ Lord, I lost so many peers, and shed so many tears." "I Ain't Mad at Cha," grieves in this same vein, and dreams of a ghetto heaven that would give rest and redemption to the most vulnerable of our world: "I beg God to make a way for our ghetto kids to breathe/ Show a sign, make us all believe." Many other songs—"I Wonder if Heaven Got a Ghetto," "Black Jesus," "Ghetto Gospel," "Only God Can Judge Me," "Hail Mary," "Are You Still Down?"—echo similar themes, as Tupac makes his voice swing between ethereal highs and mournful lows, searching for the right frequency to reach God. And Tupac is not a lone theological voice in rap: Bone Thugs-N-Harmony turns the infamous crossroads of the blues into a place where God is encountered instead of the devil; Nas cries out for the

"Holy Spirit to save me.... Cause my eyes have seen too much suffering"; and Lauryn Hill, to summon this remarkable female voice, raps about "changing the focus from the richest to the brokest.... Let God redeem you/keep your deen true."

Needless to say, for a student of religion, I was particularly intrigued by rappers who would wantonly traverse the borders of the sacred and profane in this way, and the list was a long catalog of the most distinguished rappers: Tupac, Rakim, Nas, Lauryn Hill, Public Enemy, The Geto Boys, Common, Mos Def, KRS-One, the Fugees, Wu Tang, Arrested Development, Goodie Mob, and numerous others. These figures created music that was earthy and coarse but laced with unmistakable notes of transcendence. The result was often a more mature, if tortured, spirituality than you would find in many churches—a ghetto theology so to speak. Instead of a view of God from the pulpits or ivory towers of the universities, artists in this vein were rapping about God out of the baritone depths of the human soul. From these guttural regions, they would sometimes reach surprising heights of sublimity, as they wrestled with the crushing weight of suffering, the pits of despair, and the darkness of God. Somehow they came out alive and kicking.

While my experience in the classroom at the University of Chicago was enthralling and elevating, I was also discovering at the time new streetscapes on Chicago's South Side that were unlike anything I knew in my hometown of Tucson, and the experience was like a surreal jolt that opened my eyes to the distressed parts of Chicago. In these neighborhoods, only a stone's throw away from the university, streets change with great suddenness, turning from Eden-like gardens into concrete jungles where death rates are alarmingly high. This was the Chicago described by Common, Kanye, and Lupe Fiasco more than the Chicago of Nobel Laureates. "I walk through the valley of Chi were death is," Kanye bellows, "God show me the way because the devil's trying to break me down." Kanye's Chicago is a perilous and terrifying jungle, where serpentine forces coil up in the corners, ready to snatch and claim your soul. Another Chicagoan, Common, even gives these dangers a precise location on the South Side: "Corners leave souls opened and closed/hoping for more/with nowhere to go/rolling in droves.... These are the stories told by Stony and Cottage Grove." In these renditions, hip-hop is a testimony to all the untold stories of the corners and peripheries of America. It is testimony to a Second or Third World America, where the specters of segregation seem alive and well, as if Jim Crow still rises from his grave to stalk new generations of black and brown folk.

As the years went on, hip-hop began to claim more and more territory throughout the Americas until it spread like a contagion to every part of the globe. By the late 1990s, hip-hop became widely fashionable among a variety of marginalized youth. If by reputation alone, it was seen as a music of dissent and protest, a music that gave the stage and mic to communities largely invisible to the shot-callers of politics, economics, and society. While hip-hop is hardly a mirror of ghetto life (unless it's one of those carnival mirrors that stretches, bends, and twists its image), it has given many subjugated peoples the aural canvas to sketch their own identities and troubles, dreams and nightmares, possibilities and hopes. In many instances, hip-hop has been for the poor and working classes, to quote William Jelani Cobb, what Diego Rivera's murals were for the common Mexican laborer: "With his murals, Rivera fashioned a vision of the outsized humanity pulsing within the common Mexican laborer.... What the world needs now is a rapper who can do for the common man and woman verbally what Diego Rivera was able to do with a paint brush and a blank wall.[1]

If rap music has become the sound of agitation and rebellion for many Latino youth in the Americas, then the implications for the question of "Latino" identity are considerable. At the very least, Latinos who have fallen under hip-hop's spell, and found themselves converted by its barrio gospel, have had their identities shaken and stirred, with new ingredients now added to their sense of self. In my case, the traditional Mexican music that my parents adored would be passed on to me in the milk of my mother, but I would also be nursed on African American music and this clearly blackened my mind and soul. As Gustavo Perez Firmat once said about mambos, mariachi music will not be forever.[2] And the fact that mambos and corridos have given way to hip-hop for many Cuban, Puerto Rican, and Mexican youth in the United States or Europe only illustrates the inevitability of change for Latinos in the diaspora.

In cultural studies, it's now taken for granted that human identity is never arrested in stillness, never sculpted in stone; metaphors and images that suggest mobility and mestizaje, transformation and adaptation, negotiation and revision are widely preferred over static and fixed tropes. If likened to anything, identity is now seen as a "mobile army of metaphors, metonyms, and anthropomorphisms, a sum of human relations which have been enhanced, transposed, and embellished poetically and rhetorically" to quote Nietzsche.[3] Among the many factors that converge to sculpt human identity—geographic, poetic, religious, linguistic, political, economic, cultural, and so on—music can play a considerable role, and so I propose here to consider the ways in which hip-hop has seeped into the bloodstream of many Latino youth. Though it is a diverse and heterogeneous genre, this essay focuses on the prophetic streams of hip-hop and, more specifically, the reception and reinvention of hip-hop by Latinos throughout the Americas.

## Hip-Hop in the Bronx

Leaving aside the well-known contributions in the areas of breakdancing and graffiti art, Latin music was a foundational influence in the creation of hip-hop music and culture. From a musical standpoint, it is well established that hip-hop borrowed beats and rhythms from the rich sonic world of Afro-Latin music, especially its percussive and rhythmic components (conga and bongo drums in particular).[4] Before hip-hop would exploit and develop the rich possibilities of the "break"—where the vocals and some instruments would take a break while the rhythm section of drums and bass continued—salsa and mambo music made rich use of similar ruptures in music. In the New York scene of the 1950s, legendary figures of Latin music like Machito, Tito Puente, and Tito Rodriguez all employed the break; the orchestra would stop playing in the middle of a song except for the bass line and clave beat.⁵ With the vocals and instruments suspended, the drum beats were given greater prominence and this conjured greater intensity on the dance floor. The opening created by the break, with the drums now amplified in sound, seemed to electrify the currents and rhythms of the body like nothing else, and this beckoned everyone to the dance floor. Funk music, in addition to hip-hop, is part of this heritage, and learned how to sample conga drums and other Latin percussion sounds in their music. (Ned Sublette has noted that the conga drums became one of the signature sounds of African American nationalism in the 1970s.)⁶

This principle, of course, was foundational to the hip-hop DJs of the 1970s. Kool Herc, Afrika Bambaataa, Grandmaster Flash, Charlie Chase, Grandmaster Caz, Jimmy Castor, and others recognized the possibilities that a heavily percussive "break" might offer someone trying to rock the party and, eventually, rock the mic.⁷ As in the experience of salsa and mambo music, or the bass heavy sounds of funk, the propulsive, thundering sound of the drums and bass would wash over the audience like a tide and pull them to the dance floor. And shorn of vocals, the beats would provide the MC with the perfect accompaniment to spit his or her rhymes.⁸

Recall, too, that salsa music was emerging and evolving at the same time and place as hip-hop. The Bronx of the 1970s was the matrix for both musical styles, and it gave birth to patterns of sound that would echo the marginalized, violent, and impoverished realities of black and brown America. In salsa and hip-hop alike, musical arrangements veered away from elegant and refined styles and tried to capture the aesthetics of the streets, whether in contorted and gyrating dance moves, R.I.P graffiti murals, scratching, dissonant sonics, or in lyrical portraits of urban life. In his classic reading of salsa, César Miguel Rondón highlights three major characteristics of the music: "the use of the son as the basis for its development; arrangements that were modest in terms of harmonies and innovations but markedly bitter and violent; and the imprint of the marginalized barrio. This was music produced not for the luxurious ballroom but for hard life on the streets."⁹ The same can be said about hip-hop: ghetto idioms, fashions, and sounds (with modest harmonies and strong accents on rhythm and bass) would coalesce to produce a language of rebellion and recreation. For many black and brown youth, increasingly cynical about the promises of civil rights, partying and pleasure, drums and dancing would come to have a cathartic and liberating purpose, as the story of Rubén Blades's delinquent hero, "Juan Pachanga," suggests: "Everybody swears that Juan Pachanga's really happy / But he carries the pain of betrayal in his soul / And only drink and smokes and drums can cure him."¹⁰

In 1970s New York, in fact, the curative effect of drums was a common therapy for barrio-weary youth.¹¹ Raquel Rivera points to the widespread practice of street drumming among New York Latinos, a practice that broadcast raucous and unruly drumbeats throughout the streets of the city. Sharing the same spaces that would give birth to hip-hop parties, this Afro-Latin drumming tradition was subsumed by the culture of hip-hop. "Since early hip-hop jams took place in the same spaces as street drumming," writes Joseph Schloss, "the experience of dancing to an extended, Latin-style percussion break played by a deejay in a park would have been extremely similar to the experience of dancing to live drummers in that same park.... Such moments—combining the street drumming environment with funk records—represented a cultural activity that fit equally well into both Latino and African American traditions."[12]

At this stage in hip-hop studies, appreciation for the pluralistic history of rap's origins seems well established, but it is worth recalling the transnational and intercultural influences that coalesced, condensed, and heated-up to produce the big bang explosion of hip-hop. Because so many North Americans think of the US/Mexico border as a mental wall as much as a political demarcation, the recognition of a common musical heritage throughout the Americas is frequently overlooked.[13] Whether in musical theory or cultural studies, the building of insurmountable fences between various nation-states or ethnic nationalities has a way of obscuring the mad combinations and riotous arrays of musical and cultural influences that produced black music in the Americas. And this holds true in hip-hop studies as much as anything else, where so many voices, rhythms, and loops are echoed, sampled, faded in and out, and scratched over.

Though distant echoes now, Afro-Latin music (especially salsa, mambo, and the boogaloo), Jamaican dub music (with its practice of stripping songs of their vocals and accentuating the bass and drum parts), and other Afro-Latin styles of music and dance in New York all combined forces to contribute to the invention of a new genre.[14]

## THE LATIN AMERICAN SCENE

As a key figure in the history of hip-hop, Public Enemy's Chuck D has long expressed concern about how hip-hop has developed and aged through the years: a child once so fresh and clean, a child of endless promise, now in danger of losing her soul, "talkin about popping locks, servin rocks and hittin switches, now she's a gangsta rollin with gangsta bitches...."[15] Though Common spit these lines, Chuck D has long been warning the hip-hop nation of the ruinous effect of materialism and crass hedonism on the soul of the rap world.

Besides changing the message of hip-hop—preferring the themes of booty, blunts, and bling over prophetic indictments of grinding poverty, racist legacies, and spiritual emptiness—later developments in the business of hip-hop has had the effect of severely shrinking the range of voices and perspectives in hip-hop. Now an artist must secure a corporate imprimatur in order to get any play, and this process has clearly blunted the prophetic edge. As in biblical prophecy, when a prophet works for the king and is a part of the courtly retinue, he becomes the voice of the king, not the voice of God. Something like this, according to Chuck D, has happened in hip-hop: "In the first ten to twelve years of rap recordings," Chuck D states, "rappers rapped for the people, and they rapped against the elite establishment. In the last ten or so years, rappers rap for their companies and their contracts, and they're part of the establishment now. It's two diametrically opposed ideas."[16] Because of this sea change in hip-hop, the tides have frequently turned against the most artistic and dissident voices.

Given these concerns about hip-hop's survival in a culture of self-gratification, Chuck D began to look to other parts of the world for alternatives to US rap. In a visit to South Africa in 2011, he spoke with excitement about what he experienced there, as if he had traveled through a wormhole and returned to the state of hip-hop at its "livest" infancy. "The world has parity now," he wrote, "and has surpassed the USA in all of the basic fundamentals of hip-hop."[17] For those disenchanted with the current status of hip-hop in the United States, voices from the global periphery offer refreshing alternatives: more urgent, more timely, more relevant to the convulsions and distresses of communities throughout the world.[18] In these instances, we are given glimpses of hip-hop at its most resourceful and cunning, where beats and rhymes are diamonds mined out of the ruins of poverty and social crisis, where a concern with "ends" runs deeper than "money, hos, and clothes." Instead of eliding or reinforcing the massive inequalities of the global capitalist order, these rappers raise their tongues against the powers that benefit from this discriminatory state of affairs. And they target, when necessary, all those in hip-hop that are untroubled and complacent about these facts, all the perpetrators of hip-hop, those too faded on chronic or purple drank to notice the depths of global suffering.

The study of hip-hop's global dispersion has other benefits as well: I see it as decentering and challenging the North American ego for supremacy in art and culture, reminding it of the unconscious (and sometimes blatantly conscious) prejudices that elevate this ego like a sacred chalice at the moment of consecration.[19] As Paul Gilroy insists, there is a glaring "American-centrism" in a lot of hip-hop and when this attitude prevails it tends to be silent about the struggles of anyone outside the United States, whether south of the border, across the Atlantic, or throughout the African continent for that matter.[20] In turning our attention to the global underground, not only do we get a different spin on hip-hop, but we are exposed to a more heterogeneous and chameleon-like version of "blackness" than US portraits, "blackness" as the color of pariahs and outcasts, "blackness" as a symbol of various stripes and hues of oppression.[21] And if we remember that the majority of blacks in the Western hemisphere reside in Latin America (approximately 37 percent reside in the United States), by expanding our field of vision in hip-hop studies, a new vista appears concerning the African diaspora, one that can shed light on the unions, blends, and combinations between Africa and various Spanish and Portuguese cultures, Afro-Latin hybrids.

Many Cuban hip-hop artists, I would argue, exemplify a conscious and righteous position in hip-hop. Consider EPG's simple description of their mission: "We rap about the conditions of our lives, the fact that our people, the poor, continue to get poorer while the rich get richer."[22] Or take Anónimo Consejo on a similar note: "Rap is something that is born here in your heart, with the idea of combatting injustice perpetrated by the government against immigrants, African Americans and Latinos."[23] For many Cuban rap groups—add Obsesión, Hermanos de Causa, Gente de Zona, and the Orishas to this list—hip-hop remains a revolutionary struggle, a voice of protest and peace. This engaged vision of hip-hop comes up a lot in Latin American rap groups, as if they feel obliged to mark their territory with a distinct cadence from the commercially popular rap of North America, more in keeping with a pedagogy of the oppressed than a pedagogy of ballin'. In one of their raps, "Tengo," Hermanos de Causa describes their griefs and grievances in the following verses:

> Tengo una palmera, un mapa sin tesoro
> Tengo aspiraciones sin tener lo que hace falta...
> Tengo una raza oscura y discriminada
> Tengo una jornada que me exige y no da nada
> Tengo tantas cosas que no puedo ni tocarlas
> Tengo instalaciones que no puedo ni pisarlas
> Tengo libertad entre un parenthesis de hierro
> Tengo tantos derechos sin provechos, que me encierro
> Tengo lo que tengo sin tener lo que he tenido...
>
> (I've got a palm tree, a map without a treasure
> I've got aspirations without having what I need...
> I've got discrimination because I'm black
> I've got a job that demands and gives nothing
> I've got so many things that I can't even touch
> I've got all these places I can't even step foot in
> I've got freedom in a parentheses of iron
> I've got so many rights without any benefit that I feel confined
> I've got what I have without having what I've had...)

As Alan West-Durán and Sujatha Fernandes note about this song, it is riffing on the classic poem by Nicolás Guillén, "Tengo" ("I have"), about many of the achievements of the Cuban revolution: "Tengo que ya tengo donde trabajar y ganar lo que me tengo que comer. Tengo, vamos a ver, tengo lo que tenía que tener. (I have, now, a place to work and I can earn what I have to eat. I have, let's see, I have, what was coming to me.")[24] In adopting this trope from the Cuban revolution, Guillén casts his lot with the promises and dreams of the new regime. Typical to the hip-hop generation, however, this song by Hermanos de Causa interrupts the sanguinity of the revolution's noble ideals with a disillusioned note of complaint, protest, and dissent. In line after line, the song accumulates these gripes until the regime appears deficient and defective, fragmented by the weight of these social problems, humbled by the conspicuous cracks that appear on the façade of Cuba's state apparatus. By using irreverent parody and ridicule in their raps, Hermanos de Causa holds the Revolution accountable for not making good on its promises, for writing checks with no bullion in the bank (the attitude of US rappers towards "civil rights" is similar). Though this attitude does not lead them to disown the Revolution, they also refuse to muzzle their bark at the poverty and racism that continues to hound Afro-Cubans.

In the same manner, the song targets material and consumer values: "No confundas tener más con tener cualidades" (Don't confuse having more with being better), or "Mientras más tienes más quieres y siempre más querrás. Mientras más tú tengas más ridículo serás" (The more you have, the more and more you want. The more you have, the more ridiculous you'll be). The group uses the Cuban style of *choteo*—a style of signifying—as a way of censuring and "dissing" anything that presumes innocence and sanctity, anything that claims for itself an infallible eminence, be it socialism, capitalism, or any other triumphal ideology.[25]

It's important to note here that Guillén's poetry was inspired by the rhythms and flows of Afro-Cuban *son*, and, thus, what appears in Hermanos de Causa is the *son* re-mixed for the hip-hop generation. (Incidentally, in a very interesting example of black and Latin exchanges, it was Langston Hughes, according to Arnold Rampersad, who first encouraged Guillén to make use of *son* in his poetry as Hughes had done with the blues.)[26] Many of their songs, in fact, rework the *son* in this manner, as in another rap, "Lagrimas Negras" ("Black Tears," the title of a classic *son* by the famous composer, Miguel Matamoros). The persistence of racism in Cuba is the topic:

> Siento odio profunda por tu racismo
> Ya no me confundo con tu ironía
> Y lloro sin que sepas que el llanto mío
> Tiene lágrimas negras como mi vida
>
> (I feel profound hate for your racism
> I am no longer confused by your irony
> And I cry without you knowing that my cry
> Has black tears like my life.)[27]

In this rap, the group has changed the focus from romantic abandonment and mourning, in Trio Matamoros' original version, to the legacy of racism. The song follows the plaintive and gentle tone of Matamoros's song (true to a classic Cuban *bolero*), but the lyrics are delivered with the anger and edginess of a hip-hop activist, someone who has simmered and simmered until finally reaching a boiling point. The black tears, thus, represent so much more than the agony of love: they are traces and symptoms of centuries of dishonorable behavior towards Afro-Cubans, tears that have calcified into rage and distrust.

In the Brazilian hip-hop scene, too, many of these themes—race, religion, poverty and violence—are almost always the scaffoldings on which they build their houses of language and music. Derek Pardue suggests that the youth movements of the late twentieth century—responses to the military dictatorship, 1964–1985—were used in these ways and infused rap music in Brazil with a revolutionary spirit.[28] In these versions, hip-hop is the voice of the *periferia*, the voice of slums and abandoned neighborhoods, where outlaws and the destitute live together in a common struggle. Brazilians use the perfectly apt term, *quebradas*, broken or cracked, to designate these communities, as if everything here is inoperative, wrecked, and failed, as if there is a fissure or fault line running through their hoods, ready to swallow them. One of the best-known hip-hop groups in Brazil, Racionais MCs, raps about life in these dilapidated, broken circumstances. From their early work in a compilation entitled, *Consciência Black*, and subsequent albums *Holocausto Urbano* (Urban Holocaust, 1990), and *Sobrevivendo no Inferno* (Surviving in Hell, 1997), they present harrowing portraits of life in the *periferia*, with lyrics laced with distress and determination alike, lyrics that are threads of light guiding the listener through the mazes of their hoods. From this latter album, the song "Diaro de um detento" appeared, a song about the smothering darkness of prison life.

> Hoje, tá dificil, não saiu o sol
> Hoje não tem visita, não tem futebol...
> Gracias a Deus e á Virgem Maria
> Faltam só um ano, três meses e uns dias.
> Tem uma cela lá em cima fechada
> Desde terça-feira ninguém abre pra nada
> Só o cheiro de morte e Pinho Sol.[29]
>
> (It's hard today, the sun has not come out
> There is no visitation, there is no soccer...
> Thank God and the Virgin Mary,
> There is only one year, three months and some days left.
> There's a cell block upstairs that is closed.
> Since Tuesday, nobody opens it.
> There is only the smell of death and Pine Sol.)

In this song and others, the raps move freely between the sacred and profane, the spiritual and social, stitching together a composite quilt of many emotions and concerns. As if they are wringing their souls of bitter poisons that would make for despair if contained within, their appeals to God and the Virgin Mary give them strength and grace to face the darkness without succumbing to the self-destructive temptations of drugs, violence, and nihilism. The reference here to Mary is particularly noteworthy given the importance of Marian devotion in the Caribbean and Latin America (associated with Yemanjá in Brazil, Yemayá in Cuba). Like a touch of tenderness in an otherwise hard and violent life, the image of Mary is an enlivening presence in the song, the smell of roses in an environment that reeks of death and Pine Sol.

It seems to me that these brief examples, in a world far from the Bronx, are songs true to the original spirit of hip-hop, true to the wayward spirit that once broke loose and electrified the ghettos of the world. In their efforts to produce music that summarizes the cultures, spirituality, and injustices of the global periphery, Latin American hip-hop reminds us not only of the creativity and pleasures that once gave birth to this artistic movement, but of the desperate need in our world today for sounds and lyrics that have their ears attuned to the ghettos of the world, for music that rides low and close to the streets, a music has a steely, asphalt edge to it, a music with the metallic polish of a low-rider.

## The Orishas of Hip-Hop

Since the sampling of African religion has been an essential feature of Latin American music and culture, it is not surprising that it surfaces in hip-hop as well. As a long-standing practice of Catholicism in the New World (especially among the religious guilds, or *cabildos*), African beliefs, music, and dance were coupled with Catholic rites to produce a new flavor of belief, a rich polyglot gumbo of religion and culture. Though the *cabildos* existed in fifteenth-century Seville (there were *cabildos* for gypsies, African slaves, and many other groups in Spain), the *cabildos* of the New World surpassed in number the Old World guilds and increasingly acquired African features with secret ceremonies, hermetic languages, and special musical signatures. "Isuama's *cabildo*," one researcher remarks, "preserved the chants, songs, and dances of the original Carabalí slaves."[30] Remarkable, if you think about it, that these guilds conserved such fragile treasures in oral and fleshly forms, passing on these rites without, in many cases, written records. Like curators of a dazzling heritage of sound, the *cabildos* would build living museums to these memories and styles and have an impact on the entire history of music in the Americas. The *cabildos* did nothing less than ransom the spirits of the ancestors so that they could continue to live, dance, and sing in a new land, an example of the surprising, indomitable capacity of uprooted cultures to thrive in oppressive and inhospitable circumstances.

In the cases of *son* and salsa, incantations to African gods/ancestors were frequent themes. You see this in *cantos* to the Orishas by Roberto Fonseca, Chucho Valdés, Celina González, Machito, Mercedes Valdez, Willie Rosario, Tommy Olivencia, Los Van Van, and numerous others. In Olivencia's version of "Chango 'ta Beni" (Shango is coming), for instance, the sound and lyrics capture the threatening, apocalyptic expectation of Shango, a dream that once fired the Haitian revolution.

> Chango 'ta beni, Chango 'ta beni, Chango 'ta beni.
> Con el machete en la mano, mundo va acabar, tierra va temblar.
>
> (Shango is coming, Shango is coming, Shango is coming.
> With a machete in his hands, the world is coming to an end, the world will tremble.[31]

The desperate pleas for Shango here, repeated like a liturgical chant, strike an apocalyptic tone, and are ill-omened for the masters of history. Replete with warning and eschatological expectation, the song combines threat and promise, envisaging a transformation that will redeem the lives of the degraded and disenfranchised.

For many Afro-Latinos, hip-hop continues this legacy. With the dead still haunting the young votaries of hip-hop, music is turned into an idiom of rebellion, and a portent of danger. The retrieval of the past is a subversive act, taking the community forward not backward. Consider one of EPG's raps: "We are creating hip hop using our roots. Giving you these ancestral rhythms, uncovering your mind with my fountain, showing you clearly that on my island there is a branch of hip hop that rises like a stairwell."[32] For EPG, hip-hop surely represents a break with older generations, but there is a stronger note of continuity with the past than in a lot of US rap, a resolve to constantly renew one's homage to "ancestral rhythms." In group after group you encounter similar attitudes, as in the song, "Muralla," by the Cuban rap group *Cuarta Imagen*: "Entiendan que la voz de siete rayos ya llegó / Yoruba soy Yoruba lucumí / Desde Cuba suba mi llanto Yoruba / que suba el alegre llanto / Yoruba que sale de mí" (Understand, the voice of Nsasi has arrived / I'm Yoruba, Yoruba lucumí / may my Yoruba tears rise up from Cuba / may the joyful Yoruba weeping rise out of me).[33] Besides this heartfelt description of joy and sadness in the song ("joyful weeping"), the rapper joins his voice here with the chorus of the gods from the Palo religious traditions of the Congo (the reference to the Nsasi is from the Reglas de Palo). His rap is, thus, a link in a far-reaching chain that reverses the direction of the Middle Passage and takes his listeners back to Africa, hoping to be a remedy for the maladies of cultural loss and forgetfulness. Rap in this conscious vein, to summon the line of the Philadelphia-born rapper Bahamadia, is a reproach of all "booty-ass, no grass-roots-having-ass MCs."[34]

As their name suggests, the most famous Cuban rap group, the *Orishas*, also joins these refrains. In their song "Represent," reference is made to the rich blend of musical and religious heritages in Cuba: "Ven que te quiero cantar de corazón así / la historia de mis raíces / rumba, son, y guaguancó, todo mezclado.... Represento a mis ancestros. (You'll see that I want to sing from my heart the history of my roots, rumba, son, and guaguancó, all blended together.... I represent my ancestors)." And then this song ends with a litany of praise: "Hey bro Elegua, Changó, Obatalá, Yemayá, Ochún...que mi canto suba pa' la gente de mi Cuba, mis ancestros, todos mis muerto, todo eso represento" (Hey bro Elegua, Changó, Obatalá, Yemayá, Ochún.... I pray that my song will rise and represent the people of my Cuba, my ancestors and all the dead").[35]

In this sacred hymn, it should be obvious that African gods, largely dead to US rappers, remain alive in this new generation of Latin American youth, as if they refuse the promises of the future if it means betraying the spirits of the past. If Protestant North America belongs to the future, and Latin America to the Catholic past, hip-hop in Latin America is a curious negotiation or conciliation of the two, bearing truths and beats that are simultaneously ancient and yet new. In the Cuban rap groups that I have noted, these truths are multicultural and multicolored like light seen through a stained-glass window: the cult of the saints, the black Madonna, and African spirits all shine through the mosaic patterns of their music. In one of the most explicit examples of this, the song by the Orishas, "Canto a Elewa y Changó" (Chant to Elewa/Elegua y Shango) highlights these religious themes:

> Hijo Elewa, mi santo Elewa, mi vida Elewa
> Mafareo, el rey de los caminos
> La ley de mi destino, rojo y negro como el tinto vino
> Quien me abre los caminos con su garabato ....
>
> Yo como un rayo digo loco lo que siento
> Mi voz que ruge como el viento
> Blanco y rojo represiento
> Changó virtuoso gordete como un oso

Bien perezoso, jocoso, fogoso,
Santa Bárbara bendita es tu Changó
Guía por el bien camino a tus hijos como yo
Dale la luz señora de virtud...

Tonada para los Orishas
Que llevo en el corazón con amor
Pido que me den salúd e inspiración
Y también la bendición....

Recordarás mi voz, antes que reces,
Antes que reces, reces

Son Elegua, my saint Elegua, my life Elegua,
All power to you, king of the (cross)roads
The law of my destiny, red and black like red wine
Who opens every road for me with his cane...

(Like the lightning, I say madly what I feel
My voice roars like the wind.
I represent white and red
Shango, masterful and powerful like a bear

Indolent, playful, passionate.
Holy Saint Barbara is your Shango
Guide your children, like me, on the right track.
Give them light, Lady of Virtue...

A melody for the Orishas
That I carry in my heart with love
I ask that they give me health and inspiration
And their blessings as well...

You'll remember my voice before you pray,
Before you pray, pray.)

First, take note of this reference to the union of Shango and Saint Barbara: the song takes for granted their shared identity and bond. (Their feast day is celebrated together on December 4, one of the most important festivals of the year in Cuba.) As master of lightning and fire, master of percussion-driven ritual and music, master of dance and passion, Shango is the epitome of the flashy lover of life, the exuberant performer and artist.[36] Upon first glance, it seems awfully peculiar that he would be associated with a Catholic female saint, but if you consider the ways in which Santa Barbara was celebrated in Spanish traditions—in fiery, rapturous, reveling festivity—the distance is not as remote. During the feast day of Santa Barbara and Shango, in fact, the two figures converge in carnivals of dance and music, with certain jerky, fulgurating dance moves simulating the path of lightning from heaven to earth characteristic of Shango and Santa Barbara alike. (Santa Barbara was the patroness of those who worked with explosives, those who harnessed the power of lightning.)[37] The fantastic legend of Santa Barbara—a faithful Christian woman who meets a martyr's death, but is eventually revenged by a bolt of lightning—seems to have been perfectly arranged to turn these figures into strange bedfellows, with Shango's command of lightning now given credit for avenging Santa Barbara's death, as if Shango would assail with his lightning and fire anyone who would do her harm. In these connubial embraces, with Santa Barbara and Shango rubbing, clutching, and dancing with one another, it becomes hard to tell the two apart, an allegory perhaps of a wider process of cultural eroticism and syncretism. Whatever the case, the product of this union is an eccentric, quixotic marriage of ideas and beliefs, the meeting of Yoruba and Catholic traditions at the crossroads of Hispaniola.

These cross-cultural encounters inevitably affect each tradition brought into the mix, the cultures of master and slave, colonizer and colonized. With the oblique allusions to Christian ideas and virtues in the song—the triad of faith, hope, and love is mentioned— it is clear that Christianity steals up on African culture here, changing its cast of mind to include biblical values and virtues. Given this transfiguration, the revolution that is being broadcast by the Orishas is primarily an upheaval of values before it is anything political, perhaps something in the spirit of W. E. B. Du Bois when he claimed that the stranglehold of poverty and injustice will be broken "not so much by violence and revolution, which is only the outward distortion of an inner fact, but by the ancient cardinal virtues: individual prudence, courage, temperance, and justice, and the more modern faith, hope, and love."[38] I would venture to say that vision of revolution, cultural more than political, rings true for a great number of rappers throughout the Americas.

Perhaps more striking about this song, though, Shango is plainly feminized by his contact with his other half in Santa Barbara. Now Shango is colored with the virtues associated with the goddess traditions of Catholicism. In his female avatar, in other words, he is "Lady of Virtue," a term that is unmistakably related to the female saints and, of course, to the Virgin Mary in her many apparitions in the Americas.

At the same time, though, the influence is also felt from the African side. After contact with Shango, Santa Barbara emerges from the ashes of her death as a liberator of African slaves, a fabulous and spectacular metamorphosis to say the least. As Roger Bastide has argued in the Brazilian case, Catholic saints underwent something like a transvaluation in the New World—they became confidants, protectors, and liberators of Africans.[39] Similar to the way Guadalupe was indigenized in Mexico, Santa Barbara became a patroness of many Afro-Cubans, lending her protection to the important guild, Sociedad de Socorros Mutuos Nación Lucumí de Santa Barbara. Whether it was St. Benedict the Moor in Salvador, Bahia, or St. James the Elder in Haiti, or the Virgin of Regla (associated with Yemayá), the Virgin of El Cobre (associated with Ochún), the Virgin of Mercy (associated with Obatalá), and Saint Barbara, all in Cuba, the Catholic saints underwent an apotheosis that enthroned them on every Afro-Cuban altar that was dedicated to the struggle for humanity and justice in the Americas.

We should also note that with Shango's features superimposed on Santa Barbara, it is clear that both males and females can wield power. Another line in the song, hence, appeals to the sword of Santa Barbara, cutting through the obstacles and obscurities of life to light the path of virtue. In this construal, she is strong and brave, a shield and safeguard of protection for weary workers and downtrodden communities—she is anything but a submissive, timid figure. Even with her beatific, feminine countenance, she appears in this tradition as a thunderous threat to the status quo, a lightning bolt against injustice; she appears as a figure of justice, deft with the sword, perhaps something like the biblical Judith (who famously wields the sword against Holofernes): "For thy power stands not in multitude nor thy might in strong men," Judith prays, "for thou art a God of the afflicted, a helper of the oppressed, an upholder of the weak, a protector of the forlorn, a savior of them that are without hope" (Judith 9:11).

It is clear, at any rate, that in these instances where the Orishas and santos are betrothed to each other, there is a two-way flow between African religion and Catholicism. Even when Cuban rappers are summoning the Orishas in their raps, calling on them with a ritual-like cadence, the acoustics of their world is clearly Catholic, and this creates a fusion of sound and image that could be the soundtrack of the New World. Think of this encounter like a vibrant painting in watercolor, suddenly sodden with rain so that there are smudged borders, blended pigments, amalgamated colors, jumbled images, dripping dyes, puddled paints. Now, in this postdiluvian view of culture, the original image is irretrievable, but what remains is, nonetheless, resplendent.

If we consider these Afro-Cuban religious influences on the rap scene in Cuba, we might say in sum that Cuban *raperos* know when to play the trickster, á la Elegguá, when to channel Shango's fiery dances and percussion-driven hymns, when to add Spanish and Arabic flourishes, and when, finally, to adopt African American sounds and styles. In playing with these combinations, these artists create a feast of meaning that combines the sacred and profane, the spiritual and political. Alan West-Durán sums up nicely these different themes in his reading of the song I mentioned earlier from Hermanos de Causa, "Tengo." His exegesis concerns the following lines: "Tengo de elemento, tengo de conciente, tengo fundamento" (I've got some funky elements, but I don't scare, I'm politically aware; I've got the initiation, got the foundation). "Both *conciente* and *fundamento*," he writes, "have philosophical, educational, and political meanings, with *conciente* referring to political or social consciousness and *fundamento*, speaking not only to foundations of knowledge, but also of being a *santero*. Hence, in three short lines, Hermanos de Causa reveal their situated knowledge: they 'drop science' from street experience, from their educational training, their politico-philosophical background and their religious dialogue with the Orishas."[40] In claiming *conciente* and *fundamento*, Hermanos de Causa embraces a higher order of knowledge where there is no contradiction between street smarts, social consciousness, and spiritual wisdom—each play its part in this science of the soul.[41]

## Exile and Indigenous Motifs in US Latino Rap

In compensating for the relative invisibility of indigenous struggles in US rap, Latin American rappers tend to give considerable (even principal) weight to Native American voices. Especially in parts of Latin America where the indigenous presence is most conspicuous, hip-hop has expanded its vision to encompass native histories and beliefs. In bringing these communities into bold relief, you will notice a constant preoccupation, almost obsession, with the subjects of mass displacement, exile, and migration. Music is turned into a site of aesthetical experimentation in the face of social traumas and upheavals: violence and conflict, poverty and inequality, oppression and incarceration, identity and nihilism, migration and diaspora, etc....[42] Among US Latinos, in particular, hip-hop has been a medium for many immigrants and their children to verbalize feelings of disaffection and alienation in the promise land of North America. For making so much of these themes, Latino rappers often wrap themselves around their countries of origins like a flag worn to a soccer game, and turn their music into a network of identification and alliance with slum dwellers south of the border.

Given the prominence of indigenous themes in Mexican history and culture, it should not be surprising that many rappers in this tradition travel across the US-Mexico border in search of native roots. Consider the names of some of these groups: the Funky Aztecs, Kinto Sol (an Aztec reference to the 5th sun), Ñengo el Quetzal, Aztlan Underground, the Mexakinz, Ozomatli (Aztec god of dance, fire, and music), Chhoti Maa, and Bocafloja, among others. And whether or not their name suggests it, numerous Latin groups appeal to the indigenous heritage of Latin America as a symbol of solidarity with colonized communities. This is certainly true for Immortal Technique, the Peruvian-American rapper and self-identifying "Zapatista"; for Jaas, the Mapuche *mestiza* from Chile; for Mare, the wonderful Zapotecan rapper from Oaxaca; Cypress Hill in their "Los Grandes Éxitos en Español"; or for the trailblazing Kid Frost: Almost without exception, these musicians employ hip hop as a medium for narrating indigenous memories and struggles, and for "trans-nationalizing" the hip-hop community.[43]

With Kinto Sol, these themes are pervasive. One song, "Hecho in Mexico," beams with indigenous pride: "Soy Azteca, Chichimeca, Zapoteca, (y adentro) soy Indio, Yaqui, Tarasco, y Maya."[44] The Spanish legacy of Kinto Sol's Mexican identity is hardly acknowledged in this song, as the group gives the listener a roll call of tribal filiations. In prioritizing Indian blood in this way, the group strikes a rebellious pose and derides middle-class and elite Mexicans who claim Spain as ancestor while ignoring or downplaying native roots. Kinto Sol mocks this legacy, calls these types *malinchistas* after La Malinche, the famous interpreter and mistress of Hernán Cortés. There is, of course, plenty of hyperbole in this attitude (the group consists of *mestizos,* after all, the children of La Malinche *and* Cortés), but the rhetorical excess in the song is the response to centuries of tortured memories and violent histories that have consistently belittled Indian blood. If their position is inflated for claiming Indian affiliation, it is clearly for a prophetic purpose, scathing in the manner of Bartolomé de Las Casas (notoriously profligate with his words himself).

In this same signifying, mocking tone, a song by the Funky Aztecs, "Prop 187," ridicules those Mexican Americans who turn super-patriotic when it comes to the influx of new undocumented immigrants, largely comprised of the poorest and most indigenous of Latin Americans. In solidarity with the stranger and the vulnerable, the group berates the prevailing racism in North American society, so widespread that it creeps into the hearts of every person, regardless of color. With Mexicans cast in the role of illegal alien, dope dealer, rapist, or gang member (classifications widely used in the campaign and presidency of Donald Trump), the song, "Prop 187," castigates everyone active or complicit in the racism:

> A message to the coconut: no matter how much you switch, here is what they think about you: cactus frying, long distance running, soccer playing, shank having, tortilla flipping, refried beans eating, border crossing, fruit picking, piñata breaking, lowrider driving, dope dealing, Tres Flores wearing, green card having, illiterate gang-member, go the fuck back to Mexico.[45]

If you recall, Proposition 187 in California would have denied citizenship to US-born children of undocumented immigrants as well as access to health services, public schools, and other public services. In their song, the group unrolls a long scroll of grievances about this proposition and similar initiatives, leading to this witty collection of racist epithets that have been hurled at Mexicans and other Latinos.

In another Kinto Sol's cut, "Los hijos del Maiz" (children of maize), these themes continue but now with a relentless mantra that adds up the agonies and atrocities endured by Mexican and native peoples until the hymn slowly seeps into the listener's blood. Since the narrative relates many of the hardships of the poor, and tries to extract meaning out of the misfortunes endured by the common Mexican laborer, it is not surprising that the group resorts to myth as a means of grappling with the perplexities of life. When the mind and spirit have reached an impasse, when reason is at a loss to explain or justify tribulation, myth is often the most attractive medium for guiding us through the labyrinths of life.[46]

In this particular song, the lyrics swing between a prophetic demand for action and social change, on the one hand, and a more tragic sense of disappointment and despondency. (The melancholic guitar chords and the refrain of women's voices, in particular, give the song a dirge-like feel.) Just as the group's name has apocalyptic echoes (like the four ages before, the age of the fifth sun appears to be coming to a catastrophic end), this particular song is mournful and nostalgic, dejected and eschatological. The rap bleeds with so many aggrieved memories, from the painful struggle for survival of his Tarascan grandfather in Mexico to the plight of all *hijos del maize* in diaspora.

> Esclavo del hambre, miseria, violencia,
> Trabajos no hay, dinero esta escaso
> Politicos con feria no nos hacen caso
> Esto es un fracaso cada día que paso
> Un nuevo partido es otro madrazo
> Le llaman democracia, me causa gracia
> Pero mas dolor y me deja un mal sabor
> Yo a la muerte le he perdido el temor
> No se si morir sea el remedio major

> Nuevas caras nuevas leyes, falsas ilusiones
> He pasado tanto tiempo que he llegado a conclusions
> Atencion los hijos del maize
>
> 500 años escondida la verdad
> 5 generaciones en la oscuridad
> Llego la luz termino la tempestad
> El gigante dormido vuelve a despertar
> El alma del Che me aconseja
> Villa me dice mochales la oreja
> Por fin esta lucha se encuentra pareja
> Con gusto termino con toda la nobleza…
> Llego la estapa spiritual[47]
>
> Slave of hunger, poverty and violence,
> There are no jobs, money is scarce
> Politicians with money don't pay us any attention
> Every day that passes is a disaster
> A new political party is another blow
> They call it democracy, makes me laugh
> More pain, and it leaves me with a bad taste in my mouth
> I've lost all fear of death,
> Perhaps dying is a better solution
> New faces, new laws, false illusions
> It's been a long time since I've had any answers
> Listen to me, children of maize
>
> (For 500 years, the truth has been hidden
> 5 ages in darkness
> The light has arrived, the storm has ended
> The sleeping giant will awaken again
> The soul of Che guides me
> Villa advises me to slash ears
> Finally this struggle is fair
> I will finish it with nobility…
> The spiritual era has arrived.)

The song covers a broad spectrum of emotions, a tale that seems despairing at one end and then inspired at the other. At one moment, the rapper seems resigned and melancholic, ready to submit his spirit to the earth, but then the light of Che Guevara and Pancho Villa comes to him and rallies his flagging spirit. In this valley of dry bones on earth, he suddenly visualizes a renewal and promise of justice, with the wounds of the Conquest healed and equality bestowed on the children of the sun with the same superabundance of the sun over the Sonoran Desert.

As buoyant as this hope appears in the song, it hardly obviates the tragic motifs, however. Unlike the prophetic vision, where hope for social reform remains active, the tragic attests to the losses and troubles that haunt every human effort. This tragic sensibility is present in a lot of hip-hop, marking the movement's distance from the prophetic orientation of the civil rights generation. In this specific case, Kinko Sol assumes a tragic mood, where poverty seems ineradicable, ignorance is pervasive, and death is a "better solution." Like a nightmare in which one is running and going nowhere, history seems to be running to stand still, beset on all sides by forces that impede advancement. With their invocation of Villa and Che, Kinto Sol wants to believe that the revolution can drive the "locomotive of history" forward (Marx's famous metaphor), and they want to believe in a spiritual age that would flood the world with a light of parity and truth. The conflict in the song, however, is between what their mind perceives about history—a stalled locomotive going nowhere—and a mythological dream of a more just and humane future. In this sense, the rap moves across these various borders of thought, starting with the tragic where misery seems crushing and falls on native peoples like a leaden, winter sky. And then suddenly, when things seem bleak, the heavens open up and let in rainbows of light that illuminate the earth with brilliant, colorful rays.

Notice, of course, that the dream of revolution is described here in spiritual terms not as political acts of violence. The war waged against racism and colonialism is understood to be a war of words, a strategy of music, poetry, dance, art, prayer. More like a modern shaman than a modern politician, Kinto Sol uses mythical images, tight loops, bass lines, and spell-like words to restore their patients to their lost dignity, allowing the ceremony to wash over them like a cleansing rain and rumbling thunderstorm. If we recall that the shaman, at least for many Romantics, was a poet, myth-reciter, and performance artist, Kinto Sol nicely fits the description.[48] With the rapper playing the role of shaman and soul-artist, Kinto Sol and others in this tradition call upon myth, poetry, religion, and music in the struggle to preserve the defeated memories of the past. Anonimo Consejo hits this note, too: "Here I go: silencing mouths of jealous people who want us to change. I know what I have to do. We feel the support of our dear people. In the footsteps of the Taino.... America, discovered by our indigenous people, who suffered three hard blows of the New World. When Columbus arrived, slaughter, slavery and oppression also arrived. Kokino is here though you forgot me, honoring study like Don Fernando Ortiz."[49] Besides this intriguing reference to the pioneering scholar of Afro-Cuban culture and music, Fernando Ortiz, the group leaves no doubt they are following the trail of tears and long walks of many black and indigenous communities throughout the Americas and that rap music is bread and wine for the journey: a new shamanistic medium for an ancient struggle.

In Anonimo Consejo and many others, in sum, hip-hop is a return to the sweaty and sublime roots of soul. In considering the needs and trials of the soul from the perspective of ghetto dwellers, migrants, and colored folk, hip-hop gives expression to the ills of time, to recall Nas, and to the many travails that the soul must endure in the wastelands of the modern world. But it also resists these ills. In the forms of hip-hop that we have looked at, the music mixes bitterness with sweetness: it adds the taste of anguish when needed, and the taste of solace, comfort, and joy when the former is overpowering. Religion, myth, and folklore play a key role in bestowing the music with this proper balance. By embracing religious and mythical ligatures that bind them to an ancient past, many Latin rappers work with an understanding of myth that is older and richer than what appears in the Age of Reason. For many of the rappers that we have explored, myth furnishes a poetic language that reconciles the contradictions of their lives and touches some deep part of truth that escapes the purview of scientific knowledge, some deep part of themselves, and some deep part of this astonishing universe. Far from a lie, myth lights the path of human quests for truth, sometimes in small doses like "matches struck unexpectedly in the dark," and other times, in glaring, raging illuminations.[50]

You might say, now to borrow from Aristotle on tragic poetry, that rap music effects a catharsis of artist and listener in this regard, a metamorphosis of pain into pleasure, whereby the drops or even torrents of suffering are channeled into tributaries that can nourish the soul and prevent it from corroding and rusting. As dire and distraught as some of these rap songs seem, in other words, the sheer act of composition, the pure creative achievement in making this music is surely an act of resistance against the demons of destruction and a spell against the most fatal curses. However hip-hop expresses this resistance—in bombast or boast, mourning or festivity—what consistently beats through it all is the ever-resilient pulse of life: the throbbing, flowing movement of blood through the veins. In riding the wave of these sounds and flows, hip-hop robs death of its tyranny, as joy and love prove stronger than the netherworld and more powerful than the grave. When this happens, the music offers the listener a high that is far more profound and lasting than anything a blunt can provide: dope beats, tight lyrics, and spiritual feelings so intoxicating that they allow you to lose yourself and, subsequently, gain something bigger and better. Something like this happens in Ozomatli's exuberant, boisterous song, *Cumbia de los muertos* (dance of the dead). Though the lyrics cannot convey the full richness of the song—a full band sound of percussion and horns, guitars and accordions, Latin cajónes and tablas, hip-hop beats and flows—a small piece of the song is caught in the words that follow:

> Aqui no existe la tristeza, sole existe la alegrias
> El baile de los queridos, de los queridos del pasado
> Mira como baile mi mama, bailando con mi hermano del pasado
> Sus espiritus se juntan bailando, lleno de alegria y gozando.[51]
>
> (Here, sadness doesn't exist, only joy
> The dance of loved ones, the loved ones of the past
> Look how my mother dances, dancing with my dead brother
> Their spirits joined in dance, filled with joy and delight.)

For this East LA rap group, hip-hop celebrates this dreamlike spiritual vision, where music finds the still point of the turning world and binds us—in the ancient sense of "religare"—to the community of the dead. In the case of Ozomatli, as for Latino hip-hop heads across the continent, rap music also binds its listeners to the vexed and beleaguered histories of indigenous and mestizo peoples, African Americans, Afro-Latinos, and everyone pushed to the margins of the modern world. Though flawed and imperfect, hip-hop has become a medium for the kind of poetry, cunning, spirituality, wit, and ingenuity required for the youth of these communities not only to survive these circumstances, but to subdue them, make them relent, and, in true hip-hop fashion, force them to scream their name.

## The Future of Latino Studies: Prospects and Proposals

In conclusion, I want to return to my comments earlier on the predicament of refugees and migrants in our world, and specifically, what these circumstances might mean for Latino studies. As a scholar of religious studies and hip-hop, the relationship between aesthetics and ethics, arts and justice, spirituality and politics, mysticism and prophecy remains a fundamental area of concern to me. Though one may choose to develop one element of these pairs, I myself am interested in the conjunctions and hyphens that join the two. In the cases of music, literature, dance, graffiti, or the art of rapping, for instance, there is no doubt that the aesthetic form and style of these genres are fundamental to their purpose and reason for being. The design, shape, and flair of their presentation are just as important as what is communicated, just as important as their message. At the same time, it is a wild exaggeration to suggest that the elements of hip-hop have nothing to do with basic human rights, dreams of equality and justice, and the longing for freedom. Whether in rap lyrics, a six-step in b-boying, or a RIP tag on an abandoned building or alleyway, aesthetic displays in hip-hop are frequently tributes to the invisible, discounted, or fallen in our world. It seems to me, and I follow Federico García Lorca on this, that the greatest artists possess *duende* or soul because of their ability to combine style with substance, beauty with justice. They thrill and enchant us with a form of art that is capacious and roomy, able to house a variety of emotions and concerns.

Take, for example, the question of the baroque in Latin America. Given the foundational influence of the baroque on Latin American cultures, many of the forms of religion, art, and music in the New World developed highly fertile and extravagant preoccupations with beauty, whether in rituals and myths, dances and festivals, dramas and murals, songs and poetry. Beauty has been cherished, celebrated, and adored. It is also true, however, the baroque has an ugly history in Latin America: it has often shored up hierarchical and oppressive configurations of politics and society, provided ideological legitimations of unjust societies, and promised to the masses of the poor and excluded nothing more than the hope of a better afterlife.[52] As creative and marvelous as the baroque spirit has been in Latin America, it has also shielded the rich and powerful from rebuke, which explains why so many prophetic figures in Latin America—from Las Casas to twentieth-century liberation theologians—have been critical of baroque aesthetics. Echoing the criticism of Marx, for instance, the Peruvian theologian Gustavo Gutiérrez has tended to view aesthetics and popular culture, including religion, as an opiate when they simply console and pacify without inspiring acts of justice, compassion, and social change. For him, Christian theology should stand at the crossroads of spirituality and political engagement, aesthetics and the pursuit of justice.[53]

While some of the prophetic censures of aesthetics go too far in denying the value of beauty or artistic form, their voices are important to consider even when one works on a question or topic that is clearly concerned with style and grace. While it is certainly true that hip-hop is preoccupied and even obsessed with style (and here I mean in hip-hop in the broad sense, including deejaying, emceeing, graffiti, b-boying, and fashion), there is no doubt that it is also an instrument of protest and activism, a makeshift resource used by many disenfranchised cultures to communicate their feelings of disaffection, anger, and alienation. In its best moments and best practitioners—whether sketched with graffiti, beats, and rhymes, or with the twisting moves of a b-boy—hip-hop is an anthem and manifesto on behalf of the world's poor and excluded. When it combines aesthetical creativity, pure pleasure, and ethical-political insight, it is proof that art can enlarge the human spirit.

The discipline of Latino studies would do well to heed these lessons. There is no reason that Latino studies cannot navigate the border territories of aesthetics and ethics, educating us in the rich artistic achievements of Latino heritages while speaking on behalf of border-crossers, migrants, and refugees throughout the American continent. For someone raised in the borderlands of the US Southwest, and who feels the siren call of these voices and responsibilities, intellectual life has to constantly prove its worth and relevance to these kinds of lives and experiences. When it becomes smug and self-satisfied, vain in its presumptions of superiority, it will lose not only its relevance but also its very soul. Even if it manages to achieve technical mastery or academic success, it will not have *duende*.

## Notes

1. William Jelani Cobb, *To the Break of Dawn: A Freestyle on the Hip Hop Aesthetic* (New York: NYU Press, 2008), 35.
2. Gustavo Perez Firmat, *Life on the Hyphen: The Cuban American Way* (Austin: University of Texas Press, 1994), 17.
3. Friedrich Nietzsche, *The Viking Portable Nietzsche* ed. and trans. by Walter Kaufmann (New York: Penguin Books, 1977), 46–47.
4. "Many of the bass patterns heard in today's hip hop and classic funk were nicked from Afro-Cuban bands," writes Jory Farr. See his, *Rites of Rhythm: The Music of Cuba* (New York: Regan, 2003), 7. And William Eric Perkins says the same thing in an early critical volume on hip-hop, *Droppin' Science: Critical Essays on Rap Music and Hip Hop Culture*: "I contend that the introduction of percussion beats in the dance music of the 1970s and in early hip hop were products of Latin music's powerful influence on New York and New Jersey popular culture." See *Droppin' Science: Critical Essays on Rap Music and Hip Hop Culture* (Philadelphia: Temple University Press, 1996), 6.
5. Joseph Schloss has a good description of this in *Foundation: B-boys, B-girls and Hip-Hop Culture in New York* (Oxford: Oxford University Press, 2009), 19.
6. See Joseph Schloss, *Foundation: B-boys, B-girls and Hip-Hop Culture in New York* (Oxford: Oxford University Press, 2009), 20.
7. DJ Kool Herc is usually given credit for developing and enhancing the break by using the same record on two turntables, rewinding one while the other played. This enabled him to play the break nonstop.

8. Speaking of Jimmy Castor, in particular, David Toop makes reference to the Afro-Latin influences on hip-hop: "From watching or hearing records of Latin musicians like Tito Puente, Chan Pozo and Cal Tjader, he learned to incorporate authentic Afro-Cuban rhythms and percussion, adding timbales to his vocal and multi-instrumental abilities." See David Toop, *Rap Attack #3* (London: Serpent's Tail, 2000), 24. For other classic studies of hip-hop, see Michael Eric Dyson, *Holler If You Hear Me: Searching for Tupac Shakur* (New York: Basic Civitas, 2006); Jeff Chang, *Can't Stop, Won't Stop: A History of the Hip-Hop Generation* (New York: Picador, 2005); Marcus Reeves, *Somebody Scream: Rap Music's Rise to Prominence in the Aftershock of Black Power* (New York: Farrar, Straus, and Giroux, 2009); Roni Sarig, *Third Coast: OutKast, Timbaland and How Hip-Hop Became a Southern Thing* (New York: Da Capo, 2007).
9. César Miguel Rondón, *The Book of Salsa*, trans. by Frances Aparicio (Chapel Hill: University of North Carolina Press, 2008), 16.
10. Ibid., 103.
11. Raquel Rivera, *New York Ricans from the Hip Hop Zone* (New York: Palgrave Macmillan, 2003), 35.
12. Joseph Schloss, *Foundation: B-boys, B-girls and Hip-Hop Culture in New York* (Oxford: Oxford University Press, 2009), 20.
13. Timothy Brennan, *Sacred Devotion: Afro-Latin Music and Imperial Jazz* (London: Verso, 2008), 9.
14. For a discussion of Latin influences on hip-hop origins, see Juan Flores, *From Bomba to Hip Hop: Puerto Rican Culture and Latino Identity* (New York: Columbia University Press, 2000); Raquel Rivera, *New York Ricans from the Hip Hop Zone* (New York: Palgrave Macmillan, 2003); Pancho McFarland, *The Chican@ Hip Hop Nation: Politics of a New Millenial Mestizaje* (Lansing: Michigan State University, 2013); Alejandro Nava, *In Search of Soul: Hip Hop, Literature and Religion* (Berkeley: University of California Press, 2017).
15. Common, "I Used to Love H.E.R." *Resurrection*, Relativity Records, 1994.
16. Quoted by S. Craig Watkins, *Hip Hop Matters: Politics, Pop Culture and the Struggle for the Soul of a Movement* (Boston: Beacon, 2005), 127.
17. See Hisham Aidi, *Rebel Music: Race, Empire, and the New Muslim Youth Culture* (New York: Pantheon, 2014), 255.
18. This line is a paraphrase from Greg Tate's article, "Hip Hop Turns 30: Whatcha Celebratin' For?" in *That's the Joint: The Hip Hop Studies Reader*, ed. by Murray Forman and Mark Anthony Neal (London: Routledge, 2012), 63–67.
19. Tricia Rose's work, *Black Noise: Rap Music and Black Culture in Contemporary America* (Middletown, CT: Wesleyan, 1994) foresaw the global expansion of hip-hop and the future development of polyvocal inflections of rap. In this vein, see also *Global Linguistic Flows: Hip Hop Cultures, Youth Identities, and the Politics of Language*, ed. H. Samy Alim (London: Routledge, 2008).
20. Paul Gilroy, "It's a Family Affair," in *Black Popular Culture*, ed. Gina Dent (Seattle: Bay Press, 1992), 307.
21. Manning Marable, "Race, Identity and Political Culture," in *Black Popular Culture*, ed. Gina Dent (Seattle: Bay Press, 1992), 302.
22. Quote from the hip-hop documentary, *Inventos: Hip Hop Cubano*, Eli Jacobs-Fantauzzi, Clenched Fist Productions, 2005. Quotes from this video are my translations.
23. See *Inventos: Hip Hop Cubano*, Eli Jacobs-Fantauzzi, Clenched Fist Productions, 2005.

24. Nicolás Guillén, *Yoruba from Cuba*, trans. by Salvador Ortiz-Carboneres (Leeds: Peepal Tree, 2005), 122. See Alan West-Durán, "Rap's Diasporic Dialogue: Cuba's Redefinition of Blackness," *Journal of Popular Music Studies* 16 (2004), 20. Also see Sujatha Fernandes, *Close to the Edge: In Search of the Global Hip Hop Generation* (London: Verso, 2011), 45.
25. See West-Durán, "Rap's Diasporic Dialogue: Cuba's Redefinition of Blackness," 20, for a good discussion of *choteo*.
26. This relationship between Langston Hughes and Guillén is discussed in Arnold Rampersad's biography. See also Claudia Milan, *Latining America: Black-Brown Passages and the Coloring of Latino/a Studies* (Athens: University of Georgia Press, 2013), 90–91.
27. Hermanos de Causa, "Lagrimas Negras," Mixer Music, 2008.
28. See Derek Pardue, *Brazilian Hip Hoppers Speak From the Margins* (New York: Palgrave Macmillan, 2011), 39–43.
29. Racionais MCs, "Diaro de um detento," *Sobrevivendo no Inferno*, Cosa Nostra Phonographic, 1997. I am grateful to Beatriz Carneiros, graduate student, University of Arizona, for her help in translating this song.
30. See Jory Farr, *Rites of Rhythm: The Music of Cuba* (New York: Regan Books, 2003), 215.
31. Quoted by Timothy Brennan, *Secular Devotion: Afro-Latin Music and Imperial Jazz* (London: Verso, 2008), 114.
32. *Inventos: Hip Hop Cubano*, Eli Jacobs-Fantauzzi, Clinched Fist Productions, 2005.
33. Cuarta Imagen, "La Muralla," *High Times*, 2005.
34. Bahamadia, "Spontaneity," *Kollage*, Chrysalis/EMI Records, 1996.
35. Orishas, "Represent," *A lo Cubano*, Universal Latino, 2000.
36. See David Brown, *Santería Enthroned: Art, Ritual, and Innovation in Afro-Cuban Religion* (Chicago: University of Chicago Press, 2003), 271, for an excellent discussion of Shango and other aspects of Afro-Cuban religion.
37. See David Brown, *Santería Enthroned: Art, Ritual and Innovation in Afro-Cuban Religion* (Chicago: University of Chicago Press, 2003), 67.
38. W. E. B. Du Bois, *Black Folk, Then and Now* (Oxford: Oxford University Press, 2014), last page. See also Kwame Anthony Appiah, *Lines of Descent: W.E.B. Du Bois and the Emergence of Identity* (Cambridge, MA: Harvard University Press, 2014), 135.
39. See Roger Bastide, *The African Religions of Brazil: Toward a Sociology of the Interpenetration of Civilizations*, trans. Helen Sebba (Baltimore: John Hopkins Press, 1978), 114–116.
40. Alan West-Durán, "Rap's Diasporic Dialogue: Cuba's Redefinition of Blackness," *Journal of Popular Music Studies* 16 (2004): 24.
41. Another example of this is the previously mentioned group, Obsesión. In their music, Yoruba chants are carefully layered with hip-hop beats and Afro-Cuban percussion, with an effect that seems contemporary and nostalgic, modern and traditional (as in their song, "La llaman puta," where Magia Lopez raps about the debasing and violent treatment of prostitutes in Cuba in the context of a jazz vibe and Yoruba chant). In their case, it is clear that the barrio where the rap duo is from, Regla, has left its imprint on their music. Home of one of the very first secret Abakuá societies (a black male society with origins in Nigeria), Regla today remains a center for Afro-Cuban traditions and a very popular destination for Santería pilgrims who go to visit *La Santisima Virgen de Regla*, the "black Madonna" in the town's colonial church.
42. George Lipsitz, *Dangerous Crossroads: Popular Music, PostModernism and the Poetics of Place* (London: Verso, 1994), 17.

43. Pancho McFarland, "Here Is Something You Can't Understand: Chicano Rap and the Critique of Globalization," in *Decolonial Voices*, ed. Arturo Aldama and Naomi Quiñonez (Bloomington: Indiana University Press, 2002), 308.
44. Kinto Sol, "Hecho en Mexico," *Hecho en Mexico* (Disa, 2003).
45. Funky Aztecs, "Prop 187," *Day of the Dead*, Raging Bull Records, 1995.
46. In speaking of the appeal of myth to literary modernists, specifically the Arab poet, Adonis, Talal Asad expresses this exact point: "For Adonis, myth arises whenever human reason encounters perplexing questions about existence and attempts to answer them in what can only be a non-rational way, thus producing a combination of poetry, history and wonderment." See Talal Asad, *Formations of the Secular: Christianity, Islam and Modernity* (Stanford, CA: Stanford University Press, 2003), 55. Sacvan Bercovitch also has a nice description of myth. See his *The American Jeremiad* (Madison: University of Wisconsin, 2012), xli.
47. Kinto Sol, "Los Hijos del Maize," *Los Hijos del Maize*, Univision Records, 2006.
48. See Gloria Flaherty, *Shamanism and the Eighteenth Century* (Princeton, NJ: Princeton University Press, 1992), 74–75. In particular, writes Georgi, "The litany was one favored form because its rhythms and tones affected the body directly, without appeal to the higher faculty of reason." See also Talal Asad, *Formations of the Secular: Christianity, Islam and Modernity* (Stanford, CA: Stanford University Press, 2003), 50.
49. Quote from the hip-hop documentary, *Inventos: Hip Hop Cubano*, Eli Jacobs-Fantauzzi, Clenched Fist Productions, 2005.
50. This quote is from Virginia Woolf, *To the Lighthouse* (New York: Harcourt, Brace, Jovanovich, 1989).
51. Ozomatli, "Cumbia de los Muertos," *Ozomatli*, Almo Sounds, 1998.
52. See Angel Rama's classic study of this feature of the baroque in *The Lettered City*, trans. John Charles Chasteen (Durham, NC: Duke University Press, 1996).
53. My dissertation thesis was on this topic, published as *The Mystical and Prophetic Thought of Simone Weil and Gustavo Gutiérrez* (Albany: SUNY Press, 2001).

## Bibliography

Ashon, Will. *Chamber Music: Wu-Tang and America*. New York: Faber and Faber, 2018.
Baker, Geoffrey. *Buena Vista in the Club: Rap, Reggaeton, and Revolution in Havana*. Durham, NC: Duke University Press, 2011.
Berríos-Miranda, Marisol ed, *American Sabor: Latinos and Latinas in US Popular Music*. Seattle: University of Washington Press, 2018.
Chang, Jeff. *Can't Stop, Won't Stop*. New York: St. Martin's Press, 2005.
Cobb, William Jelani. *To the Break of Dawn: A Freestyle on the Hip-Hop Aesthetic*. New York: New York University Press, 2007.
Cohn, Nik. *Triksta: Life and Death in New Orleans Rap*. New York: Vintage Books, 2005.
Flores, Juan. *From Bomba to Hip-Hop: Puerto Rican Identity and Latino Identity*. New York: Columbia University Press, 2000.
Kajikawa, Loren. *Sounding Race in Rap Songs*. Berkeley: University of California Press, 2015.
McFarland, Pancho. *Chicano Rap: Gender and Violence in the Postindustrial Barrio*. Austin: University of Texas, 2008.

Moore, Robin. *Music and Revolution: Cultural Change in Socialist Cuba*. Berkeley: University of California Press, 2006.

Nava, Alejandro. *In Search of Soul: Hip-Hop, Literature and Religion*. Berkeley: University of California Press, 2017.

Reeves, Marcus. *Somebody Scream: Rap Music's Rise to Prominence in the Aftershock of Black Power*. New York: Faber and Faber, 2008.

Rivera-Rideau, Petra. *Remixing Reggaeton: The Cultural Politics of Race in Puerto Rico*. Durham, NC: Duke University Press, 2015.

Schloss, Joseph. *Foundation: B-boys, B-girls and Hip-Hop Culture in New York*. Oxford: Oxford University Press, 2009.

Sublette, Ned. *Cuba and It's Music: From the First Drums to the Mambo*. Chicago, IL: Chicago Review Press, 2004.

# PART IV

# WHIRLING TONGUES

CHAPTER 12

# NOTES ON LATINO PHILOLOGY

ILAN STAVANS

> A word is dead, when it is said,
> Some say—
> I say it just begins to live
> That day.
>
> —Emily Dickinson, "Poem 1212" (*c.* 1872)

## On Becoming a Philologist

Words are time codes. In their essence, they contain the DNA of the people that created them.

I think of myself as a philologist, although I am well aware of how out of fashion the term has become. It used to be that anyone interested in the partnership between language and literature was called a philologist. Now these two fields are divorced. We refer to their respective endeavors with fancier terms, such as linguistics and literary criticism. It is a shame that their compatibility is no longer required. We all suffer as a result. In the Hispanic world, lexicography carries little cachet.

According to the *Oxford English Dictionary*, this branch of knowledge "deals with the structure, historical development, and relationships of a language." No language exists in a vacuum: it manifests itself in the act of telling something; to isolate language from content is to forget its true worth.

It is less controversial to become a scholar of major languages rather than of those considered minor. A major language (English, Mandarin, Spanish, French, German, etc.) is standardized; its most ideologically contested quality is that it is imperial, usurping space from other, smaller tongues. Minor languages are limited to a small number of users. They exist like an endangered species in a state of suspended continuity.

I love words just as much as I love narrative. This devotion originates from my Jewishness. I grew up in an environment where literacy was at the center of life. The way to connect to the past was through a commitment to books. I do not remember being an avid reader when I was a child; that appetite came later, when I was in my late teens. Still, my parents surrounded themselves with culture: books, plays, film, music. There was not a moment in the day when someone was not in the middle of telling a story.

Narrative is the oxygen that makes culture breathe. Narrative is not only story, though; in other words, it is not only the "what happens" but the "how it is said to happen," meaning that a narrative is always delivered in language and that form and content are one. A successful story not only depends on the sharpness of its plot; the language that plot takes is equally crucial.

Of course, language itself tells a story, too: the story of its subjects and predicates, its verbs and nouns and adjectives, its punctuation, and in equal measure, the blank space—silences—between signs within a sentence. Separating story from language is like divorcing oil from water. Yet people seldom look at the two together. They focus almost exclusively on action.

I am dismayed by the degree to which, after the basics are learned in elementary school, the study of language in all its complexity is abandoned by our education system. I am talking not only of the industrialized nations but of developing countries as well. We would do better in multiple levels if we spent more time looking at words from multiple perspectives. It would make us aware of their limitations as well as their potential. It's a tenant of life that there is much that cannot be said properly; the most challenging intellectual task we have in front of us is *to say things clearly and eloquently*.

Those two characteristics are expressions of refinement. That noun, *refinement*, unfortunately connotes elitism these days. To express oneself in convoluted fashion does not seem to be a sin anymore, although it ought to be. I am not only referring to speakers with limited education but to everyone. In fact, the situation, in my view, is worse among the educated, including academics. Ever tried reading an average literary analysis of, say, James Joyce's *Ulysses* (1920)? Joyce at least was deliberately making language more playful.

All this is understandable. Ours is an age that looks at language in utilitarian terms. Its function is to convey meaning in quick, simplistic fashion. Speaking intelligently, matching image and word, takes experience. The accumulation of that experience is what is known as "maturity." Maturity in language is linked to maturity of mind and vice versa. By the way, I am aware these comments are not politically correct. This does not make them less true.

I am not a nostalgist who believes the past is better. Quite the contrary, I am infatuated with the changes the present offers us. Being clear and eloquent is a requirement of any period. It accelerates progress.

In terms of my own intellectual trajectory, I do not remember being obsessed with words when I was young. I took them for granted. I was born into a richly textured cultural milieu where a variety of languages battled for attention. I cannot quite say how I learned to distinguish between them, to appreciate which words belonged to which code and the kind of loyalty they paid to it. In hindsight, it is easy for me to say that it was all a Babel-like chaos, but it is not true.

It was only when I became an immigrant, in the mid-1980s, that words acquired a different status for me. From Mexico, where I was raised, I traveled around the Middle East and then to Europe until I settled in the United States: New York City, to be precise, which in itself is a linguistic statement. Here, all the languages of the world converged into that small archipelago of humanity. Instead of creating confusion in me, however, I became infatuated with sounds, rhythms, and sentence structure. Surely, I had already been predisposed to such cacophony, but now I was invited to discover the infinite possibilities of every word.

In retrospect, it seems like an act of fate: New York City exists in hectic movement; to think of it as a place of meditation is counterintuitive. But that's exactly what happened to me. The environment alerted me to the labyrinthine paths of semantics. T. S. Eliot, in *Four Quartets* (1943), says: "For last year's words belong to last year's language. And next year's words await another voice." I wanted to understand the etymology of words, to trace their history, to appreciate the way they changed over time.

In other words, I have never studied philology in any formal way, mainly because no institution in the United States today offers such programs. (The word marketed in graduate school is "linguistics.")

Needless to say, my arrival to New York City did not just define me as an immigrant. All of a sudden, I also became Latino, inserting myself in a minority culture that was rapidly growing. By 2015, that minority amounted to almost a quarter of the overall population of the United States. Linguistically, this means that there are more Spanish-language speakers north of the Rio Grande than in countries like Argentina, Venezuela, and Colombia. Obviously, their crux is unique. Their tongue exists in constant contact with English, forcing it to adapt in obvious as well as unforeseen ways.

One of my first quests was to understand hybrid tongues. I became infatuated with languages in contact: Franglais (French–English), Portuñol (Spanish–Portuguese), Hebreya (Hebrew–Arabic), and so on. Should these be described as dialects? What is the difference between a language and a dialect? In what way were these manifestations the announcement of a new culture?

Eventually, I settled on Spanglish, the mix of Spanish and English. It was already preponderant in New York when I arrived. I looked into its varieties. Was there a difference between the Spanglish spoken in El Paso, Texas, and the one in Tallahassee, Florida?

My book *Spanglish: The Making of a New American Language* (2002) is in itself a composite. It opens with a lengthy essay exploring the history of Spanglish, comparing it to standardized as well as hybrid tongues. It also features a Spanglish–English dictionary of about six thousand Spanglish terms. And it concludes with a translation into Spanglish of the first chapter of Miguel de Cervantes's novel *Don Quixote of La Mancha* (1605–1615), a book that has defined me in innumerable ways.

There is an assortment of reactions to Spanglish. Since the beginning, my view has been that it's a mestizo language announcing the birth of a new civilization. In that sense, I am not altogether certain that Latinos are an immigrant group like all others before and after. My view is that as a result of a number of decisive factors—among others, a unique history, the proximity of the place once called home, restless immigration patterns, and an idiosyncrasy that keeps families together—Latinos announce a new way of being Hispanic. Any discussion of Spanglish must address this dimension.

In subsequent decades, my fascination with the brisk, still-unformed quality of Spanglish has not diminished. Since the year 2000 and even before, I have seen it flourish. It is ubiquitous in all walks of life, not only in the United States but also in the Americas.

It would not be disingenuous to suggest that my own scholarship has contributed to a more recognized status for Spanglish. While the term might have been used in the 1940s, the earliest studies of it date back to the 1970s. It was not until the first decade of this millennium when Latinos in the United States became the largest demographic and fastest-growing minority that the term "Spanglish" began to be used. Along with it came the recognition of Latinos' presence in every dimension of life: politics, the economy, religion, marketing, law enforcement, incarceration, culture, entertainment, and, naturally, language. That's when Spanglish began to be taken seriously. It suggested that, as a decisive force, the language of Latinos needed to be understood.

Other languages have been equally important to me as a philologist. In *Resurrecting Hebrew* (2008), I explored the way Eliezer Ben-Yehuda orchestrated the revival of biblical Hebrew in the framework of the late nineteenth-century Zionist movement and how that language, after the creation of the state of Israel in 1948, mutated in countless, unforeseeable ways.

I have written about the development of Yiddish in *Singer's Typewriter and Mine* (2011) and *How Yiddish Changed America and How America Changed Yiddish* (2020), and on Ladino in *The Shocken Book of Modern Sephardic Literature* (2005), and *A Critic's Journey* (2013). Although I appreciate the value of what detailed linguistic studies mean for a small cadre of specialists and have recurrently written for those audiences on these topics, my default target is the general audience. The reason, again, has to do with the adjectives I mentioned before: if something can be said clearly and eloquently, there is no reason to do otherwise.

I take this approach from Samuel Johnson, the great English polymath, whose oeuvre I thoroughly admire. Although he is referred to as "Doctor," he did not have what we call a terminal degree to hide behind. Johnson is the philologist par excellence: his essays on Shakespeare and his literary criticism in general are models of hermeneutics; his travel writings, principally those with his biographer James Boswell, are exemplary in the way the marry intellectual and experiential information; his columns for periodicals like *The Idler* and *The Rambler* showcase a mind deeply rooted in his time; and then there is *A Dictionary of the English Language* (1755), arguably the most distinctive (e.g., the most personal) of all lexicons ever published in English.

I wrote about Johnson in *Dictionary Days* (2010). And about English I have written profusely, including a regular column in the *Chronicle of Higher Education* website *Lingua Franca* and in volumes like *A Critic's Journey* and *On Self-Translation* (2018).

Having made my home since the early 1990s in a small town in New England, it is inevitable that English would be a central topic in my philological inquiries. I have always engaged in those inquiries from a comparative perspective. That's because any language that is alive is a language in contact. English is the perfect example. Such is its dominance that its survival is never in question. Yet the tongue changes every day in dramatic fashion. Shakespeare would be amazed by the way we use it today, and I am in awe by how different American English has become since I first arrived in New York in the 1990s. The barrage of youth, technological, and so-called foreign idioms that have been incorporated since then, or that have metamorphosed in plain sight, is dumbfounding.

Since I mentioned awe, consider the word *awesome*. It dates back to the late sixteenth century. Shakespeare is one of the Elizabethan writers credited for using it for the first time. It is used as a quality of the divine in the King James Version of the Bible, known as KJV, which was published in 1611. But "awesome" has been co-opted by American adolescents to refer to whatever is "excellent." Consequently, using "awesome" to talk about God feels, well, pedestrian. Some fifty years will need to pass for the term to be refurbished.

Other terms are *woke, gnome, startup, driverless, cyberspace,* and *meme*. English, as the world's dominant tongue, is a bully and a thief. It shamelessly borrows and steals and forces other languages to submit to its needs.

Most of my own philological work, however, has rotated around *el español*. This is because I am more closely linked to that language—the accident of birth—than to any other. Each of its words is a molecule waiting to be scrutinized. When did it emerge? How has it changed? What different meanings has it acquired? How do those meanings change from one landscape to another? I have said it elsewhere: it is harder for me to say I was born in Mexico than to say I was born into Spanish. From Gonzalo de Berceo to *Don Quixote de la Mancha* (1605–6015) and Gabriel García Márquez, I feel a deep connection to its millennial journey.

As I wrote in *Dictionary Days*, my personal library is packed with dictionaries of all types. A few are bilingual. Others are concerned with specific linguistic fields: slang, marketing, medicine, Shakespeare, and so forth. My collection includes many Spanish lexicons, from Sebastián de Covarrubias's *Tesoro de la lengua castellana o española* (1611) to the *Diccionario de Autoridades* (1726–1739) to the volumes edited by María Moliner (1966–1967) and Joan Corominas (1982). I spend sleepless nights browsing through them.

It is of singular interest to me that Covarrubias's thesaurus appeared in Spanish in the same year that the KJV of the Bible was released in English. Those were the two supreme empires of the period, and they were at war with each other. The KJV is a magisterial collaboration that defined the English language forever. Covarrubias's volume was less balanced. The flaws at its core announce the handicap forever cursing Hispanic philology: a derivative, non-rigorous approach to language tainted by the meddling of the Catholic Church and other powerful institutions connected with what *en español* is known as *casticismo*, the stink of Spanish pride, whose subjectivity invariably compromises the finished product.

Scholarship on Spanish philology is biased depending on the researcher's geographical location. Spain remains territorial about the language. Although only about 10 percent of Spanish speakers worldwide are in the Iberian Peninsula, the fact that its origins are there results in a distinctive tint. Hispanic Americans laugh at this attitude. There are close to 450 million users from Mexico to Argentina.

The Real Academia Española, known as RAE, has branches in every country where Spanish is the official or dominant language. Yet the matrix is in Madrid and all legislative decisions come from it. In the former colonies, looking at the RAE with suspicion is a sport. Every time an announcement is made in it, people turn it into a joke.

In comparison with English, lexicographic studies of Spanish lag behind. In the United Kingdom, dictionaries come in different types. The most respected is the *Oxford English Dictionary (OED)*, which, as its name suggests, has always been affiliated with a prestigious university. Other lexicons are also invaluable, like the one published by Merriam-Webster, in Springfield, Massachusetts, which has always been a commercial venture. Its roots go back to the eighteenth-century lexicographer Noah Webster.

A history of how these and other dictionaries came to be is well known, not only in academic circles but among general readers. Books like Simon Winchester's *The Professor and the Madman* (1998) make accessible the mythology of the first attempts, in the aftermath of the Enlightenment in Europe, to catalog words.

In contrast, the authority in charge of analyzing how dictionaries came to be in the Iberian Peninsula and its former American colonies—for instance, the *Diccionario de la Lengua Española*, first published in 1780 and reprinted periodically under the aegis of the Real Academia Española, and Andrés Bello's *Gramática de la lengua castellana destinada al uso de los americanos* (1847)—remain the domain of a few specialists and are almost totally unknown among lay readers. This is a significant limitation.

Bello is a luminary that ought to be better known. In some ways, he is the equivalent of a Doctor Johnson in Spanish: a renaissance man whose interest, from botany to diplomacy, pushed him in countless directions. My own mind works in similar ways. As much as I admire specialized interests, I am a generalist; that is, I am attracted by a plurality of things and do not see why I should reject any of them. It's the infinites connections among them that appeal to me.

Latino studies, as an area of scholarship, has grown at a rapid pace. In its essence it is interdisciplinary, combining efforts coming from history, political science, literary studies, sociology, anthropology, economics, and other established fields. Philology is the ugly duckling. On the surface, it does not appear to have any pragmatic value in the age of capital-investment education. This is nearsighted. It deserves a broader reconsideration, since just about every aspect of life can be understood through the study of the language of Latinos.

I fear Latino studies is becoming a discipline rife with sportsmanship devoted to cultural pride. Knowledge is not satisfying but perplexing. And there is no honest pursuit of knowledge without the recognition that the language it is conveyed through in is in itself complex.

# A History of the Spanish Language in Five Sentences

Knowledge is always about perspective matters, of course: we do not know things as they are but *as we are*.

Most histories of the Spanish language have been written by Iberian scholars, offering naturally disjointed views of *el español americano*. Only a few of them are in English, and even fewer have been produced in the United States by Anglo academics in the field of linguistics. That is, their target audience consists of specialists.

The only full-fledged history of Spanish written by a Latin American scholar is Antonio Alatorre's *Los 1001 años de la lengua española* (1989). Other intellectuals and scholars from the Americas have produced superb philological studies with the region's perspective that seeks to correct the imbalance created by an overabundance in Iberian perspective. These include Pedro Henríquez Ureña from the Dominican Republic; Fernando Ortiz and Lydia Cabrera from Cuba; Ángel Rosenblat from Venezuela; Raimundo Lida and María Rosa Lida de Malkiel from Argentina; and Alfonso Reyes and Gutierre Tibón from Mexico. Collectively, their pursuits have opened exciting new intellectual paths and serve as models to emulate.

To this day, no Latino (e.g., a person of Hispanic background in the United States) has ever put together a full-length volume. After Mexico, the United States has the largest concentration of Spanish-language speakers in the world. It is time for a history of global Spanish to be produced from this perspective.

I envision this history in the form of an accessible, engaging book called *A History of the Spanish Language in Five Sentences*. While the highlights of such history would remain more or less the same, the overall approach would be different: a two-millennia chronological survey, from the Roman period of the Iberian Peninsula to the ascent of the Americas as the driving force of culture. My lifelong passions, from the *Diccionario de Autoridades* to *One Hundred Years of Solitude* (1967), serve as roadmap. And philology—language plus politics, religion, and culture (literature and the arts) equals knowledge—is the driving force.

The central thesis is that Spanish, in and of itself, is tongue in eternal mutation. In its inception it was not unlike Spanglish, a hybrid used in central Spain, in the regions of Castilla and La Mancha, derided by scholars who favored Latin as the language of education. It eventually evolved into a national language when the Catholic Kings Ferdinand and Isabella consolidated their power by joining forces. From there, Spanish has evolved through imperial conquest, lending to and borrowing from other regional and international languages.

Why in five sentences? The answer is simple: why not? A dozen, eighteen, twenty-five—all numbers are random. I have opted for *cinco frases* because it is a compact, accessible number. (We use a decimal system because we have ten fingers, five on each hand.) But it's a gimmick, obviously. Each of these sentences is an excuse to reflect on another period in history, all of them interrelated.

The narrative is built around miscegenation—how disparate elements, in the proper circumstances, combined to form what Spanish is now. The first sentence in the book, "*Ya mamma, mio al-habibi*" (Your mother, my friend), symbolizes the emergence of the language as a way to orally communicate in thirteenth-century Spain. It uses a heavy dose of Arabic. It is crucial to keep in mind that for a long time the oral use of the word prevailed over its written counterpart. The *Iliad* and *Odyssey* are examples of oral tradition. In all honesty, we are uncertain who Homer was and whether indeed he was even a man. We call Homer the author of those two chronicles of Odysseus's journeys because tradition has attached them to such a name. But those tales lived for centuries in the minds of its tellers: a collective author who used memory, not parchment (let alone paper), to deliver its message.

In this section, the concept of the book as we know it (a rather recent phenomenon) is explored in the framework of Iberian history. It dates back roughly to the codification by Ezra the Scribe in the second century before the Common Era of what has come to be known as *The Five Books of Moses*. Until then, the oral word reined unchallenged, to the extent that writing things down was understood as a means of impoverishing words. Most of what is known of the Spanish language from the moment the Romans brought Vulgar Latin to the Iberian Peninsula in the year 210 before the Common Era, with the Second Punic War (until the *Glosas Emilianenses* in the ninth century), is open to conjecture since it existed mostly in oral fashion.

The narrative in *A History of the Spanish Language in Five Sentences* would reach further back, though. It would start in 218–201 BCE, as the Second Punic War takes place, in which the Romans defeat the Carthaginians and acquire the Iberian Peninsula. This is generally considered the historical moment, followed in 206 BCE with the Roman invasion of the Iberian Peninsula, when the region comes to be known as *Hispania* in the fourth century. All accounts of the development of the Spanish language, regardless of who is behind them, need to start with this beginning. The difference is in the approach. Mine would talk about invasion as a theme that is present from the start and becomes a leitmotif across centuries. The difference among imperial quests and colonial enterprises needs to be understood while also establishing an essential connection among them.

It is in 197 BCE when Hispania is officially declared a province by the Romans in following the conclusion of the Second Punic War. Soon after, in 552, Andalusía, called *Spania*, becomes part of the Byzantine Empire until 624. It is important to stress that the Roman domination of the Iberian Peninsula lasted for about four hundred years. It concluded in the 600s, leaving behind heavy traces in the region's language and culture. They are palpable in the way Latin ultimately became the source of Spanish as one of its outgrowths. As in the case of French, Portuguese, Italian, and Romanian, all Romance languages, the syntactical patterns of Spanish have a foundation in the language used by the Romans in the region.

The Roman Empire was followed by Arab invasions, including, in 711, the major one by Umayyad general Tariq ibn Ziyad conquers Hispania, resulting in the Umayyad

Caliphate, which lasted until 718. The Arab presence would ultimately become quite important as well in the shaping of Spanish. Words like *alhambre* (wire), *azotea* (roof top), and *zanahoria* (carrot) all come from the Arabic.

It was in Castilla where the earliest manifestations of a dialect that would become Spanish emerged. It is there where the language transitions from oral to written. Some of the earliest Spanish ballads are the *Las Jarchas*, a medieval lyric, written in colloquial Arabic, and inserted at the end of poetic compositions written by Islamic and Jewish troubadours. These texts, which began to flourish around 975, are considered early manifestations of the language that evolved over centuries into Spanish. Then in 1100s comes the emergence of *Glosas Silenses* and the aforementioned *Glosas Emilianenses*, glosses written as marginalia in manuscripts during the Middle Age in what is known as Vulgar Latin, a variation on the Roman Empire's language that ends up fragmenting into Romance languages. Along with *Las Jarchas*, these are early vicissitudes of Spanish. These are followed by *Libro de Alexandre*, a medieval Spanish epic poem, written around 1178–1250, about Alexander the Great, appears. Consisting of 10,770 lines and 2,675 stanzas, it is written by *Master de Clerecia*, an early anonymous series of authors from within the clerical echelons of the Catholic Church whose language is a forerunner of modern Spanish.

The message is that, like Spanglish, *el español* underwent a series of mutations. The first major figure, political as well as scholarly, that shapes Spanish was Alfonso X "El Sabio," who became king of Castile in 1252 and began his project to standardize and elevate Castilian from a vernacular to a language of knowledge and prestige. It was Gonsalo de Berceo, the first named poet of the Spanish language (d. c. 1264), who produced sonnets and other verses that began the standardization of the language, exercising enormous influence not only in the thirteenth century but across history. In terms of written material, Berceo was followed by the *Cantar del Mío Cid* written in 1195–1207. It celebrates the crusade by Rodrigo Díaz against the Arabs. And Marrano poet Juan Alfonso de Baena composed the *Cancionero de Baena*, an anthology of lyrics dedicated to King John II and Constable of Castile Álvaro de Luna. The full title was *Cancionero del Judino Juan Alfonso de Baena*. It was composed c. 1426–1430. In retrospect, these linguistic artifacts were not just important historical documents; they also set the stage for a formalized grammatical structure.

The *annus mirabilis* in Hispanic civilization is 1492. The book's second sentence, "*La compañera del imperio*" (the companion of empire), comes from that year. It included by grammarian Antonio de Nebrija in the preface to the first *Gramática de la lengua castellana*, which is considered the first attempt to look at Spanish from a serious academic perspective. Nebrija's sentence has come to be seen as an emblematic announcement of the role Spanish would take in the period of colonization, when Spain went outside itself and took control of the Americas. Nebrija, for whom I feel enormous admiration, helped consolidate a sense of pride in *castellano*, one of the peninsula's regional languages, as a unifying force in what was then known as *La Reconquista*: the attempt to unify the kingdom under one monarch, one religion, and one language. Nebrija's sentence is most controversial in its location of Spanish as a sister, a spouse, and a companion to empire.

In that crucial year, the Jews were also expelled from the Iberian Peninsula in 1492 as a result of the Edict of Expulsion, and Christopher Columbus sailed across the Atlantic, stumbling upon a new continent. Around the time, Hispania became known as *España*. But *España* was a potpourri of influences: aside from Roman, Jewish, and Arabic, the colonies, at first a source of imperial pride, would come to haunt it. In a new edition of 1496, Nebrija included the first American word known to have entered the Spanish lexicon: *canoa* (canoe). Less than four decades later, philosopher and philologist Juan de Valdés, exiled in Italy, would write his *Diálogos de la lengua* (1533), a series of conversations on the parameters of language change. Valdés's argument is indeed similar to mine: the most constant quality of language is change, he believed; and through the Spanish language one is able to understand how the Renaissance was changing at its heart.

In his chapter, I myself engage in conversation with Valdés, then move in full to the so-called Spanish *siglo de oro* (golden age) the illustrious period—in the arts as well as architecture—that as is commonly said was not quite golden, did not last a century, and was about Spain pillaging its subsidiaries in the Americas. The period is partly connected to the Spanish courts moving in 1561 from Valladolid to Madrid before it becomes Spain's official capital. Figures like Lope de Vega, Francisco de Quevedo, and Luis de Góngora wrote sonnets in precise, mathematical *español*. Lope de Vega was the most prolific *comedia* playwright of the Spanish golden age. He left behind countless sonnets and other poems as well as close to three thousand plays, the majority of them lost to posterity. As such, they became examples of how the language had already achieved tangible refinement.

Quevedo and Góngora represent two diametrically opposed aesthetic views: *culteranismo* and *conceptismo*, one looking at language as an artifice, the other employing it as a tool to explore philosophical issues. Then came the most influential work produced in that epoch and one of my two favorite Spanish-language books: Miguel de Cervantes's parody of the chivalry novels, *Don Quixote*, and *One Hundred Years of Solitude*. For many, *Don Quixote* is the apex of Spanish as an artistic, philosophical, and political language. More or less at the time Cervantes was considering writing the second part of his novel, Sebastián de Cobarruvias published his *Tesoro de la lengua española o castellana*, the first official lexicon of the Spanish language. He assembled it under the aegis of the Holy Inquisition, which, needless to say, makes it a peculiar artifact. Yet this is a record of the way Spanish was used in Cervantes's time. The two works, Cervantes's and Covarrubias's, are studied in this chapter of *A Brief History of the Spanish Language* as gateways to understanding the malleability of the language. In *Don Quixote* in particular, Sancho Panza communicated through innumerable sayings that allow a glimpse of the parlance of the poor and illiterate in the seventeenth century.

From its humble beginning as the way of communication of a small regional group in Castile, in the central part of the Iberian Peninsula, *el español* grew to be a colonizing tongue used in navigation, a tool of cultural subjugation, a conduit for literature and the arts, and a technological device essential for politics, commerce, and marketing. Sor Juana Inés de la Cruz, a Mexican nun and poet, died in 1693 in a convent where she lived most of her adult life. She left behind sonnets, *redondillas*, a defense of the rights of women, and an epistemological poem called *Primero Sueño*. Along with her, a number of crucial colonial writers in the Spanish colonies produced a literature that showcased what *mestizaje* could foster: the mixing of European and aboriginal themes. When the Spanish conquistadors arrived in the Americas in the early sixteenth century, what took place was not only a clash of civilizations but an encounter between structurally heterogeneous linguistic systems. Needless to say, that encounter was uneven. Of the two thousand or so aboriginal languages in existence on this side of the Atlantic Ocean at the time, just a handful survive today in a way that might be described as vigorous. Indigenous words in Spanish include *escuincle* (child), *compadrito* (pal), *cacahuate* (peanut), *tango, ningunear* (ignore), and *hamaca* (hammock). Some come from aboriginal languages like Nahuatl, Mayan, Quechua, and Aymara.

"*Limpia, fija y da esplendor*" (Clean, establish, and grant splendor), the third sentence in the volume, is in good measure about the origin of dictionaries in the Hispanic world, although it also focuses on pop culture. The line is the motto of the *Real Academia Española de la Lengua*, known by its acronym RAE, an institution founded in 1713, in part to compete against the *Academie française*. The motto has been the subject of much debate. In my own case, the function of the RAE is muddled by an inflexible, authoritarian approach to language that often refuses to recognize its ever-changing nature. Over the years, I have been a stern critic of the institution. That critique, handsomely articulated in these pages, starts from a simple premise: does a language need an institution to defend it? In my exploration, I also meditate on the role of dictionaries in the evolution of language in general and of Spanish in particular. The center of my attention is the *Diccionario de la Real Academia*, a proselytizing organ of the RAE.

The Royal Academy of the Spanish Language remains the most conservative institution in charge of legislating the health and continuity of the language. The *Diccionario de Autoridades* was the RAE's lexicographic foundation. Intended to purify and prescribe the use of Spanish, the *Diccionario* was started in 1726. Completed in 1739, the "authorities" of the title are an assortment of historical sources on which the lexicon builds its legitimacy. Most of them are Iberian in status; in other words, the perspective is almost anticolonial. Of course, by the beginning of the eighteenth century, ideological and cultural agitation was already taking place across the Atlantic Ocean. A period of independence fervor officially began in Latin America in 1810, in which countries seceded from Spain to become autonomous nations. Andrés Bello, the most important foundational philologist of the Spanish-speaking Americas, completed in 1847 his influential *Gramática de la lengua Española para el uso de los Americanos*, the first and still most complete grammar of Spanish ever produced in the Americas. Bello suggested simplifying the grammar of *el español* as well as adapting its syntax to the various linguistic realities in Argentina, Colombia, Mexico, and the Caribbean.

The Hispanic world in the nineteenth century is marked by the ultimate collapse of the Spanish Empire. But first, another empire needed to emerge: the United States. The Treaty of Guadalupe Hidalgo between Mexico and the United States was signed in 1848. It concluded the Mexican–American War between the two countries, with Mexico capitulating and being forced to sell two thirds of its territory for $215 million dollars. Most of this territory is known today as the American Southwest. The treaty was about the transfer of land. This is an important historical moment because the Spanish-language speakers in those lands (New Mexico, Arizona, Idaho, Utah, Nevada, etc.) suddenly became Americans, meaning they needed to start using English as their lingua franca. This marks the arrival of Spanglish.

Less than fifteen years later, in 1872 José Hernández published *El Gaucho Martín Fierro*. It became Argentina's national poem. The sequel, *La vuelta de Martín Fierro*, appears in 1879. For purposes of *A Brief History of the Spanish Language*, and for Hernández and other gaucho and *gauchesco* authors, the difference between the two has to do with the perspective the author takes. Hilario Ascasubi, Benito Lynch, Bartolomé Hidalgo, and Estanislao del Campo would use an idiosyncratic, localized Spanish that reflected life in the Pampas among the Gauchos. It is an important chapter in the development of Spanish in the Americas.

The emergence of gaucho literature and its attempt to reflect the parlance of that population was followed by the publication in 1885 of Nicaraguan *hombre de letras* Rubén Darío's *Azul...*, a collection of poems and prose pieces. It fostered the *Modernista* movement, lasting until 1915, the year before Darío's death. The *Modernista* worldview was shaped, in 1898, by the Spanish–American War, when Spain lost control of its last colonies: among these were Cuba and Puerto Rico in the Atlantic Ocean and the Philippines in the Pacific. Darío, José Martí, Lepoldo Lugones, Delmira Agustini, and other *modernistas* sought to make Spanish more like French at the beginning of the twentieth century: refined, politicized, and aware of the excesses of European colonialism. The modernistas introduced a lexicon—about *cisnes* (swans) and *pricesas* (princesses), among other foreign items—still in vogue today.

Important subsequent highlights in the development of the language are Cuban ethnographer Fernando Ortiz's *Un catauro de Cubanismos*, a lexicon of Afro-Cuban words, in 1923, which analyzed African influences in Caribbean Spanish. Likewise, Amado Alonso, working in Argentina, published *Gramática castellana* in 1938, in collaboration with Dominican essayist Pedro Henríquez Ureña. These are influential works seeking to evaluate the way Spanish in the Americas was in itself already the most powerful verbal norm, surpassing in influence what was coming from Spain at the time.

At the level of folklore, in the mid-twentieth century Mexican *carpero* (meaning: a stand-up comedian) Mario Moreno, better known as Cantinflas, appeared in the movie *Allí está el detalle* (That's the point!) in 1940. It was not his first, but it would become his most successful. He would make close to sixty movies during his prolific career. *Cantinflismo* is a style of oral Spanish that deliberately confuses grammatical structures. It has been seen as a rebellion against Iberian, upper-class Mexican, as well as Iberian linguistic patterns. Less because of what he did himself than as a result of his influence on millions, it is hard to imagine a more significant force than Cantinflas in the development of Spanish in the Americas.

The fourth sentence in the book, "*Lo bueno ya no es de nadie*" (what is good no longer has an owner), belongs to Jorge Luis Borges. It is included in his essay (or is it a poem?)

"Borges and I," originally included in his collection of poems *El hacedor* (1960). It reads in full: "*Lo bueno ya no es de nadie sino del lenguaje y la tradición*" (That which is good belongs to no one but language and tradition). In pondering this fourth sentence, my argument is that centuries of distillation culminated in a crystalline sentence in which individual ownership of words is finally renounced. This section includes meditations on Amado Alonso's *Castellano, español, idioma nacional: Historia espiritual de tres nombres*, an influential 1943 volume on the distinction between Castilian and Spanish. Alonso's book offers an intriguing argument on how Spanish went from a local language of Castilla to a global tongue.

That transition is at the heart of Pablo Neruda's *Canto General* (1950), an epic poem about Latin America that juxtaposes history with economics, psychology, and religion. From Chile to Argentina, from Mexico to Spain, the language used by Neruda, who was awarded the Nobel Prize for Literature in 1970 and was a close friend of Iberian poets like Federico García Lorca and Miguel Hernández, seeks to represent a transcontinental drive toward a common verbal force. Conversely, emphasizing the local rather than the universal, in 1950 Mexican poet and essayist Octavio Paz released his study *El laberinto de la soledad* in book form (it is a collection of previously published essays), in which he studied the Mexican collective psyche. In his book, Paz examines how *el peladito*, the Mexican streetwise guy, adapts the language to specific needs, using terms like *chingar* (to fuck), *cabrón* (badass), pendejo (asshole), and so on.

This fourth part of *A Brief History of the Spanish Language* discusses the proliferation of dictionaries in the twentieth century. Joan Corominas began publishing his *Diccionario crítico etimológico de la lengua castellana* in 1954. Along similar lines, Spanish housewife María Moliner begins publishing her *Diccionario del uso del español* in 1972. Eventually known as *Diccionario Moliner*, it became the most popular nonofficial lexicon of the Spanish language. Another lexicon is *Diccionario Clave* (2005), a popular descriptive dictionary comprising an assortment of neologisms.

The section also looks at the linguistic contribution of Colombian writer Gabriel García Márquez's *Cien años de soledad*, which becomes known as "the Bible of Latin America," as well as the verbal pyrotechnics of Cuban movie critic Guillermo Cabrera Infante's *Tres tristes tigres*, Guatemalan novelist Miguel Angel Asturias (another winner of the Nobel Prize for Literature), and Peruvian writer José María Arguedas's novel *El zorro de arriba y el zorro de abajo*, in which there is an indigenous undercurrent at the level of the style. The lexicon these three authors use in the oeuvres is either region specific or transcontinental. In some cases, it looks to replicate the jargon of specific segments of the population while in others it aspires to find a common tongue that erases differences.

In countless ways, the evolution of Spanish in the Americas is the result of migration (Italian, German, Jewish, Russian, Japanese, etc.), which became a feature of national and foreign policy in the last decades of the nineteenth and the early twentieth centuries. After the Spanish conquistadors, missionaries, and traders, the spread of the language came about from transactions across large expanses of land. And, as time went by, other migrants came to the Americas, reinvigorating Spanish with their own tongues.

*Lunfardo* and *Cocoliche* are dialects devised by Italian immigrants used in Argentina. José Hernández, Leopoldo Lugones, and Borges were among the many writers who used them in their work. There are also variants linked to Yiddish, Swedish, Japanese, Ladino, among other languages. The study of the influence of immigrant languages on Spanish is long overdue for more scholarly attention.

Those immigrant languages become essential in the last section of the book. "*In un placete of La Mancha*" (In a place of La Mancha) is the fifth sentence. It is the first line of my translation of *Don Quixote*, Part 1, chapter 1. This one reads in full: "*In un placate of la Mancha of which nombre no quiero remembrearme.*" Over a thousand-year history, the Spanish language has fostered a considerable number of variations, let alone Creolizations, from *Ladino* to Lunfardo and Cocoliche. Arguably one of its most significant is Spanglish, a driving force at the beginning of the twentieth century. Spanglish is the hybrid that results from the mixing of English and Spanish. It is used in a variety of ways by millions of people, predominantly in the United States. This last section elucidates the tension between linguistic unity and fragmentation.

There are two paths to navigate the changes the Spanish language has gone through since Antonio de Nebrija published his *Gramática* in 1492, which was among the first and arguably the most influential early lexicographic study of its kind. One path is to focus on phonological, morphological, and syntactical changes—say Alphonsine orthography, the cacophony of pronoun combination, and so on—as they take place over time. The other is to look at how the language responded to the social, economic, and political changes in Hispanic society. I have taken the second path in this book, without forgetting the first.

As I have made clear, I do not believe in purity—linguistic, racial, cultural, or otherwise. Like everything else, words exist in a state of cross-fertilization. They sharpen their appeal by interacting with others. In doing so, the change sharpens their value, which goes up and down like capital depending on the intercourse they participate in. In short, *A Brief History of the Spanish Language in Five Sentences* is a people's history of the language: how people talked, how singers sang, how actors acted, how writers wrote, and how politicians legislated. It looks at how myriad groups use and abuse the Spanish language without causing it to completely disintegrate.

Seen as a force that travels across time and space, Spanish is a hodgepodge. To talk about unity in the language is to look for commonalities in a landscape also defined by decisive differences. No matter where they find themselves, Spanish speakers miraculously understand each other: yet each of them belongs to a specific location. Such nuances are the purview of philology.

## Bibliography

Alatorre, Antonio. *Los 1001 años de la lengua española*. México City: Colegio de México and Fondo de Cultura Económica, 1989.

Alonso, Amado. *El problema de la lengua en América*. Buenos Aires: Espasa-Calpe, 1935.

Alonso, Amado. *Castellano, español, idioma nacional. Historia espiritual de tres nombres*. Buenos Aires: Espasa-Calpe, 1938.

Alonso, Amado, with Pedro Henríquez Ureña. *Gramática castellana*: Primer curso, 1938; segundo curso, 1939. Buenos Aires: Espasa-Calpe, 1940.

Alvar, Manuel. *De antiguos y nuevos diccionarios del español*. Madrid: Arco/Libros, 2002.

Asociación de Academias de la Lengua Española. *Diccionario de Americanismos*. Barcelona: Santillana, 2010.

Baily, Samuel. *Immigrants in the Lands of Promise: Italians in Buenos Aires and New York City, 1870–1914*. Ithaca, NY: Cornell University Press, 2016.

Baily, Samuel L., and Eduardo José Miguez, eds. *Mass Migration to Modern Latin America*. Lanham, MD: Rowman & Littlefield, 2003.

Bello, Andrés. *Gramática de la lengua española destinada al uso de los americanos*. Prologue by Amado Alonso. Caracas: Ministerio de Educación, 1951.

Cano Aguilar, Rafael. *El español a través de los tiempos*. Madrid: Arco/Libros, 1992.

Carreter, Fernando Lázaro. *Las ideas lingüísticas de España durante el siglo XVIII*. Barcelona: Crítica, 1949.

Carreter, Fernando Lázaro. *El dardo en la palabra*. Barcelona: Debolsillo, 1998.

Casielles-Suárez, Eugenia. "Spanglish: The Hybrid Voice of Latinos in the United States." *Atlantis: Journal of the Spanish Association for Anglo-American Studies* 39, no. 2 (2017): 147–168.

Castillo, Debra A. *Redreaming America: Toward a Bilingual American Culture*. Albany, NY: State University of New York Press, 2005.

Cobos, Rubén. *A Dictionary of New Mexico and Southern Colorado Spanish*. Santa Fe: Museum of New Mexico Press, 1983.

Coromillas, Juan, with José A. Pascual. *Diccionario crítico etimológico castellano e hispánico*. 6 vols. Madrid: Gredos, 1980–1991.

Del Valle, José, ed. *A Political History of Spanish: The Making of a Language*. Cambridge, UK: Cambridge University Press, 2013.

Diez, Miguel, Francisco Morales, and Angel Sabin. *Las lenguas de España*. 2nd ed. Madrid: Ministerio de España, 1980.

Elcock, W. D. *The Romance Languages*. Rev. ed. London: Farber and Farber, 1975.

Galván, Roberto. *El diccionario del Español Chicano*. 2nd ed. Lincolnwood: National Texbook Company, 1995.

García Mouton, Pilar. *Lenguas y dialectos de España*. Madrid: Arco/Libros, 1994.

Gerli, E. Michael. *Medieval Iberia*. London: Routledge, 2003.

Haensch, Günther. *Los diccionarios del español en el umbral del siglo XXI*. Salamanca, Spain: Ediciones Universidad de Salamanca, 1997.

Henríquez Ureña, Pedro. *La utopía de América*. Buenos Aires: Espasa-Calpe, 1925.

Henríquez Ureña, Pedro. *Seis ensayos en busca de nuestra expresión*. Buenos Aires: Espasa-Calpe, 1928.

Henríquez Ureña, Pedro. *La cultura y las letras coloniales en Santo Domingo*. Buenos Aires: Espasa-Calpe, 1936.

Henríquez Ureña, Pedro. *Sobre el problema del andalucismo dialectal de América*. Buenos Aires: Espasa-Calpe, 1937.

Henríquez Ureña, Pedro. *Corrientes Literarias en la América Hispana*. Buenos Aires: Espasa-Calpe, 1941.

Hualde, José Ignacio, et al. *Introducción a la lingüística hispánica*. 2nd ed. Cambridge, UK: Cambridge University Press, 2010.

Lapesa, Rafael. *Historia de la lengua española*. Prologue by Ramón Menéndez Pidal. 9th ed. Madrid: Gredos, 1981.

Lipski, John M. *Latin American Spanish*. London: Longman, 1994.
Lipski, John M. *Varieties of Spanish in the United States*. Washington, DC: Georgetown University Press, 2008.
López Morales, Humberto, ed. *Enciclopedia del español en los Estados Unidos*. Madrid: Instituto Cervantes-Editorial Santillana, 2009.
Menéndez Pidal, Ramón. *Orígenes del español*. 6th ed. Madrid: Espasa-Calpe, 1958.
Menéndez Pidal, Ramón. *Manual de gramática histórica española*. 14th ed. Madrid: Espasa-Calpe, 1973.
Moliner, María. *Diccionario del uso del español*. Barcelona: Espasa-Calpe, 1962.
Mondejar Cumpián, José. *Castellaño y español: Dos nombres para una lengua, en su marco histórico, ideológico y político*. Granada: Editorial Comares, 2002.
Nadeau, Jean-Benoît, and Julie Barlow. *The Story of Spanish*. New York: St. Martin's Griffin, 2013.
Noll, Volker. *Das amerikanische Spanisch: Ein regionaler und historischer Uberblick*. Tubingen: Niemeyer, 2001.
Odisho, Edward Y. "'Al'-Prefixed Arabic Loanwords in Spanish: Linguistic Implications." *Zeitschrift Für Arabische Linguistik* 33 (1997): 89–99.
Ostler, Nicholas. *Empires of the World*. New York: HarperCollins, 2005.
Penny, Ralph. *Gramática histórica del español*. Barcelona: Ariel, 1993.
Penny, Ralph. *Variation and Change in Spanish*. Cambridge, UK: Cambridge University Press, 2000.
Penny, Ralph. *A History of the Spanish Language*. 2nd ed. Cambridge, UK: Cambridge University Press, 2002.
Pharies, David A. *A Brief History of the Spanish Language*. Chicago: University of Chicago Press, 2007.
Real Academia Española. *Esbozo de una nueva gramática de la lengua española*. Madrid: Espasa-Calpe, 1973.
Real Academia Española. *Diccionario de la lengua española*. Madrid: Espasa-Calpe, 2001.
Roca, Ana, ed. *Research on Spanish in the United States*. Sommerville, MA: Cascadilla Press, 2000.
Rosenblat, Angel. *El futuro de nuestra lengua*. Caracas: Universidad Central de Venezuela, 1963.
Rosenblat, Angel. *El castellano de España y el castellano de América: Unidad y diversificación*, 2nd ed. Madrid: Taurus: 1973.
Rosenblat, Angel. *Los conquistadores y su lengua*. Caracas: Universidad Central de Venezuela, 1977.
Smead, Robert N. *Vocabulario Vaquero/Cowboy Talk: A Dictionary of Spanish Terms from the American West*. Foreword by Richard Slatta. Norman: University of Oklahoma Press, 2004.
Sokolow, Jayne A. *The Great Encounter: Native Peoples and European Settlers in the Americas, 1492–1800*. New York: M. E. Sharpe, 2003.
Stavans, Ilan. *On Borrowed Words: A Memoir of Language*. New York: Penguin, 2002.
Stavans, Ilan. *Spanglish: The Making of a New American Language*. New York: HarperCollins, 2003.
Stavans, Ilan. *Dictionary Days: A Defining Passion*. Minneapolis, Minnesota: Graywolf, 2005.
Stavans, Ilan. *Resurrecting Hebrew*. New York: Nextbook/Schocken, 2008.
Stavans, Ilan. *A Critic's Journey*. Ann Arbor: University of Michigan Press, 2010.
Stavans, Ilan. *Singer's Typewriter and Mine: Reflections on Jewish Culture*. Lincoln: University of Nebraska Press, 2012.

Stavans, Ilan. *Don Quixote: The Novel and the World*. New York: W.W. Norton, 2015.
Stavans, Ilan. *Don Quixote de La Mancha: A Graphic Novel*. Illustrated by Roberto Weil. University Park: Pennsylvania State University Press, 2018.
Stavans, Ilan. *On Self-Translation: Meditations on Language*. Albany: SUNY Press, 2018.
Stavans, Ilan. *Sor Juana: or, The Persistence of Pop*. Tucson: University of Arizona Press, 2018.
Stavans, Ilan, ed. *What Is La Hispanidad?* Austin: University of Texas Press, 2011.
Stavans, Ilan, with Iván Jaksić. *The Schocken Book of Modern Sephardic Literature*. New York: Schocken Books, 2005.
Stavans, Ilan, with Josh Lambert, eds. *How Yiddish Changed America and How America Changed Yiddish*. Brooklyn, NY: Restless Books, 2020.
Sublette, Ned. *Cuba and Its Music: From the First Drums to the Mambo*. Chicago: Chicago Review Press, 2007.
Valdés, Juan de. *Diálogo de la lengua*. Edited by Cristina Bbarbolani. Madrid: Cátedra, 1982.

# CHAPTER 13

# THE BILINGUALISMS OF LATINO/A LITERATURES

## ROLANDO PÉREZ

Before there was a Junot Díaz, there was the Nuyorican poetry movement and its founders: Miguel Algarín, Sandra María Esteves, Pedro Pietri, Miguel Piñero, and Tato Laviera. Following in their heels were writers like John Rechy, Piri Thomas, Rolando Hinojosa, Rudolfo Anaya, Tomás Rivera, Helena María Viramontes, and other authors who would come to constitute the early Latino/a literature "canon."[1] These writers wrote primarily in English and employed Spanish words whenever the matter called for it. The use of Spanish in their writing reflected their bilingualism; and they switched from one language to the other in ways that flowed out of their marginalized bicultural lives.

From the 1980s and 1990s would emerge another group of Latino/a writers such as Julia Álvarez, Gloria Anzaldúa, Giannina Braschi, Martín Espada, Sandra Cisneros, Nicholasa Mohr, Cristina García, Óscar Hijuelos, Cherríe Moraga, Ricardo Pau-Llosa, Gustavo Pérez Firmat, Ilan Stavans, and Loida Maritza Pérez. The primary language of this *bilingual* literature was also English, as these writers delinked linguistic competence from the totality of culture.

But the story of Latino/a literature does not end there—far from it. A new wave of Latino/a literature has begun to emerge in the last ten years. Unlike the Latino/a writers of the 1970s and the late 1990s, the new generation of Latino/a writers write and publish primarily in Spanish. They are bilingual; some were born in Spain, some are from a myriad of Latin American countries, and some are native to the United States. Among these writers are Carlos Aguasaco (Colombia), Marta López Luaces (Spain), Ulises Gonzáles (Peru, editor of the literary magazines *Los barbaros* and *Las bárbaras*), Miguel Ángel Zapata (Peru), Pedro Larrea (Spain), Jacqueline Herranz Brooks (Cuba), Almudena Vidorreta Torres (Spain), Lina Meruane (Chile), Marina Perezagua (Spain), Manuel Adrián López (Cuba), Gerardo Piña Rosales (Spain), Mercedes Roffé (Argentina), Claudia Salazar Jiménez (Peru), Alejandro Varderi (Venezuela; co-editor of the CUNY magazine, *Enclave*), and countless others. What is important to note about this new group of writers who are bi-cultural and bilingual (but unlike their predecessors write in Spanish instead of English) is that the Nuyorican writers and their literary heirs (e.g. Gloria Anzaldúa, Sandra Cisneros, Julia Álvarez, Esmeralda Santiago, Pablo Medina, Rosario Ferré, Junot Diaz, et al.), were the ones who paved the way for the latest wave of Latino/a literature. Now we are no longer talking about a literature, but rather about "literatures," at times linguistically bilingual in the strictest of sense of the word, at times monolingual, but always bilingual in the sense that it is the literature of writers who co-habit two languages and two cultures (if not more) at the same time. It is this brief, non-linear, and complex history that this article seeks to trace.

## Defining "Bilingualism"

For Aristotle, definitions determine the essence of objects. And because they are human constructs, definitions tend not to be objective but rather cultural and ideological in nature. Take, for example, how we think about race. As the Latin American philosopher Aníbal Quijano has argued, the concept of race was an invention of sixteenth-century Europeans who needed a way to justify the killing, enslavement, and exploitation of the colonized peoples of the "New World."[2] By defining white-skinned peoples as superior and civilized, and black and indigenous as inferior and barbaric, the Europeans could then exploit the new lands and people as they saw fit. But if clearly not all definitions are pernicious, they are, at least in many cases, ambiguous (if not downright ideological) as is the case with bilingualism.

Certainly, the generic definition of bilingualism is the capacity to speak two languages, while multilingualism, by extension, is defined as the capacity to speak more than one language. This is simple enough; for what could possibly be controversial about such a definition? We answer: nothing, except for the more problematic word, "capacity," which is often equated with competence. For what does it mean to say that someone is bilingual? Do we mean that X is capable of speaking two languages; or do we mean that X is equally grammatically competent in two languages? It was long thought that there were "scales and dichotomies" of bilingualism, such as "elite *versus* folk," and "ideal *versus* partial bilingualism."[3] The ideal bilingual, defined in such narrowly theoretical terms, was said to possess "*native-like control of two languages.*"[4] This exclusionary definition of what constitutes an ideal bilingual has led to the notion of what Suzanne Romaine has critically called "balanced bilingualism."[5] The concept of balanced bilingualism, she argues, has "followed from the assumption that bilingual persons are composed of two monolinguals."[6] But equivalence in bilingualism is virtually non-existent. The linguistic, cognitive, and socio-economic dimension of bilingualism responds to individual experiences that impact second language acquisition and the choices that the bilingual individual makes with respect to the different functions of the two languages she or he speaks. Romaine argues:

> Any society which produced functionally balanced bilinguals who used both languages equally well in all contexts would soon cease to be bilingual because no society needs two languages for the same set of functions.[7]

And later she writes: "Because of the inherent connection between proficiency and function, it is doubtful whether bilingualism per se can be measured apart from the situation in which it functions for a particular individual."[8] In other words, the ideal notion of bilingualism is always going to be problematic, inasmuch as bilingualism is culturally contextual—an object of study, as much for linguistics as for anthropology. All of which brings us to the place of bilingualism in Latino/a literatures. And here, I know of no better text to help us situate the dynamic functions of bilingualism in Latino/a literature than Gustavo Pérez Firmat's *Tongue Ties: Logo-Eroticism in Anglo-Hispanic Literature* (2003). Here Pérez Firmat, a bilingual author himself, unmoors language from culture, thereby liberating Latino/a writers from the straight jacket ideals and linguistic ideology of balanced bilingualism.[9]

Pérez Firmat dramatically begins his book with a quote from nineteenth-century Russian writer Ivan Turgenev, who once declared in a letter to a friend that a "writer who did not write only in his *mother tongue* was a thief and a pig."[10] For what writer could be so low as to betray his or her mother, or in this case, his or her "mother tongue." And yet, as it turns out, "Turgenev wrote this letter in German."[11] But in any case, Pérez Firmat's opening anecdote is a reminder that bilingualism is not only a linguistic phenomenon but also an expression of a person's affective relation to his or her languages. And it is here that he offers the reader a tripartite, bilingual conceptualization of language. For the Cuban American writer, what we call *language* in English can be broken down into (1) language as *lengua*, (2) language as *idioma*, and (3) language as *lenguaje*. He asserts that while "language as *lenguaje*" "is language detached from both person and place; that is, language as structure, as an abstract and rational system, somewhat like Saussure's *langue*," "language as *idioma*," refers to what is spoken in a specific place by a specific group of people(s).[12] Moreover, while "*idioma* reveals national or regional allegiances," "language as lengua," reveals an individual's affective relation to the language(s) he or she speaks.[13] Pérez Firmat contends:

> A tongue is language incarnate, as body part, an organ rather than a faculty. By calling our language a tongue, we highlight our bond to it, which is why we use possessives with *lengua* more often than with *lenguaje*.[14]

And a few lines further down, he reflects: "*Lenguajes* can be native and *idiomas* can be national or regional, but only a *lengua* can be familial."[15] Interestingly, this series of tongue-in-cheek and incisive reflections on language, and particularly on the affective experience of bilingualism function precisely because of the interplay between Spanish and English. If bilingualism can be studied structurally (as *lenguaje* or *langue*), the bilingualism (or more accurately, bilingualisms) of Latino/a writers ought to be considered primarily from an affective point of view, since what they create, after all, are aesthetic objects.

## The Wondrous Tribulations of Bilingualism

The introduction to *Tongue Ties* bears the title "Bilingual Bliss, Bilingual Blues," and as such, it is not only an intertextual reference to a book of poems by its author but also an intimation of the difficulties of being "bilingual." From the Latino/a college student who enrolls in a course for "heritage speakers" to renowned Latino/a writers, "ideal bilingualism," is often a source of anguish with respect to their identity. The language ideology responsible for such a definition of bilingualism determines questions of identity and how individuals are positioned or position themselves vis-à-vis such a purist, synchronic notion of what it is to be equally "competent" in two languages. What begins as an ideological issue (one that borders on questions of cultural ontology) becomes for the Latino/a writer an existential problem, which was pointed out in "What Is 'Minor' in Latino Literature."[16] It is what constitutes the experience of Pérez Firmat's "bilingual blues." Note, for example, Judith Ortiz Cofer's articulation of her Puerto Rican identity in relation to the (English) language *(lenguaje)* of her schooling and to the (Spanish) language *(lengua)* of her early childhood:

> I really resent the prevalent attitude that if you care about the Island you have to write in Spanish. It is not my fault that 95% of my education was in English in American schools...I went to the *escuela pública* (public school) for about six months; that is my total time in a school in Hormigueros. So, how can I write well in Spanish when Spanish is my second language? When I say it is my language it means that English is the language of my schooling. However, my home language was Spanish; I spoke only in Spanish with my mother.[17]

Especially significant in Ortiz Cofer's description of her bilingualism is the fact that she divorces the notion of a "mother tongue" *(lengua materna)* from linguistic competence, so that the question of her biography (what Saussure called the "diachronic" element of language) has all to do with her bilingualism: where English is the language of her linguistic competence and Spanish is the language of her innermost feelings that return her to her native town of Hormigueros. If she does not write in Spanish, she says, it is because "most of the grammar is alien" to her.[18] This does not, by any means, make her any less Puerto Rican than a Puerto Rican who lives in the island, or as she says: "Even if I cannot be geographically in the place where I was born, I consider myself a Puerto Rican the same way that anybody living on the island is a Puerto Rican *and if I could, I would write in Spanish*."[19] Though clearly Ortiz Cofer does not see herself as any less Puerto Rican than a Spanish-speaking Puerto Rican living in the island, the latter part of her statement (in italics) is expressive of the homunculus that hides in the psyche of many bilinguals who fall victim to traditional notions of a "balanced bilingualism," and the manipulative idea of "betraying" one's "mother tongue" by the "other" language.

This is why Gloria Anzaldúa declares in "Linguistic Terrorism," a section in *Borderlands/La Frontera*, that "if you want to really hurt me, talk badly about my language."[20] Or perhaps more accurately: if you want to hurt me, talk badly about *the way I speak* "my language" or "my *lengua*." In many ways, this "anxiety of betrayal" is the Latino/a writer's equivalent of Harold Bloom's "anxiety of influence." Thus, Anzaldúa's political contextualization of US bilingualism (what she calls "linguistic terrorism") helps explain the Dominican government's 2013 cultural (and politically motivated) attack on Dominican Pulitzer Prize–winning writer, Junot Díaz. In an email letter of December 2013, written, "in good faith," José Santana, the then Executive Director of the Dominican Republic's International Advisory Committee on Science and Technology, admonished the Dominican writer for meddling in Dominican political affairs (government corruption), and suggested that he should improve his Spanish before "coming" to the Dominican Republic to criticize the government.[21] Obviously, Santana's jab at Díaz's Spanish was calculated; its subtext being that linguistic competence is a requisite for political criticism and therefore, Díaz, whose Spanish was less than perfect, should stay out of Dominican politics. Targeted at what Santana deemed to be Díaz's emotional Achilles heel, the email was meant to be hurtful. In light of Santana's attack, consider for a moment Anzaldúa's summation concerning language and identity:

> Ethnic identity is twin skin to linguistic identity—I am my language. Until I can take pride in my language, I cannot take pride in myself. Until I can accept as legitimate Chicano Texas Spanish, Tex-Mex and all the other languages I speak, I cannot accept the legitimacy of myself.[22]

Plainly, then, a precondition for a rebuttal to something like Santana's attack on Díaz, requires discarding purist notions of language and promoting language and dialectal diversity. Of course, certain writers such as Judith Ortiz Cofer, Junot Díaz, Oscar Hijuelos, and others have had to deal with questions of linguistic betrayal for not writing in their mother tongue (however distant their mother tongue was from them). However, there are also those who have to contend with the same question, for opting to write in English when they could have written in Spanish instead. And here the names of Tato Laviera, Giannina Braschi, and Rosario Ferré come to mind; though for purposes of time and space, I will focus on Ferré in what follows. In her unique case, Ferré often wrote her work first in Spanish and then translated it into English, and even vice-versa—an activity for which she was highly criticized.

Born in 1928 in Ponce, Puerto Rico, into a family of considerable wealth and influence, Rosario Ferré was educated in Puerto Rico and the United States. Her father, Luis Alberto Ferré, an engineer and an industrialist, was the third Governor of the Commonwealth of Puerto Rico (1969 and 1973). And when her mother, Lorena Ramírez de Arellano, passed away in 1970, Rosario took over the role of the island's first lady. Earlier in her life (1951), Ferré was sent to study at a prep school in Wellesley, Massachusetts. And she would later earn a bachelor of arts from Manhattanville College and a PhD in Latin American Literature from the University of Maryland.

Significantly, at the tender age of fourteen, Ferré began writing articles for *El Nuevo Día*, her father's newpaper. Yet, in contradistinction to her father, who in 1968 advocated for Puerto Rican statehood, "only two years after stepping down as first lady, Ferré burst into the scene as a supporter of independence and the co-founder of *Zona de carga y descarga* ("Loading and Unloading Zone"; 1972–1975), a literary journal that radically modernized Puerto Rican letters."[23] But what made Ferré a well-known and respected literary figure were her books of essays and her fiction, particularly her novel, *Maldito amor* (1982), which she translated into English and published in 1989 as *Sweet Diamond Dust*. More controversial were *The House on the Lagoon* (1995) and *Eccentric Neighborhoods* (1998), which she first wrote in English and then self-translated and published in Spanish as *La casa de la laguna* (1997) and *Vecindarios excéntricos* (1999). This decision to write in English and later translate her work into her native tongue (her literary bilingualism, as it were) was not well received by certain sectors of Puerto Rico's intelligentsia. Ferré's answer to her detractors' accusations of cultural betrayal was to dispute the notion that language necessarily and directly correlates with identity and culture. For people who collapse one onto the other, declared Ferré in her interview with Frances Negrón-Muntaner, "Puerto Ricans 'are' the Spanish language; we 'are' Spanish." She continues:

> I disagree with that argument because I do not consider myself to "be" the Spanish language or only to be a speaker of Spanish. I am no language at all. And in addition, being Puerto Rican is more than speaking and writing a language, and more than a language. It is a culture and a way of thinking; an environment; customs, food; a very complex context.[24]

However, certain writers such as Ana Lydia Vega, who questioned Ferré's decision to give English such a prominent place in her writing, were not so much critical of her multilingualism as they were of the fact that she had reversed her position with respect to Puerto Rican independence and now advocated statehood.[25] In fact, it has been argued that the selection of *The House on the Lagoon* as a finalist for the 1995 National Book Award "demonstrates the success of Ferré's statehooding aesthetic, since the award officially recognizes the novel as 'American literature.'"[26] At any rate, what comes across in the Vega-Ferré debate is a struggle for identity where language, or more specifically bilingualism, is the postulated axis. It is interesting to note Ferré's (perhaps self-defensive) statement concerning Puerto Rican writers who write in English, when she responds to Negrón-Muntaner's request to explain how it is that "English is the link to literary modernity." To which Ferré answers:

> I believe that Puerto Ricans who are writing in English are producing more interesting work than those who are writing in Spanish. The problem is that in Puerto Rico careers are truncated, whereas in the United States, Esmeralda Santiago, continues to publish.[27]

In other words, for Ferré modernity meant the English language, just as modernity had once meant the Spanish language and culture, given that what we call *modernity*, as some Latin American philosophers and historians have argued, begins with the colonization of the indigenous peoples and lands of the Americas and the Caribbean.[28] Viewed this way, the concept of modernity is inseparable from European colonialism and everything that followed from it, up and until today's global economy. What is ironic in all its complexity is that the writing in English of Puerto Rican writers (and clearly, of other Latino/a writers as well) endorsed by Ferré is the language of the *Nuyorican* writers, who wrote in English and Spanglish, not in order to assimilate, as Lydia Vega once suggested, but rather in opposition to assimilation and marginalization through the very language of empire. Where Ferré, given her upper-class privileges, could freely choose between writing in English or Spanish, and Ana Lydia Vega could write in standard Spanish, the Nuyorican writers, stripped of their native language and culture, wrote in English (the colonial language) or Spanglish (a mixture of two colonial languages), as a political and cultural strategy.[29]

## The Counter-Colonialism of Nuyorican Spanglish or Bilingualism

Miguel Algarín begins his essay "Nuyorican Literature" in this manner: "The four-hundred-year plus history of Puerto Rico is really a very simple story of greed and amorality."[30] And as such, Algarín contextualizes the history of Puerto Rico, and by extension, the history of its literature, of which Nuyorican literature is an integral chapter as that of a colonized nation. In a just few sentences, Algarín traces the history of Puerto Rican immigration, on the one hand, back to the 1917 Jones Act that granted US citizenship to Puerto Ricans, and on the other, to Luis Muñoz Marín's "Operation Bootstrap."[31] The initiatives "made it possible for Puerto Ricans from the lower classes to come to America looking for bread, land, and liberty."[32] Without this cryptic but essential history lesson, it would be difficult to understand the origins of the Nuyorican writers.[33] Algarín, for example, was born in Puerto Rico in 1941 and immigrated with his family to the Lower East Side at the age of nine; Pedro Pietri was born in Puerto Rico in 1944 and immigrated to Spanish Harlem with his family in 1948; Miguel Piñero was born in Puerto Rico in 1946 and like Pietri immigrated with his family to the Lower East Side, at the age of four; Tato Laviera was born in Puerto Rico in 1950 and arrived in New York when he was nine; and lastly, merely in order of birthplace, Sandra María Esteves was born in the South Bronx in 1948 to a Puerto Rican father and a Dominican mother. It should not be surprising, then, that Algarín should begin his essay by referencing the Jones Act of 1917 and its superseded version of 1948, through which "the idealized trip up North" was "sold."[34]

Nuyorican writers shared the experience of either having migrated to the United States as young children or of being the children of Puerto Rican and Dominican immigrants, as in the case of Esteves. Thus, while their culture was Latino/a, the language of their upbringing, of their social interactions, and of their adulthood was English. And their writings expressed what Ed Morales has called their "Spanglish" identity (2002). Nuyorican writers wrote in English, injecting emotionally significant Spanish words into their work and inventing new terms (as others such as Anzaldúa and Díaz have done).[35] Spanish/English code-switching characterizes their writing and so does Spanglish.[36] But the bilingualism of writers who have been schooled exclusively, or almost exclusively in the United States, has often come under attack. Bilingual Latino/a writers, no less than other bilinguals, have at times given voice to this anxiety of linguistic betrayal. Take, for instance, Sandra María Esteves's poem, "Not Neither," where Esteves, though aware of her neither/nor identity, nevertheless severely judges her own linguistic competence:

Being Puertorriqueña Dominicana
Borinqueña-Quisqueyana
Taina-Africana
Born in the Bronx. Not really jíbara
*Not really hablando bien*
But yet, not gringa either
Pero ni portorra
Pero, sí, portorra too...[37]

The stanza begs the question: Who is judging "*Not really hablando bien*"? Is it Esteves herself, prey to what Anzaldúa called "linguistic terrorism"? Is it the Latino/a, linguistic purist who believes that there is only one way to speak and write Spanish? Is it the Anglo "English only" white supremacist? Is it the purist who believes in balanced bilingualism and refuses to accept code-switching as a legitimate practice who is judging Esteves's linguistic competence? Most likely, it is all of them at once, and Esteves is their victim, as Díaz was Santana's.

And yet, Nuyorican writers such as Esteves, Pietri, and Piñero innovatively understood that as a doubly colonized people, they did not have to choose—as Algarín points out—between two colonial, major languages (Spanish and English). Instead, they "trans-created," to use Juan Flores's and George Yudice's term, a mix of their own in order to avoid the trappings of assimilation and cultural colonization.[38] Their code-switching and their use of Spanglish, as Frances R. Aparicio (1994) and Regina Bernard-Carreño (2010) have suggested, should be seen as a subversive act, in opposition to colonialism. Their employment of English was a way of "using the tools of the Master, and in the process, transforming those signifiers with their cultural meanings, values, and ideologies of the subordinate sector."[39] It was a matter of transforming two major languages, into a minor language, and in that way creating a "minor literature," in the Deleuzean/

Guattarian sense.⁴⁰ And that, of course, is both a literary and a political act. Take the following examples from the work of Pedro Pietri and Miguel Piñero, respectively.

First, in "The Broken English Dream," Pietri writes:

Lápiz: Pencil
Pluma: Pen
Cocina: Kitchen
Gallina: Hen
Everyone who learns
will receive a high school equivalency diploma
a lifetime supply of employment agencies
a different bill collector for every day of the week
the right to vote for the executioner of your choice
and two hamburgers for thirty-five cents in times square…⁴¹

For Pietri, then, Latino/a access to education and the English language is only a trap to turn Latino/as into consumers, who at the end of the day, can only say "en mi casa toman bustelo."⁴² The title of the poem itself suggests two possible and concomitant meanings; one the pejorative notion of "broken English," or badly spoken and written English (a judgment), and two, the idea of the broken promises of the Marín "Muñoz Dream."⁴³

And in "A Lower East Side Poem," Piñero writes:

I don't wanna be buried in Puerto Rico
I don't wanna rest in long island cemetery
I wanna be near the stabbing shooting
gambling fighting & natural dying
& new birth crying
so please when I die.
don't take me far away
keep me near by
take my ashes and scatter them thru out
the Lower East Side…⁴⁴

Here Piñero, self-styled "Philosopher of the Criminal Mind," turns the English language against itself, while demanding to be buried among the economically imposed rubble of the Nuyorican diaspora that was the Lower East Side.⁴⁵ His cultural marginalization, which culminated in a series of prison sentences throughout his life, is given voice in Nuyorican English through an affirmation of place. To be buried in Puerto Rico, therefore, would be to somehow inauthentically erase his lived experiences and that of others like him for whom Manhattan had become "the island." Veritably, Piñero's poetics is one of alterity and displacement. Far removed from the world of someone like Rosario Ferré, Pietri's, Piñero's, Algarín's, and Esteves's English is not the result of "choice" made in the "free market" of a neoliberal economy but its opposite. For the Nuyorican writers, to be

Latino/a was to live in a state of social and economic contradictions; their bilingualism had more to do with the blues than with the bliss of Ferré and others who came after them. "The most obvious mark of this new literature emanating from the community is language: the switch from Spanish to English and bilingual writing," writes Juan Flores in *Divided Borders*. However, he cautions: "This language transfer should not be mistaken for assimilation in a wide cultural sense. As the content of the literature indicates, using English is only a sign of being here, not necessarily of liking it here or of belonging."[46] And in *Living in Spanglish*, Ed Morales, for whom Spanglish is a question of "estar" (temporal and locational), he writes: "At the root of Spanglish is a very universal state of being." Spanglish, he continues, "is a displacement from one place, home, to another place, home, in which one feels at home in both places, yet at home in neither place. It is a kind of banging-one's head against the wall state, and the only choice you have left is to embrace, the transitory (read transnational) state of in-between," and one may add, embrace difference and multiplicity.[47]

## THE INHERITORS: MORE IN THE EFFECT THAN IN THE CAUSE

At times we like to think that things are the way they are because they have been necessarily caused by some outside force: be it God, the unconscious, or political economy. And in literature, we often speak of one writer's "influence" on another writer—a notion that lies midway between necessity and freedom, so while the work of author A is said to be "influential" for author B, B's work, on the other hand, is understood to be his or her own freely written text. To add to the mix, we have philosopher Quentin Meillassoux's idea that "there is *more* in the effect than in the cause."[48] However, by the word "more," he does not mean of greater quality or quantity but simply effects that have their own intrinsic value. And I can think of no better way to describe the Latino literatures that have been produced since the Nuyorican literary movement than in this fashion. In effect, the new generation of writers who are writing exclusively in Spanish, and publishing in the United States, are often unaware that it was the Nuyorican writers (their precursors who wrote in English and Spanglish) who made this possible. But we are getting ahead of ourselves (more on this in the next and final section). For the boom in Latino/a literature that coincided, more or less, with the Latin American literary boom, began sometime in the 1970s and extends to today. And though the list is long and impressive, space not permitting, I will briefly concentrate on Gloria Anzaldúa, Giannina Braschi, Junot Díaz, Tato Laviera, and Gustavo Pérez Firmat, as their works reflect that legacy.

One of the most impressive things about the Pulitzer Prize–winning novel, *The Brief Wondrous Life of Oscar Wao*, is Junot Díaz's use of Spanish—or more accurately, his use of Spanish along with English, in a novel "that is written in English." But here I place "that is written in English" in scare quotes because the novel is actually written in both. Equally so? Of course not. But then, as mentioned earlier, balanced bilingualism in praxis is more of a myth than a lived reality. Not to mention that Díaz's English, as grammatically perfect as it is, is not the English of a Raymond Carver or of a Jonathan Franzen, just as theirs is not the English of a bilingual Dominican writer. To this point, Frances Aparicio has called the English of writers such as Díaz, Braschi, Laviera, and Pérez Firmat a "tropicalized English."[49] This "tropicalized English," Aparicio claims, has displaced the monolingual reader from his or her privileged position. Aparicio writes:

> By *metaphorically* displacing the ideal monolingual American reader and by producing texts whose poetic and cultural signifying require crosscultural competency, contemporary U.S. Latino and Latina writers are marginalizing and even potentially excluding the mono-lingual reader who has been glaringly positioned throughout history as the prototypical embodiment of cultural literacy. [50]

By placing Spanish and English sentences next to each other, without italicizing the Spanish, Díaz reminds the reader that this is what bilingualism is all about. When Oscar's mother gets angry at her son for crying over a girl, Díaz writes: "Tú ta llorando por una muchcha? She hauled Oscar to his feet by his ear."[51] Here, observably, the English is not a translation of the Spanish but instead a description of the character's own reaction to her son's behavior. This is only one example of many, where the Spanish and English occur next to each, but where the English is not the translation of the Spanish or vice versa.[52] The Nuyorican writers practiced this technique to various degrees and so did the Chicana writer Gloria Anzaldúa.

Anzaldúa's *Borderlands/La Frontera: The New Mestiza* was instrumental in clearing the path for *The Brief Wondrous Life of Oscar Wao* and other key works of Latino/a literature such as Giannina Braschi's *Yo-Yo Boing* (1998). *Borderlands/La Frontera: The New Mestiza* is written in English and in Spanish, at times in a combination of both, interspersed with poems in Spanish and entire sentences in Spanish that are not translations but mostly conceptual extensions of what came before in English. In few other works is the "mestizaje" of form and content so seamlessly executed as it is in *Borderlands/La Frontera*—a text that calls for the deconstruction of "genre and "gender" differences through language. The future, says Anzaldúa, will depend on the new "mestiza" (of the subtitle): the woman of mixed race, ethnicity, and language. That is why Anzaldúa cites entire poems in Spanish, without their translations, as she does with Violeta Parra's poem, "Arauco tiene una pena," and with one of her poems, "En el nombre de todas las madres que han perdido sus hijos en la guerra."[53] For Anzaldúa, her Chicano/a bilingualism represents an arm of resistance against both linguistic hegemony (standard Spanish) and a monoculture that demands acquiescence and one-directional translation. Anzaldúa explains:

> Presently this infant language, this bastard language, Chicano Spanish, is not approved by any society. But we Chicanos no longer feel that we need to beg entrance, that we

need always to make the first overture—to translate to Anglos, Mexicans and Latinos, apology blurting out of our mouths with every step.[54]

Hence, the Chicana mestiza "translates" La conciencia de la mestiza" into "Towards a New Consciousness" not because this is the literal translation (of chapter 7's title) but rather because this is what the emancipated future of a "cosmic race" means to her. The Chicana creates a minor language within a mayor language. Anzaldúa writes:

> For a people who are neither Spanish nor live in a country in which Spanish is the first language; for a people who live in a country in which English is the reigning tongue but who are not Anglo; for a people who cannot entirely identify with either standard (formal, Castillian) Spanish nor standard English, what recourse is left to them but to create their own language?[55]

This language, a mixture of "Standard English, Working class and slang English, Standard Spanish, Standard Mexican Spanish, North Mexican Spanish dialect, Chicano Spanish (Texas, New Mexico, Arizona and California have regional variations), Tex-Mex, [and] *Pachuco* (called *caló*)" is neither "*español ni ingles*."[56] Nonetheless, these mixtures that make up Chicano Spanish are similar to those employed by many bilingual Latino/a writers of Caribbean descent such as Tato Laviera.[57]

Born in Puerto Rico in 1950, Laviera, is the author of *La Carrerta Made a U-Turn* (1979), *EnClave* (1981), *AmeRícan* (1985), *Mainstream Ethics (Ética corriente)* (1988), and *Mixturao and Other Poems* (2008). Incidentally (or perhaps not incidentally at all) Laviera entitled one of the sections of *Mixtarao* "Fronteras," wherein appear three poems: "Español," two thirds of it written in Spanish; "Spanglish," a 50/50 code-switching poem; and "Bilingüe," a bilingual poem, with the Spanish appearing on the left side of the page and the English on the right, where the bilingualism is made to function at the affective level. However, it is in "Spanglish" that Laviera presents his poetics of Spanglish:

> pues estoy creando spanglish
> bi-cultural systems
> scientific lexicographical
> inter-textual integrations
> two expressions
> existentially wired
> two dominant languages
> continentally abrazándose
> en colloquial combate
> en las aceras del soil...[58]

As Laviera sees it, then, his Spanglish creations constitute a way of making the "two dominant languages" embrace each other or of transforming them into minor languages. This is what leads Laviera to ask the reader at the end of the poem: "Which u.s. slang do you speak?"[59] Language as *lengua* is never abstract, and slang is what is spoken "en las aceras del soil," in the streets, which brings us to Gustavo Pérez Firmat's poem, "Turning the Times Tables" from his poetry collection, *Bilingual Blues* (1995).

"Turning the Times Tables" begins with a quote from the American philosopher Charles Sanders Peirce, which reads: "I am the sum total of my language."[60] Pérez Firmat's citation is interesting for many reasons but most markedly because the original reads "my language is the sum total of myself."[61] Thus while the Cuban author has placed the individual *I* before language, Peirce, on the other hand, views humans as signs in a semiotic system, which subsumes the particular in the universal. For as Peirce argues in the sentence that precedes it, "The man and the external sign are identical, in the same sense in which the words *homo* and *man* are identical."[62] But for Pérez Firmat, for whom a speech act is constituted by *lengua*, nothing could be further from the truth. As Annabel Cox so elegantly puts it in her brilliant article on this poem and on "Bilingual Blues": "Language, the poem seems desperately to declare, is more than just a single series of signs that when placed in combinations always result in a stable and predictable outcome."[63] But as Cox does well to point out, Pérez Firmat's poetic critique of Peirce does not end there. "Turning the Times Tables" is in sociolinguistic terms an overturning of monolingualism in favor of bilingualism or multilingualism. To Peirce's statement, Pérez Firmat responds in Spanish with:

¿Y si soy dos,
o tres
o—como diría David—
un millón? [64]

Evidently, for Pérez Firmat, the notion of multilingualism (i.e., that one could be the sum of one's *languages* and that one could be the product and the producer of multiple sign systems) had not occurred to the American philosopher. But perhaps more problematic is Peirce's notion that "homo" and "man" are identical. Take the case of *dulzura* and *sweetness*: while no one would deny that they are denotatively equivalent, they are not emotionally equivalent.[65] Languages often compete with one another for our love and attention, and this jealousy or rivalry between them is what often leads a multilingual person like Laviera to have them embrace each other. To that end, the existential challenge of bilingualism is the theme of Pérez Firmat's "Bilingual Blues." He writes:

Soy un ajiaco de contradicciones
I have mixed feeling about everything.
Name your tema, I'll hedge;
name your cerca, I'll straddle it
like a cubano. [66]

That is the first stanza of the poem. The last stanza begins with a repetition of the first verse:

Soy un ajiaco de contradicciones,
un puré de impurezas...[67]

To be a set of contradictions is to be impure, to be a "number that won't square"; to be "not neither," as Sandra María Esteves said of herself. But to be an "ajiaco" is to be a mix, to be, as per Laviera, "mixturao" or as per Anzaldúa, a "mestizo." And Pérez Firmat metaphorically describes himself as an "ajiaco" of contradictions and impurities, where linguistically, for one, he is made up of multiple languages: Spanish (Cuban, African, Taino, Castilian, etc.), English (Cuban, Standard), and Spanglish, and all that this implies.[68] Those impurities or "impurezas" are best exemplified in *Scar Tissue* (2005), a book written in prose and verse, where one finds code-switching poems, poems written all in English, and poems written all in Spanish.[69] This kind of bilingual "impurity" is taken to its extreme in Giannina Braschi's novel, *Yo-Yo Boing!* (1998). For in Braschi's *Yo-Yo Boing!* the mixtures are completely deterritorialized; they are the mixtures of a yo-yo, and of the disjunctive synthesis of a *yo* and *yo*: identities that are multiplied beyond any possible recognition. The beginning section of the novel, entitled "Close Up," is almost entirely in Spanish, with some insertions of English words (most of them having to do with cosmetic products: 26–27).

In a manner that recalls the neo-Baroque literary experimentations of Severo Sarduy's novel *Cobra* (1972), Braschi's language is erotically *excessive* (in the Batailleanse sense of the word): imbued with graphic descriptions of skin, pus, blood, urine, semen, and excrement.[70] The text begins with an unidentified, nameless character, crawling on all fours, who suddenly gets it into her head to part the cheeks of her buttocks "como si fueran un bocadillo de jamón y queso," "as though they were a ham and cheese sandwich," in a scene of defecation in close up.[71]

Again, in Sarduyan fashion, Braschi's writing is a form of "writing on the body." She eroticizes even the vowels, and particularly the O, when she describes it as an open, rounded, and exclamatory letter. The next section, "Blow-Up," continues with the theme of openings, as two nameless characters: a couple standing in front of the door to their apartment carry on the following exchange in Spanglish:[72]

—Abrela tú.
—¿Por qué yo? Tú tienes las keys. Yo te las entregué a ti. Además, I left mine adentro.
—¿Por qué las dejaste adentro?
—Porque I knew you had yours.[73]

For Braschi as for Pérez Firmat with his concept of "logo eroticism," the experience of language is first bodily (*lengua*) before it becomes "lenguaje" or grammar (Peirce's system of signs). And much like Gloria Anzaldúa's *Borderlands/La Frontera*, *Yo-Yo Boing!* proposes impurity, mixture, and the *mestizaje* of words that freely flow into one another like bodily fluids. As Doris Sommer and Alexandra Vega-Merino say in their introduction to the 1998 first edition of *Yo-Yo Boing!*: "Choose and lose is one message in the madness of Giannina Braschi's *Yo-Yo Boing!* The book refuses to decide between performing in English and reveling in Spanish."[74] But it is not the book that refuses a linguistic Sophie's choice; it is Braschi who has decided much like Ferré and Laviera to remain open to English, Spanish, and Spanglish—to break down the divisive borderlands between languages. A case in point is *United States of Banana* (2011), a "mestiza" genre-bending text—a literary stew that combines essay, short story, theater, and prose poetry. Originally written in English, *United States of Banana* is a post-9/11 critique of American colonialism reminiscent of the Nuyorican literary tradition. Then there is also, of course, her collection of prose poems, *El imperio de los sueños* (1988), which she wrote in Spanish. Yet regardless of the chosen language, "all languages are dialects that are made to break new grounds," says a character in *Yo-Yo Boing!*—doubtlessly Braschi's avatar. "I feel like Dante, Petrarca and Boccaccio, and I feel like Garcilaso forging a new language. Saludo al nuevo siglo, el siglo del nuevo lenguaje de América, y le digo adiós a la retórica separatista y a los atavismos," *she* declares.

## CONCLUSION: NEW SPACES OF LATINO/A LITERATURE (BILINGUALLY IN SPANISH)

José Martí, Julia de Burgos, and Gabriela Mistral all lived in New York at different times in their lives. And whereas Martí died in the battlefield in Cuba, de Burgos and Mistral both died in New York. Yet they share the common fate of having written the majority of their works while living in the United States. They were, as Ilan Stavans's *Norton Anthology of Latino Literature* has aptly situated them, Latino/a writers.

Cut to June 6, 2016, to a meeting of ALDEEU, the association of Spanish Professionals in America, where professor and writer Tina Escaja asked a group of New York City writers to talk about their experience of writing in Spanish in the city where Julia de Burgos and Gabriela Mistral wrote and passed away. The exchange that took place at the Cervantes Institute included Raquel Abend Van Dalen, Carlos Aguasaco, Marithelma Costa, Jacqueline Herranz Brooks, Alex Lima, Abersio Núñez, Adalbar Salas Hernández, Alfredo Villanueva Collado, and myself. Implicit in Escaja's question was the idea that writing in Spanish in New York, or anywhere else in the United States, is a simple matter of choosing one language over another and that things have always been this way. But things were not always this way. Until very recently US Latino/a authors had two options: either write in Spanish and publish outside of the country, or write in English and *perhaps* publish in the United States, as did the Nuyoricans writers and their literary heirs. For the former option one needed contacts with publishing houses in Latin

America and Spain. This was more or less my own experience. When I started to publish, I knew no one in the Spanish-language literary world; I had no contact with Spanish or Latin American publishers. And though I was an avid reader of Spanish-language literature, this was not the source from which I drew my "inspiration." My world was that of philosophy, and my writings reflected that part of the cultural universe. My first major publication was *The Odyssey* (1990), a book of imaginary landscapes—or "discontinuous fables," as one reviewer called it—written in the form of plateaus. I was applying Deleuze and Guattari's notion of *plateaus* to creative writing. That was also the year I published *On An(archy) and Schizoanalyis*—what was then one of the first books in English on *Anti-Oedipus*. In subsequent years, I wrote a lot of plays, many of which were Off-Off Broadway productions, and a series of books, among them, *The Divine Duty of Servants: A Book of Worship* (1999), which was a book of creative prose based on the drawings of Bruno Schulz, followed by *The Electric Comedy* (2000), a postmodern version of Dante's *Divine Comedy*, and *The Lining of Our Souls: Excursions into Selected Painting of Edward Hopper* (2002), which was a book of prose poems based on paintings by Edward Hopper. Then when my literary work was selected for inclusion in *The Anthology of Latino Literature*.[75] I had to reflect on what it was that made or did not make my work Latino/a. And what I discovered as I reflected on it, and wrote about it in "What Is 'Minor' in Latino Literature," is that the language of my writings differs in texture from that of Anglo writers. My English vibrates in a different way; it "stutters," as Deleuze would say, and what makes it "Latino/a" is certainly not its subject matter, but rather the cadences, the rhythms, and flows of the words on the page.[76]

As such, for the exception of "H Is for Box" (1992/2005), a one-act play that deals with questions of stereotyping, few of my writings deal directly with Latino issues, though there are references to Cuba in quite a few of my writings. Happily my first publication in Spanish came about in 2017, when the Spanish publisher Amargord published *La comedia eléctrica*, a translation by Óscar Curieses of *The Electric Comedy*. Working with Curieses on the translation also made me want to revisit work that I originally wrote in English, with the idea of self-translating it and giving it another life in Spanish now that I can publish in Spanish in and outside of the United States. What I have yet to do is to write a literary work directly in Spanish (as I have done on many occasions with academic articles) and then either translate it myself into English or have someone else translate it, as in the case of Ferré and Tomás Rivera.[77]

Now, to return to Tina Escaja's ALDEEU encounter of June 2016 at the Cervantes Institute in New York, most of the writers on stage that day were writers who were born outside of the United States (Colombia, Cuba, Ecuador, Venezuela, and Puerto Rico). With the exception of one or two of these writers, they all migrated to the United States as young adults. And since Spanish was the language of their schooling (the inverse of previous Latino/a authors), these writers feel more comfortable writing in Spanish than in English. Tina Escaja, the organizer of the event, *Poetas y Narradores en Nueva York* [Poets and Narrators in New York], was born in Zamora, Spain, and writes in Spanish. A critic, poet, and playwright, some of Escaja's latest publications are *Caída libre* (2004), for which she won the Dulce María Loynaz Award in Hispanic American poetry; *Código de barras* (poetry; 2007); *Madres* (theater; 2007); *Asesinato en el laboratorio de idiomas/ Murder in the Language Lab* (novella, translated by John W. Warren in 2016); and *Manual Destructivista/Destructivist Manual* (poetry, translated by Kristin Dykstra in 2016).

For this new generation of Latino/a writers, translation has become one way of keeping alive the bilingual, Latino/a literature tradition: either by translating their own work into English or having it translated. In fact, a central figure in today's New York Latino/a literary milieu is Galician born critic, poet, novelist, and translator Marta López Luaces. Translator of the work of Robert Duncan, Ann Lauterbach, Jerome Rothenberg, and Louise Glück into Spanish, as well as co-translator of the work of contemporary Spanish poets into English (*New Poetry from Spain* 2012), few writers have done more to build bilingual bridges and tear down walls than López Luaces.[78] In 2014 she curated two literary readings at New York's Cervantes Institute, under the title *Poetry for the New Millennium*, which brought together Anglo and Latino/a writers Scott Hightower, Ann Lauterbach, Jeannette Lozano Clariond, Mercedes Roffé, Roger Santiváñez, and Don Share, among others. Since then, she has continued to promote the literary bilingualism of the United States through *Readings @ Tompkins*, a bilingual poetry series held at the Tompkins Square branch of the New York Public Library.

López Luaces is the author of the following books of poetry: *Distancia y destierros* (1998), *Memorias de un vacío, Los arquitectos de lo imaginario* (2005), *Las lenguas del viajero* (2005), *Después de la oscuridad* (2016), and *Y soñábamos con pájaros volando: antología* (2017). She has also published a collection of short stories, *La virgin de la noche* (2009), and the novel *Los traductores del viento* (2013), for which she was awarded the International Latino Book Award in 2014.

Not surprisingly, both Escaja and López Luaces have included Colombian critic and writer Carlos Aguasaco in their bilingual, bicultural readings in New York. For Aguasaco has been instrumental in forging a community of Latin American, Spanish, and Latino/a writers from all over the world, through *The Americas Poetry Festival of New York* (TAPFNY), a yearly multilingual poetry festival, he organizes with Dominican poet Yrene Santos at the Center for Worker Education of City College of the City University of New York. Since 2014 TAPFNY has brought together writers from Argentina, Chile, Colombia, Cuba, the Dominican Republic, Ecuador, El Salvador, Mexico, Peru, Puerto Rico, Spain, the United States, and even from non-Spanish-speaking countries such as Estonia, Armenia, and India. And each year Aguasaco publishes, through his own imprint, Artepoética Press, the *Multilingual Anthology [Antología Multilingüe]*, an anthology that showcases the work of the poets who attended. A poet in his own right, Carlos Aguasaco is the author of *Conversando con el ángel* (2014), *Poemas del metro de Nueva York* (2014), *Antología de poetas hermafroditas* (2014), *El viejo y el man* (2014; novel), and *Diente de plomo* (2016, prose poems). Doubtlessly his status as a poet, editor, and organizer has contributed to the success of TAPFNY.[79]

Significantly, however, in addition to readings, poetry festivals, and foreign and domestic literary presses, today's US Latino/a writers who write in Spanish have other impactful venues at their disposal, such as Ulises Gonzáles's magazine *Los bárbaros*, which after only four years since it began publishing has already garnered enough attention to be included in Jeffrey Lawrence's *Anxieties of Experience: The Literatures of the Americas from Whitman to Bolaño*.[80] *Los bárbaros*, says Lawrence, "speaks to the complex discursive mechanisms that have shaped twenty-first-century Spanish language in the United States."[81] The Latin American writers found in the pages of *Los bárbaros*, unlike the Latin American writers of the Boom (e.g., Borges and García Márquez) "are here rather than there: in New York rather than in Mexico City, Buenos Aires, or Aracataca," writes Lawrence.[82] And it is from within the United States that they are advancing beyond literary and cultural borders. The cover of the first issue, an illustration by Manuel Gómez Burns, depicts two images of Borges sitting side by side in a New York City subway train: one, the familiar Borges, sits impassively with hands atop his cane, and the other, "a much younger version of the Argentine writer, reading an English-language copy of Bolaño's *The Savage Detectives*."[83] If Lawrence has adopted Burns's illustration for the cover of his own book, it is because it captures the cross-pollination of Spanish and English languages and literatures and turns Latin American literature into Latino/a American literatures of the United States: written here but with a Latino culture that informs it. And to that extent, a publication such as *Los bárbaros* follows in the steps of the Nuyorican movement.

Then there are those who in their capacity as writers, educators, and activists have made great contributions to the post-Nuyorican literature, and to Latino/a causes in general. One such individual is the Puerto Rican poet and playwright, Nancy Mercado, author of *It Concerns the Madness* (2000), and editor of the children's anthology, *If the World Were Mine* (2003). Her work has been anthologized in *ALOUD: Voices from the Nuyorican Poets Café*; *Breaking Ground: Anthology of Puerto Rican Women Writers in New York 1980–2012/Abriendo Caminos: Antología de escritoras puertorriqueñas en Nueva York, 1980–2012*; *Looking Out, Looking In: Anthology of Latino Poetry*. And in the summer of 2017 *The Before Columbus Foundation* bestowed upon Mercado the American Book Award for Lifetime Achievement. Mercado's achievement, as well as the achievements of others already mentioned is testament to the fertile ground that was laid down by the Nuyorican writers and to which we all owe so much, even by writers like me who do not necessarily address Latino/a themes in their writings.[84]

The United States is multicultural and multilingual; it speaks/writes in many languages, not to mention countless variations written and spoken by peoples from different countries and cultures. That is why it makes little or no sense to speak either of bilingualism or of Latino/a literature in the singular. There are multiple Latino/a literatures in multiple forms of English, Spanish, and Spanglish. And they will continue to multiply.[85]

# Notes

1. My sincerest apologies to all the wonderful writers, living or dead, whose names do not appear in this article. Their absence has nothing to do with any judgment concerning the value of their work on my part. It was simply a matter of space and the particular exigencies of the subject matter. Moreover, the lists of the authors mentioned here are not in any hierarchical order, not even alphabetically; they are loose groupings by literary movements and generations.

2. Anibal Quijano, "Coloniality of Power; Eurocentrism, and Social Classification," in *Coloniality at Large: Latin America and the Postcolonial Debate*, ed. Mabel Moraña, Enrique Dussel, and Carlos A. Jáuregui (Durham, NC: Duke University Press, 2008), 182–183.
3. Suzzane Romain, "Early Bilingual Development: From Elite to Folk," in *Bilingualism and Migration*, ed. Guus Extra and Ludo Verhoeven (Berlin: Mouton de Gruyter, 1998), 62.
4. Romain, "Early Bilingual Development," 62.
5. Romain, "Early Bilingual Development," 62.
6. Romain, "Early Bilingual Development," 62.
7. Romain, "Early Bilingual Development," 63.
8. Romain, "Early Bilingual Development," 63.
9. Valdés et al., "Language Ideology: The Case of Spanish in Departments of Foreign Languages," *Anthropology and Education Quarterly* 34, no. 1 (2003).
10. Gustavo Pérez Firmat, *Tongue Ties: Logo-Eroticism in Anglo-Hispanic Literature* (New York: Palgrave Macmillan, 2003), 61.
11. Pérez Firmat, *Tongue Ties*.
12. Pérez Firmat, *Tongue Ties*, 16, 18.
13. Pérez Firmat, *Tongue Ties*, 16.
14. Pérez Firmat, *Tongue Ties*, 14.
15. Pérez Firmat, *Tongue Ties*.
16. Pérez Firmat, *Tongue Ties*.
17. Edna Acosta-Belén and Judith Ortiz Cofer, "A *MELUS* Interview: Judith Ortiz Cofer," *MELUS* 18, no. 3 (1993): 90.
18. Acosta-Belén and Ortiz Cofer, "A *MELUS* Interview: Judith Ortiz Cofer."
19. Acosta-Belén and Ortiz Cofer, "A *MELUS* Interview: Judith Ortiz Cofer."
20. Gloria Anzaldúa, *Borderlands/La Frontera: The New Mestiza* (San Francisco: Aunt Lute, 1987), 59.
21. A text of the letter can be found in the Latino Rebels website: http://www.latinorebels.com/%202013/12/03/dominican-govt-officials-email-to-junot-diaz-youre-a-fake-and-overrated-pseudo-intellectual-who-needs-to-speak-spanish-better/. December 3, 2013.
22. Anzaldúa, *Borderlands/La Frontera*, 59.
23. Frances Negrón-Muntaner and Rosario Ferré, "*Sin pelos en la lengua*: Rosario Ferré's Last Interview," *Centro Journal* 24, no. 1 (2012): 157.
24. Anzaldúa, *Borderlands/La Frontera*, 59.
25. For detailed analysis of the bilingualism in Ana Lydia Vega's famous short story, "Pollito Chicken," see Doris Sommer and Matylda Figlerowicz's insightful article, "Rhetoric and Affect in Bilingual Latinx Literature" in this volume.
26. Elena Machado Sáez, "'Latino, U.S.A,' Statehooding Puerto Rico in Rosario Ferré's *The House on the Lagoon*," *Phoebe* 16, no. 1 (2004): 23.
27. Robert Duncan, *Tensar el arco y otros poemas. Antología Poética* (1939–1987), trans. Marta. López Luaces (Madrid: Bartleby Editores, 2011), 164.
28. Enrique Dussel, "Eurocentrism and Modernity (Introduction to the Frankfurt Lectures)," *Boundary 2* 20, no. 3 (1993): 65–76; Immanuel Wallerstein, *The Modern-World System I: Capitalist Agriculture and the Origins of the European World-Economy in the Sixteenth Century* (San Diego: Academic Press, 1974).
29. "The conflicts are very many. Languages are struggling to possess us. English wants to own us completely; Spanish wants to own us completely. We, in fact, have mixed them both," from Miguel Algarín (founder of the *Nuyorican Poets' Café*, and one of the founding

members of the Nuyorican literary movement) in his 1981 essay, "Nuyorican Literature" (see Miguel Algarin, "Nuyorican Literature," in *Norton Anthology of Latino Literature*, ed. Ilan Stavans [New York: W.W. Norton, 2011], 1351–1353).

30. Algarin, "Nuyorican Literature," 1351.
31. Luis Muñõz Marín (b. 1898–d. 1980) was born in San Juan, Puerto Rico. Journalist, poet, and politician, Marín became the first governor of Puerto Rico in 1948 and is known for being the architect of the island's commonwealth status and Operation Bootstrap, which encouraged large portions of the Puerto Rican working class, mostly farmers, to leave the island in search of better opportunities in the United States. The Jones Act became a subject of debate once again in 2017, following the devastation caused by Hurricane Maria in Puerto Rico. The Jones Act, which bans foreign vessels from entering the port of Puerto Rico, initially prohibited the delivery of necessary supplies coming from non-US-registered ships. The Jones Act was temporarily waved, with great reluctance, by the Trump administration on September 28, 2017. The Jones Act is responsible to driving up the price of goods in the island and is, according to many economists, a contributing factor in Puerto Rico's national debt.
32. Algarin, "Nuyorican Literature," 1351.
33. Juan Flores, *Divided Borders: Essays on Puerto Rican Identity* (Houston, TX: Arte Público Press, 1993), 147.
34. Flores, *Divided Borders*.
35. The Latino/a "writer is not purist. He or she understands that language is primarily affective, and, as a result, often switches back and forth from English to Spanish in a way that makes English 'vibrate' in a certain kind of way." See Rolando Pérez, "What Is 'Minor' in Latino Literature?" *MELUS* 30, no. 4 (2005): 93.
36. Spanglish, a portmanteau that combines the words "English "and "Spanish," is a highly debated concept in Latino/a studies and sociolinguistics, leading to two opposing schools of thought on the matter. On the one hand, there are those who view Spanglish as a bastardization of the Spanish language. This group tends to treat the linguistic incursion of English into Spanish, as for example with Spanglish words like "lonche" for "almuerzo: lunch" or "troca" for "camión: truck," as an "invasion of Spanish by English." See Roberto González Echevarría, "Is 'Spanglish' a Language?" in *Spanglish*, ed. Ilan Stavans (Westport, CT: Greenwood, 2008), 116. For them Spanglish is badly spoken Spanish. On the other hand, there are those like Ana Celia Zentella, Ilan Stavans, and others for whom Spanglish (similar to Yiddish for Ashkenazi Jews) is a creative, linguistic enterprise that reflects the cultural hybridity of Latino immigrants. For those who hold a favorable view of Spanglish, Spanglish is a byproduct of bilingualism, and therefore, as linguistically legitimate as standard, universal Spanish.
37. For more on Sandra María Esteves's poetry and Nuyorican poetics, see William Luis's article, "Sandra María Esteves's Nuyorican Poetics: The Signifying Difference" (2004).
38. Algarin, "Nuyorican Literature," 1352.
39. Frances R. Aparicio, "On Sub-versive Signifier: U.S. Latina/o Writers Tropicalize English," *American Literature* 66, no. 4 (1994): 797.
40. "A minor literature doesn't come from a minor language; it is rather that which a minority constructs within a major language," write Deleuze and Guattari in *Kafka: Toward a Minor Literature* (16). See also this concept applied to Latino/a Literature in my article, "What Is 'Minor' in Latino Literature" from 2005.
41. Pedro Pietri, "The Broken English Dream," in *The Norton Anthology of Latino Literature*, ed. Ilan Stavans (New York: W.W. Norton, 2011), 1366.
42. Pietri, "The Broken English Dream," 1367.

43. Encouraged by Governor Luis Marín Muñoz's false promises that Puerto Ricans who immigrated to the United States would be able to find work and make a living like any other American citizen, thousands of unemployed Puerto Ricans left the island in search of a better life. Nothing of the kind occurred, and as such, for them, the United States had become "the land of 'broken English dreams,' as Pietri called it... where masses of Puerto Rican workers... [had] come to live with little prospect of either advancement or return to Puerto Rico." See Juan Flores, *Divided Borders: Essays on Puerto Rican Identity* (Houston, TX: Arte Público Press, 1993), 173.
44. Pietri, "The Broken English Dream," 1394.
45. Pietri, "The Broken English Dream," 1394.
46. Flores, *Divided Borders*, 151.
47. Ed Morales, *Living in Spanglish: The Search for a Latino Identity in America* (New York: St. Martin's Press, 2002), 7.
48. Graham Harman, "Appendix: Excerpts from *L'Inexistence divine* by Quentin Meillassoux," in *Quentin Meillassoux: Philosophy in the Making*, 2nd ed. (Edinburgh: Edinburgh University Press, 2015), 259.
49. Aparicio, "On Sub-versive Signifier," 800.
50. I would further argue that the displacement has been more than merely metaphorical, and therein lies the anti-immigration politics of President Donald Trump and the white supremacists who support him.
51. Junot Díaz, *The Brief Wondrous Life of Oscar Wao* (New York: Riverhead, 2007), 15.
52. For more on Junot Díaz's code-switching in *The Brief Wondrous Life of Oscar Wao* (2007), see Eugenia Casielles-Suárez's article, "Radical Code-Switching in *The Brief Wondrous Life of Oscar Wao*" (2013).
53. Gloria Anzaldúa, *Borderlands/La Frontera: The New Mestiza* (San Francisco: Aunt Lute, 1987), 6; Anzaldúa, *Borderlands/La Frontera*, 160–163.
54. Anzaldúa, *Borderlands/La Frontera*, v.
55. Anzaldúa, *Borderlands/La Frontera*, 55.
56. Anzaldúa, *Borderlands/La Frontera*, 55.
57. The bilingualism of New York Puerto Ricans, says Ana Celia Zentella in Chapter 3 of her book, *Growing Up Bilingual*, encompasses an entire repertory of linguistic influences from popular Puerto Rican Spanish, standard Puerto Rican Spanish, English-dominant Spanish, Puerto Rican English, African American vernacular English, Hispanicized English, to standard New York City English.
58. Tato Laviera, *Bendición: The Complete Poetry of Tato Laviera* (Houston, TX: Arte Público Press, 2014), 283–284, 289, 291.
59. Laviera, *Bendición*.
60. Gustavo Pérez Firmat, *Bilingual Blues* (Tempe, AZ: Bilingual Press, 1995), 26.
61. Charles Sanders Peirce, *Collected Papers of Charles Sanders Peirce*, ed. Charles Hartshorne and Paul Weiss (Cambridge, MA: Belknap, 1974), 5.314.
62. Sanders Peirce, *Collected Papers of Charles Sanders Peirce*.
63. Annabel Cox, "Gustavo Pérez Firmat's 'Bilingual Blues' and 'Turning the Times Tables': Language Choice and Cultural Identity in Cuban-American Literature." *Neophilologus* 91 (2007): 76.
64. Pérez Firmat, *Bilingual Blues*, 26.
65. See Pérez Firmat's treatment of Sandra Cisneros's poem, "Dulzura," in *Tongue Ties*, 14–15, 142–143, 154–155, 161).

66. Pérez Firmat, *Bilingual Blues*, 28.
67. Pérez Firmat, *Bilingual Blues*, 28.
68. Pérez Firmat's use of the "ajiaco" metaphor is a reference to Fernando Ortiz's essay "The human factors of cubanidad" where the Cuban anthropologist compares the various racial and ethnic mixtures of Cuba to that of an "ajiaco," a word of Taíno origins, which refers to a stew composed of different ingredients (Ortiz 2014, 460–461). Ortiz opposed the culinary metaphor of the "ajiaco" to that of the "melting pot," where cultural differences are made to disappear (or "melt" away) in an assimilationist cauldron.
69. *Scar Tissue* was written after the author's bout with prostate cancer and the death of his father from the same disease. In its many references to the body (blood vessels, organs, scars), and the body's fluids (semen, blood), *Scar Tissue* is a book of "impurities."
70. Severo Sarduy (1937–1993) was born in Camagüey, Cuba, and died in Paris. Along with Alejo Carpentier and José Lezama Lima, Sarduy is one of the most important Cuban writers of the twentieth century. Author of nonfiction books, novels, poetry, and radio plays, Sarduy's style is associated with the Latin American neo-baroque aesthetic.
71. Pérez Firmat, *Bilingual Blues*, 28.
72. Pérez Firmat, *Bilingual Blues*, 25 to 27.
73. The reference here is to Michelangelo Antonioni's 1966 film *Blowup*, based on Julio Cortázar's short story, "Las babas del diablo."
74. Pérez Firmat, *Bilingual Blues*, 11.
75. Ilan Stavans, ed., *The Norton Anthology of Latino Literature* (New York: W.W. Norton, 2011), 2225–2230.
76. What Doris Sommer and Matylda Figlerowicz say in "Rhetoric and Affect in Bilingual Latinx Literature" about William Carlos Williams's English could easily apply to my literary English as well.
77. For the question of language choice, and the anxiety that writing literature in Spanish, has at times provoked in someone like myself, see my conversation with Gustavo Pérez Firmat, "El dererrcho a la equivocación: Conversación con Gustavo Pérez Firmat" (2011); Tomás Rivera (b. 1935–d. 1984) wrote… *y no se lo tragó la tierra*, about the plight of Chicano/a migrant workers, in Spanish. This beautiful novella, told from the point of view of a child, was published as a bilingual edition, with a translation by Herminio Ríos in 1971 as… *y no se lo tragó la tierra/…And the Earth Did Not Devour Him*. It was retranslated into English by Evangelina Vigil-Piñón and republished in 1992 by Arte Público Press. A film, directed by Severo Pérez, was made of the novella in 1995, beating the title of the English translation.
78. *Tensar el arco y otros poemas* (2010).
79. Since its inception in 2013 Artepoética Press has published numerous books of poetry, short stories, and novels.
80. Jeffrey Lawrence, *Anxieties of Experience: The Literatures of the Americas from Whitman to Bolaño* (New York: Oxford University Press, 2018), 231–234.
81. Lawrence, *Anxieties of Experience*, 232.
82. Lawrence, *Anxieties of Experience*, 231–234.
83. Lawrence, *Anxieties of Experience*, 231–234.
84. Miguel Algarín and Bob Hallman, *ALOUD: Voices from the Nuyorican Poets Café* (New York: Henry Holt, 1994); and Myrna Nieves, *Breaking Ground: Anthology of Puerto Rican Women Writers in New York 1980-2012* (New York: Editorial Campana, 2012).
85. In memory of Rosario Ferré and Judith Ortiz Cofer.

## Bibliography

Acosta-Belén, Edna, and Judith Ortiz Cofer. A *MELUS* Interview: Judith Ortiz Cofer. *MELUS* 18, no. 3 (1993): 83–97.

Algarín, Miguel. "Nuyorican Literature." In *Norton Anthology of Latino Literature*, edited by Ilan Stavans, 1351–1353. New York: W.W. Norton, 2011.

Algarín, Miguel, and Bob Hallman. *ALOUD: Voices from the Nuyorican Poets Café*. New York: Henry Holt, 1994.

Anzaldúa, Gloria. *Borderlands/La Frontera: The New Mestiza*. San Francisco: Aunt Lute, 1987.

Aparicio, Frances R. "On Sub-versive Signifier: U.S. Latina/o Writers Tropicalize English." *American Literature* 66, no. 4 (1994): 795–801.

Bernard-Carreño, Regina. "Nuyorican Identity." *Counterpoints* 366 (2010): 77–94.

Braschi, Giannina. *El imperio de los sueños*. Barcelona: Editorial Anthropos, 1988.

Braschi, Giannina. *Yo-yo Boing!* Pittsburgh: Latin American Literary Review Press, 1998.

Casielles-Suárez, Eugenia. *Yo-Yo Boing!* Introduction by Doris Sommer and Alexandra Vega-Merino. Pittsburgh, PA: Latin America Literary Review Press, 1998.

Casielles-Suárez, Eugenia. *United States of Banana*. Las Vegas: AmazonCrossing, 2011.

Casielles-Suárez, Eugenia. "Radical Code-Switching in *The Brief Wondrous Life of Oscar Wao*." *Bulletin of Hispanic Studies* 90, no. 4 (2013): 475–487.

Cox, Annabel. Gustavo Pérez Firmat's "Bilingual Blues" and "Turning the Times Tables": Language Choice and Cultural Identity in Cuban-American Literature. *Neophilologus* 91 (2007): 63–81.

Deleuze, Gilles, and Félix Guattari. *Kafka: Toward a Minor Literature* (Dana Polan, Trans.) Minneapolis: University of Minnesota Press, 1986.

Díaz, Junot. *The Brief Wondrous Life of Oscar Wao*. New York: Riverhead, 2007.

Duncan, Robert. *Tensar el arco y otros poemas*. Antología Poética (1939–1987) Trans. Marta. López Luaces. Madrid: Bartleby Editores, 2011.

Dussel, Enrique. Eurocentrism and Modernity (Introduction to the Frankfurt Lectures). *Boundary 2* 20, no. 3 (1993): 65–76.

Esteves, Sandra María. "Puerto Rican Discovery #3: Not Neither." In *The Norton Anthology of Latino Literature*, edited by Ilan Stavans, 1398. New York: W.W. Norton, 2011.

Flores, Juan. *Divided Borders: Essays on Puerto Rican Identity*. Houston, TX: Arte Público Press, 1993.

Flores, Juan, and George Yúdice. "Living Borders/Buscando America: Languages of Latino Self-Formation." *Social Text* 24 (1990): 57–84.

González Echevarría, Roberto. "Is 'Spanglish' a Language?" In *Spanglish*. Edited by Ilan Stavans, 116–1167. Westport, CT: Greenwood, 2008.

Harman, Graham. "Appendix: Excerpts from *L'Inexistence divine* by Quentin Meillassoux." In *Quentin Meillassoux: Philosophy in the Making*, 224–287. 2nd ed. Edinburgh: Edinburgh University Press, 2015.

Laviera, Tato. *Bendición: The Complete Poetry of Tato Laviera*. Preface. Nicolás Kanellos. Introduction. Laura Lomas. Houston, TX: Arte Público Press, 2014.

Lawrence, Jeffrey. *Anxieties of Experience: The Literatures of the Americas from Whitman to Bolaño*. New York: Oxford University Press, 2018.

Luis, William. "Sandra María Esteves' Nuyorican Poetics: The Signifying Difference." *Afro-Hispanic Review* 23, no. 2 (2004): 3–12.

Luis, William, ed. *Looking Out, Looking In: Anthology of Latino Poetry*. Houston, TX: Arte Público Press, 2013.

Marian, Viorica, and Anthony Shook. "The Cognitive Benefits of Being Bilingual." *Cerebrum: the Dana Forum on Brain Science* 13 (2012): 1–12. https://www.ncbi.nlm.nih.gov/pmc/articles/PMC3583091/pdf/cer-12-13.pdf.

Mercado, Nancy, ed. *If the World Were Mine: The Young Writer's Workshop Anthology*. Newark: New Jersey Performing Arts Center Publication and United Way of Essex and West Hudson, 2003.

Morales, Ed. *Living in Spanglish: The Search for a Latino Identity in America*. New York: St. Martin's Press, 2002.

Negrón-Muntaner, Frances, and Rosario Ferré. "*Sin pelos en la lengua*: Rosario Ferré's Last Interview." *Centro Journal* 24, no. 1 (2012): 154–71.

Nieves, Myrna. *Breaking Ground: Anthology of Puerto Rican Women Writers in New York 1980-2012*. New York: Editorial Campana, 2012.

Ortiz, Fernando. "The Human Factors of Cubanidad. Preface (João Felipe Gonçalves and Gregory Duff Morton, Trans.)." *HUA: Journal of Ethnographic Theory* 4, no. 3 (2014): 445–480.

Peirce, Charles Sanders. *Collected Papers of Charles Sanders Peirce*. Pragmatism and Pragmaticism. Scientific Metaphysics. Edited by Charles Hartshorne and Paul Weiss. Cambridge, MA: Belknap, 1974.

Pérez, Rolando. "What is 'Minor' in Latino Literature?" *MELUS* 30, no. 4 (2005): 89–108.

Pérez Firmat, Gustavo. *Bilingual Blues*. Tempe, AZ: Bilingual Press, 1995.

Pérez Firmat, Gustavo. *Tongue Ties: Logo-Eroticism in Anglo-Hispanic Literature*. New York: Palgrave Macmillan, 2003.

Pérez Firmat, Gustavo. *Scar Tissue: A Memoir*. Tempe, AZ: Bilingual, 2005.

Pérez Firmat, Gustavo, and Rolando Pérez. El derecho a la equivocación: Conversación con Gustavo Pérez Firmat. *Boletín de la Academia Norteamericana de la Lengua Española* 14 (2011): 351–363.

Pietri, Pedro. "The Broken English Dream." In *The Norton Anthology of Latino Literature*. Edited by Ilan Stavans, 1393–1394. New York: W.W. Norton, 2011.

Piñero, Miguel. "A Lower Eastside Poem." In *The Norton Anthology of Latino Literature*. Edited by Ilan Stavans, 1364–1366. New York: W. W. Norton, 2011.

Quijano, Aníbal. "Coloniality of Power; Eurocentrism, and Social Classification." In *Coloniality at Large: Latin America and the Postcolonial Debate*, edited by Mabel Moraña, Enrique Dussel, and Carlos A. Jáuregui, 181–224. Durham, NC: Duke University Press, 2008.

Latino Rebels. Dominican Govt's Official's Email to Junot Díaz: You're a "Fake and Overrated Pseudo-Intellectual" Who Needs to Speak Spanish Better. 2013. http://www.latinorebels.com/2013/12/03/dominican-govt-officials-email-to-junot-diaz-youre-a-fake-and-overrated-pseudo-intellectual-who-needs-to-speak-spanish-better.

Romain, Suzzane. "Early Bilingual Development: From Elite to Folk." In *Bilingualism and Migration*. Edited by Guus Extra and Ludo Verhoeven, 61–74. Berlin: Mouton de Gruyter, 1998.

Sáez, Elena Machado. "Latino, U.S.A." Statehooding Puerto Rico in Rosario Ferré's *The House on the Lagoon*. *Phoebe* 16, no. 1 (2004): 23–38.

Sommer, Doris, and Alexandra Vega-Merino. "Introduction: Either And." In *Yo-Yo Boing!*, edited by Giannina Braschi, 11–18. Pittsburgh, PA: Latin American Literary Review Press, 1998.

Stavans, Ilan. "Tickling the Tongue." *World Literature Today* 74, no. 3 (2000): 555–558.

Stavans, Ilan. (2003). *Spanglish: The Making of a New American Language*. New York: HarperCollins.

Stavans, Ilan, ed. *Spanglish*. Westport, CT: Greenwood, 2008.
Stavans, Ilan, ed. *The Norton Anthology of Latino Literature*. New York: W.W. Norton, 2011.
Valdés, Guadalupe, Sonia V. González, Dania López García, and Patricio Márquez. "Language Ideology: The Case of Spanish in Departments of Foreign Languages." *Anthropology and Education Quarterly* 34, no. 1 (2003): 3–26.
Wallerstein, Immanuel. *The Modern-World System I: Capitalist Agriculture and the Origins of the European World-Economy in the Sixteenth Century*. San Diego: Academic Press, 1974.
Zentella, Ana Celia. *Growing Up Bilingual: Puerto Rican Children in New York*. New York: Blackwell, 1997.

CHAPTER 14

# RHETORIC AND AFFECT IN BILINGUAL LATINX LITERATURE

## MATYLDA FIGLEROWICZ AND DORIS SOMMER

BILINGUALISM is a strategy for literary creation, since writing in two languages generates otherwise unthinkable rhetorical and affective structures. Although by now bilingualism has gotten some serious academic attention as a sociological and linguistic phenomenon, an educational issue, a political point of conflict, a neurological or cognitive trait, it has not yet been the focus of much literary analysis. This is strange, or revealing, when compared with neighboring fields such as translation and exile studies. Do we still assume that expressive language naturally ends up on either side of a border, instead of straddling? Rather than an exhaustive study, this essay proposes how to read bilingual literature, offering ways that underscore its particularities. The formal and theoretical basis of this study can be extrapolated to different bi- or multilingual contexts. We focus on Latinx literature, in part, to highlight its capacity to reframe studies of creative writing in general.

The analysis of Latinx literature is impoverished if we do not first recognize bilingualism as an artistic innovation. This is what Doris Sommer proposes in *Bilingual Aesthetics*. There she grounds bilingual games in literary and linguistic forms—forms tensed and broken by the force of bilingual innovation: "The exercise needs an almost tragicomic taste for the interrupted communication that requires humility and that begs debate and negotiation. Part of bilingual gamesmanship is to train a predisposition toward feeling funny, or on edge, about language, the way that artists, activists, and philosophers are on edge about familiar or conventional uses."[1] The game we want to play here is, thus, a serious one, and we want to insist on its implications for art and politics, for philosophy and policy. This may irritate (though we hope it inspires) those many readers who consider bilingualism to be a lack of competence in either language, a purely linguistic characteristic, or a low-stakes word game. As Gustavo Pérez Firmat writes in *Tongue Ties*, "Contrary to some reports, there is no bilingualism without pain. Although bilingualists are often playful, bilingualism is not a game.... The bilingual muse is a melancholy muse; it divides and does not conquer."[2] Dividing but not conquering goes against the efficiency of speech and action, but it opens new possibilities: "The *uneconomical* effort of language learning improves general lucidity and also does something more specific: a new language opens routes of thought that can detour around decayed or clogged pathways of a first language."[3] The study of bilingualism is, thus, a perspective that allows artistic innovation to inform political thought. We hope to see in the coming years not only a greater scholarly interest in bilingualism as an aesthetic within Latinx studies, but also—considering how many contexts in the contemporary world are saturated with linguistic multiplicity—we expect the theoretical bases built in Latinx studies to play an important role in other fields, geographical and chronological.

To describe the ways in which bilingualism refreshes conventional rhetoric, maybe metonymy is the best figure to start with. Metonymy is basic to bilingual texts, which put one language (culture, reference) alongside another; and the strategy of unconventional contiguity is transformed, as we will see, in combination with other figures depending on the text that presses metonymy into new service. We will find metonymies in a geographic variant (that juxtaposes popular registers of two languages); in the dashed pleasure of unattainable desire; in collusion with over-the-top or under-the-radar expressions; as well as in the wrenching competitions between culturally coded ways to remember and to know. Starting from a rhetorical figure that morphs into variations as it relates to others puts us on the track of bilingualism as an artistic innovation. The affective structures that govern the texts are tightly connected with formal experiments, becoming the aesthetic punctum of the texts. At the same time, analyzing literary works in terms of rhetorical and affective structures is a way of tracing their interventions into the sociopolitical landscape. Following Lauren Berlant, who argues that "the aesthetic or formal rendition of affective experience provides evidence of historical processes," we can see the ways in which literary expression is linked to affective response.[4] It is our offering toward creating a record of—but also an intervention into—the experiences of bilingual communities.

Metonymy is famously described by Roman Jakobson as based on contiguity, which is the dominating logic behind the bilingual rhetorical figures.[5] In bilingual texts, the substitution of one word or phrase for another is driven by their contiguous character; it creates a competition that displaces one system by an apparently unbidden neighbor at the level of language choice. If a Spanish word is used in a predominantly English text, it holds a relation of contiguity to the words that it substitutes; but its disparity from them points toward not just a different connotation of the word but to an entire system of meaning, which opens onto a whole set of alternative connections. The interruption involves a tension between the surplus and the lack of meaning: the word used in a metonymic structure invokes additional meanings and contexts that overflow through the crack opened by its introduction. Yet the move also exposes absences and gaps because of the unnamed nuances implied in the other language. The mere insistence on contiguity reveals opportunities and risks. This makes the bilingual metonymical structure a porous space, uneven, and therefore dangerous. It is what Derrida called a "dangerous supplement," an added but unbidden element that reveals cracks in a system that had looked solid but now feels unstable.

Jacques Lacan's contribution to the definition of metonymy was to use it as the foundational figure for making meaning through language. The artificial contiguity of a word for a meaning generates communication itself, though habitual users may mistake the artifice as natural. He calls the structure the *"word-to-word"* connection: "I shall designate as metonymy, then, the one side (*versant*) of the effective field constituted by the signifier, so that meaning can emerge there."[6] Metonymy implies a dismembering of a single signifier, and a multiplication of signifiers positioned in unequal relationships to each other and to the signified. That way, the signified is a complex whole made through fragments—a whole in ways the word is used by Víctor Hernández Cruz in the title of a book of poems, *By Lingual Wholes* (1982). It can also read as "Bilingual holes." Latinx literature puts its finger in the wound (as the Spanish expression says); it locates the constitutive lack in language. The *(w)hole* signifies a polymorphous tension between absence and overflow of meaning.

The unresolved tension between more and less relates substantially to the affects generated by metonymic structures. Lacan, after all, explored language through his work in psychoanalysis. He describes the logic of contiguity governing metonymy as analogical to that of desire:

> And the enigmas that desire seems to pose for a "natural philosophy"—its frenzy mocking the abyss of the infinite, the secret collusion with which it envelops the pleasure of knowing and of dominating with *jouissance*, these amount to no other derangement of instinct than that of being caught in the rails—eternally stretching forth towards the desire for something else—of metonymy. Hence its "perverse" fixation at the very suspension-point of the signifying chain where the memory-screen is immobilized and the fascinating image of the fetish is petrified.[7]

More succinctly, Lacan writes that "desire *is* a metonymy."[8] Metonymy is an ever-expanding space, never fully encompassed. Not merely the joy of expansion nor just the threat of extensiveness, it steps away from precise answers and instead multiplies them. This way, it changes the source of pleasure, as Lacan explains. The "pleasure of knowing and of dominating" is obscured, which makes it possible for alternative pleasures of the text to arise. The change translates the sociopolitical effect of the texts by transforming the source of the readers' pleasures, from an assumed pursuit of satisfaction to the *jouissance* of unending desire. Lacan hints at the political power of metonymy to liberate us by asking "what does man find in metonymy if not the power to circumvent the obstacles of social censure? Does not this form, which gives its field to truth in its very oppression, manifest a certain servitude inherent in its presentation?"[9] Metonymy, thus, is both frustrating—like an unfulfilled yearning—and an escape valve, through which to give more than one right answer or right word.

For a good example, look at the final passage of Hernández Cruz's poem *You Gotta Have Your Tips on Fire*:

> You gotta have your tips on fire
> You never will be in the wrong place
> For the universe will feel your heat

>     And arrange its dance on your head
>     There will be a Sun/Risa
>     On your lips
>     But
>     You gotta have your tips on fire
>     Carnal.[10]

Throughout the poem, the direct apostrophes to the reader are in colloquial Spanish, which interrupts the mostly English-language text. But the Spanish itself is not solid. It juxtaposes geographic variants of informal speech. "*Carnal*" a Mexican term for buddy, is close to Puerto Rican "*pana*," and displaces it. The variations put one cultural region alongside others. This geographic variation of metonymy thickens colloquial Spanish to make it a sophisticated performance of cosmopolitan registers. Together, they construct a rhythm—the words in Spanish seem to divide the poem in stanzas, even though it is written without divisions. They create intimacy, using Spanish and its informal—yet cosmopolitan—register. But intimacy comes with a cost of distance. Who is the "you" in the poem? Where are you from, and who are your people? The words create a community, but how inclusive or exclusive? Giving readers an excess of intimate tags, the poem reduces their certainty of inclusion.

Similarly, the poem's bilingualism works the tension between pain and pleasure through a captivating but perhaps also disturbing neologism "Sun/Risa." It sounds like both "sunrise" and a "smile" (*sonrisa*), a redundant invitation to optimism. But putting the languages side by side means identifying a split—visually accented by the dash that divides them. It troubles the joy with a sign of artificial contiguity and shows desire at work as metonymy keeps sun and smile separate but present to one another. One of the following lines, the short "But," confirms the need for caution, making the dashed structure of "Sun/Risa" bear a resemblance to Wittgenstein's reflection on reading with appreciation for failure. He uses the analogy of a servant who makes a mess, carefully:

> Carefulness is a most essential part of this picture; in another the exclusion of every volition of one's own would be essential. (But take something normal people do quite unconcernedly and imagine someone accompanying in with the expression—and why not the feelings—of great carefulness.—Does that mean he is careful? Imagine a servant dropping a tea-tray and everything on it with all the outward signs of carefulness).[11]

This canny image, of dropping a tea-tray in a premeditated and careful way, is revealingly close to the metonymical structure of "Sun/Risa." It combines care and destruction: not the usual care for exactitude and correctness of language but rather a careful opening of languages. Bilingualism dissects and rearranges words, sharing the precision and the violent potential of a surgical knife.

Among the variations on metonymy, we will consider how Guillermo Cabrera Infante and Ana Lydia Vega, two Caribbean stylists, live and write inevitably at the fraying seams between English and Spanish. Their revenge on empire is to bloat the everyday abuses of "natural" languages that interfere with one another into metonymies so absurd and enthusiastic that they call attention to the colloquial games people normally play. In another approach to the rhetorical figure, William Carlos Williams and Gloria Anzaldúa juxtapose culturally coded ways of constructing knowledge and memory.

Caribbean irreverence, in Cabrera Infante and Vega, puts metonymy in the hilarious company of hyperbole or litotes. Irreverence is an enabler for these rhetorical figures as the Cuban and Puerto Rican writing mixes enthusiasm with dark humor to hover near sociopolitical commentary. In Williams and Anzaldúa, metonymic structures put in question what seems stable and well known, while operating at the fragile space of the border. The affective resonance of the rhetorical figures in these four authors resembles the two main philosophical gestures triggered by emotions according to Didi-Huberman. In *Quelle émotion! Quelle émotion?* (2013), he describes them through the metaphor of the exclamation point and the question mark: halting one in awe or in doubt. The essay also explores different temporalities. While in Cabrera Infante and Vega we find an emphasis on the relationship between present and future—which often takes the form of a fantasy—Williams and Anzaldúa highlight how past and present are mutually constructing each other. All of these authors use bilingualism to transform genres, as well as to shape the performative character of their texts. They open a new space for aesthetic pleasure and political discussion but require and form an alert audience, with new ways of reading—that's why "you gotta have your tips on fire."[12]

"*Showtime!* Señoras y señores. *Ladies and gentlemen. Muy* buenas noches damas y caballeros, tengan todos ustedes. *Good-evening ladies and gentlemen.*"[13] The opening lines of the prologue of Guillermo Cabrera Infante's *Tres tristes tigres* are a seductive invitation to a conversation on bilingualism. The prologue is an opening in many different ways. On the most immediate level of the text, it is a monologue of a host presenting a cabaret show in *Tropicana*, a club in La Habana, greeting the guests and introducing the stars of the show. This setting explains the bilingual format of the prologue, in which the host switches between English and Spanish to communicate with different parts of the audience. Yet the back and forth between the languages goes beyond an attempt to express the message to different groups. There is a dialogue established between the different parts of the text. "Estimable, muy estimado, estimadísimo público, ahora para ustedes una traducción literaria," says the host at one point when switching from English to Spanish, tellingly promising a "literary," not a "literal" translation.[14] This underscores how the bilingual form of the prologue is the foundation of its literary character, where the overlaps, the gaps, and the conflicts between what is said in each language are the strategies of creating meaning.

The opening of the show is, however, also the prologue to the novel. *Tres tristes tigres* was published in 1968, already during Cabrera Infante's European exile. It takes place in Cuba and, as the author informs us explicitly, "el libro está en cubano."[15] The specificity of the language in Cuba that the novel aims to capture is, thus, contrasted with the prologue, which through the multilingual structure produces a clash of the local setting and the exterior. The entire prologue is a direct communication with the spectators and readers—a prolonged apostrophe; yet while it seems to open to a vaster audience, its bilingualism is a game of inclusion and exclusion. Some references are clear only in one or the other language, and some only between both. At the same time, it presents the local context of the novel as openly offered to exterior, voyeuristic eyes, turning the Cuban reality into a cabaret show promised by the prologue after the host exclaims "¡Arriba el telón!... *Curtains up!*"[16] The sociopolitical commentary can be traced to specific strategies of creating meaning through the different languages, considering at the same time the tension between the performative and the written character of the text.

Switching between Spanish and English plays an important role in constructing the performative character of the prologue, making it closer to an actual opening of a show. On a more structural level, we can see it also as a structural metonymy, where the closeness of the similar parts in different languages displays the gaps and excesses of meaning. This is coupled with the rhythm of the text, which is constructed upon exclamations and apostrophes, as well as marked emphasis on certain words and phrases. The prologue is all just one paragraph, and it is difficult to divide in smaller fragments, as it seems to be all said in one breath, with every phrase flowing into the next one. This intensity and rapidity of the text are contrasted with the details of its construction, which invites us to stop at the analysis of the minutia of the wording and structure. The following passage can serve as an example of these tensions:

> Público amable, amable público, pueblo de Cuba, la tierra *más* hermosa que ojos humanos vieran, como dijo el Descubridor Colón (no el Colón de Colón, Castillo y Campanares, no... Jojojó. Sino ¡Cristóbal Colón, el de las carabelas!)... Pueblo, público, queridos concurrentes, perdonen un momento mientras me dirijo, en idioma de *Chakespeare*, en *English*, me dirijo a la selecta concurrencia que colma *todas y cada unas* de las localidades de este emporio del amor y la vida risueña. Quiero hablarle, si la amabilida proverbial de Respetable cubano me lo permite, a nuestra ENorme concurrencia americana: caballerosos y radiantes turistas que visitan la tierra de las *gay senyoritaes and brave caballerros... For your exclusive pleasure, ladies and gentlemen, our Good Neighbours, you that are now in Cuba, the most beautiful land human eyes have ever seen, as Christofry Colombus, The Discoverer, said once, you, hap-py visitors, are once and for all, welcome. WelCOME to Cuba! All of you... be WELLcome! Bienvenidos, as we say in our romantic language, the language of colonizadors and toreros (bullfighters) and very, very, but very (I know what I say) beautiful duennas. I know that you are here to sunbathe and seabathe and sweatbathe Jo jo jo.*[17]

The prologue mirrors the over-the-top aesthetics of the cabaret show it announces. It is based on multiple hyperboles, which repeatedly play an exoticizing and eroticizing role, as when they describe Cuba as "la tierra más hermosa que ojos humanos vieran," that is, "*the most beautiful land human eyes have ever seen.*" This praise of Cuba's beauty is supposedly a quotation from Columbus, which underscores the insistence on the outside gaze upon which the image of the island is constructed. At the same time, the difference between the two evocations of Columbus are telling. The one directed to the Spanish-speaking audience is an opportunity to make a local joke, evoking different places in La Habana, and flows into the announcement of the translation to English.

In English, however, the reference to Columbus allows the host as well to affirm how welcome the guests are in Cuba: "*You, hap-py visitors, are once and for all, welcome. WelCOME to Cuba! All of you... be WELLcome!*" This overly enthusiastic declaration uncovers the irony behind the hyperboles, especially since the Spanish colonization is contraposed with the tourism from the United States, thus placing "*our Good Neighbours*" in the history of Cuba's exploitation.

The host mocks the lack of individuality in the waves of tourism, offering to the crowd an impossible "*exclusive pleasure.*" He recurs again to hyperbolic irony when the foreign tourists are described as "la selecta concurrencia que colma *todas y cada unas* de las localidades de este emporio del amor y la vida risueña." Once again, not only the outside gaze directed at Cuba presents the island as an idyllic and exotic space, but also the host is ironically calling "selecta" a group that at the same time fills completely every place in Cuba. The phrasing is telling: "*todas y cada unas*" is not only emphasized by the use of italics, but also it uses "unas" instead of "una," which would be the grammatically correct form. This way, the apparent mistake is used to underscore the multiplicity of the tourists swamping the island, the hyperbole being thus brought to the level of grammatical plurality. The use of italics is interesting as well, as certain phrases in the Spanish parts of the text are emphasized through their use, but also the entire text in English is written in italics. Thus, the use of this language as such is bearing a mark of emphatic exaggeration.

Such linguistic mistakes are also an important example of how the text manages to construct a surplus of meaning through what apparently seems like a lack—in this case, a lack of command of language which, moreover, has stereotypically been connected to bi- or multilingual speakers. "Y ahora... *and now*... señoras y señores... *ladies and gentlemen*... público que sabe lo que es bueno... *Discriminatory public*" says the hosts to the audience, and the slip between "discriminating" and "discriminatory" is more than a lucky mistranslation.[18] The feigned ignorance is a way of turning the tables around and using the existing prejudice for one's own benefit. The metonymic structure of the text plays constantly with the idea of excess—the excess of contiguous words and meanings—mocking the monolithic and contained correctness.

Published almost thirty years later, in 1994, Ana Lydia Vega's short story "Pollito Chicken" offers a different way of using bilingual writing for emphatic and ironic effects. It takes place in another Caribbean island—Puerto Rico—the native land of the protagonist, Suzie Bermiúdez, who takes a trip there after ten years of living in New York and rejecting everything that connects her to the island and its culture. The use of bilingualism in the story is significantly different from the one in Cabrera Infante's text. It does not use a pretext of a setting where translation is needed, but it is based on constant code-switching between Spanish and English. This is a meaningful difference, as it responds to the contemporary everyday of many members of the Latinx community, where both languages serve as a means of communication and of construction of discourse. Significantly, there is no visual marking of the difference between the two languages in the text—such as italics—which gives the sensation of coherence and autonomy of the language formed upon code-switching.

This difference has its consequences in the way metonymy operates in the text. Rather than being a structural trait, it is present on a more basic level of particular words and phrases. When the text promises to tell us about "el surprise return de Suzie Bermiúdez a su native land tras años de luchas incesantes," the English words, introduced into a Spanish sentence structure, are contiguous to those that could be used in Spanish.[19] It is crucial from the rhetorical point of view how the code-switching manages the excess and lack of meaning. Even the surname of the protagonist is analyzable in these terms: while the actual surname is "Bermúdez," in the story it is spelled with an extra "i," which reflects the pronunciation characteristic of an English speaker. It still conserves the graphic accent on the "u," which implies a Spanish rendering of a name heard in English. This is a version of the name that puts emphasis on the intercrossing of the languages and cultures. And while not fully comprising the actual surname, it substitutes it to offer an additional meaning.

Tracing the code-switching in the story, we can see certain patterns that create meaning beyond the particular instances of it. Words that are chosen to be used in English rather than Spanish tend to either emphasize statements in an overly enthusiastic tone or offend through the use of vulgarity. For instance, Suzie decides to go to Puerto Rico because of "el breathtaking poster de Fomento que vio en la travel agency del lobby de su building," in which "los beautiful people se veían tan deliriously happy y el mar tan strikingly blue y la puesta de sol—no olvidemos la puesta de sol a la Winston-tastes-good—la puesta de sol tan shocking pink en la distancia."[20] She wants to visit the island, even though she considers the Puerto Rican community in New York as "todos esos lazy, dirty, no-good bums que eran sus compatriotas."[21] The words in English, thus, are largely based on the hyperbolic language of advertisement, projecting an image of a desired life where the intensity of experiences and of sensual stimuli takes your breath away, shocks you, and makes you delirious with happiness. At the same time, English vulgarisms introduce the same intensity in demeaning those who do not fit into this picture.

All these strong emotional expressions, inserted into a foreign linguistic structure, sound like repetitions and clichés. They repeat two different phantasmagoric discourses that are identified with the mainstream cultural and political landscape of the United States. First, the Hollywood-like feel-good story, plus the commercials and product promotion. This is intensified by the general metonymic structure of the expressions when seen in Lacanian terms—being analogical to the structure of desire, they subtly reveal the unattainability of the goals. Commodities can be thought of as having a similar structure to metonymy, being a substitute for an experience or a fulfillment: like when the taste of Winston cigarettes becomes contiguous to the view of a sunset. The second discourse captures the threat to the former, idyllic vision—the threat brought by foreigners, who show vividly the confines within the land where supposedly only the sky is the limit. Thus, a similarly powerful language constructs the discourse that justifies the inequalities.

Arguably, this bilingual structure could be described as a clash of hyperbole and litotes—as a denunciation of the fantasies through simultaneously over- and understating them.

The English words framed in Spanish phrases can be read as an understatement of what would be said in Spanish. The linguistic switch from Spanish to English makes it easier to use emotionally charged vocabulary and creates a distance between the person uttering the words and their actual meaning. Litotes is defined as "a periphrastic combination of emphasis and irony: the superlative degree of meaning intended in the *voluntas* is described by the negation of its opposite."[22] Here, rather than a negation of the opposite, we have a linguistic shift, which lowers the intensity of the words used. This is a way of further underscoring their clichéd character, and their belonging to a certain preestablished discourse. It creates also a complicity with the reader, since the displacement can only be understood when knowing not just both languages but also the context being evoked. This is a crucial feature of litotes as it "is understood in its intended meaning... on the basis of an existing, pre-established sympathy between the speaker and the listener."[23] The clash between litotes and hyperbole shows the distressing character of the fantasies, which pull toward extremes and destabilize those who pursue them.

It would not do justice to Vega's story to treat it solely as a critique of the fantasies offered by the United States and often adopted by the newcomers—the relationship that is constructed between the languages and their sociopolitical implications is more complex. While enjoying the beaches of Puerto Rico, Suzie and the bartender exchange meaningful looks. The protagonist is afraid of the sudden sexual desire she feels and escapes to her room. However, she cannot resist to call the bar and order room service. Where does this story end? We get the version of the bartender himself, which he relates to his friends, who are described as "su fan club de ávidos aspirantes a tumbagringas."[24]

> Entonces, el admirado mamitólogo narró cómo, en el preciso instante en que las platinum-frosted fingernails se incrustaban passionately en su afro, desde los skyscrapers inalcanzables de un intra-uterine orgasm, los half-opened lips de Suzie Bermiúdez producían el sonoro mugido ancestral de:
> –¡VIVA PUELTO RICO LIBREEEEEEEEEEEEEEE![25]

With this the story ends, and we are not offered any commentary from the narrator. Taken at face value, this account of the sexual encounter could be read as a victory of the native, Spanish-speaking side of Suzie, proclaiming loyalty to Puerto Rico against the imperialism of the United States, which she bought into while living in New York. And yet, this reading would obviate the phantasmagorical character of this account.[26] The masculinist and heterosexual fantasy of predatory sexuality is the basis of the bartender's bragging to his male friends. The exaggeration of the sexual abilities in describing "los skyscrapers inalcanzables," that is, the claim of reaching the unreachable, is linked with nationalistic pride, when the "intra-uterine" [sic] orgasm leads to an independentist cry. At the same time, the sexual deeds seem to be especially admired when directed at foreigners—which is why others aspire to the title of "tumbagringas."[27]

In other words, coming back to "su native land," Suzie encounters sexism and another nationalism. Rather than a self-discovery thanks to a homecoming, it presents another discourse that uses the protagonist to build its strength. Humorous and light in its tone,

Vega's short story makes a rather bitter point about different fantasies of belonging. While in Cabrera Infante's novel the use of specifically Cuban Spanish was a way of denouncing different colonialisms that exploited Cuba, in Vega's text, the last sentence, written with a mark of Puerto Rican accent, is marking another oppression. Suzie Bermiúdez, a seemingly caricaturesque character even in her name, represents the double foreignness of an immigrant who never fits in seamlessly in the country of arrival and yet can only have a fantasy of a liberation in a home waiting for her return.

Both in Cabrera Infante's and in Vega's texts, bilingualism is used to create an ironic emphasis and to generate enthusiasm, which is, however, either staged or phantasmagorical. The metonymical structures and phrases in both texts function to a great extent as described by Lacan: they are synonymous to desire. The protagonists stretch themselves from hyperbole to understatement, dislocated in their desires that can never be uttered or fulfilled. Yet they mimic enthusiasm by playing along: they do not just buy into the narrative of the fantasy, they take it to its very end: and by this exaggeration make it shatter. The higher the text can take it, the more painful the dissonance and the fall. Lauren Berlant discusses similar violence of fantasies in *Cruel Optimism*: "Fantasy is the means by which people hoard idealizing theories and tableaux about how they and the world 'add up to something.' What happens when those fantasies start to fray—depression, dissociation, pragmatism, cynicism, optimism, activism, or an incoherent mash?"[28] Bilingualism is formed by, and responds to, the experiences that shatter the good-life fantasies: such as colonialism, immigration, and capitalism. The literary forms that are developed can be seen as one of the "multiple modes of attachment, endurance, and attunement to the world and to the contemporary world of spreading precarity and normative dissolution."[29] The texts offer a moment of ecstatic laughter, a saturated feeling, which nonetheless leaves a void after it passes. Not fitting into the preexisting narratives, bilingual forms show the impossibility of participation in the fantasies of fulfillment in life. Yet the desire they express opens a new space, which, while not satisfying the fantasies, makes it possible to understand and cope with the loss.

Bilingualism, therefore, opens a new space within language and text, an opportunity not just to broaden the scope of the discussion but to alter forms of aesthetic expression and of constructing knowledge. Gloria Anzaldúa's texts explore these possibilities, through different displacements of languages, genres, and discourses. Concerned mostly with the Mexican and Chicano identities, in *Borderlands/La Frontera* (1987) Anzaldúa frames this opening space in terms of a wound: "The U.S.-Mexican border *es una herida abierta* where the Third World grates against the first and bleeds" Anzaldúa denounces not just the violence of the border but also the premises of the division it creates[30]—she describes the US borderlands as Aztlán, the Aztec mythical homeland, thus marking it as an inherently Mexican territory. This broader description of the borderlands is intertwined with the more particular conceptualization of Anzaldúa's own identity, which allows her to denounce the situation of marginalized groups, such as women or queer people, in the already discriminated Chicano community.[31]

As Anzaldúa is one of the most widely read Chicanx authors and scholars, there has been a lot of discussion around her work. While widely praised, it was also criticized for its essentializing and oversimplifying character. Some denounced Anzaldúa's texts for their way of referencing Indigenous cultures, which reduces the Indigenous presence to a mythical past.[32] Other scholars argue that as much as the border is described by Anzaldúa as a wound, it does not fully recognize its asymmetry and the subsequent disparity in the way border studies are conceptualized on either side.[33] While these critical responses are well founded, it can be argued that the form of Anzaldúa's works pushes against the oversimplifying claims that it makes. The languages and genres are used in a way that poses more complex questions and problematizes the interpretations of the texts. Anzaldúa's use of bilingual metonymy shows it is not just a figure of breakage but also of collage, allowing the different signifiers to reform the signified.

The text, though dominated by English, introduces multiple phrases in Spanish—sometimes translated, sometimes not—as well as some terms in Nahuatl, mostly when referring to Aztec mythology. This could be seen as analogic to the use of different genres: while we could see texts such as *Borderlands/La Frontera* as scholarly essays, their form combines academic writing with poetry, short stories, or memoirs. This is a way of constructing scholarship based on different genres and learning from oral tradition and storytelling. Bilingual literature shows a tendency and a capacity of defying the rules of genres—like we have seen in Cabrera Infante's *Tres tristes tigres*, where the prologue is playing both with genres and the orality of the text. In that sense, Anzaldúa's scholarly writing, informed by literary creation, proposes a new way of constructing knowledge using different modes of thinking and founded upon different traditions of creating meaning. This is something she addresses openly in some of her later texts such as *Light in the Dark/Luz en lo oscuro*, where she describes her process of "attempting to create new epistemological frameworks"—which, tellingly, she analyzes in bilingual terms, finding its origins in the Spanish verb *idear*.[34]

An example of these different tensions can be the way Anzaldúa conceptualizes home and homecoming—it shows the problematic aspects of her work, as well as the creative and philosophical potential of it. In *Borderlands/La Frontera* Anzaldúa argues that Mexican immigrants have a right to live in the US territory that used to be part of Mexico, since it is a kind of homecoming, and of claiming the Indigenous ancestry: "*El retorno* to the promised land first began with the Indians from the interior of Mexico and the *mestizos* that came with the *conquistadores* in the 1500s. Immigration continued in the next three centuries.... Today thousands of Mexicans are crossing the border legally and illegally; ten million people without documents have returned to the Southwest."[35] The use of the terminology such as the "promised land" and "Aztlán" privileges a mythical past, while not naming, for instance, the Indigenous communities that actually inhabit today the territories that are referenced. Nonetheless, the metonymical reformulation of immigration as *el retorno*—while easily understandable for different readers, given its closeness to the English word *return*—shifts the discussion to a different ground, with a different order of rights to the land. It is not a right that is recognized in the dominant discourses or from the legal viewpoint, and so it is introduced in Spanish, a language that in the borderlands does not have the institutional power of English.[36] It shows the key term as not a straightforward, easily applicable notion: not being in the dominant language of the place—and of the text—*el retorno* underscores how the experience of crossing the border is not seamless and how believing in a right to inhabit a place does not automatically create a sense of belonging.[37]

Disbelonging is problematized further when Anzaldúa tells the anecdote of a friend who thought *homophobia* meant "fear of going home."[38] Not accepted within her community mostly because of being a queer woman, Anzaldúa perceived how meaningful this misunderstanding was. This fruitful mistake fits so tightly within the text also because of its structure of a linguistic twist, treating language as a moldable matter, which shapes and textures invite creative reorganizations. This resembles the way Anzaldúa uses bilingualism: to question what we think is obvious and to redefine what is well known. To put it in terms of rhetorical figures, it could be seen as an aphorismus, a figure of argumentation, which is "a form of refutation that questions the use of some word or phrase."[39] In other words, it focuses attention on the meaning of something seemingly clear, provoking both an inside reflection and outreaching change. Phonetically similar to aphorism, aphorismus is, philosophically, rather its opposite. Instead of "a short statement of truth or principle characterized by its depth of thought," aphorismus is a refutation of unshakable truths and principles.[40] The concept of *el retorno* showed how bilingualism, through metonymy, opens new paths for aphorismus—the displacement into a different language adds a series of particular sociopolitical concerns but also of theoretical and formal questions. Bilingualism permits new ways of constructing knowledge—rethinking concepts, genres of scholarship, and sources of research. This is apparent as well when reading scholarship on how studies on intelligence of the bilingual people were conducted. As Suzanne Romaine shows in her study, many of such projects were marked by prejudice against the command of language and mental skills of bilingual individuals. Yet studies that recognized the creative potential of bilingualism not only refuted these preconceptions, but also made it possible to subvert rigid standards of what intelligence is and of how it can be measured.[41]

Anzaldúa uses bilingualism to talk about identity and belonging in a very open way, thematized within the text. In William Carlos Williams's poetry, similar preoccupations are expressed through different strategies, yet are also strongly dependent on bilingualism. While Anzaldúa describes an open wound, Williams's poetry opens a crack that might, however, run deeper. Even though studied within the canon of poetry in English, Williams has also been read as a bilingual author, especially since Julio Marzán's *The Spanish American Roots of William Carlos Williams*.[42] Marzán pays close attention to Williams's upbringing in a Spanish-speaking home—which he sees as fundamental to the poet's creation—where he grew up hyper-aware of the social negativity toward bicultural immigrants.[43]

Williams's poetry is renowned for its spontaneous yet precise use of language. In one of his earliest collections of poems, *Al Que Quiere!* (1917), he creates what we could see as perfect objects—following Williams's imagery we could say, objects glazed with words. Bilingualism is what disturbs this seemingly solid and smooth surface, not taking away any of the precision and virtuosity of the language but making its use more problematic and the words themselves more porous. Already the title of this book of poetry poses a problem: while in Spanish—and using a grammatical structure typical for the language that is difficult to translate—it follows English orthographic rules (omitting the first exclamation mark, capitalizing all the words of the title). In the collection, we find the following poem, "El Hombre":

> It's a strange courage
> you give me ancient star:
> Shine alone in the sunrise
> toward which you lend no part![44]

The title of the poem is one of the few instances of a direct usage of Spanish in Williams's poetry. Marzán sees it as a way of showing the necessity of reading deeper into the text, acknowledging its multiple layers: "The Spanish title, then, was more than decorative; the use of Spanish called attention to an encoding, in a secret style that gravitated to the conceit, the pun, the enciphering that obliged Williams's reader, as Góngora expected of his, to 'remove the bark.' This claim, of course, contradicts Williams's reputation of the spontaneous, spoken idiom—a legacy that fits neatly into his busy biography divided between doctoring and writing."[45] It could be read as another instance of bilingual aphorismus, a questioning of notions that might appear clear—the meaning of being a man, and of language in its capacity of expressing it.

In a mere four lines the poem collapses the ungraspable past with the personal present. The voice of the poem establishes an intimate relationship with the ancient star, to which he directs himself with the words "you give me." The "courage" the star gives is "strange" and based on loneliness and on not participating in the unstoppable event that is occurring: the sunrise. This courage is coming from a combination of strength and weakness: the star is ancient yet it disappears with each sunrise (at least for the man), and it cannot break this cycle. It is the courage of disbelonging—*of* rather than *for*. The poem constructs a history for disbelonging, for solitude and for the temporal, ephemeral character of a human being. Inscribed in a duration that is not personal, this disbelonging—marked from the beginning by the use of Spanish in the title—belongs in history, led by the courage of being while not being part of.

To see how the bilingual strategies work in a different type of Williams's poem, we can read this piece with "The Desert Music": while "El Hombre" is small and compact like a stone, "The Desert Music," written almost forty years later, resembles a multipart dance. The poem struggles with many identity questions, and its setting oscillates between El Paso and Juarez. The impulse for its creation is, according to the text itself, its opening image. This image is itself a kind of an aphorismus; it is an image of estranged perception, of the surprise at the human figure, transformed by the position it is forced into:

> – the dance begins: to end about a form
> propped motionless – on the bridge
> between Juarez and El Paso – unrecognizable

```
            in the semi-dark
                                        Wait!
            The others waited while you inspected it,
            on the very walk itself.
                                        Is it alive?
                                                            – neither a head,
            legs nor arms!
                            It isn't a sack of rags someone
            has abandoned here              .       torpid against
            the flange of the supporting girder     ?
                                                    .
                            an inhuman shapelessness,
            knees hugged tight up into the belly
                    Egg-shaped!
                                                What a place to sleep!
            on the International Boundary. Where else,
            interjurisdictional, not to be disturbed?
            How shall we get said what must be said?
            Only a poem (1954, 71–72)
```

This figure, the dehumanized person turned into an unidentifiable shape, shows the violence of the in-betweenness. This violence of the border, while denounced and estranging, impels to question one's identity. The questions of national or ethnic belonging are asked, together with the question about the meaning of being a poet. All the parts of the identity that are being explored are conceptualized through performance: "the dance begins" together with the poem. The lyrical persona performs being an American, cowboy-like, macho figure, adopting a stereotypical vision of Mexico and the United States: the description of the border and the Mexican territory paints it as a seedy place, with shabby strip clubs; it is a place where numerous Mexicans ask for money on the streets, while American tourists wander around looking for bargains.[46] At one point of the poem, its protagonist detaches himself straightforwardly from the Latin American, forming a complaint that starts with "What else, Latins, do you yourself / seek but relief"—not only does "you" create a sense of excluding oneself from this group, but it is also stressed by the following "yourself," so there is no space left to doubt.[47] Yet he sabotages his own performance, showing the cracks in it. When performing being overly American, "tequila" is deliberately—and exaggeratingly—misspelled as "techilla."[48] However, a phrase in Spanish is introduced seamlessly and without mistakes: "– paper flowers (para los santos)."[49] The main voice of the poem introduces in his speech verbal constructions that are not idiomatic in English, but are based on Spanish grammar or vocabulary. We read about the stripper he is watching:

```
                                            in her mockery of virtue
            she becomes unaccountably virtuous.
                                            though she in no
            way pretends it. (83)
```

The last line does not fit any of the standard uses of the word "pretend." However, saying "no lo pretende" in this context would be a common phrase in Spanish, implying a lack of aspiration to virtue on the part of the performer. Similarly, we read about a woman "inciting her man," which echoes the Spanish "incitar," but is a dissonance in English, where one would rather speak about "provoking" or "teasing."[50] Or, in the complaint of the lyrical persona "My feet are beginning to ache me" we see a transposition of the Spanish reflexive form of expressing pain, "*me* duelen los pies."[51] These subtle irruptions of Spanish are concentrated in verbs, which is meaningful, given the orientation towards action and motion of the poem. The second to last stanza of the poem reads:

> Now the music volleys through as in
> a lonely moment I hear it.                     Now it is all
> about me.                The dance!            The verb detaches itself
> seeking to become articulate                   . (90)

The verb that detaches itself, and articulates what we can see as a performance of the self, also shows the complexities of the performance, thanks to the bilingual play that the verbs are entangled in. This metonymic swapping of words leads to displacement within the performance displayed. Marzán writes that "Williams' Latin half revealed itself as his spiritual center. His major creative achievement was his translating the exotic voice of that core into the voice of an Anglo persona amenable to a reading public that conventionally held in low regard that most important component of his historical person."[52] "The Desert Music" shows the relationship as more complex: the presence of the Spanish does not really exoticize the text; rather, it reveals itself in a subtle yet structurally crucial manner. The performance of the US-American is questioned through it, putting both identities in crisis, stressing the disbelonging.

Anzaldúa and Williams both alter and combine forms: different genres and registers of writing, the spoken word and oral tradition, and musical rhythms. In both, moreover, the visual plays a major role. Anzaldúa's essays oscillate between different rhythms of prose and poetry, which are clearly visible on the page as in this passage of the poem opening the first chapter of *Borderlands/La Frontera*:

> 1,950 mile-long open wound
> dividing a *pueblo*, a culture,
> running down the length of my body,
>     staking fence rods in my flesh
>     splits me                                  splits me
>             me raja                            me raja
> This is my home
> this thin edge of
>         barbwire (2–3)

The poem's phrases are cut into uneven verses, also separated inside of them by long blank spaces. The spatial organization of the poem seems to visualize the central verb of the stanza, *rajar*, crucial to the notion of *la herida abierta* introduced by Anzaldúa in this essay and important for the tradition of debates on Mexican identity.[53] *Rajar* condenses in itself multiple concepts Anzaldúa discusses in her work: the discrimination of women, who become themselves an open wound, converges with the description of the boarder as *la herida abierta*, where the penetration between the inside and the outside becomes the central conflict. It brings to mind another image used by Anzaldúa: in *Light in the Dark/Luz en lo oscuro* she uses Coyolxauhqui as a metaphor for her writing:

> I am often driven by the impulse to write something down, by the desire and urgency to communicate, to make meaning, to make sense of things, to create myself through this knowledge-producing act. I call this impulse the "Coyolxauhqui imperative": a struggle to reconstruct oneself and heal the sustos resulting from woundings, traumas, racism, and other acts of violation que hechan pedazos nuestras almas, split us, scatter our energies, and haunt us.[54]

While—as discussed previously—the use of mythological figures in Anzaldúa's writing is problematic, seen from the point of view of art history, rather than mythology, this image is another interesting translation of the verb *rajar* into visual terms.[55] Coyolxauhqui's dismembered body was represented in Templo Mayor of Tenochtitlan. It was a round relief, in which Coyolxauhqui's body was represented in pieces, which seem to spin in a constant circular movement. As Matos Moctezuma describes, when the human sacrifices were made on the altar of Huitzilopochtli, the blood streamed down the stairs onto the figure of Coyolxauhqui, thus reenacting the mythological narration.[56] Architecture, sculpture, and ritual meet: writing makes use of it, and the poem in the beginning of *Borderlands/La Frontera* is composed of similarly dismembered words, words that come to pieces because *se rajan*; they split, they open. Bilingualism splits words: they are no longer coherent, compact, or united. Yet, this way, they are constantly actualized into a flowing narration.

In Williams, similarly, it is the visual composition of the poems that creates their rhythm: the way the verses are cut and enclosed into forms. It is not the meter changing, just the spatial organization; yet it indicates different voices or changes in place and atmosphere. Not all the poem's words start from the same point, nor come to end along the same axis. The spaces and periods become loquacious.

```
              - paper flowers (para los santos)
    baked red-clay utensils, daubed
    with blue, silverware,
    dried peppers, onions, print goods, children's
    clothing               .        the place deserted all but

    for a few Indians squatted in the
    booths, unnoticing (don't you think it)
    as though they slept there       . (76)
```

It this passage, the first verse starts with a visual line, as if marking a lost beginning of the phrase. After the enumeration of the objects and colors, the space divided by a period can stand for both multiplicity and nothingness: the list could be continued, but the blank space prepares us already for the desertion of the place. The spatialization of the poem makes the parenthesis regain its visual meaning, estranging it from its usual usage through the plasticity of the poem. The brackets enclose the words as a container would, marking them as second or secondary thoughts. They impede them from spilling throughout the text—limiting the Spanish words, or the words that reveal worry and unease. The last period of the stanza is distanced from the last word, implying a hesitation rather than a closure. The visuality of the poem forces the reader to see and hear it differently, letting more voices filter in.

Williams and Anzaldúa are both concerned with time and space: they give their words plasticity, try to connect the "ancient star" to themselves, or to see the wound through a mythical eye. Both situating themselves in the fragile and violent space of the border, they give different responses to the experience of disbelonging: a more violent one in the case of Anzaldúa, a more uneasy one in the case of Williams. The texts show also a desire for belonging: in Anzaldúa, a constant and open attempt to affirm the existence of a home; in Williams's poetry, an insistent performance of the belonging that constantly subverts itself, showing the complexity and beauty of a failed performance. It produces a certain resentment: the indignation and bitterness coming from the frustration of the desire. Resentment, however, also in the sense of the strength of the feeling—if we look at the etymology of the word *resent*, it comes from the French "sentir," to feel, strengthened by the prefix "re," signifying intensity. While in previously analyzed texts, the strength of feelings was let loose through an uncontrollable—though neatly calculated in its exaggeration—enthusiasm, here it causes an implosion of the words, which need to be reconstructed in bilingual, or multilingual, constellations. Redefining concepts and redrawing images is also a way of looking at a complicated, traumatic past. Heather Love proposes a way of looking at such a past:

> A central paradox of any transformative criticism is that it dreams for the future are founded on a history of suffering, stigma, and violence. Oppositional criticism opposes not only existing structures of power but also the very history that gives it meaning.... For groups constituted by historical injury, the challenge is to engage with the past without being destroyed by it. Sometimes it seems it would be better to move on—to let, as Marx wrote, the dead bury the dead. But it is the damaging aspects of the past that tend to stay with us, and the desire to forget may itself be a symptom of haunting. The dead can bury the dead all day long and still not be done.[57]

Love writes about constructing the past of queer communities, yet her theory can prove to be productive in this context as well. This approach goes against the logic of progress—similarly as we could see in Cabrera Infante and Vega, who dismantled fantasies of the future. It offers a look back, initiating a painful yet constructive process. The destruction of words leads to destruction of discourses, but this is also opening a space and allowing redefinitions, while the metonymic structures remind one constantly of the existence of the unattainable.

In these texts, identity is at stake, since it is closely linked with belonging. Love discusses similar issues in terms of queer identities: "Homosexual identity is indelibly marked by the effects of reverse discourse: on the one hand, it continues to be understood as a form of damaged or compromised subjectivity; on the other hand, the characteristic forms of gay freedom are produced in response to this history."[58] A similar process occurs in the bilingual texts—even though they do not hide the pain and suffering brought by the disbelonging, they open different spaces of freedom. In his poem *Convocación de palabras* (1994), Tino Villanueva introduces, in the predominantly Spanish text, foreign words that he had to learn when he tried to integrate into US society. All the foreign words are in italics, marking their strangeness. The last word of the poem, *libertad*, though Spanish, is also stressed by the use of italics.[59] This subtle, visual note that ends the poem responds to this need of a new freedom and encourages the formation of this space. Ana Lydia Vega's short story opens with the words of Albert Memmi: "Un homme à cheval sur deux cultures est rarement bien assis."[60] In the analyzed texts, straddling two cultures or languages indeed provokes discomfort. Yet the authors take advantage of this position. They manage to transform being torn apart into an opening space, where more movements are possible.

There are many reasons for the strangeness of the knight's move, the main one being the conventionality of art, about which I am writing.

The second reason lies in the fact that the knight is not free—it moves in an L-shaped manner because it is forbidden to take a straight road.[61]

Bilingual authors move like the knight described by Victor Shklovsky. The knight is not free, yet it has Williams's "strange courage," which gives the knight a strange freedom. Their road is not straight, the two horses make it only less comfortable, but this does not stop them from taking it.

## Notes

1. Doris Sommer, *Bilingual Aesthetics: A New Sentimental Education* (Durham, NC: Duke University Press, 2004), xiii.
2. At the same time, following Wittgenstein, we can trace the serious and philosophical "language games," which are at play in bilingualism. See Doris Sommer, *Bilingual Aesthetics: A New Sentimental Education* (Durham, NC: Duke University Press, 2004).
3. Sommer, *Bilingual Aesthetics*, xix–xx.
4. Lauren Berlant, *Cruel Optimism* (Durham, NC: Duke University Press, 2011), 16.
5. Roman Jakobson, *Fundamentals of Language* (The Hague: Mouton, 1971), 90–96.
6. Jacques Lacan, "The Agency of the Letter in the Unconscious or Reason Since Freud (1957)," in *Écrits: A Selection*, trans. Alan Sheridan (New York: W.W. Norton, 1977), 156.
7. Lacan, "The Agency of the Letter in the Unconscious or Reason Since Freud (1957)," 169–170.
8. Lacan, "The Agency of the Letter in the Unconscious or Reason Since Freud (1957)," 175.
9. Lacan, "The Agency of the Letter in the Unconscious or Reason Since Freud (1957)," 158.

10. Víctor Hernández Cruz, *Snaps* (New York: Random House, 1969), 8.
11. Ludwig Wittgenstein, *Philosophical Investigations* (Oxford: Basil Blackwell, 1968), 71.
12. These bilingual strategies are inscribed in the history of colonialism and imperialism, and as such could be also seen in relation to Homi Bhabha's theory of mimicry, which he defines based on the axis of metonymy and metaphor. See Homi Bhabha, "Of Mimicry and Man: The Ambivalence of Colonial Discourse," *October* 28 (1984): 125–133.
13. Guillermo Cabrera Infante, *Tres tristes tigres* (Barcelona: Biblioteca de Bolsillo, 1991), 15.
14. Cabrera Infante, *Tres tristes tigres*, 16.
15. Cabrera Infante, *Tres tristes tigres*, 9.
16. Cabrera Infante, *Tres tristes tigres*, 19.
17. Cabrera Infante, *Tres tristes tigres*, 15–16.
18. Cabrera Infante, *Tres tristes tigres*, 19.
19. Ana Lydia Vega, "Pollito Chicken," in *Vírgenes y mártires*, ed. Ana Lydia Vega and Carmen Lugo Filippi, 73–80 (Río Piedras, Mexico: Editorial Antillana, 1994), 75.
20. Vega, "Pollito Chicken," 75.
21. Despite a seemingly third-person narration, the narrator's voice is intermingled with Suzie's own thoughts in a way that makes it impossible to separate them in a clear fashion.
22. Heinrich Lausberg, *Handbook of Literary Rhetoric: A Foundation for Literary Study* (Leiden: Brill, 1998), 268.
23. Lausberg, *Handbook of Literary Rhetoric*, 269.
24. Vega, "Pollito Chicken," 79.
25. Vega, "Pollito Chicken," 79.
26. So far, many scholars read this ending of a story—both right after its publication and more recently—as a viable and trustworthy account of what happened, and thus have analyzed it as an actual expression of the protagonist's feelings or views that were suppressed. See, for instance, Diana L. Vélez, "*Pollito Chicken*: Split Subjectivity, National Identity and The Articulation of Female Sexuality in a Narrative by Ana Lydia Vega," *The Americas Review* 14, no. 2 (1986): 73; and see Megan Jeanette Myers, "Ana Lydia Vega's *Pollito Chicken*: Stripped to the Bone," *Caribe: Revista de Cultura y Literatura* 15, no. 1 (2012): 47–66. Vélez argues that "the laughter at the end, the reader's pleasure, comes from the literal undermining of Suzie's self-hating discourse by another voice, one which has been denied entry into the text as spoken." It can be argued, however, that the pleasure coming from the text is more complex and problematic.
27. Scholars have underscored Vega's importance in denouncing sexism. For instance, Juan G. Gelpi writes: "Con la narrativa de Ana Lydia Vega se cruza un límite, una frontera: en ella estamos decididamente fuera del canon paternalista" (1993, 96). Juan G. Gelpi, "Ana Lydia Vega: Ante el debate de la cultura nacional de Puerto Rico." *Revista Chilena de Literatura* 42 (1993): 95–99.
28. Berlant, *Cruel Optimism*, 2.
29. Berlant, *Cruel Optimism*, 13.
30. Gloria Anzaldúa, *Light in The Dark/Luz en lo oscuro: Rewriting Identity, Spirituality, Reality* (Durham, NC: Duke University Press, 2015), 25.
31. We could read Anzaldúa's text in refernce to the tradition of the theoretical and political vindication of Hélène Cixous's "Le Rire de la Méduse" (1975). Her description is alike in its assertion of political and artistic rights of women and of diversity of sexualities but also uses similar strategies to attain it, referring to the bodily aspect of writing and making

reference to mythical cultural foundations. In Cixous's case this means returning to Greek mythology, while for Anzaldúa it means looking back to Aztec mythology.

32. See Josefina Saldaña-Portillo, "Who's the Indian in Aztlán? Re-Writing Mestizaje, Indianism, and Chicanismo from the Lacandón," in *The Latin American Subaltern Reader*, ed. Ileana Rodríguez (Durham, NC: Duke University Press, 2001), 402–423. Saldaña-Portillo writes, "We must take seriously the Zapatista movement's critique of mestizaje and indigenismo as parallel ideologies that incorporate the figure of Indian in the consolidation of a nationalist identity in order to effectively exclude contemporary Indians. Thus, in our Chicano reappropiation of the biologized terms of mestizaje and indigenismo, we are also always recuperating the Indian as an ancestral part rather than recognizing contemporary Indians as coinhabitants not only of this continent abstractly conceived, but of the neighborhoods and streets of hundreds of U.S. cities and towns." Saldaña-Portillo shows also that the apparent attempt to recuperate the Indigenous culture, such as the Aztec myths, is a repetition of a state-sponsored campaign of restitution of mythic elements of the past, as a substitute for dealing with the contemporary Indigenous communities.

33. The authors of *Border Women. Writing from La Frontera* claim that "Anzaldúa's book, despite its multiple crossings of cultural and gender borders—from ethnicity to feminisms, from the academic realm to the work of blue-collar labor—tends to essentialize relations between Mexico and the United States. Her third country between the two nations, the borderlands, is still a metaphorical country defined and narrated from a First World perspective" (see Debra A. Castillo, Tabuenca Córdoba, and María Socorro, "Reading the Border, North and South," in *Border Women: Writing from La Frontera*, ed. Debra A. Castillo and María Socorro Tabuenca (Minneapolis: University of Minnesota Press, 2002), 1–32. These scholars argue that Anzaldúa's texts try and construct memory based on myth and attempt to offer a catharsis, while the wound cannot be closed—especially not one-sidedly.

34. Anzaldúa, *Light in The Dark/Luz en lo oscuro*; similar strategies, like the use of different genres, have been taken up by other scholars, especially within Chicano studies, for instance, in Alberto Arteaga's 1997 *Chicano Poetics*.

35. Anzaldúa, *Light in The Dark/Luz en lo oscuro*, 33.

36. The text problematizes, however, the status of Spanish as well, since it recalls the Spanish conquest, which led to the exploitation of the Indigenous population and resulted in their displacement to what is now the US Southwest.

37. It is interesting to contrapose diverse attempts of resignification linked to the (post-) colonial experience of different Latinx and Latin American groups. A good example to contrast with Anzaldúa's text would be the work of Luz María De la Torre Amaguaña's, who in "¿Qué significa ser mujer indígena en la contemporaneidad?" (2010) uses similar strategies yet proposes a different project in terms of the perspective of Indigeneity and construction of identity.

38. Anzaldúa, *Light in The Dark/Luz en lo oscuro*, 19–20.

39. Jack Myers, *Dictionary of Poetic Terms* (Denton: University of North Texas Press, 2003), 22.

40. Myers, *Dictionary of Poetic Terms*, 22.

41. Suzanne Romaine, *Bilingualism* (Cambridge, MA: Blackwell, 1995), 107–119.

42. Julio Marzán, *The Spanish American Roots of William Carlos Williams* (Austin: University of Texas Press, 1994), 6.

43. Nowadays, we can observe a certain duality in the way Williams is studied: while he still forms part of the canon of poetry in English, he also appears in publications such as anthologies of Latinx literature.
44. William Carlos Williams, "Al Que Quiere!" in *The Collected Poems of William Carlos Williams*, ed. A. Walton Litz and Christopher MacGowan, vol. 1. (New York: New Directions, 1986), 76.
45. Marzán, *The Spanish American Roots*, 4.
46. Williams has been described by many scholars as a poet crucial for the construction of American modernism, responding to and performing many aspects of what is seen as the core of the US-American and the modern (see Laleh Atashi, "The Status of William Carlos Williams in American Modernism," *Messages, Sages, and Ages* 3, no. 2 (2016): 54–63.
47. William Carlos Williams, *The Desert Music and Other Poems* (New York: Random House, 1954) 88.
48. Williams, *The Desert Music and Other Poems* 75.
49. Williams, *The Desert Music and Other Poems* 76.
50. Williams, *The Desert Music and Other Poems*, 84.
51. This operation is similar to the "mistakes" that appeared in Cabrera Infante's work. While for some readers these expressions might simply sound strange, others will see in them a bilingual wink. This shows again the diversification of both the pleasures and the audiences of the texts—as argued in *Bilingual Games*, "the days of the one ideal reader have been numbered and spent in our segmented societies. A 'target audience' today can mean the target of exclusion or confusion." See Doris Sommer, "Introduction," in *Bilingual Games: Some Literary Investigations*, ed. Doris Sommer (New York: Palgrave Macmillan, 2003), 1–18.
52. Marzán, *The Spanish American Roots*, xi.
53. See Octavio Paz, *El Laberinto de la Soledad* (Mexico City: Fondo de Cultura Económica, 1998), 10. Paz writes at length about the concept of *rajar*, describing how "el lenguaje popular refleja hasta qué punto nos defendemos del exterior: el ideal de la 'hombría' consiste en no 'rajarse' nunca. Los que se 'abren' son cobardes. Para nosotros, contrariamente a lo que ocurre con otros pueblos, abrirse es una debilidad o una traición. El mexicano puede doblarse, humillarse, 'agacharse,' pero no 'rajarse,' esto es, permitir que el mundo exterior penetre en su intimidad. El 'rajado' es de poco fiar, un traidor o un hombre de dudosa fidelidad, que cuenta los secretos y es incapaz de afrontar los peligros como se debe. Las mujeres son seres inferiores porque, al entregarse, se abren. Su inferioridad es constitucional y radica en su sexo, en su 'rajada,' herida que jamás cicatriza."
54. Anzaldúa, *Borderlands/La Frontera*, 1.
55. In this case, also the choice of the figure itself is problematic. Coyolxauhqui tried to kill her mother because she was pregnant with an unknown person, thus incarnating a certain normative and conservative force; this force was then overcome by the new sibling that was born. Eduardo Matos Moctezuma, "Archaeology & Symbolism in Aztec Mexico: The Templo Mayor of Tenochtitlan," *Journal of the American Academy of Religion* 53, no. 4 (1985): 797–813.
56. Anzaldúa, *Borderlands/La Frontera*, 199–200.
57. Heather Love, *Feeling Backward: Loss and the Politics of Queer History* (Cambridge, MA: Harvard University Press, 2007), 1.
58. Love, *Feeling Backward*, 2.

59. Tino Villanueva, "Convocación de palabras," in *The Multilingual Anthology of American Literature: A Reader of Original Texts with English Translations*, ed. Marc Shell and Werner Sollors (New York: New York University Press, 2000), 678.
60. Vega, "Pollito Chicken," 75.
61. Victor Shklovsky. *Knight's Move* (Normal, IL: Dalkey Archive Press, 2005), 3.

## Bibliography

Anzaldúa, Gloria. *Borderlands/La Frontera. The New Mestiza*. San Francisco: Aunt Lute, 1987.
Anzaldúa, Gloria. *Light in The Dark/Luz en lo oscuro. Rewriting Identity, Spirituality, Reality*. Durham, NC: Duke University Press, 2015.
Arteaga, Alberto. *Chicano Poetics. Heterotexts and Hybridites*. Cambridge, UK: Cambridge University Press, 1997.
Atashi, Laleh. "The Status of William Carlos Williams in American Modernism." *Messages, Sages, and Ages* 3, no. 2 (2016): 54–63.
Berlant, Lauren. *Cruel Optimism*. Durham, NC: Duke University Press, 2011.
Bhabha, Homi. "Of Mimicry and Man: The Ambivalence of Colonial Discourse." *October* 28 (1984): 125–133.
Cabrera Infante, Guillermo. *Tres tristes tigres*. Barcelona: Biblioteca de Bolsillo, 1991.
Castillo, Debra A., Tabuenca Córdoba, and María Socorro. "Reading the Border, North and South." In *Border Women. Writing from La Frontera*, edited by Debra A. Castillo and María Socorro Tabuenca, 1–32. Minneapolis: University of Minnesota Press, 2002.
Cixous, Hélène. "Le Rire de la Méduse." *L'Arc* 61 (1975): 39–54.
De la Torre Amaguaña, Luz María. "¿Qué significa ser mujer indígena en la contemporaneidad?" *Mester* 39, no. 1 (2010): 1–25.
Didi-Huberman, Georges. *Quelle émotion! Quelle émotion?* Montrouge: Bayard, 2013.
Gelpi, Juan G. "Ana Lydia Vega: Ante el debate de la cultura nacional de Puerto Rico." *Revista Chilena de Literatura* 42 (1993): 95–99.
Hernández Cruz, Víctor. *Snaps*. New York: Random House, 1969.
Hernández Cruz, Víctor. *By Linugal Wholes*. San Francisco: Momo's, 1982.
Jakobson, Roman. *Fundamentals of Language*. The Hague and Paris: Mouton, 1971.
Lacan, Jacques. "The Agency of the Letter in the Unconscious or Reason Since Freud (1957)." In *Écrits: A Selection*, translated by Alan Sheridan, 146–175. New York: W.W. Norton, 1977.
Lausberg, Heinrich. *Handbook of Literary Rhetoric: A Foundation for Literary Study*. Leiden: Brill, 1998.
Love, Heather. *Feeling Backward. Loss and the Politics of Queer History*. Cambridge, MA: Harvard University Press, 2007.
Marzán, Julio. *The Spanish American Roots of William Carlos Williams*. Austin: University of Texas Press, 1994.
Matos Moctezuma, Eduardo. "Symbolism of the Templo Mayor." In *The Aztec Templo Mayor*, edited by E. Boone, 185–210. Washington DC: Dumbarton Oaks, 1987.
Myers, Jack. *Dictionary of Poetic Terms*. Denton: University of North Texas Press, 2003.
Myers, Megan Jeanette. "Ana Lydia Vega's *Pollito Chicken*: Stripped to the Bone." *Caribe: Revista de Cultura y Literatura*, 15, no. 1 (2012): 47–66.
Paz, Octavio. *El Laberinto de la Soledad*. Mexico City: Fondo de Cultura Económica, 1998.
Pérez Firmat, Gustavo. *Tongue Ties. Logo-Eroticism in Anglo-Hispanic Literature*. New York: Palgrave Macmillan, 2003.

Romaine, Suzanne. *Bilingualism*. Cambridge, MA: Blackwell, 1995.

Saldaña-Portillo, Josefina. "Who's the Indian in Aztlán? Re-Writing Mestizaje, Indianism, and Chicanismo from the Lacandón." In *The Latin American Subaltern Reader*, edited by Ileana Rodríguez, 402–423. Durham, NC: Duke University Press, 2001.

Shklovsky, Victor. *Knight's Move*. Normal, IL: Dalkey Archive Press, 2005.

Sommer, Doris. "Introduction." In *Bilingual Games: Some Literary Investigations*, edited by Doris Sommer, 1–18. New York: Palgrave Macmillan, 2003.

Sommer, Doris. *Bilingual Aesthetics: A New Sentimental Education*. Durham, NC: Duke University Press, 2004.

Vega, Ana Lydia. "Pollito Chicken." In *Vírgenes y mártires*, edited by Ana Lydia Vega and Carmen Lugo Filippi, 73–80. Río Piedras, Mexico: Editorial Antillana, 1994.

Vélez, Diana L. "*Pollito Chicken*: Split Subjectivity, National Identity and the Articulation of Female Sexuality in a Narrative by Ana Lydia Vega." *The Americas Review* 14, no. 2 (1986), 68–76.

Villanueva, Tino. "Convocación de palabras." In *The Multilingual Anthology of American Literature: A Reader of Original Texts with English Translations*, edited by Marc Shell and Werner Sollors, 678. New York: New York University Press, 2000.

Williams, William Carlos. *The Desert Music and Other Poems*. New York: Random House, 1954.

Williams, William Carlos. *Al Que Quiere!* In *The Collected Poems of William Carlos Williams*, edited by A. Walton Litz and Christopher MacGowan, Vol. 1. New York: New Directions, 1986.

Wittgenstein, Ludwig. *Philosophical Investigations*. Oxford: Basil Blackwell, 1968.

CHAPTER 15

# ALWAYS IN TRANSLATION
## Ways of Writing in Spanish and English

### REGINA GALASSO

In the early 2000s, as a doctoral student at Johns Hopkins University, my research interests were strongly tied to taking the scholarship of the early twentieth-century New York literary production of writers from Spain and Latin America beyond a study of a single author or single national group. I wanted to look beyond the foundational authors associated with the city such as José Martí (b. 1853–d. 1895) and Federico García Lorca (b. 1898–d. 1936), spotlight overlooked authors and texts, and identify how the city influenced their work as something more than a fascinating physical site to describe. I was also determined to identify how the city was present in their literature besides being a place that inspires a love-hate relationship with its dwellers. At the same time, I wanted to examine what the synergies might be among the literature of writers from Spain and Latin America in the context of a city that produced the most pan-Hispanic periodicals in the world according to Nicolás Kanellos (b. United States, 1945–) and Helvetia Martell, an aspect of the city's dynamic culture that further was endorsed in 2010 by Mexican-born New York–based author Carmen Boullosa (b. Mexico, 1954–) in her essay "Notes on Writing in Spanish in New York."[1]

As a result, my early research recovered texts that fell outside the established boundaries within the discipline of Spanish and Latin American literary studies as practiced in the United States. For instance, the pages from the early years of the Spanish-language daily newspaper *La prensa* tried to transcend national boundaries in a variety of ways. They brought together announcements and news about writers from all over Spain, Latin America, and the United States. Writers competed against each other in literary contests and made the headlines when they arrived at the docks in New York harbor. *La prensa* also made room to welcome beginning speakers of Spanish by offering language lessons within the newspaper's own pages. In its early years, *La prensa* had a notably inclusive nature welcoming all speakers of Spanish including individuals interested in learning the language. Further, I studied the New York writing of Julio Camba (b. 1884–d. 1962) and José Moreno Villa (b. 1887–d. 1955), who as writers from Spain visited the city in the first half of the twentieth century, hidden in the shadow of Lorca's visit and his resulting *The Poet in New York and Other Poems* (1940). Intended for an audience in Spain, their work engaged the sounds of the city along with English and other languages in constructive ways for thinking about how a city is put into words for faraway readers. Additionally, I studied two texts that depict the immigrant experience in the city: *Lucas Guevara* (1914) by Alirio Díaz Guerra (b. Colombia, 1862–d. New York, ca. 1925), and *La vida real* (1986) by Miguel Barnet (b. Cuba, 1940–). Although *Luca Guevara* is said to be the first novel of the Latin American immigrant experience to the United States written in Spanish (Browitt) and *La vida real* is authored by one of the foundational authors of novelas de testimonio and about a Cuban who moves from the countryside to Havana and then on the Florida and New York, neither example of immigrant literature had a visible place among the texts endorsed by the discipline. Originally published in New York City in 1914, *Lucas Guevara* had fallen out of circulation until Kanellos found a copy of it at the New York Public Library and reprinted it in 2001 via his publishing house Arte Público Press and subsequently commissioned its English translation by Ethriam Cash Brammer de González, published in 2003. *La vida real* being the fourth in Barnet's series of novelas de testimonio was released in 1986, a few years prior to the release of Cristina Garcia's *Dreaming in Cuban* (1992), a book in English that deservingly took the spotlight of the Cuban experience in the United States as well as that of Latino literature.

When I state that my general research interests involve Spanish-language writers in the United States and more specifically in New York, I am repeatedly asked about Latino literature. However, when I initially embarked on customizing my research interests, my main goal was to broaden how we understand the relationship between New York and Spanish and Latin American literary production. Not only did I want to look beyond individual, mostly canonical writers, or single national literatures, but I also wanted to see how New York City has been part of the Spanish-speaking world beyond its landmark place in Latino literature. Strong connections surfaced among the directions of my work and Latino literature. For example, Lorca figured prominently in the writing of Jaime Manrique (b. Colombia, 1949–). The New York–based writer, educator, and translator authored two novels that feature Lorca: *My Night with / Mi noche con Federico García Lorca* (1995), published as a bilingual edition with English translations by Edith Grossman and Eugene Richie, and *Maricones eminentes (Arenas, Lorca, Puig and Me)* (1999), first published in English and a year later translated by Juan Camacho and published in Spanish. *La prensa* eventually became what is today's New York *El diario*, a newspaper read by a largely Latino audience. *Lucas Guevara*, although not widely studied, is one of the foundational texts of Latino literature. *La vida real* was published at a time when Latino studies became an established part of departments and programs at universities in the United States, and further diversified representations of sentiment toward Cuba held by Cubans living in the United States who were born in Cuba. Given my scholarly desire to explore the literature of Spain within a pan-Hispanic framework of New York, the most provoking encounter between my early research and Latino literature came when I learned about Felipe Alfau (b. Spain, 1902–d. 1999), author of the novel *Chromos*. *Chromos* received a nomination for the 1990 National Book Award alongside *Paradise* by Elena Castedo (b. Spain, 1937–), who was born in Barcelona, raised in Chile, and later moved to the United States. During the same year *The Mambo Kings Play Songs of Love: A Novel* by Oscar Hijuelos (b. United States, 1951–d. 2013) won the Pulitzer Prize for Fiction, and Octavio Paz (b. 1914–d. 1998) won the Nobel Prize for Literature, making 1990 a notable year for writers of Spanish-speaking descent.

## Intralingual Translation

*Chromos* focused on a group of characters from Spain living in New York as they went about their daily life, mostly ruminating about language, place, expression, and storytelling. *Chromos*, however, was not written in or close to the 1990s. Alfau wrote it about forty years earlier, during the 1950s, when he was well settled in New York after having lived with his family in the Basque Country, the Philippines, and the Caribbean. He and his family reached New York around 1916, when the Barcelona-born Alfau was about fourteen years of age. Alfau came from a family of writers and politicians. His parents were Antonio Abad Alfau Baralt, "influyente abogado y orador" 'influential lawyer and public speaker" and Eugenia Galván Velázquez.[2] His maternal grandfather Manuel de Jesús Galván (b. 1834–d. 1910) was a Dominican diplomat, journalist, politician, and novelist, best known for the historical novel *Enriquillo*, published in 1879. Vicki L. Ruiz and Virginia Sánchez Korrol note that *Enriquillo* is "one of the better-known and best-regarded *indianista* (idealize Indian-themed) novels in the Spanish Caribbean and Latin America."[3] Alfau's sister Jesusa Alfau Galván de Solalinde (b. 1890–d. 1943), like her grandfather, has been associated with Dominican literature. Mostly writing in Spanish, she authored the novel *Los débiles*, published in Spain in 1912, while a teenager and later wrote essays "meant to interpret for many in the Latino communities, within and outside the United States, customs and values of North American culture" for *Las Novedades*, published in the United States and edited by her father.[4] In New York the Alfau siblings engaged with the Iberian and Latin American communities. Jesusa and Felipe's family socialized with the family of the Uruguayan painter and writer Joaquin Torres García (b. 1874–d. 1949). Jesusa married Spanish-born Antonio G. Solalinde (b. 1892–1937), a distinguished professor of Hispanic studies. Felipe took classes, possibly with Professor Federico de Onís (b. 1888–d. 1966), one of the pillars of US Hispanism as founder of the Spanish Department at Columbia and was involved with the *La Pred. nsa*. Just like his sister, Felipe contributed to the Spanish-language New York daily. Though unlike his sister he bypassed providing explanations about US culture for a curious audience abroad. Instead, he wrote music criticism demonstrating an investment in the local scene. These pieces for *La Prensa* and his poetry are the only known writing that Felipe produced in Spanish. Felipe published more in English than Jesusa. In 1929, he authored a book of children's stories *Old Tales from Spain* in English and his two novels, *Locos* (1936) and *Chromos*, were also in English. During his day job, he moved between

Spanish and English as a translator at Morgan Bank in lower Manhattan for many years. Immersed in a professional context with the Spanish language within the city of New York during the twentieth century and socializing with speakers of Spanish from different regions of the Spanish-speaking world exposed Felipe and Jesusa to the different variants of Spanish, not to mention the other languages that must have influenced their own writing and expression. Therefore, intralingual translation, "an interpretation of verbal signs by means of other signs of the same language" or interpreting one variant of Spanish so that it is understood by users of another, was a part of Jesusa's and Felipe's life in New York City, and that should be noted in critical considerations of their writing.[5]

In *Across the Lines: Travel, Language, Translation*, translation theorist and scholar Michael Cronin suggests that intralingual translation "is often disguised by writers and critics to create the illusion of linguistic transparency."[6] Further as intralingual translation happens within the same language, it has the potential to be seen as an uncomplicated task. This overlooked mode of translation, however, is an ever-present characteristic within Spanish in New York and other Spanish-speaking communities throughout the United States. One of Alfau's successors, Eduardo Lago (b. Spain, 1954–), the New York–based scholar, writer, and translator into Spanish of Junot Díaz (b. Dominican Republic, 1968–) among others, won Spain's Premio Nadal for *Llámame Brooklyn* in early 2006. Despite the novel's cast of characters that includes speakers of different variants of Spanish, critics do not note dramatic alterations in the Spanish of *Llámame Brooklyn*. On the contrary, Lago confesses that when he travels to Spain, his "accent seems distorted," and that he sometimes makes lexical choices associated with Mexican or Chilean Spanish (Rodríguez Martorell). Along with fellow Spanish-speaking, New York–based writers Carmen Boullosa (b. Mexico, 1954–), José Manuel Prieto (b. Cuba, 1962–), Naief Yehya (b. Mexico, 1963–), Sylvia Molloy (b. Argentina, 1938–), and Eduardo Mitre (b. Bolivia, 1943–), Lago founded Café Nueva York, a group of writers who work in Spanish and live in New York, and wrote the "Manifiesto Neoyorkino" calling for greater attention to the long tradition of writers from Latin America and Spain who have lived in the New York City. Thus, interacting with Spanish speakers from four different countries calls for intralingual translation as a large part of his communication.

When Lago enters the literary scene, New York is incomparably diverse with regard to the Spanish language. Antonio Muñoz Molina, who spends about half of his time in New York, in a 2007 essay describes the city as the "mejor atalaya para entender la lengua Española...en Estados Unidos...best observation point from which to understand the Spanish language" in his essay "Paisajes del idioma: Spanish in New York: A Moving Landscape."[7] Muñoz Molina says that the city serves as a place "donde confluyen todos los ríos del idioma, todos los acentos" (n.p.) or rather a "confluence for all rivers of the language, for every accent."[8] Besides listing the variations from Cuba, Mexico, the Dominican Republic, Puerto Rico, Guatemala, Colombia, River Plate, Bolivia, and Chile, Muñoz Molina adds that one is able to hear "la más rara, la más antigua de las hablas españolas, el judeoespañol que algunos hijos y nietos—nietos sobre todo—de emigrantes llegados del antiguo imperio otomano quisieran nostálgicamente recobrar" and "the rarest, the oldest of Spanish argots, the Judeo-Spanish that some of the children and grandchildren—especially the grandchildren—of immigrants from the old Ottoman Empire now nostalgically wish to recover."[9] Muñoz Molina expresses that such a linguistic situation does not call for confusion. On the contrary, in the city:

> Todas las variantes son inmediatamente inteligibles para cualquiera que hable la lengua: en vez de limitarla, la enriquecen, porque nos enseñan formas de nombrar las cosas que son distintas de las nuestras y sin embargo nunca nos niegan su significado, con sólo prestar un poco de atención.
> Each and every variation is immediately intelligible for anyone who speaks the language: Instead of limiting it, they enrich it, because they teach us ways of calling things that are different from our own and yet never deny us their meaning—as long as we are paying attention.[10]

Intralingual translation is an integral part of Spanish-speaking communities in New York and an act that highlights language choice and often calls for justification and linguistic and cultural growth, as speakers are asked to provide definitions, rephrase, and expand their vocabulary. Sherry Simon, a literary scholar who writes about translation and the urban experience, in her book *Cities in Translation: Intersections of Language and Memory* says that "accents, code-switching and translation are to be valued for the ways in which they interrupt the self-sufficiencies of 'mono' cultures."[11] Thus, one dynamic dimension of the Latino cultural and literary experience includes interruption within the Spanish language, or a space to negotiate among the multiple variants of Spanish in the US context.

## Interlingual Translation

English also interrupts Spanish in Latino contexts just as Spanish interrupts English. These interruptions are healthy for literary creation and innovation. In *Bilingual Aesthetics: A New Sentimental Education*, Doris Sommer states that "noticing the interruptions of one language by another could cure some of the cramps in conventional expectations about the good and the beautiful with the remedy of acknowledging that alter-nation is normal everyday practice."[12] For Latino writers, in addition to maneuvering among the different variants of Spanish in writing, English plays a huge role from its participation in Spanglish to being the language of choice for some writers. Complications, of course, do arise from this dual language situation. Vanessa Pérez along with Vivien Cao share that:

> U.S. Latino/a literature is deeply preoccupied with language. Latino/a authors through their characters often reveal the anxiety many Latinos/as feel around language as they are expected to speak two languages. English to claim their sense of belonging to the United States, and Spanish to identify as Latino/a and remain connected to their home countries.[13]

Because of these expectations, regardless of a Latino author's decision to use Spanish or English, for whatever reason, the other language is considered even if it does not visibly present itself on the page. In other words, whatever the choice may be, the presence or the absence of the other language is a constant of Latino literature. Spanish is always present, and so is English. Regardless of the knowledge of and strength in either language, creative writing is a translational act as the choice of language, and its justifications are spotlighted in the context of Latino writing. Although writing may happen in one language, the other never leaves the writer. Translators work in the same way: as they bring a text into one language, they do not dismiss the language from which they are translating. The two languages are present, although one is notably absent.

One of today's most prominent Latino writers, the Dominican-born, New Jersey–raised Junot Díaz (b. Dominican Republic, 1968–), writes in English and is employed by an English creative writing program at the Massachusetts Institute of Technology. His writing does not dismiss the use of Spanish. Italics have long been the way in which a text acknowledges the inclusion of foreign words. In Latino literature, as Isabel Espinal points out, "neither language is really foreign"; thus, Díaz does not mark the difference between the two languages in his writing with the use of italics or quotations and shows that Spanish is part of US English in the twenty-first century.[14] In his own words, he explains:

> For me allowing the Spanish to exist in my text without the benefit of italics or quotations marks a very important political move. Spanish is not a minority language. Not in this hemisphere, not in the United States, not in the world inside my head. So why treat it like one? Why "other" it? Why de-normalize it? By keeping Spanish as normative in a predominantly English text, I wanted to remind readers of the mutability of languages. And to mark how steadily English is transforming Spanish and Spanish is transforming English.[15]

Díaz not only normalizes the flexible use of the two languages together, but he also prioritizes the experience of the bilingual English-Spanish reader as speakers of both languages have a more complete experience reading the text than the monolingual speaker of English.

Moreover, the title of Díaz's Pulitzer Prize–winning novel *The Brief Wonderous Life of Oscar Wao* (2008) also plays with the notion of how language is heard. If read aloud, *The Brief Wonderous Life of Oscar Wao* sounds like the "Spanglish pronunciation of Oscar Wilde, whom [the main character] is said to resemble when dressed up in his Doctor Who costume for Halloween."[16] Readers of Latino literature have an advantage if they know both Spanish and English even if they are reading a monolingual text as the presence and influence of Spanish happens in several ways. With other titles of Latino literature, there are titles in English, and titles in Spanish, and titles that do not make the language of the novel so obvious such as the previously mentioned *Lucas Guevara* by Díaz Guerra, *Felicita* (1990) by Nicholasa Mohr (b. New York, 1938–), and *Soledad* (2001) by Angie Cruz (b. New York, 1972–). Additionally, Felipe Alfau's *Locos* and *Chromos* make the reader wonder if the books themselves are in Spanish or English. Further because of the expectations of Spanish or English in Latino literature, it might not be clear to outsiders which version came first when a book is published in a bilingual edition or a subsequent edition of a translation is published as a separate book. For example, some of today's outsider readers might believe that the 1994 translation *De cómo las muchachas García perdieron el acento* by Jordi Gubern or the 2007 translation with the same title by Mercedes Guhl might have preceded *How the García Girls Lost Their Accent* (1991) by Julia Álvarez (b. United States, 1950–). What is more, the title page of Guhl's edition says that Ruth Herrera revised the translation. It is not often that a reviser's name of the translation is included on the title page, let alone the translator's name.

The Spanish translation of Álvarez's novel is an example of interlingual translation, or *translation proper*, "an interpretation of verbal signs by means of some other language."[17] Because Spanish and English are heavily ingrained in the text, regardless of the text's main language, moving it into another language presents the translator with unique challenges. In discussions about her translation process, Edith Grossman (b. United States, 1936–), one of today's most prominent English translators of Spanish texts, some of them works of Latino literature, discusses the process of translation as the relationship between hearing the text in one language and speaking it in another. In her own words, she explains:

> The unique factor in the experience of translators is that we not only are listeners to the text, hearing the author's voice in the mind's ear, but speakers of a second text—the translated work—who repeat what we have heard, though in another language, a language with its own literary tradition, its own cultural accretions, its own lexicon and syntax, its own historical experience, all of which must be treated with as much respect, esteem, and appreciation as we bring to the language of the original writer.[18]

The history, context, and experience, and the options that Latinos have regarding how they use Spanish and English, call for the translator to develop a creative strategy that results in careful considerations of both languages. For example, in my own English translation *A True Story: A Cuban in New York* (2010) of Barnet's *La vida real*, a novela de testimonio about a Cuban who moves from the countryside to Havana and then on to Tampa and New York City, told from New York, where the narrator-protagonist has lived for many years, I encountered welcome and enriching interruptions between the two languages when trying to speak the text in my English translation. *La vida real* is mainly in Spanish with a sprinkle of words in English. On a few occasions, Julián Mesa, the narrator-protagonist, says a short phrase in English. Moreover, Julián occasionally talks about his resistance to the use of English in New York. Even so, when as a literary translator trying to make this text available to English readers and as someone who has lived in New York City and the area for many years, I can perfectly imagine Julián confidently speaking a particular variant of Latino English with a Cuban accent. I could not get the sounds of what I imagined Julián's English to be like out of my head. However, my translation would not be effective if English readers unfamiliar with that variant of the language could not appreciate it. I settled on a casual English that included some Spanish words, with the purpose of not distracting readers too much from the telling of the incredible events of Julián's story.

If I were to translate this text again, one of the things I would do would be to surround myself with native Cuban Spanish speakers of Julián's age when he tells the story, who learned English in their late twenties in Manhattan, in order to be able to write a particular branch of Latino English for my translation. As a result, this process would not only involve the goal of producing an interlingual translation but also include what might be an even more intense task, intralingual translation. The process which Achy Obejas (b. Cuba, 1956-) carried out when she made the Spanish translation of *The Brief Wonderous Life of Oscar Wao* is exemplary. Díaz chose Obejas, a Cuban American writer, translator, and professor, to do the translation, which he wanted to be in Dominican Spanish. Obejas, a translator who goes from Spanish to English and English to Spanish, never having stepped foot in the Dominican Republic before, engaged in a careful and thorough process. In fact, when asked by Natalie Díaz for PEN America what the most "daring thing you ever put into words" was, she discusses her translation of Díaz's novel:

> I thought the translation into Spanish of Junot Díaz's *The Brief Wondrous Life of Oscar Wao* was particularly loaded, though: First, Junot is my friend, and it had to be just right. Second, we'd made a decision to give the translation a very Dominican/Caribbean bent, and I'm Cuban, not Dominican, so I knew off the top it would be flat-out unacceptable in some circles. I worried that in trying to get close to Junot's voice—to really try to capture his voice in Spanish, not just translate—it would be seen, not only as not very conventional—no big deal on that!—but also, perhaps, as falling short. In the end, the translation got raves, and Junot was happy, so all was good in my world.[19]

In order to produce a successful translation, Obejas altered her everyday life by changing her cable package to include multiple Dominican channels, which she never turned off, listening to Dominican radio talk shows from New York and Santo Domingo ("UNCORKING"). Additionally, she had Díaz and some of his friends read drafts of the translation as she worked.

Those conditions, ideal for her project, however, are seldom available to the translator due to time constraints, publishing pressures, and the lack of financial sources. Therefore, the demands that many examples of Latino literature place on interlingual translation highlight the work, research, and collaborative efforts of the translator and additionally require an intralingual translation thus inviting creative efforts for translation. Whether a Latino character or book is functionally bilingual, monolingual, or multilingual, the relationship to Spanish and English is repeatedly present. Many layers of translation are an integral part of the Latino literary experience.

## Alfau's Intervention

Felipe Alfau's *Chromos* further pushes the relationship between English and Spanish in the context of writing in the United States. Alfau's experience in several locations gave him exposure to multiple languages, and variations of those languages, thus complicating Alfau's placement within a national literature and his relationship to language and creative writing. As a Barcelona-born writer living in a dominantly English-speaking city, he had to reconcile Spanish and English within his literature. Such a trajectory, at least regarding the use of language, shares traits with immigrant and Latino writers. Attention to Alfau's literary language, specifically that of his prose, presents another face of life among two languages and its implications for creative writing. As a candidate for the National Book Award, *Chromos* was, of course, in English. Alfau wrote all of his known literary prose in English, and in Spanish music criticism and poetry. He produced literature in both Spanish and English, although never relying on Spanglish or heavy code-switching, "the mixing or switching of two static language codes."[20] As such, outside readers might wonder which texts are translations and which are originals, something that, like some titles of Latino literature, is not indicated by the books' titles.

Alfau demonstrated to be strong in both English and Spanish and was a professional translator between the two languages. There were other translators in his family. His other sister Montserrat Alfau translated and collaborated with on scholarly projects with her husband Felipe Teixador (b. Barcelona, 1895–d. Mexico City, 1980). Teixador translated from French and English. Alfau tells that Montserrat "did translations" and that she was going to translate *Locos*, although it never happened.[21] Ilan Stavans asked Alfau if he ever attempted to translate his own work, and his response was "Never. Why would I?"[22] Although Alfau's response is disappointingly short, Stavans's provocation to get Alfau to discuss the literary phenomenon of self-translation, or *autotraducción*, is appropriate given Alfau's personal and creative trajectory. But in the context of Latino literature, Eva Gentes and Trish Van Bolderen point out that "few Latino self-translators are recognized as such" and further indicate that "research into literary self-translation among Latino authors in the United States is nonetheless lacking." In their study of self-translation, Gentes and Van Bolderen consider instances of self-translation to be "an author translating their own literary work into another language and text."[23] Such a definition of self-translation fails to acknowledge the relationship most Latino writers have with language. Javier Calvo (b. Spain, 1973–), author of the recent book *El fantasma en el libro: La vida en un mundo de traducciones* (2016) in Spanish on translation for a general audience, proposes a more nuanced approach to self-translation:

> En términos históricos, la autotraducción es resultando de la proliferación de autores emigrados o itinerantes, aunque su distribución en el mundo también viene determinada por factores geopolíticos. El domino global del inglés, por ejemplo, ha hecho que muchos autores se trasladen a países anglosajones y una vez allí se traduzcan a sí mismos al inglés o bien lo adopten como idioma literario.

Historically speaking, self-translation is a result of the proliferation of emigrant and itinerant authors, even though their distribution throughout the world is also determined by geopolitical factors. English's global dominance, for example, has made many authors move to Anglophone countries and once there, they translate themselves into English or they adopt it as a literary language.[24]

While self-translation can come in the form of translation proper, Calvo suggests that an adopted literary language is also an act of self-translation. In Alfau's case, translation was already part of his original writing and thus in no need for further transformation on his part.

A writer of children's literature and novels, a poet, and a music critic, Alfau never authored a literary translation that we know of, perhaps because he understood all too well the frustrations involved. In 1991, a year after *Chromos* had been nominated for the National Book Award, it was translated into Spanish by María Teresa Fernández de Castro and published in Spain with the prominent Barcelona publisher Seix Barral. In an interview, Alfau reported to Stavans that he was not fond of the Spanish translation:

> When I read the lousy Spanish translation, made in Barcelona, of *Chromos*, I thought my message had been deformed, my intentions inverted. The translator often misunderstands a sentence. Unfortunately, the mistakes are not rare. The art of translation is difficult, to say the least. One cannot substitute one word in a language with its equivalent in another. The task is to make two cultures find a common path, a bridge. I think translators must be anthropolinguists if they want to succeed in their profession.[25]

Yes, translation is difficult. Here, Alfau is evaluating a text that is considered a result of interlingual translation: the English-language text was transformed into a Spanish language text. Each literary text presents a unique challenge for its translator. The particular challenge *Chromos* presents is with regard to the way in which it deals with Spanish and English. In Gregory Rabassa's review of *Chromos*, he comments that "the very language of [Alfau's] narration is perfectly good English, and yet it is not English. Nor is it Spanish either in a free or in a literal translation."[26] Rabassa, a keen bilingual English-Spanish reader and a literary translator, pinpoints that the origin of the uniqueness of Alfau's language fuses Spanish and English. In Alfau's own words: "My English is Iberian—an acquisition. It's half English and half my own creation, the result of an immigrant experience."[27] Although being half-and-half, Alfau's "Iberian English" does not have a hyphen. His English maintains the Spanish but does not give it an equal space. In this way, Alfau's language is distinct because it refuses to surrender to choosing between Spanish or English, but rather holds on to Spanish while being visibly English. The language of *Chromos* has captured translation. As a result, *Chromos* is outstanding according to Rabassa "not only for what it says, but also for what it is struggling to say."[28] Alfau's literature in English presents another way of living among the two languages as it opts out of code-switching and injects English with a Spanish influence. In her essay "*El incansable juego / The Untiring Game*: Dominican Women Writing and Translating Ourselves," Isabel Espinal (b. United States, 1964–) discusses her experience translating Yrene Santos (b. Dominican Republic, 1963–) from Spanish to English. Her description of her own English could well represent the English of Alfau's *Chromos*: "I have learned to be comfortable with an English that may somehow still sound like the Spanish it is not supposed to be."[29] Writing in the mid-twentieth century about the context of the cohabitation of Spanish and English in New York City, *Chromos* begins with the sentence "The moment one learns English, complications set in" noting that transformations begin with the very first words.[30]

Felipe's sister Jesusa "wrote in Spanish and valued her Iberian background," and has been accepted as a part of the Dominican/Hispanic family of writers in the United States, in part because she was embraced by the scholar and college president Daisy Cocco De Filippis (b. Dominican Republic, 1949–), who edited a collection of Jesusa's novel and articles.[31] In *Latinas in the United States: A Historical Encyclopedia* (2006), Ruiz and Sánchez Korrol note that Alfau Galván de Solalinde's work in Spanish on the United States continues the path of what José Martí and Pachín Marín (b. 1863–d. 1897) had done before her, and further state that her "life and work are early precursors of what became the diasporic Dominican/Hispanic family in the twentieth century."[32] Seven Jesusa died outside the Iberian Peninsula, in 1943 in Mexico, after leading a life that took her to several places, including New York and Wisconsin. Like Jesusa, Felipe Alfau never returned to Spain to live. He remained a resident of New York City until his death in a retirement home in Queens in 1999. The name Felipe Alfau has not been a stranger to critical writing on Latino literature. However, as Silvio Torres-Saillant notes, at least in the context of Dominican literature "no existe similar interés en reclamar."[33] What is more, Silvio Torres-Saillant finds no place for him in Latino writing given negative comments he made about "citizens from the Caribbean and Hispanic America" and the lack of traces of his Dominican background.[34] About a decade prior to the publication of Ruiz and Sánchez Korrol's book, and five years after Alfau's nomination for the National Book Award, Ilan Stavans placed Alfau within the genealogy of Latino Literary Studies in *The Hispanic Condition: Reflections on Culture and Identity in America*.[35] At the time, critical work on Alfau was limited. In fact, the majority of critical work on Alfau belonged to Stavans, who at the time was most noted for his work on Latin American and Latino culture. Stavans had made previous efforts in 1993 to gain an audience for Alfau and through the publication of a special issue of *Review of Contemporary Fiction* shared with Georges Perec (France, 1936–1982), the work and life of Alfau did not go entirely into the abyss of unknown authors. Since then Stavans, as general editor of the *Norton Anthology of Latino Literature* (2010), included Alfau among the tome's pages and continues to push for Alfau's place within Latino writing. Indeed, it is difficult to talk about Alfau, who "wrote in English, did not display ethnic solidarity, and held reactionary views" in the context of Latino literature.[36] In an interview, Stavans himself confronted Alfau about his political and religious views, and his response was passive, claiming that he lived in other times isolated from the rest of the world, suggesting that whatever he would have to say would have little influence on anything.

The backgrounds and experiences of Latinos are vast, and determining exactly where, if, and how Alfau fits on the spectrum is unproductive. However, something is to be gained from the attempts that Stavans has made to introduce Alfau to a Latino studies audience. Regardless of Alfau's inclusion or not in Latino literature, Stavans appreciated the many facets of translation at play in Alfau's work as they open new paths for thinking about multilingual writing, and more specifically writing that springs from a context in which Spanish and English exist, thus forging the connections with Latino literature. Alfau presents a theory about writing in a strong bilingual context via a language of translation. Alfau shows that the synergies of Spanish and English are never dormant although one of the languages might not be visible. In her recent essay "The Perils of Polyglossia" (2018) when citing an interaction between Roy Harris and an audience member at a lecture at Princeton University, the scholar, translator, and educator Esther Allen reminds us that translations contain a "*critique* or *theory*" of the original.[37] If the value of Alfau's writing is to be found, not in the content of his writing but rather in his literary language that carefully represents a situation in which Spanish and English exist, this is where I believe Alfau can make the most productive intervention and connection with Latino literature. His literature presents another way of living among the two languages that relies on a state of translation that is only clear to speakers of both languages. In an interview, Karen Cresci asked Junot Díaz if he enjoyed working with translators. He responded, "We exist in a constant state of translation. We just don't like it. We don't like to be reminded that we are translating this experience. Translators remind us of our relationship with language the way not everyone is comfortable with."[38] Because Latino literature emerges from a situation of continuous movement in and out of Spanish and English and variants of those languages, translation is part of a vivid process of communication and creation. Questions of translation expand the value of Latino writing and appreciation for the relationship between Spanish and English and its literary use.

The contemporary poet, performer, and educator Urayoán Noel (b. Puerto Rico, 1976–) provides one of the most innovative and active ways of making the process of translation visible in Latino literary production. His bilingual book of poems *Buzzing Hemisphere / Rumor Hemisférico* (2015) is an experimentation in self-translation in which the majority of the poems have a Spanish and an English version. His ongoing series of wokitokiteki, accessible via internet with an invitation for others to submit their own creations, is described as "poems [that] are generated spontaneously by speaking into a smartphone while walking around urban and/or natural landscapes, yet over the years patterns appear: landscapes with which the poet is socio-spatially and/or biographically enmeshed (the Bronx, New York; Río Piedras, Puerto Rico) as well as accompanying *lang*scapes and mindscapes."[39] The language of Noel's wokitokitekis is a response to the poet's surroundings. Most wokitokitekis include Spanish and English, but moreover, the two languages respond to each other in order to keep the poetry in motion as seen in "CHIC AGONISTIC CHIC AGOTADO": "AND DID I MENTION THE 7-ELEVEN? LOS QUE SE VEN Y LOS QUE NO SE VEN LOS QUE SE ELEVAN Y TODO LO QUE CONLLEVA CAMINAR ONE FOOT AND THEN ANOTHER."[40] Further, the poet plays with the sounds of language. For example, "LLUVIA (YOU BE A...)," welcomes listeners of Spanish and English, and audibly and visibly displays different ways of hearing the same utterance. Although responding to the immediate sounds and space, Noel's poems also brings to the present literary texts of the past. For example, in "CHIC AGONISTIC CHIC AGOTADO":

> I TOLD YOU THERE WAS A STARBUCKS NO STARS AND FEWER BUCKS BUT REFULLS MAYBE AND REFILLS MAYBE AND AFTER THE BATONS THE HYBERBATONS THE BETANCES'S AND THE MARTÍ'S AND THE LOLAS AND THE LOLITAS AND THE JUAN-MIGUEL-MILAGROS-OLGA-MANUEL NO NERVOUS BREAKDOWN ON THESE STREETS.[41]

Here, the reader is reminded of foundational texts of Latino literature such as the poem "Puerto Rican Obituary" (1973) by Pedro Pietri (b. Puerto Rico, 1944–d. 2004) and the memoir *Down These Mean Streets* (1967) by Piri Thomas (b. 1928–d. 2011) as well as familiar names. Noel's poems, as well as Latino literature, would not be possible without Spanish and English, their presences and absences, their variants, their interactions, their presents and pasts, and their translations.

One day at a child's birthday party, in a mostly English-speaking setting, I heard a mother whose first language was Spanish, say in English to her son "How do you say _____ in Spanish?" I cannot recall the word in question because it was the situation itself that was more memorable. When the child did not produce the word in Spanish right away, the mother quickly criticized her son on his lack of knowledge of Spanish to the other adults gathered around. It was clear that the boy did know how to come up with a word for her. He searched her face for a few seconds and waited for her to say something more. He hesitated because he did not know in which context his mother wanted to use the word, not because he could not translate the single, random word thrown his way. However, when he heard his mother tell the group that he could not do it, he quickly lost interest and continued to play with his friends. I do not blame the mother, as a similar exchange happens in many bilingual situations. I share this anecdote to illustrate the anxieties felt by Latinos surrounding language. A more widespread understanding of language and translation, or how words belong to contexts, might make individuals more attune to the complexities of asking for a single-word translation and thus undo ideas about an individual's deficiencies in English and Spanish. In the coming years, scholars, publishers, and reviewers should support scholarly work that deals with the intersection of Translation studies and Latino studies. An increase in monographic essays and books that focus on an author's work across languages, their translation work, their involvement with other authors, and their translators would offer more access to the contexts, connections, and complexities of Latino writing, while at the same time working to bring visibility to the integral role of translation and translators at large. An exploration of self-translation in Latino literature that goes beyond seeing translation as a result and more as a process could also open doors to the intricacies of literary texts themselves. At the same time, Latino studies could lead the way to acknowledgment of translation as a process and to looser dimensions of translation that could expand our understanding of the role of language in contemporary multilingual contexts.

## Notes

1. All translations are mine unless otherwise noted; Nicolás Kanellos and Helvetia Martell, *Hispanic Periodicals in the United States, Origins to 1960: A Brief History and Comprehensive Bibliography* (Houston, TX: Arte Público Press, 2000), 72.
2. Silvio Torres-Saillant, "Pereginaciones antillanas: Sobre el saber hegemónico y la identidad diaspórica," *Revista iberoamericana* 79, no. 243 (2013): 515.
3. Vicki L. Ruiz and Virginia Sánchez Korrol, *Latinas in the United States: A Historical Encyclopedia*. Vol. 1. (Bloomington: Indiana University Press, 2006), 37.
4. In 1930, a second edition of *Los débiles* was "prepared for use as a textbook in intermediate to advance Spanish-language courses" ("Jesusa"). Prentice Hall in New York published it with an introduction, notes, exercises, and vocabulary by J. Horace Nunemaker. It also includes original drawings by the author (Ruiz and Sánchez Korrol, *Latinas in the United States*, 37).
5. Roman Jakobson, "On Linguistic Aspects of Translation," *On Translation*, ed. Reuben A. Brower (Cambridge, MA: Harvard University Press, 1959), 233.
6. Michael Cronin, *Across the Lines: Travel, Language, Translation* (Cork, Ireland: Cork University Press, 2000), 3.
7. This translation is by Dan Newland, published in *Hispanic New York: A Sourcebook*, ed. Claudio Iván Remeseira (New York: Columbia University Press 2010), 356.
8. Newland, *Hispanic New York*, 356.
9. Newland, *Hispanic New York*, 356.
10. Newland, *Hispanic New York*, 356.
11. Sherry Simon, *Cities in Translation: Intersections of Language and Memory* (New York: Routledge, 2012), 1.
12. Doris Somer, *Bilingual Aesthetics: A New Sentimental Education* (Durham, NC: Duke University Press, 2004), 164.
13. Vanesa Pérez and Vivien Cao, "The CUNY-NYSIEB Guide to Translanguaging in Latino/a Literature," *CUNY-NYS Initiative on Emergent Bilinguals*, January 2015, iv.
14. Isabel Espinal, "*El incansable juego* / The Untiring Game / Dominican Women Writing and Translating Ourselves," *Translocalities-Translocalidades: Feminist Politics of Translation in the Latin-a Américas*, ed. Sonia E. Alvarez (Durham, NC: Duke University Press, 2014), 105.
15. Cited in Evelyn Nain-Ming Ch'ien, *Weird English* (Cambridge, MA: Harvard University Press, 2005), 204.
16. A. O. Scott, "Dreaming in Spanglish," Review of *The Brief Wonderous Life of Oscar Wao*, by Junot Díaz. *The New York Times Book Review*, September 30, 2007.
17. Jakobson, "On Linguistic Aspects of Translation," 233.
18. Edith Grossman, *Why Translation Matters* (New Haven, CT: Yale University Press, 2010).
19. PEN.org.
20. Pérez and Cao, "The CUNY-NYSIEB Guide to Translanguaging in Latino/a Literature," iv.
21. Ilan Stavans, "Anonymity: An Interview with Felipe Alfau," *The Review of Contemporary Fiction* 13, no. 1 (1993), 146.
22. Stavans, "Anonymity," 151.

23. Eva Gentes and Trish Van Bolderen, "Self-Translation," in *Oxford Bibliographies in Latino Studies* (Oxford: Oxford University Press, 2017), DOI: 10.1093/OBO/9780199913701-0104.
24. Javier Calvo, *El fantasma en el libro: La vida en un mundo de traducciones* (Barcelona: Seix Barral, 2016), 66.
25. Stavans, "Anonymity," 150.
26. Gregory Rabassa, "The Power of *Chromos*," *The Review of Contemporary Fiction* 13, no. 1 (1993): 224.
27. Stavans, "Anonymity" 151.
28. Rabassa, "The Power of *Chromos*," 224.
29. Espinal, "*El incansable juego* / The Untiring Game / Dominican Women Writing and Translating Ourselves," 104.
30. Felipe Alfau, *Chromos* (Elmwood Park, IL: Dalkey, 1990), 1.
31. Torres-Saillant, "Dominican-American Literature," in 424.
32. Ruiz and Sánchez Korrol, *Latinas in the United States*, 38.
33. See Silvio Torres-Saillant, "Pereginaciones antillanas: Sobre el saber hegemónico y la identidad diaspórica," *Revista iberoamericana* 79, no. 243 (2013): 501–522 for more details about the life of Jesusa.
34. Torres-Saillant, "Dominican-American Literature," 425.
35. Ilan Stavans, *The Hispanic Condition: Reflections on Culture and Identity in America* (New York: HarperPerennial, 1995), 175.
36. Torres-Saillant, "Dominican-American," 424.
37. Emphasis in original; Esther Allen, "The Perils of Polyglossia," in *The Fictions of Translation*, ed. Judith Woodsworth (Amsterdam: John Benjamins, 2018), 67.
38. See Junot Díaz, "Junot Díaz: 'We Exist in a Constant State of Translation. We Just Don't Like It," interview by Karen Cresci, *The BAR Buenos Aires Review*, May 4, 2013, n.p.
39. Urayoán Noel, *Buzzing Hemisphere / Rumor Hemisférico* (Tuscon: University of Arizona Press, 2015).
40. Urayoán Noel, "LLUVIA (YOU BE A…)," *Wokitokiteki*, July 14, 2016.
41. Noel, "LLUVIA (YOU BE A…)," n.p.

## Bibliography

Alfau, Felipe. *Chromos*. Elmwood Park, IL: Dalkey, 1990.
Alfau, Felipe. *Locos: A Comedy of Gestures*. Prologue Felipe Alfau. Afterword Mary McCarthy. Elmwood Park, IL: Dalkey, 1988.
Alfau, Felipe. *Old Tales from Spain*. Illust. Rhea Wells. Garden City, NY: Doubleday, Doran & Company, 1929.
Alfau Galván de Solalinde, Jesusa. *Los débiles*. Madrid: José Blass y Cia, 1912.
Alfau Galván de Solalinde, Jesusa. *Los débiles*. Edited by J. Horace Nunemaker. New York: Prentice-Hall, 1930.
Allen, Esther. "The Perils of Polyglossia." In *The Fictions of Translation*, edited by Judith Woodsworth, 67–82. Amsterdam: John Benjamins, 2018.
Alvarez, Julia. *How the García Girls Lost Their Accent*. New York: Algonquin, 1991.
Barnet, Miguel. *La vida real*. Madrid: Alfaguara, 1986.
Boullosa, Carmen. "Notes on Writing in Spanish in New York." In *Nueva York, 1613–1945*, edited by Edward J. Sullivan, 122–135. London: Scala, 2010.

Browitt, Jeffery. "En híbrida mezcolanza: Exile and Cultural Anxiety in Alirio Díaz Guerra's *Lucas Guevara*." *Portal: Journal of Multidisciplinary International Studies* 2, no. 1 (2005).

Calvo, Javier. *El fantasma en el libro: La vida en un mundo de traducciones*. Barcelona: Seix Barral, 2016.

Castedo, Elena. *Paradise*. New York: Grove Press, 1990.

Ch'ien, Evelyn Nain-Ming. *Weird English*. Cambridge, MA: Harvard University Press, 2005.

Cronin, Michael. *Across the Lines: Travel, Language, Translation*. Cork, Ireland: Cork University Press, 2000.

Cruz, Angie. *Soledad: A Novel*. New York: Simon & Schuster, 2002.

Díaz Guerra, Alirio. *Lucas Guevara*. Introduction by Nicolás Kanellos and Liz Hernández. Houston, TX: Arte Público Press, 2001.

Díaz Guerra, Alirio. *Lucas Guevara*. Trans. Ethriam Cash Brammer de González. Introduction by Nicolás Kanellos and Liz Hernández. Houston, TX: Arte Público Press, 2003.

Díaz, Junot. *La breve y maravillosa vida de Óscar Wao*. Translated by Achy Obejas. New York: Vintage Español, 2008.

Díaz, Junot. *The Brief Wonderous Life of Oscar Wao*. New York: Riverhead Books, 2007.

Díaz, Junot. "Junot Díaz: 'We Exist in a Constant State of Translation. We Just Don't Like It.'" Interview by Karen Cresci. *The BAR Buenos Aires Review*, May 4, 2013.

Espinal, Isabel. "*El incansable juego* / The Untiring Game / Dominican Women Writing and Translating Ourselves." *Translocalities-Translocalidades: Feminist Politics of Translation in the Latin-a Américas*. Edited by Sonia E. Alvarez, 95–106. Durham, NC: Duke University Press, 2014.

Fernández de Castro, María Teresa. *Cromos*. Barcelona: Seix Barral, 1991.

Galasso, Regina, trans. *A True Story: A Cuban in New York*. By Miguel Barnet. New York: Jorge Pinto Books, 2010.

Galván, Manuel de Jesús. *Enriquillo: Novela histórica o crónica novelada*. Ed. Marina Galváz Acero. Madrid: Biblioteca Literaria Iberoamericana y Filipina. Vol 2: República Dominicana. Agencia Española de Cooperación Internacional, Ediciones de Cultura Hispánica, 1996.

García, Cristina. *Dreaming in Cuban*. New York: Ballantine Books, 1992.

García Lorca, Federico. *The Poet in New York and Other Poems*. Translated by Rolfe Humphries and introduced by José Bergamin. New York: W.W. Norton, 1940.

Gentes, Eva, and Trish Van Bolderen. "Self-Translation." In *Oxford Bibliographies in Latino Studies*. Oxford: Oxford University Press, 2017.

Grossman, Edith. *Why Translation Matters*. New Haven, CT: Yale University Press, 2010.

Gubern, Jordi, trans. *De cómo las muchachas García perdieron el acento*. By Julia Alvarez. Barcelona: Ediciones B, 1994.

Guhl, Mercedes, trans. *De cómo las muchachas García perdieron el acento*. By Julia Alvarez. New York: Vintage Español, 2011.

Hijuelos, Oscar. *The Mambo Kings Play Songs of Love: A Novel*. New York: HarperCollins, 1992.

Kanellos, Nicolás, and Helvetia Martell. *Hispanic Periodicals in the United States, Origins to 1960: A Brief History and Comprehensive Bibliography*. Houston, TX: Arte Público Press, 2000.

Jakobson, Roman. "On Linguistic Aspects of Translation." In *On Translation*, edited by Reuben A. Brower, 232–239. Cambridge, MA: Harvard University Press, 1959.

"Jesusa Alfau Galván de Solalinde." *Latinas in History*. 2008. Web.

Lago, Eduardo. *Llámame Brooklyn*. Barcelona: Destino, 2006.

Lago, Eduardo, et al. "Manifiesto Neoyorkino." *Letralia Tierra de Letras: La revista de los escritores hispanoamericanos en Internet*. 18 dic. 2006.

Manrique, Jaime. *Eminentes maricones: Arenas, Lorca, Puig y yo*. Translated by Juan Camacho. Madrid: Síntesis, 2000.

Manrique, Jaime. *Maricones eminentes (Arenas, Lorca, Puig and Me)*. Madison: University of Wisconsin Press, 1999.

Manrique, Jaime. *My Night with / Mi noche con Federico García Lorca*. Translated by Edith Grossman and Eugene Richie. Hudson, NY: The Groundwater Press, 1995.

Martín Gaite, Carmen, ed. *Cuentos de antaño*. Prólogo Carmen Martín Gaite. Il. Rhea Wells. Barcelona: Siruela, 1991.

Mohr, Nicholasa. *Felicita*. Illustrated by Ray Cruz. New York: Bantam, 1990.

Muñoz Molina, Antonio. "Paisajes del idioma." *El País*, March 24, 2007.

Newland, Dan, trans. "Spanish in New York: A Moving Landscape." *Hispanic New York: A Sourcebook*. Edited by Claudio Remeseira, 355–358. New York: Columbia University Press, 2010.

Noel, Urayoán. *Buzzing Hemisphere / Rumor Hemisférico*. Tuscon: University of Arizona Press, 2015.

Noel, Urayoán. "CHIC AGONISTIC CHIC AGOTADO." *Narrative Northeast*. August 25, 2015.

Noel, Urayoán. "LLUVIA (YOU BE A…)." *Wokitokiteki*. July 14, 2016.

Noel, Urayoán. *Wokitokiteki*. Web. July 12, 2018.

Obejas, Achy. "The PEN Ten with Achy Obejas." Interview by Natalie Díaz. *Pen America*. October 6, 2015. Web.

Obejas, Achy. "UNCORKING CUBA: One Hundred Bottles, a Literary Conversation with Achy Obejas." Interview by Eduardo Aparicio. Austin, Texas. 2011.

Pérez, Vanesa, and Vivien Cao. "The CUNY-NYSIEB Guide to Translanguaging in Latino/a Literature." *CUNY-NYS Initiative on Emergent Bilinguals*. January 2015.

Pietri, Pedro. *Pedro Pietri: Selected Poetry*. Edited by Juan Flores and Pedro López Adorno. San Francisco: City Lights, 2015.

Rabassa, Gregory. "The Power of *Chromos*." *The Review of Contemporary Fiction* 13, no. 1 (1993): 223–224.

Rodríguez Martorell, Carlos. "Eduardo Lago—An Ode to Brooklyn." *Críticas Magazine* 15 (2006).

Ruiz, Vicki L., and Virginia Sánchez Korrol. *Latinas in the United States: A Historical Encyclopedia*. Vol. 1. Bloomington: Indiana University Press, 2006.

Scott, A. O. "Dreaming in Spanglish." Review of *The Brief Wonderous Life of Oscar Wao*, by Junot Díaz. *The New York Times Book Review*, September 30, 2007.

Simon, Sherry. *Cities in Translation: Intersections of Language and Memory*. New York: Routledge, 2012.

Somer, Doris. *Bilingual Aesthetics: A New Sentimental Education*. Durham, NC: Duke University Press, 2004.

Stavans, Ilan. "Anonymity: An Interview with Felipe Alfau." *The Review of Contemporary Fiction* 13, no. 1 (1993): 146–157.

Stavans, Ilan. *The Hispanic Condition: Reflections on Culture and Identity in America*. New York: HarperPerennial, 1995.

Stavans, Ilan, ed. *Norton Anthology of Latino Literature*. New York: W.W. Norton, 2010.

Stavans, Ilan, trans. *Sentimental Songs (La poesia cursi)*. Elmwood Park, IL: Dalkey, 1992.

Thomas, Piri. *Down These Mean Streets*. New York: Vintage, 1997.

Torres-Saillant, Silvio. "Dominican-American Literature." *The Routledge Companion to Latino/a Literature*. Edited by Suzanne Bost and Frances Aparicio. New York: Routledge, 2013.

Torres-Saillant, Silvio. "Pereginaciones antillanas: Sobre el saber hegemónico y la identidad diaspórica." *Revista iberoamericana* 79, no. 243 (2013): 501–522.

CHAPTER 16

................................................................................

# SPANGLISH

*Current Issues, Future Perspectives, and Linguistic Insights*

................................................................................

### SILVIA BETTI AND RENATA ENGHELS

To have another language is to possess a second soul.

—Charlemagne

LINGUISTS typically only encounter a few research topics in their lifetime that really spark their interest.[1] This is the case not only because these topics are often complex and encompass various issues at different levels but also because they are still often underexposed, as uncharted territory waiting to be explored. Spanglish is one of those topics. This may come as a surprise to some, since Spanglish has been hotly debated during the last two to three decades. Nevertheless, the statement still holds true because of two noticeable trends in the literature.

First, more than other linguistic phenomena, Spanglish has triggered numerous and at times emotionally charged debates in almost every possible respect. Some of these debates have involved the following issues:

- the negative and positive attitudes toward the phenomenon itself: Spanglish as a threat to the future of Spanish or English in the United States versus Spanglish as a dynamic and creative hybrid form of communication;[2]
- the terminology: "Spanglish"[3] versus "espanglish" or "popular Spanish of the US";[4]
- its linguistic status: Spanglish as a new language or a dialect, for example.[5]

It goes without saying that writing a state-of-the-art review on Spanglish, in all its complexity and contradictions, is quite challenging. However, the main goal of the present study is not to present a literature review but to rather show that what many of the debates ignore is that the phenomenon—however it may be labeled or perceived—responds to a unique set of properties characterizing exceptional human communicative abilities. In fact, this brings us to the second common divisor of the Spanglish library. Spanglish has rightly been treated as a socially, politically, and culturally relevant research domain and has been the topic of many sociolinguistic studies. Questions concerning where and by whom it is spoken have been tackled on several occasions.[6] However, much less is known about what really happens in the minds of Spanglish speakers. Recently, López García-Molins has contributed to resolving this puzzle by proposing a neurolinguistics model that explains the mental processes behind Spanglish.[7] However valuable and inspiring, this model still suffers from the same restriction of previous sociolinguistic approaches, in that it focuses on only one of the two dimensions that constitute language, namely cognitive and social aspects. In the recent literature, the need for a more interdisciplinary approach has been stated more explicitly.[8] This is also the starting point of the present analysis.

Specifically, this article studies a series of issues identifying Spanglish as a unique form of communication. The section *A Tentative Definition of Spanglish* discusses why Spanglish has been a growing topic of interest—and controversy—ever since it first attracted the attention of specialists, be it from a linguistic, literary, or sociocultural perspective. It is shown that over the last decades, the study of Spanglish has become an increasingly popular topic and that this is mainly due to the changing social and political context in which the *hispanounidenses* live. This section also briefly addresses the main challenges that are expected in the (near) future. Next, we will argue that Spanglish is a unique form of bilingualism. Moreover, it is demonstrated that Spanglish offers valuable insights into the main characteristics of human language, including basic principles such as iconicity, economy, creativity, and productivity.

# A Tentative Definition of *Spanglish*

## The Nature of Language Contact

The history of Spanish in contact with English in the United States is neither a recent nor understudied phenomenon. In her classic text *Borderlands/La frontera: The New Mestiza*, Anzaldúa already provides an example of this linguistic cohabitation and its profound significance and exceptional evolution:

> Spanish is a border tongue which developed naturally. Change, *evolución, enriquecimiento de palabras nuevas por invención o adopción* have created variants of Chicano Spanish, *un nuevo lenguaje. Un lenguaje que corresponde a un modo de vivir.* Chicano Spanish is not incorrect, it is a living language... A language which they [*Chicanos*] can connect their identity to, one capable of communicating the realities and values

true to themselves—a language with terms that are neither *español ni inglés*, but both. We speak a patois, a forked tongue, a variation of two languages.⁹

Indeed, in the twenty-first century it is not possible to preserve cultures or languages intact because as people integrate into a culture, they adopt certain aspects of that culture, resulting in inevitable enrichment. The *mestizaje* and hybridization are the expression of cultural maturity because people have adapted to new ways of living, and different individuals live together and share multiple competences, moving between different cultural and linguistic spaces.¹⁰ During the inauguration act of the third *Congreso Internacional de la Lengua Española*, Fuentes defended the *mestizo* Spanish in the globalized world with the following words: "Todos llegamos de otra parte. Y nadie llegó con las manos vacías" [We all come from different places. And nobody came with empty hands.]¹¹

Within this global and *mestizo* landscape, the American territory constitutes a particular case in point. The continuing migrations of Hispanics northward have changed the profile of the United States, not only from a cultural, social, and economic viewpoint but also because of the linguistic contact between English and Spanish. In this particular context, the relationship between English and Spanish is characterized by many interchanges, which generates a situation of interpenetration—and, one might say, mutual dependency.

Actually, according to the US Census Bureau, among the 321 million people who lived there in 2015, approximately 56.6 million (or 17.8% of the total population) were Hispanics. Planning offices foresee a possible increase of this number to 106 million in 2050, as a consequence of which the Hispanics would represent about a quarter (26.6%) of the total number of inhabitants (398 million) (US Census Bureau; *Pew Research Center* 2015; *The Economist* 2015).¹²

From a linguistic perspective, Spanish is the most spoken language in the United States, after English. Jenkins observes that:

> De los 50.5 millones de hispanos que viven en el país, 35.4 millones de ellos hablan español en casa. De todos los países hispanohablantes, es el quinto donde más se habla español, tiene más hablantes de la lengua española que Venezuela, Perú, Chile, Bolivia, Ecuador, Paraguay, Uruguay y cualquier país antillano o centroamericano... [Of the 50.5 million Hispanics that live in the country, 35.4 million speak Spanish at home. Of all Spanish speaking countries, it is the fifth where Spanish is most frequently spoken; it has more speakers of Spanish than Venezuela, Perú, Chile, Bolivia, Ecuador, Paraguay, Uruguay or any Antillean or Central American country.]¹³

And the Observatory of the Instituto Cervantes in Harvard highlights that "Estados Unidos se sitúa como el segundo país del mundo con más hispanohablantes en número absoluto, solo superado por México (112.3 millones), y por delante de países como Colombia (47.5 millones), España (46.7 millones) y Argentina (41.6 millones)."¹⁴ [The United States constitutes the second country in the world with the most Spanish speakers in absolute numbers, only surpassed by Mexico (112.3 million), and ahead of countries such as Colombia (47.5 million), Spain (46.7 million) and Argentina (41.6 million).]

Naturally, as is well known, this phenomenon of language contact is not an exclusive US trait but arises whenever two (or more) languages share the same territory, as in the case of *franglais* (the mixing of French and English) or *chinglish* (combining Chinese with English), among many others. However, these cases have not been the object of much polemic because the speakers involved are far less numerous than the *hispanounidense* group. In the matter that is of interest here, contact between English and Spanish may occur at various levels among which there are borrowings—which are most common and arise with various degrees of adaptation to Spanish as in *aplicar* "solicitar," *aplicación* "solicitud," *lonche* "lunch," *bildin* "building," and so on—and syntactic calques, but the most noticeable phenomenon is code-switching.[15]

## The Notion of Spanglish and Its History

The contact between Spanish and English generates what is commonly defined as Spanglish. This phenomenon has raised a great interest both within and out of the United States. Its history is not recent, but, according to different sources, goes back to 1848 when, as a result of the Guadalupe Hidalgo Treaty, Mexico surrendered various territories of the Southwest to the United States. In these areas, there was a strong intensification of bilingual intercourse by Hispanics who were obliged to use English as a language for commerce and education. This contact continued, and still continues, because of migration streams to the United States. In the beginning, Spanglish was considered as the "hijo de la calle," only spoken in the suburbs of big northern American cities (eastern Los Angeles, Spanish Harlem, Miami, etc.), but starting in the mid-1980s, it further developed, for instance, in literature and music, also due to the so-called fiebre latina (Latin fever). Today, the vitality of the phenomenon persists because of its frequent use in the media, on social media, in advertising, and in music created for the young *hispanounidenses*.

In December 2016, Ros publishes an article with the meaningful title "El futuro cercano de EEUU es mestizo y se escribe en Spanglish" [The near future of the US is mestizo and will be written in Spanglish],[16] in which Spanglish is defined as a phenomenon with an assured future. But can a phenomenon that has been so disdained or that has even been defined as inexistent constitute a reality? We dare to write that it does. Hispano American speakers are very well aware of the fact that both languages define their daily lives, and they do not worry too much about the exact denomination of these linguistic exchanges.

The Real Academia Española (RAE), which in the past had never considered the term *Spanglish*, decides in 2012 to record it in its dictionary. The definition of the term *espanglish* (with the prothetic Spanish e-) enters the online version of the *Diccionario de la Academia DRAE* (nowadays known as DLE) for the first time in 2012, and its definition generates a great polemic:[17]

> *Artículo nuevo. Avance de la vigésima tercera edición* (*DRAE on line*)
> **espanglish.**

(Del ingl. *Spanglish*, fusión de *Spanish* "español" y *English* "inglés").
1. m. Modalidad del habla de algunos grupos hispanos de los Estados Unidos, en la que se mezclan, deformándolos, elementos léxicos y gramaticales del español y del inglés."

These criticisms arise due to the use of the form "deformándolos," unacceptable for the majority of linguists who condemn the unscientific nature of this definition, which seems to neglect the large bibliography on the topic. Therefore, Del Valle and Zentella decide to write a series of open letters to the RAE, the Asociación de Academias de la Lengua Española (ASALE), and the Academia Norteamericana de la Lengua Española (ANLE).[18] The ANLE forcefully disputed this inopportune gerund and due to its continuous efforts, the definition of *espanglish* was modified in the printed *Diccionario Real Academia Española* (today, the DLE), published in the fall of 2014, eliminating the gerund *deformándolos*:

*espanglish*. (Fusión de *español* y el ingl. E*nglish* "inglés"). m. Modalidad del habla de algunos grupos hispanos de los Estados Unidos en la que se mezclan elementos léxicos y gramaticales del español y del inglés.[19]

Indeed, from a semiotic viewpoint, as an instrument of communication, all forms are valid. In the words of Zentella, Spanglish is "a graphic way of saying 'we speak both because we are both.'" And also: "We embrace Spanglish with open and frank discussions of its roots and problems, just as we embrace expanding our repertoires of English and Spanish, all part of *el habla del pueblo*" (author's emphasis).[20]

The phenomenon has been studied from different perspectives by many authors, without the following list being exhaustive.

Zentella has dedicated her (academic) life to the study of Spanglish.[21] Then you have Morales, Fairclough, Stavans, Lipski, Ardila, Otheguy, Moreno Fernández, López García Molins, López Morales, Dumitrescu, Betti, Mayor Marsán, Torres, and others.[22]

However, because of its polymorphic and ever-changing nature, the phenomenon is hard to explain. The term has been used to refer to very different phenomena such as bilingual code-switching (adapted or non-adapted borrowings), calques from English, neologisms, varieties of "anglicized" Spanish, and "hispanized" English, as is the case of Chicano Spanish and Porto Rican English. It was the Puerto Rican journalist Salvador Tió who in his column "Teoría del Espanglish" published on October 28, 1948, in *El Diario de Puerto Rico* used the term *espanglish* (with the prothetic Spanish e-) for the first time, in an attempt to describe the phenomenon that he considered to be "contaminante, perjudical y peligroso" [contagious, detrimental and dangerous]. But Spanglish constitutes a reality.

Consider, for instance, that in a Hispanic family living in the United States, the father may properly speak English and Spanish, the mother may speak excellent Spanish and regular English, the grandparents may speak hardly any English, but the children can speak better English than Spanish. Within one and the same family there are different levels of command of both languages, and here the use of Spanglish may be particularly beneficial. Whereas some *Hispanos* indicate that they have an emotional connection with Spanish, some identify more with Spanglish, because it is the language they speak with other *Hispanounidenses*. Spanglish may also symbolize a kind of protective barrier, or a linguistic and cultural conscience. Although President Trump shut down the Spanish page of the White House in January 2017, and wants to continue the building of the border wall, it will be impossible to stop the usage of a linguistic tool already consolidated between Hispano-American families but also between friends, in schools, in universities, and in daily life. In addition to being a communicative practice, for many Latinos it is also a form of identity, of multiculturalism, that in the United States can indeed represent perfectly those who live between these two realities.[23] This contact of languages is, in a certain sense, a refuge from homesickness and nostalgia and a kind of protection against the social marginalization and incomprehension by the host society, which may cause a feeling of alienation or confrontation.[24]

Newly arrived migrants cannot participate in the normal flow of life, exchange values everyday, have their family next door, and, above all, have no access to knowledge, to the source of information. But every migrant is a thinking person, a bearer of culture and vital experiences, emotional, not a blank page, and so often feels displaced, helpless in the host society, and acquiring a new way of communicating requires a complete Location in both spaces: their life before and their current life. As Zentella points out: "Para los hispanos bilingües, hablar el español, el inglés, y el Spanglish con los amigos y la familia *es una forma de expresar, disfrutar, y compartir su identidad bicultural.*" [For the bilingual *hispanos*, speaking Spanish and English, and Spanglish with friends and family is a form of expressing, enjoying, and sharing their bicultural identity.][25]

From a sociohistorical viewpoint, Spanglish develops in the heart of what is considered the "minoría hispánica," composed, however, by numerous heterogeneous groups integrated by people of different ethnicities and social classes. From a sociological viewpoint, this group is exceptionally dynamic—meaning that it brings in a different culture, world vision, and sensitivity—and is therefore able to resist complete assimilation to the dominant English-speaking group. Although recently Trump has spoken ill of the Mexican Hispanics and the Spanish language in general, "estas condiciones adversas no van a frenar el movimiento de la minoría hispana" [these adverse conditions will not slow down the movement of the Hispanic minority].[26] Its culture spreads across the country through a language that is constantly renewed.

## Spanglish Today

We are living in the era of mestizaje, multiculturalism, and plurilingualism, which constitute a richness, an advantage. Thanks to language, you get to know the culture and the possibility of comparing and contrasting different civilizations. Speaking two languages benefits *hispanounidenses* in particular in the near future, and as a consequence of the globalization process. In March 2015[27] the Pew Research Center published the results of a survey (authored by Krogstad and Gonzalez-Barrera) called "A majority of

English-speaking Hispanics in the U.S. are bilingual" according to which: "Fully 87% said Latino immigrants need to learn English to succeed. At the same time, nearly all (95%) said it is important for future generations of US Hispanics to speak Spanish." It was also observed that "due in part to bilingualism, in 2013 Spanish was the most spoken non-English language in the US, used by 35.8 million Hispanics in the US plus an additional 2.6 million non-Hispanics. Overall, three-in-four Hispanics (73%) ages 5 and older speak Spanish in their homes, when including those who are bilingual." And the following was reported with regard to Spanglish: "And as a sign of the times, Spanglish, an informal hybrid of both languages, is widely used among Hispanics ages 16 to 25. Among these young Hispanics, 70% report using Spanglish, according to an analysis we did in 2009." Among the comments of that survey, it stands out that famous scholar Ana C. Zentella criticized the data with the following words (emphasis of the author of the commentary):[28]

> I agree that the title and the opening paragraph are inaccurate, and confusing. The 62% refers to ALL Hispanics, and is the result of adding up Mainly English (25%) and Bilingual (36%). Their English ability is clear. BUT only 50% of the second generation is bilingual, and the loss of bilingualism in the third generation is worrisome [23%]. Of course, we can argue that the metric used by the study to determine BILINGUALISM, i.e. equivalent ability to converse AND READ in Spanish is too stringent. (author's emphasis)

To summarize, the data are often hard to interpret, and it is important to pursue the necessary investigations in order to pinpoint the linguistic situation in a country that is so wide and diverse. As concerns Spanglish, using it is favorable to interculturality, to opening oneself to another culture through a flexible and diversified mental structure.[29] López García-Molins observes:

> Despacharlo como un caso más de contacto de lenguas me parece altamente reduccionista. Sus tornasolados teóricos resultan bastante intrincados y lo constituyen en objeto digno de estudio por sí mismo, con independencia de que su dimensión empírica y político-social (al fin y al cabo, en EE.UU. hay cincuenta millones de personas expuestas al spanglish) lo aconsejen igualmente. [Selling it as just another case of language contact appears to me as a simplification. Its theoretical variations are rather complicated and make it a worthwhile object of study, independently of what its empirical (after all, in the US 50 million people are exposed to Spanglish) and political and social dimensions also suggest.][30]

In the era of Trump, the multicultural nature of the United States is at stake. Still, in a comment on the decision of the Trump Administration to suppress the accounts in Spanish of the social networks used by the Government, the new director of the Instituto Cervantes, Bonet, stated that "no reconocer el carácter plurilingüe de los Estados Unidos, es no respetar la realidad. 55 millones de hispanohablantes no es una minoría, o si acaso, una gran minoría" [failing to recognize the plurilingual character of the United

States, is not respecting reality. 55 million Hispanic speakers is not a minority, or, if you wish, a big minority.][31]

This further confirms that the phenomenon of Spanglish is still alive as a communicative need of *mestizo* coexistence that wants to take on a complex society's messages. The Hispanics who live in the United States, who speak Spanish, identify with their Latin side, maintain a cultural baggage that connects them, and at the same time being part of the Anglo-Saxon community, take from that culture what they need. Villanueva, the current director of the RAE, writes that "El 'spanglish' no es enemigo del español. Es una expresión de la mezcla entre dos lenguas y los órganos de comunicación de la comunidad hispana ofrecen expresión en un español que es entendido por todos" ["Spanglish" is not the enemy of Spanish. It is the expression of a mixing between two languages and the communication methods of the Hispanic community provide an expression in Spanish that can be understood by all.][32]

The contacts with other cultures and ways of life, the hybridization of languages, cultures, and lifestyles serve to confront differences, to understand them, accept them, live them. García Canclini[33] on these issues underscores that:

> Así como circulan con fluidez en una misma frase entre español e inglés, mezclan información de las costumbres y fiestas de sus culturas tradicionales con los espectáculos mediáticos. Sus artesanías muestran calendarios aztecas, últimas cenas, personajes disneylandescos y se van renovando con la iconografía del cine y la televisión. Por eso, pueden comunicarse con habitantes comunes que atraviesan ese lugar, artistas que reelaboran símbolos históricos, como el caballo troyano, alusiones complejas a los modos en que estadounidenses y mexicanos penetran en el territorio de los otros. O presentan la superposición del fútbol y el baloncesto, y obtienen el eco festivo de espectadores acostumbrados a esas hibridaciones e interferencias. [Just as they shift fluently in the same sentence between Spanish and English, they mix information about the customs and festivals of their traditional cultures with media shows. Their crafts show Aztec calendars, last suppers, Disneyland characters and they are renewed with the iconography of cinema and television. That is why they can communicate with common inhabitants who cross that place, artists who rework historical symbols, such as the Trojan horse, complex allusions to the ways in which Americans and Mexicans penetrate the territory of others. Or they present the superposition of football and basketball, and they obtain the festive echo of spectators accustomed to those hybrids and interferences.]

Likewise, Spanglish is an expressive strategy open to change, a reflection of that dual identity in motion, a way of being in the middle of two worlds and visions of the world. Giannina Braschi writes very lucidly about Spanglish:

> Existe y está vivo—ahora más que nunca. La realidad bilingüe está a punto de decidir las elecciones en Estados Unidos... Spanglish fue un movimiento cultural que se convirtió en una realidad política. Hoy en día más de la mitad de los puertorriqueños se han mudado a Estados Unidos y decidirán las elecciones, junto a los mexicanos y otros inmigrantes latinoamericanos que irán a las urnas mañana. Hay dos

movimientos en la historia de la colonización: invasión e inmigración. La emigración es una reacción a una invasión. Emigran porque han sido invadidos. Se trata de cambiar la perspectiva desde el punto del colonizador al punto de vista del colonizado. [It exists and it is alive—now more than ever. The bilingual reality is about to decide the elections in the United States [...] Spanglish was a cultural movement that became a political reality. Today more than half of Puerto Ricans have moved to the United States and will decide the elections, along with Mexicans and other Latin American immigrants who will go to the polls tomorrow. There are two movements in the history of colonization: invasion and immigration. Emigration is a reaction to an invasion. They emigrate because they have been invaded. It is about changing the perspective from the point of the colonizer to the point of view of the colonized.][34]

The elections have decided otherwise, but this does not mean that the bilingual reality does not continue to be dynamic.

## Spanglish Tomorrow

Indeed, in a recent conference in Barcelona, Stavans has defended the following idea:

La fortaleza del espanglish está, ha estado y estará en la calle, y nosotros en las universidades debemos salir a la calle y tratar de entender lo que está pasando allá. La calle siempre estará un paso por delante. El idioma es de la gente, no de los académicos. Por más que nosotros tratemos de estandarizarlo, de conceptualizarlo, de catalogarlo, en última instancia la gente hace con el idioma lo que quiere y nosotros tenemos que seguir esa trayectoria popular. [The strength of espanglish is, has been and will be on the streets, and those of us in the universities have to go to those streets and try and understand what is happening there. The streets will always be one step ahead. Language is property of common people, not of academics. No matter how much effort we put into trying to standardize, conceptualize, and register it, eventually people will do with language what they want, and we have to follow up on this popular trajectory.[35]]

In this citation, Stavans uses the future form "estará," which exemplifies the power of Spanglish. I believe that as scholars we should not fossilize ourselves with one term. I understand the positions of those who consider that word as something harmful, as something that underestimates the real knowledge of the speakers. But if that word after its birth has prospered, it means that it explains and captures defining features of a culture that is Spanish-speaking and English-speaking; *Hispanoactuante* and *Angloactuante*. Spanglish, both as a term and as a phenomenon, has not disappeared; on the contrary, it is still alive and vital. Already in 2002 Valdés observed: "A large percentage of Hispanic teens, especially foreign-born teens, speak Spanish at home, speak some form of 'Spanglish' and Spanish with their Latino friends, and speak English with their non-Latino peers."[36]

The task of educators, scholars, artists, and intellectuals is to spread correct Spanish and English, and to give a presence to Spanglish as something natural and as a sign of hybridization (or something else), of a new identity *in-between*. As has been emphasized on other occasions, Spanglish does not represent either Spanish *in* the United States or Spanish *of* the United States, but rather a form of family communication, a natural expressive strategy, a reflection of a society and the people who speak it. It is a more complex phenomenon than it seems, as seen, for example, in the literature of many Latino/a writers, where this "third code" channels its *mestizaje* in a broad sense.[37] In fact, Spanglish does not exist without both Spanish and English but is born as a result of this contact. López García-Molins puts forward the idea that "los hablantes de spanglish tienen que hablar, mejor o peor, español e inglés para poder hablar spanglish. No existe un sistema lingüístico del spanglish independiente de los del español y del inglés: por eso se puede afirmar que el spanglish no es, tan solo se practica." [Speakers of Spanglish need to speak, for better or for worse, Spanish and English in order to be able to speak Spanglish. There is no Spanglish system, independent from Spanish and English; therefore it can be claimed that Spanglish does not exist, but is only used.][38]

Moreno Fernández, meanwhile, in a March 2017 article, explains that the situation of the language in the United States "is analyzed as a diglossic complex, in the form of diglossia of double-scheme." This author writes that "this interpretation makes compatible a US Spanish with Spanglish, both of them in connection and continuity. The work also points out the importance of Education and the Media for the constitution of a US Spanish." Moreno Fernández continues: "The elaboration of a proper standard for US Spanish, respectful of its identity, requires a knowledge of the language in all its sociolinguistic complexity." For this reason, a dictionary of Anglicisms of US Spanish appeared in January 2018 (*DAEE: Diccionario de anglicismos del español estadounidense*) and a nationwide lexical study is actually being prepared.[39]

To finish this paragraph, I consider the illuminating words of Ana C. Zentella, which, despite the years, remain valid:

> Los críticos ignoran la extensión de nuestros logros lingüísticos, culturales, educativos, organizacionales y económicos; nuestros bodegueros (dueños de bodegas/tiendas de provisiones), poetas, músicos, maestros, médicos, trabajadores de la industria textil, activistas comunitarios, etc., no se mencionan en los libros de historia.[40]
>
> A pesar de que una patria colonizada usó nuestra emigración y esterilización como "válvulas de escape", y de las políticas sociales y económicas inhóspitas en la nueva tierra que nos construyó como inadaptados patológicos semilingües, dejamos una marca indeleble en Nueva York. La voz de esa marca es el Spanglish, un nombre incorrecto si da la impresión de que se ha creado una tercera lengua. En su lugar, como Algarín notó en su introducción a la reconocida antología *Nuyorican Poetry*, "el Nuyorican promedio tiene un dominio funcional de ambas [inglés y español] y normalmente usa ambas lenguas simultáneamente" [...] Básicamente, el Spanglish es una manera colorida de alternar entre variedades de inglés y español, adoptada porque "la novedad en la lengua crece a medida que las personas hacen y aprenden cosas nunca antes hechas o aprendidas." Critics ignore the extent of our linguistic,

cultural, educational, organizational and economic achievements; our winemakers (owners of warehouses/grocery stores), poets, musicians, teachers, doctors, workers of the textile workers, community activists, etc., are not mentioned in the history books.

In spite of the fact that a colonized country used our emigration and sterilization as "escape valves," and of the inhospitable social and economic policies in the new land that built us as pathological semi-lingual misfits, we left an indelible mark in New York. The voice of that brand is Spanglish, an incorrect name if it gives the impression that a third language has been created. Instead, as Algarin noted in his introduction to the well-known anthology *Nuyorican Poetry*, "the average Nuyorican has a functional domain of both [English and Spanish] and usually uses both languages simultaneously" [...] Basically, Spanglish is a colorful way of alternating between varieties of English and Spanish, adopted because "novelty in the language grows as people make and learn things never before done or learned."

## COGNITIVE, FUNCTIONAL, AND COMMUNICATIVE DIMENSIONS OF SPANGLISH

After this detailed definition of the phenomenon, the present section will start from the idea that Spanglish, as a unique form of bilingualism, can best be understood by means of a cognitive and functional viewpoint on language. This perspective establishes a direct link between specific linguistic phenomena and structures, on the one hand, and the way language is represented in the mind, on the other. It also takes other cognitive abilities (e.g., perception) into account and considers how language is used in daily discourse, with its numerous social functions. Besides critically revising (in *Spanglish in the Eye of a Linguistic Storm*) the main issues that the phenomenon under scrutiny has created—namely, the question of whether Spanglish is a worthy research topic for linguists (and, if so, what kind of language phenomenon is it?)—most of this section is dedicated to showing that these questions are irrelevant when seen from a cognitive-functional perspective (*An Economical Linguistic System with Maximum Performance*). Studying Spanglish—and by extension different kinds of code-switching—offers insight into the main characteristics of human language, including basic principles such as symbolism, economy, and iconicity.

### Spanglish in the Eye of a Linguistic Storm

*In and Out of (Linguistic) Textbooks*

Ever since the phenomenon has been identified and labeled, many different voices have been heard on the question whether Spanglish constitutes a natural manifestation of human language that is worthy of be inclusion in (socio)linguistic studies and textbooks.[41] When we analyze the arguments in favor and against, two trends become apparent.

First, authors contradict each other by using the exact same arguments but from different perspectives. Second, most arguments in favor are based on both sociocultural and linguistic motivations, whereas most negative ones use only sociolinguistic arguments and disregard linguistic ones.

To capture the general mood among committed researchers, consider the following descriptions of Spanglish, which can be organized into a set of antonym pairs: (a) to some, Spanglish is a *sickness* caused by the hybridization of English and Spanish, bringing decay and deterioration to those languages, while to others it constitutes a dynamic, fertile system; (b) sometimes, Spanglish is regarded as a *threat* to the cultures associated with both languages while at other times it is seen as an opportunity to preserve the Latino identity.[42, 43, 44, 45]

Similar contrasting views can be found in more systemic linguistic accounts of the phenomenon: some see Spanglish as a sign of the linguistic ignorance and mediocrity of its speakers,[46] while others feel that it attests to the richness of the (Spanish) language and can only be produced by people who have the skills to perform advanced communication strategies.[47] It has repeatedly been argued that the use of Spanglish is a direct reflection of the lack of linguistic competence of its speakers, who in fact want to speak English but are unable to.[48] This has been related to linguistic confusion in children in the process of language acquisition. Silva-Corvalán, for example, is generally positive toward Spanglish but still concludes that the "simplified grammar" used by Spanish children raised and living in Los Angeles is the result of incomplete language acquisition.[49] As such, the lack of competence has directly been associated with a simplified linguistic system. Tió Montes de Oca already compared the development of Spanish in Puerto Rico with that of Papiamento, a Creole language.[50] As a consequence, in the absence of a system, the road lies open to linguistic chaos, an image conjured up by González Echevarría: "The last thing we need is to have each group carve out its own Spanglish, creating a Babel of hybrid tongues."[51] This is confirmed by Marcos-Marín, who refers to Spanglish as an individual and high-fashion form of expression.[52]

An entirely different story is told among Spanglish supporters, who instead hypothesize that the code-switching nature of Spanglish is not harmful to the speakers' monolingual competence in Spanish or English. On the contrary, it represents "a third linguistic system," rule-governed and full of remarkable regularities, which can only be produced by speakers with a high level of "bilingual dexterity and grammatical knowledge"[53]

## *Language, Dialect, or Speech Manifestation of a Third Kind?*

Linguists who consider Spanglish to be a valuable research subject typically engage in a discussion on the exact nature of the phenomenon: is it a new language, a dialect, or a different kind of speech manifestation? Essentially, the problem is that Spanglish can hardly be called a language based upon purely linguistic arguments (especially if a standardized grammar is considered, as is argued later). Instead, it seems more plausible to refer to it as a dialect.[54] In that case, however, what other dialect has received such attention and propagation in both academia and the media?

Most authors are rather reluctant to use the term "language," exceptions being Stavans and Álvarez Martínez. The latter defines Latin Americans in the United States as "transculturated people" who create an entirely new language to reflect their hybridity, and the author firmly states that Spanglish is "yet another authentic language of the Americas."[55] Stavans adopts a more moderate viewpoint, believing that as Spanglish is "in the process of standardizing its syntax," it will further solidify its status as a language in the future.[56]

Indeed, the lack of a codified and normalized lexicon and grammar is the main argument to withhold from Spanglish the full status of a language. Indeed, several authors have listed many local varieties, such as Cubonics, Domininicanish, Chicano, or Tex-Mex, which would suggest that it is a dialect.[57] In that case, a new question arises: is Spanglish a dialect of Spanish, a dialect of English, or something else entirely? Only a few authors, such as Marcos-Marín, situate Spanglish closer to the English pole than the Spanish one.[58] Otheguy, by contrast, is one of the most ardent defenders of the idea that the phenomenon is to be defined as popular Spanish of the United States, thereby rejecting the notion of Spanglish itself.[59]

López-García Molins presents a more nuanced picture, stating that the exact classification of the phenomenon depends on the viewpoint that is taken: from a cultural viewpoint, Spanglish is closer to the Anglo-American pole, whereas linguistically speaking, it would certainly be closer to Spanish.[60] The phenomenon in itself is essentially hybrid: Spanglish not only represents a process of convergence toward English but also a general tendency to recover Spanish as a heritage language, which in turn would constitute a process of divergence from English. Moreover, traditional criteria of a dialect are not easily applied to Spanglish: as it is spoken across the whole of the United States, it cannot be defined as a spatial dialect; because it is produced by speakers of all diastratic levels, it cannot be a social dialect; and since it appears in diverging discourse genres (from spoken to written language), it is not a register dialect either. Taking into account these restrictions, López García-Molins defines Spanglish as a psycholinguistic, fused, and porous dialect of Spanish. It is a psychological dialect because its speakers use mixed (i.e., fused) neural networks and porous because, like a sponge, the Spanish language is soaked in English and fills any (lexical or grammatical) gaps in its system with English elements.[61]

Parallel to this discussion on the language versus dialect status, the idea has persisted that Spanglish is something else entirely and that the traditional distinction does not account for its complexity. Hernández-Sancristán, for instance, describes Spanglish as a syncretic expressive "speech modality" whose main function is to establish continuity between the normative poles of Spanish and English.[62] This idea contrasts sharply with former accounts that have attempted to define it as a dialect of one of the two languages and effectively creates a neutral space between different linguistic and cultural models. Spanglish is authentic because of its noncodified nature and subjective because it depends on the emotional and physical conditions of the speakers.

This study further elaborates on this idea and aims to show that discussions on the exact status of Spanglish can be reconciled within a broader, integrated view on language as a window to its speakers' emotions and cognitive processes. Moreover, from such a perspective, the code-switching nature of Spanglish does not imply a simplified system but quite the opposite, as it adds an extra dimension to the already complex set of mechanisms that interact with language use.

## Spanglish as a Unique Manifestation of the Human Language Faculty

### The Cognitive-Functional Framework in a Nutshell

Before discussing the basic characteristics of Spanglish, this section briefly explains what the cognitive linguistics enterprise stands for.[63] This framework was developed in the 1980s by key figures such as Langacker and Lakoff, as a reaction to generative Chomskyan linguistics that almost exclusively examined formal and (morpho)syntactic phenomena and considered language to be a faculty independent from other forms of cognition. The cognitive-functional approach, in contrast, studies language in a completely opposite way and is based on three tenets: integration, symbolization, and observation.[64]

First, the principle of integration implies that language is processed in a parallel way to other cognitive abilities such as memory, the motor system and, more important, experience and perception of the world. Just as we are able to see entities and events from different angles, with varying degrees of granularity and from different levels of salience, different language structures can present the same message from different perspectives, in more or less detail, foregrounding or backgrounding particular aspects of the information. Second, syntax, semantics, morphology, and phonetics are claimed to constitute a continuum of symbolic structures, or form-meaning pairings. These symbolic units can be more or less complex and function at different levels, ranging from words to entire constructions. The focus lies mainly on linguistic meaning (including encyclopedic knowledge, pragmatic and semantic meaning), which is believed to interact with formal structures in a fundamental way. Finally, cognitive linguistics is mainly usage based, which means that the framework does not refer to universal, innate principles but posits that language is acquired through real discourse. As a consequence, linguistic phenomena should not be analyzed based on a researcher's intuition, but through corpus studies of authentic (spoken or written) data.[65]

To summarize, Figure 16.1 represents the different levels of representation of language structure, as conceived by cognitive-functional models. This overview is further developed and explained throughout our analysis of the nature of Spanglish.

This cognitive perspective leads to four fundamental characteristics of language, which, in the following sections, will be shown to apply to Spanglish as well:

- Language is systematic and has rules of usage. Systematic patterns found in language may reflect conceptual structures (see next section).
- Language is also flexible. Linguistic rules are not perfect and are, to some extent, speaker-dependent. They can be violated or bended (see next section).

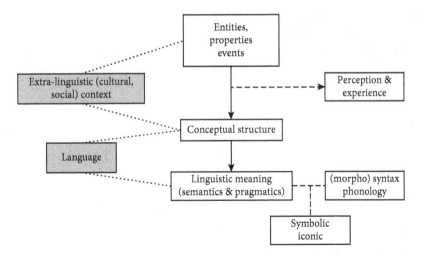

FIGURE 16.1. Levels of representation of cognitive-functional models.

- Language is a social and cultural phenomenon. Its nature and structure depends on its users, their contexts, and the purpose of their communication acts (see *An Integrated Human Faculty*).
- Language is symbolic and therefore a construct of form-meaning pairings. Each symbol has meaning, be it a word, a construction, or, as is shown later, a code-switching structure (see *An Integrated Human Faculty*).

## An Economical Linguistic System with Maximum Performance

One of the fundamentals of language is that, above all, it obeys the principle of economy. The human language faculty optimally strives for a good management of the available resources, thus implying a minimum amount of effort to obtain a maximum result. This can only be achieved by its rule-based nature: in a linguistic system, symbols do not combine in arbitrary ways to infinity but follow more or less general or language-specific rules that apply recursively and together constitute the "grammar" of (a) language. As a result, the question whether Spanglish—and, by extension, all manifestations of code-switching—is governed by its own grammar is a legitimate one. Most linguists working in different frameworks actually agree that Spanglish (and code-switching) is not simply a chaotic way of speaking but follows a series of rather clear-cut linguistic patterns. How should these patterns be defined? (Do they mimic the grammar of one of the two languages or a third grammar?) And where are they to be situated in the language architecture, at the syntactic level, in the lexicon, or somewhere else? These questions are still matters of great controversy.

A constant throughout different approaches is that they tend to focus on rules of code-switching at the intrasentential level (i.e., codeswithes within a sentence). Lipski, for instance, provides the following list of restrictions: there can be no code-switching between a pronominal subject and its verb (1a), between a verb and anteposed or postposed clitics (1b), between an interrogative word and the remainder of the sentence (1c), or between a negation word and the sentence part it applies to (1d).[66]

(1) a. **Él* lives in Chicago.
    b. *Juan *lo* did.
    c. **When* vas a hacerlo?
    d. *El médico *no* recommends that.

Restrictions also apply to verb clauses, as code-switching cannot occur between an auxiliary verb and a past participle (2a), except when the auxiliary verb is *to be* (2b) or *estar* (2c).

(2) a. *María *ha finished* her meal.
    b. Mary *is revisando* su informe.
    c. María *está checking* her answers.

On the other hand, Zentella paints a less restrictive and more positive image of code-switching by providing a large list of contexts, situated at different syntactic levels, in which the phenomenon operates as a rule-based system.[67] To illustrate, in her data, code-switching often occurs between a verb and its object or subject NP (3a–b), adverbial phrase (3c), or prepositional phrase (3d). The phenomenon also frequently occurs in exclamations (4a), imperatives (4b), and tags (4c).

(3) a. She went to the *entierro*.
    b. My *pollina* is longer then hers.
    c. I'ma put it *al revéz*.
    d. I'm going with her *a la esquina*.

(4) a. Y era un nene, *embarrassing*!
    b. It's full already, *mira*!
    c. E/h/to e/h/ una peseta, *right*?

The generative viewpoint, according to which switching patterns such as the ones that have just been described for Spanglish are formed on the basis of a syntactic hierarchy, has long been dominant. The Equivalence Constraint and the Free Morpheme Constraint[68] by Poplack and Sankoff are among the most widespread theories and illustrate that code-switching is governed by an overarching third grammar that governs the mixture of the two monolingual grammars.[69] Other approaches also focus on the (hierarchical) complement relation that governs sentence structures, without suggesting the existence of a third grammar. According to Mahootian, just as the head of a phrase governs the position of its complements in monolingual contexts, in code-switching contexts the language of the head determines the internal structure of a phrase.[70] Minimalistic models (such as that in MacSwan) dismiss the idea of a control structure or third grammar for code-switching systems such as Spanglish.[71] They claim that bilinguals have two separate lexicons with idiosyncratic differences, each with their own morphosyntactic rules. Code-switching is then the result of simply mixing these two lexicons, combined within the invariant computation system of human language.[72]

On numerous occasions, these generative models have been criticized on empirical grounds. Specifically, they do not always predict the right restrictions. Some subject pronouns, for instance, can appear in another language than that of the main verb, thus breaking the generally accepted rule (see example [1c]):

(5) *Él y Alberto* sleep during the day.[73]

The alternating position (and language) of an adjective within a noun phrase (NP), anteposed or postposed to the noun, is another interesting case in point. Within a generative approach,[74] code-switching is not allowed between an adjective and a noun because of the non-equivalent word order of this phenomenon in Spanish and English: in the former, postposition of an adjective is predominant although anteposition is not impossible (e.g., *un fenómeno interesante* but also *un interesante fenómeno*), whereas in the latter, anteposition of the adjective is the only option (e.g., *an interesting phenomenon* vs. \**a phenomenon interesting*).[75] However, several early counterexamples can be found in the literature.[76]

(6) a. I want a motorcycle *verde*.[77]
    b. Miguel vió (sic) un *green* pájaro.[78]

In (6a), a Spanish adjective is inserted within an English NP, following the Spanish adjective word order. The opposite holds for (6b): there is code-switching toward English, following the English grammar rule for adjective position.

An important model that has attempted to reconcile these empirical observations is the Markedness model of Myers-Scotton.[79] The Matrix Language defines the position in the surface structure for both content words and functional categories. The decision which language functions as the Matrix Language is susceptible to continuous change.

As a restricted case study for the question whether Spanglish has its "own" grammar, and how this would have originated, an analysis of the word order within the NP is conducted in Susana Chávez-Silverman's volume of essays *Killer Crónicas*.[80] The analysis shows that in most cases there is code-switching between a Spanish noun and an English adjective (79.5 percent, e.g., *an interesting pregunta*, p. 63), whereas code-switching between an English noun and a Spanish adjective is much less common (20.5 percent, e.g., *los ridículos, amateurish "professional" musicians*). Given that the noun is to be defined as the nucleus of the NP, Spanish would be expected to be the Matrix Language determining not only the language in which the noun appears but also the word order and adjective position in the NP. Still, adjectives are usually anteposed to the noun (87.5 percent) (e.g., *esa tiny, casi breaking down lavadora*), thus following English word order, which is, however, also frequent in Spanish. Postposition, only possible in Spanish, only occurs in 12.5 percent of the cases (e.g., *había visto mucho nature espectacular*). In other words, word order is not strictly defined by the grammar of the Matrix Language. However, the word order in the Spanglish NP is not strictly determined by the grammar of the adjective's language either: 84 percent of the anteposed adjectives are in English (e.g., *un pale yellow sobre*) (compared to 16 percent in Spanish, e.g., *un fornido gringo housepainter*), but, more important, 60 percent of the postposed adjectives are also in English (e.g., *esas florcitas pink*) (versus 40 percent in Spanish, e.g., *6 kitchen workers africanas*).

To conclude, just like any other language, Spanglish grammar pursues linguistic economy and is therefore characterized by rules and recursivity. However, these rules are not watertight but are quite flexible. The case study on adjective position shows that in Spanglish, word order in the NP can be determined by factors other than the grammar of English or Spanish, which supports the idea that Spanglish syntax is indeed governed by a third grammar. The following section discusses the possible characteristics of such a grammar.

## An Integrated Human Faculty

It has often been argued that Spanglish grammar, including the phenomenon of code-switching obviously, is determined by external factors (i.e., the social context and culture in which the speakers live). It is the expression *par excellence* of a bicultural yet unitary identity.[81]

In fact, this idea ties in with the basic tenet of cognitive linguistics according to which language is not an isolated phenomenon but an integrated language faculty. This means that language directly relates to a speaker's conceptual system and the way his or her perceptions of the world, including his or her sociocultural experience, are structured and organized in the mind).[82] As mentioned previously (*The Cognitive-Functional Framework in a Nutshell*), the cognitive framework is built upon the idea that linguistic meaning and structure reflect patterns of our internalized conceptual systems, are encyclopedic, and include sociocultural beliefs. Metaphor research constitutes a prototypical example of how this theoretical principle translates into research: linguistic metaphors (e.g., *he is feeling down today*) are analyzed as expressions of how abstract concepts (i.e., emotional feelings) are structured in terms of conceptual domains determined by our physical experience (i.e., vertical position and motion.[83] This is also known as the "embodiment" thesis: the human mind, including language, relates to the ways in which the body interacts with the environment in which it lives.[84]

A cognitive-functional approach to language therefore takes sociocultural and psycholinguistic findings into account. Note that, as a result of this premise, if we want to better understand what is mentally happening in bilingual discourse, we should not only focus on larger units such as societies and communities but also on individual speakers. This is defined as "individual multilingualism" and can help to understand the contradictory indications in the literature on what is and is not allowed in code-switching contexts (see, e.g., *supra An Economical Linguistic System with Maximum Performance*), as well as the idea that there are various "Spanglishes."[85]

The relationship between a bilingual's language use and the context in which (s)he lives has been confirmed by numerous studies. The Cultural Frame Switching framework, for instance, has been developed to investigate whether bilinguals express different personalities when they speak in different languages, and whether these personalities are consistent with cultural differences. Ramírez-Esparza et al. argue that Spanish-English bilinguals express greater concern about interpersonal agreement and group identity when they speak Spanish and exhibit more energetic and effective behavior and language use in English.[86] The Spanish language has indeed been defined as a "we code," a language of intimate, informal activities between relatives or friends, whereas English is seen as a "they code," used in formal, often work-related circumstances.[87] This is also known as "metaphorical codeswitching."[88] Put differently, in a code-switching context, Spanish can be defined as the language of subjectification and English as the language of objectification.

Still, let us go back to the integrated language model of cognitive linguistics (see Figure 16.1). In fact, the model does more than posit a relationship between language structures and conceptual structures; it is built upon the principle that different levels of linguistic analysis (i.e., [morpho]syntax, semantics, and pragmatics) are inseparable. The focus is on the meaning of linguistic elements (thus reflecting conceptual meaning), but this meaning is always paired with a particular form.[89] Hence the symbolic and iconic nature of human language.

Consequently, to understand Spanglish grammar, it is important to realize that instead of being exclusively determined by morphosyntactic and hierarchical factors (see, e.g., *An Integrated Human Faculty*), code-switching is also influenced by the speakers' cognitive calculations and rational choices. Following the principle of iconicity, speakers choose a particular form (thus the language or code) for their conversational contribution, which indexes a set of (social) rights and obligations associated with that form (and code) or fills particular pragmatic and communicative needs. Montes-Alcalá distinguishes the following functions of code-switching:[90]

- a speaker unconsciously switches to another language to insert linguistic routinized elements such as idioms and discourse markers;
- a speaker can switch languages for the sake of clarification: (s)he wants to further elaborate on or explain concepts or ideas, sometimes by repeating or inserting a parenthetical comment;
- a bilingual speaker may codeswitch for stylistic reasons, such as the desire to portray informal speech in a more realistic way;
- within the same vein of ideas, code-switching can serve emphatic purposes: the speaker wants to capture the attention of the interlocutor by foregrounding a linguistic item;

- in a direct quote or paraphrase, the speaker may use the original language (which may imply shifting to that language) of a third party;
- speakers may codeswitch due to a lexical need, meaning that they switch for particular "culturally-charged items."

In a study on the alternating use of discourse markers such as *you know/sabes (qué)* in Susana Chávez-Silverman's *Killer Crónicas*, Enghels shows how the Spanish markers appear in emotionally loaded (subjective) contexts related to the author's youth, whereas the English equivalents mostly relate to objective metadiscursive functions, such as introducing examples or adding extra information.[91] In paragraph (7a), the author refers to her restricted knowledge of California and the world in her younger years. The use of the Spanish marker ¿*Pero sabes qué*? could then be interpreted as a strategy to capture the interlocutor's attention by emphasizing Chávez-Silverman's emotional reminiscence of her youth. In contrast, the English marker *you know* is used most frequently with an epistemic meaning. In these cases, the author explicitly calls upon the knowledge of the interlocutor ("do you understand what I am saying?," "do you know what I mean?") to further elaborate on a newly introduced item. In (7b), Susana Chávez-Silverman explains to her interlocutor Pierre what the plant jacarandá looks like and provides some objective information.

(7) a. Ugh, había pensado years before, una vez cuando me desviaron al Ontario Airport, right smack en medio del Evil, en vez del John Wayne Airport de Orange County. I'd never even heard of "Ontario, California." I couldn't believe such a bleached-out, tumbleweeded, rascuache sprawl was even part of California! ¿*Pero sabes qué*? What did I know? Lo único del southland que conocía up to then eran los lush orange groves and suburban lawns del San Fernando Valley de mi infancia, before we moved north por el glaucoma de daddy, y para que yo y mis hermanas wouldn't turn into Valley Girls.[92]

b. Anyway, no me acuerdo haber visto, antes de Sudáfrica, un jacarandá. Sultry yet somehow insouciant too, durante el resto del año, con esas dark green, frilly leaves—casi como una de esas sensitive plants, *you know*, the ones that curl up y se ponen all shy cuando les tocas las hojas con la yema del dedo o con un lápiz, well, like that, pero en gigante—y sus weird, flat, walnut-colored pods.[93]

To conclude, the code-switching processes at the very bottom of Spanglish respond to an economic system, determined by morphosyntactic but also largely socio-pragmatic functions. This corresponds with cognitive and functional studies of language and overrules any questions on the exact status of Spanish (dialect vs. language, closer to English or closer to Spanish). The examples and case studies described in these sections clearly show that labels such as "a lack of linguistic competence," "simplified systems," or "linguistic chaos" lose track of the fact that Spanglish fully complies with the basic characteristics of the general human language faculty.

## Conclusion

Spanglish is a sensitive research topic because of its denomination as well as its linguistic, cultural, social, economic, and emotional characteristics. This text has offered some reflections on this communicational and cultural reality of the United States and other territories. As an expression of the universal human language faculty, Spanglish is a dynamic, polymorphic phenomenon that belongs to its speakers, not to the linguists who try and shape it by imposing rules and norms. The Spanish of today is a "lengua en ebullición" [a language in phase of ebullition] as Emilio Lorenzo pointed out.[94] The complex and multifaceted nature of the Hispanic community in the United States has given rise to a fascinating hybrid reality, which is the result of different mixings.[95] Because of this heterogeneous condition and those composed identities, other ways of being an American have been created, which could imply that assimilation to the mainstream (linguistic) norms may not be desirable.[96] We are convinced that bilingual and bicultural (as well as intercultural) education has to be supported because it constitutes an added value from a linguistic, cultural, and sociological viewpoint.

At this point, it is impossible to factually assert that Spanglish has become the future language of the United States. However, we need to recognize and respect the wishes of those who want to use this form of communication: that is to say, who want to express themselves in the way that best suits them.[97] To retain this form of bilingualism and biculturalism, it is important to preserve the Hispanic language and culture in the United States. To conclude, Spanglish, as the fruit of those lives lived between two languages, cultures, and sensibilities, can be a tool for many Hispanics to express themselves in certain contexts, traversing different worlds to create a new "panlatino" identity, an identity that makes them different from *other* Americans.[98] An appropriate concluding statement might be the following: "For a people who cannot entirely identify with either standard (formal, Castilian) Spanish nor standard English, what recourse is left to them but to create their own language?"[99]

## Notes

1. This is a collaborative paper. It is worth mentioning that Silvia Betti has authored the section: "A Tentative Definition of Spanglish" (translated by Renata Enghels and Silvia Betti) and the section "Conclusion", whereas Renata Enghels was responsible for the "Introduction" and the section "Spanglish in the Eye of a Linguistic Storm." The bibliography and notes correspond to the parts indicated. This article appears as a chapter in the *Oxford Handbook of Latino Studies* (9780190691202). The authors wish to thank Laurie Piña Rosales, Frank Nuessel, and Giannina Braschi for their valuable suggestions.
2. Ilan Stavans, ed., *Spanglish* (Westport, CT: Greenwood, 2008); Dennis Baron, *The English-Only Question: An Official Language for Americans?* (New Haven, CT: Yale University Press, 1990).

3. Silvia Betti, *El Spanglish ¿medio eficaz de comunicación?* (Bologna, Italy: Pitagora Editrice, 2008).
4. Francisco A. Marcos-Marín, "De lenguas y fronteras: el espanglish y el portuñol." *Nueva Revista de Política, Cultura y Arte* 74 (2001): 70–79; Ricardo Otheguy, "El llamado espanglish," in *Enciclopedia del español en los Estados Unidos*, ed. Humberto López Morales (Madrid: Instituto Cervantes/Santillana, 2009), 222–223.
5. Ángel López García-Molins, *Teoría del Spanglish* (Valencia, Spain: Tirant lo Blanch, 2015), 83–84; and Stephanie Álvarez Martínez, "¡¿qué, qué?!—Transculturación and Tato Laviera's Spanglish Poetics," in *Spanglish*, ed. Ilan Stavans (Westport, CT: Greenwood, 2008), 106.
6. Betti, *El Spanglish*; Stavans, *Spanglish*.
7. García-Molins, *Teoría del Spanglish*, 83–84.
8. Eva Rodríguez-González and M. Carmen Parafita-Couto, "Calling for Interdisciplinary Approaches to the Study of 'Spanglish' and Its Linguistic Manifestations," *Hispania* 95, no. 3 (2012): 461–480; Antonio Torres Torres, "El español estadounidense, entre el 'spanglish' y el español internacional," in *Nuevas voces sobre el Spanglish: Una investigación polifónica*, ed. Silvia Betti and Enrique Serra Alegre (New York and Valencia, Spain: ANLE/Universidad de Valencia, 2016), 131–147; and *Spanish-English codeswitching in the Caribbean and the U.S.*, ed. Rosa E. Guzzardo Tamargo et al. (Amsterdam: John Benjamins, 2016), 12–35.
9. Anzaldúa, *Borderlands/La Frontera*, 77.
10. Silvia Betti, "Reflexiones sobre el contacto lingüístico: el spanglish y el caso de la revista estadounidense *Latina*," in *Rumbos del hispanismo en el umbral del Cincuentenario de la AIH*, ed. Patrizia Botta and Sara Pastor, vol. 8 (Rome: Bagatto Libri, 2012), 538–548.
11. Carlos Fuentes, *Discurso de inauguración III CILE en Rosario*. 2004, accessed March 21, 2017, congresosdelalengua.es/rosario/inauguracion/fuentes_c.htm.
12. US Census Bureau 2015a, 2015b. Jens M. Krogstad and Mark H. Lopez, "Hispanic Population Reaches Record 55 Million, but Growth Has Cooled." *Pew Research Center*, 2015. http://www.pewresearch.org/fact-tank/2015/06/25/u-s-hispanic-population-growth-surge-cools/.
13. Devin L. Jenkins, "El suroeste creciente: un breve análisis sociodemográfico de la población hispanohablante de los Estados Unidos," in *El español en Estados Unidos. E Pluribus Unum? Enfoques multidisciplinarios*, ed. Domnita Dumitrescu and Gerardo Piña-Rosales (New York: Academia Norteamericana de la Lengua Española, 2013), 31–45.
14. Hernández-Nieto y Gutiérrez, http://cervantesobservatorio.fas.harvard.edu/sites/default/files/mapa_hispano_2017sp.pdf, accessed August 30, 2017.
15. According to Carli, there is a fundamental difference between code-switching and code-mixing. The former implies the ability to switch from one language to another depending on the situation and the speaker. The latter, code-mixing, provides the transfer of linguistic elements from one language to another and corresponds to the lexical field as much as to the grammatical.
16. http://www.hispanopost.com/el-futuro-cercano-de-eeuu-es-mestizo-y-se-escribe-en-spanglish. Accessed July 2017.
17. Silvia Betti, "La definición del spanglish en la última edición del *Diccionario de la Real Academia* (2014)," *Glosas* (Academia Norteamericana de la Lengua Española) 8, no. 8 (2015): 6.
18. José Del Valle and Ana Celia Zentella, "Lengua y política: el espanglish y las deformaciones de la RAE," *Revista Cronopio* 55 (October 2014), accessed May 21, 2017, http://www.revistacronopto.com/?p=14411.

19. *Diccionario Real Academia Española* 2014: 945.
20. Zentella, "Spanglish: Language Politics vs *el habla del pueblo*," in *Spanish-English Codeswitching in the Caribbean and the U.S.*, ed. Rosa E. Guzzardo Tamargo et al. (Amsterdam: John Benjamins, 2016), 12–35.
21. Zentella, "Spanish and English in Contact in the United States: The Puerto Rican Experience," *Word* 33, no. 1–2 (1982): 41–57; Zentella, "La hispanofobia del movimiento "Inglés oficial" en los Estados Unidos por la oficialización del inglés, *Alteridades* 5 (10), 1995: 55–65; Zentella, *Growing up Bilingual: Puerto Rican Children in New York* (Oxford: Blackwell, 1997); Zentella, "Would You Like Your Children to Speak English and Spanish?" / "¿Quieren que sus hijos hablen el inglés y el español?" 1998, accessed December 14 2016, http://www.spanishdict.com/answers/170367/would-you-raise-your-children-to-speak-spanish-if-that-language-isnt-part-of-your-family-heritage; and Zentella, "The Grammar of Spanglish," in *Spanglish*, ed. Ilan Stavans (Westport, CT: Greenwood, 2008), 42–63; Zentella, "Spanglish: Language Politics," 12–35.
22. Ed Morales, *Living in Spanglish. The Search for Latino Identity in America* (New York: St. Martin's Press, 2002); Marta Fairclough, "El (denomidado) Spanglish en los Estados Unidos: Polémicas y realidades," *Revista Internacional de Lingüística Iberoamericana* 1, no. 2 (2003): 185–204; Ilan Stavans, *Spanglish: The Making of a New American Language* (New York: Harper Collins, 2003); Stavans, *Spanglish*; Lipski, "La lengua española en los Estados Unidos: Avanza a la vez que retrocede", 2004, accessed May 21, 2017, http://www.personal.psu.edu/jml34/SEL.PDF; Lipski, "El español de América en contacto con otras lenguas." In *Lingüística aplicada del español*, edited by Manel Lacorte, 309–345 (Madrid: Arco Libros, 2007); Lipski, *Varieties of Spanish in the United States* (Washington DC: Georgetown University Press, 2008); Lipski, "¿Existe un dialecto estadounidense del español?" *La proyección internacional de la lengua española*. Congreso Internacional de Valparaíso (CILE), 2010, accessed September 10 2016, http://congresosdelalengua.es/valparaiso/ponencias/america_lengua_espanola/lipski_john_m.htm; Lipski, "Hacia una dialectología del español estadounidense," in *El español en Estados Unidos. E Pluribus Unum? Enfoques multidisciplinarios*, ed. by Domnita Dumitrescu and Gerardo Piña-Rosales (New York: Academia Norteamericana de la Lengua Española, 2013), 107–127; Lipski, "El español en Estados Unidos: lo que es y lo que no es," *El español en el mundo. Unidad y diversidad.* Congreso Internacional de Puerto Rico (CILE), 2016, accessed September 10 2016, http://congresosdelalengua.es/puertorico/mesas/lipski-john.htm; Alfredo Ardila, "Spanglish: An Anglicized Spanish Dialect," *Hispanic Journal of Behavioral Sciences* 27 (2005): 60–81; and Otheguy, "El llamado espanglish," 222–223; Ricardo Otheguy and Nancy Stern, "On So-called Spanglish," *International Journal of Bilingualism* 15, no. 1 (2010): 85–100; Francisco Moreno-Fernández, "Dialectología hispánica de los Estados Unidos," in *Enciclopedia del español en los Estados Unidos*, ed. Humberto; López Morales (Madrid: Instituto Cervantes/Santillana, 2009) 200–221; Moreno-Fernández, "Panorama interdisciplinario del español en los Estados Unidos," *Tribuna Norteamericana*, Instituto Franklin, 14 (October 2013): 1–6; Moreno-Fernández, "El español en los Estados Unidos y el Instituto Cervantes en Harvard," *Anuario del Instituto Cervantes 2014*, 2014: 375–392; Moreno-Fernández, "La estandarización del español estadounidense," *Blog del Instituto Franklin*, June 17 2015a, accessed September 10, 2016, http://dialogoatlantico.com/2015/06/la-estandarizacion-del-espanol-estadounidense; Moreno-Fernández, "Lexicografía del español estadounidense. Propuesta de diccionario de anglicismos," *Glosas* (Academia Norteamericana de la Lengua Española) 8 (2015b): 39–54, accessed September 10, 2016 http://www.anle.us/132/Glosas;

and Moreno-Fernández and Domnita Dumitrescu (dirs.), *Bibliografía lingüística del español en los Estados Unidos / Linguistic Bibliography of Spanish in the United States* (Cambridge, MA: Instituto Cervantes at Harvard University—ANLE, 2016); Ángel López García-Molins, *Teoría del Spanglish* (Valencia, Spain: Tirant lo Blanch, 2015); López García-Molins, *El español de Estados Unidos y el problema de la norma lingüística* (New York: Academia Norteamericana de la Lengua Española, 2014); Humberto López Morales, ed., *Enciclopedia del español en los Estados Unidos* (Madrid: Instituto Cervantes/Santillana, 2009); Domnita Dumitrescu, "La alternancia de lenguas como actividad de imagen en el discurso hispanoundense/Code-switching as face-work in the discourse of US Hispanics," *Pragmática sociocultural/ Sociocultural Pragmatics* 2, no. 1 (2014): 1–34; Dumitrescu, "Spanglish, estadounidismos y bilingüismo vestigial: ¿Qué es qué?" in *Visiones europeas del spanglish*, ed. by Silvia Betti and Daniel Jorques-Jiménez (Valencia, Spain: Uno y Cero Ediciones, 2015), 26–40; Betti, "La ilusión de una lengua: el spanglish entre realidad y utopía," in *El español en Estados Unidos. E Pluribus Unum? Enfoques multidisciplinarios*, ed. Domnita Dumitrescu and Gerardo Piña-Rosales (New York: Academia Norteamericana de la Lengua Española, 2013), 189–216; Betti, "La definición del spanglish en la última edición del *Diccionario de la Real Academia* (2014)," *Glosas* (Academia Norteamericana de la Lengua Española) 8, no. 8 (2015): 5–14; M. Mayor Marsán, ed., *Español o Espanglish ¿Cuál es el futuro de nuestra lengua en los Estados Unidos?* (Miami: Ediciones Baquiana, 2008); Torres Torres, "El español estadounidense, 131–147; Torres Torres, "El Spanglish, un proceso especial de contacto de lenguas," *1st International Conference on Spanglish*, Amherst, 2004, accessed September 10 2016, www.amherst.edu/~spanglish/Torres.htm; and Torres Torres, "Sobre el *spanglish* en los Estados Unidos: implicaciones de un caleidoscopio de perspectivas," in *Visiones europeas del spanglish*, edited by Silvia Betti and Daniel Jorques-Jiménez, 96–109 (Valencia, Spain: Uno y Cero Ediciones, 2015).

23. Silvia Betti, *El Spanglish*; Betti, "La definición del spanglish en la última edición del *Diccionario de la Real Academia* (2014)," *Glosas* (Academia Norteamericana de la Lengua Española), 8, no. 8 (2015): 5–14; Betti and Jorques-Jiménez, eds., *Visiones europeas del Spanglish* (Valencia, Spain: Uno y Cero Ediciones, 2015); and Betti and Serra Alegre, eds., *Nuevas voces sobre el spanglish: una investigación polifónica* (Valencia, Spain: Universidad de Valencia, 2016).

24. Silvia Marcu, "Fronteras de cristal de la inmigración. Visión de los inmigrantes del este europeo en España," *ARBOR Ciencia, Pensamiento y Cultura* 186, no. 744 (July/August 2010): 721–736.

25. Ana Celia Zentella, "Would You Like Your Children to Speak English and Spanish?" / "¿Quieren que sus hijos hablen el inglés y el español?" http://www.spanishdict.com/answers/170367/would-you-raise-your-children-to-speak-spanish-if-that-language-isnt-part-of-your-family-heritage. Accessed December 14, 2016.

26. Dario Villanueva, "La actitud de Trump va en contra de la evolución del mundo," *La Razón.es*. http://www.ultimahorapress.com/item/47909_dar-amp-iacute-o-villanueva-quot-la-actitud-de-trump-va-en-contra-de-la-evoluci-amp-oacute-n-del-mundo-quot. Accessed January 30, 2017.

27. http://www.pewresearch.org/fact-tank/2015/03/24/a-majority-of-english-speaking-hispanics-in-the-u-s-are-bilingual/ (last accessed August 2017).

28. Zentella, in the comments about the survey: http://www.pewresearch.org/fact-tank/2015/03/24/a-majority-of-english-speaking-hispanics-in-the-u-s-are-bilingual/#comments.

29. In the United States, Spanglish is active at various levels of language, including pragmatics, and is in need of studies that take into account the demographic tendency of the

Hispanics being the most numerous "minority," which also sees its economic power increasing and has particular cultures and traditions. It is a communicative modality that writers and singers have used in their works with manifested speakers. However, it has been described sometimes as dangerous and harmful for Spanish and English, or a sign of linguistic ignorance.

30. López García-Molins, *Teoría del Spanglish*.
31. In Valentina Proust Iligaray, "El español en tiempos tempestuosos," *El Mercurio*, February 19, 2017.
32. Villanueva, "La actitud de Trump va en contra de la evolución del mundo."
33. Néstor García Canclini, "Malentendidos interculturales en la frontera México-Estados Unidos," Coord. Ascensión Barañano and José Luis García, *Culturas en contacto. Encuentros y desencuentros* (Ministerio de Educación. Cultura y Deporte de España, 2003). http://nestorgarciacanclini.net/index.php/hibridacion-e-interculturalidad/70-fragmento-qmalentendidos-interculturales-en-la-frontera-mexico-estados-unidosq, Accessed September 20, 2015.
34. Braschi, personal communication, November 2016.
35. http://www.ub.edu/web/ub/es/menu_eines/noticies/2015/entrevistes/stavans_ilan.html).
36. Isabel Valdés, *Marketing to American Latinos. A Guide to the In-Culture Approach (Part 2)* (New York: Paramount Market, 2002), 95.
37. Lipski, "La lengua española en los Estados Unidos."
38. García-Molins, *Teoría del Spanglish*, 83–84.
39. The *Diccionario de anglicismos del español estadounidense* (2018: 19) explains Moreno Fernández "is a repertoire of words defined by the characteristics specified in the title." And "as its title indicates, compiles Anglicisms used in the Spanish of the United States and provides descriptive information of its social, geographic, and stylistic use. It is, in fact, a dictionary that is descriptive, differential, and of the usage of United States Spanish, [...]."
40. Ana C. Zentella, "Recuerdos de una Nuyorican", *Ínsula, El español en Estados Unidos y Puerto Rico*. Número 679-680. Julio/Agosto 03, https://www.insula.es/sites/default/files/articulos_muestra/INSULA%20679-680.htm, Accessed September 20, 2015. Algarín, Miguel, "Introducción", Miguel Algarín and Miguel Piñero (eds.), *Nuyorican Poetry*, Nueva York, W. Morrow, 1975.
41. As this section does not aim at establishing an exhaustive overview of the state of the art on Spanglish, bibliographic references are included on an illustrative basis.
42. Gonzalo Sobejano, "El Spanglish no es algo gracioso, es una corrupción del lenguaje," *La Voz Digital*, accessed December 14 2016, http://www.lavozdigital.es.
43. Stavans, *Spanglish*.
44. Roberto González Echevarría, "Hablar spanglish es devaluar el español," *New York Times*, 1997.
45. Betti, *El Spanglish*; Moreno-Fernández, "Dialectología hispánica de los Estados Unidos," 200–221; Ángel López García-Molins and Ricardo Morant-Marco, "El spanglish como fundamento del nacionalismo latino en EE.UU," in *Visiones europeas del spanglish*, ed. Silvia Betti and Daniel Jorques-Jiménez, 86–95 (Valencia, Spain: Uno y Cero Ediciones, 2015).
46. Fernando Lara, "El espanglish," *Boletín Editorial del Colegio de México* 85 (2000): 23–27.
47. Betti, *El Spanglish*; Ángel López García-Molins, *Teoría del Spanglish* (Valencia, Spain: Tirant lo Blanch, 2015); López García-Molins and Morant-Marco, "El spanglish como fundamento del nacionalismo latino en EE.UU," 86–95; Ángel López García-Molins, "El

Spanglish como dialecto psicológico," in *Nuevas voces sobre el spanglish: Una investigación polifónica*, ed. Silvia Betti and Enrique Serra Alegre, 105–116 (Valencia, Spain: Universidad de Valencia, 2016); Torres Torres, "El español estadounidense, entre el 'spanglish' y el español internacional," in *Nuevas voces sobre el Spanglish: Una investigación polifónica*, ed. Silvia Betti and Enrique Serra Alegre (Valencia, Spain: Universidad de Valencia, 2016), 131–147.

48. Marcos-Marín, "De lenguas y fronteras: el espanglish y el portuñol," 70–79; Marcos-Marín, *Los retos del español*.
49. Carmen Silva-Corvalán, "El español de Los Ángeles: ¿Adquisición incompleta o desgaste lingüístico?," in *Estudios sociolingüísticos del español de España y América*, ed. Ana María Cestero Mancera, Isabel Molina Martos, and Florentino Paredes García, 121–142 (Madrid: Arco Libros, 2006).
50. Creole languages are generally defined as languages that arise from mixtures of other languages. Compared to pidgins, they have a more complex morphosyntactic and lexico-semantic system. But still, their grammar is simpler than that of the languages they derive from (see Derek Bickerton, *Roots of Language* [Ann Arbor: Karoma, 1981]; Salvador Tió Montes de Oca, "Teoría del Espanglish," in *A fuego lento, cien columnas de humor y una cornisa* (Rio Piedras: University of Puerto Rico, 1954).
51. González Echevarría, "Hablar spanglish es devaluar el español."
52. Marcos-Marín, *Los retos del español*.
53. Carmen Silva-Corvalán and Kim Potowski, "La alternancia de códigos (Codeswitching)," in *Enciclopedia del español en los Estados Unidos*, ed. Humberto López Morales, 272–276 (Madrid: Instituto Cervantes/Santillana, 2009); Zentella, "Spanglish: Language Politics vs el habla del pueblo," 12.
54. A dialect is defined as "any distinct variety of a language, especially one spoken in a specific part of a country or other geographical area." From *The Concise Oxford Dictionary of Linguistics*, http://www.oxfordreference.com/view/).
55. Stephanie Álvarez Martínez, "¡¿qué, qué?!—Transculturación and Tato Laviera's Spanglish Poetics," in *Spanglish*, ed. Ilan Stavans, 106 (Westport, CT: Greenwood, 2008).
56. Stavans, *Spanglish*, 71.
57. Stavans, *Spanglish*; Betti, *El Spanglish*.
58. Marcos-Marín, "De lenguas y fronteras: el espanglish y el portuñol," 70–79; Marcos-Marín, *Los retos del español*.
59. Ricardo Otheguy, "El llamado espanglish," in *Enciclopedia del español en los Estados Unidos*, ed. Humberto López Morales, 222–223 (Madrid: Instituto Cervantes/Santillana, 2009).
60. Angel López García-Molins and Ricardo Morant-Marco, "El spanglish como fundamento del nacionalismo latino en EE.UU," in *Visiones europeas del spanglish*, ed. Silvia Betti and Daniel Jorques-Jiménez (Valencia, Spain: Uno y Cero Ediciones, 2015), 86–95; and López García-Molins, "El Spanglish como dialecto psicológico," 105–116.
61. López García-Molins, *El español de Estados Unidos*.
62. Carlos Hernández-Sacristán, "Principio retórico de continuidad en el Spanglish y sus implicaciones cognitivas," in *Visiones Europeas del Spanglish*, ed. Silvia Betti and Daniel Jorques-Jiménez (Valencia, Spain: Uno y Cero Ediciones, 2015), 41–51.
63. In fact, the cognitive linguistics framework unites several theories and approaches that share a set of guiding principles and research strategies.

64. Vyvyan Evans and Melanie Green, *Cognitive Linguistics: An Introduction* (Edinburgh: Edinburgh University Press, 2006); Renata Enghels, *Les modalités de perception visuelle et auditive: Différences conceptuelles et répercussions sémantico-syntaxiques en espagnol et en français* (Tubingen, Germany: Niemeyer, 2007); and John R. Taylor and Jeanette Littlemore, *The Bloomsbury Companion to Cognitive Linguistics* (London: Bloomsbury, 2014).
65. Note that this is problematic for Spanglish, as almost no corpora are available, with the exception of corpora including transcriptions of speech produced by Spanish speakers in the United States (e.g., *Corpus of Mexican Spanish in Salinas (California), Español hablado en el suroeste de los Estados Unidos, Spanish in Texas*). As a consequence, researchers turn to alternative data collection methods such as conducting surveys or experiments or analyzing texts written in Spanglish.
66. John M. Lipski, "El español de América en contacto con otras lenguas," in *Lingüística aplicada del español*, edited by Manel Lacorte, 309–345 (Madrid: Arco Libros, 2007), 333. For a more detailed analysis of the possibilities of intrasentential code-switching including pronouns, see Kay González-Vilbazo and Bryan Koronkiewicz, "Tú y Yo Can Codeswitch, Nosotros Cannot. Pronouns in Spanish-English Codeswitching," in *Spanish-English Codeswitching in the Carribean and the US*, ed. Rosa E. Guzzardo Tamargo, Catherine M. Mazak, and M. Carmen Parafita Couto (Amsterdam: John Benjamins, 2016), 237–260.
67. Zentella, *Growing up Bilingual*; Zentella, "The Grammar of Spanglish," 45–46.
68. These constraints are defined by MacSwan as follows: "Codes will tend to be switched at points where the surface structures of the languages map into each other" and "A switch may occur at only point in the discurse at which it is possible to make a surface constituent cut and still retain a free morpheme" (38).
69. Shana Poplack, "Sometimes I'll Start A Sentence in Spanish y termino en español: Towards a Typology of Codeswitching," *Linguistics* 18 (1980): 581–618; David Sankoff and Shana Poplack, "A Formal Grammar for Codeswitching," *Papers in Linguistics* 14, no. 1 (1981): 3–46.
70. Shahrzad Mahootian, "A Null Theory of Codeswitching" (PhD diss., Northwestern University, 1993).
71. Jeff MacSwan, "The Architecture of the Bilingual Language Faculty: Evidence from Intrasentential Code Switching," *Bilingualism: Language and Cognition* 3, no. 1 (2000): 37–54.
72. For more information on general constraints, see Carol W. Pfaff, "Constraints on Language Mixing: Intrasentential Codeswitching and Borrowing in Spanish/English," *Language* 55 (1979): 291–318.
73. González-Vilbazo and Koronkiewicz, "Tú y Yo Can Codeswitch, Nosotros Cannot," 244.
74. Shana Poplack, "Sometimes I'll Start A Sentence in Spanish y termino en español: Towards a Typology of Codeswitching," *Linguistics* 18 (1980): 581–618.
75. See also Rosaura Sánchez, "Our Linguistic and Social Context," in *Spanglish*, ed. Ilan Stavans (Westport, CT: Greenwood Press, 2008), 36: "Shifts seem to occur where there are similarities in structures but not in cases where the surface structures are entirely different."
76. Mónica Moro, "The Universality of Syntactic Constraints on Spanish-English Codeswitching in the USA," *Language and Intercultural Communication* 15, no. 3 (2015): 398.
77. Erica F. McClure, "Aspects of Code-switching in the Discourse of Bilingual Mexican-American Children," in *Latino Language and Communicative Behavior*, ed. Muriel Saville-Troike (Washington DC: Georgetown University Press, 1977), 98.
78. Nicholas J. Sobin, "On Code-switching Inside NP," *Applied Psycholinguistics* 5 (1984): 303.

79. Carol Myers-Scotton, *Social Motivations for Code-Switching* (Oxford: Oxford University Press, 1993); Carol Myers-Scotton, "A Theoretical Introduction to the Markedness Model," in *Codes and Consequences Choosing Linguistic Varieties*, ed. Carol Myers-Scotton. (Oxford: Oxford University Press, 1998), 18–40.
80. For a detailed explanation as to why this literary work can be treated as a valuable source of information for the linguistic analysis of code-switching in Spanglish, see Enghels (in press). The case study on variable adjective position and language has been conducted in collaboration with Laura Van Belleghem.
81. José Luis Blas Arroyo, *Sociolingüística del español* (Madrid: Cátedra, 2005); Betti, *El Spanglish*.
82. Ronald W. Langacker, *Foundations of Cognitive Grammar: Theoretical Prerequisites* (Stanford, CA: Stanford University Press, 1987); Evans and Green, *Cognitive Linguistics*; and Taylor and Littlemore, *The Bloomsbury Companion*.
83. See, e.g., George Lakoff and Mark Johnson, *Metaphors We Live By* (Chicago: University of Chicago Press, 1980).
84. George Lakoff and Mark Johnson, *Philosophy in the Flesh: The Embodied Mind and its Challenge to Western Thought* (New York: Basic Books, 1999).
85. Karoline Kühl and Kurt Braunmüller, "Linguistic Stability and Divergence: An Extended Perspective on Language Contact," in *Stability and Divergence in Language Contact. Factors and Mechanisms* (Amsterdam: John Benjamins, 2014), 13–38; and García-Molins, *Teoría del Spanglish*.
86. Nairán Ramírez-Esparza, Samuel D. Gosling, Verónica Benet-Martínez, Jeffrey P. Potter, and James W. Pennebaker, "Do Bilinguals Have Two Personalities? A Special Case of Cultural Frame Switching," *Journal of Research in Personality* 40 (2006): 99–120.
87. John Gumperz, "Conversational Code-Switching," in *Discourse Strategies* (Cambridge, UK: Cambridge University Press, 1982), 59–99; Yvette Bürki, "La alternancia de códigos en la literatura neorriqueña," *Revista Internacional de Lingüística Iberoamericana* 1, no. 2 (2003): 79–96; and Linda Ohlson, "'"Baby I'm Sorry, te juro, I'm Sorry". Subjetivización versus objetivización mediante el cambio de código inglés/español en la letra de una canción de bachata actual,'" in *Spanish in Contact: Policy, Social and Linguistic Inquiries*, ed. Kim Potowski and Richard Cameron (Amsterdam: John Benjamins, 2007), 173–189.
88. Monica Heller, *Codeswitching: Anthropological and Sociolinguistic Perspectives* (Berlin: Mouton de Gruyter, 1988); Laura Callahan, *Spanish/English Codeswitching in a Written Corpus* (Amsterdam: Benjamins, 2004).
89. Langacker, *Foundations of Cognitive Grammar*.
90. Cecilia Montes-Alcalá, "Code-Switching in US-Latino-Novels," in *Language Mixing and Code-Switching in Writing*, ed. Mark Sebba, Shahrzad Mahootian, and Carla Jonsson (New York: Routledge, 2012), 74–75.
91. Susana Chávez-Silverman, *Killer Crónicas: Bilingual Memories/Memorias Bilingües* (Madison: University of Wisconsin Press, 2004).
92. Chávez-Silverman, *Killer Crónicas*, 8.
93. Chávez-Silverman, *Killer Crónicas*, 6.
94. Emilio Lorenzo, *El español de hoy, lengua en ebullición* (Madrid: Gredos, 1971).
95. Silvia Betti, "La vida entre dos lenguas y culturas: Reflexiones sobre el fenómeno del Spanglish," *Boletín de la ANLE* (Academia Norteamericana de la Lengua Española), 12–13 (2009–2010): 130–180.
96. Montserrat Guibernau, "¿Qué significa 'ser americano'?" *La Vanguardia*, March 8, 2008.
97. Betti, "La vida entre dos lenguas y culturas," 130–180.

98. Zentella, "La hispanofobia del movimiento "Inglés oficial" en los Estados Unidos por la oficialización del inglés." *Alteridades* 5, no. 10 (1995), 63; Montserrat Guibernau, "¿Qué significa 'ser americano'?" *La Vanguardia*, March 8, 2008; and Betti, "La vida entre dos lenguas y culturas," 130–180.
99. Anzaldúa, *Borderlands/La Frontera*, 77.

# Bibliography

Alvar, Manuel. *Por los caminos de nuestra lengua*. Alcalá de Henares, Mexico: Servicio de Publicaciones de la Universidad de Alcalá de Henares, 1995.

Álvarez Martínez, Stephanie. "¡¿qué, qué?!—Transculturación and Tato Laviera's Spanglish Poetics." In *Spanglish*, edited by Ilan Stavans, 88–109. Westport, CT: Greenwood, 2008.

Anzaldúa, Gloria. *Borderlands/La Frontera. The New Mestiza*. San Francisco: Aunt Lute, 1987.

Anzaldúa, Gloria. *Borderlands/La Frontera: The New Mestiza*. San Francisco: Aunt Lute, 2007.

Ardila, Alfredo. "Spanglish: An Anglicized Spanish Dialect." *Hispanic Journal of Behavioral Sciences* n 27 (2005): 60–81.

Baron, Dennis. *The English-only Question: An Official Language for Americans?* New Haven, CT: Yale University Press, 1990.

Betti, Silvia. *El Spanglish ¿medio eficaz de comunicación?* Bologna: Pitagora Editrice, 2008.

Betti, Silvia. "La vida entre dos lenguas y culturas: reflexiones sobre el fenómeno del *spanglish*." *Boletín de la ANLE* (Academia Norteamericana de la Lengua Española), 12–13 (2009-2010): 130–180.

Betti, Silvia. "Reflexiones sobre el contacto lingüístico: el spanglish y el caso de la revista estadounidense *Latina*." In *Rumbos del hispanismo en el umbral del Cincuentenario de la AIH*, edited by Patrizia Botta, and Sara Pastor, vol. 8, Lengua, 538–548. Rome: Bagatto Libri, 2012.

Betti, Silvia. "La ilusión de una lengua: El spanglish entre realidad y utopía." In *El español en Estados Unidos. E Pluribus Unum? Enfoques multidisciplinarios*, edited by Domnita Dumitrescu, and Gerardo Piña-Rosales, 189–216. New York: Academia Norteamericana de la Lengua Española, 2013.

Betti, Silvia. "La definición del spanglish en la última edición del *Diccionario de la Real Academia* (2014)." *Glosas* (Academia Norteamericana de la Lengua Española) 8, no. 8 (2015): 5–14.

Betti, Silvia, and Daniel Jorques-Jiménez, eds. *Visiones europeas del spanglish*. Valencia, Spain: Uno y Cero Ediciones, 2015.

Bickerton, Derek. *Roots of Language*. Ann Arbor, MI: Karoma, 1981.

Blas Arroyo, José Luis. *Sociolingüística del español*. Madrid: Cátedra, 2005.

Bürki, Yvette. "La alternancia de códigos en la literatura neorriqueña." *Revista Internacional de Lingüística Iberoamericana* 1, no. 2 (2003): 79–96.

Callahan, Laura. *Spanish/English Codeswitching in a Written Corpus*. Amsterdam: Benjamins, 2004.

Carli, Augusto. "Il fenomeno della commutazione di codice." *SSLM-Miscellanea* 3, Università degli Studi di Trieste, Scuola Superiore di Lingue Moderne per Interpreti e Traduttori (1996): 127–146.

Chávez-Silverman, Susana. *Killer Crónicas. Bilingual Memories/Memorias Bilingües*. Madison: University of Wisconsin Press, 2004.

Del Valle, José, and Ana Celia Zentella. "Lengua y política: el espanglish y las deformaciones de la RAE." *Revista Cronopio* 55 (October 2014). http://www.revistacronopto.com/?p=14411.

Dumitrescu, Domnita. "La alternancia de lenguas como actividad de imagen en el discurso hispanoundense/Code-switching as face-work in the discourse of US Hispanics." *Pragmática sociocultural/ Sociocultural Pragmatics* 2, no. 1 (2014): 1–34.

Dumitrescu, Domnita. "Spanglish, estadounidismos y bilingüismo vestigial: ¿Qué es qué?" In *Visiones europeas del spanglish*, edited by Silvia Betti and Daniel Jorques-Jiménez, 26–40. Valencia, Spain: Uno y Cero Ediciones, 2015.

Enghels, Renata. *Les modalités de perception visuelle et auditive: Différences conceptuelles et répercussions sémantico-syntaxiques en espagnol et en français*. Tubingen, Germany: Niemeyer, 2007.

Enghels, Renata, forthcoming. "Socio-pragmatic Functions of Code-Switching in Latino Essays: A Case Study on Bilingual Pragmatic Markers in Susana Chávez-Silverman's *Killer Crónicas* (2004)." *Bulletin of Hispanic Studies*.

Evans, Vyvyan, and Melanie Green. *Cognitive Linguistics: An Introduction*. Edinburgh: Edinburgh University Press, 2006.

Fairclough, Marta. "El (denomidado) Spanglish en los Estados Unidos: Polémicas y realidades." *Revista Internacional de Lingüística Iberoamericana* 1, no.2 (2003): 185–204.

Fuentes, Carlos. *Discurso de inauguración III CILE en Rosario*. 2004. http://www.congresosdelalengua.es/rosario/inauguracion/fuentes_c.htm.

González Echevarría, Roberto. "Hablar spanglish es devaluar el español." *New York Times*, 1997.

González-Vilbazo, Kay, and Bryan Koronkiewicz. "Tú y yo can codeswitch, nosotros cannot. Pronouns in Spanish-English codeswitching. In *Spanish-English Codeswitching in the Carribean and the US*, edited by Rosa E. Guzzardo Tamargo, Catherine M. Mazak, and M. Carmen Parafita Couto, 237–260. Amsterdam: John Benjamins, 2016.

Guibernau, Montserrat. "¿Qué significa 'ser americano'?" *La Vanguardia*, March 8, 2008.

Gumperz, John. "Conversational Code-Switching." In *Discourse Strategies*, edited by John Gumperz, 59–99. Cambridge, UK: Cambridge University Press, 1982.

Guzzardo Tamargo, Rosa E., Catherine M. Mazak, and M. Carmen Parafita Couto. *Spanish-English Codeswitching in the Carribean and the US*. Amsterdam: John Benjamins, 2016.

Heller, Monica. *Codeswitching: Anthropological and Sociolinguistic Perspectives*. Berlin: Mouton de Gruyter, 1988.

Hernández-Nieto, Rosana, and Marcus C. Gutiérrez. Francisco Moreno-Fernández (dir.). "Mapa hispano de los Estados Unidos 2017." *Informes del Observatorio / Observatorio Reports*. 035-11/2017SP, 2017, http://cervantesobservatorio.fas.harvard.edu/sites/default/files/mapa_hispano_2017sp.pdf , accessed August 30, 2017.

Hernández-Sacristán, Carlos. "Principio retórico de continuidad en el Spanglish y sus implicaciones cognitivas." In *Visiones Europeas del Spanglish*, edited by Silvia Betti and Daniel Jorques-Jiménez, 41–51. Valencia, Spain: Uno y Cero Ediciones, 2015.

Jenkins, Devin L. "El suroeste creciente: un breve análisis sociodemográfico de la población hispanohablante de los Estados Unidos." In *El español en Estados Unidos. E Pluribus Unum? Enfoques multidisciplinarios*, edited by Domnita Dumitrescu and Gerardo Piña-Rosales, 31–45. New York: Academia Norteamericana de la Lengua Española, 2013.

Krogstad, Jens M., and Mark H. Lopez. "Hispanic Population Reaches Record 55 Million, but Growth Has Cooled." *Pew Research Center*, 2015. http://www.pewresearch.org/fact-tank/2015/06/25/u-s-hispanic-population-growth-surge-cools/.

Krogstad, Jens M., and Ana González-Barrera. "A Majority of English-speaking Hispanics in the U.S. are Bilingual." *Pew Research Center*, 2015, http://pewrsr.ch/19MGhgV, accessed March 31, 2017.

Kühl, Karoline, and Kurt Braunmüller. "Linguistic Stability and Divergence. An Extended Perspective on Language Contact." In *Stability and Divergence in Language Contact: Factors and Mechanisms*, edited by Karoline Kühl and Kurt Braunmüller, 13–38. Amsterdam: John Benjamins, 2014.

Lara, Fernando. "El espanglish." *Boletín Editorial del Colegio de México* 85 (2000): 23–27.

Lakoff, George, and Mark Johnson. *Metaphors We Live By*. Chicago: University of Chicago Press, 1980.

Lakoff, George, and Mark Johnson. *Philosophy in the Flesh: The Embodied Mind and Its Challenge to Western Thought*. New York: Basic Books, 1999.

Langacker, Ronald W. *Foundations of Cognitive Grammar. Theoretical Prerequisites*. Stanford, CA: Stanford University Press, 1987.

Lipski, John M. "La lengua española en los Estados Unidos: Avanza a la vez que retrocede," 2004. http://www.personal.psu.edu/jml34/SEL.PDF, accessed May 21, 2017.

Lipski, John M. "El español de América en contacto con otras lenguas." In *Lingüística aplicada del español*, edited by Manel Lacorte, 309–345. Madrid: Arco Libros, 2007.

Lipski, John M. *Varieties of Spanish in the United States*. Washington, DC: Georgetown University Press, 2008.

Lipski, John M. "¿Existe un dialecto estadounidense del español?" *La proyección internacional de la lengua española*. Congreso Internacional de Valparaíso (CILE), 2010, http://congresosdelalengua.es/valparaiso/ponencias/america_lengua_espanola/lipski_john_m.htm, accessed September 10 2016.

Lipski, John M. "Hacia una dialectología del español estadounidense." In *El español en Estados Unidos. E Pluribus Unum? Enfoques multidisciplinarios*, edited by Domnita Dumitrescu and Gerardo Piña-Rosales, 107–127. New York: Academia Norteamericana de la Lengua Española, 2013.

Lipski, John M. "El español en Estados Unidos: lo que es y lo que no es". *El español en el mundo. Unidad y diversidad*. Congreso Internacional de Puerto Rico (CILE), 2016, http://congresosdelalengua.es/puertorico/mesas/lipski-john.htm, accessed September 10 2016.

López García-Molins, Ángel. *El español de Estados Unidos y el problema de la norma lingüística*. New York: Academia Norteamericana de la Lengua Española, 2014.

López García-Molins, Ángel. *Teoría del spanglish*. Valencia, Spain: Tirant lo Blanch, 2015.

López García-Molins, Ángel, and Ricardo Morant-Marco. "El spanglish como fundamento del nacionalismo latino en EE.UU." In *Visiones europeas del spanglish*, edited by Silvia Betti, and Daniel Jorques-Jiménez, 86–95. Valencia, Spain: Uno y Cero Ediciones, 2015.

López García-Molins, Ángel. "El Spanglish como dialecto psicológico." In *Nuevas voces sobre el spanglish: Una investigación polifónica*, edited by Silvia Betti, and Enrique Serra Alegre, 105–116. Valencia: Universidad de Valencia, 2016.

Lorenzo, Emilio. *El español de hoy, lengua en ebullición*. Madrid: Gredos, 1971.

MacSwan, Jeff. "The Architecture of the Bilingual Language Faculty: Evidence from Intrasentential Code Switching." *Bilingualism: Language and Cognition* 3, no. 1 (2000): 37–54.

Mahootian, Shahrzad. *A Null Theory of Codeswitching*. PhD diss., Northwestern University, 1993.

Marcos-Marín, Francisco A. "De lenguas y fronteras: el espanglish y el portuñol." *Nueva Revista de Política, Cultura y Arte*, 74 (2001): 70–79.

Marcos-Marín, Francisco A. *Los retos del español*. Madrid: Iberoamericana, 2006.

Marcu, Silvia. "Fronteras de cristal de la inmigración. Visión de los inmigrantes del este europeo en España." *ARBOR Ciencia, Pensamiento y Cultura* 186, no. 744 (July–August 2010): 721–736.

Mayor Marsán, Maricel, ed. *Español o Espanglish ¿Cuál es el futuro de nuestra lengua en los Estados Unidos?* Miami: Ediciones Baquiana, 2008.

McClure, Erica F. "Aspects of Code-Switching in the Discourse of Bilingual Mexican-American Children." In *Latino Language and Communicative Behavior*, edited by Muriel Saville-Troike, 92–115. Washington, DC: Georgetown University Press, 1977.

Montes-Alcalá, Cecilia. "Code-Switching in US-Latino-Novels." In *Language Mixing and Code-Switching in Writing*, edited by Mark Sebba, Shahrzad Mahootian, and Carla Jonsson, 68–88. New York: Routledge, 2012.

Morales, Ed. *Living in Spanglish: The Search for Latino Identity in America*. New York: St. Martin's Press, 2002.

Moreno-Fernández, Francisco. "Dialectología hispánica de los Estados Unidos." In *Enciclopedia del español en los Estados Unidos*, edited by Humberto López Morales, 200–221. Madrid: Instituto Cervantes/Santillana, 2009.

Moreno-Fernández, Francisco. "Panorama interdisciplinario del español en los Estados Unidos." *Tribuna Norteamericana*, Instituto Franklin, 14 (October 2013): 1–6.

Moreno-Fernández, Francisco. "El español en los Estados Unidos y el Instituto Cervantes en Harvard." *Anuario del Instituto Cervantes 2014*, 2014: 375–392.

Moreno-Fernández, Francisco. "La estandarización del español estadounidense." *Blog del Instituto Franklin*, http://dialogoatlantico.com/2015/06/la-estandarizacion-del-espanol-estadounidense/, accessed September 10, 2016.

Moreno-Fernández, Francisco. "Lexicografía del español estadounidense. Propuesta de diccionario de anglicismos." *Glosas* (Academia Norteamericana de la Lengua Española) 8, no. 8, (2015): 39–54, http://www.anle.us/132/Glosas, accessed September 10 2016.

Moreno-Fernández, Francisco, and Domnita Dumitrescu (dirs.). *Bibliografía lingüística del español en los Estados Unidos*. Cambridge, MA: Instituto Cervantes at Harvard University—ANLE, 2016.

Moro, Mónica. "The Universality of Syntactic Constraints on Spanish-English Codeswitching in the USA." *Language and Intercultural Communication*, 15, no. 3 (2015): 391–406.

Myers-Scotton, Carol. *Social Motivations for Code-Switching*. Oxford: Oxford University Press, 1993.

Myers-Scotton, Carol. "A Theoretical Introduction to the Markedness Model." In *Codes and Consequences Choosing Linguistic Varieties*, edited by Carol Myers-Scotton, 18–40. Oxford: Oxford University Press, 1998.

Observatorio de la lengua española y las culturas hispánicas en los Estados Unidos. Harvard: http://cervantesobservatorio.fas.harvard.edu/es.

Ohlson, Linda. ' "Baby I'm sorry, te juro, I'm sorry'. Subjetivización versus objetivización mediante el cambio de código inglés/español en la letra de una canción de bachata actual.' " In *Spanish in Contact. Policy, Social and Linguistic Inquiries*, edited by Kim Potowski and Richard Cameron, 173–189. Amsterdam: John Benjamins, 2007.

Otheguy, Ricardo. "El llamado espanglish": In *Enciclopedia del español en los Estados Unidos*, edited by Humberto López Morales, 222–223. Madrid: Instituto Cervantes/Santillana, 2009.

Otheguy, Ricardo, and Nancy Stern. "On So-called Spanglish." *International Journal of Bilingualism* 15, no. 1 (2010): 85–100.

Pew Research Center. *Modern Immigration Wave Brings 59 million to the U.S., Driving Population Growth and Change Through 2065*, 2015, http://pewrsr.ch/1KKz4rY, accessed March 21 2017.
Pfaff, Carol W. "Constraints on Language Mixing: Intrasentential Codeswitching and Borrowing in Spanish/English." *Language* 55 (1979): 291–318.
Poplack, Shana. "Sometimes I'll Start a Sentence in Spanish y termino en español: Towards a Typology of Codeswitching." *Linguistics* 18 (1980): 581–618.
Proust Iligaray, Valentina. "El español en tiempos tempestuosos." *El Mercurio*, February 19, 2017.
Ramírez-Esparza, Nairán, Samuel D. Gosling, Verónica Benet-Martínez, Jeffrey P. Potter, and James W. Pennebaker. "Do Bilinguals Have Two Personalities? A Special Case of Cultural Frame Switching." *Journal of Research in Personality* 40 (2006): 99–120.
Real Academia Española. *Diccionario de la lengua española (Edición del Tricentenario)*. Madrid: Espasa, 2014.
Rodríguez-González, Eva, and M. Carmen Parafita-Couto. "Calling for Interdisciplinary Approaches to the Study of "Spanglish" and Its Linguistic Manifestations." *Hispania* 95, no. 3 (2012): 461–480.
Ros, Jorge. "El futuro cercano de EE. UU. es mestizo y se escribe en Spanglish." *Hispanopost*, December 13, 2016, http://www.hispanopost.com/el-futuro-cercano-de-eeuu-es-mestizo-y-se-escribe-en-spanglish, accessed December 14 2016.
Sánchez, Rosaura. "Our Linguistic and Social Context." In *Spanglish*, edited by Ilan Stavans, 3–41. Westport, CT: Greenwood, 2008.
Sankoff, David, and Shana Poplack. "A Formal Grammar for Codeswitching." *Papers in Linguistics* 14, no. 1 (1981): 3–46.
Silva-Corvalán, Carmen. "El español de Los Ángeles: ¿Adquisición incompleta o desgaste lingüístico?" In *Estudios sociolingüísticos del español de España y América*, edited by Ana María Cestero Mancera, Isabel Molina Martos, and Florentino Paredes García, 121–142. Madrid: Arco Libros, 2006.
Silva-Corvalán, Carmen, and Kim Potowski. "La alternancia de códigos (Codeswitching)." In *Enciclopedia del español en los Estados Unidos*, edited by Humberto López Morales, 272–276. Madrid: Instituto Cervantes/Santillana, 2009.
Silvia Betti, and Enrique Serra Alegre, eds. *Nuevas voces sobre el spanglish: Una investigación polifónica*. Valencia, Spain: ANLE y Universidad de Valencia, 2016.
Sobejano, Gonzalo. "El Spanglish no es algo gracioso, es una corrupción del lenguaje." *La Voz Digital* 2007, http://www.lavozdigital.es., accessed December 14, 2016.
Sobin, Nicholas J. "On Code-Switching Inside NP." *Applied Psycholinguistics* 5 (1984): 293–303.
Stavans, Ilan. *Spanglish: The Making of a New American Language*. New York: Harper Collins, 2003.
Stavans, Ilan, ed. *Spanglish*. Westport, CT: Greenwood, 2008.
Taylor, John R., and Jeanette Littlemore. *The Bloomsbury Companion to Cognitive Linguistics*. London: Bloomsbury, 2014.
Tió Montes de Oca, Salvador. "Teoría del Espanglish." *A fuego lento, cien columnas de humor y una cornisa*. Rio Piedras: University of Puerto Rico, 1954.
The Economist. *America's Hispanics: From Minor to Major*, 2015, http://econ.st/1x06jaO, accessed March 24 2017.
Torres, Lourdes. "In the Contact-Zone: Code-Switching Strategies by Latino/-a Writers." *Melus* 32, no. 1 (2007): 75–96.

Torres Torres, Antonio. "El Spanglish, un proceso especial de contacto de lenguas." *1st International Conference on Spanglish*, Amherst, 2004. www.amherst.edu/~spanglish/Torres.htm., accessed September 10 2016.

Torres Torres, Antonio. "Miradas sobre la identidad latina en los Estados Unidos." *Revista Pecios*, December 5, 2007, https://pecios.wordpress.com/2007/12/05/miradas-sobre-la-identidad-latina-en-los-estados-unidos/., accessed March 21 2016.

Torres Torres, Antonio. "Sobre el spanglish en los Estados Unidos: Implicaciones de un caleidoscopio de perspectivas." In *Visiones europeas del spanglish*, edited by Silvia Betti and Daniel Jorques-Jiménez, 96–109. Valencia, Spain: Uno y Cero Ediciones, 2015.

Torres Torres, Antonio. "El español estadounidense, entre el 'spanglish' y el español internacional." In *Nuevas voces sobre el Spanglish: una investigación polifónica*, edited by Silvia Betti and Enrique Serra Alegre, 131–147. Valencia, Spain: Universidad de Valencia, 2016.

US Census Bureau. *Population Estimates*, 2014, http://1.usa.gov/1Ov6iTw, accessed March 21, 2017.

US Census Bureau. *Newsroom: Hispanic Heritage Month*, 2015a, http://bit.ly/2actQO1, accessed March 21 2016.

US Census Bureau. *Quick Facts United States*, 2015b, http://bit.ly/2aeQwoO, accessed March 21, 2016.

Valdés, Isabel. *Marketing to American Latinos: A Guide to the In-Culture Approach (Part 2)*. New York: Paramount Market, 2002.

Villanueva Darío. "La actitud de Trump va en contra de la evolución del mundo." *La Razón.es*, January 29, 2017, ltimahorapress.com/item/47909_dar-amp-iacute-o-villanueva-quot-la-actitud-de-trump-va-en-contra-de-la-evoluci-amp-oacute-n-del-mundo-quot., accessed January 30, 2017.

Zentella, Ana Celia. "Spanish and English in Contact in the United States: The Puerto Rican Experience." *Word* 33, no. 1–2 (1982): 41–57.

Zentella, Ana Celia. "La hispanofobia del movimiento 'Inglés oficial' en los Estados Unidos por la oficialización del inglés." *Alteridades* 5, no. 10 (1995): 55–65.

Zentella, Ana Celia. *Growing up Bilingual: Puerto Rican Children in New York*. Oxford: Blackwell, 1997.

Zentella, Ana Celia. "Would You Like Your Children to Speak English and Spanish?" / "¿Quieren que sus hijos hablen el inglés y el español?" http://www.spanishdict.com/answers/170367/would-you-raise-your-children-to-speak-spanish-if-that-language-isnt-part-of-your-family-heritage, accessed December 14 2016.

Zentella, Ana Celia. "The Grammar of Spanglish." In *Spanglish*, edited by Ilan Stavans, 42–63. Westport, CT: Greenwood, 2008.

Zentella, Ana Celia. "Spanglish: Language Politics vs. *el habla del pueblo*." In *Spanish-English Codeswitching in the Caribbean and the U.S.*, edited by Rosa E. Guzzardo Tamargo et al., 12–35. Amsterdam: John Benjamins, 2016.

# PART V
## WAYS OF BEING

CHAPTER 17

# LATINX POP CULTURAL STUDIES *HOY!*

FREDERICK LUIS ALDAMA

Latinxs are the largest growing demographic in the United States.[1] At 18 percent of the US population, Latinxs are the majority minority. And, in some regions of the United States like the Southwest, Latinxs are the majority. With this proverbial "Browning of America" it should come as little surprise, then, that we're seeing Latinx experiences and identities reconstructed in all variety of pop cultural phenomena: from TV, webisodes, film, and music, to street art, comic books, video games, viral Internet performances, among others. However, what is surprising is that Latinxs continue to be underrepresented and egregiously misrepresented in the mainstream pop cultural imaginary—and with devastating material consequences and effects on Latinx peoples.

Many contemporary Latinx scholars seek to enrich our understanding of mainstreaming of Latinx identity and experience as well as how Latinx creators distill and reconstruct in complex and rich ways such identities and experiences. Launched in the late twentieth century by scholars such as Frances Aparicio and Susana Chávez-Silverman (*Tropicalizations*), we see the study of Latinx pop culture come to prominence in the early twenty-first century with scholars such as Juan Flores (*From Bomba to Hip-Hop*), Alicia Gaspar de Alba (*Velvet Barrios*), Michelle Habell-Pallán and Mary Romero (*Latino/a Popular Culture*), Angharad N. Valdivia (*A Latina in the Land of Hollywood*), Arlene Dávila (*Latinos, Inc.*), Frances Negrón-Muntaner (*Boricua Pop*), and Charles Tatum (*Chicano Popular Culture*) setting sights on this type of excavatory work.[2] In *Velvet Barrios*, for instance, we see the systematic analysis of altars, music (boleros, rap, and hip-hop), sports, lowrider magazines, quinceañeras, among others to identify queer and feminist borderland spaces of resistance to mainstream and *machista* Latinx cultural phenomena. Other scholars seek to critically open eyes to how mainstream pop culture negatively impacts (cultural heritage, body, phenotype, and language) the daily existence of Latinxs. In *A Latina in the Land of Hollywood*, Angharad N. Valdivia forcefully calls attention to those Victoria's Secret and Frederick's of Hollywood catalogs that *normalize* white, middle-class ideals of beauty.[3] And, in her book *Latina/os and the*

*Media* she analyzes how accented-Spanish English and phenotype forever *foreign-ize* Latinxs such as Salma Hayek, Eva Mendes, Jennifer Lopez, Eva Longoria, and America Ferrera.[4] And in Isabel Molina-Guzmán's *Latina and Latinos on TV* she demonstrates how even though we're seeing more Latinxs in front of the TV camera, shows like *Modern Family* and *The Office* continue to deepen the xenophobia and racism that pervades US society today.[5]

In their introduction to *Latino/a Popular Culture*, Habell-Pallán and Romero identify the pop cultural landscape as a "mosaic of contradictions."[6] That is, for all the negative stereotypes and restrictive ways that the mainstream boxes in Latinxs, we see Latinx musicians, writers, artists, comic book creators, and performers actively metabolizing all cultural phenomena to clear positive spaces of empowerment and to *make* new perception, thought, and feeling about Latinx identities and experiences. Scholars such as Mary Beltrán, Camilla Fojas, Cruz Medina, Pancho McFarland, Phillip Penix-Tadsen, Enrique García, Mauricio Espinoza, Osvaldo Cleger, Guisela Latorre, Laura Pérez, Peter J. García, Chon Noriega, María Elena Cepeda, Charles Ramírez Berg, Paloma Martínez-Cruz, Charles Tatum, William Nericcio, Deborah Paredez, Priscilla Ovale, Richard T. Rodriguez, and so many others have analyzed Latinx musicscapes, film- and mediascapes, performative, digital, and art spaces, videogames, sports, and the list goes on. For instance, Cruz Medina's *Reclaiming Poch@ Pop* analyzes the work of Lalo Alcaraz (Pocho.com and Pocho Hour of Power), Guillermo Gomez-Peña (*Codex Espangliensis*), blogger Romeo Guzman (*Pocho in Greater Mexico*), and photographer Pocho-One to show how they variously clear sites of Latinx empowerment through their pop cultural creations through the pop cultural productions of Latinos who self-identify as poch@.[7] In several of my coauthored books with Ilan Stavans, we analyze pop cultural creations as they surface then travel across both sides of the US/Mexico border.[8] In Pancho McFarland's *Toward a Chican@ Hip Hop*, we see how Latinx hip-hop can powerfully interweave indigenous traditions (sacred *maiz* narratives) and identities.[9] And we see this same excavatory impulse in scholarship with a purposefully pedagogical aim. I think of the capacious scholarly sweeps made in Charles Tatum's *Chicano Popular Culture*, Patricia M. Montilla's edited *Latinos and American Popular Culture*, and my edited *The Routledge Companion to Latino/a Pop Culture* that also provide roadmaps for those teaching Latinx pop culture in undergraduate classes for the first time.[10]

As this brief overview of the Latinx pop culture scholarly terrain indicates, there has been (and continues to be) much work done to identify the cultural phenomena that oppressively restrict and that vitally affirm the complex, intersectional (race, gender, sexuality, class, region) ways Latinxs exist in the United States. This article for the *Oxford Handbook of Latino Studies* continues this stereoscopic work: (1) to explore the ways the mainstream pop culture restricts and often destructively simplifies; (2) to examine how a range of Latinx pop cultural creations not only willfully mirror Latinx identities and experiences but also actively transform everyday life for Latinx peoples.

What is meant by Latinx pop culture? For some this might be the artificial division between mass or lowbrow culture and highbrow culture; or this could mean the difference between Alisa Valdez's breezy *Dirty Girls Social Club* (2003) and Salvador Plascencia's metafictional *People of Paper* (2005); or it could mean the difference between graffiti street art and that which appears in sanctified museum spaces. Valdez's *Dirty Girls* is created to entertain the masses and participates in global capitalist circuits of production and consumption; some might argue, too, that it smokescreens neoliberal processes of exploitation and oppression. For the purposes of this article—and to mirror the intellectual approach by many of the Latinx scholars mentioned earlier—while there's certainly an *intent* that needs to be considered on the part of creating respective cultural phenomena, once it's out of the hands of the creator, there's no telling how it will be used in the making of new cultural phenomena. Think of Blatinx (Haitian/Puerto Rican) artist Jean-Michel Basquiat's art that appeared on cardboard, walls, trains, and whatever else he could get his hands on. This art is now exhibited in sanctified high-art museum spaces.

While Latinx pop cultural studies has come into its own in the twenty-first century, pop culture by and about Latinxs began rising to prominence in the late twentieth century; of course, this culture has been an important part of larger US culture since the signing of the Treaty of Guadalupe Hidalgo (1848) through the early twentieth century in the form of newspapers, magazines, cartoons, and radio shows. However, it is during and after the various Latinx activist movements and the increased demographic and urbanization of Latinxs that we begin to see pop cultural phenomena explode. During the 1980s, for example, we witnessed a tremendous outpouring of music and films by Latinxs. I think of Gloria Estefan and the *Miami Sound Machine* along with films of Luis Valdez such as *Zoot Suit* (1981) and *La Bamba* (1987) as well as Gregory Nava's *El Norte* (1984) and Cheech Marín's *Born in East LA* (1987). There were TV shows like Paul Rodriguez's *a.k.a Pablo* that continued to grow (as had already begun in the 1970s with *Chico and the Man*) the presence of Latinx characters with more agency and range than the caricatures seen in *I Love Lucy* and *Speedy Gonzales*. This trend to foreground complex Latinx identities and experiences continued to gain traction in the 1990s with TV shows like *House of Buggin* and *First Time Out*, the popularization of musicians like Santana, Jon Secada, Selena, Marc Anthony, J-Lo, and Ricky Martin, and the success with Latinx and non-Latinx audiences of films like *American Me* (1992), *El Mariachi* (1992), *Mi Vida Loca* (1994), *I Like It Like That* (1994), *Mi Familia* (1995), and *Selena* (1997).

Latinx pop culture continued to grow in leaps and bounds in the twenty-first century. In film, we see Latinx actors in mainstream and Latinx films, playing Latinx-identified characters as well as ethnoracially ambiguous characters. Rosario Dawson moved from the indie margins (Larry Clark's 1995 *Kids*) to the mainstream with her appearance in Barry Sonnenfeld's *Men in Black 2* (2002) and Peter Berg's *The Rundown* (2003). And we see Zoe Saldana's play Latinx dancer Eva Rodriguez in Nicholas Hytner's *Center Stage* (2000) followed by a string of action-hero roles in films like *Avatar* (2009), *Colombiana* (2011), and the *Guardians of the Galaxy* (2014) franchise. Also in 2000, Michelle Rodriguez plays Brooklyn-raised Latinx boxer Diana Guzman, in Karyn Kusama's *Girlfight* (2000) followed also by a string of action-hero roles in, for instance, the *Fast & Furious* franchise (2001–), *Avatar*, *Machete* (2010) and *Machete Kills* (2013), and *Alita: Battle Angel* (2018). And we see Latinx actors like Jessica Alba in films like John Duigan's *Paranoid* (2000) as well as in roles like *migra*-cum-activist Sartana in Robert Rodriguez's *Machete* series. We see America Ferrera play the Los Angeles Chicanx Ana Garcia in Patricia Cardosa's *Real Women Have Curves* (2002) and her in the role of Hedy Galili in Todd Berger's *It's a Disaster* (2012). We see actors like Gabriel Chavarria in Latinx-focused films like *Lowriders* (and TV shows like *East Los High*) as well in mainstream films like *War of the Planet of the Apes* (2017). I think, too, of Eiza González who plays the role of Monica "Darling" Costello in *Baby Driver* (2017) and the role of Santanico Pandemonium in Robert Rodriguez's cable-TV serialized *From Dusk Till Dawn* (2014–2016) and as Nyssiana in Rodriguez's cyberpunk sci-fi movie *Alita: Battle Angel* (2018). We see former Nickelodeon star Isabela Moner as Izabella in *Transformers: The Last Knight* (2017) as well as in the role of Nina Simone in Cynthia Mort's biopic *Nina* (2016). Since his role in *Gone in 60 Seconds* in 2000, Michael Peña has starred in Paul Haggis's *Crash* (2004), Oliver Stone's *World Trade Center* (2006), Edward James Olmos's *Walkout* (2006), David Ayer's *End of Watch* (2012), David O. Russell's *American Hustle*, Ayer's *Fury* (2014), Ridley Scott's *The Martian* (2015), Diego Luna's *Cesar Chavez* (2015), and Peyton Reed's *Ant-Man* (2015) and *Ant-Man and the Wasp* (2018), to mention just a few.

In the twenty-first century we also see a greater screen presence among Latinx actors playing characters of all ages, genders, sexualities and from a variety of Latinx ancestral heritages and class backgrounds. For instance, queer Latinx teens appear in primetime shows like *Glee* (2009–2015) with Naya Rivera playing Santana, as well as *Ugly Betty* with Mark Indelicato playing Justin Suarez; we also had queer Latinx characters in shows like *Grey's Anatomy* with Dr. Callie Torres (Calliope Iphegenia), *The Office* (2005–2012) with Óscar Martínez (Oscar Nunez), and in *True Blood* (2008–2014) with Jesus Velasquez (Kevin Alejandro). With shows like *Desperate Housewives* (2004–2012) and *Modern Family* (2009–), we see the appearance of upper and middle-class Latinx families. And with shows like *Devious Maids* (2013–2016), *Jane the Virgin* (2014–), *Cristela* (2014–2015), and *Ugly Betty* (2006–2010) we have Latinx middle- and working-class families represented. And with digital streaming platforms coming into their own in the twenty-first century, we see other shows produced that focus nearly exclusively on Latinx communities such as Hulu's *East Los High* (2013–).[11]

All of these shows certainly complicate the Latinx representational terrain. However, when we begin to scratch the surface of many of these films and TV shows, an uncritical reproduction of simplistic and negative stereotypes often can be discerned. For instance, in *Desperate Housewives* we see the upper-middle-class Solis family deal with issues typical of those living on Wisteria Lane such as deceit and infidelity. But the show also distinguishes them from the Anglo families. The Solis family are hot tempered, oversexed, and, finally, downwardly mobile. They are the family that slips into a non-country-club-going group when Carlos (Ricardo Antonio Chavira) goes blind, loses his job, and takes up massage therapy. Rather than pass through the front doors of the country club, they find themselves welcome only by way of the servant's entrance—an indication generally of their lower status in the community now that they are no longer members of the professional, bourgeois class. In *Ugly Betty*, the show focuses on the upward mobility of Betty (America Ferrera) whose smarts (street and book) and a modicum of coincidence lead to her arrival in the upper-middle professional class romancing the Anglo boss.

While there's much importance placed on food (Mexican), dance, and code-switching (especially during heightened emotional moments and by the older generation represented by the father who peppers his English with "Dios mio!" and "mija," and so on) as expressions of their Latinidad, the show subordinates this to its fairytale vision of the Latinx family: that hard work and the pursuit of one's passion will lead to a Cinderella-like, socioeconomic transformation. *Modern Family* also plays into the upward mobility and assimilationist fantasy and takes viewers back to the kind of histrionics seen in *I Love Lucy* shows of the 1950s. The show writes the Latina character, Gloria (Sofía Vergara), as the malapropism-prone (heavily Spanish-accented English) buffoon and butt of all the punchlines. Indeed, according to Dolores Inés Casillas and colleagues, the show's mocking of Gloria's accent privileges non-accented English and erases the struggles of those Latinxs who struggle with English in an English-language-dominant nation.[12]

This is not to say there are not primetime TV shows that critically rupture the televisual imaginary constructed by shows like *Ugly Betty* and *Desperate Housewife*. In *Scrubs* (2001–2010), note the interaction between the nurse Carla Espinosa (played by Judy Reyes) and her significant other—the African American character Christopher Turk (played by Donald Faison). It's not so much the show's depiction of her as hot tempered, gossipy, and sassy that is innovative, but rather it is the way the show uses Reyes's mixed, Afro-Latinx features to disrupt stereotypes. While television viewers learn over the show's eight seasons that she's of Dominican origin, having migrated to Chicago as a child, others including Turk constantly try to pigeonhole her as something else: Mexican, Puerto Rican, you name it (but not Blatinx). In so doing, the show also calls into question the very construction of Latino as a category: who is included and who is not.

And in *The George Lopez Show* (2001–2007) there is great emphasis in casting and writing a show about the everyday interactions of a mixed Mexican-Cuban intergenerational family: George (George Lopez) is Mexican Latinx, and his wife Angie (Constance Marie) is Cuban Latinx. Angie's father, Vic, speaks English with a pronounced Spanish accent, but he's not made the butt of jokes by family members or the show's audience. The show is a comedy, but it's also a show that reconstructs the complex and culturally varied ways that Latinxs exist in the United States.

It's important to understand that Latinxs in the twenty-first century consume all variety of cultural phenomena: from *Modern Family* to *telenovelas* like *Eva Luna* (2010–2011) to shows like *Lost* (2004–2010) and film franchises like *Ant-Man* and *Star Wars*. In exercising our varied tastes, we also represent a huge trillion-dollar purchasing power. This translates into both cinema ticket sales (Latinxs see the most films of any demographic in the United States) and TV viewing numbers as well as the buying of toys and the like. For corporate America, the Latinx demographic represents a huge consumer demographic. Viewed with somewhat cynical and skeptical eyes, the increased representation of Latinxs in the entertainment industry is a result of this push to capture the Latinx consumer market. Here's where we might skeptically ask: Was Marvel's introduction of Miles Morales as the Afro-Latinx Spidey in its Ultimate comics series done to enrich the comic book universe, or simply to take advantage of the purchasing power of the two largest minority populations in the United States: African Americans and

Latinxs? Was the Latino-focused content in a special bilingual issue of *Rolling Stone* (November 22, 2012) that included pieces on Latino musicians Pitbull and Calle 13 as well as fiction by Junot Díaz a *new* way to engage its readership or a marketing ploy directed at Latinos? We might ask the same when we see Latinxs cast in mainstream action films: Saldana in the *Guardians* franchise films, Oscar Isaac as Poe Dameron in the latest *Star Wars* films, Michal Peña in *Ant-Man* (2015) and *Ant Man and the Wasp* (2018), and Jay Hernandez as El Diablo in David Ayer's *Suicide Squad* (2016), among many others.

Within this schema, Latinx actors are rarely cast as the protagonists. Skeptically speaking, they are present *enough* to get that Latinx filmgoer into a cinema seat; they are the spicy brown peppering that adds meaning to an otherwise homogenized Anglo dish. Think of the Latinx characters Julio (Diego Luna) and Frey (Alice Braga) whose presence launches the Anglo protagonist, Max (Matt Damon), on a mission to save all Latinxs and humanity at large.

As was mentioned at the beginning of this chapter, however, Latinx subjects are not passive consumers of this mainstreamed Latinx fodder. There's an active metabolizing and critical redeployment of these narratives as well as the fashioning of entirely new cultural phenomena. So, while we can and should be critical when Anglo Robin Williams is voice-cast to play the animated Latinx character, Ramon, in the *Happy Feet* (2006), we can now see creators like Jorge Gutierrez cast Latinxs to voice Latinx charters—and complex ones at that—in TV shows like *El Tigre* (2007–2008) and films like *The Book of Life* (2014). As Laura Fernández analyzes and discusses in "Canta y no llores," Gutierrez's creates a Latinx empowered, borderland film that purposefully appeals primarily to a Latinx audience—especially Latinx youth increasingly forgotten by educators across the nation.[13] He creates a feature-length animation that entertains *and* affirms Mexican myth and ritual.

Latinx (and some non-Latinx) filmmakers are working in the realist, motion-photographic mode to push back and clear new spaces for Latinx subjectivities and experiences. For instance, in *Gun Hill Road* (2011) director Rashaad Ernesto Green focuses on intergenerational struggle between a Puerto Rican father and son; this time, however, the son Michael (Harmony Santana) is rejected because she identifies as Vanessa. In Peter Bratt's *La Mission* (2009), Latinx (and secondarily non-Latinx) filmgoers are immersed in the Latinx community of San Francisco, encountering the *machista* violence of a Latinx father, Che (Benjamin Bratt), toward his gay son, Jes (Alex Hernandez). The film ends with a reconciliation after Che experiences a symbolic rebirth in and through his connection with his indigenous ancestral heritage. As Cecilia Aragon argues in "Performing Mestizaje," *La Mission* makes vitally new age-old communal, anticolonial mestizaje rituals such as *la danza Azteca*, linking Latinx communities today with our indigenous pasts.

Latinx filmmakers are innovating in the pop cultural space of music videos. With today's relatively low production costs, availability of Kickstarter and other fund-raising platforms, and Internet distribution sites, we are seeing a proliferation of Latinx creators and performers in music video spaces. There are the activist music videos of Alex Rivera:

"El Hielo" and "Wake Me Up." Rivera's music videos entertain *and* educate audiences about the oppression and exploitation of undocumented peoples.[14] There are J-Lo's mainstream music videos such as "I Luv U Papi" that inform audiences about the ways Latinas are hypersexualized and animalized in mainstream pop culture. It opens with J-Lo and friends being told by a record label executive that her new music video should be filmed in a water park or a zoo. They object. The music video instead reverses the male sexualizing gaze of Latina bodies, with J-Lo as agent of the narrative and gaze. And let us not forget how today's social media and Internet platforms turned Sarai Gonzalez into a music video superstar with the Spanish-language "Soy Yo" music video by Bomba Estéreo. When it was released on September 7, 2016, it logged over 6.5 million views. And Malu Trevejo's garnering of a huge Internet audience led to the recording of her hit single, "Luna Llena" and her signing with label In-Tu Línea, a division of Universal Music Latino.

Saria and Malu have used the Internet and social media platforms to find and build huge Latinx audiences. Other twenty-first-century Latinx creators use the Internet (YouTube, blogs, and social media, for instance) to construct star personas and personal brands. Here we see how Latinx digital spaces function as profit-driven reified spaces as well as a creative space for making new content to convey the richly layered aspects of being Latinx.[15]

Relative low production costs in other areas such as music and comic books have led to a tremendous outpouring of Latinx pop cultural creation in these areas. There's raza rock 'n' roll and punk, techno, hip-hop, and hard rock musicscapes that can and do create pop cultural spaces that affirm all variety of Latinx identities and build communities of resistance.[16] And in the realm of comic books we also see an intense and constant productivity among Latinxs. Latinx comic book authors create stories of all genres. We have those such as Frank Espinosa (*Rocketo*) and Los Bros Hernandez (*Citizen Rex*) who carry readers into the future with their epic sci-fi story worlds. We have those who choose noir as their storytelling style such as Rafael Navarro (*Sonambulo*) and Gilbert Hernandez (standalones like *Julio's Day*). There are youth-oriented, coming-of-age (and coming out) stories such as Ivan Velez Jr. (*Tales of the Closet*), Graciela Rodriguez's *Lunatic Fringe* (2010), and Liz Mayorga's *Outgrowing Plastic Dolls* (2013). We have those who choose the life-education journey (or *Bildung*) story such as Rhode Montijo (*Pablo's Inferno* and *Tartamudo*) and Wilfred Santiago (*In My Darkest Hour*). Then there are those who choose the superheroic mode such as Fernando Rodriguez (*Aztec of the City*), Richard Dominguez (*El Gato Negro*), Laura Molina (*Cihualyaomiquiz, the Jaguar*), Carlos Saldaña (*Burrito*), Rafael Navarro (*Sonambulo*), and Javier Hernandez (*El Muerto*), among many others. We have those working in the satirical mode like Lalo Alcaraz (*La Cucaracha*), Oscar Garza and Rolando Esquivel (*Mashbone & Grifty*), and Ilan Stavans and Robert Weil (*Mr. Spic Goes to Washington*). Others work in the horror mode such as Crystal Gonzalez (*In the Dark*), Liz Mayorga (*Monstrous Love Stories*), Kelly Fernandez (*The Ciguapa*), and Emil Ferris (*My Favorite Thing Is Monsters*). We also have comics aimed at the younger set such as Sebastian Kadlecik (*Quince*), Gilbert Hernandez (*The Adventures of Venus*), and Fernando de Peña and Rodrigo Vargas (*Elisa y Los Mutantes*).

And we have Latinx creators who choose the nonfictional graphic mode such as Inverna Lockpez (*Cuba My Revolution*), Ilan Stavans and Santiago Cohen (*Angelitos*), and Alberto Ledesma (*Diary of a Reluctant Dreamer*). We also have those who choose the biographical form, such as Wilfred Santiago (his masterful *21: The Story of Roberto Clemente*), those who choose the historical form such as Ilan Stavans (writer) and Lalo Alcaraz (artist) in the making of *Latino U.S.A: A Cartoon History*, and authors like Daniel Parada who choose to give a graphic narrative form to pre-Columbian history in *Zotz: Serpent and Shield*. Today, we have more and more Latinx creators creating characters with all sorts of intersectional identities. For instance, in the comics of Kat Fajardo, Breena Nuñez, Vicko, Serenity Sersección, and Christa R. Road, we encounter powerful narratives of Latina experiences and identities that open eyes to different ways of understanding race, sexuality, gender, and class identities and experiences. With pencil, ink, and paper along with scanners, tablets, and the Internet, these Latinx creators have been able to reach and grow Latinx and non-Latinx audiences. Comics have become a pop cultural space filled with Latinx storytellers. It offers all variety of tensions and harmonies between its visual and verbal ingredients.[17]

This article has touched on but a few areas where we see the creation, distribution, and consumption of pop culture by and about Latinxs. There is, of course, much more to this story, including important scholarly work done in the areas of video games, street art, performance art, spoken-word poetry, lowrider culture, sports, quinceañeras, religious ritual, literature, theater, and much more.[18]

Every year I teach an introductory course on Latinx studies. I do so through the lens of Latinx pop culture. I have found that I can take the students on a journey of deep learning about how race, class, gender, and sexuality operate in and through an analytical lens that focuses on film, comic books, music, blogs, Latinx Tweet fiction, music videos, and much more. I also remind the students that Latinx creators and consumers of pop culture are *active* in their creating and consuming. That is, while there is much for us to be critical of in terms of the mainstream imaginary and its simplistic and destructive reconstructions of Latinidad, we are not passive, absorptive sponges. Where cultural phenomenon guides the imagination of Latinxs is not predetermined. Latinxs actively metabolize all that comes our way into newly imagined and real cultural phenomena. This in turn can and does positively impact the shaping of Latinx lives. Of course, this does not excuse the pop cultural phenomena associated with Latinxs that reproduce destructive stereotypes. We can and should call attention to this: in its evaluation, we can learn much about racist, sexist, classist material histories and social practices. Finally, I use pop culture by and about Latinxs to remind them that Latinx experiences and identities are at once varied and have commonalities. No matter whether Mexican, Central America, Latin American, Cuban, Dominican, Puerto Rican, Chumash Indian, or other indigenous groups of origin as US Latinxs, we share common ground in terms of language, religious practice, food, and *cariños*; that is, there's something tangible about how we have grown our culture in terms of our shared education of the senses: touch, smell, taste, and sound. We share histories of conquest and internal colonial mentalities within families, pre-Columbian ancestry and tradition, culture, history.

There is still much work to be done analyzing Latinx pop cultural phenomena. We have only just begun the work of excavating the rich ways that indigeneity across the Américas and Caribbean informs the shaping of Latinx pop cultural creations. The study of Latinx pop cultural phenomena will continue to deeply enrich our understanding of all the resplendent ways that Latinxs exist in the United States—as well as how Latinxs are agents of progressive change in the everyday lives of all denizens of the United States.

## Notes

1. I use the term "Latinx" throughout this essay to be inclusive of all genders and sexual orientation as well as to embrace a term generated and deployed by new generations of Latinxs in the United States. This does not mean that I erase the history and politics that inform the term "Latino/a." However, I side with those who consider this a powerful bottom-up claiming of language in ways that demonstrate inclusivity. In "What's in an 'x'? An Exchange about the Politics of 'Latinx'," Sandra L. Soto-Santiago succinctly states: "The 'x', the '@', and whatever may come after this, are an invitation to question language and those who impose those rules upon us" (91). She concludes how the category Latinx "dismantle[s] what exists and invites us to re-think how individuals with different ideologies, perspectives, and identities are included or rejected from different spaces or communities through language."
2. Juan Flores, *From Bomba to Hip-Hop: Puerto Rican Culture and Latino Identity* (New York: Columbia University Press, 2000); Alicia Gaspar de Alba, ed., *Velvet Barrios: Popular Culture & Chicana/o Sexualities* (New York: Palgrave Macmillan, 2003); Michelle Habell-Pallán and Mary Romero, eds. *Latino/a Popular Culture* (New York: New York University Press, 2002); Angharad N. Valdivia, *A Latina in the Land of Hollywood and Other Essays on Media Culture* (Tucson: University of Arizona Press, 2000); Arlene Dávila, *Latinos, Inc.: The Marketing and Making of a People* (Berkeley: University of California Press, 2001); Frances Negrón-Muntaner, *Boricua Pop: Puerto Ricans and the Latinization of American Culture* (New York: New York University Press, 2004); Charles Tatum, *Chicano Popular Culture: Que Hable el Pueblo* (Tucson: University of Arizona Press, 2001).
3. Valdivia, *A Latina in the Land of Hollywood*, 2000.
4. Angharad N. Valdivia, *Latina/os and the Media* (Cambridge, UK: Polity Press, 2010).
5. Isabel Molina-Guzmán, *Latinas and Latinos on TV: Colorblind Comedy in the Post-Racial Network Era* (Tucson: The University of Arizona Press, 2018).
6. Habell-Pallán and Romero, *Latino/a Popular Culture*, 2.
7. Cruz Medina, *Reclaiming Poch@ Pop: Examining the Rhetoric of Cultural Deficiency* (New York: Palgrave, 2015).
8. See Frederick Luis Aldama and Ilan Stavans, *¡Muy Pop! Conversations on Latino Popular Culture* (Ann Arbor: University of Michigan Press, 2013) and *Laughing Matters: Conversations on Humor* (San Diego: San Diego State University Press, 2016).
9. Pancho McFarland, *Toward a Chican@ Hip Hop* (New York: Routledge, 2018).
10. Tatum, *Chicano Popular Culture*; Patricia Montilla, ed., *Latinos and American Popular Culture* (Santa Barbara, CA: ABC/CLIO, 2013); Frederick Luis Aldama, ed., *The Routledge Companion to Latina/o Popular Culture* (London: Routledge, 2016).
11. For more on digital spaces for Latinx televisual programming, see Mary Beltrán's "Televisual, Reel, Animated, Comic, Digital & Speculative Pop Spaces." In *The Routledge*

Companion to Latina/o Popular Culture, edited by Frederick Luis Aldama (London: Routledge, 2016), 23–33.
12. See Dolores Inés Casillas, Juan Sebastian Ferrada, and Sara Veronica Hinojos, "The Accent on Modern Family Listening to Representations of the Latina Vocal Body," *Aztlán: A Journal of Chicano Studies* 43, no. 1 (Spring 2018): 61–87.
13. Laura Fernández, "Canta y no llores: Life and Latinidad in Children's Animation," in *The Routledge Companion to Latina/o Popular Culture*, edited by Frederick Luis Aldama (London: Routledge, 2016), 68–75.
14. See Frederick Luis Aldama, "Toward a Transfrontera-LatinX Aesthetic: An Interview with Filmmaker Alex Rivera," *Latino Studies* 15, no. 50 (2017): 373–380.
15. See Kathryn M. Frank, "Beyond the 'Digital Divide': Digital Media and Latina/o Pop Culture," in *The Routledge Companion to Latina/o Popular Culture*.
16. See the work of Josh Kuhn, Peter J. Garcia, Pancho McFarland, and Nicholas Centino.
17. See Frederick Luis Aldama, *Your Brain on Latino Comics: From Gus Arriola to Los Bros Hernandez* (Austin: University of Texas Press, 2009) and *Latinx Comic Book Storytelling: An Odyssey by Interview* (San Diego: San Diego State University Press, 2016), among others as well as the work of Enrique García.
18. See Aldama, *The Routledge Companion to Latino/a Pop Culture*.

# Bibliography

Aldama, Frederick Luis. Ed. *Latinx Ciné in the Twenty-First Century*. Tucson: University of Arizona Press, 2019.

Aldama, Frederick Luis. *Latino/a Children and Young Adult Writers on the Art of Storytelling*. Pittsburgh: University of Pittsburgh Press, 2018.

Aldama, Frederick Luis. *Latinx Superheroes in Mainstream Comics: The Documentary Film*. 2018. https://www.amazon.com/Latinx-Superheroes-Mainstream-Comics-Daniel/dp/B07JJYNCZK.

Aldama, Frederick Luis. *Latinx Superheroes in Mainstream Comics*. Tucson: University of Arizona Press, 2017.

Aldama, Frederick Luis, ed. *Critical Approaches to the Films of Robert Rodriguez*. Austin: University of Texas Press, 2015.

Aldama, Frederick Luis. *The Cinema of Robert Rodriguez*. Austin: University of Texas Press, 2014.

Aldama, Frederick Luis, ed. *Latinos and Narrative Media: Participation and Portrayal*. New York: Palgrave Macmillan, 2013.

Aldama, Frederick Luis, ed. *Multicultural Comics: From Zap to Blue Beetle*. Austin: University of Texas Press, 2010.

Aldama, Frederick Luis, and William Nericcio. *Talking #browntv: Latinas and latinos on the screen*. Columbus: Ohio State University Press, 2019.

Aldama, Frederick Luis, and Christopher González. *Reel Latinxs: Representation in US Film & TV*. Tucson: University of Arizona Press, 2019.

Aldama, Frederick Luis, and Christopher González. *Latinx Studies: The Key Concepts*. New York: Routledge, 2018.

Aldama, Frederick Luis, and Christopher González. *Graphic Borders: Latino Comic Books Past, Present, and Future*. Austin: University of Texas Press, 2016.

Aldama, Frederick Luis, and Christopher González. *Latinos in the End Zone: Conversations on the Brown Color Line in the NFL*. New York: Palgrave Macmillan, 2013.

Aparicio, Frances, and Susana Chávez-Silverman, eds. *Tropicalizations: Transcultural Representations of Latinidad*. Hanover, NH: University Press of New England, 1997.

Fojas, Camilla. *Border Bandits: Hollywood on the Southern Frontier*. Austin: University of Texas Press, 2008.

Fregoso, Rosa Linda. *The Bronze Screen: Chicana and Chicano Film Culture*. Minneapolis: University of Minnesota Press, 1993.

Martínez-Cruz, Paloma. *Food Fight! Millennial Mestizaje Meets the Culinary Marketplace*. Tucson: University of Arizona Press, 2019.

Mendible, Myra, ed. *From Bananas to Buttocks: The Latina Body in Popular Film and Culture*. Austin: University of Texas Press, 2007.

Molina-Guzmán, Isabel. *Dangerous Curves: Latina Bodies in the Media*. New York: New York University Press, 2010.

Noriega, Chon, and Ana M. López, eds. *The Ethnic Eye: Latino Media Arts*. Minneapolis: University of Minnesota Press, 1996.

Ovalle, Priscilla. *Dance and the Hollywood Latina: Race, Sex, and Stardom*. New Brunswick, NJ: Rutgers University Press, 2011.

Paredez, Deborah. *Selenidad: Selena, Latinos, and the Performance of Memory*. Durham, NC: Duke University Press, 2009.

Ramírez Berg, Charles. *Latino Images in Film: Stereotypes, Subversion, & Resistance*. Austin: University of Texas Press, 2002.

Ramírez, Catherine. "Afrofuturism/Chicanafuturism: Fictive Kin." *Aztlan: A Journal of Chicano Studies* 33, no. 1 (2008): 185–194.

Rodriguez, Richard T. *Next of Kin: The Family in Chicano/a Cultural Politics*. Durham, NC: Duke University Press, 2009.

Stavans, Ilan. *Sor Juana: Or, The Persistence of Pop*. Tucson: University of Arizona Press, 2018.

Stavans, Ilan, and Frederick Luis Aldama. *Laughter Matters: Conversations on Humor*. San Diego: San Diego State University Press, 2016.

Tatum, Charles. M. *Chicano Popular Culture, Second Edition: Que Hable el Pueblo*. Tucson: University of Arizona Press, 2017.

Valdivia, Angharad N. *Latina/os and the Media*. Malden, MA: Polity Press, 2010.

CHAPTER 18

# REFLECTIONS ON LATINA/O THEATER

DEBRA CASTILLO

"Theater," modified by the adjective "Latina/o," like any other genre of human expression, is extraordinarily rich. It includes the legacy and continuing vitality of varied and often conflicting aesthetic projects. For some, the story starts with El Teatro Campesino [farmworker theater]—beginning in 1965, inspired by the Mexican carpa [tent] tradition, and archetypically figuring social justice performances by Luis Valdez and his troupe on flatbed trailers alongside the marches by striking members of the National Farmworkers Union. It includes, also from the 1960s, Miriam Colón's Teatro Rodante Puertorriqueño [Puerto Rican traveling theater], which later merged with Rosalba Rolón's Bronx-based Pregones Theater[1]). This theater group was founded with the goal of educating wider audiences about the contributions of Latina/os to the theater arts. There were the influential María Irene Fornés workshops of the 1980s at INTAR in Manhattan, the long-running Festival Latino at Chicago's Goodman Theatre, and the even longer-running (since 1986) Festival Internacional de Teatro Hispano in Miami. There were the evolving series of festivals organized since the 1980s under the rubric of TENAZ (Teatro Nacional de Aztlán/National Theatre of Aztlán); the productions of the more recent (since the 1990s) indigenous troupes such as the Coatlicue Theater Company (founded by Chichimec Otomi sisters Elvira and Hortensia Colorado) that perform in many languages throughout the vast geographical and cultural expanses of Abya Yala ("continent of life": the Kuna term for what most of us call "the Americas"). In a modest way, it also includes university-based organizations such as Teatrotaller, the troupe I have collaborated with since its founding in 1993, which has produced over eighty shows to date, including classic and contemporary drama, as well as—increasingly—creative collection projects focusing on issues of interest to my students. The range also includes Jorge Monje's twenty-first-century "Microteatro"—fifteen-minute plays performed for an audience of fifteen in Spanish-speaking Miami—and Pulitzer Prize–winning works by Nilo Cruz and Quiara Alegria Hudes.

And then in 2015 came *Hamilton*, and it changed everything.

The story of Lin-Manuel Miranda's wildly successful Broadway follow-up to his highly successful *In the Heights* (2005; with book by Quiara Alegria Hudes) is well known. Inspired by Ron Chernow's biography of this founding father, Miranda reimagined American Revolutionary history spotlighting Alexander Hamilton heading a multiracial cast backed by the kinetic energy of hip-hop music (itself a Latino-infused form derived from musical collaborations between African American, Jamaican/Caribbean, and Latina/o artists in New York's South Bronx in the 1970s). *Hamilton* has been sold out since its move to Broadway and has won every possible award in the United States, including only the third Pulitzer Prize given to a Latina or Latino playwright. It stopped cold the discussion of changing the face on the $10 bill. It reinvigorated discussions about the "Latino boom," the "sleeping giant," and in reactionary circles, "the brown peril."

More important, *Hamilton* disrupts the familiar academic history of Latina/o theater largely based on the imagined unity of identity between a Latino or Latina author and their topics. A Latina/o presumably writes about what he or she knows and only knows about recognizably Latino/a themes and topics. The plays will highlight Latino/a characters, albeit most often in a form that derives from the unspoken unities of European play structure. Lin Manuel Miranda's genius was to rewrite the most intractably WASPian elements of US history, giving a Latino edge to the founding myths and doing so with an aesthetic and a formal shakeup that is blindingly local, Latino, and contemporary.

Nonetheless, at the current time, a discussion framed as one about Latina/o theater necessarily (even grammatically) presumes an undertaking in which a shared concern about identity is considered both fundamental and somehow revelatory. Yet it would include work as historically and geographically disparate as an *acto* by Teatro Campesino, a fifteen-minute Spanish-language play in Miami, and a pull-out-all-the-stops Broadway musical with Latina/o actors but no Latino characters. So what do we mean by Latina/o in the twenty-first century, anyway?

In most discussions of the Latina/o canon, the answer is implicit, if slightly incoherent. In their own ways, Coatlicue Theater and *Hamilton* are putting pressure on the received understandings of this term and asking us to rethink our facile answers to this question.

There will be more about the challenges posed by Coatlicue and *Hamilton* at the end of this chapter, but first we need to set the background.

For many people, Latina/o theater is circumscribed by its politics of identity and a clear statement of ethical responsibilities to a particular, well-defined community. These principles have been succinctly (if somewhat austerely) articulated by W. E. B. DuBois in 1926, when talking about African American theater as *by, for, about,* and *near* the community. DuBois writes: "The plays of a real Negro theatre must be: 1. About us. That is, they must have plots which reveal real Negro life as it is. 2. By us. That is, they must be written by Negro authors who understand from birth and continual association just what it means to be a Negro today. 3. For us. That is, the theatre must cater primarily to Negro audiences and be supported and sustained by their entertainment and approval. 4. Near us. The theatre must be in a Negro neighborhood."[2]

As Jon Rossini notes, the continuing pertinence of DuBois's admittedly essentialist framing of the goals of ethnic theater reside in the "importance of maintaining a space for racially and ethnically marked theater within the United States in the face of a language of multiculturalism that sometimes works to erase difference."[3] Rossini's take on the question is filtered largely through an academic lens, and his argument is sustained by a rigorous academic analysis. Brian Eugenio Herrera asks an analogous question from a practice-based point of view in his article, "But Do We Have the Actors for That?" Herrera notes that the question about casting often signals unaddressed tensions around issues of diversity, inclusion, and best practices in theater production. Raising the question of ethnically appropriate casting is a somewhat hypocritical way for ostensibly liberal decision makers not to stage diverse plays in settings where the directors struggle to find student actors of a particular ethnicity. His response is that there needs to be a distinction between the goals of an educational institution (where questions of linguistic fluency, cultural competence, and creative coalition are part of the learning process, and nontraditional casting can bring more Latina/o plays to more university stages) and a professional theater where ethnically analogous performers are expected.

In any case, the footprint of what we understand as Latina/o theater is generally marked by its most recent incarnations. In this case, the 1960s model still prevails: that of Latino/a theater as the product of activist writer/performers deeply committed to the struggles of the civil rights era and to issues of presence and representation in all aspects. This is social movement theater that has provided a blueprint for other performance traditions that stress a mission of advocacy. Street performance, consciousness raising, and political and social activism went hand in hand. *By, for, about,* and *near* described an aesthetic practice derived from and functioning in collaboration with political necessity. One could, for instance, trace one version of this history of activism directly from *La carreta* (René Marqués's 1953 play about Puerto Rican immigration to New York, the signature production of the Teatro Rodante Puertorriqueño, where Miriam Colón had it translated into English for a wider audience) or *Las dos caras del patroncito* (which Teatro Campesino developed in 1965 out of an improvisation during that year's grape strike by the United Farmworkers in Delano, California). It is no coincidence that both these plays are originally in Spanish, even though the most familiar forms of Latina/o theatrical production these days are in English, with perhaps a few Spanish words to indicate an ethnic alliance or origin.[4]

Because "Latina/o" makes an identity claim, cultural production associated with Latinidad is generally understood to be authored by a person with ancestry linking him or her to countries in the Americas previously colonized by Spain. This is a tortuous definition based on a problematic assumption that breaks apart under the slightest pressure. As a result, we do not often look at it too closely. First of all, this country-of-origin imaginary version of identity leaves out vast swathes of the Americas, including, most obviously, Brazil but also Belize, Guyana, Suriname, French Guiana, and many islands/nations in the Caribbean: Jamaica, Barbados, Trinidad and Tobago, among others. Haitian authors, curiously enough, are often linked to Latinidad along with writers from

Cuba, Puerto Rico, and the Dominican Republic (perhaps because Haitians share the island of Hispañola).

Secondly, much like the United States, all the independent nations of the Americas (except for Colombia, as of 2002) have birthright citizenship laws. This means that all children of immigrants to most countries in this hemisphere are also citizens. Lebanese immigrants are Mexicans. Italian immigrants are Argentine. Japanese immigrants are Peruvian. If they or their children then move to the United States, they and their descendents are Latina/os, no matter how mixed their backgrounds were on arrival or subsequently become through later generations. Obvious cases in point include the distinguished Latina playwright Caridad Svich, born in the United States to Cuban-Argentine-Spanish-Croatian parents; California-born Milcha Sanchez Scott, whose background is Indonesian, Chinese, Dutch, and Colombian, and who spent her early years in Colombia, Mexico, and London; or Ruth Behar (whose *Translated Woman* was adapted for the stage by Pregones), of Sephardic Turkish, Ashkenazi Polish, and Russian ancestry. Behar, in a famous essay, "Juban America" (1995), describes herself as Cuban, because her Jewish ancestors were refused admission to the United States, although while in Cuba her family was and always would be called Polish. They became Cuban, and American, once family members arrived in the United States. This was because post-Castro Cubans were given preferential admission, resident visas, and an easy path to naturalization.

The founder of Miami's "Microteatro," Jorge Monje is in this sense only ambiguously and sometimes considered a Latino. While he had deep connections and an international network in Peru, Costa Rica, Mexico, and Argentina he was an immigrant from Spain, not Spanish-speaking Latin America. And Spaniards, no matter how integrated into the community they are, come from the colonizer country. And Houston-born Aaron Burns reminds everyone that cultural mixture continues in the United States; his dark comedy, *Blacktino* (2011), tells the story of a half-black, half-Latino boy who finds refuge and support in his high school's theater program.

The standard syllabus for Latina/o theater courses begins with Teatro Campesino and traces a predictable geo-ethnic course, pairing the Southwest and West with Mexican Americans, the Southeast with Cuban Americans, and the Northeast with Puerto Rican theater production. This is often imagined as if it were a family tree, or a kind of intellectual genealogy, something that is certainly true of the most cited of these projects: the INTAR workshops run by María Irene Fornés. Yet many of these sites and troupes were disconnected from each other, with idiosyncratic projects invented/reinvented by theater practitioners as they immigrated to the United States at different stages of their lives and careers. Whether we can call this discontinuous history a "genealogy" at all is highly contentious, although it is a useful concept for coalition building.

Fundamentally, despite the typical university syllabus and *pace* DuBois, the kind of political project that he imagined in 1926 takes on a much different hue nearly a hundred years later, when the ethnoracial silos that purportedly helped us understand theatrical production have long since been broken down. Today, scholars and critics move outside the classroom and back into the material conditions of performance today, in our theaters and on our streets. This could mean—as is the case of Jimmy Noriega—advising United We Dream on performance techniques to strengthen their protest and advocacy work; or it could mean scholars working with community members and students to tell their stories, in their own way, for their local audiences.

At the same time, it is crucial to recognize that these ethnic studies courses and programs, established thirty, forty, or perhaps fifty years ago, have created the familiar histories that help US audiences recognize a generalized performance category called "Latina/o," that is distinct and nonwhite and that allows contemporary performers to both evolve within and step outside these presumed boundaries.

So, what, specifically is the timeline? While the *by, for, about*, and *near* of people of Latin American descent creating theater in what would become the United States begins long before there was such a country, most scholars and teachers begin the timeline in earnest with the ferment of the civil rights era in the 1960s. In most scholarly accounts, this loose chronology is divided two ways: by geographical region and by affinity groups based on countries of ancestral origin, often limited to "the big three": Mexico, Puerto Rico, and Cuba (this division never quite works, as examples such as Sánchez-Scott and Svich already suggest). The term "Latino" itself, furthermore, is a 1990s product of the reaction against the earlier agglutinating word "Hispanic," rejected for its connection with the Iberian Peninsula and even more for its official use on the US census. Even later, dating to the 1990s and into the 2000s, are the tussles with Spanish grammar in the service of greater inclusivity that gave us "Latina/o," "Latina," and "Latinx."

In this rough genealogy, the timeline gestures toward a longer history of native and immigrant theater in Spanish before the dawn of the twentieth century (sometimes well before): at times as a local, community building activity, other times—and frequently highlighting the participation of international performers—as a high culture event. Jumping from the eighteenth or nineteenth century to the 1960s means not just privileging a period of general civil rights consciousness raising but also a forged consciousness of a shared history of oppression (rather than, say, as a mainstream cultural project with a deep past, in the way that mainstream US theater continues to present Shakespeare) that united Latina/os and gave force to their expression in many genres, including theater. Thus, although the Chamizal Siglo de Oro Festival in the National Memorial Theater near El Paso has been celebrated annually since 1975, the standard timeline for Latina/o theater skips over this rich period of Spanish theater, contemporaneous with Shakespeare, and generally gives pride of place to twentieth-century collective creation projects by (originally) nonprofessional troupes, rather than high culture performances in repertoire by professionally trained actors. The story is further consolidated and given greater prominence in emphasizing the contributions of projects such as El Teatro Campesino, whose signature early form were the *actos* that spoke to California farmworkers about their condition and gave them tools to change it.

El Teatro Campesino, lead by Luis Valdez, also re-imagined traditional folk forms— in 1975 they created and performed a Christmas *Pastorela* (still produced biannually in the Mission at San Juan Bautista in northern California, and filmed in 1991 for PBS). Valdez increasingly separated his individual work from the collective that he helped found and began to write full-length plays anchored in signal moments of Chicano/a history. In 1977 his imaginative take on the 1942 Sleepy Lagoon murder case, *Zoot Suit*, was produced by the Mark Taper Forum in Los Angeles. This play was later taken to Broadway, although it was not successful there and had a short run. He filmed the play in 1981, where it has the distinction of being the first full-length Chicano feature film made in Hollywood. Even more successful was his second Hollywood film. In 1987 he filmed *La Bamba*, a biopic about the rock-and-roll star Ritchie Valens, who died in a plane crash in 1959, with the movie propelling the hit song "La Bamba" to number one on the music charts for the second time: the only song to date to ever accomplish this feat and the only song in a language other than English to become a major Billboard hit. Valdez has not been able to repeat these mainstream successes; his only other major film credit is for the 1994 made-for-TV movie, *Cisco Kid*, about a pair of heroes riding around nineteenth-century Mexico and dealing with injustices they find on the road, itself a remake and homage to a 1950s television series.

After more than fifty years of continuous work, El Teatro Campesino continues to be a landmark organization and remains vital and active as an ensemble theater, with a playhouse located in the northern California mission town of San Juan Bautista. In the standard timeline, though, most scholars highlight the early work noted above rather than their later plays, or this much longer history of continuous production. In the abbreviated story of Latina/o theater, El Teatro Campesino represents two moments: first, the informal activist theater of the 1960s, a scrappy history of collective creation and street theater, done in the context of resistance to establishment politics; and second, the 1970s consolidation and institutionalization of key Latina/o theater troupes into professional organizations, with their own spaces, often supported at key points by NGOs. In the case of Valdez, for instance, it was a 1977 Rockefeller Foundation grant that underwrote the production of *Zoot Suit*.

The civil rights movement was largely male dominated, and in the 1980s, in this condensed timeline, women scholars, activists, and theater professionals more forcefully asserted the need to open spaces for other considerations than the narrowly political ones of the era—of gender and sexuality, along with race—as crucial human issues. While thinkers such as Gloria Anzaldúa, in *Borderlands/La Frontera* famously articulated the tenets of a mestiza consciousness, the decade also brought more attention to women playwrights. Among the most cited we must include Cherríe Moraga (San Francisco), Milcha Sanchez-Scott (Chicago and elsewhere), and Maria Irene Fornés (New York). These women famously put women characters front and center in some of their most celebrated plays, and it is not coincidental that their passionate feminist appeals for greater inclusivity of human experience in theater also go hand in hand, in Moraga, Anzaldúa, and Fornés's cases, with their lesbianism. Key interventions from the period that speak to this emergent gender consciousness include Milcha Sanchez Scott's 1980 *Latinas*; Cherríe Moraga's *Shadow of a Man*, written in 1983–1984 when she was studying with Maria Irene Fornés; and Fornes's own *Fefu and Her Friends* (1977).

In this succinct version of the timeline, the geography would shift from California in the 1960s to New York in the 1980s, highlighting Fornés's fundamental influence both as a playwright and as director of INTAR's (International Arts Relations) Hispanic Playwrights in Residency workshops from 1981 to 1992. She was a major influence on the next generation of Latina/o playwrights who studied or worked with her at INTAR: Milcha Sanchez Scott, Edwin Sánchez, Migdalia Cruz, José Rivera, Nilo Cruz, Josefina Lopez, among many other distinguished playwrights.[5] Many of these playwrights have gone on to mentor other younger Latina/os, and in this prominent context we can see a true, multigenerational genealogy that is now three or four generations deep. As a *New York Times* quote prominently cited on the INTAR website says, "There's scarcely a Latino artist in America who has not been supported or trained or produced by INTAR." As such, her influence cannot be overstated.

At the same time, the DuBoisian recommendation of *for, by, about, near* is given a twist. INTAR celebrates its role in helping to shape playwrights and support the careers of over 175 Latina/o artists; at the same time, its mission statement emphasizes that one of their primary goals is to "make accessible the diversity inherent in America's cultural heritage," presumably expanding the "for" not just to mainstream America but, in its project of developing "theater arts without borders," to sharing Latina/o work internationally, which is not at all "near." Thus, if the 1960s is a time of collective action, the 1970s of institutional consolidation, the 1980s represent a moment of crossover in many senses: to more attention to the wider range of human experience, to broader visibility for more diverse audiences. As Alberto Sandoval-Sánchez somewhat harshly writes: "Since the 1980s... attention in Latino theater and (mainstream) regional playhouses and productions has been drawn to marketing, accessibility to the general public, theatrical and artistic professionalization, identifying targeted audiences for sponsorship, and crossing over in order to cater to Anglo-American audiences in English only."[6] Jumping forward in time, the current Hispanic Playwrights in Residency Laboratory Director at INTAR is Caridad Svich, who is also the creator of the international NoPassport virtual and live theater project, and whose driving impetus is broadly international as well.

There was no single institution in the 1990s with the overwhelming influence of either INTAR or Teatro Campesino, and that is definitely a positive development. Instead we celebrate the resurgence and expanding vitality of regional Latina/o theaters, many of them established much earlier, such as Pregones and Repertorio español, which are the most prominent among the numerous New York City Latino/a theaters. There is also Teatro de la Luna in Virginia, as well as more recent organizations—all founded in the year 2000—for example, Teatro Bravo in Phoenix, Teatro Luna in Chicago (an all-Latina theater), and Teatro Vivo in Austin. Each of these thriving regional theaters has its own mission statement and range of productions; many of them also support internships, playwriting workshops, classes, and community events. They pair classic Latina/o and Hispanic world repertoire with premier global productions. By the turn of the millennium, Latina/o theater had greater visibility than ever, and twenty-first-century playwrights are now the fourth-generation inheritors of a tradition they can trace to the mid-twentieth century.

If these significant troupes serve as one way of defining a timeline and a genealogy of Latina/o theater, other lenses into this history come from other kinds of institutional memories: the burgeoning scholarship by academic thinkers, the consolidation of knowledge and its passing on through university courses (often taught in ethnic studies contexts as well as theater programs), and key professional organizations. And here we need to think about what is taught, where it is taught (in English, Spanish, or theater departments), and what plays are performed—whether on the season or in more casual, workshop environments. For example, most of Teatrotaller's productions were sponsored by the Spanish program; the theater program—while praising the work—said they had no room in their schedule and no space in their theaters for these plays. This is something that has only changed within the last decade when closer collaboration became the norm.

In the second decade of the twenty-first century, playwrights both share and incorporate knowledge from those ethnic studies contexts (many of which were founded in the early 1970s) and respond to the growing demands of a contemporary Latina/o middle-class audience for mainstream, high-quality theatrical experiences (see, in this respect.[7] Latina/o theater, then, is often bifurcated into an unstable and diverse artistic field traced through the histories and practices of long-running and emergent theaters and troupes on the one hand and institutional structures for understanding theater in academic settings on the other.

Luis Valdez articulated one of the early manifesto-like appreciations of Latina/o theater in his 1970 "Notes on Chicano Theatre," where he writes that "Chicano theatre, then, is first a reaffirmation of LIFE," and he continues: "That is what all theatre is supposed to be, of course; but the limp, superficial, gringo seco productions in the 'professional' American theatre (and in the college and university drama departments that serve it) are so antiseptic, they are antibiotic (anti-life)."[8] His argument is grounded in aesthetics: "The nature of Chicanismo calls for a revolutionary turn in the arts as well as society. Chicano theatre must be revolutionary in technique as well as content... a teatro of ritual, of music, of beauty and spiritual sensitivity."[9] Ironically, given his later success as a grant writer, he is passionate about the need for this theater to be independent: "Above all, the national organization of teatros Chicanos would be self-supporting and independent.... The corazón de la Raza cannot be revolutionized on a grant from Uncle Sam."[10]

Valdez has never been an academic, of course, but his passion for thinking about a specifically Latina/o aesthetics is echoed in the small but growing group of academically based Latinas and Latinos who come from a background in theater practice, from senior scholars such as Jorge Huerta and Carlos Morton to younger ones such as Brian Eugenio Herrera, Coya Paz, and Jimmy Noriega. Likewise, it has been heartening to see our bookshelves beginning to groan under the weight of thoughtful analyses of Latina/o theater and performance in the United States. These studies begin with helpful overviews in readers such as those by Rossini, Orchard, Danielson, Arrizón, and Martínez Cruz, where the authors show a breathtakingly broad command of the field and offer clear, succinct, and thoughtful outlines of a complex history.

For a rich dialogue on contemporary debates, the dossier edited by Luis A. Ramos-Garcia, *The State of Latino Theater in the USA* (2002), provides a wide-ranging set of studies by scholars and practitioners who explore and historicize Latina/o theatrical work as well as give rich contexts for individual artists. Contributors read like a who's-who in the field, including articles by Beatriz Rizk, Alberto Sandoval-Sánchez, Jossiana Arroyo, Eduardo Cabrera, Patricia González, Tamara Underiner, and many others. In his introduction, Ramos-García writes, "As Latin American and Latino theaters have always been places of political expression, the voices represented in this volume address the questions of why theater has been perceived as the principal disseminator of dominant ideology and why it has become a common place for intellectual scorn, collective response, and even societal upheaval."[11] The explicit goal of this volume is to counter such misperceptions with a "more rigorous"[12] understanding of a body of artistic expression that reflects a broad range of cultures, values, and forms of expression.

Likewise, the March 2017 special issue of *Theatre Topics*[13] on "Latinx Performance" offers a wonderful introduction to current issues. The dossier includes scholarly articles by some of the most active and influential scholars writing in the second decade of the twenty-first century: Brian Eugenio Herrera, Jimmy Noriega, Patricia Ybarra, Matthieu Chapman, Noe Montez, Teresa Marrero, and Patricia Herrera, as well as a conversation with playwrights Elaine Romero and Anne García-Romero and an overview of the Latinx Theatre Commons by Maria Enriquez and Christopher Goodson. The introductory note from the editor of the journal, Gwendolyn Alker, laments the oversight—the prejudice—that had previously sidelined the vital contributions of Latina and Latino theater artists and scholars even in the pages of seemingly progressive journals like this one. She writes: "Latinx theatre in this country has always been at the lead of the various fields of applied theatre (for example, through the work of Augusto Boal), practice-based research, and community-based theatre (such as with Teatro Campesino and Culture Clash, a group that is frequently discussed in this special issue), although they may use differing labels to describe their work. Through the work of Maria Irene Fornes and her students, Latinxs have had one of the most rigorous and successful lineages of playwriting pedagogy, cohering through the work of Nilo Cruz, Migdalia Cruz, and Quiara Alegría Hudes, as well as many others. In short... an effort must be made both to recognize this and acknowledge the ways in which such communities of color are often disregarded from the more mainstream nationalist histories of US performance."[14]

Among book-length studies on anyone's list of important references is Nicolás Kanellos's classic 1990 survey of the deep history of Latina/o performance practice in the United States, *A History of Hispanic Theatre in the USA: Origins to 1940*. Other books that speak to the continental reach of Latina/o theater include Herrera's *Latin Numbers*, Rossini's *Contemporary Latino/a Theater*, and Patricia Ybarra's forthcoming book, *Latino/a Theatre in the Time of Neoliberalism*. There are, of course, many other substantial studies on individual theater troupes such as Teatro Campesino, as well as useful analyses of theater and performance in specific geographical areas, alongside books about playwrights sharing a particular country of origin or of descent. Anthologies and publications in journals help readers keep abreast of playwrights and performances across the country.

Academics share their work mostly with their peers through these kinds of publications, but many of them are also active in other kinds of public scholarship and community building. In 2010 *latinopia* published online a beautifully illustrated timeline: "100 years of Latino Theatre," which opens with productions by the Cuban American community in Ybor City and Tampa, Florida, in 1900 and closes with the 2010 New Los Angeles Theater Center production of Evelina Fernandez's play *Dementia*, directed by one of the twenty-first century's top Latino directors, and a leader in the larger Latina/o theater community, José Luis Valenzuela. Another online contribution, also encyclopedic in scope, is Tlaloc Rivas's 2013 contribution to *Café Onda*, "101 Plays by The New Americans, or on Latinidad." Rivas begins his meditation with a reflection on the 2013 Boston gathering of members of the Latinx Theatre Commons and their shared concern about the need for a catalogue of plays by Latina/o authors, as well as a curated list of the most important and influential ones. In this article, Rivas offers his own comprehensive list of 101 plays and invites collaborators to chime in, add others, and point out favorites.

These shared online sites provide significant platforms for intellectual and practice-based work. One of the most exciting and promising is the Latinx Theatre Commons (LTC on the HowlRound site). LTC has a sixty-plus-member steering committee, and a loose organization of working committees under a "producer" (currently Abigail Vega) and task-oriented volunteer subcommittees, each with one or two "champions," who report to the producer on a monthly basis (see Marrero for more detail). The site includes a rich and growing body of contributions, many of them in both Spanish and English. LTC hosts calls for convenings, information about the collective effort "El Fuego," designed to provide material support for productions of Latina/o plays in theaters across the country, and artist lists to help producers get in touch with Latina/o designers, stage managers, dramaturgs, choreographers, and other technicians (visitors to the site are invited to add their names). It also sponsors an online journal, *Café Onda* (where Rivas's essay appeared), which hosts essays, blogs, livestream video, and thoughtful critique. (And it's where one can read an extended blog piece by veteran Chicano playwright and scholar Carlos Morton on "Reviving *Zoot Suit* in the Time of Trump.") There is even a shop where one can purchase a Latinx Theatre Commons tote bag or donate to the organization, alongside other HowlRound books, T-shirts, and other products.

While not exclusive to a US Latina/o focus, there is much to learn from the deep archives of text and video at the Hemispheric Institute website, a project coordinated by NYU professor Diana Taylor. The Hemispheric Institute has always been transnational and transversal in many other ways in its programming, and while it supports cutting-edge theater by Latina/os and other emerging artists, its focus has always been more on performance art rather than on theater per se. The program now has two main centers: one in New York City, the other in San Cristóbal de las Casas, Mexico. The former center is particularly relevant, including ongoing workshops, lectures, and performance events in the EMERGENYC series, under the leadership of George Emilio Sánchez.

Many of these scholars (and some practitioners) cross paths at the annual meetings of the two main US theater organizations, ATHE and ASTR, or the smaller meetings hosted by the *Latin American Theatre Review*. ATHE sponsors the active "Latinx,

Indigenous, and the Americas" focus group. Their 2016 conference, for instance, hosted a preconference meeting organized by Coya Paz and Courtney Elkin Mohler ("Urgent Matters: Bodies at Work, Bodies at Risk") with a special focus on Latina/o and indigenous theater. The ATHE 2017 theme is "Spectacle: Balancing Education, Theory, and Praxis," and organizers Jimmy Noriega and Noe Montez note particularly the tremendous growth in attention to Latina/o theater in recent years, calling attention to formerly invisible and marginalized theater scholarship and performance, while reminding members of the need to be attentive to a history of oppressive practices that offer only an illusion of empowerment without substance.

For its part, in ASTR, two of the three program chairs for its 2017 conference are prominent Latina/o scholar-practitioners: Jimmy Noriega and Analola Santana. ASTR's conferences are always organized around workshop sessions proposed by members and have a strong recent history of emphasis on diversity. ASTR has recently announced a multiyear funded initiative named after (and supporting the goals of) one of the most prominent scholars of Latina/o performance: José Estéban Muñoz. The announcement says, in part: "The José Esteban Muñoz Targeted Research Working Sessions is a multi-year funded project which supports, promotes, and features the production of research by and about people of color at ASTR. To commemorate and celebrate the late performance theorist José Esteban Muñoz, these working sessions aim to foster and forward intersectional work that also attends to and includes LGBTQ communities, disability communities, and scholars without institutional support."

Another highly visible way that scholars make their contributions to the discussion and promotion of Latina/o theater—in addition to print and online scholarship, collaboration in professional organizations, and (sometimes) working as directors, actors, and other theater practitioners in plays—is through their classroom teaching and workshops. Noe Montez has a novel approach to his Latina/o theater classroom: he encourages his students to think of scholarly work as activism and online technology as a resource for teaching and research. He has his students write Wikipedia pages for underrepresented artists as class assignments. The challenges the students faced in meeting the Wikipedia requirements for verification through secondary sources (when secondary materials on many of these artists are almost nonexistent) helped him make a pedagogical point, while the students' commitment to overcoming these difficulties could only result in a more complete encyclopedia.

In general, though, theater/plays are taught in one of two places: literature classes and the theater program. Orchard's article in particular focuses on the place of Latina/o theater in the literature classroom and points out the challenges of including even token representation in a crowded syllabus where professors worry about historical coverage, as well as introducing students to a variety of genres. Orchard's two case-study plays are Josefina Niggli's *Soldadera* (1936) and Irene Fornés's *The Conduct of Life* (1985).

While the article gives useful tips on how to incorporate these two plays into a more general course, Orchard's approach also reminds us of the challenges, many of which have already been well articulated by Jorge Huerta in 2004. Because Latina/o theater is bilingual, and universities tend to be discipline driven, it poses a problem to both

English-based literature and theater programs and, in a different way, to Spanish departments. On the one hand, there is the problem of access to the plays in English and a dearth of translations; on the other, there is a limited relation to Spanish departments for work that comes from outside the traditional geographical purview of Spain and Spanish-speaking Latin America. And in either case, literature programs have little access to the trained staff or to the funding required for even the most bare-bones production; thus, they tend to focus heavily on literary readings of plays, perhaps with a bit of scene work to give students a sense of how this genre is different from reading a novel. For theater departments it is almost worse, especially when thinking of production on the all-important theater season; if the play is bilingual, or involves code-switching, it is seen as inaccessible to most and—as Herrera argues in his article about casting—difficult for non Latina/o, non-bilingual directors to imagine producing.

My own survey of syllabi from many colleges and universities suggests that Latina/o theater rarely shows up in Spanish courses (on theater or any other literary genre) and—more surprisingly—has only a modest presence in Latina/o culture studies courses. In the majority of theater departments, Latina/o theater, when it appears at all, is given two weeks of attention in the department's designated "diversity" course: this generally means attention to Luis Valdez and Teatro Campesino for one week, and in the next week, a couple of playwrights from the limited pool of world-renowned Latina/o names such as Milcha Sánchez Scott, Luis Alfaro, María Irene Fornés, or Cherríe Moraga. A theater department course combining Latina/o and Latin American theater is a familiar option: half of the syllabus is generally relegated to playwrights from the United States—which, of course, means covering the other thirty-three countries with the rest of the syllabus; there are no good choices in these Procrustean situations. Theater department courses that focus on Latina/o theater have a surprisingly small list of playwrights in the shared canon, and most of them are common to the vast majority of syllabi. In outlining a generic syllabus, the typical course will include a hefty amount of space to Chicana/o theater: Luis Valdez, Cherríe Moraga, Guillermo Gómez Peña, Luis Alfaro, and Culture Clash. They then switch geographical zones and include works by Milcha Sánchez Scott; Cuban-Americans Coco Fusco, Nilo Cruz, Carmelita Tropicana (Alina Troyano), and Maria Irene Fornés; Puerto Rican José Rivera, Nuyorican Miguel Piñero, and Migdalia Cruz (South Bronx), along with wild cards such as Caridad Svich and Colombian American John Leguizamo. Almost no syllabi include Pulitzer Prize winners Lin Manuel Miranda or Quiara Alegria Hudes or senior canonical figures such as Carlos Morton. Few include Elaine Romero, Josefina Lopez, Marga Gomez, Guillermo Reyes, Octavio Solís, or Dolores Prida—to mention only a few more of the most canonical names represented in academic studies. This standardization of the classroom syllabus suggests a huge gap between what we think is important in scholarship and what we think is necessary and representative in our teaching. Hardly anyone includes playwrights or troupes that bridge the intersections of Latina/o and indigenous identities, though this is a current major focus of the biggest US scholarly societies; almost no courses include work by the Latina/o millennials (Generation Y).

Here is where we should return to the issue raised earlier about the two ends of the spectrum signaled by Coatlicue Theatre Company and *Hamilton* and the challenges they pose, definitionally, aesthetically, as we think about how Latina/o theater has been imagined, what stories it tells us, and where it is going next.[15]

From another perspective on Latinidad, one that breaks through both institutional canons and practical experience, troupes such as the Coatlicue Theatre Company remind us that indigenous peoples claim their right to space for their cultures and languages outside of any of the colonial histories of the Americas, especially when those histories are told by and through European-framed languages and structures. Nonetheless, in US categories of identity, if they are descendents of people inhabiting countries formerly colonized by Spain where Spanish is an official language, they are also considered Latina/os, regardless of whether they or their ancestors spoke that colonial language (there are, for example, Oxnard Mixtec immigrants from Mexico who are bilingual in English and Mixteco and bypassed Spanish entirely). For other indigenous theater practitioners, the choice of using the European colonizer languages of English or Spanish to reach their audiences means a choice of two enemy languages and two genocidal histories. And yet they persevere, with languages that stick in their throats, presenting to audiences that imagine their people are extinct. To make a claim about Abya Yala, rather than later colonial impositions and political-geographical divisions, is also to disrupt the understanding of how we think about Latina/o and its relation to these colonial histories: histories that are otherwise (and often) challenged in the socially activist realms of many plays' content.

Thus, for instance, indigenous theater, including theater by people who have immigrated to the United Staters from countries where Spanish is the official language, is often a theater that understands itself as emerging from within a long tradition coming from outside European performance norms or colonial languages such as Spanish, French, and English. In many of these traditions, performance is not understood to be "playing" a role but embodying the ancestors and the gods as a constituent aspect of the work: this is a kind of transubstantiation (to use the Christian term evoked by Underiner in her study) in which history is made present, and the audience is assumed to include the living, the dead, and the divine.[16] Alongside the colonial passion plays and other Christian spectacles that often incorporate indigenous elements and themes as a kind of resistant subtext, other native performance traditions continued, often in underground fashion. Sometimes they blended together over the centuries in projects that use a Western structure or characters to tell a local story that draws on millennial traditions.

This is the theater of a people "scheduled to disappear" but that maintains a robust presence, often more visible and recognized in the countries of origin and arrival than that of their native counterparts in the United States.[17] Aymara and Quechua are official languages of both Bolivia and Peru (along with several dozen other indigenous languages in the case of Bolivia). Paraguay is a bilingual country, and both Guaraní and Spanish are official languages. Colombia recognizes sixty-five languages; Mexico has no official language, and although most of the inhabitants speak Spanish, there are at least fifty-five other languages spoken in the country. The United States, by the way, has traditionally had four official languages (English, Spanish, French, and Hawaiian): three colonial, and only one of them native.

For indigenous Latina/o playwrights, alliances with other language groups in Abya Yala are vital. If a Paraguayan audience could be expected to appreciate a play in Guaraní, and Chiapanecan highlanders would best appreciate humor in Tsotsil, the same would not be true in the United States: this is a place where even Spanglish is suspect, much less theater that incorporates linguistic elements from indigenous cultures with native speakers in the thousands rather than millions. It is crucial to remember, though, that for most of these performers, there is a tacit or explicit understanding of presenting their work for a bifurcated audience, of which only the smaller group may be native and who will come out of the performance with very different understandings of what they experienced. Thus, Underiner claims, "What is new about this era of indigenous-language theatre... is the question of authorship, theme, and point of view, with indigenous people themselves writing about their vital experiences for audiences who are also (but not exclusively) indigenous."[18] Thus, the border-straddling Tohono O'odham in Arizona/Mexico, thus also the work of the Coatlicue Theater Company, which has learned from—and offered—workshops in indigenous communities in Chiapas, Mexico, working among other millennial inhabitants of Abya Yala (with whom they do not share a single word in common in their first languages).

Lin Manuel Miranda's *Hamilton* makes yet another claim. For Julissa Catalan, *Hamilton* "is huge for all minorities. For Latinos who are first generation Americans like myself, this is our nation's story being told, and now we can see ourselves personified in it for the first time."[19] More than representation, *Hamilton* reminds us that we need to shake up our theoretical and aesthetic positions and that Latina/o theater does not fit into neat and predictable boxes about oppressed subjects and minority/marginalized discourse. Theater scholars and historians tend to look at content rather than form, especially for works associated with ethnically marked playwrights. We often read plays by Latina/os as if they were ethnographic documents rather than aesthetic ones (see, e.g., Ybarra 2017 on this issue). For Ybarra, the damning lack of cultural competence among many mainstream scholars and critics means that we tend to imagine Latina/o performance as if it comes from a mysterious continent we do not have to evaluate fully; hence, we can pigeonhole and "celebrate" any contributions to form an aesthetics as either telenovelesque or magic realist, according to whichever of these two alternative flavors of being Latin(o) American happens to appeal.[20]

*Hamilton* speaks to a cultural competence shared by anyone who has gone to elementary school in the United States and half-slept through history classes about illustrious forefathers in the Revolutionary War, or watched any of the recent films we confuse with history, or wondered who that guy with the good handwriting was on the $10 bill—and then absentmindedly Googled him. It engages the cultural competence of second-generation rap lovers for whom hip-hop was always around and always assumed to be solely African American in genesis. Hamilton, says Lin Manuel Miranda, reminds him of Tupac. When he says this, his audience is not thinking of Tupac Amaru I, the last emperor of the Andean realm of Tawantinsuyu and leader of an unsuccessful rebellion against the Spanish in 1572, or the man who claimed to be his descendent, Tupac Amaru II, who rebelled against Spanish rule in the late eighteenth century. Miranda's reference is to Tupac Amaru Shakur, the West Coast rapper who was murdered in 1996. And yet all of the Tupacs shared a common, fatal, flaw: they were confrontational and did not back down—and it eventually cost them their lives. And for Miranda, Alexander Hamilton had the same problem and had the same dazzling potential cut short.

At the same time, this play is making a strong claim for political recognition as well as cultural citizenship. A *New Yorker* article by Rebecca Mead quotes Oskar Eustis, the director of the Public Theater, who comments that "by telling the story of the founding of the country through the eyes of a bastard, immigrant orphan, told entirely by people of color, he is saying 'This is our county. We get to lay claim to it.'"[21] This assertion is echoed by actor Daveed Diggs (who plays Jefferson) along other lines. Diggs speaks about the importance of the musical style: "Rap is the voice of the people of our generation, and of people of color, and just the fact that it exists in this piece, and is not commented on, gives us a sense of ownership."[22] The implications are significant. It is not, in this case, that "theater," modified by the adjective "Latina/o," can argue its place into an American canon (albeit on the diversity card) but rather that works by Latinas and Latinos are central to US theater (unmodified) and fundamental to its formal shapes, its aesthetic challenges, and its technical achievements, whether we are thinking of social movement activist projects or Broadway musicals. Any US theater history that does not take into account these accomplishments is simply incomplete and, as Luis Valdez said in 1970, antibiotic. *Hamilton*, and other works like it, create the antibodies that preserve life.

## Notes

1. Both "theatre" and "theater" are accepted spellings of the word. I use the variant depending on the official name of the theatre/er or the material quoted.
2. W. E. B. DuBois, "Krigwa Players Little Negro Theatre," *Crisis* 32, no. 3 (1926): 134–136.
3. Jon D. Rossini, *Contemporary Latina/o Theater: Wrighting Ethnicity* (Carbondale: Southern Illinois University Press, 2008), 11.
4. One could, of course, argue that the earliest theatrical productions in any European language in what is now the United States were in Spanish—especially the religious plays used by Spanish missionaries: the Moors and Christians plays, the pastorelas (shepherd), and passion plays that inculcated Christianity via performance as early as the sixteenth century and were as much *against* as *for* the community. Los Angeles, New York City, Tampa, and San Antonio all had thriving Hispanic theaters in the nineteenth century. To use either of these as origin points would significantly rewrite the genealogy. Whether or not they are "Latino" is another question.
5. INTAR, which produces Latina/o plays in English, was founded by Max Ferrá in 1966. Admittedly, the standard timeline has its chronological challenges.
6. Jose Sandoval-Sánchez, *José, Can You See: Latinos On and Off Broadway* (Madison: University of Wisconsin Press, 1999), 118.
7. Rossini, *Contemporary Latina/o* 14–15.

8. Luis Valdez, *Early Works* (Houston, TX: Arte Público, 1990), 6.
9. Valdez, *Early Works*, 7, 9.
10. Valdez, *Early Works*, 10.
11. Luis Ramos-Garcia, ed., *The State of Latino Theater in the USA* (New York: Routledge, 2002), xiv.
12. Ramos-Garcia, *The State of Latino Theater in the USA*, xxiii.
13. *Theatre Topics* is one of the two official journals of the Association for Theatre in Higher Education (ATHE), along with *Theatre Journal*. ATHE is one of the two main academic theatre organizations in the United States, along with the American Society for Theatre Research (ASTR), whose official journal is *Theatre Survey*.
14. Boal, of course, is Brazilian; see Gwendolyn Alker, "A Note from the Editor," *Theatre Topics* 27, no. 1 (2017): xi.
15. For those who are keeping track, Elvira and Hortensia Colorado are from the baby-boom generation; Lin Manuel Miranda is Generation Y.
16. Tamara Underiner, "Burning Texts: Indigenous Dramaturgy on the Continent of Life," in *Indigenous North American Drama: A Multivocal History*, ed. Birgit Däwes (Albany: State University of New York Press, 2013), 66.
17. Jean Franco, *Decline and Fall of the Lettered City* (Cambridge, MA: Harvard University Press, 2009), 24.
18. Underiner, "Burning Texts," 68.
19. From Miranda's *Hamilton*. http://www.hamiltonbroadway.com/.
20. Patricia Ybarra, "How to Read a Latinx Play in the Twenty-First Century: Learning from Quiara Alegria Hudes," *Theatre Topics* 27, no. 1 (2017): 49–59.
21. Rebecca Mead, "All About the Hamiltons," *The New Yorker*, February 9, 2015. http://www.newyorker.com/magazine/2015/02/09/hamiltons.
22. Mead, "All About the Hamiltons."

## Theaters and Other Resources

"100 years of Latino Theatre." (2010). Latinopia.com. http://latinopia.com/latino-theater/100-years-of-chicanolatino-theatre/

American Society for Theatre Research. http://www.astr.org/

Association for Theatre in Higher Education. http://www.athe.org/page/General_Information

Coatlicue Theatre Company. http://www.hemisphericinstitute.org/hemi/en/modules/itemlist/category/168-coatlicue

Festival internacional de teatro hispano en Miami. http://www.teatroenmiami.net/index.php/articulos-teatro/8135-32-festival-internacional-de-teatro-hispano-de-miami

Goodman Theatre. https://www.goodmantheatre.org/

*Hamilton*. http://www.hamiltonbroadway.com/

Hemispheric Institute of Performance and Politics. http://www.hemisphericinstitute.org/

INTAR. http://www.intartheatre.org/

Latinx Theatre Commons. http://howlround.com/latinx-theatre-commons

Microteatro Miami. https://microtheatermiami.com/en/
NoPassport. http://nopassport.org/
Pregones Theater. http://pregonesprtt.org/
Repertorio español. http://repertorio.nyc/#/
Teatro Bravo. http://www.teatrobravo.org/
Teatro Campesino. http://elteatrocampesino.com/
Teatro de la luna. http://teatrodelaluna.org/homes/institucional.htm
Teatro Luna. http://www.teatroluna.org/current.html
Teatrotaller. https://courses.cit.cornell.edu/spanl301/

# Bibliography

Alker, Gwendolyn. "A Note from the Editor." *Theatre Topics* 27, no. 1 (2017): ix–xi.
Anzaldúa, Gloria. *Borderlands/La Frontera: The New Mestiza*. San Francisco: Spinsters/Aunt Lute, 1987.
Arrizón, Alicia. "Performance Art and Theater." *Latino and Latina Writers*. Edited by Alan West-Durán. Vol 1. Farmington Hills, MI: Gale, 2004.
Behar, Ruth. "Juban America." *Poetics Today* 16, no. 1 (1995): 151–170.
*Burns, Aaron, dir. Blacktino*. Fist Pick Films, 2011.
Catalan, Julissa. "Why Hamilton Is So Important to the Latino Community." Sheknows.com. (2016). http://www.sheknows.com/entertainment/articles/1120535/why-hamilton-is-so-important-to-the-latino-community.
Danielson, Marivel T. "Teaching US Latino/a Performance." In *Latino/a Literature in the Classroom*, edited by Frederick Luis Aldaa, 150–158. New York: Routledge, 2015.
DuBois, W. E. B. "Krigwa Players Little Negro Theatre." *Crisis*. 32, no. 3 (1926): 134–136.
Franco, Jean. *Decline and Fall of the Lettered City*. Cambridge, MA: Harvard University Press, 2009.
Godinez, Henry D., and Ramon H. Rivera-Servera, eds. *Goodman Theater's Festival Latino*. Evanston, IL: Northwestern University Press, 2013.
Herrera, Brian Eugenio. *Latin Numbers: Playing Latino in Twentieth Century US Popular Performance*. Ann Arbor: University of Michigan Press, 2015.
Herrera, Brian Eugenio. "'But Do We Have the Actors for That?': Some Principles of Staging Latinx Plays in a University Theatre." *Theatre Topics* 27, no. 1 (2017): 23–35.
Huerta, Jorge. "From the Margins to the Mainstream: Latino/a Theater in the US." *Studies in Twentieth and Twenty-First Century Literature* 32, no. 2 (2008): Article 13. https://doi.org/10.4148/2334-4415.1687.
Huerta, Jorge. "Teaching and Producing Latina/o and Latin American Plays in US Colleges and Universities." *Theatre Journal* 56, no. 3 (2004): 472–474.
Kanellos, Nicolás. *A History of Hispanic Theatre in the USA: Origins to 1940*. Austin: University of Texas Press, 1990.
Marrero, Teresa. "The Latinx Theatre Commons." *Theatre Topics* 27, no. 1 (2017). doi: *https://doi.org/10.1353/tt.2017.0013*
Martínez Cruz, Paloma. "Performance Pedagogy in the Latino Literature Classroom." In *Latino/a Literature in the Classroom*, edited by Frederick Luis Aldama, 159–167. New York: Routledge, 2015.

Mead, Rebecca. "All About the Hamiltons." *The New Yorker*, February 9, 2015. http://www.newyorker.com/magazine/2015/02/09/hamiltons.

Montez, Noe. "Decolonizing Wikipedia Through Advocacy and Activism." *Theatre Topics* 27, no. 1 (2017). doi: https://doi.org/10.1353/tt.2017.0012

Noriega, Jimmy. "Don't Teach These Plays!" *Theatre Topics* 27, no. 1 (2017): 37–48.

Orchard, William "Theater in the Latino/a Literature Classroom." In *Latino/a Literature in the Classroom*, edited by Frederick Luis Aldama, 141–149. New York: Routledge, 2105.

Ramos-Garcia, Luis A., ed. *The State of Latino Theater in the USA*. New York: Routledge, 2002.

Rivas, Tlaloc. "101 Plays by The New Americans, or on Latinidad." HowlRound.com. 2013. http://howlround.com/101-plays-by-the-new-americans-or-on-latinidad.

Rossini, Jon. D. *Contemporary Latina/o Theater: Wrighting Ethnicity*. Carbondale: Southern Illinois University Press, 2008.

Rossini, Jon. D. "Teatro." In *The Routledge Companion to Latino/a Literature*, edited by Suzanne Bost and Frances R. Aparicio, 275–284. New York: Routledge, 2013.

Sandoval-Sánchez, José. *José, Can You See: Latinos On and Off Broadway*. Madison: University of Wisconsin Press, 1999.

Svich, Caridad. "US Polyglot Latino Theatre and Its Link to the Americas." *Contemporary Theatre Review* 16 (2006): 189–197. http://dx.doi.org/10.1080/10486800600587179.

Underiner, Tamara. "Burning Texts: Indigenous Dramaturgy on the Continent of Life." In *Indigenous North American Drama: A Multivocal History*, edited by Birgit Däwes, 62–73. Albany: State University of New York Press, 2013.

Valdez, Luis. *Early Works*. Houston, TX: Arte Público, 1990.

Ybarra, Patricia. "How to Read a Latinx Play in the Twenty-first Century: Learning from Quiara Alegria Hudes." *Theatre Topics* 27, no. 1 (2017): 49–59.

CHAPTER 19

# TRANSCOLONIAL GOTHIC AND DECOLONIAL SATIRE IN RAMÓN EMETERIO BETANCES

### IVONNE M. GARCÍA

In her study of the transamerican origins of Latinx literature, in which she reclaims "Spanish as a literary language of the United States," Kirsten Silva Gruez argues that nineteenth-century Latinx writers "were constituted not only by the cultural and linguistic forms of their Hispanophone place of origin, but by those of the Anglophone United States as well."[1] Within that context of clashing empires, Silva Gruez finds that Latinx "subjectivity is produced in no small part by the web of political maneuvers [by the United States] designed to control, or to acquire outright, the territories Spain had once claimed in the hemisphere" (xi). Along similar lines, Ilan Stavans has noted how Latinx people are "a byproduct of the age of empire: transplanted, uprooted, in a process of constant reinvention" (lxiv). For Stavans, Latinx writers are "birthed from the confrontation" of at least two worlds, and thereby tend to inhabit "a liminal zone," existing "in multiple states of being at the same time."[2] Silva Gruez and Stavans are key voices in the continually emergent field of Latinx studies, which has been fueled by the impetus not only to recover a literary legacy in at least two languages but also to document "the immense regional and national diversity" of this heritage along with its "new literary categories and as yet unexplored critical/theoretical approaches."[3] My essay on two of Ramón Emeterio Betances's literary works—published originally in French and only recently available in their Spanish translation—contributes to this effort of recovery by making these little-studied works accessible to a non-Spanish-speaking audience and introducing new critical frameworks into our wider field.

In 1859, Betances published in Paris a short story titled "*La vierge de Borinquen*" (The Virgin of Borinquen).[4] Influenced by Edgar Allan Poe's "The Oval Portrait," which Betances read in its French translation and from which he took the story's epigraphs, Betances's tale is set in an insane asylum where an Antillean physician—the narrator—arrives for a visit.⁵ There he is taken to see a person the guide describes as his "compatriot," a demented young man who asks the visitor whether he knew the beloved woman he still mourns, because the doctor has said he hails from the Antilles. The deranged man tells of how he asked his young betrothed to join him abroad and how "ella vino toda sonriente a encontrarse con él en los países donde las pesadas brumas velan los esplendores infinitos" [she came, all smiles, to meet him in the countries where the heavy mists shroud the infinite splendors].⁶ But "antes de que hubiera terminado de nombrarla 'Virgen de Borinquen', una noche se hallaron ambos...como en una tumba!" [before he had finished naming her the "Virgin of Borinquen" [the indigenous Taíno name for the island of Puerto Rico], one night they both found themselves...as if in a tomb!].⁷ The young man, who believes he has a dagger in his empty right hand with which he repeatedly tries to stab himself, exclaims: "¡Yo la he visto fría como al agua del río! ¡Verde como las hojas de la ribera! ¡Yo he escuchado el suspiro de la muerte! ¡He perdido a mi triste virgen adorada!" [I have seen her cold, like the river's water! Green, like the leaves at the river's edge! I have heard the sigh of death! I have lost my adored sad virgin!].⁸

When the young man regains some lucidity and realizes anew that he cannot kill himself, he tells the doctor about his tormenting nightmares, filled with bats, crows, tarantulas, and serpents, whose purpose is to seize and destroy the scattered pages on which he has written his thoughts in an effort to reorder his mind and regain his sanity. He then confesses to the doctor that his mission in life now is to "estudiar ciencias desconocidas y descubrir el mundo que ELLA habita" [study unknown sciences and discover the world where SHE inhabits], suggesting that he seeks the secrets to how he can bring her back from the dead (166). Thus, he says, he searches for that "Spirit" who can teach him what he needs to know to free his beloved from the grip of death. An old woman, another patient in the asylum, ridicules the young man, pointing to him and mocking him after hearing his purpose; she notes that he is unworthy of his mission and predicts he will fail. Her words enrage the young man, who curses her but then falls dead at the doctor's feet.

This gothicized melodrama not only shows the transatlantic reach of the American gothic in the nineteenth century but also how Betances drew from his own autobiographical experiences to craft an anti-colonial cautionary tale.⁹ In early 1859, the same year of the story's publication, Betances (in his early thirties) had proposed marriage to his twenty-year-old niece, María del Carmen Henri Betances, and she traveled from Puerto Rico to France to marry him. At the time, Betances was living in exile to avoid being arrested by Spanish authorities in Puerto Rico because of his abolitionist activities. Because of the blood relation, the engaged couple had to wait for approval from the Pope; once it was received, they scheduled the wedding for early May. But in April, three days before her birthday, Lita (as she was familiarly known) died of typhoid fever, leaving Betances in a state of maddened despair and regret. Tormented by guilt at having asked Lita to come to France and at having been unable to save her despite his medical training, Betances draws on the gothic because of the genre's distinct position at the crossroads between fact and fiction.¹⁰

The story, as scholars have noted, moves from the elegiac to the allegorical by representing the "virgin" as the symbol of Puerto Rico. Emma Rivera-Ramago has argued that the little-studied story "[e]s el cuento en honor de su 'virgen adorada', pero también es el texto que la sacraliza como emblema sagrado de la nación" [the story is in honor of his "adored virgin" but this is also the text that establishes her as the sacred emblem of the nation].[11] In her introduction to the first publication of the story's Spanish translation in 1981, Ada Suárez Díaz also notes how the story "[e]s un eco de su drama existencial" [resembles his existential drama] and adds how "[a]lgunas experiencias de la vida de Betances durante ese período parecen emanar de la fantasía de Poe" [some experiences in Betances's life during that period appear to arise from Poe's fantasy].[12] Finding resonance in Poe's story, Betances uses his own personal experience as inspiration for this gothicized account to immortalize not only Lita, but also his *patria*, Puerto Rico.

This article focuses on Betances's autobiographically gothic story and on his 1889 novella, *Los viajes de Escaldado* [*The Travels of Escaldado*], also published in French and later translated into Spanish (the English translations of the cited passages of *Escaldado* here are my own). Particularly interesting is how these literary works articulate Betances's defining transcolonial perspective within the larger nineteenth-century transamerican imaginary. Sarah E. Johnson has described "transcoloniality" as emerging from the "communication networks that flourished in the interstices of empires."[13] She defines "transcoloniality as both a geopolitical and a methodological concept" that articulates "the conflicts and collaborations that occurred between the residents of American territories governed by separate political entities." A transcolonial methodology, Johnson suggests, "provides a counternarrative to the linguistically and disciplinarily isolated fields of American and Caribbean studies that still tend to compartmentalize the region according to [colonially based] categories." Here we use the term "transcolonial" to identify Betances's struggle within the historical moment of competing and interconnected empires and also to categorize the methods he used to represent and critique imperialism across different geopolitical contexts.

Further, Betances's writings reflect a decolonial vision, one that challenges and undermines the discourses of coloniality by privileging the Antillean experience over that of the colonizer.[14] In that way, Betances's texts aim to decolonize knowledge, engaging in what Aníbal Quijano has described as "decoloniality," or the act of discursive liberation from "the prison of coloniality" as "part of the process of social liberation from all power organized as inequality, discrimination, exploitation, and as domination."[15] Significantly, because Betances's decolonial vision arises within the context of an emergent US empire, both of the texts I examine here rewrite US literary works—Poe's nightmarish gothic and Benjamin Franklin's self-congratulatory autobiography, respectively. In doing so, Betances trains his critical eye on influential literary texts from the rising nation-empire to craft both a transcolonial gothic that shows the Poesque consequences of colonial transplantation and to articulate a decolonial satire that mocks foundational US ideologies. In both of these works, Betances wields literature as a weapon against the shared coloniality of multiple imperialisms.

Betances's nineteenth century was an era of rampant and clashing imperialisms, a time when Europe was "slicing up the world and the U.S. was preparing to dispute them its piece."[16] Within this geopolitical context, a variety of emerging ideals—such as liberalism, republicanism, and nationalism—contributed to what Benedict Anderson describes as that era's characteristic "globe-stretching" and "nation-linking."[17] These discursive connections at a global level were further facilitated by major technological innovations, such as the telegraph, the international mail system, steamships, and railways, which fueled international travel and communications.[18] Also importantly, by the late 1880s most of the world, including Brazil and Cuba, the last remaining "slave states," had abolished slavery.[19] This shift from slave labor and agriculture-based economies to greater industrialization and mechanization propelled the historical shift in the long-standing rivalries between the old empires of Britain, France, and Spain as new empires-to-be emerged, such as Germany, Italy, Japan, and the United States. Because of the junctures created by the fierce competition among flagging and emergent empires, Anderson describes this historical moment as one of "early globalization."[20] The global awareness in the contested geopolitical context of his time is clearly present in Betances's writings.

Born in 1827 in the southwestern town of Cabo Rojo, Puerto Rico, Betances was the youngest child and only son of a wealthy, slave-owning immigrant from Santo Domingo and a *criolla* from Cabo Rojo.[21] In 1837, after his mother's death, his father sent him to study in Toulouse, France, where he completed two bachelor's degrees, one in sciences and one in literature. Betances returned briefly to Puerto Rico in 1848, after participating in the revolt in Paris that year and then went back to France to study medicine. He did not return to Puerto Rico until 1856, when he distinguished himself as a physician during a cholera epidemic. Also during those early years in Puerto Rico, Betances became a fervent abolitionist, founding a secret anti-slavery society and dedicating himself to publicly redeeming slave children, which did not endear him to Spanish authorities. That is when he was forced into his first exile in 1858, which set the stage not only for his long-standing role as a newspaper correspondent but also for the events he fictionalized in "The Virgin of Borinquen." In 1865 Betances returned to Puerto Rico to practice medicine, and he continued his anti-colonial subversion against Spanish domination in the Antilles. His separatist activities took him to New York City, where Cubans and Puerto Ricans had joined in their revolutionary efforts against Spain.[22]

Before Martí coined the phrase "our America" as a hemispheric anti-imperialist call to action, Betances, identified by Spain as its most dangerous subversive, had developed a transcolonial vision for the Antilles—one that saw all the islands united against empire. Martí's hemispheric vision foresaw a united America against US imperialism, while Betances focused on a pan-Antillean union, believing that the Antilles (including French-speaking Haiti) should become a larger nation, a new *Gran Patria*.[23] A sworn anti-imperialist, Betances dedicated his entire life to the cause of independence and armed revolution for Puerto Rico, Cuba, and Santo Domingo, and also supported and tried to arm the rebels in the Philippines. Like Martí, who endured exile because of his words, writings, and actions, Betances had to flee Puerto Rico several times during his lifetime and was persecuted by spies, detained, deported, and continually harassed by Spanish authorities. But unlike Martí, who died on Cuban soil defending his island's independence, Betances died exiled in France a few months before the United States invaded Puerto Rico.

In "The Virgin of Borinquen," one of his earliest literary works, Betances drew inspiration from his own Poesque experience with death and madness at the loss of his betrothed to construct a gothic tale in which he splits his authorial self into two characters—that of the rational Antillean doctor and that of his crazed compatriot.[24] In his introduction to the 2017 edition of Betances's complete works by Félix Ojeda Reyes and Paul Estrade, Félix Córdova Iturregui notes that the narrative voice shifts within the story so that even the madman "se autorretrata como si fuera otro" [represents himself as if he were an *other*].[25] In establishing a gothic duality to reflect his own life experiences, Betances also portrayed his betrothed—just like the madman in his story—as symbolically embodying his own beloved island.[26] In a June 1859 letter, one of the dozens Betances wrote recounting Lita's death that year, he states that Lita was "mi patria idolatrada" [my idolized *patria*], adding that "La llamábamos la Borinqueña y era el tipo perfecto, el ideal adorable, la personificación misteriosa de nuestro caro país" [We called her *la Borinqueña*—the woman from Borinquen—and she was the perfect type, the adorable ideal, the mysterious personification of our dear country].[27] Betances figures Lita as his worshipped idol and combines that idolatry with the love of his country, Puerto Rico, gendering the island in traditional terms as the "ideal" woman and making them one and the same. Similarly, this doubling reflects Betances's transcolonial experience of persecution by Spain and exile in France, as represented by the two Antillean men. In the story, these two characters are brought together, not in their common island—from which they are both estranged—but in France, where they are both "strangers," as the visiting doctor tells the madman.

In Betances's case, the displacement from the Spanish-dominated colonial site of Puerto Rico to France's center of colonial power in Paris is produced by the forces of empire since Betances could not get married and live in Puerto Rico because he was persecuted by Spanish authorities and becomes the implicit catalyst for the tragic results. The tragedy of the fictionalized story is not only that the unnamed young woman dies because she has left her native island for inhospitable shores but also that the young man himself dies once he realizes that he can never see her again. Moreover, the story—in a meta-fictional way—shows us how the deranged man's attempts to write himself back into sanity are thwarted by the gothic symbols of sentient evil: the bats, snakes, spiders, and crows that steal his dispersed notes. His struggle to wrest the pieces of his writing from the fearful creatures who keep taking them away from him ends when: "Luego, cayendo unos sobre otros, se despedazaron—y toda su sangre manaba de sus heridas—y era negra—y a medida que caía, gota a gota, se transformaba en vapor de obscuridad—y todo desapareció ante mis ojos—y mis ideas permanecieron en caos" [Later, falling one upon the other, they tore each other apart—and all their blood gushed from their wounds—and it was black—and as it fell, drop by drop, it transformed in a fog of darkness—and everything disappeared before my eyes—and my ideas remained in chaos].²⁸ At this moment, the young man echoes Betances's own sense, as reflected in his letters, that he is lost to the world and to himself because he cannot control the forces that prevent him from overcoming the deepest of despairs.

Then the gothic narrative takes a turn that builds on its transcolonial perspective, one that aims to teach the Antillean doctor listening to the narrative—and the reader—the most significant lesson. Just when the crazed young man believes that all has been lost, he finds himself "junto al cadáver sagrado de mi prometida—y un cirio santo ardía a la cabecera de 'la Virgen de Borinquen'. Y era ella quien me había libertado—y luego de mi liberación, escondiendo su rostro divino bajo un velo de lágrimas, desapareció—y yo... yo me quedé solo! ¡solo para siempre!" [next to the sacred corpse of my betrothed—and a holy candle burned at the head of "the Virgin of Borinquen." And it was she who had freed me—and after my liberation, hiding her divine face behind a veil of tears, she disappeared—and I... I was left alone! Alone forever!].²⁹ Although the young man is desperate because he will forever be without her, he realizes that his Puerto Rican "virgin" freed him from the torments of his prison. In functioning as an allegory of Betances's colonized *patria*—patriarchally figured as sexually untouched and thereby granted a sort of divine—the young woman symbolizes the nascent nation on the verge of realizing its sovereignty, just as Lita was to assume the cultural vestments of full womanhood by becoming Betances's wife.³⁰ Similarly, the fate of his island, still a "virgin" to freedom and sovereignty, becomes the inspiration that saves Betances himself from succumbing to madness. Like the Antillean doctor who is the story's main narrator, Betances (unlike the young man who cannot piece his thoughts together) writes the story to retain his sanity and to represent the tragic consequences of colonial dislocation.

Indeed, the story functions as an eerie foreshadowing, because Betances died in exile in Paris, ill, impoverished, and heartbroken only months after Puerto Rico was invaded by US forces in 1898, as he had feared. Ultimately, Betances refashions Poe's gothicized representations to tell a story that merges the personal and the political and that moves beyond the psychological horror faced by its characters (and author) to underline—in gothically dramatic ways—the repercussions of displacement. Betances's transcolonial vision borrows from US and British gothic texts to represent the impact of multiple colonialisms at both national and personal levels. In "The Virgin of Borinquen," Betances draws from Poe's gothic style of psychological horror not only to explore his own personal torment at the tragic death of his young fiancée but also to allegorize his love for his nation seeking to overcome personal devastation to live to fight another day.

Thirty years later, in 1889, Betances drew from another genre—satire—for his novella *The Travels of Escaldado*, which is both transcolonial in scope and decolonial in purpose.³¹ A rewriting (and continuation) of Voltaire's *Histoire des voyages de Escarmentado*, first published in 1756, Betances's satire is decolonial because it transcends the critique of only one colonial context, revealing the prevailingly imperialistic, and thereby global character of the world in which he lived and wrote.³² Nevertheless, Betances's satire also is particularly national and regional because it is specifically concerned with Puerto Rico and Latin America. In this novella, Escaldado (whose name in Spanish means "scalded") tells *"El Antillano"* (or The Antillean, which was Betances's alias as a newspaper correspondent) about his recent travels after leaving his native country of Venezuela. Escaldado, who identifies himself as hailing from "una pequeña república de América del Sur" [a small republic in South America] tells how he is a direct descendant on his mother's side of "la señora Escarmentada" [Mrs. Escarmentada, or Mrs. Chastised], a direct descendant of Voltaire's character, Scarmentado.[33]

When the young Escaldado reaches the age of twenty, his father, who had seen in his country, "tantas guerras civiles, tantas batallas, masacres, ruinas, aventureros convertidos en generales...; generales erigidos en presidentes, presidentes transformados en tiranos enriquecidos sin escrúpulos" [so many civil wars, so many battles, massacres, ruinations, adventurers turned into generals...; generals propped up as presidents, presidents transformed into enriched and unscrupulous tyrants], decides to send the young man on a trip to Europe. The purpose of the journey, Escaldado says, is "para adquirir allí la cortesía, la moderación y la cultura que sólo otorga el espectáculo de una civilización depurada" [so that I could acquire there the courteousness, the moderation, and the culture that is only bestowed by the spectacle of a purified civilization].[34] Following his father's wishes, Escaldado promptly leaves for Paris.

As Betances sets the scene in the first few paragraphs of the story, we perceive his satirical play on names because Escarmentado (which means "chastised") becomes Escaldado, which refers to being scalded. Thus, the suggestion is that the protagonist does not benefit from a legacy of progress but the reverse—and that his fate is to be ultimately injured or burned. Further, we learn that although he comes from a republic in the New World, "three times larger than France," as Escaldado notes, it is a country wracked by political unrest, corruption, and tyranny, as well as military interventions in politics.[35] Like Martí, who in "Our America" criticized the Latin American republics for their unstable political systems, Betances anticipates the same theme in this satirical novella. Similar to those Latin Americans who Martí criticized in 1892 for looking toward Europe and imitating its ways, Escaldado's father sets his son on the road back to the Old World where he is to be "civilized." Betances deploys the opposition between savagery and civilization, casting the New World as the former, in Escaldado's father's view, and the Old World as the source of civilization that will enlighten his son.

Escaldado arrives in Paris, adopts Parisian dress (a habit of Latin American youth that Martí criticized three years later in "Our America"), and establishes himself at a grand hotel, "muy dispuesto a admirar las bellezas de esa noble capital, llamada por un francés el cerebro del mundo" [well disposed to admire the beauties of that noble capital city, called by a Frenchman the brain of the world].[36] He settles himself in his hotel, where he begins to receive visitors, mostly industrialists who want to involve him in some kind of trade or business enterprise. Among the visitors there is a journalist who brings him a copy of his newspaper. Escaldado finds him amusing: "el cual encontré lleno de ingenio, aunque sin sentido" [which I found full of ingenuity but no sense]. When the journalist reads him an article about Venezuela, the narrator listens in astonishment because "todo ese escrito probaba tan gran ignorancia de los asuntos de los cuales hablaba y era totalmente contrario a la verdad" [the entire document was proof of such great ignorance of the issues that it addressed and was totally contrary to the truth].[37] Escaldado accuses the journalist of publishing falsehoods, the journalist gets insulted, and Escaldado ends up being challenged to a duel. While he states that "jamás he sido hombre de espada" [he has never been a man of swords], he is persuaded by his friends "que debía honrar mi nacionalidad, adoptar las costumbres del país en donde tenía la ventaja de hallarme y hacerme degollar" [to honor my nationality, adopting the customs of the country where I had the advantage of being and getting my throat cut].[38] Escaldado clumsily fights the duel, receiving a deep wound to his chest that nearly kills him and puts him in the hospital for three weeks: "Me costó bien caro" [it was very costly].[39]

Once he is out of the hospital, Escaldado walks to the Latin Quarter where he sees young students and "sabios" [wise men] trying to drown a woman for selling patriotic medals, and then he attends an assembly in Belleville where a group of anarchists attack him after he questions their desire to end the world so they can begin it anew. Escaldado narrates how

> desgarrado y completamente herido, corrí al hotel, cerré mis baúles y decidí partir hacia Inglaterra, seguro de encontrar en los flemáticos hijos de Albión, la moderación que conviene a un pueblo cristiano, episcopal, metodista y civilizador.
>
> [all torn up and totally wounded, I ran to the hotel, closed my trunks and decided to leave for England, where I was sure that I would find, in the sanguine sons of Albion, the moderation that is proper for a Christian, Episcopal, Methodist and civilizing people.][40]

After being attacked twice in France for pointing out the falsehoods in the press and the absurdity of the anarchists' plans, Escaldado is driven out of that country and looks to England as the true civilized nation. In neither the "fourth estate" nor in politics, Escaldado finds anything to emulate in France.

Escaldado then confesses that before deciding on England, he had thought of going to Germany, "pero veía al imperio germánico tan erizado de sables y de bayonetas y tan rodeado de cañones, de fosas y de fortalezas, que temía esa visita" [but I saw the Germanic empire so prickly with sables and bayonets and so surrounded by cannons, moats and fortresses, that I feared that visit].[41] After getting shot at in the border between France and Germany, he decides to change course toward "la libre Albión" [free Albion], and he eventually arrives in London. There he also witnesses a group of people discussing "el asunto de Irlanda" [the Irish question], which suggests the same colonial question Betances raised about his native island. As Escaldado readies himself to side with the rebels, and yells: "¡Viva Irlanda!" [Long live Ireland], he is caught by police and is sent to prison in Dublin, where he spends a month until the Venezuelan consul ("a cuyos oídos no sé cómo llegó este asunto" [I don't know how he heard about this]) frees him.[42] Escaldado then decides to book passage to the United States, specifically to New Orleans, "a buscar refugio en la República coloso, República modelo, al abandonar la monarquía parlamentaria por excelencia" [searching for refuge in the colossus Republic, the model Republic, by abandoning the most excellent parliamentary monarchy] of England.[43] By this point Escaldado's travels have brought him full circle back to the New World. In the Old World he witnesses intransigence, anarchism, militarism, and imperialism (in both Germany and England), and he is ready to return to a republic like his own.

But the republic to end all republics, the one that he anticipatorily describes as a "Colossus," suggesting it will eventually overpower the rest by sheer force, fares no better. Upon his arrival to the United States, he notices a crowd gathering excitedly for some kind of happy spectacle, and he rushes along with them. But he finds himself among several hooded men, and Escaldado soon notices that

> algunos sostenían cuerdas y otros golpeaban con palos a un desgraciado negro que habían arrancado del banco de los acusados y que arrastraban, seguidos por la muchedumbre con gritos de:—¡Muerte! ¡Línchenlo!
> [some held ropes and others had sticks, with which they were beating a poor black man whom they had wrested from the defendant's chair and whom they were dragging, followed by the mob, chanting:—Death! Lynch him!]   (237)

Escaldado is told that "ese criminal había tenido la audacia de hacerse amar por una joven blanca, y el pueblo en masa hacía acto de justicia ejecutando la ley Lynch" [the criminal had the audacity to be loved by a white woman, and the people en masse were doing an act of justice by enforcing the Lynch law].[44] In a gesture "tan tonto como instintivo" [as foolish as it was instinctive], Escaldado attempts to defend the victim, but he is immediately captured and tied up. His neck is noosed, and he is going to be hung from the other side of the rope tied to "[el] infortunado Yoyo" [the unfortunate Yoyo] when another Venezuelan consul who is watching the spectacle recognizes Escaldado and saves him from the mob.

Thus, Escaldado leaves this republic of republics, after finding out that a vitriolic racism trumps political rights in that nation. It is significant in Betances's novella that the black man is being lynched because a white woman fell in love with him. In this passage, Betances turns the rhetorical tables on the stereotype of the black man as dangerous to the virtue of white women by representing white women (and white US society in general) as a danger to the black man and to his allies. The fact that he calls the black man Yoyo, which we can read as a repetition of the self-identifying "me" or "I" in Spanish, suggests that the colonized subjectivities of the black man (despite his living in "a free country") and of Escaldado (despite his hailing from "a free country") are the same.

Promptly fleeing the United States, Escaldado had heard of "una pequeña isla afortunada, especie de paraíso terrenal…donde…no se ha visto un toro embestir hombre ni mujer, aún vestidos de rojo, en donde las mismas serpientes no pican, y en donde los hombres, que nunca han peleado por la libertad, se ocupan, sobre todo, de procrear" [a small fortunate island, a kind of earthly paradise…where…bulls do not charge men or women, even if they are dressed in red, serpents do not bite, and where men, who have never fought for freedom, are mostly occupied in procreating].⁴⁵ On he goes toward "la colonia española de Puerto Rico" [the Spanish colony of Puerto Rico], and impressed by "la belleza del país y del carácter humilde y dulce de estos isleños" [the beauty of the country, and the humble and sweet character of those islanders].⁴⁶ Once there, Escaldado goes to a café looking for some refreshment and respite from the tropical heat. However, once in the café, he is asked whether he supports the *secos* or the *mojados* [the dry ones or the wet ones], to which he answers that "me daba lo mismo, con tal de que fuesen frescos" [he could go either way, as long as they were fresh].⁴⁷ While Escaldado believes he is being asked to choose between two kinds of baked goods, he is actually being interrogated by a Spanish sympathizer who demands to know whether he is in favor of Spanish rule (the *secos*, meaning those hailing from dry Castile) or of autonomy for Puerto Ricans (the *mojados*, or those descended from the Spaniards who crossed the sea). He is accused of making fun of his interlocutor, grabbed by a civil guard, and taken to be tortured by Spanish military officials. Escaldado then recounts a series of horrible tortures, including being hung by his foot (near another similarly tortured man) and then both bodies being pushed against each other: "Cada choque de nuestros dos cuerpos nos hacía dar gritos desgarradores" [Each collision of our bodies would make us scream in agony].⁴⁸

The tortures described by Betances are historically recorded as the *compontes*, Inquisition-like tortures instituted by Spanish authorities in 1887 against anyone in Puerto Rico suspected of being a separatist or an autonomist.⁴⁹ Escaldado notes how

> y yo, que no había tenido idea de los procedimientos contundentes de la Inquisición, nada más que aplicados a los asuntos de la fe católica y que los creía abolidos, comprendí que la causa por la cual se les empleaba había sólo cambiado, y que si habían servido hasta finales del siglo XVIII para hacernos agradables a la religión, aún servían al final del siglo XIX—siglo del teléfono y de los globos no-dirigibles (sic)—para hacernos amar la política conservadora.
>
> [I, who had had no idea of the actual procedures of the Inquisition, except were applied to issues of the Catholic faith, and who believed they had been abolished, realized that only the reason for which these procedures were used had changed, and that if they had served until the end of the eighteenth century to make us agreeable to religion, they were still useful at the end of the nineteenth century, the century of the telephone and of the non-dirigible airships, to force us to love conservative politics.]   (240)

Alluding to the Inquisition to describe the persecution of autonomists and *soberanistas* (those who wanted freedom from Spanish rule) in Puerto Rico, Betances's satire compares the tortures that forced people to submit to Catholic dogma with those that forced Puerto Ricans to submit to Spanish colonial rule.

Betances also addresses the fact that while the late nineteenth century symbolized modernity and progress because of new communication technologies and modes of transportation, the causes of oppression (whether religious, political, national, or racial) had not changed but had merely found different vestments with which to dress themselves. Finally, Escaldado escapes Puerto Rico and travels to Madrid, where he wants to register complaints about how he was treated, only to find himself escorted by gendarmes to the border, "rogándome que presentara mis querellas en otra parte" [who begged me to take my complaints somewhere else] (240). Defeated in his attempts to find civilization in any of the countries—empires, republics, and colonies—that he visited, Escaldado returns to his native country to some forest land he owns. In a move that demonstrates Betances's decolonial rewriting of US texts, Escaldado decides to "reanudar los experimentos de Franklin para alcanzar la perfección moral" [renew the experiments of (Benjamin) Franklin to reach moral perfection] (241). Thus, Escaldado chooses twelve groups of animals, "de los cuales cada uno representaba una de las virtudes buscadas por el filósofo, y los instalé cómodamente alrededor de mi morada" [each of which represented one of the virtues searched for by the philosopher, and I installed them comfortably around my house] (241). Living among these animals, Escaldado is constantly reminded of the virtues hailed by Franklin in his autobiography.[50]

Escaldado lists the virtues in the same order as Franklin does in his autobiography, but instead of the descriptive sentences that Franklin adds to define what each virtue means, Escaldado includes the animal that embodies the virtue. Escaldado lists:

1. Temperance—the camel
2. Silence—the carp
3. Order—the beaver
4. Resolution—the hummingbird
5. Frugality—the ant
6. Industry—the ox
7. Sincerity—the dog
8. Moderation—the lamb
9. Cleanliness—the swan
10. Tranquility—the elephant
11. Chastity—the parrot
12. Humility—the donkey

The major difference between Escaldado's and Franklin's lists is that while Franklin enumerates thirteen virtues, Escaldado lists only twelve because he argues that justice is a virtue "demasiado noble para investir a ninguno de los seres que me rodeaban" [too noble to be represented by any of the beings that surrounded me].[51] Here, the reader notes that while Escaldado did not find any of these virtues in any of the places he traveled to, he has, however, found them represented in animals.

In this tale of political (not only personal) development, inspired by Voltaire and a rewriting of Franklin, Escaldado's conclusion is that tolerance (and thereby justice) cannot be found where empires or republics or colonies clash—they can only be forged by individuals within their own limited spheres of action. Because he judges himself unworthy of representing the virtue of tolerance, Escaldado decides to "inscribir [la palabra Tolerancia] en letras de oro en la entrada de un pequeño pabellón central adonde venían a resolverse ante mí todos los asuntos en litigio de los miembros de la familia" [inscribe the word Tolerance in golden letters at the entrance of a small central building where family members came to me to solve any issue under litigation].[52] But Escaldado notes that he does not expect "que en los países más civilizados, esa gran virtud fuera empleada en todos los quehaceres de la inteligencia humana, no antes de seis mil u ocho mil años" [that the more civilized countries will employ that virtue in all of the to-dos of human intelligence before six thousand or eight thousand years have passed].[53]

Escaldado fails to find the virtues praised by Franklin, Enlightenment philosopher and Founding Father of the United States, in his own country. There, the nation's evident racism (an aspect that Martí also highlighted in his writings on the United States) fully contradicts the nation-building myths of equality and democracy of the republic. This critique is decolonial in both form and content, since Escaldado not only rewrites Franklin's paradigms but also satirizes them. Moreover, Escaldado does not find civilization in Europe, where his father has sent him to go looking for models to imitate. Instead, Escaldado must (like Martí concluded in his essay) eschew all ideas of mimetism, and instead must follow his own American (in the hemispheric sense) ideas of justice and civilization, including pairing moral virtues with industrious animals, such as the ant. The political and social commentary in this short novella is delivered through a biting transcolonial satire, one that cuts across imperial and colonial contexts to comment on the human nature that promotes, subjects itself, and rebels against colonialism.

Betances's gaze is focused not only on the imperial powers of Britain, France, Germany, and the United States but also on a politically unstable Latin America and on his own colonial Puerto Rico, where the people are more interested in "procreating" than in fighting for their freedom. The transcolonial perspective of Betances's story challenges the positivist ideals represented by Franklin by showing how imperialism and colonial rule ultimately defeat both the hope for and the application of justice. The freedoms of expression and of association, which Escaldado heroically strives to uphold throughout his visits to all these countries, are only possible once he returns to his own native land: but only in the space that he controls, which is his own native forest. This return to the land, a place where Escaldado can be sovereign, operates as a metaphor for Betances's pro-independence activism against both Spain and the United States. Still, in Betances's narrative, Escaldado chooses to wait until the time is ripe for history to change, after taking a protagonist role everywhere he goes: getting pummeled in France, almost killed in Germany, imprisoned in England, nearly lynched in the States, tortured in Puerto Rico, and deported from Spain.

Betances's writings show how the relationship between rising and waning empires throughout the nineteenth century enabled the emergence of transcolonial discourses that although born in different geocultural contexts shared a significant synchronicity. This highly volatile time helped propel anti-colonial writers, including Betances in Puerto Rico and Martí in Cuba, who articulated a transcolonial subjectivity and a global self-awareness within the threat of multiple imperialisms. Years before Martí's famous 1891 essay "Our America," Betances's political and literary works articulated a transcolonial viewpoint, establishing him as a major cultural theorist within the global Latin/o Americas. In their writings, both Betances and Martí foresaw (and cautioned against) the rise of the US empire at the close of the nineteenth century. Because their goals moved beyond politics toward theory and philosophy, Betances and Martí remain perceptive and relevant cultural and political theorists of transcoloniality. Specifically, in his own writings, Betances not only anticipated the global reach of imperialism but also envisioned ways in which literary works could be used to combat their colonialist influence.

Betances deployed a transcolonial view in his speeches, letters, and essays to attack Spanish colonial domination in both the Caribbean and the Pacific. But it is through his literature, which still remains largely understudied, that we see Betances deploy the transcolonial gothic and decolonial satire that reveals the world as an imperialist playground within which the currently or formerly colonized are imperiled. In *The Virgin of Borinquen*, two lives are lost to the forces of colonial persecution and displacement, while the Antillean narrator, who remains behind to bear the burden of the gothic narrative, must learn—like the reader—to heed its cautionary lesson. The Antillean narrator—the double of Betances—must live to continue the fight for the freedom of Borinquen, whose embodied "virgin" has died far from its shores. Years later, in his short novella's recasting of Voltaire through the imagined travels of Escaldado, Betances suggests that the time will come when a decolonial answer will be found. Both stories reflect the multiply colonial contexts in which Betances lived and composed them, and just as importantly, they are both lessons in decoloniality—or in the process of fighting against "all power organized as inequality, discrimination, exploitation, and as domination."[54] While Betances may have died believing he was politically defeated, once the United States grabbed its place as a rising empire in the hemisphere, his transcolonial and decolonial perspectives have lost none of their subversive and persuasive power—especially in the twenty-first century.

In these troubled times, when our communities find themselves increasingly embattled, the field of Latinx studies has an even more significant role in showing how we are not just a "recent phenomenon" and that the so-called American imaginary is—and has consistently been—transamerican in scope and transcolonial in awareness.[55] By demanding "a reconsideration of the national demarcations of the American literary canon," and by underlining "the need to diversify the American imaginary," we also should continue to reclaim the noun "American" as solely hemispheric.[56] Our terminology should actively reflect the inclusive, as opposed to colonialist, ways to understand the multilingual, multivocal, multiperspectival, and multiply connected literary history of the Americas as a whole. Within that backdrop, the recovery and the translation into English of Betances's writing aims to be a decolonial act that not only acknowledges the diverse points of departure from which the Latinx experience originated but also points to the future of our now-three-decades-old field as we continue to make inroads in decolonizing the knowledge we produced and that has been produced about us.

# The Virgin of Borinquen[57]

## by Ramón Emeterio Betances

—To the glory of my angel

The Three Kings are leaving,
Glory be to God!
They come and go
And we don't!
*Chants populaires de Noel*

She was a maiden of rarest beauty, and not more lovely than full of glee. And evil was the hour when she saw, and loved, and wedded the painter.

And he was a passionate, and wild, and moody man, who became lost in reveries... Yet she smiled on and still on, uncomplainingly, because she saw that the painter... took a fervid and burning pleasure in his task.[58]

We then walked into a room where several men were gathered. They were seated around a long table. Some rested their elbows on it and hid their foreheads and their eyes in their hands and their fingers were contorted in their hair. Others, looking at these men, smiled with a mocking laugh. Others had their backs to the table and murmured incomprehensibly to themselves, without moving their lips. Suddenly, one of them, seated at the center of the gathering, stood up. He was the very image of the long-haired Christ and he magestically extended his arms: "Here is my blood"—he said—"take it and drink!"

—"That is not the most curious among them," the doctor told me. "You are going to meet your compatriot, and if you know how to interrogate him, he himself will tell you his story. I was his friend, but he doesn't recognize me anymore; he even treats me with a certain disdain, believing me incapable of helping him in his endeavors."

In one of the corners of the room, seated at the end of a bench, was a slim, tall, dusky, wasted man whose sunken eyes would emit sinister rays and then just as suddenly reveal the most painful melancholy. Sometimes, the end of his breath was confused with a slight piercing sigh and then he would turn as if he heard a voice from beyond. He convulsively gripped his right arm with his left hand, just above his wrist, with so much force that, despite his tanned skin, a white and red ribbon would appear around the pressed part. He looked around him, and then he fixed his eyes on the floor. He was thus when we approached. He rose before me, driving two lightning strikes into my eyes, all in one motion.

— "Are you Egyptian?"

— "No"—I said—"but I am, like you, a stranger to these parts. What do you wish for?"

— "Regardless, you look like you must descend from the Egyptian race. What do you have to teach me?"

— "I come from the Antilles."

— "Ah!"—he exclaimed, and his voice took on a sweet and sad tone—"Did you know her, undoubtedly?"

— "Maybe I'll say yes, with the condition that you should make me her portrait."

—"Her portrait?...She was a beneficent genie...She was a happy, sweet, and tender young woman, very modest and burning in love, beautiful like a star and guileless like a flower, sometimes thoughtful and serious. Adored by children and loved by the old, she possessed the joys of innocence and gave advice like a wise person. Her words carried the treasures of an infinite kindness and her long radiant looks revealed the understanding of a great intelligence. Do you recognize her? Have you seen her?"

—"She was"—I said with respect— "pure Reason and venerated Love!"

—"Yes"— said the poor madman, profoundly saddened, while he,...he was a sad and silent dreamer. He ardently searched for her happiness, unrelentingly, but he searched far from the country where Love lives in the light, and he wanted the will of his betrothed to be combined with his, and he asked her to come, and she came all smiles to meet him in the countries where heavy mists shroud the infinite splendors, and before he had finished naming her as the "Virgin of Borinquen," one night they both found themselves...as if in a tomb!

The madman said these last words with a melancholy so moving that I felt how my eyes filled with tears. I turned my face. Until that moment, he had spoken while always pressing his right arm with his left hand, as if the hand and the arm belonged to two different people. With his last words, they separated without any effort. Then, the man exclaimed: "I have seen her cold like the river's water! Green like the leaves at the river's edge! I have heard the sigh of death! I have lost my adored sad virgin!"

In that instant, he raised his right hand to the heavens. I saw the doctor blanch as he saw his friend, unable to understand what fear agitated him. Suddenly, the madman fixed his eyes on his hand, saw it free, and smiling, hit at his heart and fell as if wounded by a lightning strike.

—"He believes he has a dagger that he drives into himself irresistibly each time that he lets the hand go"—the doctor told me, with a voice that trembled, filled with compassion—"I fear those hits to the chest and I would prefer to see his right hand atrophy under the constant pressure of his left hand."

The madman, at the same time, returned his hands to their habitual position. Returning to himself, he got back on his feet, saying:

—"It's true! My task is not yet accomplished!"

—"Listen"— said the doctor quietly—"After what's happened, he is still mad."

—"Yes, it's true"—the madman continued, addressing me and impressed, undoubtedly, by my creole figure—"if it is true that you are Egyptian, you will understand this story of desolation and darkness and will dedicate yourself, as I do, to studying the sciences that reveal the worlds beyond."

An old woman, with a face like a mummy, had walked quietly through the room and had come to sit herself in front of the madman. She then erupted into a cackle of diabolic incredulity, but silenced herself immediately under the gaze of full authority that the creole gave her. She remained impassive, nailed to her place, and with her small lashless eyes fixed on him.

"I found myself"— he said—"in a room whose dimensions were all of thirteen feet. It had thirteen walls without exit and I had been locked in there by the same maleficent, blind, and destructive genie who, as part of its games, had killed my betrothed, and had taken her where thought cannot penetrate. The deepest darkness, the thick and impenetrable night, ruled to the level where the tip of my longest hair could reach; beyond was the living light, splendid, sparkling. I remained blind at the bottom of my nightly prison, but in the luminous atmosphere I would see the flutter of somber birds, like my prison, bats and crows, while on the white ceiling horrible tarantulas chased black spiders, and snakes with round, glassy eyes, unmoving though alive, irresistibly drew to them blind and heavy moles, around which they coiled themselves while they hung their infernal sibilant heads towards me. I could not see any part of my body, and if I raised my hand toward the light, the darkness would rise like a tide to the tip of my extended fingers. I made fruitless efforts to pass from that level. Then I felt that the length of my fingers diminished; they sank into my hand and my hand disappeared into my abbreviated arm. Horrified, I diverted my gaze from the repugnant objects I was allowed to see; my thought would return to myself and I contemplated my interiority. Suddenly, I was overcome by an irresistible chill. An immeasurable cold overcame me. The hair on my head stood on end and floated as if in soapy water. I felt that I was sinking to the bottom and, as I sank, the cold slithered on my body, always rising, rising. When it reached my heart, I drowned (ah, what anxiety!). Then, it reached my brain, which froze. I saw my bony face, naked. The vault of my skull opened and closed again with a rough noise, and then a frightening wind blew followed by the rumor of dry leaves snatched as they gyrated upon themselves. The wind blew from top to bottom and I saw an infinity of white paper squares, irregularly ripped, each bearing an inscription, which twirled in the midst of the astonished bats and the crows. All my ideas had flown from my brain, like the birds from their nest! Each one of them appeared inscribed over another of the fluttering sheets. I felt bemused!... Slowly, everything returned to silence and the sheets became impregnated with the heavy mist distilled by the darkness, falling again to the back of the room. Then I was taken over by vertigo. I wanted to pick up and collect my ideas. Each time a paper fell, I ran toward it; I searched, probing on the floor, and, if I found it, I would press it between the index and middle finder, I would bring it to the light. I wanted to read my thought there. The darkness extended itself over everything that came in contact with any part of my body, but the paper overcame this and remained in the light. I was almost to the point of recovering my lost idea when a bat, passing, issued a sharp cry, swatted the paper with its wing and made it fall. I ran to recover it, but a crow, batting its wings over the paper, cawed and snatched it with its beak. Then, a spider, hanging from an imperceptible thread, fell fast like a rock, running speedily over the floor of darkness, took the writing and, while ascending, twisted and creased it between its legs; a snake, sinking the three darts of its tongue into the ceiling, remained suspended and balanced its body while it writhed in the air; then it lashed its tail so terribly that the paper stuck to it and when it touched my hand I trembled from the cold. I arduously continued with my endless task. My persistence did not in any way appease the relentlessness of my enemies; their cold figures, impassive, immutable, began to affect me. I felt drenched in cold sweats. My heart beat with such a great acceleration that I could not count its movements. I collapsed, exhausted!"

"Darkness and light mixed and conflated themselves. The birds and the snakes fell avidly upon the insects and the moles and devoured them. Later, falling one upon the other, they tore each other apart—and all their blood gushed from their wounds—and it was black—and as it fell, drop by drop, it transformed in a fog of darkness—and everything disappeared before my eyes—and my ideas remained in chaos. Later, when passing my hand over my eyes, I could not distinguish but a small luminous spot and an unmoving body—and I found myself next to the sacred corpse of my betrothed—and a holy candle burned at the head of 'the Virgin of Borinquen.' And it was she who had freed me—and after my liberation, hiding her divine face behind a veil of tears, she disappeared—and I… I was left alone! Alone forever!"

I had listened to this story with all the interest that can be inspired by great despair, so deeply felt. The unfortunate young bride who was about to enjoy so much love, herself loving with a sublime devotion, the emotion of the lover who told his dream, the death of these two intelligences, were sufficiently powerful motives to move a sensitive heart. To all this, there was added a scene that left me with the most profound sadness.

"And now"—the madman added with anxiety—"do you have something to teach me? This dagger that you see in my hand is ready to plunge into me. I would release it, but I still should study the unknown sciences and discover the world which SHE inhabits. If I set free this hand, I will die without seeing the Spirit I seek, and to deeply explore those sciences, I cannot leave her chained. That's why I go on asking those who pass by: 'Do you have something to teach me? Pour upon me your knowledge!' It is said,"—he continued—"that other men have discovered impenetrable worlds and have communicated with powers that have all of life and all of science. I will do the same for HER!"—the lover concluded proudly.

"Listen! Listen!"—said the old woman with scorn, as she moved away pointing her finger at the creole—"Ha! Ha! Ha! Not just anyone can travel to Corinth."

The young man's eyes became inflamed. A convulsive tremor took hold of him and he yelled:

—"Sybil of desperation, I curse you!"

And he fell dead, suddenly.

The Christ came to kneel next to him while praying and murmuring:

… "Because they had loved much!"

Charenton, Holy Friday, April 22, 18…, midnight.

## Notes

1. Kirsten Silva Gruez, *Ambassadors of Culture The Transamerican Origins of Latino Writing* (Princeton, NJ: Princeton University Press, 2001), xvii, xi.
2. Ilan Stavans, ed., "Introduction: The Search for Wholeness," *The Norton Anthology of Latino Literature* (New York: W.W. Norton, 2010), lxviii.
3. Erlinda Gonzales-Berry and Chuck Tatum, eds., "Introduction," *Recovering the U.S. Hispanic Literary Heritage, Volume 2* (Houston, TX: Arte Público, 1995), 13.
4. The English translations of Betances's texts analyzed here are my own. The Spanish translation of the French original is by José Emilio González as included in *Betances: Obras Completas, Escritos Literarios Vol. III*, ed. Félix Ojeda Reyes y Paul Estrade (San Juan, PR: ZOOMIdeal, 2017), 159–166. González's translation appears in Ada Suárez Díaz's *La Virgen de Borinquen y Epistolario Intimo*, published in 1981 by the Instituto de Cultura Puertorriqueña, which also includes the French original.
5. In Poe's "The Oval Portrait," a young painter marries a beautiful woman but neglects her health as he starts to fervently paint her portrait, failing to notice that she withers as the painting becomes more lifelike. At the moment he finishes the portrait, his beloved dies. Ada Suárez Díaz notes that Poe's stories began to be translated into French in 1845 but that it was Charles Baudelaire's translations in 1857 that were the most significant and the ones Betances likely read. Suárez Díaz also notes that Poe was popular in France at the time Betances was there. See Suárez Díaz, "Introducción," *La Virgen de Borinquen y Epistolario Intimo*, vii.
6. Betances, "La virgen de Borinquen," 162.
7. Betances, *The Virgin*, 166.
8. Betances, *The Virgin*, 166.
9. Elma Beatriz Rosado wonders whether Betances was "expiando sus angustias para sacarlas de su organismo y evitar el riesgo de que puedan perturbar su mente debido al profundo golpe emocional que está viviendo? ¿Cómo saberlo?" [atoning for his suffering so he could remove it from himself and escape the danger of mental illness from the deep emotional blow he experienced? How could we know?] Elma Beatriz Rosado, ""La virgen de Borinquen, Betances y el anillo nupcial," *80 grados:Prensa sin prisa*. 6 mayo 2018, 14. Translation mine.
10. Suárez Díaz notes how Betances read Poe in the French translation by Charles Baudelaire published in 1858, from where he took the epigraphs for the story (vii).
11. Emma Rivera-Ramago, "Amor Prohibido: La Mujer y la Patria en Ramón Emeterio Betances." PhD diss. (Amherst: University of Massachusetts, 1998), 93.
12. Suárez Díaz, "Introducción," vi, vii. All translations of Rivera-Ramago's and Suárez Díaz's work from Spanish to English are mine.
13. Johnson, *The Fear of French Negroes*, 2–3.
14. See Aníbal Quijano, "Coloniality and Modernity/Rationality," *Globalization and the Decolonial Option*, ed. Walter D. Mignolo and Arturo Escobar (London: Routledge, 2010).
15. Johnson, *The Fear of French Negroes*, 31, 32.
16. See Irma Rivera Nieves, *Cambio de Cielo: Viaje, Sujeto y Ley en Ledrú, Hostos y Rizal* (San Juan, PR: Postdata, 1999), 181.
17. Benedict Anderson, *Under Three Flags: Anarchism and the Anti-Colonial Imagination* (New York, Verso, 2005), 1.
18. Anderson, *Under Three Flags*, 3.
19. Anderson, *Under Three Flags*, 142.

20. Anderson, *Under Three Flags*, 3.
21. Suárez Díaz, *El Antillano*, 13. As a person of mixed race, Betances's birth was originally recorded in the Baptismal Book of *"Pardos"* (people of mixed race) as opposed to the *"Libro de Blancos"* [Book of Whites], but his family had the record transferred to the "white" book in 1840.
22. For a biography of Betances, see Ada Suárez Díaz, *El antillano: biografía del Dr. Ramón Emeterio Betances, 1827–1898* (San Juan, PR: Centro de Estudios Avanzados de Puerto Rico y el Caribe, 1988).
23. See Irma Reyes-Santos, "On Pan-Antillean Politics: Ramón Emeterio Betances and Gregorio Luperón Speak to the Present," *Callaloo* 36, no. 1 (2013): 142–157.
24. Although Betances buried Lita's body in Mennecy, France, shortly after her death, in July he decided to take her back to Puerto Rico and have her body exhumed. He transported her body by ship first to Saint Thomas, which meant forty days of crossing the Atlantic, and finally to Puerto Rico, where she was finally laid to rest in November 1859. See Suárez Díaz, "Introducción," vi (translation mine).
25. Félix Córdova Iturregui, "Poética y revolución: La voz literaria de Ramón Emeterio Betances," *Betances: Obras Completas, Vol. 3* (San Juan, PR: ZOOMIdeal, 2017), 15–42. 37. Translation mine.
26. Ada Suárez Díaz, *La virgen de Borinquen y Epistolario Intimo* (San Juan: Instituto de Cultura Puertorriqueña, 1981).
27. Suárez Díaz, "Introducción," 88.
28. Betances, *La virgen de Borinquen*, 10.
29. Betances, *La virgen de Borinquen*, 10.
30. Betances, *La virgen de Borinquen*, 36.
31. Ojeda Reyes and Estrade note that *Voyages de Scaldado, récit recueilli par "El Antillano"* was published in Paris in 1888, and then translated into Spanish and published in 1894 by Luis Caballer. Ojeda Reyes and Estrade use the 1982 translation by Carmen Lugo Filippi. All English translations here are mine. See Ojeda Reyes and Estrade, *Betances*, 231.
32. Carmen Lugo Filippi argues that Betances's satire is in the European style of Erasmus, Rabelais, or Voltaire "que no se conforman con ser meramente satíricos ingeniosos, sino que se empeñan en blandir la invectiva a diestra y siniestra, como estrategas hábiles y despiadados y hacen uso de la mordacidad, de la ironía, del ataque de costado y de las terribles insinuaciones" [who did not conform themselves to merely being ingenuous satirists but also insisted on wielding invective left and right, as able and implacable strategists, and [to this end] deployed mordacity, irony, attacks from the side and terrible insinuations]." See Lugo Filippi, "Betances satírico," *Revista Cuadrivium* 1 (1998): 35–37, http://www.uprh.edu/~ivelez/p35lugofilippi.html. Translation mine.
33. Betances, *Escaldado*, 231. See Voltaire, *The History of the Voyages of Scarmentado: A Satire*, translated from the French of M. de Voltaire (London, 1757).
34. Betances, *La virgen de Borinquen*, 232.
35. Betances, *La virgen de Borinquen*, 231.
36. Betances, *La virgen de Borinquen*, 232.
37. Betances, *La virgen de Borinquen*, 233.
38. Betances, *Escaldado*, 233.
39. Betances, *Escaldado*, 234.
40. Betances, *Escaldado*, 235.
41. Betances, *Escaldado*, 236.

42. Betances, *Escaldado*, 237.
43. Betances, *Escaldado*, 237.
44. Betances, *Escaldado*, 237.
45. Betances, *Escaldado*, 238.
46. Betances, *Escaldado*, 238.
47. Betances, *Escaldado*, 238.
48. Betances, *Escaldado*, 239.
49. For a description of the tortures, see Luis M. Díaz Soler, *Puerto Rico desde sus orígenes hasta el cese de la dominación española* [History of Puerto Rico: Origins to the end of Spanish rule] (Río Piedras: Editorial Universidad, 1999), 642. "The three detained farm hands later said they were tied by their feet and hands, whipped and abandoned, unconscious, at a rundown warehouse... where they spent two or three days at the mercy of rats and vermin. [Others] told of how they were slapped in the face and were tortured with *palillos* (sticks) [wooden sticks with nails used to pressure fingers and hands together]. [A carpenter] reported that he was beaten [by a Spanish sergeant], who ordered that he be taken to a cane field and shot, an order that was not complied with." Another person, like Escaldado, was hung by his feet.
50. Franklin's list of thirteen virtues includes temperance, silence, order, resolution, frugality, industry, sincerity, justice, moderation, cleanliness, tranquility, chastity, and humility. See *The Autobiography of Benjamin Franklin* (Boston: Houghton, Mifflin, 1888), 102–104.
51. Betances, *Escaldado*, 241.
52. Betances, *Escaldado*, 241.
53. Betances, *Escaldado*, 241.
54. Quijano, "Coloniality," 31.
55. Gonzales-Berry and Tatum, *Recovering*, 19.
56. Gonzales-Berry and Tatum, *Recovering*, 19.
57. English translation by Ivonne M. García and Lance K. Oliver from the 1981 Spanish translation by José Emilio González published in Félix Ojeda Reyes and Paul Estrade's *Betances: Obras Completas, Escritos Literarios Vol. 3*.
58. From Edgar Allan Poe's "The Oval Portrait," 1850.

## Bibliography

Anderson, Benedict. *Under Three Flags: Anarchism and the Anti-Colonial Imagination*. New York: Verso, 2005.

Betances, Ramón Emeterio. "La virgen de Borinquen." In *Betances: Obras Completas, Vol. 3, Escritos literarios*. Edited by Félix Ojeda Reyes and Paul Estrade, 159–166. San Juan, PR: ZOOMIdeal, 2017.

Betances, Ramón Emeterio. "Viajes de Escaldado." In *Betances: Obras Completas*, 1889, 231–241.

Córdova Iturregui, Félix. "Poética y revolución: La voz literaria de Ramón Emeterio Betances." In *Betances: Obras Completas, Vol. 3*. San Juan, PR: ZOOMIdeal, 2017.

Díaz Soler, Luis M. *Puerto Rico desde sus orígenes hasta el cese de la dominación española*. Río Piedras, PR: Editorial Universidad, 1999.

Franklin, Benjamin. *The Autobiography of Benjamin Franklin*. New York: Houghton, Mifflin, 1888.

Gonzales-Berry, Erlinda, and Chuck Tatum, eds. "Introduction." *Recovering the U.S. Hispanic Literary Heritage. Vol. 2*. Houston, TX: Arte Público, 1995.

Johnson, Sara E. *The Fear of French Negroes: Transcolonial Collaboration in the Revolutionary Americas*. Berkeley: University of California Press, 2012.

Lugo Filippi, Carmen. "Betances satírico." *Revista Cuadrivium* 1 (1998): 35–37, http://www.uprh.edu/~ivelez/p35lugofilippi.html.

Ojeda Reyes, Félix, and Paul Estrade. *Betances: Obras Completas, Escritos Literarios Vol. 3*. San Juan, PR: ZOOMIdeal, 2017.

Quijano, Aníbal. "Coloniality and Modernity/Rationality." In *Globalization and the Decolonial Option*. Edited by Walter D. Mignolo and Arturo Escobar. London: Routledge, 2010.

Rivera Nieves, Irma. *Cambio de Cielo: Viaje, Sujeto y Ley en Ledrú, Hostos y Rizal*. San Juan, PR: Postdata, 1999.

Rivera-Ramago, Emma. "Amor Prohibido: La Mujer y la Patria en Ramón Emeterio Betances." PhD diss., University of Massachusetts Amherst, 1998.

Rosado, Elma Beatriz. "La virgen de Borinquen, Betances y el anillo nupcial." *80 grados:Prensa sin Prisa*. 6 mayo 2018. http://www.80grados.net/la-virgen-de-borinquen-betances-y-el-anillo-nupcial/#_edn35. 1–22.

Silva Gruez, Kirsten. *Ambassadors of Culture The Transamerican Origins of Latino Writing*. Princeton, NJ: Princeton University Press, 2001.

Stavans, Ilan, ed. "Introduction: The Search for Wholeness." *The Norton Anthology of Latino Literature*. New York: W.W. Norton, 2010.

Suárez Díaz, Ada. "Introducción." *La Virgen de Borinquen y Epistolario Intimo*. San Juan, PR: Instituto de Cultura Puertorriqueña, 1981.

Suárez Díaz, Ada. *El antillano: Biografía del Dr. Ramón Emeterio Betances, 1827–1898*. San Juan, PR: Centro de Estudios Avanzados de Puerto Rico y el Caribe, 1988.

Voltaire. *The History of the Voyages of Scarmentado: A Satire*. London: Paul Vaillant, 1757.

CHAPTER 20

# A BORDERLANDS HISTORY OF LATINX CINEMA

PAUL A. SCHROEDER RODRÍGUEZ

STUDIES of Latinx cinema typically take one of two approaches: identifying, analyzing, and evaluating mainstream media's representations of Latinxs since the silent period; or tracing the emergence and development of a cinema made by, for, and about Latinxs since the 1970s. Allen Woll's pioneering *The Latin Image in American Films* (1977) is still a relevant study that focuses on mainstream representations: clearly written and argued, it gives readers a breakdown of the major Latinx and Latin American stereotypes (greaser, Latin Lover, Mexican Spitfire) as they crystallized, disappeared, and sometimes reemerged under new guises, from the silent period until the mid-1970s, when the book was published; while Mary C. Beltrán's more recent *Latina/o Stars in U.S. Eyes* (2009) completes the picture by focusing on the construction of Latinx stardom in film and television since the silent period. The second approach is exemplified by Rosa Linda Fregoso's *The Bronze Screen* (1993), a cultural studies and feminist take on Chicana and Chicano cinematic culture from its origins in the Chicanx civil rights movement of the 1960s through the early 1990s. Chon Noriega's edited volume *Chicanos and Film: Representation and Resistance* (1992) includes both approaches in one tome: Part I includes essays on Chicanxs in Hollywood and in the Mexican film industry, while Part II includes essays on films made by, for, and about Chicanxs. This double approach also characterizes *The Bronze Screen*, a documentary that shares the title of Rosa Linda Fregoso's book, though not its content. Instead, as the liner notes state, the documentary honors the past, illuminates the present, and opens a window to the future of Latinos in motion pictures. From silent movies to urban gang films, stereotypes of the Greaser, the Lazy Mexican, the Latin Lover, and the Dark Lady are examined. Rare and extensive footage traces the progression of this distorted screen image to the increased prominence of today's Latino actors, writers, and directors.

The extensive use of footage effectively shows what academic studies have amply demonstrated: that representations of Latinxs on the big screen are dominated by negative stereotypes. This article, however, does not focus on stereotypes, but rather on the relatively small number of films that explore the complexities, nuances, and contradictions of the Latinx experience of living in the B/borderlands, regardless of the films' country or origin or the ethnicity of the filmmakers. As such, it offers a novel perspective in a field where much of the research continues to focus either on stereotypes/representations of individual Latinx characters, or on Latinx artists (directors, actors, etc.) who increasingly work in a media landscape where traditional format films have become a small part of a wide range of audiovisual narratives available online via streaming services such as Netflix and YouTube.

This shift in content and viewing practices from cinema to media is amply reflected in recent scholarship. Consider this year's announcement that *Cinema Journal*, the foremost academic journal in the field, will change its name to *JCMS: Journal of Cinema and Media Studies*. Or that this year's Latinx Studies Conference featured only one session focused specifically on film, but five on media, including a plenary session titled "Latinx Media Now!" Three exemplary anthologies trace this shift over the past twenty years: *The Ethnic Eye: Latino Media Arts*, *Latin Looks: Images of Latinas and Latinos in U.S. Media*, and *Latinos and Narrative Media: Participation and Portrayal*.[1] All have "media" in their titles, but whereas the first privileges essays on film, the essays in Rodríguez's anthology are more or less equally divided between film and other media, and Aldama's anthology clearly privileges non-film media. Other anthologies with "media" in their title go even further by not including a single essay on film (e.g., *Contemporary Latina/o Media: Production, Circulation, Politics*) or by including only one (*The Routledge Companion to Latina/o Media*).[2]

This does not mean that film studies is fast disappearing into media studies. This year's Conference of the Latin American Studies Association, for example, featured a film festival and over forty panels specifically on film, while the 2018 Conference Program of the Society for Cinema and Media Studies mentions "media-" and "film-" in almost equal measure. And yet, recent books specifically focused on Latinx cinema are few and far between, including *Heroes, Lovers, and Others: The Story of Latinos in Hollywood*, *Latino Images in Film: Stereotypes, Subversion and Resistance*, *The Promotion and Distribution of U.S. Latino Films*, *The Cinema of Robert Rodríguez*, and *Cinema Between Latin America and Los Angeles: Origins to 1960*.[3]

Given these recent trends in the scholarship, it might be that cinema has become to media what poetry has long been to literature: a minority form valued for its artistic pedigree (the film-as-seventh-art argument); for the ease with which it can be incorporated into a variety of courses; and for its historical depth when compared to other media. This essay makes the most of this last point, to evaluate how the Latinx experience of the B/borderlands has been understood and represented audio-visually over the past one hundred years.

## Borderlands

As a physical space, the first Latinx borderlands emerged in the 1830s in Texas, with a series of conflicts that included the Battle of the Alamo (1836) and grew into an all-out war between Mexico and the United States. The war officially ended in 1848 with Mexico's loss of approximately half of its territory, but clashes along the border have persisted into the twenty-first century, "*una herida abierta* where the Third World grates against the first and bleeds."[4] A powerful metaphor, *una herida abierta* also describes subsequent Latinx physical borderlands generated in the wake of US expansionism and imperialism elsewhere, particularly in the Caribbean and in the Philippines since 1898. But borderlands are also psychological. Anzaldúa calls them an uncomfortable place to live in, a landscape whose prominent features are hatred, anger, and exploitation but also as a place of creation, where the switching of codes and their mixture creates "a new language, the language of the Borderlands" (iii–iv). Throughout her book *Borderlands/La Frontera*, Anzaldúa associates lowercase borderlands with destructive confrontations, and uppercase Borderlands with productive transformations.[5] For example, some of the words she uses to describe borderlands with a lowercase *b* include rape, maiming, tension, strangling, gassing, shooting, ambivalence, unrest, and death; copping out, assimilation, and inner struggle; and tragic, lynching, burning, and pillage.[6] For Borderlands with an uppercase *B*, on the other hand, she uses words such as intimacy, mixing, and new; creating, giving birth, transformation, and numinous experience; and confluence, malleability, cross-pollination, and *mestiza*consciousness.[7] The most powerful images of the Borderlands with an uppercase *B* are reserved for the poem titled "To Live in the Borderlands Means You," where the poetic voice concludes that:

> To survive the Borderlands
> you must live *sin fronteras*
> be a crossroads.[8]

Here we have two clearly distinct conceptualizations of the B/borderlands: one, with a lowercase *b*, is a space of exploitation, keeper of the dualistic status quo, a space marked by coercion and sometimes fatal force; the other, with an uppercase *B*, is not its opposite, its "counterstance," but rather "queer," the expression of a new mestiza consciousness:

> The work of mestiza consciousness is to break down the subject-object duality that keeps her a prisoner and to show in the flesh and through the images in her work how duality is transcended.... A massive uprooting of dualistic thinking in the individual and collective consciousness is the beginning of a long struggle, but one that could, in our best hopes, bring us to the end of rape, of violence, of war.[9]

In effect, two conceptions of the B/borderlands anchored to two distinct worldviews: one dualistic, split between two mortal combatants; the other dialogical, a way of life that does not react to dominant culture, but acts from within its own rootedness at the crossroads.

By this double definition, cinematic representations of the Latinx experience of the borderlands with a lowercase b have always dominated the big screen in mainstream narrative films, where Latinx characters are either negative stereotypes or simply absent. But even as early as the silent period there have been attempts to also represent the complex and oftentimes contradictory perspectives of the Latinx experience of the Borderlands with a capital *B*, where the switching of cultural, cinematic, and linguistic codes creates a new language: the language of a Borderlands cinema. These attempts never quite reach Anzaldúa's ideal of living *sin fronteras*, but the attempts do exist and merit a closer look, and indeed a more thorough theorization.

Anzaldúa distinguishes between borderlands and Borderlands but does not elaborate on the power dynamics between them beyond a recognition that to reach the ideal of the Borderlands requires those with more power to cede some of it: "Chicanos no longer feel that we need to beg entrance, that we need always to make the first overture...Today we ask to be met halfway."[10] Fernando Ortiz, the foremost Cuban anthropologist of the twentieth century, developed an analogous theory of culture for a context similarly marked by conflict between two cultures in close proximity, European and African, out of which a new culture emerges. Ortiz called his theory transculturation, and did in fact elaborate on the power dynamics between the cultures involved:

> I am going to take the liberty of employing for the first time the term transculturation, fully aware of the fact that it is a neologism. And I venture to suggest that it might be adopted in sociological terminology, to a great extent at least, as a substitute for the term acculturation, whose use is now spreading...I am of the opinion that the word transculturation better expresses the different phases of the process of transition from one culture to another because this does not consist merely in acquiring another culture, which is what the English word acculturation really implies, but the process also necessarily involves the loss or uprooting of a previous culture, which could be defined as deculturation. In addition, it carries the idea of the consequent creation of new phenomena, which could be called neoculturation. In the end, as the school of Malinowski's followers maintains, the result of every union of cultures is similar to that of the reproductive process between individuals: the offspring always has something of both parents but is always different from each of them.[11]

Some, like Alberto Moreiras, have read transculturation as a adialectical process where neoculturation is the final synthesis of a conflict between acculturation and deculturation. Yet neoculturationbcan be seen bot as the culmination of a real or symbolic conflict between acculturation and deculturation, or between modernization and tradition, but as one position within a transculturation dynamic model where cultures are marked by their position relative to one another and not by any stable essence or identity. This requires a minor adjustment to Ortiz's theory, so that instead of deculturation (Ortiz's term), this article will speak of counter-culturation. Transculturation, in this revised model, is therefore the combined interaction between three clearly identifiable cultural positions: (A) one hegemonic or acculturating (i.e., with the power to assimilate others into its own culture); (B) one counterhegemonic or countercultural (with the will to confront hegemonic culture head on); and (C) one transactional, marked by a willingness, as Anzaldúa puts it, to meet the other halfway (see Figure 20.1).

The arrows in this model represent a multidirectional dynamic that can shift across time and space, instead of a unidirectional mechanism that is applicable across time and space, as Marx's dialectic would have it.

Applied to Anzaldúa's B/borderlands, we would have two opposing borderlands with a lowercase *b* (A and B), and a Borderlands (C) that combines elements of the opposing sides, as in Figure 20.2.

These two models are clearly simplifications of a much more complex cultural dynamic. They are, one might say, two-dimensional renderings of a three-dimensional reality that, when mapped onto cultural groups, fails to account for additional cultures involved in the mix and for important variations within any given culture. Ironically, these very limitations facilitate an analysis of cinema's representations of the Latinxs B/borderlands because films, especially commercial ones, tend to reduce the three-dimensional Latinx reality to two dimensions (via formulas that include stereotypes of different kinds), instead of the complex, contradictory, and nuanced real-life individuals who participate in more than one culture in multiple ways. That said, the model provides sufficient theoretical grounding to facilitate asking ourselves how cinema has represented the transcultural Latinx experience of the B/borderlands, and just as important, how these representations are bound to the material possibilities of production in five distinct periods: silent cinema (1900s–1920s), commercial sound cinema (1930s–1960s), social problem films (1930s–1950s), New Latinx cinema (1970s), mainstream televisual cinema (1980s–1990s), and cinema in the digital age (2000s–present).

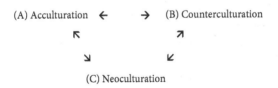

FIGURE 20.1. Ortiz's model of transculturation, with "deculturation" replaced by "counterculturation."

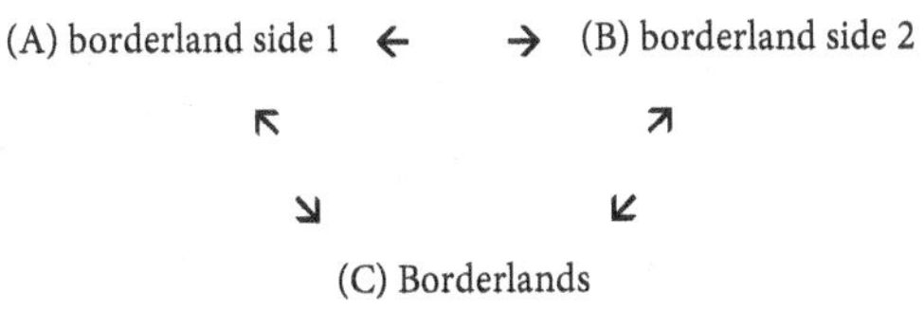

(A) borderland side 1 ← → (B) borderland side 2

(C) Borderlands

FIGURE 20.2. Anzaldúa's B/borderlands model of culture.

## Silent Cinema (1900s–1920s)

The first moving images of the US–Mexico borderlands were recorded fifty years after the creation of the physical borderland, when the first moving picture cameras were brought to the area from New Jersey (Edison's Kinetoscope) and France (the Lumieres' Cinématographe). It is impossible of course to say which films were the first to focus on the Latinx experience of the borderlands, since so many silent films have disappeared or been destroyed. However, we do know that the first Westerns date to the first decade of filmmaking, and that the Hollywood Western quickly crystallized a stereotype of Mexicans as a type of bandit so degraded and vile they were no longer called simply bandits, but "greasers." "The typical 'greaser'," writes Allen Woll,

> was violent and prone to murder... While the normal villain would primarily murder or steal, the Mexican greaser often carried his occupation to excess... Despite [their] innate sense of violence... the greasers had one had one chance to redeem themselves. Namely, they had to forsake their Mexican brethren, and ally themselves with either the Americans, the landowners, or the business executives when they were threatened by a horde of attacking greasers. In this respect, the "good greaser" becomes the equivalent of the "Uncle Tom" figure that has been seen in films about blacks. The loyalty is to the master, the dominant race or nation, and never to fellow blacks or Mexicans.[12]

There are other Latinx stereotypes that first emerged during the silent period (the Caucasian Caballero/Latin Lover, the Dark Lady/Mexican Spitfire, and the Mexican bracero who realizes that life in Mexico will always be better than in the United States), but they pale in comparison to the greaser in importance and longevity, in part thanks to its reemergence as the Latinx urban gangster (oftentimes Puerto Rican) since the 1960s. The persistence of such negative representations can effectively be explained as a strategy on the part of the hegemonic cultural apparatus to acculturate Latinxs by first dehumanizing them, a process whereby Latinx subjects reject their own culture as inferior and accept the only available alternative in sight. In this process, Latinxs need not be greasers, they can be other stereotypes so long as these stereotypes are sufficiently negative that Latinx viewers do not identify with them and instead identify with the mainstream characters and their culture.

An exception in the silent period to this lamentable practice is a compilation film that Félix Padilla, scion of an El Paso-Juárez family of film distributors and exhibitors, constructed using material culled from existing films. *La venganza de Pancho Villa* (1930–1936) was widely exhibited in small towns on both sides of the US–Mexico border to enthusiastic Mexicans and Mexican Americans who would sometimes celebrate the film's reconstruction of Villa's life as a popular Mexican hero with shouts of "¡*Viva Villa! ¡Mueran los gringos!*"[13] The film was recently added to the Library of Congress National Film Archive, and even though it is still under restoration, we can get a good sense of it in Gregorio Rocha's documentary *Los rollos perdidos de Pancho Villa* (2003), where he includes about twenty minutes' worth of the film. As Rocha explains it, Félix Padilla's point of departure was the Hollywood episodic film *Liberty: A Daughter of the U.S.A.* (1916). Padilla did not like how *Liberty* represented Mexicans, so he proceeded to completely turn the original on its head by cutting and splicing it and other films into a new narrative where Mexicans were the heroes and the Anglos were the villains. Liberty, the protagonist played by Marie Wallencamp, became a secondary character. The villainous Pancho López, played by Raymond Nye, became the heroic protagonist Pancho Villa. And to fill in the inevitable gaps in his new story of the last years of Villa's military career, Padilla created new intertitles and incorporated some sequences taken from other films like the biopic *The Life of General Villa* (William C. Cabanné, 1914) and the now lost Mexican documentary *Historia de la Revolución Mexicana* (Julio Lamadrid, 1928). In later versions of *La venganza de Pancho Villa*, Félix Padilla's son Eduardo even incorporated original footage he shot with family members as actors, to represent additional scenes in the life of Pancho Villa (Figure 20.3).

What is most fascinating about *La venganza de Pancho Villa* is how it transforms negative stereotypes of Pancho Villa and of Mexicans as greasers into (oftentimes) positive stereotypes as national heroes. For example, *Liberty* centers around Villa's real-life 1916 attack on Columbus, New Mexico, from the perspective of the Anglos: Villa and the Mexicans are savages while the villagers and the Anglo soldiers camped nearby are martyrs.

**FIGURE 20.3.** Reconstruction of the assassination of Pancho Villa, filmed by the Padillas for *La venganza de Pancho Villa* (*The Vengeance of Pancho Villa*, Félix Padilla and Eduardo Padilla, 1930–1936). Rocha, Gregorio. *Los rollos perdidos de Pancho Villa* https://www.youtube.com/watch?v=YrawE8Xxz74.

In Padilla's recreation, however, the attack on Columbus is a mere antecedent to the film's climax, which now takes place during the subsequent US incursion into Mexican territory to capture Villa. In this new climax, a heroic Pancho Villa becomes the defender of Mexico's sovereignty and territorial integrity, calling on Mexicans to rise up in arms to resist the impending US invasion and then successfully defeating a group of Pershing's soldiers in a historical battle with no military significance. However, in Padilla's hands this becomes countercultural vengeance against Hollywood's belittling of the Mexican male.

Like the physical borderlands where it was edited and exhibited, *La venganza de Pancho Villa* is marked by mixture, transformation, and cross-pollination. And even though it still functions at the level of stereotypes (not surprising given the source material and the film's countercultural spin of that source material), Gregorio Rocha is right to call it "the first border film," a film that "slips across the borders of two countries and two cultures, between the greaser and the gringo, between the politically correct and incorrect, between reality and fiction...an open film."

# Commercial Sound Cinema (1930s–1960s)

The coming of sound in the late 1920s forced Hollywood studios to think seriously about language. Before sound, Hollywood could easily export a film to non-English-speaking countries by creating new intertitles in the target languages. That ended with the arrival of sound, whereupon Hollywood experimented with several options, including subtitling, dubbing, the production of multiple language versions of the same film, and the production of single-version Spanish-language B-films, mostly by small studios that never managed to produce more than a handful of films each. In this brave new world, many Spanish-speaking actors, technicians, assistant directors, and behind-the-scenes professionals saw the coming of sound as an opportunity to apply their skills to the production of Spanish-language films back in their countries of origin. Not all Spanish speakers returned to their countries, of course, and many were Spanish speakers from the United States. But regardless of where they worked—Mexico, Spain, Puerto Rico, Hollywood—Spanish-speaking filmmakers sought to fill the growing demand for Spanish-language films with productions that highlighted local customs and manners through a reduced number of proven genres such as musicals, comedies, and melodrama. This strategy did not favor complex explorations of the B/borderlands, and even on the few occasions when Spanish-language films made in the United States set the action in the physical borderlands of the US Southwest, they reproduced Hollywood and Mexican stereotypes in films like *El hombre malo* (dir. William McGann, 1931; a Western about a Mexican bandit/caballero who helps an Anglo rancher save his ranch), *El milagro de la calle mayor* (dir. Steven Sekely, 1939; a *cabaretera* melodrama set in the Mexican neighborhood of Los Angeles where Margo—that was her stage name—plays a sacrificial wife and mother), and *Cuando canta la ley* (dir. Richard Harlan, 1940; a Western musical starring Tito Guízar as a Mexican secret agent *charro*). Unlike English-language Hollywood films, these Spanish-language Hollywood films did not represent Latinxs negatively, but neither did they go beyond positive stereotypes that narratively functioned to help Anglos or Caucasian Mexicans win the day. In this regard, they also served as vehicles of assimilation into hegemonic culture and its class and racial value system.

The practice of representing the Latinx B/borderlands experience from a decidedly Anglo or Mexican perspective continued well into the end of the studio era. This happened in otherwise exceptional English-language Hollywood films such as *High Noon* (dir. Fred Zinnemann, 1952), where Mexican actress Katy Jurado delivers the performance of a lifetime as Helen Ramírez, the morally upright mistress who sees through the hypocrisy of her Anglo lovers; *Touch of Evil* (dir. Orson Wells, 1958), an ensemble film-noir where the main Mexican character is played by conservative actor Charlton Heston in brownface; and *West Side Story* (dir. Jerome Robbins and Robert Wise, 1961), the cinematic adaptation of the Broadway show about gangs in New York. The film famously earned Puerto Rican actress Rita Moreno an Academy Award for Best Supporting Actress as a Puerto Rican spitfire who sings the praises of consumerist America, opposite Natalie Moore as the puritanical Latina whose innocence wins her the love of the Anglo lead.

In Mexican commercial films of the same period, the Latinx experience of the borderlands barely went beyond narratives of Mexican migrants as tragic figures who can only be redeemed by returning to Mexico (cf. *Pito Pérez se va de bracero*, dir. Alfonso Patiño Gómez, 1947), or the negative representation of Chicanos as working-class *pochos* whose embrace of American cultural practices and values puts them in a limbo between the Anglo culture that still rejects them and the Mexican culture that no longer recognizes them as one of their own (cf. *El pocho*, dir. Eulalio González, 1964).

## SOCIAL PROBLEM FILMS (1930S–1950S)

Even though they are fairly rare, social problem films produced during the sound studio period deserve to be discussed separately because their representation of the Latinx experience of the B/borderlands is more nuanced. At least eight such films were made in the United States on Mexican Americans, including *Bordertown* (dir. Archie Mayo, 1938), *The Lawless* (dir. Joseph Losey, 1954), *A Medal for Benny* (dir. Irving Pichel, 1945), and *Salt of the Earth* (dir. Herbert Biberman, 1954). A handful of such films deal with the juvenile delinquency in the Puerto Rican borderlands of New York City, including *City Across the River* (1949) and *Blackboard Jungle* (1955). And in Mexico, two social problem films that deal with Mexican migrants in the United States stand out: *Espaldas mojadas* (dir. Alejandro Galindo, 1954) and *Los desarraigados* (dir. Gilberto Gazcón, 1958). Of these, the most notable are *Bordertown*, *Espaldas mojadas*, and *Salt of the Earth*.

Charles Ramírez Berg calls *Bordertown* "the first Hollywood sound film to deal with a Mexican American's attempt to enter the mainstream and participate in the American Dream."[14] The film tells the story of Johnny Ramírez (Paul Muni), a poor Mexican

American fresh out of night law school who in his first court case loses his temper and is disbarred from the profession. He finds work in a rundown border town casino, turns it around with the help of the casino owner's wife (Bette Davis), and having made it financially, proposes to a socialite who rejects his marriage proposal. "Marriage isn't for us," she tells him. "You belong to a different tribe, Savage." Just then she dies in an accident, Johnny sells the casino, and returns to the barrio, "back where I belong… with my own people." This synopsis makes clear that the film is a Hollywood melodrama, as does its high production values, its use of stars, a tight script filled with reversals of fortune, and a narrative arc driven by the characters' emotions. But Ramírez Berg is correct to also read it as a "paradigmatic example of the entire class of Chicano social problem films" where Chicanos' desire to enter the mainstream is represented as a threat, even if that margin is embodied as an intelligent, resourceful, and ambitious Mexican American like Johnny who does not question the values and structures of the dominant culture. Johnny's return to the barrio therefore signals that "the best course of action is for ethnic/immigrant/class/gender Others to go home to their old ethnic neighborhood, the locus of all that is good and true. Abandoning their aspirations of mainstream integration and success, these characters can remain content in the knowledge that they have gained morality, a prize far greater than fame or fortune."[15]

*Espaldas mojadas* gives both Mexican and Mexican American viewers a similar warning, only this time the barrio to return to is Mexico. Filmed in the tradition of Italian Neorealism, the film's plot revolves around Rafael Améndola (David Silva), a Mexican rural worker forced to flee the country after confronting the local landowner. In the United States he goes from job to job without any real chance of social mobility because his undocumented status is exploited by both Anglos and Chicanos. The only good thing that happens to Rafael is that he falls in love with María del Consuelo (Martha Valdés), a Chicana who explains to him that "I am not Mexican, I am a *pocha*. We're worse off than Blacks. They stay united and do not feel the pull of another country. But we're not loved by Mexicans and the Anglos look down on us." Director Alejandro Galindo wrote that he made *Espaldas mojadas* in order to "convince Mexicans not to go to the United States," and this warning seems to extend to Mexican Americans in reverse, for at the end of the film it is clear that Rafael and María "redeem one another by crossing to Mexico."[16] Yet from a B/borderlands perspective, *Espaldas mojadas* still stands out because it sympathetically represents the complicated Chicanx sociocultural position vis-à-vis Anglos, Mexicans, and blacks. In so doing, it complicates accepted cultural binarisms even as it fails to represent any relationships between Chicanxs and blacks, and even as it proposes that the only way forward for Chicanxs is to "become Mexican," as Rafael tells María.

*Salt of the Earth* radically breaks with these and other ideological limitations of the Latinx social problem film of the period through a combination of forms that look back to Italian Neorealism's focus on the everyday life of workers, and back as well to Eisenstein's use of types and montage within the frame. The film also "prefigures the genre of docudrama that was still twenty years into the future," in no small measure by going beyond Neorealism's focus on male-centered narratives (the film centers on the struggles of working Latina women); and by going beyond Eisenstein's reductive use of types, with two leads who suffer exploitation by the town's sole employer as workers, yes, but also as ethnic subjects who must also confront conflict within their union and within their very own household.[17] The likely reason for the film's many breakthroughs is its unlikely production, having been commissioned by the International Union of Mine Mill and Smelter Workers; and written, produced, and edited by members of the Hollywood Group of Ten, so-called because they had been blacklisted by the House Un-American Activities Committee at the height of McCarthyism.

The film begins with the protagonist Esperanza Quintero (Rosaura Revueltas) cutting wood and building a fire to heat water for household chores, and a superimposed title:

> Our scene is NEW MEXICO
> Land of the free Americans
> who inspired this film
> Home of the brave Americans
> who played most of its roles.

Shortly thereafter we hear Esperanza in voiceover: "How shall I begin my story that has no beginning?... Our roots go deep in this place... deeper than the mine shafts" to a time when the town was called "San Marcos... not Zinc Town, U [pause] S [pause] A." In less than five minutes, *Salt of the Earth* has already broken ground on several fronts: it represents a mestiza by the name of Esperanza (the name means "hope" in Spanish) as a physically strong lead narrator who is as freedom loving and as brave as any other person, and whose family history stretches back to a time before the Anglos, back even to a time before the Europeans, when New Mexico was peopled by indigenous groups like the Hopi, the Pueblo, and the Navajo.

The rest of the film centers on a strike by Mexican American miners for equality with their Anglo peers in a nearby mine, the discussions on whether or not to let their wives take over the picket line after an injunction prohibits miners from striking, and how the women successfully take over the picket line. As the women's leadership roles grow, tensions rise within the union and at home, and when Esperanza's husband, Ramón, (Juan Chacón) has all but given up hope, she links the aspirations of the strikers to her own aspirations as a woman:

> Why are you afraid to have me at your side? Do you think you can have dignity only if I have none?... The Anglo bosses look down on you, and you hate them for it. "Stay in your place, you dirty Mexican" .... But why when you say to me "Stay in your place," do you feel better having someone lower than you?... I don't want anything lower than I am. I am low enough already. I want to rise and to push everything up with me. And if you don't understand this you are a fool. Because you can't win this strike without me. You can't do anything without me!

Initially, Ramón interprets Esperanza's words as an affront to his masculinity, and almost strikes her (Figure 20.4).

FIGURE 20.4. Ramón (Juan Chacón), the oppressed mineworker, in turn oppresses his wife Esperanza (Rosaura Revueltas) in *Salt of the Earth* (Herbert Biberman, 1954). *Salt of the Earth*. 1999. DVD. Directed by Herbert Biberman. [United States]: Pioneer Entertainment.

The next day, however, his recollection of Esperanza's powerful words leads to a turning point in the narrative, the mining company signals they will settle, and Ramón tells all those gathered, "Thanks, sisters, and brothers... Esperanza, for your dignity. You were right. Together, we can push everything up with us as we go." Tellingly, the script saves the last words for Esperanza in a voiceover, shot in close-up from below: "Then I knew we had won something they could never take away. Something I could leave to my children, and they, the Salt of the Earth, would inherit." This simple and compelling idea of radical equality proved too dangerous for the US government, which banned the film and effectively disinherited a whole generation of working-class Latinxs of the first film to portray them as complex human beings with a deep-rooted past, a dignified present, and a future of hope.

## New Latinx Cinema (1970s)

The civil rights movement of the 1960s and 1970s transformed Latinx cinema. The Chicano Movement, the farmworkers' struggle, the Young Lords in Chicago and New York, feminism's second wave, the gay rights movement, and the anti–Vietnam War protests—all of these profoundly marked a group of filmmakers who began their careers during this period: Luis Valdez (b. 1940), Sylvia Morales (b. 1943), Jesús Rodríguez-Soltero

(b. 1943), Lourdes Portillo (b. 1944), Efraín Gutiérrez (b. 1946), Jesús Salvador Treviño (b. 1946), and Henry Gamboa Jr. (b. 1951), among others. Like their counterparts of the New Latin America cinema, this generation of Latinx filmmakers was galvanized by the Cuban Revolution's early promise for radical, progressive change, and felt inspired by Cuban filmmakers' effective use of low-cost documentaries to raise political awareness and mobilize people against their oppressors. Given the revolutionary discourse and Latin Americanist outlook of this generation, it is best to approach their collective work transnationally, as one of the "national" cinemas that make up the New Latin American Cinema NLAC: the New Latinx cinema.

According to David Maciel, the most recurrent themes in Chicanx documentaries of the 1960s and 1970s include "the representation of the Chicano Movement and its historical roots, the cultural traditions of the community, criticism of the stereotypes that contribute to Chicano discrimination and oppression, and the condition of the Chicana."[18] These themes are in full display in three relatively well-known documentaries: *Yo soy Joaquín* (dir. Luis Valdez, 1969), *Yo soy chicano* (dir. Bill Nye, 1972), and *Chicana* (Sylvia Morales, 1979). *Yo soy Joaquín* is an adaptation of Rodolfo "Corky" Gonzales's 1967 work of the same title, a landmark epic poem that traces the history of Chicanos from their origins in the indigenous cultures of Meso-America, through the conquest and colonization under Spanish rule, Mexican independence, the Mexican Revolution, the Mexican American War, and into the present situation of oppression under Anglo capitalism. The film begins poetically, with images of indigenous artwork and a melodious soundtrack of indigenous wind instruments; then the tempo slowly increases until it culminates with a montage that reveals the pull Cuban documentarist filmmakers, especially Santiago Álvarez's agit-prop use of found photographs and footage, had on Latinx filmmakers of this period. Significantly, by the end of the film a Spanish guitar plays along with the indigenous flute, underscoring the poem's thesis that Chicanx culture is a mixture of indigenous and Spanish elements that stands steadfastly and enduringly against "that monstrous, technical / industrial giant called Progress and Anglo success." *Yo soy chicano* continues where *Yo soy Joaquín* left off by focusing on the activists who are fighting that struggle against Anglo capitalism in the present: Dolores Huerta and the California-based Farmworkers' Union, Rodolfo "Corky" Gonzalez and his civil rights organization Crusade for Justice in Colorado, José Ángel Gutiérrez and his Texas-based Raza Unida Party, Reies López Tijerina and his struggle to reclaim New Mexico lands owed to Mexican descendants under the Treaty of Guadalupe, and Salomán Baldenegro, one of the founders of the Mexican American Studies Program at the University of Arizona. Finally, *Chicana* uses aesthetics and narrative strategies similar to those found in *Yo soy Joaquín* to provide a much-needed feminist retort to the androcentrism found in *Yo soy Joaquín*, by highlighting the central role that all women have played in Chicanx history, whether they are anonymous (Figure 20.5), little-known (like soldadera-turned-general Carmen Robles and the grassroots organizer Francisca Robles), or famous (like Sor Juana Inés de la Cruz and Dolores Huerta).

The first feature-length feature Chicano film is *Please, Don't Bury Me Alive!* (dir. Efraín Gutiérrez, 1975), a low-budget independent film that "broke the Mexican film industry's

FIGURE 20.5. An anonymous farmworker in *Chicana* (Sylvia Morales, 1979). *Chicana*. 1989. VHS. Directed by Sylvia Morales. New York, NY: Women Make Movies.

monopoly on the Spanish-language theater circuit in the United States ... [and] inspired a Mexican independent movement in the late 1970s."[19] The film tells the story of Alejandro Hernández (Efraín Gutiérrez), a young Chicano from San Antonio, Texas, who lost his brother to the Vietnam War.

Alejandro tries to do the right thing by his family and his community but also engages in petty crimes, and one day he is framed for drug possession. In court, the same white judge who sentences him to ten years in prison paroles an Anglo for essentially the same crime; hence, the film's title. *Don't Bury Me Alive!* is a perfect example of what Cuban filmmaker and theorist Julio García Espinosa called imperfect cinema:

> Imperfect cinema finds a new audience in those who struggle, and it finds its themes in their problems ... Imperfect cinema is no longer interested in quality or technique. It can be created equally well with a Mitchell or with an 8mm camera, in a studio or in a guerrilla camp in the middle of the jungle. Imperfect cinema is no longer interested in predetermined taste, and much less in "good taste." ... The future lies with folk art. But let us no longer display folk art with demagogic pride, with a celebrative air. Let us exhibit it instead as a cruel denunciation, as a painful testimony to the level at which the peoples of the world have been forced to limit their artistic creativity.[20]

*Don't Bury me Alive!* does all of this and more. It created a new audience of Chicanx moviegoers in the US–Mexico borderlands; it found its themes in its audiences' real-life problems with a discriminatory criminal justice system, and it is visibly not interested in achieving the high production values of Hollywood or auteur cinema. Just as important, it claimed the Borderlands with a capital *B* as a worthy objective for Chicanxs, in a soliloquy by Alejando that "signals the *cinematic* and *rhetorical* climax of the film, and to that extent... becomes something of a manifesto for the director":

> I am old enough now to know that what I really want is some way of bringing together both my worlds. There's a lot to be said for living in a nice track house, or for pulling out of the barrio and heading for the suburb. The thing is, I do not want that. That may be hard for some of you to believe, but I really like being Chicano. But it's only been in the last few years that so many of us have had the guts to own up to the fact that we are Chicanos, and we're going to stay that way. Now, how the hell am I going to be Chicano and compete in an Anglo world with you pushy people. Well, that's part of a problem. That's part of a big problem. Who the hell said we had to be the same? That is ridiculous. There must be room in this country for me to be Chicano in dignity. Americano in my own way.[21]

Clearly countercultural, the manifesto also has an aesthetic dimension, in effect saying, "Who the hell said Chicanx cinema had to aspire to look like Hollywood or auteur cinema?" Henry Gamboa Jr.'s experimental video art of the 1980s and 1990s continues in this low-budget and highly critical tradition, and while video art is outside the scope of this essay, no history of Latinx cinema writ large would be complete without his videos, a selection of which the UCLA Chicano Studies Research Center published in DVD format in 2004.

In the other major Latinx borderland at the time, New York City, two independently produced features stand out. *Short Eyes* (dir. Robert M. Young, 1977) is a drama based on Nuyorican Miguel Piñero's play of the same name, and set, quite tellingly, in a prison where inmates segregate themselves according to their "race": blacks, whites, and the Puerto Ricans who navigate between the two groups. *El Súper* (dir. León Ichaso, 1979), on the other hand, tells the story of a working-class Cuban family divided between the parents who dream of one day returning to Cuba "after Fidel," and the daughter who feels right at home in the city. But by far the most interesting films of the Latinx B/borderlands in New York during this period are the experimental shorts by José Rodríguez Soltero, in particular *Lupe* (1966). A tribute to Hollywood star Lupe Vélez (a.k.a. the Mexican Spitfire), *Lupe* reimagines Vélez's last attempts at finding love, her suicide, and a triumphant resurrection that evokes Baroque paintings of the Virgin Mary's ascension to heaven (Figure 20.7).

*Lupe* is clearly rooted in New York City's underground cinema movement of the 1960s: it is visually striking, with bold, saturated colors; while narratively, it is every bit as transgressive as comparable films by Andy Warhol and Jack Smith, the two artists most often associated with this movement. But its soundtrack, filled with songs by the likes of Mexican Javier Solís and the Afro-American group Martha and the Vandellas, in addition to the superb acting by drag queen Mario Montez (an artistic name that pays tribute to Dominican-born María Montez, a.k.a. the Queen of Technicolor), anchors *Lupe* to an Afro-Latinx, popular, and eminently queer Borderlands culture that oscillated between shame and pleasure, irony and belief.[22] It is a culture that Brazilian artist Hélio Oiticica, in a tribute to Mario Montez, fittingly called "Tropicamp."

FIGURE 20.6. Alejandro (Efraín Gutiérrez, left) attends his brother's funeral in *Please, Don't Bury Me Alive!* (Efraín Gutiérrez, 1975). *Please, Don't Bury Me Alive!* 2007. DVD. Directed by Efraín Gutiérrez. Los Angeles: UCLA Chicano Studies Research Center.

FIGURE 20.7. Lupe (Mario Montez) dances carefree after death in *Lupe* (José Rodríguez Soltero, 1966). *Lupe*. 2016. DVD. Directed by José Rodríguez Soltero. New York, NY: Filmmakers' Co-op.

## Mainstream Televisual Cinema (1980s–1990s)

The 1980s witnessed a marked shift away from the experimentalism and militancy of the New Latinx Cinema, to films that consciously seek to engage a wider audience by mixing mainstream entertainment formulas and politics. The foundations of this shift were laid during the 1970s, by media advocacy organizations such as Carisma, Chicano Cinema Colalition, Justicia, National Latino Media Coalition, NOSOTROS, and Jamás, which often included Latinxs of different ethnic backgrounds.[23] Thanks to their pioneering work, a number of public television stations began to produce Latinx-themed programs such as *Canción de la Raza*, *Acción chicano* [sic], *Bienvenidos*, and *Realidades*. These programs nurtured a whole generation of Latinx media technicians, producers, and managers, and they also attracted filmmakers who found in these television stations a new and more reliable source of funding for their films. This, if only partly, explains why Latinx cinema shifted away from the countercultural militancy and aesthetics of the 1960s and 1970s (preponderance of long shots and omniscient voiceover to represent historically grounded collective characters who are socially motivated) to a more televisual aesthetics (preponderance of medium and close shots and dialogue to represent individualized characters who are psychologically motivated). In other words, the shift in focus from collective struggle to individualized struggles aligned better with the liberal-pluralist values that guided (and still guides) public television. In this view, the United States is made up of distinct cultural groups whose place in the national mosaic/quilt/melting pot (choose your metaphor) is fixed. The underlying idea is that groups are analogous to individuals, and just as individuals are inevitably separated from one another by their impermeable skins, so are cultural groups within the nation separated by impermeable physical and cultural borders

For example, *Raíces de sangre* (dir. Jesús Salvador Treviño, 1977) is an homage to *Salt of the Earth*, and the first Chicano film to be financed by the Echeverría government in Mexico as part of a new policy (aligned with US liberal pluralism) that sought to include Chicanos in a national imaginary composed of more or less socially stable individuals and groups. *¡Alambrista!* (dir. Robert M. Young, 1977) is an award-winning drama financed by public television station KCET in Los Angeles. It holds the honor of being the first feature film to center on the struggles of Mexican undocumented workers, including their unfair working conditions and the heavy handedness of the Immigration and Naturalization Service, all from the perspective of likeable characters whose efforts to fight injustice hardly go beyond the level of the individual action. *The Ballad of Gregorio Cortez* (dir. Robert M. Young, 1981), based on Américo Paredes's *With a Pistol in His Hand: A Border Ballad and Its Hero*, was partially financed by PBS and by the National Council of La Raza, and uses the Western as a vehicle to celebrate the life of the title's namesake as an exceptional Mexican American hero. *Seguín* (dir. Jesús Salvador Treviño, 1982) is a historical drama set during the years of the Texas Republic in the

1830s. It was produced by KCET and explores the origins of Mexican Americans' subaltern condition through (improbably) the eyes of a landowning Mexican individual who sides with the Anglos and later regrets it. And *El norte* (dir. Gregory Nava, 1983), the best-known film of this group, was also funded by PBS and uses reversals of fortune and character types worthy of a telenovela to tell the story of Central American migrants to the United States who must break with their indigenous past in order to become culturally and economically integrated.

Ironically, given the preponderance of publicly funded Latinx films in the early 1980s, the quintessential Latinx film of this period was not produced by public television but by a major Hollywood studio. *Zoot Suit* (dir. Luis Valdez, 1982) adapts a Broadway musical that Valdez wrote and directed in 1979, itself an adaptation of a play he had written and directed to great acclaim in 1978 in Los Angeles. In fact, filming was done entirely indoors in the same Los Angeles theater where the play had been staged in 1978, keeping the essential elements of the original play (the use of character types and of Chicanx folklore, language, and dress), as well as certain elements of the Broadway musical (choreographed musical numbers and high production values), but adding film-specific elements such as a streamlined narrative arc, the strategic use of close-ups, and *chiaroscuro* lighting. The film tells the story of the Zoot Suit riots of 1943 from the perspective of Hank Reyna (Daniel Valdez), a fictional character based on Hank Leyvas, one of hundreds of Chicano gang members who were falsely accused for the riots and sent to prison. But the film's most memorable character is El Pachuco (Edward James Olmos), a doppelgänger that allows Valdez to explore Hank's many psychological conflicts in terms that are specific to the Chicano culture. Thus, the Pachuco neither looks nor acts like a Mexican spirit nor an Anglo ghost but is instead a corporealized, sleek alter ego who continually challenges Hank using the kind of Spanglish, distinctive body language, and visual symbols that characterize the pachuco culture in the Los Angeles Borderlands, not least its stylized constructions of gender (Figure 20.8).

In an assessment of this aspect of the film, Fregoso concludes that "[t]he cultural-nationalist strategy re-articulated in *Zoot Suit*... interpellates all subjects, Chicanas and Chicanos, into... inhabiting the brotherhood of Chicanismo," a brotherhood that privileges a masculine essence "buried deep within the inner psyche, or, more significantly, in the mythic Aztlán."[24] Alternatively, one could do a psychological reading of the Pachuco character as Hank's anima, the feminine that lives in all male subjects, if we consider that the first time that the Pachuco appears in a play by Valdez, he did so as the moon, with a sequined suit and "very light surrealistic make-up."[25] The feminine-lunar origins of this Pachuco are not lost in the film, for the costume design makes it easy to imagine a queer production of the play with a transvestite in the Pachuco role. Regardless, the film's undeniably high artistic value and the fact that it can generate multiple and even contradictory interpretations helps to explain why the film has stood the test of time so well.

Toward the end of the decade, the balance between politics and entertainment tipped in favor of entertainment thanks to the unprecedented commercial success of *La Bamba* (dir. Luis Valdez, 1987), a musical biopic of Chicano rock and roll star Ricardo Valenzuela

FIGURE 20.8. El Pachuco (Edward James Olmos) heals Hank (Daniel Valdez) in *Zoot Suit* (Luis Valdez, 1982). *Zoot Suit*. 2003. DVD. Directed by Luis Valdez. Universal City, CA: Universal Studios.

(a.k.a. Ritchie Valens) that offered audiences an assimilationist narrative whereby "the more one is culturally assimilated, the greater the possibility of social mobility, as in the case of Ritchie."[26] The film achieves this not only through Ritchie's adoption of rock and roll and his desire for a white girlfriend but also through the characterization of his non-assimilated brother Bob (Esai Morales) as an abusive and drug-dealing gang member. Predictably, the facile binarism turns Ritchie's narrative death into a cathartic moment that reaffirms the dominant culture's negative perceptions of non-assimilated Chicanxs such as Bob. Other prominent films that directly or indirectly represent this assimilationist ideology via the uncritical use of mainstream genres include *My Family* (dir. Gregory Nava, 1995) and *Selena* (dir. Gregory Nava, 1997). *My Family*, for example, is so bound to the formulas of melodrama that even the mass deportation of Mexicans in the 1930s is represented as a minor reversal of fortune for the Sánchez family in an overall narrative arc that so closely follows the dominant narrative arc of European migrants to the United States that someone as perceptive as Roger Ebert could call the film "the great American story, told again and again, of how our families came to this land and tried to make it better for their children," even though no other migrant group in the history of the United States has suffered mass deportations. *Selena*, for its part, shares with *La Bamba* being a musical biopic of a crossover Chicanx pop sensation, but unlike *La Bamba*, it does not even attempt to explore the complex negotiations of a minority subject gone mainstream, opting instead to show a Selena, in Nava's own words, "as American as Apple pie."

Gloria Anzaldúa published *Borderlands* in 1987, a time of intense debates about the kind of mainstreaming of Latinx culture that these films encode. "We Chicanos," writes Anzaldúa, "no longer feel that we need to beg entrance, that we need always to make the first overture—to translate to Anglos, Mexicans and Latinos [i.e., Latin Americans], apology blurting out of our mouths with every step. Today we ask to be met halfway."[27] By uncritically adopting mainstream forms such as the family saga and the musical biopic and translating into mainstream codes everything that is specific to Latinx culture, these films in effect make the first overture and put the needs of non-Latinx audiences first. *Born in East L.A.* (dir. Cheech Marin, 1987), by contrast, asks non-Latinx audiences to meet its protagonist halfway by not translating its many references to Tin-Tan, the great Mexican film comedian; by focusing its narrative on the deportation of its protagonist Rudy (Cheech Marin); and by redefining what it is to be an American from a decidedly Chicanx perspective, as when Rudy, asked by a coyote to teach a group of Asians how to behave and speak like Americans, proceeds to show them how to walk, dress, and speak like a Chicano from East Los Angeles. Most important, Rudy casts his lot with poor migrants from different nationalities and ethnicities, at one point giving up his seat so that another migrant may enter the United States; and afterward, he leads hundreds of migrants across the border in a heroic march that symbolically replaces the mainstream representation of American identity as highly individualized and European, with a collective representation that is transnational, multiethnic, and popular. Consequently, even though *Born in East L.A.* is a Hollywood production, its worldview is closer to that of contemporaneous independent productions like *La ofrenda* (dir. Lourdes Portillo, 1988), a documentary about the Day of the Dead that beautifully explores the Latinx experience of living in the crossroads of the Borderlands between life and death, past and present, Mexico and the United States; *El Jardín del Edén* (dir. María Novaro, 1995), a Mexican drama set in Tijuana that explores the difficult cross-cultural interactions between characters from both sides of the border; and *Lone Star* (dir. John Sayles, 1996), a mystery Western and the decade's most sophisticated treatment of the B/borderlands.

*Lone Star* tells the story of the aptly named Frontera, a small border town in Texas with a hidden past. An ensemble film, it includes characters as diverse as Chris Wade (Kris Kristofferson), a bigoted, corrupt, and universally despised sheriff who takes a monthly cut out of every business transaction in town; Hollis Pogue (Clifton James), the deputy sheriff and later Major of Frontera who killed Wade in order to stop him from murdering a young black Seminole who did not want to let Wade in on a cut of a side business (Otis Payne, played by Gabriel Casseus when young and by Ron Canada as an older man); Buddy Deeds (Matthew McConaughey), the assistant sheriff who witnesses Wade's death and decides to cover it up, becomes a legendary sheriff, and uses the office in more accommodating ways; his son Sam Deeds (Chris Cooper), brought back to town to become sheriff because of his last name; Pilar Cruz (Elizabeth Peña), Sam's first love and currently a high school history teacher; and Mercedes Cruz (Miriam Colón), Pilar's mother and onetime lover of Buddy Deeds (Figure 20.9).

The story unfolds in the late 1990s, with extensive use of flashbacks to fill in information about the past, including how Wade was killed not by Buddy Deeds, as people thought, but by Pogue; the fact that Buddy Deeds is Pilar's father (and therefore Pilar and Sam are siblings in an incestuous relationship); and how Mercedes, who continually berates the migrant Mexican workers in her restaurant for not being sufficiently American, had herself crossed into the United States as an undocumented migrant.

FIGURE 20.9. High school sweethearts Sam Deeds (Chris Cooper) and Pilar Cruz (Elizabeth Peña) meet once again as adults at the border river, in *Lone Star* (John Sayles, 1996). *Lone Star*. 1999. DVD. Directed by John Seyles. [California]: Warner Home Video.

Just as important, the collective history of Frontera and of Texas is also explored, during a heated PTA meeting where Anglos make it clear they do not agree with how Pilar is teaching local history:

ANGLO MAN: The men who founded this state have the right to have their story told.
HISPANIC MAN: The men who founded this state broke from Mexico because they needed slavery to be legal to make a fortune in the cotton business.
PILAR CRUZ: I think that's a bit of an oversimplification....
ANGLO MAN: You call it history, I call it propaganda. I'm sure they've got their own account of the Alamo on the other side, but we're not on the other side and our schools shouldn't teach it that way.
PILAR CRUZ: Excuse me. I've only been trying to get across part of the complexity of our situation here. Cultures coming together in both negative and positive ways.

Indeed, the film as a whole is an extended exploration of the complexity of the B/borderlands. As Otis Delmore tells his estranged son Delmore Payne (Joe Morton), newly arrived in Frontera as the Coronel charged with closing the military base there, "It's not like there's a borderline between the good people and the bad people. You're not on either one side or the other." This idea applies to practically all of the relationships in town, quite visibly in father–son relationships (Buddy and Sam, Otis and Delmore, Delmore and his son Chat) but also in the mother–daughter relationship between Mercedes and Pilar, the sibling rivalry between Pilar's upright daughter and wayward son, the people on both sides of the US–Mexico border; and most dramatically, in the incestuous relationship between Sam and Pilar, who only find out about their blood ties at the very end of the film, at which point Pilar asks, "We start from scratch?"

SAM: Yeah.
PILAR: Everything that went before, all that stuff, that history—the hell with it, right?... Forget the Alamo.

Because we as viewers learn this information at the same time the characters do, and because the film ends at this point, we are left to make sense of this unexpected and morally fraught crossing of boundaries. Are we to read the crossing literally, as a taboo that cannot be justified, or as a metaphor of cultural transgression? In the first reading, Sam and Pilar may want to forget the Alamo but would nevertheless have to face the town's rejection, not to mention the reality that incest is a third-degree felony in Texas.[28] This reading, while accurate, is limited and limiting, especially when compared to a much richer metaphorical reading that allows us to view the incest as one of many equally complex border crossings throughout the film: between legality and legitimacy, past and present, Anglo and Hispanic, Mexican and Mexican American, black and Indigenous, Anglo and black. In fact, the overabundance of such crossings suggests that *Lone Star* is as much a mystery about origins as it is murder mystery, for in the end, the fact that Pilar and Sam are siblings provides an alternative conceptualization of the B/borderlands where all of the seemingly separate communities and histories of the B/borderlands are really the closest of kin, and not the more or less isolated groups that liberal pluralism sees as occupying fixed geographical and cultural spaces. From this perspective, Sam and Pilar are, like the black Seminoles, the embodiment of a Borderlands identity and culture, no longer Mexican or Anglo or black or Indigenous but rather Mexican *and* Anglo *and* black *and* Indigenous; and Pilar's entreaty to forget the Alamo is not an invitation to forget history tout court but to forget that version of history that sees the different communities in the Borderlands as adversaries irreparably bound to loathe and hurt one another.

# Cinema in the Digital Age (2000s–Present)

The rise to prominence of private television since the early 1990s, along with the emergence of digital technology in late 1990s and its democratization since the mid-2000s, has accelerated the process of audiovisual diversification so much that the audiovisual sphere today can no longer be said to privilege feature-length narrative films and documentaries. This, along with the fact that we are currently in the middle of a new period in the history of Latinx cinema, makes it difficult to say which trends will emerge as the important ones in the long term. Nevertheless, we can say with certainty that contemporary Latinx cinema is enjoying steady growth in terms of production and that this growth has been accompanied by a growing diversification in content matter and in forms, even as most films continue to rely on character types, if not outright stereotypes. Some of the films that do not fall into these narrative traps include *Bread and Roses* (dir. Ken Loach, 2000); *Girlfight* (dir. Karyn Kusama, 2000), *Señorita Extraviada* (dir. Lourdes Portillo, 2001), *Real Women Have Curves* (dir. Patricia Cardoso, 2002), *Walkout* (dir. Edward James Olmos, 2006), *Quinceañera* (dir. Richard Glatzer and Wash

Westmoreland, 2006), *María Full of Grace* (dir. Joshua Marston, 2006), *Sin Nombre* (dir. Cary Fukunaga, 2009), and *Sleep Dealer* (dir. Alex Rivera, 2009), by far the most innovative film of the group.

One of only a few science fiction Latinx films, *Sleep Dealer* is set in a dystopic future where the manual labor in the United States is performed by robots controlled remotely from maquiladoras in Tijuana, and presumably elsewhere in the Third World. Rivera first presented this concept in *Animaquiladora/Why Cybraceros?* (1997), a five-minute promotional that spoofs one produced by the California Grower's Council in the 1940s. Rivera's mock promotional features a guardedly excited female voice that explains:

> Picking, pruning, cutting, and handling farm produce are all simple but delicate tasks, work that requires such attention to detail that it remains a challenge for farm technologists, and as of yet, cannot be automated. As the American workforce grows increasingly sophisticated, it is harder to find the hand labor to do these grueling tasks, which is why the United States Department of Labor is excited to announce a new program to get the job done. It's known as the Cybracero Program... [T]he presence of braceros [in the mid-twentieth century] contributed to a climate of racial and economic suspicion. Evidence of major tension was not hard to find. But soon, such concerns will no longer be an issue. Under the Cybracero Program, American farm labor will be accomplished on American soil but no Mexican workers will need to leave Mexico. Only the labor of Mexicans will cross the border... Sound impossible? Using high speed internet connections directly to Mexico, American farms and Mexican laborers will be directly connected. These workers will then be able to remotely control robotic farmworkers, known as cybraceros from their village in Mexico... Using a series of simple commands, a Mexican worker can, from Mexico, watch their internet feed, decide which fruit is ripe, which branch needs pruning, and which bush needs watering. To the worker it's as simple as point and click. For the American farmer, it's all the labor without the worker. In Spanish, cybracero means a worker who operates a computer with his arms and hands. But in American lingo, cybracero means a worker who poses no threat of becoming an American citizen. And that means quality products at low financial *and* social cost to you, the American consumer.

*Sleep Dealer* takes this premise to its logical conclusion by having cybraceros work not just in the fields but also in construction, transportation, and even babysitting, using more advanced technology that connects robots directly to workers' nervous system via nodes implanted on their arms, shoulders, and backs (Figure 20.10). On the US side, the same technology is used by the military to control drones that strike against "aqua-terrorists" who try to destroy the dams that multinational companies own throughout the world.

The film's narrative follows Memo (Luis Fernando Peña), a young man from Oaxaca who dreams of leaving the farming life behind, including the daily trips he and his father must make to the nearby dam in order to get just enough water for their milpa, at ever-increasing prices. During his free time, Memo plays around with computers. When he is

FIGURE 20.10. Memo (Luis Fernando Peña, right) working as a cybracero in *Sleep Dealer* (Alex Rivera, 2009). *Sleep Dealer*. 2009. DVD. Directed by Alex Rivera. Los Angeles: Maya Entertainment.

able to connect to the outside world, he intercepts and interrupts communication between drones that are about to kill some "aqua-terrorists" in the nearby dam. After the drone company identifies Memo's house as the source of the interruption, it announces its destruction on *Drones*, a reality show that allows viewers to see what drone pilots see during their missions. The strike is handled by Rudy Ramírez (Jacob Vargas), a newly graduated Mexican American cyber-soldier who always wanted to be a soldier like his father, but who begins to have doubts about it after killing Memo's father. These two seemingly opposing characters end up joining forces to destroy the dam but only after Memo leaves Oaxaca to find a job as a cybracero in Tijuana and falls in love with Luz Martínez (Leonor Valera), an aspiring writer who unwittingly helps bring the two men together. After the strike, Rudy cannot return to the United States and decides to go south, while Memo decides he will stay in Tijuana, where

> maybe there's a future for me... on the edge [orilla] of everything. A future with a past [cut to Memo watering his personal milpa]. If I connect [cut to him and Luz walking together]. And fight [cut to a long shot of the border fence with drones flying overhead].

This powerful conclusion defines the Borderlands as a liminal space with the potential to transform social relations that are currently mediated by both capital and technology into social relations of the kind that Memo learned growing up in Oaxaca: these are relations based on love and respect for one another and for the earth that sustains us. It is a Borderlands currently torn by real physical borders that viewers, pace Memo, can nevertheless destroy, using the very tools that uphold them, as the last shot suggests.

## Conclusion

For over a century now, cinema has mediated the complex process of Latinx transculturation in the US B/borderlands, oftentimes privileging representations of acculturation, and less often, representations of counterculturation and neoculturation. For the first half of the twentieth century, representations of acculturation prevailed, as mainstream cinema, both in the silent era and during the sound studio era, positioned Latinx viewers to identify with positive stereotypes of Anglo heroes and heroines and not with their own culture. This was a culture often represented by greasers and buffoons in the case of men, and by servants and spitfires in the case of women. The silent found-footage film *The Vengeance of Pancho Villa* consciously inverts this practice by positioning viewers to identify with a positive stereotype of Pancho Villa and against negative stereotypes of Anglo characters—most of the time. Indeed, the partly negative, partly positive representation of both Pancho Villa and Anglo characters saves the film from becoming a simplistic exercise of stereotype inversion.

During the sound studio era, a number of social problem films sought to explore the Latinx experience of the B/borderlands from within. The most important of these was *Salt of the Earth*, not only because of its many artistic merits but also because Mexican American men and women played complex protagonist roles as individuals and as a collective force to be reckoned with. Ten years later, a New Latinx Cinema continued where *Salt of the Earth* left off by shifting the accent from a class-based politics to an ethnic Latinx politics that is informed by a shared historical past rooted in Indo-Latin America (as evidenced in *Yo soy Joaquín* and *Chicana*) and that guides political action in the present, as *Yo soy chicano* makes clear. *Please Don't Bury Me Alive!* and *Lupe*, for their part, expanded the range of Latinx cinema by exploring the contradictory desires that Latinxs in the margins of mainstream Latinx culture face in their daily lives.

The New Latinx Cinema's countercultural politics and aesthetics was short lived, as Latinx cinema became more and more mainstream starting in the late 1970s. The process is linked to the rise of public television, which required content producers to align their product with the liberal pluralism of the funding government agencies. That is to say, unlike the countercultural, non-assimilationist perspective represented in the New Latinx Cinema, films of the 1980s and 1990s tend to favor the integration of Latinx characters into a United States that is conceived as a multicultural mosaic in the tradition of liberal pluralism. Films of this period grapple with the contradictions of this ideology by denouncing cases where the invitation to be part of the national mosaic is not being honored, as in *Seguín*, *¡Alambrista!*, and *Zoot Suit*; celebrating cases where it is, as in *La Bamba* and *Selena*; or calling into question the central metaphor of liberalism of groups-as-individuals, as *Born in East L.A.* and *Lone Star* successfully do.

In many ways, films of the past two decades continue to grapple with the contradictions of this invitation, as the democratization of the medium has allowed more filmmakers to expand the range of form and subject matter via films such as *Girlfight*, *Real Women*

*Have Curves*, and *Quinceañera*, all of which add a much-needed feminist and/or queer perspective to the male-dominated narratives of the twentieth century. Yet at the same time, Latinx cinema has also begun to register the growing crisis of liberal pluralism in films like *Sin nombre* and *Sleep Dealer*, which share a preoccupation with the dehumanization generated by the intertwined realities of war and global capitalism.

Where, then, is Latinx cinema headed? To answer this question, consider Anzaldúa's definition of the Borderlands, as "present wherever two or more cultures edge each other, where people of different races occupy the same territory, where under, lower, middle and upper classes touch, where the space between two individuals shirks with intimacy."[29] A Latinx Borderlands cinema, then, would be a cinema that foregrounds narratives where differences based on race and class shirk with intimacy. By this definition, much of Latinx cinema of the past twenty years is a borderlands cinema with a lowercase *b*, a cinema that eschews rather than shirks intimacy, most visibly via graphic violence that is often gratuitous. Think of *The Three Burials of Melquíades Estrada* (dir. Tommy Lee Jones, 2005) or *Machete* (dir. Robert Rodríguez, 2010), technically excellent films that nevertheless reproduce the stereotype of the borderlands as incorrigibly violent.[30] Could it possibly be that a corporate giant such as Disney Studios points the way out of this dead end? Judging by the financial and critical success of *Coco* (dir. Lee Unkrich, 2017), an animated film that explores the Borderlands between the living and the dead with references to both US and Mexican popular culture, that might just be the case.

## Notes

1. Chon Noriega and Ana M. López, eds., *The Ethnic Eye: Latino Media Arts* (Minneapolis: University of Minnesota Press, 1996); Clara E. Rodríguez, ed., *Latin Looks: Images of Latinas and Latinos in U.S. Media* (Boulder, CO: Westview Press, 1997); and Frederick Luis Aldama, ed., *Latinos and Narrative Media: Participation and Portrayal* (New York: Palgrave Macmillan, 2013).
2. Arlene Davila, and Yeidi M. Rivero, eds., *Contemporary Latina/o Media: Production, Circulation, Politics* (New York: New York University Press, 2014); Maria Elena Cepeda and Dolores Inés Casillas, eds., *The Routledge Companion to Latina/o Media* (New York: Routledge, 2016).
3. Clara Ramírez, *Heroes, Lovers, and Others: The Story of Latinos in Hollywood* (New York: Oxford University Press, 2008); Charles Ramírez Berg, *Latino Images in Film: Stereotypes, Subversion and Resistance* (Austin: University of Texas Press, 2002); Henry Puente, *The Promotion and Distribution of U.S. Latino Films* (New York: Peter Lang, 2011); Frederick Luis Aldama, *The Cinema of Robert Rodríguez* (Austin: University of Texas Press, 2014); and Colin Gunkel, Jan-Christopher Horak, and Lisa Jarvinen, eds., *Cinema Between Latin America and Los Angeles: Origins to 1960* (New Brunswick, NJ: Rutgers University Press, 2019).
4. Gloria Anzaldúa, *Borderlands / La Frontera* (San Francisco: Aunt Lute Book Company, 1987), 3.
5. In the first edition (1997), lowercase uses of borderlands appear fourteen times on pages i (twice), iii (four times), 3 (twice), 4 (once), 61 (once), 62 (once), 63 (once), and 90 (twice);

while uppercase uses of Borderlands appear twelve times on pages iii (once), iv (once), 73 (twice), 77 (once), 194 (five times), and 195 (twice). This is not counting the times that the word appears as part of a title because in those cases it may not correspond to the definitions mentioned earlier. For example, on p. 20, Borderlands is used with a capital *B* because it is part of a section title, but its use corresponds to the first definition of borderlands with a lowercase *b*.

6. Anzaldúa, *Borderlands / La Frontera*, 3–4; Anzaldúa, *Borderlands / La Frontera*, 61–63; Anzaldúa, *Borderlands / La Frontera*, 90.
7. Anzaldúa, *Borderlands / La Frontera*, iii–iv, 73, 77.
8. Anzaldúa, *Borderlands / La Frontera*, 195.
9. Anzaldúa, *Borderlands / La Frontera*, 78, 80.
10. Anzaldúa, *Borderlands / La Frontera*, iv.
11. Fernando Ortiz, *Cuban Counterpoint: Tobacco and Sugar* [1940], trans. Harret de Onís (Durham, NC: Duke University Press, 1995), 97, 102–103.
12. Allen Woll, *The Latin Image in American Film* (Los Angeles: UCLA Latin American Center Publications, 1980), 8–9.
13. Gregorio Rocha, "La venganza de Pancho Villa: A Lost and Found Film," in *F Is for Phony: Fake Documentary and Truth's Undoing*, edited by Alexandra Juhasz and Jesse Lerner (Minneapolis: University of Minnesota Press, 2006), 56.
14. Ramírez Berg, *Latino Images in Film*, 113.
15. Ramírez Berg, *Latino Images in Film*, 116–117.
16. Claire Fox, *The Fence and the River: Culture and Politics in the U.S.-Mexico Border* (Minneapolis: University of Minnesota Press, 1999).
17. Herbert Biberman, *Salt of the Earth: The Story of a Film* (New York: Harbor Electronic, 2003), 11.
18. David Maciel, "Latino Cinema," in *Handbook of Hispanic Culture in the United States Literature and Art*, edited by Francisco Lomelí (Houston, TX: Arte Público Press, 1993), 317. https://www.ejumpcut.org/archive/onlinessays/JC20folder/ImperfectCinema.html.
19. Chon A. Noriega, "The Migrant Intellectual." *Aztlán: A Journal of Chicano Studies* 32, no. 1 (2007), 17.
20. Julio García Espinosa, "Towards an Imperfect Cinema" [1969], trans. Julianne Burton, *Jump Cut* 20 (1979): 24–26.
21. Noriega, "The Migrant Intellectual," 12.
22. Arnaldo M. Cruz-Malavé, "Between Irony and Belief: The Queer Diasporic Underground Aesthetics of José Rodríguez-Soltero and Mario Montez," *GLQ* 21, no. 4 (2015): 585–615. doi:10.1215/10642684-3123701.
23. Maciel, "Latino Cinema," 315.
24. Rosa Linda Fregoso, *The Bronze Screen: Chicana and Chicano Film Culture* (Minneapolis: University of Minnesota Press, 1993), 37–38.
25. Luis Valdez, "*Zoot Suit*: The Man, the Myth, Still Lives (A Conversation with Luis Valdes)," Interview with Gregg Barrios, *Bilingual Review / La Revista Bilingüe* 10, no. 2 (1983): 162.
26. Fregoso, *The Bronze Screen*, 46.
27. Anzaldúa, *Borderlands / La Frontera*, iv.
28. Margaret E. Montoya, "Lines of Demarcation in a Town Called Frontera: A Review of John Sayles' Movie *Lone Star*," *New Mexico Law Review* 27 (Winter 1997): 239.
29. Anzaldúa, *Borderlands / La Frontera* (San Francisco: Aunt Lute Book Company, 1987), iii.
30. Camila Fojas, *Border Bandits* (Austin: University of Texas Press, 2009).

# Bibliography

Aldama, Frederick Luis, ed. *Latinos and Narrative Media: Participation and Portrayal.* New York: Palgrave Macmillan, 2013.

Aldama, Frederick Luis. *The Cinema of Robert Rodríguez.* Austin: University of Texas Press, 2014.

Anzaldúa, Gloria. *Borderlands / La Frontera.* San Francisco: Aunt Lute Book Company, 1987.

Beltrán, Mary C. *Latina/o Stars in U.S. Eyes: The Making and Meanings of Film and TV Stardom.* Chicago: University of Illinois Press, 2009.

Biberman, Herbert. *Salt of the Earth: The Story of a Film.* New York: Harbor Electronic, 2003.

de los Santos, Nancy, Susan Santos, and Alberto Domínguez, dirs. *The Bronze Screen.* Questar Entertainment, 2003.

Cepeda, Maria Elena, and Dolores Inés Casillas, eds. *The Routledge Companion to Latina/o Media.* New York: Routledge, 2016.

Cruz-Malavé, Arnaldo M. "Between Irony and Belief: The Queer Diasporic Underground Aesthetics of José Rodríguez-Soltero and Mario Montez." *GLQ* 21, no. 4 (2015): 585–615. doi:10.1215/10642684-3123701.

Dávila, Arlene, and Yeidi M. Riverso, eds. *Contemporary Latina/o Media: Production, Circulation, Politics.* New York: New York University Press, 2014.

Ebert, Roger. Review of *My Family*. https://www.rogerebert.com/reviews/my-family-1995.

Fojas, Camila. *Border Bandits.* Austin: University of Texas Press, 2009.

Fox, Claire. *The Fence and the River: Culture and Politics in the U.S.-Mexico Border.* Minneapolis: University of Minnesota Press, 1999.

Fregoso, Rosa Linda. *The Bronze Screen: Chicana and Chicano Film Culture.* Minneapolis: University of Minnesota Press, 1993.

Gamboa, Harry Jr. *Gamboa, Harry Jr.: Early Video Art.* Los Angeles: UCLA Chicano Studies Research Center, 2004.

García Espinosa, Julio. "Towards an Imperfect Cinema" [1969] Trans. Julianne Burton. *Jump Cut* 20 (1979): 24–26.

Gunkel, Colin, Jan-Christopher Horak, and Lisa Jarvinen, eds. *Cinema Between Latin America and Los Angles: Origins to 1960.* New Brunswick, NJ: Rutgers University Press, 2019.

Maciel, David. "Latino Cinema." Translated by Rhonda Osmun Hayworth. In *Handbook of Hispanic Culture in the United States Literature and Art.* Edited by Francisco Lomelí, 312–331. Houston, TX: Arte Público Press, 1993. https://www.ejumpcut.org/archive/onlinessays/JC2ofolder/ImperfectCinema.html.

Montoya, Margaret E. "Lines of Demarcation in a Town Called Frontera: A Review of John Sayles' Movie *Lone Star*." *New Mexico Law Review* 27 (Winter 1997): 223–240.

Moreiras, Alberto. *The Exhaustion of Difference.* Durham, NC: Duke University Press, 2001.

Noriega, Chon A., ed. *Chicanos and Film: Representation and Resistance.* Minneapolis: University of Minnesota Press, 1992.

Noriega, Chon A. "The Migrant Intellectual." *Aztlán: A Journal of Chicano Studies* 32, no. 1 (2007): 1–20.

Noriega, Chon, and Ana M. López, eds. *The Ethnic Eye: Latino Media Arts.* Minneapolis: University of Minnesota Press, 1996.

Oiticica, Hélio. "Mario Montez, Tropicamp." [1971] *Afterall: A Journal of Art, Context and Enquiry* 28 (Autumn/Winter 2011): 16–21. doi:10.1086/662967.

Ortiz, Fernando. *Cuban Counterpoint: Tobacco and Sugar* [1940]. Trans. Harret de Onís. Durham, NC: Duke University Press, 1995.

Puente, Henry. *The Promotion and Distribution of U.S. Latino Films*. New York: Peter Lang, 2011.

Ramírez, Clara. *Heroes, Lovers, and Others: The Story of Latinos in Hollywood*. New York: Oxford University Press, 2008.

Ramírez Berg, Charles. *Latino Images in Film: Stereotypes, Subversion and Resistance*. Austin: University of Texas Press, 2002.

Rocha, Gregorio. *Los rollos perdidos de Pancho Villa* https://www.youtube.com/watch?v=YrawE8Xxz74.

Rocha, Gregorio C. "La venganza de Pancho Villa: A Lost and Found Border Film." In *F Is for Phony: Fake Documentary and Truth's Undoing*. Edited by Alexandra Juhasz and Jesse Lerner, 50–58. Minneapolis: University of Minnesota Press, 2006.

Rodríguez, Clara E., ed. *Latin Looks: Images of Latinas and Latinos in U.S. Media*. Boulder, CO: Westview Press, 1997.

Valdez, Luis, "*Zoot Suit*: The Man, The Myth, Still Lives (A Conversation with Luis Valdes)." Interview with Gregg Barrios. *Bilingual Review / La Revista Bilingüe* 10, no. 2 (1983): 159–164.

Woll, Allen, *The Latin Image in American Film*. Los Angeles: UCLA Latin American Center Publications, 1980.

CHAPTER 21

# TELEVISION AND ITS IMPACT ON LATINX COMMUNITIES

## MARI CASTAÑEDA

TELEVISION is the principal storyteller of the modern era; and although it has been broadcasting news and entertainment programming nearly nonstop since the late 1950s, the role and presence of Latinx people on the most pervasive and persuasive communications medium in the United States continues to be relatively invisible as well as stereotypical across a multitude of English-language television outlets.[1] Federico Subervi-Vélez[2] predicted in the late 1990s that bias in news and entertainment would continue to be an issue for Latinos if a rigorous policy and research agenda was not put in place for intentionally including Latinx lived experiences on television and media more generally. The lack of non-biased inclusion has in many ways created an audiovisual vacuum that permits the visual dehumanization of Latinos, the rise of anti-immigrant discourse, and the construction of a perceived reality that Latinos are uneducated or not law-abiding citizens. The impact of such televisual representations should not to be minimized. In a study published in *Latino Studies*, Eileen McConnell found that articles published by a regional Atlanta newspaper—which were then often repeated on local television news outlets—portrayed the demographic changes produced by newly arriving Latino and Asian families as a negative shift despite migration to the local area by African American and white families taking place at the same rate.[3] Consequently, journalists and media creators in Atlanta circulated and sustained media discourses that privileged a white-black racialized hierarchy and reproduced a narrative of nonexistent Latino contributions despite the fact that the community had positively impacted social and economic spheres across the South in recent decades. Research by the Pew Research Center concurred that the migration of Latinx communities to the South was in some cases saving the housing rental market and public schools from closing down, since Latino families were moving into low population areas. The changes taking place led to the term "New Latino South" and were viewed by economists as a productive change given the need for workers in the agricultural and textile industries. Yet this narrative is not what has generally circulated about Latinos, and the passage of anti-immigrant legislation in Georgia, Alabama, Tennessee, and North Carolina in recent years underscores the role television media has played in misrepresenting and scapegoating Latinos. Given this unsettling situation, is there any hope for media, and television in particular, to adequately represent the diverse ways of life of US Latinx communities? What has been the historical impact of television on Latinx communities, and what can we expect in the future for television's ability to provide a meaningful picture of the wide-ranging positionalities that exist within these communities?

In an effort to address this problematic issue, the chapter will focus on five important areas pertaining to the intersection of television with Latinx communities and the ways in which the evolving televisual context is mediating diasporic translatinidades: (1) the role of Latinas in television set manufacturing, (2) the representation of Latinos in mainstream television, (3) the rise of Spanish-language television, (4) the importance of telenovelas in global television, and (5) the emergence of TV streaming as a new venue for translatinidades. Taken together, these five topics complete a framework that allows for a comprehensive investigation of television and how it constitutes social, political, economic, and cultural lived experiences; television is thus more than merely a glowing screen in living rooms worldwide. Ultimately, the goal of this chapter is to investigate how television and its relationship with Latinx communities must be recognized as a multilayered and evolving formation that is culturally embedded as well as closely interconnected to market power.

Currently, the Latinx population constitutes 18 percent of the US population, but they represent less than 6 percent of all television and film characters, news anchors, producers, directors, and writers even after nearly seventy years of a burgeoning mainstream television industry, one that now includes online streaming and hundreds of cable and satellite channels.[4] Even when Latinos gain employment access to media industries, they often experience what Hector Amaya calls the "Latino public sphere parado," since such access does not guarantee access to political power. Media activists and communication scholars have indeed confirmed that the complicated political, economic, and cultural nature of television (and media more generally) means that inclusion does not always lead to televisual transformation.[5] As Dan Schiller argues, the US media and its related telecommunications sectors continue to be embedded in a web of commodity arrangements that are shaped by persistent structural disparity.[6] Therefore, it is essential to examine television through a transcultural political economy framework, which aims to understand the intersections between macro and micro processes and practices. Further, to have a lens that emphasizes a Latinx critical communication (LatCritComm) analyses, which centralizes Latinx experiences, can be fruitful in their provision of a broader theoretical and conceptual framework for examining television and its impact on Latinx communities.[7] These theoretical underpinnings are especially important for explaining Latinx labor in the production of television, which ranges from programming development to the factory floor where actual consumer electronic screens are manufactured. We now turn our attention to the issue of production in order to better understand how the making of television for the North American consumer market has affected Latinx communities.

## SITUATING THE MAKING OF TELEVISION

Television is historically perceived as a window into the world that often renders Latinos as either invisible or as existing within a deficit discourse.[8] It is still amazing how an audiovisual flickering screen—and increasingly a small mobile device—can profoundly shape how we see ourselves and other people, places, and practices across national and global contexts. The power of the audiovisual medium is not innocuous or insignificant, and in fact it is an important factor in how racial and ethnic populations have been treated symbolically and materially over time.[9] The film documentary *Latinos Beyond Reel* (2013) demonstrates how the representations of Latinos, on both TV and movie screens, have created an uncharitable narrative in which Latinx communities are often demonized, sexualized, scapegoated, or discredited within the US imaginary, despite the fact that there are almost 650 million Latinos and Latin Americans across the Americas. Notwithstanding the growth in population, the expansion of on-screen images that represent a wide range of lived experiences—that is evidently present within the population itself—has not occurred. According to the featured scholars in *Latinos Beyond Reel*, such as Isabel Molina-Guzmán, Otto Santa Ana, and Angharad Valdivia, television has historically worked as an ideological tool that limits the representation of Latinos as change agents. Similar to African Americans, Latinos are not consistently regarded as legitimate citizens capable of building the nation. In fact, more often than not, they are questioned as to whether they belong in the nation and are viewed as embodying a dubious citizenship. Thus, they are a population needing to be monitored in relationship to dominantly white democratic society.[10]

Yet from the very start of the US television industry, Latinos aimed to carve out a space for creating agency in representation, ownership, and audience support.[11] Similar to what had occurred in broadcast radio, the English-language mainstream commercial sector was entrenched in culturally biased policies and customs that discriminated against people of color, and created few opportunities for Latino images and voices across the mainstream mass media, including the television and film industries.[12] Like radio, television for Spanish-speaking audiences also began as an effort to tap into the potential of a future broadcast market in the United States, particularly since Mexico and other Latin American countries were already creating their own extensive mass media industries. Latino broadcasters thus envisioned a role for Spanish-language information, music, and entertainment not only in the US media landscape but one that was able to flow transnationally. As América Rodriguez notes, the transnational structure of the emerging Spanish-language cultural production industries was intimately connected to the rise of transnational audiences, products, and consumers.[13]

Interestingly, the emergence of the Spanish-language television sector in the United States also coincided with the rise of the transnational maquiladora industry along the US-Mexico border. The making of television sets by maquila factories would eventually become the global platform for television set production. As Spanish-language television and Latinos made their way on both the US and Latin American/Caribbean airwaves, Mexican maquila workers become central to the manufacturing of television sets for the consumer market across the Americas. As more consumers bought into the imaginaries created by television entertainment, advertising, and news, the need for more television sets became crucial—especially as television viewing became ubiquitous in homes and businesses alike.

The US public as a whole knows very little about the roles that Latinos (Mexicans in particular) have played and continue to play in the production of television sets. Although consumer electronic maquiladoras have been producing television sets for the past fifty years, most consumers are unaware that their TV screens are manufactured across the US-Mexico border. When transborder manufacturing began to intensify in the mid-1960s and early 1970s, there was indeed extensive discontent from largely white factory workers located in the Northeast and Midwest who worked for companies such as Panasonic, General Electric, and RCA but were now losing their jobs because of the relocating of the television manufacturing industry to the US-Mexico border. Narratives about "Mexicans stealing US workers' jobs" abounded at that time, and such narratives have not abated as new industries have reduced their US labor force and transferred to offshore production, especially after the North American Free Trade Agreement (NAFTA) in 1994. Yet rather than blaming the free market ethos that threatens to upend the capacity of all workers, US media narratives have accentuated the role of Latin American workers in transnational manufacturing, and this attribution has also impacted how Latino immigrant workers are treated in the United States. Manuel Casas and Ana Cabrera argue that the negative perceptions often attributed to Latino workers are creating a context where anti-immigration laws, policy, and actions are being promoted and enacted.[14] Such perceptions and policies unfortunately fail to recognize the historical geopolitical context and the broader reality that workers south of the border are facing as well.

For instance, in the context of Mexican maquila workers, women constitute the largest percentage of the television set manufacturing workforce in the Americas, and it is on the backs of their labor that the United States now has access to inexpensive digital television sets. Companies such as Sony and Ericsson produce digital television sets along the US-Mexico border with a largely female workforce comprising Latinas between the ages of thirteen to twenty-five. Latinas are the largest makers of television sets because they are stereotypically perceived to be submissive, quiet workers willing to work for low wages; however, it is often the violent working conditions and economic strife that forces these women to endure inhospitable treatment. Elvia Arriola also emphasizes that Mexican women are not the only maquila workers: women from Honduras, Nicaragua, Guatemala, and El Salvador have also been compelled to leave their countries due to social and political unrest yet are unable to cross into the United States from Mexico.[15]

As a result, they have become part of the Mexican border's migrant labor population. Over four thousand companies have maquila factories in the border region, and television set and consumer electronics production have become some of the largest manufacturing sectors in the region. This is a byproduct of the fact that more than 40 million television sets are manufactured in Mexico annually, and this production supplies 90 percent of the TV products that are sold in the US market every year.

Interestingly, the twin sister plants of maquiladoras located in California, Texas, and Arizona also mainly comprise Latina workers, which is ironic since their voices, images, and issues are not frequently heard or seen on mainstream airwaves. As the primary producers of television sets, Latina television set makers are an invisible labor force whose media representations are nonexistent. Where are the audiovisual commentaries that show the labor conditions that many of these women endure, or narratives describing the paradox that women maquila workers experience when they become the primary breadwinners and consequently can challenge patriarchy through their material agency? Maura Toro-Morn states that these kinds of stories, which magnify our understanding of Latina labor contributions, are consistently ignored in the media despite the fact that coverage would do much to humanize Latinx populations.[16] On the contrary, what the general population in the United States largely sees are stereotypical representations. Latina lived experiences are portrayed from the standpoint of maids, prostitutes, and undocumented single mothers. They are not viewed as the hardworking technical specialists they are required to become across the maquiladora industry. Rather what we continue to be exposed to are problematic representations of Latinos on mainstream US television, as the following section will discuss.

## Representing Latinos on Broadcast Television

The long-standing representations of Latinos on US broadcast television are historically negative, with images characterizing Latinos as violent offenders, dim-witted laborers, or sexual deviants. According to Mary Beltrán, such images serve the racial hegemony that has influenced the founding of America and allows for the reinforcement of social norms that sustain the exoticization and exploitation of Latino communities within the broader societal context.[17] To say that these images do nothing is to lack an understanding of media power and the impact such discourses have in shaping the public's worldview. Indeed, Otto Santa Ana argues that the constant barrage of derogatory images of Latinos on television and media more generally indicates a value system of the United States that oppresses communities of color.[18] The long history of these images in the United States has thus succeeded in maintaining a level of social distance and fear about Latinos, especially if they do not speak English. It is important to acknowledge that the anxiety over Latinos is tied to the history of colonialism and exploitative labor in the

United States.[19] Consequently, by marginalizing non-white communities, dominant structures can write these communities out of history as well as hinder their capacity for political-economic agency. Despite the liberal democratic principles of free and open airwaves that presumably belong to the public, scholars have shown that the media, especially broadcasting, have utilized programming and policy processes to protect the entrenched political and racialized status quo as represented through communication content. Dana Mastro and Elizabeth Behm-Morawitz have demonstrated that television is a site of cultural politics that rarely challenges the hegemonic messages about Latinos that have permeated mass media for decades.[20] Vicki Mayer also contends that both stereotypical images and the invisibility of Latinos work as a form of mediated, latent racism that has the potential to undermine a multicultural sensibility that values non-white communities.[21]

Therefore, by reinforcing a white supremacist and pro-capitalist ideology in news and entertainment programming, forms of social control can be maintained in which Latinos and people of color are more generally perceived as embodying the negative racial and ethnic stereotypes that are continuously reproduced about them. Consequently, these populations become unworthy of upward mobility or educational resources, and the subtle (and sometimes very direct message) becomes that the Latinos best belong in kitchens, agricultural fields, prisons, and increasingly outside the boundaries of the United States. They are believed to not belong in positions of power; and if they do occupy such positions, the expectation is that they must reinforce a free-market ideology. Conservative xenophobic agendas only deem Latinos as acceptable when they are considered white, legal, and capitalist. Latinos, regardless of citizenship status, are continuously marked with the televisual narrative of requiring deportation and imprisonment. David Manuel Hernández shows that assumptions about criminality abound when it comes to Latinos, especially Latino immigrants, and these presumptions are asserted over and over again by xenophobic politicians and ratings-hungry television programs—which are then concurrently consumed by audiences who fail to question the televised biased orientations.[22] For the television industry, these imaginative imperatives are viewed as merely political and economic actions (and ostensibly not racist) because they are simply reflecting the ways of the world and not necessarily passing judgment.

Yet as Ediberto Roman demonstrates, for Latinos there are undeniable destructive and insidious legal and political effects that the constant televising of racial and ethnic stereotypes has on the community in terms of stigma and the perpetuation of damaging myths.[23] These in turn bolster the idea that Latinos, Mexicans, and Mexican Americans in particular do not belong in the United States and are unworthy of its resources.[24] Television images create meaning, and as the demographics in the United States and across the Americas continue to shift toward more people of color, those images will mean the difference between intersectional inclusion and violent exclusion. On mainstream English-language television, the moments of acceptance toward Latinos (which are expressed when Latino characters or stories are permitted on the screen) are then turned into ambivalence when those same stories fail to represent a humanized or complex characterization. The persistent media narratives of Latinos, especially immigrants, as threatening the cultural and social fabric of society in the United States is what ultimately comes to represent the Latino diaspora.[25]

The impact of television is not only evident in the persuasive and pervasive narratives that it creates over time but also in the psychological effects wrought upon Latinos and non-Latinos alike. Multiple studies have demonstrated the cognitive and social impact that television has on everyday people, especially children.[26] Research projects examining the impact of television on Latino youth have demonstrated that there are negative effects that television exposure has on people's sense of self-worth, identity formation, educational attainment, and overall well-being. Research by Rocío Rivadeneyra, Monique Ward, and Maya Gordon found that the exclusion of Latinos from television had the powerful potential of diminishing the self-confidence of Latino audiences, especially young women.[27] Additionally, "the repeated exposure to stereotypical portrayals of Latinos as lazy, violent, uneducated, and criminal could lead viewers of all races to believe that these attributes characterize Latinos in the real world…In this way, it is believed that Latino viewers may come to think of themselves and their own group in these negative ways, thereby diminishing the self-esteem of individual Latino viewers."[28] Television invisibility and negative characterizations not only affect people's ability to function successfully at school, work, or in civic settings but also have the potential to impact the collective structure of feeling. As more research continues to be conducted, it is increasingly evident that media is a key force in the social development and the misrepresentation of Latinos, and examining its impact through television is crucial.

For instance, researchers are studying the longitudinal mental health effects of feeling inconsequential and unimportant as a result of television images, which also reinforce the television studies conjecture that stipulates, "If it doesn't exist in the media, then it doesn't exist." And if marginalized communities do appear on television, then they are considered suspect.[29] Thus, Latinos are rarely portrayed as possibly having the capacity to embody middle-class lives as professors, judges, school teachers, car mechanics, or business owners, since those characterizations are virtually non-existent on US communications platforms; rather, Latinos are viewed through unfavorable frames.[30] In 1980, the scholar Felix Gutierrez submitted a report to the US Department of Health in which he described the historical portrayal and employment statistics of Latinos in US media and quoted Ruben Salazar, the murdered *Los Angeles Times* journalist, as observing: "The media, having ignored the Mexican Americans for so long, but now willing to report on them, seem impatient about the complexities of the story…It's as if the media, having finally discovered the Mexican American, is not amused that under the serape and sombrero is a complex Chicano instead of a potential Gringo."[31] In point of fact, mainstream television has struggled to understand and properly portray the complexity of Latinidad. Yet analyzing the television representation of Latinos is critical because Latinos, especially the youth, are also the heaviest consumers of mass media of all ethnic and racial groups in the United States. Additionally, over time Latino children become adults whose values are in part shaped by a television system that seems to devalue who they are as political, economic, and cultural agents and only celebrates their contributions if it is related to food, music, or sexual prowess.

Jennifer Willis's study of "Latino Night" in a small town in Ohio demonstrates the ways in which Latinos are celebrated for their cultural exoticization through music and dance but are criticized if efforts to assimilate fall short and Latinos aim for political agency.[32] Such agency is viewed with suspicion since it is believed Latinos will want to legitimize issues that are believed to be contrary to the "American way" such as bilingualism. There is actually palpable fear about Latinos becoming significant change agents in civil society. This great fear has become especially evident since the 2016 presidential elections, and television news has increasingly become the repetitive mouthpiece for conservative xenophobes. And the material consequences are real. For instance, the rise of virulent racist taunts and physical fights at K–12 schools during the presidential primaries and after the national elections this past fall, particularly at sporting events, is the direct result of a political media landscape that utilizes the persuasiveness and pervasiveness of communication systems to espouse a white supremacist ideology that aspires to delegitimize Latinos and people of color in general as social and political actors. The limited Latinx representations and diversity on the televisual landscape not only create limited understanding of the social world but have the potential to produce real violence against underrepresented and historically marginalized communities.

Jack Levin and Jack MacDevitt confirm that broadcast media have helped fuel the rising toward tide of bigotry and hate crimes against people of color, including Latinos.[33] The enduring stereotypes that are perpetuated in television narratives then become the portrayals and pictures in our heads that then shape whether and how other people should be treated, and even despised and/or victimized.[34] Hateful rhetoric has particularly impacted the immigration debates during the last decade, and Kevin Johnson and Joanna Cuevas Ingram argue that such racially charged discourse is not just producing physical violence against Latinos; it is also shaping the practices and architecture of immigration enforcement laws as communities of color, literally and figuratively, change the racial and ethnic demographics of the United States.[35] The anti-immigrant discourses and physical attacks as well as the non-stop ICE deportations have emboldened a plethora of hate speech via the broadcast airwaves, and thus hate crimes against undocumented Latino immigrants have continued to rise. Although the television industry argues that media effects are minimal and its industry has no power to create real material effects in the world (i.e., it is simply reflecting what is already taking place), it chooses to turn a blind eye to the data amassed over the years demonstrating otherwise.[36] While it is true that one specific program may not necessarily produce a violent reaction by an individual, it is the persistent long-term audiovisual messaging that makes television a powerful medium for the systematic production of certain narratives. George Gerbner, Larry Gross, and Michael Morgan demonstrate through cultivation analysis that audiences who spend more time living in the world of television are more likely to perceive "the 'real world' in the terms of the images, values, portrayals, and ideologies that emerge through the lens of television."[37]

Consequently, the impact of Latino invisibility, according to researchers, must not be underestimated; yet the television industry does not feel any responsibility to provide adequate representation: after all, it is a commercial business and not a social service venue.[38] Nevertheless, there is little doubt that television irresponsibly over-represents Latinos as parasites and non-contributors to our society. And in that sense, the mainstream television industry is making a choice, certainly one rooted in the profit motive, to represent Latinos more negatively than positively and to act largely as a commercial agent to the detriment of society as a whole. And since the airwaves are meant to be public and only loaned to them (assuming they are servicing the needs of local communities adequately), they should thus be held accountable for their misrepresentation of Latinos. This is particularly crucial, since Latinos will become the largest consumer group by 2050, and television's survival will be dependent on this population.[39]

This fact explains a new trend that researchers are also investigating, which is the whitening and whitewashing of Latinos in order to make them more palatable to the mainstream and correspondingly encouraging Latinos to see themselves as white or at least in color-blind ways. Arlene Dávila argues that this growing shift toward a marketable Latinidad is connected to whiteness, colorblindness, and neoliberalism at a time when the state is extracting itself from providing social welfare initiatives and relying more on privatization. Since Latinos are perceived to be the greatest threat to the normativity of whiteness, their emerging (albeit slow) transformation into acceptable American citizen/subjects is ultimately tied, as Dávila states, "to a larger racial project entailing the very reconfiguration of how we talk or do not talk about race and racial hierarchies in an increasingly racially diversified society."[40] Although the earlier discussion seems to suggest a gloomy future, that is not necessarily the case.

The recent presence of Latino characters, directors, writers, and producers in some of the most popular television shows, such as *How to Get Away with Murder*, *Jane the Virgin*, and *Grey's Anatomy*, demonstrate the potential to shift the televisual narrative about Latinos' creative and political potential. Certainly, the gradual increase of Latinos into the mainstream television industry is taking place within the larger reality of news and entertainment, yet negative characterizations of Latinos continue to dominate. But scholars believe there is hope for the future of Latinos in English-language television, whether it is on the traditional broadcast venues or online streaming outlets. Increasingly, Latino television leaders are attempting to also retain some level of cultural heritage, bilingualism, and racial identity even as they are pressured to homogenize the diasporic translatinidad experience. Both Eva Longoria and America Ferrera, along with a slew of other Latinx Hollywood insiders, have called out the television and film industries for their "casual racism" of Latino actors and storytelling; the most recent challenge was live during the 2016 Golden Globes ceremony. Additionally, Latinos are in constant negotiation between an imagined framework of diasporic latinidad and their specific mestizaje, which is not always articulated in national terms.[41] This perhaps illustrates the difficulty of adequately representing Latinos on mainstream television: they are not one cultural or national group but constitute multiple racial/ethnic identities. Thus, the diverse Latinx communities cannot be pigeonholed. This is a challenge for an industry so dependent on the lowest common denominator in terms of social experience and commercial imperatives that are easy to categorize on TV. Therefore, the rise of digital media is creating opportunities for counter-narratives and providing a sliver of hope that gender, sexuality, class, and the diversity of Latinidades is possible and accessible through the future of television beyond the airwaves.

## Streaming Television as the Future

There is growing optimism about the power and accessibility of streaming television, not only for creating programming outside of the mainstream but also providing more possibilities for developing Latinx images and narratives that otherwise do not exist. It is through this technology and the multiple platforms that researchers are finding the prospect of developing something different in terms of Latino representation through the new forms of televisual production, distribution, and consumption.[42] For example, new television shows not featured on traditional broadcast outlets but on small-screen formats such as Netflix and Amazon (e.g., the remake of *One Day at a Time*, the Gael Garcia Bernal series, *Mozart in the Jungle*, and the new series *Vida*) are becoming popular and are lauded as examples of Latinos becoming a valuable community (and commodity) worthwhile of representation. These streaming TV shows are mediating diasporic translatinidades by using familiar tropes to present new ways of understanding Latino lived experiences. The newest show, *One Day at a Time* by showrunner Gloria Calderon Kellet, now in its second season, is a remake of a 1970s broadcast television program that in this newest iteration features an extended Cuban American family in order to account for how today's Latinx families are often structured in the United States. The fact the show is featured online gives producers a wide landscape in which to explore issues that are often considered too touchy or political for advertiser-supported mainstream broadcast television.

Other networks on cable—CW, for example—push boundaries with television programming and are taking advantage of the wider latitude and addressing topics such as immigration, Latina motherhood, and extended families. These topics are in fact central to the story line for CW's award-winning program, *Jane the Virgin*. This television program not only provides alternative and more complex narratives about Latinos (although it still sometimes alludes to stereotypes), it still aims to express narratives that are traditionally left out of the televisual conversation on mainstream TV. Additionally, it also includes digital modes of storytelling by displaying texting on the screen as part of the show; this demonstrates a willingness to move outside traditional broadcast television production norms. Researchers are finding that these alternative streaming spaces are creating opportunities not only to develop alternative storytelling but also to boost Latinx creative labor, which is often shut out of mainstream broadcast television.

Vittoria Rodriguez and Mary Beltrán have found that the rise of the digital web series platform is a "burgeoining new frontier for creative expression where Latina/o storytelling is part of the norm rather than the exception."[43] In their study, they examined a slew of web series in which Latina/Latino subjectivities are the core of televisual productions that ranged from drama to satiric comedy and included narratives about Latina feminist superheroes, undocumented youth, and family angst. Despite the financial limitations of such productions, Rodriguez and Beltrán ultimately conclude that "as digital media production tools, mobile devices, and streaming media platforms [like Hulu and YouTube] become more broadly accessible and make digital production and exhibition easier, Latina/o producers and others who have traditionally been excluded from television production may increasingly utilize these tools to tell their stories."[44] The hope is that these new digital platforms will positively impact how Latinx communities are represented and perceived, thus changing the relationship between media and historically underrepresented communities. Yet the reality of accessing financial resources for developing widely accessible digital creative media productions should not be undervalued, and political economic connections continue to be one of the largest barriers to Latino entry into the television and media industries. It is unfortunate that so much of the US entertainment and news industries are based on significant fiscal patronage, peer networks, college backgrounds, and social capital; and yet it is a reality that few people discuss openly because it demonstrates that access to the television industry is not merely about media creativity and talent but also advantageous socioeconomic credentials. Hector Amaya concurs that Latina/Latino creative professionals have a hard time gaining access to employment opportunities in the television industry due to these perceived credentialed requirements but also because of the enduring bias that permeates so much of the media.[45]

Additionally, since the deregulatory turn at the Federal Communications Commission in 1996, it has also been difficult to apply EEOC policies to an industry that is rooted in the First Amendment. For many Latinos, the educational, cultural, and financial components that are often necessary to embark on a television career are out of reach because emerging Latino media innovators are either first-generation college graduates or below the socioeconomic ladder that allows for families to support young creatives in their budding television careers. Thus, the extensive financial resources that are needed for developing networks or getting a college education (and especially at universities and colleges that industry folks consider up to par) is extremely difficult and thus leaves hundreds of potential Latinx television creators out of the landscape where new programming can be produced or where they can find employment within one of the television sectors. The rise of diversity employment programs within the television industry and work by NALIP (National Association of Latino Independent Producers) and NHMC (National Hispanic Media Coalition) are certainly helping to improve the situation. These organizations along with established industry insiders are calling for more inclusion of Latinos, since the population will constitute 35 percent of the US population by 2050.

Unfortunately, at the rate of hiring taking place, Latinos will constitute less than 10 percent of the television creative and production workforce; outside of manufacturing television sets, this is a real problem that needs to be addressed. In *The Latino Gap*, a report focusing on the minimal representation of Latinos in front of and behind the camera, Frances Negrón-Muntaner noted that Latinos were voracious media consumers yet their exclusion from the television and media industries was equal to the population of California and Illinois combined: in other words, given the number of Latino audience members and the population as a whole, over 50 million Latinos were being left out of media employment.[46] The report concludes that "Latino presence in mainstream media remains extremely low and changing at a very slow pace in relation to the demographic changes sweeping the country. We have called this conundrum the Latino media gap: as Latino consumer power grows, relative Latino media presence shrinks."[47] This is unacceptable if we are to have a truly inclusive media environment and if Latinos are to make a significant sociocultural impact in the direction the country is headed, especially one that is accepting of (undocumented) immigrants. Thus, streaming television via Hulu, Netflix, or YouTube has become an interesting alternative for bypassing the old (white) boy network in order to get Latino voices heard and aired on television. Scholars are finding that Latinos, however, are still rarely considered for employment in the traditional media venues; when they do get jobs in the industry, they are often relegated to manual or menial labor. Rarely are they hired to be a part of the creative teams that produce the alternate realities and counter-narratives necessary for offsetting the negative perceptions of Latinos that currently dominate the US and global imaginary. Showrunners like Tanya Saracho are attempting to change this structural reality by hiring primarily Latinx writers for series such as Starz's *Vida*, which also streams through Amazon and was renewed for a second season.

Furthermore, before becoming too enthusiastic about the potential of digital television, it is important to note that technologies in and of themselves are not neutral apparatuses, and their development and distribution are very much embedded in political, economic, and sociocultural networks of power. Despite the growing accessibility of computerized devices, these same digital technologies by themselves will not upend historical systems of oppression. Likewise, Jose Luis Benitez and Vivana Rojas and her colleagues have each found that digital divide and digital inclusion, especially of Latino communities, continued to be significant issues even as information communication technologies increasingly become critical mechanisms for class mobility, civic engagement, and cultural expression.[48] Certainly, this broader context forces us to be cautious of blindly celebrating the potential of advanced communications; yet there is no doubt that new forms of television have the potential to interrogate conventional (and stereotypical) cultural productions of diasporic translatinidades. In some ways, the US Spanish-language television industry has worked to become a space that can provide an assemblage of affirmative narratives about Latinos, some of which offer alternatives to the mainstream English-language sector.

# Spanish-Language Television as an Alternative

Spanish-language television is uniquely situated within the broader discussion of television's power. It lies at the intersection of debates over Latino immigration and the role of US communications in shaping the nation's politics. It is the last surviving ethnic broadcast media in the United States and with time has grown and become available in the majority of metropolitan areas across the country.[49] Certainly, the growth of the Latino population has spurred the sustainability of the Spanish-language television industry and has in the twenty-first century become an important venue for representing the political, economic, and social issues that are impacting Latinos.[50] In its early history, the US Spanish-language television sector was dominated by Mexico's media conglomerate Televisa until a competitor, Telemundo (originally from Puerto Rico), challenged the ownership structure of the industry, especially Univision. Its parent company, Televisa, was viewed as an alien entity and thus in violation of the Communication Act of 1934, which specified that US broadcast licenses could not be owned by foreign companies. Even in the television industry, Mexican-related entities were viewed with suspicion and regarded as a threat to US communications and national security.[51] Unlike Telemundo, which was owned and operated by a company residing on US territory, Univision was challenged for being majority-owned by non-US business interests.

By the late 1980s, the Spanish-language television industry was largely owned by US companies that were increasingly interested in attracting a Latino consumer audience and developing synergistic media corporate alliances in order to cover the multiple communication spaces that Latinos occupy. For instance, Telemundo is now owned by NBC Universal, which in turn is owned by Seagrams Universal. Seagrams has as part of its long list of media properties several entities that speak to the diasporic translatinidad experience. Over the years, other Spanish-language television networks have emerged across cable and satellite TV platforms such as Azteca America and Estrella TV. Alan Albarran has also noted that Spanish-language television is now a cultural arbiter that has profoundly remade the media industries in all the Latin American countries as well as in Spain.[52] Spanish-language television is thus a global phenomenon that must be understood within that context as well.

In the United States, the growing demand for Latino consumers has vaulted the expansion of the Spanish-language television sector, and the demand from Latino audiences for more diverse offerings has also influenced its growth. Additionally, the racially charged immigration debates of the past year, and the most recent presidential executive orders that have empowered ICE more than ever to target Latino communities, have also inspired Spanish-language radio and television to take an even bigger stand against the growing xenophobia toward Latinos in and outside the United States.[53] Jorge Ramos from Univision's nightly national news program, Noticiero, has become a particularly outspoken advocate for addressing Latino issues on news programming as it relates to the US political landscape. His forthright style when asking questions during the presidential primaries was viewed with both awe and aversion because Ramos was willing to ask specific questions about the apparent racist policies certain candidates were espousing as part of their presidential campaign platforms.[54] There is actually a long history of research that has examined the ways in which Spanish-language media, and television news more recently, has committed itself to engaging with the Latino issues that English-language television programming often ignores: especially when it has to do with the human and violent impact of immigration and the political-economic uncertainties of Latin America and the Caribbean.[55]

Additionally, Yann Kereval (2011) notes that "the effect of using Spanish-language media serves to promote a sense of group consciousness among Latinos by reinforcing roots in Latin America and the commonalities among Latinos of varying national origin."[56] On the other hand, in terms of entertainment on Spanish-language television, there is still more to do with the representation and creation of alternative narratives of women, sexuality, and race.[57] Indeed, sexism, homophobia, and racism can still be found in Spanish-language television, and telenovelas are some of the clearest examples of these enduring problematic practices. Yet there are clear efforts to challenge such ideologies within the Spanish-language media industry, and although it is a slow movement, the need for a more inclusive environment is undeniable as the broader social context shifts toward a broader engagement with race, class, and sexuality. For many Latino communities at the conservative end of the political and religious spectrum, the ideological and social changes underway—and those represented on the televisual landscape—will be difficult to grapple with. They will require more in-depth research in terms of the longitudinal impact on diasporic translatinidades.[58] Telenovelas, on the other hand, have the potential to demonstrate other lived realities and thus challenge, through pro-social educational entertainment messaging, long-held beliefs about race, class, sexuality, gender, and religious beliefs.

## Telenovelizing Television

There is a large body of scholarship about telenovelas and their role in US and global television. There is also emerging research examining the ways in which telenovelas have reenergized the mainstream television landscape in the United States. For instance, *Ugly Betty* and *Jane the Virgin* have been extremely successful in their reinterpretation of the telenovela genre, their role as cultural translators, and their willingness to engage with issues having to do with the dignity and complexity of undocumented immigration.[59] According to Courtney Brannon Donoghue, the global popularity of the *Ugly Betty* "franchise [and its] adaptation in the US illustrates how the telenovela format is a fluid and flexible product with the ability to incorporate the complicated history of national border crossing, immigration and the Latino experience within the United States."[60] Although the cultural flexibility of the telenovela genre does not automatically produce a successful cultural translation, as was the case with some telenovela adaptations in other parts of the world, Spanish-language telenovela stories have proven to be profitable television commodities with the power to attract millions of viewers. Hence, the adoption of a telenovela-style narrative by *Jane the Virgin* is an attempt to also tap into bilingual Latino audiences that have historically tuned into telenovelas, the highest-rated programs on Spanish-language television in the United States.

The well-established transnational flow of telenovelas from Mexico, Venezuela, Brazil, and Colombia into US Spanish-language television, and thus the US cultural imaginary, have also impacted the awareness and acknowledgment of the telenovela genre as a legitimate televisual form. It is true that most people associate telenovelas as representing over-the-top drama and dramatic themes relating to sex, violence, family secrets, business backstabbing, community intrigue, and at times humor to name a few, telenovela as a term has also become increasingly accepted as a term connoting (zany) drama.[61] Interestingly, recent mainstream English-language magazine and newspaper stories have used the term to signify high drama at a high school, workplace, and government agency. It is indeed fascinating that the word "telenovela" is now becoming part of the English vernacular. Increasingly, people refer to the term "telenovela" rather than "soap opera" when describing a complicated and outlandish situation in their lives. Thus, as telenovelas continue to flow transnationally on Spanish-language television and abroad, there will be continued attempts to adopt the telenovela genre to US mainstream television because it is such a globally recognized genre.

The success of telenovelas has also inspired global television, and many telenovela products have been reinvented for television landscapes across the world such as Korea, Italy, Israel, and Ghana. Scholars have noted in multiple studies how telenovelas have impacted television production on an international scale, especially since it has proven to be successful in its inclusion of pro-social messaging and educational entertainment. In a study of Mexican telenovelas, Julee Tate found that telenovelas with pro-social messages against homophobia and intolerance were in fact successful productions that raised awareness and promoted open-minded behaviors toward same-sex relationships.[62] Similarly, the film documentary *Novela, Novela* (2004)—which highlighted a youth oriented telenovela from Nicaragua that discussed sexual orientation, domestic violence, and educational access—noted that this feminist-inspired telenovela was extremely successful in incorporating pro-social messages, providing informational resources for seeking help, and budging the entrenched negative attitudes toward queer identities.

Although it is important to acknowledge the limitations of telenovelas, and their use as commodities circulating in a global capitalist pop culture, we cannot lose sight of the fact that popular telenovelas are redubbed and rebroadcast internationally, and many national television industries have adopted and expanded upon the styles and techniques to produce their own homegrown telenovela-influenced TV programs. Some of these programs are progressive adaptations, while others are not.[63] Ultimately, Latinx scholars have pointed to a variety of ways in which the telenovela genre has mediated diaporic translatinidades and altered the televisual engagement of Latino and non-Latino audiences alike worldwide.[64] Quite possibly we will continue witnessing the telenovelizing of television, especially mainstream English-language television as traditional sitcom structures evolve to include telenovela narratives and styles and online media platforms become spaces for such experimentation and increased access.

## CONCLUSION

There is no doubt television occupies an important cultural, political, and economic space in both the material and scholarly worlds. Latinx scholars have engaged with the technology, practices, and policies surrounding television and have developed a wealth of research that points to the persuasive and pervasive power of a communications medium that is now evolving faster than ever. In actuality, television is profoundly changing due to the rise of digital technologies and the proliferation of media access. Consequently, the most productive intersection between Latinx representation and television will occur in this era of digitalization.[65] We are currently witnessing some successes of Latinx-influenced television programs through streaming services (such as *Vida* and *Mozart in the Jungle*), as well as locally produced public television and YouTube-distributed programs that vault Latinx images, issues, and voices into a globalized communications sphere no longer limited by the mainstream broadcast airwaves. The Latino-themed bilingual program *Presencia* on WGBY in Springfield, Massachusetts, for instance, is watched more through its video-on-demand platform than through the airwaves, and the program recently won a public-TV award for its treatment of Latino history and the community's diversity in western New England in the past two years. In some ways, increasing Latinos' access to the television industry may be one way of alleviating the distortions often generated about these communities.

The same holds true for US Spanish-language television where racial, gender, and LGBTQ representation haven been historically underrepresented and at times demeaned. Those voices are slowly making their way into the bilingual broadcasting world, yet there is still more work to be done in this area as well. Nonetheless, the emergence of online venues for cultural and social expression has provided opportunities for challenging the invisibility of Latinx people that currently exists in traditional televised spaces. From bloggers to meme creators to cultural critics discussing, for example, what it means to be a Latinx "undocuqueer," these digital platforms have made available an audiovisual venue that calls into question the traditional television structures of content creation, programming prioritization, and audience procurement. The rise of streaming technologies has opened the possibilities of Latinx representation on the televisual sphere, which is critical given the seemingly anti-Latino rhetoric that currently dominates the broadcast news. Spanish-language television has also become an important venue for challenging the xenophobic treatment of Latinos that have historically permeated mainstream English-language television. The telenovelizing of television has also emerged as a notable shift that Latinx scholars have pointed to as an abiding cultural force. Lastly, Latinx labor in television production is rarely acknowledged, and yet Latina workers in particular have been essential in the manufacturing of traditional and digital television sets and consumer electronics. This chapter attempted to document such Latinx labor as well as how the topics of representation, streaming platforms, Spanish-language TV, and telenovelas have deeply influenced television's impact on

Latinx communities. As the demographics in the United States shift toward an increasingly larger Latino population, it will be more important than ever to conduct scholarly investigations of the televisual landscape and its relationship with diasporic Latinidades well into the future.

## Notes

1. Dana E. Mastro and Elizabeth Behm-Morawitz, "Latino Representation on Primetime Television," *Journalism & Mass Communication Quarterly* 82, no. 1 (2005): 110–130; Mari Castañeda, Martha Fuentes-Bautista, and Felicitas Baruch, "Racial and Ethnic Inclusion in the Digital Era: Shifting Discourses in Communications Public Policy," *Journal of Social Issues* 71, no. 1 (2015): 139–154.
2. Federico A. Subervi-Vélez, "The Mass Media and Latinos: Policy and Research Agendas for the Next Century," *Aztlan: A Journal of Chicano Studies* 24, no. 2 (1999): 131–147.
3. Eileen Diaz McConnell, "An 'Incredible Number of Latinos and Asians:' Media Representations of Racial and Ethnic Population Change in Atlanta, Georgia," *Latino Studies* 9, nos. 2–3 (2011): 177–197.
4. Stacy L. Smith, Marc Choueiti, and Katherine Pieper, *Comprehensive Annenberg Report on Diversity in Entertainment* (Los Angeles: Institute for Diversity and Empowerment at Annenberg, USC, 2016); UCLA, *Hollywood Diversity Report: Business as Usual?* (Los Angeles: Bunche Center for African American Studies, UCLA, 2016).
5. Mari Castañeda, "¡Adelante! Advancing Social Justice Through Latina/o Community Media," in *Media and Social Justice*, ed. J. Pooley, S. C. Jansen, and L. Taub (New York: Palgrave Macmillan, 2011), 115–127.
6. Dan Schiller, *Digital Depression: Information Technology and Economic Crisis* (Urbana-Champaign: University of Illinois Press, 2014).
7. Claudia Anguiano and Mari Castañeda, "Forging a Path: Past and Present Scope of Critical Race Theory and Latina/o Critical Race Theory in Communication Studies," *Review of Communication* 14, no. 2 (2014): 107–124.
8. Tara J. Yosso, "Critical Race Media Literacy: Challenging Deficit Discourse about Chicanas/os," *Journal of Popular Film and Television* 30 no. 1 (2002): 52–62.
9. Adriana Olivarez, "Studying Representations of US Latino Culture," *Journal of Communication Inquiry* 22, no. 4 (1998): 426–437.
10. Leo Chavez, *The Latino Threat: Constructing Immigrants, Citizens, and the Nation* (Stanford, CA: Stanford University Press, 2013).
11. Felix F. Gutierrez and Jorge Reina Schement, "Spanish International Network: The Flow of Television from Mexico to the United States," *Communication Research* 11, no. 2 (1984): 241–258.
12. Chon Noriega, "El Hilo Latino: Representation, Identity and National Culture," *Jump Cut* 38 (1993): 45–50.
13. América Rodriguez, *Making Latino News: Race, Language, Class* (Los Angeles: SAGE, 1999).
14. Manuel J. Casas and Ana P. Cabrera, "Latina/o Immigration: Actions and Outcomes Based on Perceptions and Emotions or Facts?" *Hispanic Journal of Behavioral Sciences* 33, no. 3 (2011): 282–303.

15. Elvia R. Arriola, "Voices from the Barbed Wires of Despair: Women in the Maquiladoras, Latina Critical Legal Theory, and Gender at the US-Mexico Border," *DePaul Law Review* 49 (1999): 729–816.
16. Maura I. Toro-Morn, "Beyond Gender Dichotomies: Toward a New Century of Gendered Scholarship in the Latina/o Experience," in *Latinas/os in the United States: Changing the Face of America*, ed. H. Rodríguez, R. Sáenz, and C. Menjívar (Boston: Springer, 2008), 277–293.
17. Mary Beltrán, "The Hollywood Latina Body as Site of Social Struggle: Media Constructions of Stardom and Jennifer Lopez's Cross-over Butt," *Quarterly Review of Film and Video* 19, no. 1 (2002): 71–86.
18. Otto Santa Ana, *Brown Tide Rising: Metaphors of Latinos in Contemporary American Public Discourse* (Austin: University of Texas Press, 2002).
19. Mari Castañeda, "La lucha sigue: Latina and Latino Labor in the US Media Industries," *Kalfou* 1, no. 2 (2015): 203–220.
20. Mastro and Behm-Morawitz, "Latino Representation on Primetime Television," 110–130.
21. Vicki Mayer, "From Segmented to Fragmented: Latino Media in San Antonio, Texas," *Journalism & Mass Communication Quarterly* 78, no. 2 (2001): 291–306.
22. David Manuel Hernández, "Pursuant to Deportation: Latinos and Immigrant Detention," *Latino Studies* 6, no. 1 (2008): 35–63.
23. Ediberto Roman, "Who Exactly Is Living *la vida loca*: The Legal and Political Consequences of Latino-Latina Ethnic and Racial Stereotypes in Film and Other Media," *Journal of Gender, Race & Justice* 4 (2000): 37–68.
24. Mari Castañeda, "The Importance of Spanish-language and Latino Media," in *Latina/o Communication Studies Today*, ed. A. Valdivia (New York: Peter Lang, 2008), 51–68.
25. Adalberto Aguirre, "Arizona's SB1070, Latino Immigrants and the Framing of Anti-Immigrant Policies," *Latino Studies* 10, no. 3 (2012): 385–394.
26. Rocío L. Rivadeneyra, Monique Ward, and Maya Gordon, "Distorted Reflections: Media Exposure and Latino Adolescents' Conceptions of Self," *Media Psychology* 9, no. 2 (2007): 261–290; Hayley Dohnt and Marika Tiggemann, "The Contribution of Peer and Media Influences to the Development of Body Satisfaction and Self-Esteem in Young Girls: A Prospective Study," *Developmental Psychology* 42, no. 5 (2006): 929–936; Bradley S. Greenberg and Dana E. Mastro, "Children, Race, Ethnicity, and Media," in *The Handbook of Children, Media, and Development*, ed. S.L. Calvert and B.J. Wilson (Malden, MA: Wiley-Blackwell, 2008), 98–120.
27. Ibid.
28. Rocío Rivadeneyra and L. Monique Ward, "From Ally McBeal to Sábado Gigante: Contributions of Television Viewing to the Gender Role Attitudes of Latino Adolescents," *Journal of Adolescent Research* 20, no. 4 (2005): 453–475.
29. Franklin D. Gilliam Jr. and Shanto Iyengar, "Prime Suspects: The Influence of Local Television News on the Viewing Public," *American Journal of Political Science* 44, no. 3 (2000): 560–573.
30. Xae Alicia Reyes and Diana I. Rios. "Imaging Teachers: In Fact and in the Mass Media," *Journal of Latinos and Education* 2, no. 1 (2003): 3–11.
31. Felix F. Gutierrez, *Latinos and the Media in the United States: An Overview*. Report to the US Department of Health (Washington, DC: US Department of Health, 1980), 7.
32. Jennifer L. Willis, "'Latino Night': Performances of Latina/o Culture in Northwest Ohio," *Communication Quaterly* 45, no. 3 (1997): 335–354.

33. Jack Levin and Jack MacDevitt, *Hate Crimes: The Rising Tide of Bigotry and Bloodshed* (New York: Plenum, 2013).
34. Fredrick Aldama, ed., *Latinos and Narrative Media: Participation and Portrayal* (New York: Palgrave Macmillan, 2013).
35. Kevin R. Johnson and Joanna E. Cuevas Ingram, "Anatomy of a Modern-Day Lynching: The Relationship Between Hate Crimes Against Latina/os and the Debate over Immigration Reform," *North Carolina Law Review* 91 (2012): 1613–1656.
36. Jennings Bryant and Mary Beth Oliver, *Media Effects: Advances in Theory and Research* (New York: Routledge, 2009).
37. George Gerbner et al., "Growing up with Television: Cultivation Processes," in *Media Effects: Advances in Theory and Research*, 2nd ed., B. Jennings and D. Zillman, eds. (London: Lawrence Erlbaum, 2002), 43–68.
38. Rose M. Kundanis, *Children, Teens, Families, and Mass Media: The Millennial Generation* (New York: Routledge, 2003).
39. Castañeda, "La lucha sigue: Latina and Latino Labor in the US Media Industries," 203–220.
40. Arlene Dávila, *Latino Spin: Public Image and the Whitewashing of Race* (New York: NYU Press, 2008), 5.
41. Noriega, "El Hilo Latino," 45–50.
42. Arlene Dávila and Yeidy M. Rivero, eds. *Contemporary Latina/o Media: Production, Circulation, Politics* (New York: NYU Press, 2014).
43. Vittorio Rodriguez and Mary Beltrán, "From the Bronze Screen to the Computer," in *The Routledge Companion to Latina/o Media*, M.E. Cepeda and D.I. Casillas, eds. (New York: Routledge, 2017), 156–170.
44. Rodriguez and Beltrán, "From the Bronze Screen to the Computer," 156–170.
45. Hector Amaya, "Citizenship, Diversity, Law and Ugly Betty," *Media, Culture & Society* 32 no. 5 (2010): 801–817.
46. Frances Negrón-Muntaner, *The Latino Media Gap*, The Center for the Study of Ethnicity and Race, Columbia University. http://www.columbia.edu/cu/cser/downloads/AdvancedExectutiveSummary.pdf. 2014.
47. Ibid., 6.
48. Jose Luis Benitez, "Transnational Dimensions of the Digital Divide Among Salvadoran Immigrants in the Washington DC Metropolitan Area," *Global Networks* 6, no. 2 (2006): 181–199; Viviana Rojas et al., "Communities, Cultural Capital and Digital Inclusion: Ten Years of Tracking Techno-Dispositions and Techno-Capital," in *Inequity in the Technopolis: Race, Class, Gender, and the Digital Divide in Austin*, J. Straubhaar, J. Spence, Z. Tufekci, and R.G. Lentz, eds. (Austin: University of Texas Press, 2012), 223–264.
49. Kenton T. Wilkinson, "Collective Situational Ethnicity and Latino Subgroups' Struggle for Influence in U.S. Spanish-language Television," *Communication Quarterly* 50, nos. 3–4 (2002): 422–443.
50. Jillian Báez and Mari Castañeda, "Two Sides of the Same Story: Media Narratives of Latinos and the Subprtime Mortgage Crisis," *Critical Studies in Media Communication* 31, no. 1 (2014): 27–41.
51. G. Cristina Mora, *Making Hispanics: How Activists, Bureaucrats, and Media Constructed a New American* (Chicago: University of Chicago Press, 2014).
52. Alan Albarran, *The Handbook of Spanish Language Media* (New York: Routledge, 2009).
53. Veronica Zavala, *Venimos a Triunfar! A Discourse Analysis of Spanish Language Radio Piolín por la Mañana* (PhD diss., University of California, Santa Barbara, 2013).

54. Ronald Bishop, "An Unimaginable Combination: Journalists React to the Jorge Ramos-Donald Trump Confrontation," *International Journal of Hispanic Media* 8, no. 38 (2015): 122–140.
55. Regina Branton and Johanna Dunaway, "English-and Spanish-Language Media Coverage of Immigration: A Comparative Analysis," *Social Science Quarterly* 89, no. 4 (2008): 1006–1022; Kristin C. Moran, "Is Changing the Language Enough? The Spanish-Language 'Alternative' in the USA," *Journalism* 7 no. 3 (2006): 389–405; and Rodriguez, *Making Latino News*.
56. Yann P. Kerevel, "The Influence of Spanish-Language Media on Latino Public Opinion and Group Consciousness," *Social Science Quarterly* 92, no. 2 (2011): 509–534.
57. Teresa Correa, "Framing Latinas: Hispanic Women Through the Lenses of Spanish-Language and English-Language News Media," *Journalism* 11, no. 4 (2010): 425–443.
58. Marisa Abrajano, "Are Blacks and Latinos Responsible for the Passage of Proposition 8? Analyzing Voter Attitudes on California's Proposal to Ban Same-Sex Marriage in 2008," *Political Research Quarterly* 63, no. 4 (2010): 922–932.
59. Juan Piñón, "*Ugly Betty* and the Emergence of the Latina/o Producers as Cultural Translators," *Communication Theory* 21, no. 4 (2011): 392–412.
60. Courtney Brannon Donoghue, "Importing and Translating Betty: Contemporary Telenovela Format Flow within the Unites States Television Industry," in *Soap Operas and Telenovelas in the Digital Age: Global Industries and New Audiences*, Diana I. A. Ríos and Mari Castañeda, eds. (New York: Peter Lang, 2011), 271–283.
61. Kristin C. Moran, "Beyond the Market" in *The Routledge Companion to Latina/o Media*, M.E. Cepeda and D.I. Casillas, eds. (New York: Routledge, 2017), 88–102.
62. Julee Tate, "Laughing All the Way to Tolerance? Mexican Comedic Telenovelas as Vehicles for Lessons Against Homophobia," *The Latin Americanist* 58, no. 3 (2014): 51–65.
63. Mari Castañeda, "¡Adelante! Advancing Social Justice Through Latina/o Community Media," in *Media and Social Justice*, ed. J. Pooley, S. C. Jansen, and L. Taub (New York: Palgrave Macmillan, 2011), 115–127.
64. Ilan Stavans, ed., *Telenovelas* (Santa Barbara, CA: Greenwood, 2010).
65. Mari Castañeda, Martha Fuentes-Bautista, and Felicitas Baruch, "Racial and Ethnic Inclusion in the Digital Era: Shifting Discourses in Communications Public Policy," *Journal of Social Issues* 71, no. 1 (2015): 139–154.

## Bibliography

Aguirre, Adalberto. "Arizona's SB1070, Latino Immigrants and the Framing of Anti-Immigrant Policies." *Latino Studies* 10, no. 3 (2012): 385–394.

Albarran, Alan. *The Handbook of Spanish Language Media*. New York: Routledge, 2009.

Aldama, Fredrick, ed. *Latinos and Narrative Media: Participation and Portrayal*. New York: Palgrave Macmillan, 2013.

Anguiano, Claudia, and Mari Castañeda. "Forging a Path: Past and Present Scope of Critical Race Theory and Latina/o Critical Race Theory in Communication Studies." *Review of Communication* 14, no. 2 (2014): 107–124.

Báez, Jillian, and Castañeda, Mari. "Two Sides of the Same Story: Media Narratives of Latinos and the Subprtime Mortgage Crisis." *Critical Studies in Media Communication* 31, no. 1 (2014): 27–41.

Beltrán, Mary. "The Hollywood Latina Body as Site of Social Struggle: Media Constructions of Stardom and Jennifer Lopez's Cross-over Butt." *Quarterly Review of Film and Video* 19, no. 1 (2002): 71–86.

Beltrán, Mary. "Latina/os on TV!: A Proud (and Ongoing) Struggle over Representation and Authorship." In *The Routledge Companion to Latina/o Popular Culture*, edited by Frederick L. Aldama, 23–33. New York: Routledge, 2016.

Branton, Regina, and Johanna Dunaway. "English-and Spanish-Language Media Coverage of Immigration: A Comparative Analysis." *Social Science Quarterly* 89, no. 4 (2008): 1006–1022.

Brayton, Sean. "Mexican Labor in the Hollywood Imaginary." *International Journal of Cultural Studies* 11, no. 4 (2008): 459–476.

Castañeda, Mari. "The Importance of Spanish-language and Latino Media." In *Latina/o Communication Studies Today*, edited by Angarhard Valdivia, 51–68. New York: Peter Lang, 2008.

Castañeda, Mari. "¡Adelante! Advancing Social Justice Through Latina/o Community Media." In *Media and Social Justice*, edited by Jefferson Pooley, Sue Curry Jansen, and Lora Taub, 115–127. New York: Palgrave Macmillan, 2011.

Castañeda, Mari. "La lucha sigue: Latina and Latino Labor in the US Media Industries." *Kalfou* 1, no. 2 (2015): 203–220.

Castañeda, Mari, Martha Fuentes-Bautista, and Felicitas Baruch. "Racial and Ethnic Inclusion in the Digital Era: Shifting Discourses in Communications Public Policy." *Journal of Social Issues*, 71, no.1 (2015): 139–154.

Chavez, Leo. *The Latino Threat: Constructing Immigrants, Citizens, and the Nation*. Stanford, CA: Stanford University Press, 2013.

Correa, Teresa. "Framing Latinas: Hispanic Women Through the Lenses of Spanish-Language and English-language News Media." *Journalism* 11, no. 4 (2010): 425–443.

Dávila, Arlene M. *Latinos, Inc: The Marketing and Making of a People*. Berkeley: University of California Press, 2001.

Dávila, Arlene. *Latino Spin: Public Image and the Whitewashing of Race*. New York: New York University Press, 2008.

Dávila, Arlene, and Yeidy M. Rivero, eds. *Contemporary Latina/o Media: Production, Circulation, Politics*. New York: New York University Press, 2014.

Dixon, Travis Lemar, and Daniel Linz. "Overrepresentation and Underrepresentation of African Americans and Latinos as Lawbreakers on Television News." *Journal of Communication* 50, no. 2 (2000): 131–154.

Donoghue, Courtney Brannon. "Importing and translating Betty: Contemporary telenovela format flow within the Unites States television industry." In *Soap Operas and Telenovelas in the Digital Age: Global Industries and New Audiences*, edited by Diana I. A. Ríos and Mari Castañeda, 271–283. New York: Peter Lang, 2011.

Gutierrez, Felix F. *Latinos and the Media in the United States: An Overview*. Report. Washington, DC: US Department of Health, 1980.

Hamann, Edmund T., and Jenelle Reeves. "CE Raids, Children, Media, and Making Sense of Latino Newcomers in Flyover Country." *Anthropology & Education Quarterly* 43, no. 1 (2012): 24–40.

Hernández, David Manuel. "Pursuant to Deportation: Latinos and Immigrant Detention." *Latino Studies* 6, no. 1 (2008): 35–63.

Johnson, Kevin R., and Joanna E. Cuevas Ingram. "Anatomy of a Modern-Day Lynching: The Relationship Between Hate Crimes Against Latina/os and the Debate over Immigration Reform." *North Carolina Law Review* 91 (2012): 1613–1656.

Kerevel, Yann P. "The Influence of Spanish-Language Media on Latino Public Opinion and Group Consciousness." *Social Science Quarterly* 92, no. 2 (2011): 509–534.

Olivarez, Adriana. "Studying Representations of US Latino Culture." *Journal of Communication Inquiry* 22 no. 4 (1998): 426–437.

Mastro, Dana E., and Elizabeth Behm-Morawitz. "Latino Representation on Primetime Television." *Journalism & Mass Communication Quarterly* 82. no. 1 (2005): 110–130.

Mayer, Vicki. "From Segmented to Fragmented: Latino Media in San Antonio, Texas." *Journalism & Mass Communication Quarterly* 78, no. 2 (2001): 291–306.

McConnell, Eileen Diaz. "An 'Incredible Number of Latinos and Asians:' Media Representations of Racial and Ethnic Population Change in Atlanta, Georgia." *Latino Studies* 9, no. 2–3 (2011): 177–197.

Molina-Guzmán, Isabel. "# OscarsSoWhite: how Stuart Hall Explains Why Nothing Changes in Hollywood and Everything is Changing." *Critical Studies in Media Communication* 33, no. 5 (2016): 438–454.

Mora, G. Cristina. *Making Hispanics: How Activists, Bureaucrats, and Media Constructed a New American*. Chicago: University of Chicago Press, 2014.

Moran, Kristin C. "Beyond the Market." In *The Routledge Companion to Latina/o Media*, edited by María Elena Cepeda and Dolores Inés Casillas, 88–102. New York: Routledge, 2017.

Negrón-Muntaner, Frances. *The Latino Media Gap*. The Center for the Study of Ethnicity and Race, Columbia University. http://www.columbia.edu/cu/cser/downloads/AdvancedExectutiveSummary.pdf (2014).

Noriega, Chon. "El hilo Latino: Representation, Identity and National Culture." *Jump Cut* 38 (1993): 45–50.

Piñón, Juan. "Ugly Betty and the Emergence of the Latina/o Producers as Cultural Translators." *Communication Theory* 21, no. 4 (2011): 392–412.

Retis, Jessica. "The Portrayal of Latin American Immigrants in the Spanish Mainstream Media: Fear of Compassion." *The International Journal of Hispanic Media* 9, no. 1 (2016): 32–45.

Rivadeneyra, Rocío, L. Monique Ward, and Maya Gordon. "Distorted Reflections: Media Exposure and Latino Adolescents' Conceptions of Self." *Media Psychology*, no. 2 (2007): 261–290.

Rodriguez, América. *Making Latino News: Race, Language, Class*. Los Angeles: SAGE, 1999.

Rodriguez, Vittoria, and Mary Beltrán. "From the Bronze Screen to the Computer." In *The Routledge Companion to Latina/o Media*, edited by María Elena Cepeda and Dolores Inés Casillas, 156–170. New York: Routledge, 2017.

Rojas, Viviana, et al. "Communities, Cultural Capital and Digital Inclusion: Ten Years of Tracking Techno-Dispositions and Techno-Capital." In *Inequity in the Technopolis Race, Class, Gender, and the Digital Divide in Austin*, edited by Joseph Straubhaar, Jeremiah Spence, Zeynep Tufekci, and Roberta G. Lentz, 223–264. Austin: University of Texas Press, 2012.

Roman, Ediberto. "Who Exactly is Living *la vida loca*: The Legal and Political Consequences of Latino-Latina Ethnic and Racial Stereotypes in Film and other Media." *Journal of Gender, Race & Justice* 4 (2000): 37–68.

Santa Ana, Otto. *Brown Tide Rising: Metaphors of Latinos in Contemporary American Public Discourse*. Austin: University of Texas Press, 2002.

Smith, Stacy L., Marc Choueiti, and Katherine Pieper. *Comprehensive Annenberg Report on diversity in entertainment*. Institute for Diversity and Empowerment at Annenberg (IDEA), USC: Los Angeles, CA, 2016.

Stavans, Ilan, ed. *Telenovelas*. Santa Barbara, CA: Greenwood, 2010.

Tate, Julee. "Laughing All the Way to Tolerance? Mexican Comedic Telenovelas as Vehicles for Lessons Against Homophobia." *The Latin Americanist* 58, no. 3 (2014): 51–65.

Treviño, Jesús Salvador. "Latino Portrayals in Film and Television." *Jump Cut* 30 (1985): 14–16.

Willis, Jennifer L. "'Latino Night': Performances of Latina/o Culture in Northwest Ohio." *Communication Quaterly* 45, no. 3 (1997): 335–354.

Yosso, Tara J. "Critical Race Media Literacy: Challenging Deficit Discourse about Chicanas/os." *Journal of Popular Film and Television* 30, no. 1 (2002): 52–62.

Zavala, Veronica. *Venimos a Triunfar! A Discourse Analysis of Spanish Language Radio Piolín por la Mañana*. PhD diss., University of California, Santa Barbara, 2013.

CHAPTER 22

# LATINO/AS AND SPORTS

## JORGE IBER

In the late 1990s, the publication of Samuel O. Regalado's *Viva Baseball: Latinos and Their Special Hunger* and Mario Longoria's *Athletes Remembered: Chicano/Latino Professional Football Players, 1929–1970* provided some of the first opportunities to examine critically the extensive and socially significant history of the participation of Spanish-surnamed athletes in the United States's two principal sports and professional leagues: Major League Baseball (MLB) and the National Football League (NFL).[1] These two publications supplied the impetus for other writers, both academic and popular, to pursue supplementary avenues of research into this understudied but important topic. For example, it is essential to consider the academic studies of Adrian Burgos and Jose Alamillo, among others. A recent introductory effort to capture the totality of the impact of Latino/as' historical presence in American sport appeared in 2011 with the publication of *Latinos in U.S. Sports: A History of Isolation, Cultural Identity, and Acceptance*.[2] On the more popular side of the equation, readers should look to the contributions of writers such as David Maraniss, Bruce Markusen, and Tim Wendel, among others.[3] Much of the historical ground that will be discussed briefly in various subsections of this essay draws from such authors.

Of course, the "traditional" sports in the United States, and the role of Latino/as in them, will be considered. Thus, there will be individual categories focused on the sports of baseball, football, basketball, softball, soccer/*futbol*, boxing, hockey, tennis, and others. The numerous competitive levels of the various games will be examined; as some work has been done (though much more is needed) over the past decade on how *atletas* played sports not just at the professional level but also in their local communities and educational institutions.[4] What did these games, teams, and players mean to their "people's" struggles/daily existence as well as to the broader society? Given the demographic and geographic changes that have been taking place in the United States over the past few decades, these are not inconsequential inquiries.

While a not unsubstantial amount of historical research has been done, it is also important to move the conversation forward by focusing on areas that are just now becoming significant aspects of the participation of Latino/as in American athletics (both on the field and in the business sense of the undertaking). For example, how are those with Spanish surnames, who are increasingly present in "non-traditional" areas, interacting with (and even changing) the sporting scene in locales from the Deep South to the Midwest? How are Latinos being targeted for their dollars by leagues, collegiate athletic programs, and consumer product advertisers tied to watching American sports? Given the burgeoning of this population, why are Latino/as still severely underrepresented on the playing fields of America's largest academic institutions of higher learning? Finally, as more and more individuals of Spanish-speaking backgrounds intermarry/intermingle with "whites" or African Americans, how does the surrounding society react to individual players (e.g., the recent hullabaloo caused by Marcus Stroman's decision to play for the United States [and not the Puerto Rican team] in the World Baseball Classic) who are "part" Latino/a, yet do not have Spanish surnames? All of these topics will be addressed.

## Overview

An appropriate way to commence this essay is to present a brief overview of how the athletic and related intellectual capabilities (or lack thereof) of persons of Latino background were perceived by many in the broader American society. An appropriate place to start is with the 1920s works of Elmer Mitchell, a scholar of physical education, an early proponent of intramural sports, and a coach at major collegiate institutions in Michigan. Here was an academician who drew attention to the dispositional and physical "deficiencies" of this population. Of the fifteen "races" discussed in three essays from that year, the persons we would today call Latino/as (which he referred to as "South Americans") were portrayed degradingly as being thoroughly "undisciplined" and not having the proper "physique," "environment," and "disposition" to be successful in modern American sporting competition. In brief, they did not have what it took to become "champion" athletes. Mitchell summarized his "groundbreaking" research by noting that "the Indian in him chafes at discipline and sustained effort, while the Spanish side is proud to a fault {and thus his} disposition makes team play difficult."[5]

With regard to the intellectual competencies, works from the early decades of the 1900s provide similar arguments. For example, the works of Lewis Terman, primarily focused on persons of Mexican ancestry, argued that students of this background must be "segregated in special classes and be given instruction which is concrete and practical." His overall assessment was that such persons "cannot master abstractions, but they can be made efficient workers" and that overall "their dullness seems to be racial, or at least inherent in the family stock from which they come."[6] Thus, many in the larger society believed, given this poor genetic material, little could be expected in terms of athletic ability and strategic aptitude necessary in order to participate in the "complex" sports popular in contemporary American society.

As historians and authors have shown, this was not the case. In reality, Latino/as have always embraced American sports and have used them to create unity in their community, to bring honor and recognition to local schools, to reach out to other ethnics in friendly competition, and to claim a share of societal space. We now turn to individual sports, starting with the American game that has attracted the largest and widest following among Latinos, the "national pastime" of baseball.

## Baseball

By this stage of the historiographical game the stories of important individual ballplayers, most significantly Roberto Clemente, have been examined. There are other works that deal with more obscure individuals who nevertheless have historical significance. Among recent works in this area are studies on the life and times of Al Lopez, Armando Marsans, Tony Oliva, and minor leaguer Leo Najo. All of these works provide glimpses into the various racial, ethnic, and social realities that surrounded these players' lives (Lopez was Spanish-Cuban from Florida, Marsans and Oliva were Cuban born, Najo was Mexican American). While the works noted are noteworthy, there are many other athletes in this sport with Spanish-speaking backgrounds who merit serious academic study. It is hoped that summaries such as this will inspire even more work in this field.[7]

The role that Latinos have played in the sport has been scrutinized (since Regalado's initial work) by important writers, with Adrian Burgos at the forefront. His works such as *Playing America's Game: Baseball, Latinos, and the Color Line* and *Cuban Star: How One Negro-League Owner Changed the Face of Baseball* are required reading for anyone pursuing serious study of this topic. These studies, along with Burgos's continuing efforts on the website La Vida Baseball provide not only a summary of action on the field and in the boardrooms of the Negro Leagues and MLB but also shed light on how players and management navigated the color line, racial insensitivity, and off-the-field language and cultural issues at the professional level.[8] For a further examination of racial and economic matters, and how these relate to Spanish speakers in the highest levels of baseball, it is also necessary to consult projects by Mark Kurlansky and Rob Ruck on the sport in the Caribbean.[9] Two works that provide broad coverage and are worth noting take us in very different directions: first, the history of Cuban baseball (the ambassadors of the sport among other Spanish speakers) is beautifully recounted in Roberto Gonzalez Echevarria's masterful *The Pride of Havana: A History of Cuban Baseball*; and second, a more tragic tale is presented concerning the treatment of Latino ballplayers in the academy system by Arturo J. Marcano Guevara and David P. Fidler in *Stealing Lives: The Globalization of Baseball and the Tragic Story of Alexis Quiroz*.[10] Another recent trend worth noting at the MLB level is the publication of several autobiographies (for a mass audience, not "youth editions") by individual athletes (usually upon their retirement). Among notable projects in this category are those by David Ortiz, Mariano Rivera, and

Jorge Posada. A more scholarly version of such biographical studies is a book on former MLB pitcher Mike Torrez by Jorge Iber.[11]

While an examination on how Latinos have fared at the highest echelons of baseball is critical to an overall understanding of this group's significant role in American sport, it is imperative to acknowledge that the game has as much (if not greater) significance to communities/*comunidades* at the local level. One of the most important contributions to an understanding of this history can be found in the dozen or so books compiled under the leadership of Richard Santillan over the past decade. The most recent effort focuses on the sport in El Paso, with others already in the pipeline. In alliance with the Baseball Reliquary (located in Monrovia, California), Santillan and various collaborators have collected hundreds of photographs that capture the story and significance of the sport to communities in myriad locales. While these are picture books, they provide a sense of the sport's importance to cultural sustenance/maintenance and civil rights struggles by Mexican Americans. Santillan is currently working with the Smithsonian Institution to create an exhibit in Washington DC, as well as a traveling display to help make even more photos, game equipment, and oral histories accessible to the general public.[12]

In addition to Santillan's efforts, there are other studies that deal with baseball in various locales: for example, Sam Regalado and Jose Alamillo have both produced wonderful essays that detail the role of baseball in community and cultural maintenance, as well as how the sport was used in efforts to attract membership to unions and civil-rights organizations in Southern California. After all, at this level the game is more than just recreational sport and a chance to enjoy a Sunday afternoon. A more recent endeavor along these lines is by John Fraire, who recounts the importance of baseball to his hometown of Indiana Harbor and its Mexican American community. Likewise, the *Sports Illustrated* article on the 1949 El Paso Bowie Bears state title baseball team (comprising mostly Mexican Americans) shows how playing the sport helped to challenge assumptions about physical and intellectual limitations widely held by the broader Texan society at that time. There are also some works that highlight the role of Mexican American women in playing both baseball and softball during the years shortly after World War II.[13]

While a substantial amount of spade work has been completed on the study of Latinos and baseball, there remains much to do. For example, to follow up on Wolff, it is significant to examine how baseball at the high school level in places such as El Paso, the Rio Grande Valley of Texas, parts of Florida, New Mexico, and elsewhere impacted the lives of Latinos. This endeavor remains virtually unexamined. A recent publication by Joel S. Franks, on the importance of (among other issues) high school sports among Asian Americans in the Santa Clara Valley, can serve as an excellent model in this regard.[14] What about the stories of early Latinos playing baseball at the collegiate level? The case of Rafael Palmeiro and his experiences at Mississippi State in the 1980s would be quite instructive. How did the folks in Starkville react to the arrival of a Cubano in their midst? There is virtually no substantial research being done in this particular area. Finally, what about the role of Latinas? With the presence of Jessica Mendoza on ESPN baseball broadcasts, it is necessary to recognize this historical connection as well. While Mendoza made her mark in softball, there is a bit of work on this topic—though more is certainly needed. For example, please see the chapter on Veronica Alvarez in Jennifer Ring's *A Game of Their Own: Voices of Contemporary Women in Baseball*.[15]

## FOOTBALL

Given that the sport of football began in America's most elite universities, it is not surprising to note that this endeavor took a bit longer to become popular among Latinos (especially those of lower social/economic standing). There are writers, however, who have examined how the sport spread to various other ethnic groups, such as the works of Gerald Gems on the proliferation of the game among Eastern and southern Europeans, as well as Native Americans; but Spanish speakers have been generally overlooked.[16] Although the sport was not unknown by the latter part of the nineteenth century among the those with Spanish surnames, it would take time to spread to places such as Texas (available information notes that the first game of football took place in Galveston in 1892, and high schools—in the most heavily Mexican American regions—were playing in El Paso by 1895 and Laredo and the Rio Grande Valley by the 1910s), California (high schools were playing by the late 1880s), and New Mexico (early 1900s) before we would begin to note the (miniscule) presence of athletes of this background.

Football did move on to the nations of Cuba and Mexico by the latter part of the nineteenth century, however. Michael Wood, currently teaching at the University of Alabama, documents the history of the sport on the island nation. Jorge Iber has contributed an article to an anthology entitled *Touchdown: An American Obsession* that builds upon Wood's work and presents a basic overview of the movement of the game into Mexico (and much later, to other parts of Central and South America). In both cases, the game remained the purview of the elites and middle class. Thus, the number of Cubans or Mexicans who came to the United States and played the sport was limited in the early decades of the 1900s.[17]

There have been studies that discuss the value of football as a tool to change the way that Latinos are perceived by the majority. Among these are essays by Douglas E. Foley and Mark A. Grey, as well as a master's thesis by Cesar Torrico. A brief way to summarize these endeavors is that the scholars see limitations in the power of sports to change how ethnics are viewed by the broader society. A more balanced discussion can be found in a dissertation by Rafael E. Romo, which seeks to provide clues as to the development of a support system so that more Latino (Mexican Americans in particular) football players can move on and succeed at the collegiate level. The fact that so few (percentage wise) are playing collegiate sports will be mentioned later. A recent article on collegiate football in Texas, however, does note that more Latinos are playing but at lower division schools such as Incarnate Word University in San Antonio.[18]

The most extensive general research done on the relationship between the gridiron and Latinos comes from the work of Mario Longoria (mentioned earlier). In his 1997 study, this author, in collaboration with the National Football Hall of Fame, the NFL, the

Canadian Football League, and various university athletic programs, compiled an impressive list of collegiate and professional athletes who played between the 1920s and the AFL-NFL merger of 1970. Longoria is currently working with Jorge Iber on a project designed to integrate research on high school athletes from Texas, New Mexico, California, Florida, and elsewhere into this overarching narrative. Additionally, the authors are working to update the collegiate and professional information.

At the local/regional level, a plethora of information can be found in the extensive research of Greg Selber in the Rio Grande Valley of Texas. Selber's book *Border Ball: The History of High School Football in the Rio Grande Valley* is an excellent example of the type of study that should be done in regard to other sports (such as the issue with baseball mentioned previously). Also worth noting is a dissertation by Joel Huerta entitled *Red, Brown and Blue: A History and Cultural Poetics of High School Football in Mexican America*, from the University of Texas and Jorge Iber's article on the only team from the valley to ever win a state title in football: the 1961 Donna Redskins.

While not specifically focused on football, a publication by Jose Angel Gutierrez on the Chicano Movement in Crystal City, Texas, does draw connections between this civil rights struggle and the game and pageantry surrounding the sport. There is also documentation of the development of a truly unique tradition in the Rio Grande Valley that examines the development of *corridos* for various high school football teams. These songs have been played for more than four decades and are part of a distinctively Mexican American football call-in show that broadcasts from McAllen. From California, there is a wonderful movie, *Symbol of Heart*, that details one of the most important (and predominantly Mexican American) football rivalries in the country: the yearly battle between the Garfield High Bulldogs and the Roosevelt High Roughriders (known as the East Los Angeles Classic). A similar story is told from a New Mexico perspective in *Cruces Divided: A Historical Football Rivalry*, which recounts the rivalry between the Las Cruces Bulldogs and the Mayfield Trojans.

During the time of the Chicano Movement, there is also an intriguing story that deals with a Latina who broke a barrier by playing football for a small high school in New Mexico. There is precious little that details the relationship between Latinas and this sport, though a recent story/video from ESPN notes how one young Mexican American woman helped save a football season by suiting up to play for a six-player team in the small town of Harrold, Texas. Finally, from a "regional/local" perspective, it is important to note that there are now a few works dealing with football players in "new" locales of Latino/a concentration, such as Iowa and Georgia. Please see articles by Wayne Drehs and Josiah Schlatter on these stories.[19]

There are a few autobiographical offerings on Spanish-surnamed athletes and coaches in this sport. For example, Tom Florez, Jim Plunkett, and Barry Alvarez (who is of Spanish descent) have all coauthored such books. Additionally, there are articles in the popular press on individual coaches such as Juan Castillo (currently with the Bills) and Ron Rivera (head coach of the Carolina Panthers). Probably the most significant effort in terms of an autobiography by a Mexicano football player comes from the writings of Dr. Jorge Prieto, who learned the game while his family lived in Southern California in the 1920s. He then went on to play college football in his homeland of Mexico. This work provides a unique perspective of the passion and importance of football on both sides of the border.[20]

The fervor that Latinos have for football is not only displayed on the field itself. There are many articles that discuss the relationship between such communities and teams. For example, a recent essay appearing in *Texas Monthly* described the enthusiastic support for the Dallas Cowboys among most Mexican Americans in the Rio Grande Valley. A similar discussion can be found (in both non-academic and academic writings) with regard to the Oakland/Los Angeles/Las Vegas Raiders. Surprisingly, there is not a similar study on the Miami Dolphins, although there are studies dealing with how the team's fans reacted to Colin Kaepernick's recent stint in the city. Not surprisingly, Dolphin linebacker and Cuban American Kiko Alonso spoke for many of his co-ethnics when the 49ers visited southern Florida during the 2016 campaign. Finally, there are many articles that have appeared in recent years dealing with marketing efforts by schools and professional teams to reach out to Latino fans, including works on the reborn Los Angeles Rams.[21] Perhaps the most significant contribution to the study of Latinos and football is found in the publication of Frederick Luis Aldama and Christopher Gonzalez's *Latinos in the End Zone: Conversations on the Brown Color Line in the NFL*. This work details the experiences of Latinos in both the NFL and CFL and deals with the question of why there are not more players of this ethnic background at the professional level. Finally, the work proffers in-depth interviews with legendary *jugadores* such as Joe Kapp, Jim Plunkett, and Tom Flores.[22]

## BASKETBALL

The story of basketball's ties with Spanish speakers begins shortly after the game's invention in 1891 as the YMCA began expanding into Latin America, with substantial information available about early hoop-related events in Mexico and Puerto Rico. Shortly after the commencement of operations in Mexico City in 1902, one YMCA official noted that "basketball and handball were introduced and immediately took root." One estimate was that by 1930 there were approximately forty thousand aficionados of the sport in Monterrey alone. In addition to international efforts, there were endeavors to present the game to Latino/as within the United States as well during the early decades of the 1900s. Thus, by the 1920s, there were established clubs and leagues in places such as Los Angeles and El Paso. On the island colony of Puerto Rico, the first YMCA opened in San Juan in 1913; and three years later, *boriquas* had established their own tournament and eventually the San Juan Basketball League. Among the authors who have written about this subject in this early era are Jose Alamillo, Manuel Bernardo Ramirez, and Glenn Avent.[23]

With regard to the game and Latino/as in the United States, we can look at the work of Christine Marin and Michael Innis-Jimenez, which explains to readers how the game impacted Spanish-surnamed athletes in both rural and urban settings. Marin's essay focuses on the story of the Miami (Arizona) basketball team, which had a substantial Mexican American component, and how it earned a national reputation as a scoring dynamo during the early 1950s. The team garnered much positive attention for the community as well as a statewide dominance. Further, Marin argues, the players recognized that their ability to succeed went well beyond the court, as several went on to get college degrees and became successful. Not only did the success of the Vandals challenge stereotypes about physical, cultural, and intellectual limitations, it also helped change the lives of many Mexican American families in this mining community. Likewise, Innis-Jimenez presents a story with many similarities but based in inner-city Chicago between the years of World War I and World War II. One interesting tidbit that this author discussed dealt with how playing basketball made it possible for many Mexican Americans to get out of their barrio, see other parts of their home city, and interact with competitors of other ethnic backgrounds.[24]

While there is nowhere near as much research on Latinos and basketball as on baseball and football, three recent studies do excellent work in connecting the sport with the civic and cultural existence of Mexicans and Mexican Americans. The first project is part of an anthology forthcoming from Texas Tech University Press and edited by Greg Selber. Beyond his work with Rio Grande Valley football, this scholar has also spent time documenting the history of hoops in this region. First, he published an overview of the history of the sport at what is now the University of Texas-Rio Grande Valley (for many years the institution went by University of Texas Pan American). There is much material therein that discusses the story of local Mexican Americans who played for the (then) Broncos (now the Vaqueros). Chief among these athletes is a legendary Texas hoopster named Jesus "Chuy" Guerra. Beyond his work with UTRGV, Selber has also documented the role of basketball in the lives of Texas Latinas. Here, he examines how and why many Spanish-surnamed women were not given the opportunity (for cultural and economic reasons) to participate and how that trend has changed over the past quarter century. This is indeed good news, as just a decade or so ago, there was an important article in *USA Today* that bemoaned the limited opportunities for Latinas to play basketball (as well as other sports) due to cultural and socioeconomic issues. Another contribution comes in the form of a dissertation by Bernardo Ramirez Rios entitled *Culture, Migration, and Sport: A Bi-National Investigation of Southern Mexican Migrant Communities in Oaxaca, Mexico and Los Angeles, California* wherein the author examines the importance of basketball in maintaining cultural traditions among Oaxacans north of the border, and how tournaments in southern California (and now, elsewhere) help to maintain a connection to families and traditions back in Mexico.[25]

A final but crucial book to consult with regard to US-based Spanish speakers and basketball is *When Mexicans Could Play Ball: Basketball, Race, and Identity in San Antonio, 1928–1945* by BYU professor Ignacio Garcia. This work is exemplary and captures the totality of what research on Latinos and sport should accomplish. It is an examination of a school (Lanier High), a barrio, the development of the sport in the community, the "place" of Mexican Americans in Texas education at that time, and (most significantly) how the success on the court of a group of Latinos (and a legendary coach of the same background) provided an impressive challenge to the assumptions of most in the majority population of the Lone Star state concerning the capabilities of the Spanish surnamed. If there is only one book consulted on this topic, this should be the one.[26]

## SOFTBALL

There are two distinct historical aspects of this sport that have connections to the Latino/a experience: that of young women playing the game, mostly at the high school and collegiate levels, and that of older men who have played the sport. Fortunately, there is research on both topics.

A good recent essay on how young women from such backgrounds are moving into the collegiate sport is by Andrea Canales of ESPN. In 1999 Katherine M. Jamieson, of Michigan State University, completed a dissertation that analyzed the presence of Latinas in collegiate softball. A few years later, she fleshed out some of her results in an article entitled "Advance at Your Own Risk: Latinas, Families, and Collegiate Softball" for an anthology. While discussing some of the action on the diamond, Jamieson's principal focus in both endeavors was to articulate why Latinas were often held back from playing the sport, how they had to navigate treacherous waters of (when going to college) leaving home and family, as well as entering into predominantly white (and often elite) institutions of higher learning. The discipline required to gain attention of a collegiate program was often not sufficient to overcome some of these other obstacles. Further, for those who succeeded on the field and in the classroom, there were still other matters to deal with. How did families and barrio dwellers deal with women who had gone against "the expected" (staying home, getting married, and beginning families) and gotten an education simply by "playing a game." All of these matters are of great consequence to current and future players (such as those mentioned in the Canales piece noted earlier). Certainly, as with the basketball players discussed in Selber's study, there has been progress made, but there are still critical roadblocks to Latina participation in softball (and other athletic endeavors) to be overcome. The works presented by Jamieson are informative touchstones that will help point the way to greater opportunities in the future.

As a final note in this section, it would seem reasonable to wonder why there has not been a study on the life, career, and significance of one of the greatest players of all time in this sport: the half-Cuban/half-Puerto Rican legend, Lisa Fernandez.[27]

The story of Latinas playing softball is significant, and we have documentation of such athletes playing the sport since the 1930s and 1940s. Likewise, there has been much research on the significance of the sport among (predominantly) Mexican American men, particularly in the postwar years. As noted by Jorge Iber in his book on former MLB pitcher Mike Torrez, not all of the diamond-based talent in that family played baseball. Mike's older brother, John (known as "Johnny-Boy"), is a living legend among those who are familiar with the history of softball in the Midwest. Thanks to the research of both Ben Chappell of the University of Kansas and regional scholar Gene Chavez, there are now extensive oral histories, articles, and collected materials that document this socially and athletically significant tale. In 2017, for example, the longest-running Mexican American softball tournament, based in Newton, Kansas, will celebrate its sixty-ninth anniversary. What began as a humble event to support the local Catholic parish has now become a major happening that attracts players from across the United States.

Another key element of the current format has been how to deal with the ethnic makeup of players. When Newton (and others) first started, they were exclusively "Mexican" in composition. Given demographic changes, should such tournaments retain this requirement? The answer, as discussed by Johnny Boy Torrez and Chappell, is a definite *no*. The Torrez clan, for example, in both "Mexican" softball and basketball tournaments has dealt with the fact that in their own clan there are athletes who are of Mexican descent but are not Spanish surnamed.[28]

## Soccer/*Futbol*

The historical trajectory of the relationship between Latino/as and *futbol* in the United States has been documented in various works. Among the authors who have examined this topic are Juan Javier Pescador and Jose Alamillo. These writers have noted the significance of the game to communities as varied as New York City, San Antonio, Los Angeles, and parts of the Midwest. One common element to be found among these clubs was a connection to Latino-based sporting associations and the bearing of team names that demonstrated national/ethnic pride. An example of this trend can be seen in the history of the Aztecas in Southern California during the 1930s, as well as Club Necaxa from Chicago in the 1940s. As Pescador argued, "Necaxa enabled a healthy competition to develop between Mexicans and ethnic Europeans... {and} played a prominent role in shaping recreational and social activities for people of Mexican descent in Chicago." Even more clubs appeared and became prominent participants in local leagues during the 1960s and 1970s. More recently, works have detailed the development of soccer leagues as a way to claim "space" in places such as Washington, DC; Garden City, Kansas; Kansas City, Missouri; Siler City, North Carolina; Portland, Oregon; and even in Birmingham, Alabama. Needless to say, wherever Latinos have gone, the beautiful game has moved with them.[29]

There is mention of Latinas and soccer in some of the works noted previously. For example, Quinones's book detailing Mexicano/Latino life in Garden City does discuss the development of a girls' squad at the local high school. Likewise, building upon his book on Siler City, Paul Cuadros has also authored a work that sheds light on how Latinas in the "new" South are utilizing the sport to claim greater autonomy for themselves, as well as seeking a recreational opportunity as a respite from their often stressful lives in meat/chicken processing plants and demanding home environments. Other efforts to document such stories can be found in a documentary by Maria Finitzo entitled *In the Game* about Latinas on a Chicago-area high school team, the difficulties confronted by cultural beliefs and economic circumstances, and articles on individual players such as two-time Olympic gold medalist Amy Rodriguez.[30]

A final area of discussion necessary in this subsection deals with some of the articles that have been generated to articulate how Major League Soccer (MLS) has, from its inception, sought out this particular demographic to support its endeavors. A recent essay on this topic is by Luis Miguel Echegaray. Here, the author interviews individuals associated with the Kansas City franchise and finds there has been a drastic change in attendance and interest in the club since the late 1990s as a result of targeting Latino/as specifically. Another important piece that details the relationship between the MLS and Spanish speakers from a negative perspective can be seen in an intriguing study by Ric Jensen and Jason Sosa entitled "The Importance of Building Positive Relationships Between Hispanic Audiences and Major League Soccer Franchises: A Case Study of Public Relations Challenges Facing Houston 1836." This essay discusses a franchise's move to the Bayou City and the results of neglecting the concerns of (mostly) Mexican/Mexican Americans in the potential fan base when naming a side. It is almost comical to encounter the naiveté of management "surprised" by the fact that individuals of this background would not be pleased with their local franchise being named after the year that Texas seceded from Mexico. The team was quickly rechristened "Dynamo," and it has been a successful addition to the league. Other authors who have written about this commercial/branding/marketing topic include Todd R. Jewell and David Molina, Emmanuel Ayim, Fernando Delgado, and Yara Simon.[31]

## Boxing

There are several authors who have examined the historical ties between Latino/as and the sport of boxing. Most of these works deal with the importance of the sport to the poor and as a mechanism for cultural retention. Among important contributors to this research are studies by Enrique Encinosa, Benita Heiskanen, Gregory S. Rodriguez, and Tom I. Romero. Two recent works deal with the significance of the career and death of Benny "Kid" Paret and the complex racial identity of Kid Chocolate, a black Cubano who was claimed by both African Americans and Latinos in New York during the early 1900s. Finally, a new book by Troy Rondinone on the life and career of Gaspar "Indio" Ortega discusses not only goings on in the ring but how this particular pugilist helped to improve the perception of Mexicanos among Americans during the heyday of the sport on television. There are also recent articles, both academic and popular, dealing with the presence of Latinas in the ring.[32]

Although boxing has had a long run as the "sport of the poor" in the United States, it has certainly lost substantial appeal, particularly with the "mainstream." For most of the twentieth century, pugilism was an important part of the lives of recent immigrants, and there have been times when African Americans (as well as fighters of other ethnic backgrounds) have dominated. This is certainly no longer the case. It is not an exaggeration to state that Latinos have been mostly responsible for maintaining the viability of the sport (particularly at the lower divisions). Since the 1990s, promoters have noted the Latino market's indispensability to boxing's economic survival.

The reliance is both a positive and a negative. It is of great benefit to have a major sport so focused on this market segment. For example, in the early twenty-first century the commentator Richard Hoffer asserted that "Hispanic immigration, which is now penetrating Kansas and Iowa and Michigan and lots of places east of the Mississippi, will have a far more profound impact on boxing than the waves of Jews and Irish and Filipinos that preceded it." However, other commentators have remarked on the extreme overdependence of boxing on this one group. If boxing cannot find athletes who can "cross over," the sport will become even less relevant. Does the Latino market have enough demand to sustain the sport of boxing, or is it doomed to fade?

Various essays provide further information on these trends. The two essays by Hoffer and Hoffer deal directly with the significant role of Latinos (primarily Mexicans) as a target audience for pay-per-view boxing sales. The author looks at how a substantial percentage of a typical pay-per-view audience consists of Latino consumers. A still more recent offering by Hoffer goes on to detail how Oscar De La Hoya has parlayed this love of boxing into an economic empire that includes promotion, publishing, and land development. Although De La Hoya's success can be seen as his achievement of the American Dream, his attempts to cross over into the broader market have cost him, generating consternation among some Latinos in academia as well as in the community at large, as noted in Delgado and Rodriguez. Finally, *Street and Smith's Sports Business Journal* features an interview with the chief executive officer of Golden Boy Promotions, Richard Schaefer, in which he indicates that although the sport is having difficulties reaching out to other groups, the increased demand for boxing among Latinos and for the attendant products advertised is still growing and will continue to do so for the foreseeable future.[33]

# Tennis, Hockey, and Other Sporting Endeavors

The limited writings on other sports include a few primers on track and field by Dyreson and Mendoza, a sport in which many Latinos (particularly Mexican Americans) have excelled since the 1930s. The majority of works discussed in this article cover the roles of Latinos and sport, with studies having been published on Latinas; although a recent article on Brenda Martinez perhaps shows the way toward more done in this area. A study on minor-league hockey by Boyd explained how Latinos were being courted by teams in "new" sports. While successful for a while, minor league franchises in heavily

Mexican American markets (Laredo and the Rio Grande Valley) ultimately failed. Another issue to bring up here mirrors what was mentioned regarding Lisa Fernandez in the softball subsection: how is it that no one has written a book on the life, career, and significance of NHLer Scott Gomez? There is, recently, a new Latino to cheer for on the ice: Austin Matthews of the Toronto Maple Leafs. Yes, he is Latino, all the way down to having his mother stay with him while he played in Sweden so that she could make him his favorite meal: tortilla soup![34]

Works on collegiate and Olympic wrestling by Cejudo and Plaschke and Iber and Maril, on golf by Garcia (at the high school level) and Trevino and Blair, and on tennis by Metcalf and Alamillo will hopefully spur further interest in the Latino/a role in these pursuits. A recent article by Rita Liberti in her anthology on San Francisco/Bay Area sports on the significance of Rosie Casals is an excellent example of what can and should be done in this regard. Such efforts should provide an impetus for scholars to do research on athletes in less studied sports. Finally, there have been many articles over the past decade or so that deal with the attempt by NASCAR to attract this potential clientele to their sport (with mixed results).[35]

# New Directions

As is evident by now, there has been a great deal of research done on the participation of Latino/as in American sport: both as athletes and as consumers of various forms of athletic competition. Where do we go from here? Here are several key areas that merit discussion and study. First, it is necessary to do more work on to how sport is making it possible for Latino/as to integrate into "new" areas of concentration. While we do have documentation of the positives from such athletic interactions (like the article on Latinos in Iowa high school football noted earlier), is this an isolated incident, or is it a trend? A recent article that deals with overt/controversial activities that took place at a high school football game in South Carolina may indicate that not all is positive. The controversy surrounded students waving an American flag and making disparaging/taunting remarks against a team with a substantial number of Latinos.[36]

A second topic that merits continued research was mentioned previously: how do various athletic organizations interact with Latino/as in order to attract them as customers? The work of Michelle Gacio-Harrolle is instructive in this regard, and it is a good starting point for those who wish to learn more about this topic.[37] Perhaps more research into such matters would reduce the risk of incidents such as the one with the Houston 1836s noted earlier. Unfortunately, not all marketing professionals have gotten this message. For example, see the story about a recent disastrous attempt to "reach" Latinos by a minor league hockey team.[38] A more critical perspective concerning the significance/value/benefit of Latino marketing comes from the work of Arlene Davila, who argues that increased attention by marketers does not necessarily indicate that Latino/as are accepted by the broader society.[39]

Third, research needs to be conducted into why Latino/as are not represented in proportional numbers in collegiate sports. Two recent articles have helped to lay the groundwork for such efforts. In "Game Delay: Latinos Not Yet Scoring with College Athletics," Paul Ruffin argues that there are important obstacles to increasing these numbers. Among these are an overrepresentation of Spanish-surnamed students at community colleges (which often do not field football teams); issues with the application process for athletic scholarships; (as noted earlier) overreliance on youths to help provide financial support to families (particularly among more recent immigrants); and the scarcity of role models. An article by Juan Vidal in *Rolling Stone* echoed these issues. Until there are better avenues for Latinos to pursue a four-year collegiate education, it is likely that this population will not be accurately represented in at this level of competition.[40]

Finally, a recent article on Toronto Blue Jays pitcher Marcus Stroman, whose father is African American and mother is Puerto Rican, noted that he encountered substantial blowback after he decided to play for Team USA in the recent World Baseball Classic. The fact that Stroman pitched against Puerto Rico in the final game only added to the debate.[41] How should such matters be handled? There have been many athletes in the past (e.g., Dolphin great Manny Fernandez) who have Spanish surnames but do not consider themselves Latinos. Likewise, there are those such as Eric Hosmer of the San Diego Padres who have Anglo surnames but are proud of their Latino (in his case, Cuban) heritage. Who gets to make the determination as to who is Latino/a? What are the implications of this discussion? More research needs to be done in this regard.

In summary, this essay has merely scratched the surface of the work that can be done in a variety of academic fields (as well as in popular literature) concerning the ties between Latino/as and American sport. As is evident, we have been in the game for a long time, and we will only become a larger part of US athletics as we move further into the twenty-first century.

The area of participation in sports can be a fruitful topic for scholars in the field of Latino studies. As noted, the topic has generated relatively little scrutiny from academicians, though the field is on the verge of blossoming. When I first approached colleagues in the department of history at Texas Tech University almost twenty years ago with the notion of examining the historical experiences of Mexican American athletes in southern Texas, many scoffed at the notion. Sports was too "popular" and did not examine "significant issues," they claimed. As this essay, and the plethora of articles, anthologies, and books written since then demonstrate, they could not have been more incorrect in their assertion.

Sport, as a vehicle for understanding the Latino/a experience in the United States, is a rich vein of academic gold that has been barely tapped. What young scholars in this field need to do is to pursue a "bottom-up" approach to sports. Sure, we would all love to be able to write about professional athletes, but those are relatively few in number. There needs to be a focus on schools with a substantial Latino/a presence throughout the nation: regardless of whether that presence be of long-standing history or a more recent development. Texas, California, and Florida are no longer the only places that need to be examined. Schools in various parts of Arkansas, for example, now field teams that are up to one-third Latino. Certainly there is a story there that cries out for research and study. For example, the history of the Garfield/Roosevelt rivalry in East Los Angeles/Boyle Heights has generated two films (with the recent addition of *The Classic*, directed by Billy McMillin) does justice to *Symbol of Heart* but gives the story a more contemporary element. While the older movie provides a history of the game and the communities (obviously a worthwhile endeavor), McMillin goes one step further and provides an overview of the history but also follows the current lives and struggles of various players involved in the game. Here is a sports movie that deals with issues of immigration, economic disparity, and the difficulty of continuing to play a sport when matters outside of the field intervene in the lives of players and their families. Another wonderful example of such research comes from ESPN and the excellent short film *The Lettermen*, which examines the relationship between (mostly) Latino players and their Japanese American head coach and an interesting mechanism to build up pride in players and their families. Who will be the first to capture a similar story in a place such as Springfield, Arkansas?

This is but the tip of the iceberg for the possibilities of this research. Other areas that might be valuable to pursue include research in the field of education and sociology, examining contemporary issues in the classroom and the barrio concerning why Latino/as are not represented proportionally in collegiate athletics. Given that Latinos are the largest minority group in the nation, why is it that a 2017 study by TIDES (The Institute for Diversity and Ethics in Sport), at the University of Central Florida, noted that in Division I football, only 2.4 percent of athletes were of Latino background during the 2016 campaign. Overall, Latinos made up only 5.5 percent of all collegiate athletes at levels down to Division III. For Latinas, the figure was 5.1 percent.[42] So as to get a better sense of why good athletes cannot pursue athletic opportunities at the collegiate level, we need to get "down in the weeds," and that means pursuing studies at the high school and local levels. In summary, it is not just what happens on the field that matters, it is what takes place off the field (in this case, what prevents our youth from benefiting from athletics) that must be understood. Questions such as these should help guide young scholars in the near future. Sports have always been a key element in the daily lives of Spanish-surnamed people in the United States. It is time that we viewed it as an element worthy of study, just as much as we discuss other topics such as religion, race, class, and gender.

## Notes

1. Samuel O. Regalado, *Viva Baseball: Latin Major Leaguers and Their Special Hunger* (Champaign: University of Illinois Press, 1998); and Mario Longoria, *Athletes Remembered: Mexicano/Latino Professional Football Players, 1929-1970* (Tempe, AZ: Bilingual Press, 1997).
2. Jorge Iber, Samuel O. Regalado, Jose M. Alamillo, and Arnoldo De Leon, *Latinos In U.S. Sports: A History of Isolation, Cultural Identity, and Acceptance* (Champaign, IL: Human Kinetics, 2011).
3. The following list is by no means exhaustive: Adrian Burgos, *Playing America's Game: Baseball, Latinos and the Color Line* (Berkeley: University of California Press, 2007); Jose M. Alamillo, "Peloteros in Paradise: Mexican American Baseball and Oppositional Politics

in Southern California, 1930–1950," *Western Historical Quarterly* 34, no. 2 (Summer 2003): 191-211; David Maraniss, *Clemente: The Passion and Grace of Baseball's Last Hero* (New York: Simon and Schuster, 2006); Bruce Markusen, *The Team That Changed Baseball: Roberto Clemente and the 1971 Pittsburgh Pirates* (Yardley, PA: Westholme, 2006); and Tim Wendel, *Far from Home: Latino Baseball Players in America* (Washington, DC: National Geographic, 2008).

4. See, for example: Jorge Iber, "Latina/os in the American High School, Collegiate and Community Sporting Landscape," in *The Routledge Companion to Latina/o Popular Culture*, ed. Frederick Luis Aldama (New York: Routledge, 2016), 345-353.

5. Iber, Latina/os in the American High School, 346. See also *The Michigan Alumnus*, Volume XXVI, October 1919–August 1920, 33.

6. See the following: Carlos Kevin Blanton, "'They Cannot Master Abstractions, But They Can Often Be Made Efficient Workers': Race and Class in the Intelligence Testing of Mexican Americans and African Americans in Texas during the 1920s," *Social Science Quarterly* 81, no. 4 (December 2000): 1014-1026. Quotes are from pages 1017 and 1018; and Miroslava Chavez-Garcia, "Intelligence Testing at Whittier School, 1890-1920," *Pacific Historical Review* 76, no. 2 (May 2007): 193-228. Quotes from 217 and 227.

7. Wes Singletary, *Al Lopez: The Life of Baseball's El Senor* (Jefferson, NC: McFarland, 1999); Peter Toot, *Armando Marsans: The First Cuban Major League Baseball Player* (Jefferson, NC: McFarland, 2003); Thom Henninger, *Tony Oliva: The Life and Times of a Minnesota Twins Legend* (Minneapolis: University of Minnesota Press, 2015); and Noe Torres, *Baseball's First Mexican American Star: The Amazing Story of Leo Najo*.

8. Adrian Burgos, *Playing America's Game: Baseball, Latinos and the Color Line* (Berkeley: University of California Press, 2007) and *Cuban Star: How One Negro-League Owner Changed the Face of Baseball* (New York: Hill and Wang, 2011).

9. Rob Ruck, *Raceball: How the Major Leagues Colonized the Black and Latin Game* (Boston: Beacon, 2011) and Mark Kurlansky, *The Eastern Stars: How Baseball Changed the Dominican Town of San Pedro de Macoris* (New York: Riverhead, 2010).

10. Roberto Gonzalez Echevarria, *The Pride of Havana: A History of Cuban Baseball* (New York: Oxford University Press, 1999); and Arturo J. Marcano Guevara and David P. Fidler, *Stealing Lives: The Globalization of Baseball and the Tragic Story of Alexis Quiroz* (Bloomington: Indiana University Press, 2002).

11. David Ortiz with Michael Holley, *Papi: My Story* (Boston: Houghton Mifflin, 2017); Mariano Rivera with Wayne Coffey, *The Closer: My Story* (New York: Little, Brown, 2015); Jorge Posada, *The Journey Home: My Life in Pinstripes* (New York: HarperCollins, 2015); and Jorge Iber, *Mike Torrez: A Baseball Biography* (Jefferson, NC: McFarland, 2016).

12. Richard Santillan et al., *Mexican American Baseball in El Paso: Images of Baseball* (Charleston, SC: Arcadia, 2017).

13. See the following: Jose Alamillo, "*Peloteros* in Paradise: Mexican American Baseball and Oppositional Politics in Southern California, 1930-1960," *Western Historical Quarterly* 34, no. 2 (2003): 191-211; Samuel O. Regalado, "Baseball in the Barrios: The Scene in East Los Angeles since World War II," *Baseball History* 1, no. 2 (Summer, 1986): 47-59; John Fraire, "Mexicans Playing Baseball in Indiana Harbor: Ethnic Identity Development Among Mexican Youth in Indiana Harbor, Indiana, 1920-1942," PhD diss., Union Institute and University, 2013; Alexander Wolff, "The Barrio Boys," *Sports Illustrated*, June 27, 2011; and Jorge Iber, Samuel O. Regalado, Jose M. Alamillo, and Arnoldo De Leon, *Latinos In U.S. Sports: A History of Isolation, Cultural Identity, and Acceptance*, 124.

14. Joel S. Franks, "Off the Bench: Asian Americans and Sports in the Santa Clara Valley during the Mid-Twentieth Century," in *San Francisco Bay Area Sports: Golden Gate Athletics, Recreation and Community*, ed. Rita Liberti and Maureen Smith (Fayetteville: University of Arkansas Press, 2017), 113–128.
15. Jennifer Ring, *A Game of Their Own: Voices of Contemporary Women in Baseball* (Lincoln: University of Nebraska Press, 2015), 121–138.
16. Gerald Gems, *Sport and the Shaping of Italian American Identity* (Syracuse, NY: Syracuse University Press, 2013); and Gerald Gems, *For Pride, Profit and Patriarchy: Football and the Incorporation of American Values* (Scarecrow Press, 2000).
17. Michael T. Wood, "American Football in Cuba: L.S.U. vs. University of Havana, 1907," https://ussporthistory.com/2015/12/31/american-football-in-cuba-l-s-u-vs-university-of-havana-1907/; and "American Football in Cuba: A Brief Introduction," https://ussporthistory.com/2015/07/30/american-football-in-cuba-a-brief-introduction/. See also Jorge Iber, "American Football in Latin America," in *Touchdown: An American Obsession*, ed. Gerald Gems (Great Barrington, MA: Berkshire, 2017).
18. Douglas E. Foley, "The Great American Football Ritual: Reproducing Race, Class and Gender Inequality," *Sociology of Sport Journal* 7 (1990): 111–135; Mark A. Grey, "Sport and Immigrant, Minority and Anglo Relations in Garden City (Kansas) High School," *Sociology of Sport Journal* 9 (1992): 255–270; Cesar Torrico, "The Effects of Sports Participation on the Chicano Athlete," master's thesis, San Jose State University, 1999; Rafael E. Romo, "A Phenomenological Study of the Perceptions and Experiences of Mexican Americans Participating in Collegiate Football" (PhD diss., Capella University, 2009); and David Flores, "Wheels of Progress Are Turning for Hispanic College Football Players in Texas," accessed September 3, 2009, http://www.mysanantonio.com/sacultura/conexion/article/Wheels-of-progress-are-turning-for-Hispanic-857997.php.
19. Greg Selber, *Border Ball: The History of High School Football in the Rio Grande Valley* (Deer Park, NY: Linus, 2009); and Joel Huerta, "Red, Brown, and Blue: A History and Cultural Poetics of High School Football in Mexican America" (PhD diss., University of Texas, 2005); Jorge Iber, "On Field Foes and Racial Misperceptions: The 1961 Donna Redskins and Their Drive to the Texas State Football Championship," *International Journal of the History of Sport* 21, no. 2 (March 2004): 237–256; Jose Angel Gutierrez, *We Won't Back Down: Severita Lara's Rise From Student Leader to Mayor* (Houston, TX: Arte Publico, 2005); Lynn Brezosky, "Tex Mex Songs Part of Pigskin Pride," *Laredo Morning Times*, November 2, 2005, 1; "Breaking the All-Male Barrier," *La Luz* 5, no. 1–2 (March 1976): 26; Elizabeth Merrill, "Six Man Forever," http://www.espn.com/espn/feature/story/_/id/20229005/high-school-girl-saves-football-season-fading-texas-town; Wayne Drehs, "Cultures Are Teammates at Iowa High School," accessed October 2006, http://sports.espn.go.com/espn/print?id=2618295&type=story; and Josiah Schlatter, "Que pass-a: Georgia High School Football Squad Using Spanish Snap Counts," accessed October 29, 2010 http://offthebench.nbcsports.com/2010/10/29/que-pass-a-georgia-high-school-football-squad-using-spanish-snap-counts.
20. Tom Flores and Frank Cooney, *Fire in the Iceman: Autobiography of Tom Flores* (Bonus Books, 1992); Jim Plunkett and Dave Newhouse, *The Jim Plunkett Story: The Saga of a Man Who Came Back* (Arbor House, 1981); Barry Alvarez and Mike Lucas, *Don't Flinch: Barry Alvarez, The Autobiography* (Champaign, IL: KCI Sports, 2006); Evan Mazza, "Juan Castillo is Leaving the Ravens to Join the Buffalo Bills Coaching Staff," https://www.baltimorebeatdown.com/2017/1/12/14258250/juan-castillo-is-leaving-the-ravens-to-join-the-buffalo-bills-coaching-staff; and Pat Yasinkas, "Rivera Embraces Role as Pioneer,"

http://www.espn.com/nfl/story/_/page/OneNation-NFL121009/nfl-ron-rivera-was-hispanic-pioneer-coach-player; Jorge Prieto, *The Quarterback Who Almost Wasn't* (Houston, TX: Arte Publico, 1994).

21. Cecilia Balli, "How 'America's Team' Became South Texas's Team," accessed January 15, 2017, http://www.texasmonthly.com/the-culture/americas-team-became-south-texass-team/; Maliik Obee, "The Oakland Raiders: The NFL's Most Transcendent Franchise," https://justblogbaby.com/2016/12/02/the-oakland-raiders-the-nfls-most-transcendent-franchise/; Brendan Weber, "Quedate en Oakland: Raider Fans Advance Fight to Keep Team Away from Las Vegas," http://www.nbcbayarea.com/news/local/Quedate-en-Oakland-Stay-in-Oakland-Fight-Mexico-City-402267595.html; Elliot Almond, "Raiders Go Deep for Hispanic Fans: Why Latinos Love the Silver and Black," accessed January 11, 2003, http://www.geoscape.com/pageimages/Raiders_Go_Deep_Hispanic_Fans_Bay.pdf; Armando Salguero, "Kiko Alonso turns 'bad blood' for Colin Kaepernick into great performance," accessed November 27, 2016, http://www.miamiherald.com/sports/spt-columns-blogs/armando-salguero/article117426693.html. With regard to marketing, see Bill Redeker, "NFL Capitalizes on Hispanic Football Fever," accessed February 1, 2012, http://abcnews.go.com/WNT/story?id=129236; Richie Matthews and Carlos Vassallo, "Opinion: Move over Futbol, the NFL Scores Big with Latinos," accessed January 3, 2012 http://abcnews.go.com/WNT/story?id=129236; and Andrea Canales, "The Rams Are Back, but Los Angeles Has Changed," accessed September 15, 2016, http://www.espn.com/blog/onenacion/post/_/id/5222/the-rams-are-back-but-los-angeles-has-changed.

22. Frederick Luis Aldama and Christopher Gonzalez, *Latinos in the End Zone: Conversations on the Brown Color Line in the NFL* (New York: Palgrave Macmillan, 2014).

23. Jorge Iber, Samuel O. Regalado, Jose M. Alamillo, and Arnoldo De Leon, *Latinos in U.S. Sports: A History of Isolation, Cultural Identity, and Acceptance*, 98 and 99. See also Glenn Avent, "A Popular and Wholesome Resort: Gender, Class, and the Young Men's Christian Association in Porfirian Mexico" (Master's thesis, University of British Columbia, 1992); Jose Alamillo, "Playing Across Borders: Transnational Sports and Identities in Southern California and Mexico, 1930–1945," *Pacific Historical Review* 79, no. 3 (2010): 360–392; and Manuel Bernardo Ramirez, "El Pasoans: Life and Society in Mexican El Paso, 1920–1945" (PhD diss., University of Mississippi, 2000).

24. Michael Innis-Jimenez, "Beyond the Baseball Diamond and the Basketball Court: Organized Leisure in Interwar Mexican Chicago," in *More Than Just Peloteros: Sport and US Latino Communities,* ed. Jorge Iber (Lubbock: Texas Tech University Press, 2015), 66–94; and Christine Marin, "Courting Success and Realizing the American Dream: Arizona's Mighty Miami High School Championship Basketball Team, 1951," in *More Than Just Peloteros: Sport and US Latino Communities,* ed. Jorge Iber (Lubbock: Texas Tech University Press, 2015), 150–183.

25. Greg Selber, *Bronc Ball: The History of College Basketball at Texas-Pan American* (Edinburgh, TX: UT Pan American Press, 2013); Greb Selber, "Hills to Climb: An Historical Analysis of Latina Participation in Texas High School Basketball," in *More Than Just Peloteros: Sport and US Latino Communities,* Vol. 2, ed. Jorge Iber (Lubbock: Texas Tech University Press, forthcoming); and Mary Jo Sylwester, "Culture, Family Play Role in Sports for Latina Girls," accessed March 29, 2005, http://usatoday30.usatoday.com/sports/2005-03-28-hispanic-tradition_x.htm; and Bernardo Ramirez Rios, "Culture, Migration, and Sport: A Bi-National Investigation of Southern Mexican Migrant Communities in Oaxaca, Mexico and Los Angeles, California" (PhD diss., Ohio State University, 2012).

26. Ignacio M. Garcia, *When Mexicans Could Play Ball: Basketball, Race, and Identity in San Antonio, 1928–1945* (Austin: University of Texas Press, 2013).
27. Andrea Canales, "Latinas Are Embracing Softball," accessed April 3, 2017, http://www.espn.com/blog/onenacion/post/_/id/7216/latinas-are-embracing-softball. See also: Katherine M. Jamieson, "A Qualitative Analysis of Latinas in Collegiate Softball," doctoral dissertation, Michigan State University, 1999; and "Advance at Your Own Risk: Latinas, Families, and Collegiate Softball," in *Mexican Americans and Sports: A Reader on Athletics and Barrio Life*, ed. Jorge Iber and Samuel O. Regalado (College Station: Texas A&M University Press, 2007): 213–232; and Jorge Iber, Samuel O. Regalado, Jose M. Alamillo, and Arnoldo De Leon, *Latinos in U.S. Sports*, 276–278.
28. Ben Chappell, "Mexican American Fastpitch," in *More Than Just Peloteros: Sport and US Latino Communities, Vol, II*, ed. Jorge Iber (Texas Tech University Press, 2018), and Jorge Iber, *Mike Torrez: A Baseball Biography* (Jefferson, NC: McFarland, 2016). There are many websites that document this story as well. Here are just a few: https://www.neh.gov/events/2015/07/31/building-communities-mexican-american-fast-pitch-softball-leagues; http://www.elcentroinc.com/event/mexican-american-fast-pitch-softball-exhibit/; http://harveycountynow.com/sports/143; and http://harveycountynow.com/sports/mexican-american-softball-prepares-for-68th-tourney.
29. Jorge Iber, Samuel O. Regalado, Jose M. Alamillo, and Arnoldo De Leon, *Latinos In U.S. Sports: A History of Isolation, Cultural Identity, and Acceptance* (Champaign, IL: Human Kinetics, 2011), 131–133, 210–214, and 256–261. See also Juan Javier Pescador, "Los Heroes del Domingo: Soccer, Borders, and Social Spaces in Great Lakes Mexican Communities, 1940–1970," in *Mexican Americans and Sports: A Reader on Athletics and Barrio Life*, ed. Jorge Iber and Samuel O. Regalado (College Station: Texas A&M University Press, 2007): 73–88. See also Marie Price and Courtney Whitworth, "Soccer and Latino Cultural Space: Metropolitan Washington Futbol Leagues," in *Hispanic Spaces, Latino Places: Community and Cultural Diversity in Contemporary America*, ed. Daniel D. Arreola (Austin: University of Texas Press, 2004): 167–186; Sam Quinones, *Antonio's Gun and Delfino's Dream: True Tales of Mexican Migration* (Albuquerque: University of New Mexico Press, 2008); Natalia Suarez Montero, "The Expression of Latinidad at Soccer Games in Kansas City" (Master's thesis, University of Kansas, 2010); Paul Cuadros, *A Home on the Field: How One Championship Team Inspires Hope for the Revival of Small Town America* (New York: Harper Collins, 2006); and Steve Wilson, *The Boys from Little Mexico* (Boston: Beacon, 2010); and Matt Zeigler, *Total Football: Latin American Soccer in Alabama* (Amazon Digital Services, 2012).
30. See the following: Paul Cuadros, "We Play Too: Latina Integration Through Soccer in the 'New South,'" *The Southeastern Geographer* 51, no. 2 (Fall 2011): 227–241; emezcla.com/lists/culture/in-the-game-documentary-soccer-latina-kelly-high-school-world-channel/; Candace Bucker, "Hispanic Girls Face Many Obstacles to Playing Sports," accessed July 9, 2009, http://hispanic-marketing.com/hispanic-girls-face-many-obstacles-to-playing-sports/; and Elayna Fernandez, "Everyday Masters: Amy Rodriguez Hopes Her World Cup Win Inspires Latinas in Soccer," accessed October 8, 2015, http://www.latina.com/lifestyle/inspiring-latina/amy-rodriguez-everyday-masters-interview.
31. Luis Miguel Echegaray, "How MLS Embraced Latinos: 'We View the Hispanic Market as Part of Our DNA,'" accessed September 15, 2016, https://www.theguardian.com/football/2016/sep/15/mls-latinos-hispanic-community-dna; Ric Jensen and Jason Sosa, "The Importance of Building Positive Relationships Between Hispanic Audiences and Major League Soccer Franchises: A Case Study of Public Relations Challenges Facing Houston

1836," *Soccer and Society* 9, no. 4 (2008): 477–490; Todd R. Jewell and David J. Molina, "An Evaluation of the Relationship between Hispanics and Major League Soccer," *Journal of Sports Economics* 6, no. 2 (2005): 160–177; Emmanuel Ayim, "An Examination of Sport Identity amongst Youth Soccer Participants: Implications for MLS Marketing" (PhD diss., University of Nevada-Las Vegas, 2009); Fernando Delgado, "Sports and Politics: Major League Soccer, Constitution, and (the) Latino Audience(s)," *Journal of Social and Sport Issues* 23, no.1 (1999): 41–54; and Yara Simon, "When It Comes to Connecting with Latinos, US Sports Leagues Can Learn from MLS," http://remezcla.com/lists/sports/mls-latinos-fans/.

32. Enrique Encinosa, *Azucar y Chocolate: Historia del Boxeo Cubano* (Miami, FL: Ediciones Universal, 2004); Benita Heiskanen, "The *Latinization* of Boxing: A Texas Case Study," *Journal of Sport History* 32, no. 1 (2005): 45–66; Gregory S. Rodriguez, "Palaces of Pain—Arenas of Mexican-American Dreams: Boxing and the Formation of Ethnic Mexican Identities in Twentieth-Century Los Angeles" (PhD diss., University of California, San Diego, 1999); Tom I. Romero II, "Wearing the Red, White and Blue Trunks of Aztlan: Rodolfo "Corky" Gonzales and the Convergence of American and Chicano Nationalism," in *Mexican Americans and Sports: A Reader on Athletics and Barrio Life*, ed. Jorge Iber and Samuel O. Regalado (College Station: Texas A&M University Press, 2007), 89–120; Christina D. Abreu, "The Story of Benny "Kid" Paret: Cuban Boxers, the Cuban Revolution, and the U.S. Media, 1959–1962," *Journal of Sport History* 38, no.1 (Spring 2011): 95–113; Enver M. Casimir, "A Variable of Unwavering Significance: Latinos, African Americans, and the Racial Identity of Kid Chocolate," in *More Than Just Peloteros: Sport and US Latino Communities*, ed. Jorge Iber, 39–65; Troy Rondinone, *Friday Night Fighter: Gaspar "Indio" Ortega and the Golden Age of Television Boxing* (Urbana: University of Illinois Press, 2013); Christi Halbert, "Tough Enough and Woman Enough: Stereotypes, Discrimination, and Impression Management among Women Professional Boxers," *Journal of Sport and Social Issues* 21, no. 1 (1997): 7–36, Alfonso Felix, "Meet Marlen Esparza and Jajaira Gonzalez: Two Badass Boxers on the Road to the US Olympic Team," http://remezcla.com/features/sports/marlen-esparza-jajaira-gonzalez-two-badass-latina-boxers-us-olympics/.

33. Fernando Delgado, "Golden but Not Brown: Oscar De La Hoya and the Complications of Culture, Manhood, and Boxing," *International Journal of the History of Sport* 22, no. 2 (2005): 196–211; Richard Hoffer, "Viva Mexico," *Sports Illustrated*, July 1, 2002, http://sportsillustrated.cnn.com/vault/article/magazine/MAG1026151/index.htm; "Fight-Game Inferno," *Sports Illustrated*, March 10, 2003; "Taking Care of Business," *Sports Illustrated*, December 11, 2006, http://sportsillustrated.cnn.com/vault/article/magazine/MAG1028195/index.htm; http://sportsillustrated.cnn.com/vault/article/magazine/MAG1114577/; and "Plugged In," *Street and Smith's SportsBusiness Journal*, October 1, 2012, http://www.Sportsbusinessdaily.com/Journal/Issues/2012/10/01/People-and-Pop-Culture/Plugged-In.aspx?hl=Hispanics&sc=0; and Greory S. Rodriguez, "Saving Face, Place, and Race: Oscar De La Hoya and the 'All-American' Dreams of U.S. Boxing," in *Sports Matters: Race, Recreation and Culture*, ed. John Bloom and Michael Nevin Willard (New York: University Press, 2002), 279–298.

34. Mark D. Dyerson, "The Foot Runners Conquer Mexico and Texas: Endurance Racing, *Indigenismo*, and Nationalism," in *Mexican Americans and Sports: A Reader on Athletics and Barrio Life*, ed. Jorge Iber and Samuel O. Regalado, 19–49; Alexander Mendoza, "Beating the Odds: Mexican American Distance Runners in Texas, 1950–1995," in *Mexican Americans and Sports: A Reader on Athletics and Barrio Life*, ed. Jorge Iber and

Samuel O. Regalado (College Station, TX: Texas A&M University Press, 2006), 188–212; Maria Jose Sada, "Rio 2016: Latina Track Star Brenda Martinez Defeats All Odds in Pursuit of Her Olympic Career," accessed August 11, 2016, http://www.foxnews.com/sports/2016/08/11/latina-track-star-defeats-all-odds-in-pursuit-her-olympic-career.html; Bill Boyd, *All Roads Lead to Hockey: Reports from Northern Canada to the Mexican Border* (Lincoln: University of Nebraska Press, 2006); and, "Austin Matthews, Hockey's Newest Star, has Latino Heritage," accessed 13 October 2016, http://www.espn.com/blog/onenacion/post/_/id/5746/auston-mathews-hockeys-newest-star-has-latino-heritage.

35. Henry Cejudo and Bill Plaschke, *American Victory: Wrestling, Dreams, and a Journey toward Home* (New York: Celebra, 2010); Jorge Iber and Lee Maril, *Latino American Wrestling Experience: Over 100 Years of Wrestling Heritage in the United States* (Stillwater, OK: National Wrestling Hall of Fame, 2014): http://nwhof.org/latinowrestling/; Humberto G. Garcia, *Mustang Miracle* (Bloomington, IN: AuthorHouse, 2010); Lee Trevino and Sam Blair, *They Call Me Super Mex* (New York: Random House, 1982); John Metcalf, "Invaders from Below the Equator: Latinos at Wimbledon," *Sports Illustrated*, July 13, 1959, 14–16; Jose M. Alamillo, "'Bad Boy' of Tennis: Richard "Pancho" Gonzalez, Racialized Masculinity, and the Print Media in Postwar America," in *More Than Just Peloteros: Sport and US Latino Communities*, ed. Jorge Iber (Champaign, IL: Human Kinetics, 2011), 121–149; and Rita Liberti, "Rebel with a Racket: Rosie Casals," in *San Francisco Bay Area Sports: Golden Gate Athletics, Recreation, and Community*, 221–234; Michael B. Edward, Derek H. Aldeman, and Steven G. Estes. "An Appraisal of Stock Car Racing's Economic and Geographic Development in North America: NASCAR as Flexible Accumulation," *Journal of Sports Marketing and Management* 8, no. 1–2 (2010): 160–179; Barry Janoff, "Can NASCAR Be Numero Uno with Hispanic Fans, Marketers?" *Brandweek* 48, no. 29 (6–13 August 2007): 10; Tripp Mickle, "NASCAR, Track Appeals to Hispanics," *Street and Smith's SportsBusiness Journal*, August 29, 2011, 4; and, Tripp Mickel, "NASCAR Gains Traction with L.A. Strategy," *Street and Smith's SportsBusiness Journal*, April 29, 2013, 34.

36. Colin Ward-Henninger, "South Carolina High School Bans American Flags from Football Game," accessed August 29, 2016, https://www.cbssports.com/general/news/south-carolina-high-school-bans-american-flags-from-football-game/; and Ariel Zibler, "American Flag Banned from South Carolina High School Football Games Because Principal Says They Were Used to Taunt Hispanic Students," August 29, 2016, http://www.dailymail.co.uk/news/article-3764060/American-flag-BANNED-South-Carolina-high-school-football-games-principal-says-used-taunt-Hispanic-students.html.

37. Michelle Gacio Harrolle and Galen T. Trail, "Ethnic Identification, Acculturation and Sports Identification of Latinos in the United States," *International Journal of Sports Marketing and Sponsorship* 8, no. 3 (2007): 234–253; Michelle Gacio Harrolle, "Sport Spectator Conative Loyalty: A Comparison of Latino Subgroups and Non-Latino Consumers" (PhD diss., University of Florida, 2007).

38. Adrian Carrasquillo, "Hockey Team's Controversial Latino Promotion Moves Forward Minus Dora and Plus Latino Veterans," NBC Latino, 2012; and Julio Ricardo Varela, "Opinion: Hockey Team's Promotion Featuring Dora, a Sombrero and Maracas Is a Major Fail," NBC Latino, 2012.

39. Arlene Dávila, *Latino Spin: Public Image and the Whitewashing of Race* (New York: New York University Press, 2008).

40. Paul Ruffins, "Game Delay: Latinos Not Yet Scoring with College Athletics," accessed October 5, 2010, http://diverseeducation.com/article/14216/; and Juan Vidal, "Why Does

American Sports Have a Latino Problem?," accessed September 16, 2016, http://www.rollingstone.com/sports/news/why-does-american-sports-have-a-latino-problem-w440069.
41. Robert Sanchez, "Dream Chaser: For Marcus Stroman, a Little Extra Edge is Always Easy to Find," accessed May 3, 2017, http://www.espn.com/espn/feature/story/_/id/19293493/toronto-blue-jays-ace-marcus-stroman-looking-build-wbc-success.
42. Richard Lapchick, "The 2016 Racial and Gender Report Card: College Sports," 5-6 http://nebula.wsimg.com/38d2d0480373afd027ca38308220711f?AccessKeyId=DAC3A56D8FB782449D2A&disposition=0&alloworigin=1.

## Bibliography

Abreu, Christina D. "The Story of Benny "Kid" Paret: Cuban Boxers, the Cuban Revolution, and the U.S. Media, 1959–1962." *Journal of Sport History* 38, no. 1 (Spring 2011): 95–113.

Alamillo, Jose M. "Playing Across Borders: Transnational Sports and Identities in Southern California and Mexico, 1930–1945." *Pacific Historical Review* 79, no. 3 (2010): 360–392.

Alamillo, Jose M. "Peloteros in Paradise: Mexican American Baseball and Oppositional Politics in Southern California, 1930–1960." *Western Historical Quarterly* 34, no. 2 (2003): 191–211.

Aldama, Frederick Luis, and Christopher Gonzalez. *Latinos in the End Zone: Conversations on the Brown Color Line in the NFL*. New York: Palgrave Macmillan, 2014.

Balli, Cecilia. "How 'America's Team' Became South Texas's Team." *Texas Monthly*, January 15, 2017. http://www.texasmonthly.com/the-culture/americas-team-became-south-texass-team/.

Burgos, Adrian. *Playing America's Game: Baseball, Latinos and the Color Line*. Berkeley: University of California Press, 2007.

Cuadros, Paul. *A Home on the Field: How One Championship Team Inspires Hope for the Revival of Small Town America*. New York: HarperCollins, 2006.

Dávila, Arlene. *Latino Spin: Public Image and the Whitewashing of Race*. New York: New York University Press, 2008.

Drehs, Wayne. 2006. "Cultures Are Teammates at Iowa High School." ESPN.com, accessed October 11, 2006. http://sports.espn.go.com/espn/print?id=2618295&type=story.

Garcia, Ignacio M. *When Mexicans Could Play Ball: Basketball, Race, and Identity in San Antonio, 1928–1945*. Austin: University of Texas Press, 2013.

Heiskanen, Benita. "The Latinization of Boxing: A Texas Case Study." *Journal of Sport History* 32, no. 1 (2005): 45–66.

Iber, Jorge. *Mike Torrez: A Baseball Biography*. Jefferson, NC: McFarland, 2016.

Iber, Jorge. "On Field Foes and Racial Misperceptions: The 1961 Donna Redskins and Their Drive to the Texas State Football Championship." *International Journal of the History of Sport* 21, no. 2 (March 2004): 237–256.

Iber, Jorge, Samuel O. Regalado, Jose M. Alamillo, and Arnoldo De Leon. *Latinos in U.S. Sports: A History of Isolation, Cultural Identity, and Acceptance*. Champaign, IL: Human Kinetics, 2011.

Jamieson, Katherine M. 1999. "A Qualitative Analysis of Latinas in Collegiate Softball." PhD diss., Michigan State University.

Jensen, Ric, and Jason Sosa, "The Importance of Building Positive Relationships Between Hispanic Audiences and Major League Soccer Franchises: A Case Study of Public Relations Challenges Facing Houston 1836." *Soccer and Society* 9, no. 4 (2008): 477–490.

Longoria, Mario. *Athletes Remembered: Mexicano/Latino Professional Football Players, 1929–1970*. Tempe, AZ: Bilingual Press, 1997.

Price, Marie, and Courtney Whitworth. "Soccer and Latino Cultural Space: Metropolitan Washington Futbol Leagues." In *Hispanic Spaces, Latino Places: Community and Cultural Diversity in Contemporary America*, edited by Daniel D. Arreola, 167–186. Austin: University of Texas Press, 2004.

Ramirez Rios, Bernardo. 2012. "Culture, Migration, and Sport: A Bi-National Investigation of Southern Mexican Migrant Communities in Oaxaca, Mexico and Los Angeles, California." PhD diss., Ohio State University.

Regalado, Samuel O. *Viva Baseball: Latin Major Leaguers and Their Special Hunger*. Champaign: University of Illinois Press, 1998.

Rondinone, Troy. *Friday Night Fighter: Gaspar "Indio" Ortega and the Golden Age of Television Boxing*. Urbana: University of Illinois Press, 2013.

Ruck, Rob. *Raceball: How the Major Leagues Colonized the Black and Latin Game*. Boston: Beacon, 2011.

Selber, Greg. *Border Ball: The History of High School Football in the Rio Grande Valley*. Deer Park, NY: Linus, 2009.

Sylwester, Mary Jo. "Culture, Family Play Role in Sports for Latina Girls." http://usatoday30.usatoday.com/sports/2005-03-28-hispanic-tradition_x.htm.

Vidal, Juan. "Why Does American Sports Have a Latino Problem?" http://www.rollingstone.com/sports/news/why-does-american-sports-have-a-latino-problem-w440069.

Wilson, Steve. *The Boys From Little Mexico*. Boston: Beacon, 2010.

Wood, Michael T. "American Football in Cuba: A Brief Introduction." July 2015. https://ussporthistory.com/2015/07/30/american-football-in-cuba-a-brief-introduction/.

# Appendix

# Does Latino Literature Matter? A Conversation

## ILAN STAVANS AND CHARLES HATFIELD

*Charles Hatfield*: Enough time has passed since *The Norton Anthology of Latino Literature* (2011) was first published for us to reflect on some of the different things it has meant and done. I am also interested in thinking through the questions the anthology leads us—sometimes intentionally, sometimes not—to ask not only about Latino/a literature but also about literature as such.

But before we get to those questions, I would like to ask you about the place you imagine for *The Norton Anthology of Latino Literature* in relation to the many anthologies of Latino/a literature that preceded it, including those that were co-edited by you and Harold Augenbraum.

At the outset of one of the anthologies you and Augenbraum edited—*Lengua Fresca: Latinos Writing on the Edge* (2006)—Augenbraum suggested that some of your earlier anthologies had "reflected a moment in the polity of the United States and US-Latino culture: a focus on bringing new voices to the table, a temporary pushing of one's way into notice." But, Augenbraum, argued, "that time has passed." In his view, Latinos now "have their place at the table," and there is in contemporary Latino/a writing even a "post-Latino consciousness," or at least "a different vantage point."

To be sure, many early anthologies of Latino/a literature from the 1970s were in different ways a response to the socioeconomic marginalization of Latinos and the literary marginalization of Latino/a writing. Setting aside the question of whether Latinos or Latino/a literature have actually entered the mainstream or "have a seat at the table," my question is this: if the starting point for an anthology of Latino/a literature is that both Latinos and Latino/a literature have entered "the mainstream," what work do you imagine that an anthology of Latino/a literature needs to do?

*Ilan Stavans*: My answer, at first at least, requires a short trip through the labyrinthine paths of etymology.

The term "Latino" came about in the late 1980s. It replaced "Hispanic," which was used in government documents during the Nixon administration. These two terms represented a consolidation, and maybe an erasure, of traditions. For throughout the twentieth century, the minority we know today under these rubrics was made of Puerto Ricans in the mainland, Cubans in exile, particularly after Castro's revolution in 1958–1959, and *mexicanos*, who themselves were a rainbow made of *Californios*, Tejanos, Chicanos, and other types, which were names frequently referring to the same people. Many now call it "Latinx literature," but it was not so then. The anthologies from the 1950s to the 1970s focused on Puerto Ricans, Cubans, etc., as separate, self-sufficient traditions. As soon as the terms "Hispanic" and "Latino" were used, the minority was seen as a sum of parts.

In 1993, Augenbraum and I edited *Growing Up Latino*. It was published by Houghton Mifflin. The endeavor came about serendipitously. Augenbraum's wife was friends with the daughter of Marc Jaffe, an editor there. A year earlier, Augenraum and I had received a grant from the NEH to put together a symposium about Latino literature at The Mercantile Library, where he served as director. He mentioned it to Jaffe, who said he was interested in bringing out a collection of memoirs and stories. We made the selection but coming up with the volume's title was not easy. A few authors resisted the idea of having their work in an anthology calling them "Hispanic" because the term was seen at the time was coming from outside the minority, specifically from the government. Others wanted "Mestizo." A few more suggested using "a/o" in either "Latino" or "Mestizo." The debate showcased the degree to which terminology balkanized the landscape. I chose the final title.

*Growing Up Latino* became enormously successful. It went through numerous printings. It was adopted in high school and college classrooms. Its purpose was to push for a place in the mainstream. That was the period when Sandra Cisneros, Ana Castillo, Julia Alvarez, and Denise Chavez were being picked up by major houses like Farrar, Straus, and Giroux; Knopf; Norton; and others. Oscar Hijuelos won the Pulitzer Prize for *The Mambo Kings Play Songs of Love* (1989). The feeling was that Latino literature was hot. Since the anthology continued to sell handsomely, Houghton Mifflin decided to repackage it. It came out with a fresh new cover, a preface, and so on. They also convinced us to do another anthology, *Lengua Fresca*, which introduced a young crop of Latino writers.

The cultural climate had changed by then. With the exception of one or two—primarily Junot Díaz, whose novel *The Brief Wondrous Life of Oscar Wao* (2007), the only other Pulitzer Prize winner in the tradition, was about to appear the following year—Latino writers were no longer the new kid on the block. At least not from the perspective of publishers. Mainstream houses did not think there was a Latino readership to be found that compared to say the vigorous black readership. And interest among non-Latino readers was difficult to sustain. In any event, the fad had chilled.

More or less at the same time, the rise of Latino studies manifested itself in academia. In the early 1990s, the number of positions in the field was minuscule. Schools, undergraduate and graduate, did not have specialized programs. Mexican studies prevailed in the Southwest while Caribbean studies dominated the Northeast. A few locations were able to zoom, of course: in Florida, it was Cuban studies; in New York, Puerto Rican studies. It was only with the new millennium that a consciousness attached to "Latinidad" manifested itself. I signed up to do the *Norton Anthology of Latino Literature* in 1997. Bill Clinton was president. It took me thirteen years to complete it. It came out with Obama in the White House. The nation's priorities had changed dramatically by then. So had Latinos. We were no longer seen as outsiders. In fact, in 2011 we became the largest minority, surpassing blacks. We were also the fastest growing. It was announced that year that by 2025, one out of every four Americans would claim a Latino ancestry.

In direct response to your question, anthologies exist to perform all sorts of tasks. They push for recognition. Or showcase the development of a tradition. Or evaluate a phenomenon. Or call for a new assessment. For instance, a story by Henry James in an anthology of psychological literature will be received differently than the same story in an anthology of ghost stories. With his close friend the Dominican man of letters Pedro Henríquez Ureña, Borges once edited an anthology of Argentine literature. The purpose was to emphasize a side of Argentinean literature that in the editors' view had not been sufficiently valued. He also edited anthologies of fantastic literature, of dreams, or non-existent creatures, and of visions of heaven and hell. Umberto Eco made parallel anthologies that combined texts and images, one about beauty, the other about ugliness. Angela Carter edited an anthology of women's fairy tales. Over the years, doing anthologies has been a pleasure of mine. For instance, I did *The Oxford Book of Jewish Stories* (1998). And *The FSG Book of Twentieth-Century Latin American Poetry* (2011), which, as it happens, came out simultaneously with *The Norton Anthology of Latino Literature*.

Changes in the market and in the way literature is distributed these days have made the art of editing anthologies somewhat redundant. Borges, to the best of my knowledge, never paid permissions for his anthologies. Permission costs now can make a project prohibitive. People also can download text online, which makes banking on an edited volume unfeasible. All of which is valuable yet the role of anthologies, in my view, is still important. Editors are curators as well as safe-keepers, not to mention historians.

*Charles Hatfield:* *The Norton Anthology of Latino Literature* was, I believe, a monumentally important and useful project for a number of reasons, not least of which is the breadth of what it includes within "Latino/a literature." But it seems that the anthology's broad generic, historical, and thematic inclusiveness—ranging from colonial Latin American *crónicas* to song lyrics by Ricky Martin—might cut two ways. On the one hand, the anthology celebrates the fact that people we might plausibly call Latino/a have been writing in and about the United States for the last five hundred years, and it also calls our attention, in the case of someone such as William Carlos Williams, for example, to how deeply a consciousness of Latinidad extends into the most canonical US American poetry. On the other hand, it might be said that the anthology's inclusiveness occludes a clear vision of the contours of Latino/a literature itself and leaves us to wonder when and where, exactly, it begins and ends.

It is probably a strange way of getting at the point, but I wonder what you would say to a student who said, "Professor Stavans, my goal is to write something that might someday find its way into a future edition of *The Norton Anthology of Latino Literature*."

What I am getting at is a distinction between literature written by people who we would identify as Latino/a and/or who self-identify as Latino/a and a body of literature that could be labeled "Latino/a literature," and what I have in mind is something along the lines of Jorge Volpi's distinction between "Latin American literature" as "a literature" and literature that happens to be produced by writers who come from Latin America. As Volpi puts it, there are undoubtedly "hundreds or thousands of Latin American writers [...] or better said, hundreds of thousands of Chilean, Honduran, Dominican, Venezuelan (et cetera) writers," but there is no "uniquely [Latin American] literary body endowed with recognizable characteristics." We can set aside Volpi's polemic about Latin American literature if you want, but the distinction he draws between texts written by Latin Americans and "Latin American literature," even if he happens to want to eschew one of the two, would seem to be an important one.

Volpi, of course, is not the only person who thinks that reflecting on this sort of difference is important—Kenneth Warren's *What Was African American Literature?* (2011) makes the point that "the mere existence of literary texts does not necessarily indicate the existence of a literature" and issues a warning about the perils of failing to distinguish between "the existence of writers from an ascriptive group (even writers whose merit is broadly acclaimed) and the conceptualization of works by multiple authors from this group as *a literature*."

I would be very interested in knowing your thoughts about how pertinent this distinction might be in relation to Latino/a literature.

**Ilan Stavans**: Volpi, who is a good friend, is wrong on at least a couple of fronts. Using a Platonic framework, he endorses the particular at the expense of the universal. The world is full of chairs of all kinds, big and small, four-legged or one-legged, comfortable or uncomfortable, and so on, but, in concrete terms, there is no such thing as "a prototype of the chair." That is because prototypes are abstractions. They exist in the mind, as summations. When we look at a modernistic object that is compact and that appears to be useful for people to sit down, we say it resembles a chair because we can invoke in our mind the varieties of chairs we have seen throughout life and conclude that this object somehow fits into this pattern even if it looks strange and untraditional.

When writers in the United States talk about "the great American novel," they do the same: throw into one basket their conception of what a novel is, what American is, and what could be considered canon reshaping—and put it forward as an ideal target. That is because the concepts of nation and novel and literary greatness can be mixed. Likewise, Latin American literature. The models we have from the past, ranging from Fernández de Lizardi's The *Itching Parrot* (1830) to the books that are part of the MacOndo movement in the 1990s, create a prototype in our mind. It is not a fixed, unmovable prototype but one that keeps on changing; and it is based on a small sample of recognized items that over time have become trend setters.

If a student comes to me with the question you have asked, "My goal is to write something that might be considered for inclusion in the next edition of *The Norton Anthology of Latino Literature*," it is clear that the Platonic prototype is already set. The cumulative effect of what Latino literature has been over the centuries is encouraging new generations to define themselves. That definition will be based on rejections and embraces. For instance, it is a well-known fact that, figuratively speaking, in order to supersede your role model, you first need to kill. Thus, my first response is: learn as much as you can from your precursors, then kill them; only then will you find your place alongside them.

Volpi is also wrong in that literature is not only what writers write but what readers read. Strictly speaking, the manuscript of the great Latino novel that is sitting in a drawer accumulating dust is not worth a dime; only when someone finds it and publishes it and readers engage with it does it become part of reality. Readers, therefore, are the ultimate consummators of literature; without them, there is nothing. And among readers, there are those who, for better or worse, take upon themselves to establish a lineage.

I am talking here of the act and art of canonization. *The Norton Anthology of Latino Literature* is a concerted attempt to understand how the mechanics of the tradition work: who might be said to have started it, who has been influenced by whom, what kinds of motifs have traveled through generations, what kinds of rivalries have been fruitful, in what sense has language been renewed and how has that language come to be in terms of style and economy and politics, etc. A literary tradition is always seen in retrospect, with an eagle's eye. It is, inevitably, about authority, although it is not authoritarian. And it is subjective as well as subjected to change.

Of course, any tradition is made of drastically different stages. Fray Bartolomé de Las Casas or Eusebio Chacón, José Martí or even Julia de Burgos are not Latino writers until their work is appropriated by successive generations. It is the game of genealogical sequencing. No one wants to be an orphan, not even orphans.

*Charles Hatfield:* Having used *The Norton Anthology of Latino Literature* in at least a couple undergraduate courses I have taught, I can attest to how powerful it is for students—even (or maybe especially) here in Texas—to discover that some of the very first texts written in many parts of the territory that comprises the present-day United States were actually written by Spanish-speaking people (e.g., Cabeza de Vaca). The fact that Cabeza de Vaca wrote in what is now the United States also raises productive questions about what it means to talk about American literary history, and connects twentieth-century Latino/a writing to a deep archive that has been embraced by some twentieth-century writers and that is also obviously very much a part of the larger historical process behind twentieth-century Latino/a writing. (Américo Paredes's *With His Pistol in His Hand* reminds us how important it is to understand the long story of how we got here if we are to understand where we are).

However, the inclusion of sixteenth-century writers such as Cabeza de Vaca or Las Casas in an anthology of Latino/a literature constitutive of "the origins" of a Latino/a literary tradition represented by Tato Laviera and Richard Rodriguez might end up turning a historically specific, socially constructed political category into a trans-historical, natural, and non-political one.

Even if "Latino" had existed as a category in the sixteenth or seventeenth centuries, we can be certain that membership in that group would not have operated under the same criteria that it did in 1850, 1950, or 2018. If we then claimed that present-day Latinos and seventeenth-century Latinos were members of the same group, I think we would be forced to say, problematically, that Latinidad is not actually a social or historical construction but actually something that supersedes the vicissitudes of history and social construction (i.e., that there is a transhistorical Latino essence).

It is not hard to see how this line of thinking quickly leads to a much narrower frame for an anthology of Latino/a literature that perhaps would consist primarily of post-WWII texts that grapple with Latinidad as such in some way (a quintessential example would be Cristina García's *A Handbook to Luck* from 2007).

I am thinking about Rolena Adorno's recent *Colonial Latin American Literature: A Very Short Introduction*, where she begins by pointing out that "colonial Latin American literature" is a "misnomer." The misnomer, she suggests, does not involve the "colonial" part of the term, which "has a clear temporal referent: the more than three centuries of Spanish domination in the Americas." Rather, the misnomer involves the characterization of the texts discussed in her book as both "Latin American" and as "literature."

On the one hand, as Adorno points out, the term "Latin America" only appeared "after independence," and on the other hand, "the eighteenth-century concept of literature had not yet emerged." Thus, Adorno's study of Colonial Latin American literature begins with the recognition that much of what gets called "colonial Latin American literature" is neither, strictly speaking, Latin American nor literature. Nevertheless, Adorno proposes that the term colonial Latin American literature is not only a "misnomer" but also a "useful" one.

If we are too scrupulous about the "misnomer," we end up with a history of "Latin American literature" as something that would begin, at the earliest, in the middle of the nineteenth century and take shape with *modernismo*. We would lose, perhaps, a more expansive sense of "Latin American literature," but could we gain something else important?

*Ilan Stavans*: What is Latinidad? A convenient, empowering rubric. It will last for a while but it is not eternal. Its uses depend on the people who congregate around it. At some point other rubrics will become attractive and this one will cede. Needless to say, a rubric is a mask. We get tied to them, feeling they are a kind of capital. Living without them is harder.

I want to move to another topic: the centrality of classics. Ours is a time in which books matter little, certainly less than they did a generation ago. We have moved into the realm of images. We traffic with them: static images, moving images; pure images and adulterated images. For better or worse, images now contain our memory.

In my view, *The Norton Anthology of Latino Literature* was produced as an era was coming to an end. I very much wanted to produce this one—to invest countless hours, to let my mind lose in the annals of history—because I believe that a classic, among other things, is a book around which a nation comes together. Think of *The Iliad* and *The Odyssey*. Think of the Hebrew Bible and of the King James Version of it, of Shakespeare and Milton, the Mahabharata and the *Popol Vuh*. Think even of *Le Chanson de Roland* and *Don Quixote* and *Leaves of Grass* and Borges's essays and stories. For instance, we know what Argentineness is because of the latter, even if they are not exclusively about Argentina.

I am mixing, on purpose, sacred and secular books in my list. I do not believe classics need to be connected with the divine in order to agglutinate a population around them. *The Norton Anthology of Latino Literature* is a compendium of classics. As such, it is a statement of a particular time and place, but hopefully it also transcends these coordinates. I say this with uttermost humility. My role was to map it, to gather the pieces that make it, to build the transitions between one entry and another. In short, to create a semblance of continuity, which is, after all, what traditions are about. The objective was to foster conversation, to generate a sense of place and belonging. And in so doing, to push Latinidad forward.

But aside from the fact that the book as an object is losing importance, Latinos—I say this with a heavy heart—are not passionate readers. It is said that the *Popol Vuh* and similar documents should be credited for the invention of Mesoamérica in the colonial period. It is what scholars believe. But is it true? To what extent was it a read—meaning a contested—artifact around which a community spread? I am interested in this indigenous book because I am in the process of retelling it. Not translating it but rewriting it. I am using the core as a foundation but the words I am employing are mine. My impression is that upon publication, it will be mostly non-Latinos who will be drawn to it.

This generates in me an urgent question: when it is not a book what creates a nation, what is it? My answer: outside forces. To a large extent, Latin America, in its modern incarnation, is the by-product of foreigners who landed it with preconceived ideas. They wanted the region to be like the places they knew or they were coming from: Europe, Asia, Africa, the United States, and so on. That outsider's perspective made Latin America what it is.

Bizarrely, what comes to my mind is a book Jean-Paul Sartre wrote called *Anti-Semite and Jew* (1946). It is terrible, yet I am obsessed with it. Sartre's argument is that Jews exist because of anti-Semites and vice versa. You need an enemy to find your sense of being. If not an enemy, at least what academics today call "the other."

It is terrific to know that *The Norton Anthology of Latino Literature* is broadly read. But is it a tool among many that Latinos might use to explore who they are? Only a minuscule portion, let us be honest. Telenovelas do that far more effectively. As does popular music. And *fútbol*. Is the volume a depository of memory? Yes, but so are all the other items I just mentioned. We just are not a literate civilization. Our sense of self does not rotate around the written word. It is not that illiteracy runs high. It does, for sure. It is just that, as a general rule, we don't articulate thought narrative. You will tell me, and rightly so, that I am a pessimist and that we surely do. What about Neruda? What about *One Hundred Years of Solitude* (1967)? What about the rich literature we have produced, in Latin America as well as in the United States? And I will answer: what about it? Does it really have an impact? If so, it is small, really small.

*Charles Hatfield*: I think what you are calling the impact of these texts—*Canto General* or *One Hundred Years of Solitude*—was probably always a lot less than most of us who teach literature are comfortable admitting, and most of us would probably be even more uncomfortable with the notion that their importance is separate from their "impact," although I happen to think that is the case. But I want to get to what I think is an especially interesting set of points you make as they pertain to *The Norton Anthology of Latino Literature*. On the whole, you are concerned that literature as such is not doing the work you want it to do, and you worry that *The Norton Anthology of Latino Literature* is perhaps not functioning as "a tool among many that Latinos might use to explore who they are."

But in order for us to lament the decline or absence of the literary—in Latin America, in US Latino/a culture, or wherever—do we not have to have some sense that the literary can do things that other cultural forms cannot, or at least a sense that the literary does something *better* or *more effectively* than other cultural forms (such as telenovelas or popular music)? In other words, do we not have to believe that there is something at least special (if not entirely unique) about literary discourse as such?

To be sure, I think that *The Norton Anthology of Latino Literature* does, and will continue to do, a great deal of important work in the world not just by making available Tato Laviera or Rolando Hinojosa to readers but also by putting Laviera and Hinojosa in dialogue with Julia de Burgos and Richard Rodriguez and all the other writers anthologized. But without diminishing the importance of that work, I do think it is important to reflect on what the anthology has to say about Latino literature *as literature*. The anthology, for example, begins and ends with non-literary texts: *crónicas* on the front end and *dichos*, *chistes*, and *reggaetón* on the back end. In between, non-literary texts (e.g., speeches by Cesar Chavez and Luis Muñoz Marín) are presented seamlessly alongside poems and short stories, etc.

So, one might say that even as *The Norton Anthology of Latino Literature* does important work for Latino/a literature and the Latino/a writers it anthologizes, it blows up the category of the literary, or is at least indifferent to the difference between what is literature and what is not. Just to be clear: I am not saying that Muñoz Marín—or *reggaetón*—and literature *no tienen nada que ver*, only that the anthology's indifference to the differences among them could be said to get us further away from seeing literature as the kind of thing whose absence or decline it might make sense to lament. What do you say?

*Ilan Stavans*: I sense a hint of defensiveness in your words, Charles: what can literature do that other cultural forms can't? I could make a long list and so could you. But this kind of question only arises, I am convinced, when the function of literature is threatened. Thus, there is a need to over-emphasize its qualities, to distinguish them from music, TV, film, theater, dance, graffiti, etc. What attracts me to literature, however, and to art in general, are precisely their porous edges.

Let me give you an out-of-context example. Unlike my friends who decried the awarding of the Nobel Prize in Literature to Bob Dylan in 2016—ouch! There are so few ways literature is able to get worldwide recognition, the Nobel Prize principally among them, plus, does Dylan really need another $1,000,000?—as a waste as well as a concession to the pervasiveness of popular culture, I thought it was a magisterial move by the Nobel Committee. To me Dylan is a contemporary troubadour, an inheritor of Homer's mantle. His lyrics are poems, their impact enormous.

I say this because I don't believe literature starts and ends on the page. In fact, the page might be a kind of imprisonment. Just as the first manifestations of Spanish literature are the *jarchas* and the *Mester of Juglaría* and *Clerecía* and the *Cancionero de Baena*, early iterations of oral rhyme done by itinerant songwriters, a few connected with the ecclesiastical structure of the Catholic Church, we must look at literature today without borders, not only in the national sense but by way of platforms.

Slam poetry, improvised *décimas*, online recitations, and so on. I say this in the same way I believe that Banksy's sudden street graffiti is as valuable as Picasso's *Guernica*. A number from Lin-Manuel Miranda's *In the Heights* and Paul Simon and Derek Walcott's *The Capeman* me are as valuable as William Carlos Williams's "This Is Just to Say." I don't believe in the division between highbrow and pop culture. Yet because we are over that artificial delineation, literature has lost its gravitas.

There used to be a time when any new book by Saul Bellow or Gabriel García Márquez would push people to bookstores. You have that type of frenzy with J.K. Rowling among adolescents, which is inspiring. But adults are in a state of retrenchment. And in Latino literature, the dire situation is worse. When Junot Díaz was accused of sexual misconduct and bullying, it was fascinating to see the reaction of both non-Latinos and Latinos.

In my impression, the impact was stronger among the former. In the latter, it was restricted to academics: scholars of different types who cried excess because a brown man was again being portrayed as a sexual predator in the media. Were there any average readers outside the world of academia that were inflamed by Díaz's purported behavior? If so, they were outside my radar. In other words, Díaz is not quite read, I mean spontaneously; he is assigned, which means a teacher (like me) compels students to delve into his fiction.

We are lost when the *only* realm for literature to be active is the classroom. Then authors are tailoring their craft to teachers, not to the lay public, which means their content must satisfy a certain aesthetics and political viewpoints.

To me ethnic literature in particular is at a dangerous point. Don't get me wrong! I am enormously proud of *The Norton Anthology of Latino Literature*. But I also fear that literature is losing ground, that literacy has been largely achieved across economic backgrounds, but the written word has lost enormous ground. Writing is a form of suffering to many people today, followed only by reading. Which is a disgrace because writing is thinking. In order to learn how to think clearly, writing is a good first step. And reading the second.

I want to return to a previous point: Latinos are not really part of a literary culture. Music is the glue. If you want to know what the community thinks, how it lives, what its dreams are, listen to salsa, merengue, bachata, cumbias, tangos, *corridos, rancheras,* mariachis, *regatón, canción de protesta*, and many other melodic manifestations. That is why *The Norton Anthology of Latino Literature* includes numerous pieces of music. And do you know which of the numerous sections of the volume was the hardest to put together? Those related to music. Let me tell you a secret: the last part of the anthology, the one including lyrics, was much larger.

I don't remember exactly but it could have been five times what it ended up being, maybe ten. I had written headnotes for all them. But guess what? Permission prices were either prohibitive or impossible to locate. The music industry, as you know, is notoriously cumbersome when it comes to keeping copyright provenances. The Norton permissions editor got lost in more than one labyrinth, and I along with her.

I don't want to confuse realms. This, obviously, was meant to be an anthology of literary artifacts. Lyrics were an addition to the menu, never the main course. In projects such as the two-volume encyclopedia of *Latin Music* (2015), I explored that dimension fully. Still, in the Norton project my intension was to cross-fertilize because that is what I believe literature does so beautifully. And because the heart of Latinos is there.

*Charles Hatfield:* You said that "if you want to know what the community thinks, how it lives, what its dreams are, listen to salsa, merengue, bachata, cumbias." I agree with you in a sense, but what I would like to know is what we think literature—and Latino literature, in particular—can do once we have accepted that it is not the most reliable documentary source, or once we see it as a bad/incomplete window onto the culture from which it emerges?

*Ilan Stavans:* Do not get me wrong! To me without literature there is no life. But I do not live with the false impression that literature matters considerably. Truth is, it is more marginal by the day. The poetry that has social impact is the one adapted to songs. Now if we are not interested in emphasizing social impact, literature, in its solipsism, is an enchanting way to escape. In fact, the narrative that matters these days—I am thinking of best-sellers—are intrinsically escapists.

*Charles Hatfield:* I think escaping does not have to be solipsistic or an alternative to social impact—Martín Espada's "Imagine the Angels of Bread" (to cite a favorite example) is an escape, in a sense, to an imagined future where "the food stamps / of adolescent mothers / are auctioned like gold doubloons." And Espada's poem is, technically, also indifferent not only to what we might call its "impact" or effects but also to our perception or participation as readers, by which I mean that it does not really invite us to do or feel much of anything and mostly reports a series of transformations that are announced as if they were certain and imminent: "this is the year that the hands / pulling tomatoes from the vine / uproot the deed to the earth that sprouts the vine."

There is, to my mind, a radical politics in all this, in part because the poem is committed to the notion that "the shutdown of extermination camps / began as imagination of a land / without barbed wire or the crematorium," but primarily because the world that the poem imagines will be brought about not by our feeling differently about "adolescent mothers" or "the hands / pulling tomatoes from the vine" but rather by material redistribution ("food stamps" become "gold doubloons," workers get "the deed to the earth" or end up owning the cannery).

I could say more, but the point I am trying to make is both that Espada's poem, as a poem, gives us a vision of a world that is not easily available elsewhere and also, more important, that in its turning into itself as a poem and turning its back on its effects on its readers—refusing its porous edges—gives us a vision of the sorts of transformations that will not bring that world about.

Before we get to this, I want to ask you one question: we have talked a lot about *The Norton Anthology of Latino Literature* in terms of Latinos as both its readers and authors, but of course one of the powerful implications of the anthology seems to be that the works it contains are particularly important *as literature*: that Latino/a literature (however we define it or demarcate it) is both particular and particularly interesting as a literature. Would you agree?

*Ilan Stavans*: Of course: both as literature and as historical document.

*Charles Hatfield:* I am still thinking about your concerns about how widely literature—and by extension Latino/a literature—is read. Could not it be said that the minute we are concerned with how widely literature is read, we are also going to be on the road to wanting to get beyond literature in some way? At no moment in the twentieth century was literature the best way to reach the greatest number of people, and if we say that Dylan's poems are to be celebrated because of the enormity of their impact, are not we just turning literature into a commodity in the most absolute sense? If we are selling widgets, obviously success means people buying them (the more people buy them, the more successful we are). But if we are writing poems, we can imagine that our sense of what a successful poem looks like might happily coexist with an awareness that not many people want it. And what if literature, for precisely this reason, offers us a possibility of something that is not structured by the market?

*Ilan Stavans*: My point is that literature exists today in conjunction (e.g., in competition) with a plethora of artistic manifestations that exercise such power on the imagination, literature is almost an afterthought. This is good if we see it as marginal. It is the ancient paradigm of the tree that falls in a lonely forest. If a great poem is written but no one reads it, is it a poem? And it is great? It is important, in my view, to be fully cognizant of the diminishing relevance of literature.

*Charles Hatfield:* I disagree, and to get back to something you said earlier: I do not think it is in the least bit defensive to talk about what literature can do that other cultural forms can't—rather, I would say it is a prerequisite for making sense of why we have such a thing as literature in the first place.

Without some notion of literature's specificity—some notion of what literature can do that other cultural forms cannot—how do we make sense of how or why, for example, Pedro Pietri wrote "Puerto Rican Obituary" *as a poem*? Pietri's poem is a useful example not just because it is a great poem but also because it is not in the least bit invested in distinctions between high and low, and it is worth noting the equally obvious fact that the poem is intensely political. In an interview, Pietri talked about a lot of the things you have mentioned: for example, *radio-novelas*, popular music, a childhood and secondary education that gave no privilege to literature, the fact that it was not until he got a job working in the library at Columbia that he started reading poetry, etc.

But how can we begin to make sense of "Puerto Rican Obituary" without first having to make sense of the literary form Pietri takes on? Ultimately, could we not say that the real work Pietri's poem is doing can be found in its poem-ness? "Puerto Rican Obituary" gives us a vision of the world in which everything revolves around labor and commodities: "They worked / They worked / They worked / and they died / They died broke / They died owing"; Miguel who "died hating Milagros because Milagros / had a color television set / and he could not afford one yet" and Olga who "died dreaming about real jewelry" and all who live to "keep the morticians employed." The freedom from what the poem is offered by the poem itself as a poem, which is to say, the poem gives us a vision of a new, different set of rules— "where beautiful people sing / and dance and work together."

What if, in other words, the work of the poem takes place in the places where Pietri, in his commitment to writing *a poem as such*, responds to a set of aesthetic demands that resist, and give him freedom from, the demands that govern the subjects in the poem? And is not Pietri demonstrating in some sense some commitment other than communicating to "the lay public" inasmuch as he might have been the first to tell us that the lay public does not give a damn about poetry? Another way of putting this would be to say that whereas "dial soap commercials" must satisfy the demands of consumers, poems must satisfy the aesthetic demands of poetry?

*Ilan Stavans*: The aesthetic demands of poetry require readers to exist. Not only is the existence of those readers at peril today; their sophistication is, too. Anthologies, in mysterious ways, are manuals of reading. They deliver texts not in isolation but in context. They either invent a tradition or they refurbish it. And they are depositories of memory. In return, they expect—patiently, I should add—their own type of reader, one capable of reading critically as well as cumulatively. Reading critically is reading with an eye as well as an "I," doing it intelligently, knowing how to discriminate between useful and useless information. Reading cumulatively is reading a piece against what came before and what comes after; that is, reading longitudinally. In that sense, anthologies are about re-reading. They ask us to return, to reconsider, to make choices. That is because their ideal reader is active, engaged, inquisitive. The best anthology reader is an editor in waiting.

As I tell you all this, I am aware that I am delivering a kind of manifesto. Reading for me is the equivalent of breathing: without it, I die. If I matter, it is because of what I have read has impacted my life. I understand now, in my fifties, how one grows as a reader. I could never be the same reader I was at eighteen or at thirty-three? With age comes patience as well as discernment. Needless to say, all this applies to you as well, my friend. One cannot understand the concept of poem-ness without having read countless poems, otherwise Pietri's "Puerto Rican Obituary" would simply be an arbitrary configuration of words and sentences and thoughts and propositions. That is what a reader's life does: it detects and concludes, imagines and refutes. The exact same type of dedication is needed when one appreciates the value of say Juan Luis Guerra's "*Ojalá que llueva café*" (1989) or when binge-watching a Netflix series. You might do these quickly, without consideration. Or you might approach them with reverence, pondering where they come from, what they mean, and what they say beyond the surface. My feeling is that as the art of reading goes down—because it is an art, after all—the capacity of discernment is moving to other realms. And not slowly, I should add, but rather quickly.

I am not a fatalist, though. Truth is, literature, in its written manifestation, has never been for everyone. It takes labor. In other words, it is elitist. It shuns people out because that *all* citizens should be part of its club, which makes it bizarrely undemocratic. At a time when populism is the order of the day, people hate these concepts—elitist. But that is what literature is at its core: by and for the few. Elites are small pockets of uniqueness that safeguard a certain mode of life that benefits everyone.

# Index

aborigines 26
Abya Yala 53, 394, 406–407
Academia Norteamericana de la Lengua Española (ANLE) 351
*Acción chicano* [sic] 449
acculturation 49–50, 128–129, 436–438, 457
Acoma Pueblo 26
Acosta-Belén, Edna 163
Acosta, Oscar Zeta 143
*Across the Lines: Travel, Language, Translation* 333
activism xiii
Adams, John Quincy 32
Adelitas, Las 137
Adorno, Rolena 513
"Advance at Your Own Risk: Latinas, Families, and Collegiate Softball," 493
*Adventures of Venus, The* 389
Africa 16, 43
Afrika Bambaataa 240
Afro-Americans 31–32
Afro-Latin Project 76
Agua Bendita 113
Aguasaco, Carlos 282, 296, 298
Agustini, Delmira 276
Aja, Alan A. 165
*a.k.a Pablo* 385
*¡Alambrista!* 449, 457
Alamillo, Jose 485, 488, 491, 494, 497
Alarcón, Norma 152
Alba, Jessica 385
Alba, John Cutler 111
Albarran, Alan 474
Alberdi, Juan Bautista 21, 210
Alcarez, Lalo 389–390
Alcoff, Linda 209–211
Aldama, Frederick Luis xiv, xviii–xix, 491
Aldema, Frederick 82
Alejandro, Kevin 386

Alex, Stacey M. xiv
Alfaro, Luis 405
Alfau Baralt, Antonio Abad 332
Alfau, Felipe xviii, 331–333, 335, 338–340
Alfau Galván de Solalinde, Jesusa 332–343
Alfau, Montserrat 338
Alfonso X, King ("El Sabio") 273
Algarín, Miguel xvii, 282, 288–290, 356–357
*Alita: Battle Angel* 385–386
Alker, Gwendolyn 402
Allen, Esther 341
*Allí está el detalle* (That's the point!) 276
*Alma América: Poemas indo-españoles* 18–19
Alonso, Amado 276–277
Alonso, Kiko 491
*ALOUD: Voices from the Nuyorican Poets Café* 299
*Al Que Quiere!* 318–319
Alurista 129, 136, 143
Alvarado, Esteban 30
Alvarez, Barry 490
Álvarez, Julia 168, 282–283, 336, 510
Álvarez Martínez, Stephanie 359
Alvarez, Veronica 489
Amaya, Hector 463, 472
*AmeRícan* 293
*American Catholic, The* 222
American Folklore Society (AFS) 63
*American folktales: from the collections of the Library of Congress* 67
*American Hustle* 386
*American Me* 385
*American Midwest, The: an interpretative encyclopedia* 67
American Society for Theater Research (ASTR) 403–404
*Americas Poetry Festival of New York, The* (TAPFNY) 298
Amparo Ruiz de Burton, Maria 159

Ana (character in *Real Women Have Curves*) 167
Anaya, Rudolfo 104–118, 143, 282
Anderson, Benedict 414
Andrade, Oswaldo de 7–8
*Angelitos* 390
Angelou, Maya 31–32
*Angelus Novus* 6
*Animaquiladora/Why Cybraceros?* 455
Anthony, Marc 385
*Anti-Semite and Jew* 514
*Ant-Man/Ant-Man and the Wasp* 386–388
*Antología de poetas hermafroditas* 298
Antonio Maceo brigade 97–98
*Anxieties of Experience: The Literatures of the Americas from Whitman to Bolaño* 298–299
Anzaldúa, Gloria xviii, xx, 7, 67, 107, 152–153, 161–162, 168, 221, 282–283, 286, 291–293, 311, 316–318, 321–323, 348–349, 399. *See also* borderlands; *Borderlands/La Frontera*
Aparicio, Frances R. 289, 291–292, 383
Aquino, Maria Pilar 227
"Arab Steeds of the Conquerors, The," 18
Aragon, Cecilia 388
"Arauco tiene una pena," 292
Arcos, Jorge Luis 94
Ardila, Alfredo 351
"Are You Still Down?," 237
Argentina 21–22
Arguedas, José María 277
*Ariel* 7, 23
*arquitectos de lo imaginario, Los* 298
Arrested Development 238
Arriola, Elvia 465
Arrizón, Alicia xv–xvi, 401
Arroyo, Jossiana 402
"Artes de Cuba: From the Island to the World," 97–98
arts, Latinx representation in, and arts access 79–81
Ascasubi, Hilario 276
*Asesinato en el laboratorio de idiomas/Murder in the Language Lab* 297–298
Asia 19

Asociación de Academias de la Lengua Española (ASALE) 351
Asociación de Licenciados y Doctores Españoles en Estados Unidos (ALDEEU) 296–297
assimilation 52
Association for Theater in Higher Education (ATHE) 403–404
Asturias, Miguel Angel 277
*Athletes Remembered: Chicano/Latino Professional Football Players, 1929–1970* 485
Augenbraum, Harold 509–510
*Avatar/Avatar Machete* 385
Avent, Glenn 491
Ayers, David 386, 388
Ayim, Emmanuel 495
*Aztec of the City* 389
Aztlán 129–130, 139, 251, 316–317
*Azul* 276

*Baby Driver* 386
Baca, Judy 143
Baena, Juan Alfonso de 273
Baldenegro, Salomán 445
*Ballad of Gregorio Cortez, The* 449
Ballet Folklorico Tepehuani Nelli (True Conqueror in Nahuatl) 77
*Bamba, La* 385, 399, 450–451, 457
Barbara, Saint 247–250
*bárbaros, Los* 298–299
Barela, Casimiro 27
Barnet, Miguel 331, 336
barrio
  Barrio de las Empacadoras (Back of the Yards) 74
  *Barrio Dreams: Puerto Ricans, Latinos, and the Neoliberal City* 181
  "barrioization," 182
  *Barrio-Logos: Space and Place in Urban Chicano Literature and Culture* 182
  music 236–257
Barton, Paul 230
*Bases y puntos de partida para la organización política de la República Argentina* 21
Basquiat, Jean-Michel 385
Bastide, Roger 249

Batalla de Caseros 22
Batallón de Pardos y Morenos 22
Beauvoir, Simone de 165
*Before Columbus Foundation, The* 299
Behar, Ruth xv, 397
Behm-Morawitz, Elibabeth 467
belief and cognition, in thaumaturgic reasoning 44–49
Bello, Andrés 270, 275
Beltrán, Mary 433, 466, 471–472
Benedict the Moor, Saint 249
Benitez, Jose Luis 473
Benjamin, Walter xiii, 3, 6, 15
Ben-Yehuda, Eliezer 268
Berceo, Gonsalo de 273
Berger, Todd 386
Berg, Peter 385
Berlant, Lauren 308, 316
Bernard-Carreño, Regina 289
Betances, Ramón Emeterio 159, 412–428
Betti, Silvia xviii, 351
*Beyond El Barrio* 180
*Bienvenidos* 449
bilingualism xviii, 168, 282–299, 307–324. *See also* literature, bilingual; rhetoric; Spanglish
  *Bilingual Aesthetics: A New Sentimental Education* 307, 334
  *Bilingual Blues* 294–295, 384
  capitalism, colonialization and 316
  defined 283–284
  tribulations of 285–288
Birthright Israel 97–98
Black 107–108
  Jesus 237
  Manifesto 225
  soldiers 22
*Blackboard Jungle* 441
Blackmon, Douglas 36
*Blacktino* 397
Blades, Rubén 240
Blair, Sam 497
Blanco, Richard 95, 97
Bland, Sandra 74
*Bless Me, Ultima* 113
Bloom, Harold 286
"blowouts," 132–133

Blum, Lawrence 203
Boal, Augusto 402
Bocafloja 251
Bolaño, Roberto 299
Bolívar, Simón 20, 210
bondage 33. *See also* slavery
Bonet, Juan Manuel (Juan Miguel) 353–354
Bone Thugs-N-Harmony 237
Bonilla-Silva, Eduardo 206
*Book of Life, The* 388
*Book of Negro Folklore* 114–115
*Border Ball: The History of High School Football in the Rio Grande Valley* 490
borderlands 435–442
*Borderlands/La Frontera: The New Mestiza* xx, 7, 107, 153, 286, 292, 296, 321–322, 348–349, 399, 435–437
*Bordertown* (film) 441–442
Borges, Jorge Luis 276–278, 299, 511
Borges, Julia de 515
*Boricua Pop* 383
Borinqueña, La 159
*Born in East L.A.* 385, 452, 457
Boswell, James 268
Botello, Rufugio 30
Boullosa, Carmen 330, 333
Bourke, John Gregory 116
Boyarin, Daniel and Jonathan 91
Boyd, Bill 496
Bracero Program 65
Brammer de González, Ethriam Cash 331
Brannon Donoghue, Courtney 475
Braschi, Giannina 90, 282, 291–292, 295, 316–318, 354–355
Bratt, Peter 388
Brazil 22
*Bread and Roses* 454
*Breaking Ground: Anthology of Puerto Rican Women Writers in New York 1980–2012/ Abriendo Caminos: Antología de escritoras puertorriqueñas en Nueva York, 1980–2012* 299
*Bridges to Cuba/Puentes a Cuba* 92, 94
*Brief History of the Spanish Language in Five Sentences, A* xvii
*Brief Wonderous Life of Oscar Wao, The* 291–292, 335–336, 510

*Bronze Screen, The* 433
Bros Hernandez, Los 389
Brown Berets 230
Brown, Michael 13
Bruce-Novoa, Juan 105–106
buffalo 28–29
Bunge, Carlos Octavio 17
Burgos, Adrian 485, 487
Burgos, Julia de 296, 512–513
*Burlador de Sevilla y convidado de piedra, El* (The prankster of Seville and his stone guest) 150
Burns, Aaron 397
*Burrito* 389
Busto, Rudy 228
"But Do We Have the Actors for That?," 396
Butler, Judith 148
*Buzzing Hemisphere / Rumor Hemisférico* 341
Byam, Melanie 158
*By Lingual Wholes* 309

Cabeza de Baca Gilbert, Fabiola 160
Cabeza de Vaca, Álvar Nunez 513
*cabildos* 246
Cabrera, Ana 465
Cabrera, Eduardo 402
Cabrera Infante, Guillermo 277, 310–313, 316–317
Cabrera, Lydia 271
Caesar, Julius 38
*Café Onda* 403
*Cahier d'un retour au pays natal/ Notebook of a Return to my Native Land* 104
*Caída libre* 297
Calderón, Héctor 110
Calderon Kellet, Gloria 471
Calhoun, John C. 32–33, 38
*Calle 13*, 388
*Calligraphy of the Witch* 118
*caló* 128, 293
Calvo, Javier 338
Camba, Julio 330–331
Campo, Estanislao del 276
Campos, J. Alberto 79
Canales, Andrea 493
*Canción de la Raza* 449

*Cancionero de Baena (Cancionero del Judino Juan Alfonso de Baena)* 273, 516
Candace, Queen 45
Cannabrava, Euryalo 211
"Cannibalist Manifesto," 7–8
*Cantar del Mío Cid* 273
"Canta y no llores," 388
Cantinflas (Mario Moreno) 276
*Cantinflismo* 276
"Canto a Elewa y Changó," (Chant to Elewa/ Elegua y Shango) 247–248
*Canto General* 277, 515
Cantú, Norma 68
Caotlalopeuh 153
Cao, Vivien 334
*Capeman, The* 516
Cardosa, Patricia 167, 386
Caribbean (Hispanic) 12
Carisma 449
Carlisle, Pennsylvania, Indian School at 49–51
Carlos, Alfredo 190
Carpentier, Alejo xv, 104, 114–115
Carrasco, Brabara 143
Carrasco, David 221
*carreta, La* 396
Carreto, Vicereine Leonor 157
Carrillo, Joe 80
Carter, Angela 511
Casal, Lourdes 97–98
Casas, Bartolomé de Las 251
Casas, Manuel 465
"Case FOR 'Latinx,' The: Why Intersectionality is Not a Choice," 165
Casillas, Dolores Inés 387
Castañeda, Carlos 222
Castañeda, Mari xx
Castedo, Elena 332
*Castellano, español, idioma nacional: Historia espiritual de tres nombres* 277
*casticismo* 269
Castillo, Ana 118, 168, 510
Castillo, Debra xix
Castillo, Juan 490
Castor, Jimmy 240
Castro, Fidel 92
Castro, Raul 95

Castro, Sal 132
Catalan, Julissa 407
*catauro de Cubanismos, Un* 276
Catholicism. *See also* Barbara, Saint;
    Guadalupe, La; Inquisition; Virgin
  culture and 150, 245–250
  European source of 5
  Hispanic philology and 269–273
  Latina/os and 220–223, 226–230
  Spanish 25–26, 48, 271
*Católicos Por La Raza* 226
Cavazzi, Antonio 116
ceiba tree 99
Cejudo, Henry 497
*Celebrating Latino Folklore: An Encyclopedia of Cultural Traditions* 68
*Center Stage* 385
Cepeda, Maria Elena 384
Cervantes, Miguel de 267, 274
Césaire, Aimé 104
*Cesar Chavez* 386
Cetina Gutierréz, Rita 158
Chacón, Eusebio 512–513
"Chango 'ta Beni," (Shango is coming) 246
Chapman, Matthew 402
Chappell, Ben 494
Charles V, King, 42, 49
Charrería culture 71–72
Charruá Indians 23–24
Chase, Charlie 240
Chaurand, Juan Carlos, Andres, and Maria 75
Chavaria, Gabriel 386
Chávez, César 131, 143, 223–224, 515
Chavez, Denise 510
Chavez, Gene 494
Chavez Jr., Tomas 225
Chávez-Silverman, Susana 363, 366, 383
Chernow, Ron 395
Chhoti Maa 251
Chiang, Joe 31
*Chicana* 445, 457
Chicanismo 128, 136–137, 163, 401
Chicano 134–136
  antiwar movement 140–142
  *Chicano Popular Culture* 384
  "Generation," 127–131, 134, 138, 141
  history 129–131
  identity 128–129
  movement xv, 7
  politics 137–140
  *Popular Culture* 383
  Power 129
  renaissance 143
  struggle for educational justice 132–134
  as a term 128–129
Chicano Cinema Colalition 449
*Chicanos and Film: Representation and Resistance* 433
Chi, Enrique and Diego 75–76
China/Chinese 16, 30–31, 43
*Chingado/Chingada* 151, 155, 167
Chocano, José Santos 18–19
*choteo* 243–244
Christianity 27, 37–49, 53, 256
  Coatlicue and 154
  La Malinche and 152
  political engagement and 256
  race/slavery and 12–18
  Santuario Chimayó and 221
  spectacles and 406
  Tonantzín and 153–154
  white 220–225
*Chromos* 332–333, 335, 338–340
*Chronicle of the Narváez Expedition* 9
Chuck D 241–242
*Cien años de soledad* 277
*Ciguapa, The* 389
Cihuácoatl 153–154
*Cihualyaomiquiz* 389
cinema
  *Cinema Between Latin America and Los Angeles: Origins to 1960* 434
  *Cinema of Robert Rodríguez, The* 434
  in the Digital Age 454–457
  history of Latinx 433–458
  imperfect 446
  mainstream televisual 449–454.
    *See also* television
  new Latinx 444–448
  silent 438–440
  social problem films 441–444
  sound 440–441
*Cisco Kid* 399

Cisneros, Sandra xvii, 168, 282, 283, 510
*Cities in Translation: Intersections of Language and Memory* 334
*Citizen Rex* 389
*City Across the River* 441
Civil War 33
*Clansman, The* 45
class
   oppression 15–23. *See also* slavery
   stratification 16–23
*Classic, The* 499
Cleger, Osvaldo 384
*Clerecia, Mester de* 273, 516
Clifford, James 91
Clinton, Hillary 13
Coatlicue 153–154
Cobarruvias, Sebastián de 274
*Cobra* 295
Cocco De Filippis, Daisy 340
*Coco* 458
*Cocoliche* 278
*Code* (of Mesopotamian law) 14
code-switching 289, 293, 295, 313–314, 334, 338–339, 360–365, 387
*Codex Espangliensis* 384
*Código de barras* 297–298
Cody, William 28–29
cognitive-functional models 361f16.1
Cohen, Santiago 390
Coleman, Benjamin 51
*Colombiana* 385
Colonial Atlantic, and Anaya 112–117
colonialization/conquest 12–13, 16–54
*Colonial Latin American Literature: A Very Short Introduction* 513
Colón, Miriam 394, 396
Colorado 27
Columbus, Christopher 47
comics 387–390
Common 238
Communication Act of 1934 474
*conceptismo* 274
*consciente* 250
*Conduct of Life, The* 404
*Conflicto y armonía de las razas* 21–22
Congo, imperial xv
Congress for the New Urbanism (CNU) 178

*Consciência Black* 244
Consejo, Anonimo 254
Constraints, Equivalence, and Free Morpheme 362
*Contemporary Latino/a Theater* 402
*Conversando con el ángel* 298
conversion, cultural 49–54
convict leasing 35–36
*Convocación de palabras* 324
*corazón de México, El* 78
Cordero, Celestina and Rafael 159
Corlett, Angelo 211
Corominas, Joan 269, 277
"corrido de Kiansis, El," 73
corridos xiv, 73–77
Cortés, Hernán 151
*Cosmic Race, The* 7
Costa, Marithelma 296
Costa Rica (1891 railway contract) 19–20
Costas, Orlando 220
Cotera, Maria Eugenia 63
counterculturation 436, 447
Covarrubias, Sebastián de 269
Cox, Annabel 294
Coyolxauhqui 322
*Crash* 386
"creative city," 178–179
Creative Class (CC) 178–179, 185–186
Creek War 23
Crenshaw, Kimberly 161
Creolization 63
Cresci, Karen 341
*crise de la conscience européenne, La: 1680–1715* 46
Crisostomo, Paula 132
*Cristela* 386
*Critic's Journey, A* 268
*Crónica de una muerte anunciada/ Chronicle of a Death Foretold* 114, 116–117
*Crónica Inmigrante* 74–75
*Crónica, La* 160
Cronin, Michael 333
*Cruces Divided: A Historical Football Rivalry* 490
*Cruel Optimism* 316
Crusade for Justice 445
Cruz, Angie 335

Cruz Blanca, La 160
Cruz, Juana de la 199
Cruz, Migdalia 402, 405
Cruz, Nilo 394, 402, 405
Cruz, Sor Juana Inéz de (Juana Inéz de Asbaje y Ramírez de Santillana) 155–158, 210, 274–275
Cuadros, Paul 494
*Cuando canta la ley* 440
*Cuarta Imagen* 247
"Cuba and Its Diaspora," 91
Cuba/Cubans xv, 91–99
*Cuban Star: How One Negro-League Owner Changed the Face of Baseball* 487
CubaOne Foundation 97–98
*Cucaracha, La* 389
Cuevas Ingram, Joanna 469
Cuevas, Teresa 62–63
*culteranismo* 274
Cultural Frame Switching 365
Culture Clash 402, 405
*Culture, Migration, and Sport: A Bi-National Investigation of Southern Mexican Migrant Communities in Oaxaca, Mexico and Los Angeles, California* 492
cumbia 73–77
*Cumbia de los muertos* (dance of the dead) 255–256
Cush 43
Cypress Hill 251

dance, folkloric, in Ohio 77–79
Danielson, Marivel T. 401
Dario, Rubén 276
Dávila, Arlene 181, 383, 470, 497
Davis, Mike 181
Davis, Roger P. 65
Dawson, Rosario 385
*débiles, Los* 332
decoloniality 414
*De cómo las muchachas García perdieron el acento* 336
deculturation 436
De La Hoya, Oscar 496
de las Casas, Bartolomé 199
Delgadillo, Theresa 65, 106, 221
Delgado, Fernando 495, 496

Del Valle, José 351
*Democrates Secundus* 42, 49
Dence, Carmen 79
de Oñate, Juan 26
Derrida, Jacques 308
*desarraigados, Los* 441
"Desert Music, The," 319–321
*Desperate Housewives* 386
*Después de la oscuridad* 298
developmental topographical disorientaion 3
*Devious Maids* 386
*Dew on the Thorn* 26
*Dialectic of Sex, The* 149
*Diálogos de la lengua* 274
*Dialogos: Placemaking in Latino Communities and Latino Placemaking* 182
*diario, El* 331
"Diaro de um detento," 245
*Diary of a Reluctant Dreamer* 390
diaspora 91, 93–94, 99. *See also* Cuba/Cubans
*Diaspora: A Journal of Transnational Studies* 91
Diaz, David 181–182, 185
Díaz Guerra, Alirio 331, 335
Díaz, Junot xviii, 283, 286, 291–292, 333, 335, 341, 388, 510
Díaz, Natalie 336
Díaz, Rodrigo 273
dictionaries
   *Diccionario Clave* 277
   *Diccionario crítico etimológico de la lengua castellana* 277
   *Diccionario de anglicismos del español estadounidense (DAEE)* 356
   *Diccionario de Autoridades* 269, 271
   *Diccionario de la Lengua Española* 270
   *Diccionario del uso del español (Diccionario Moliner)* 277
   *Diccionario Real Academia Española (DLE)* 351
   *Dictionary Days* 268–269
   *Dictionary of the English Language, A* 268
Didi-Huberman, Georges 311
*Diente de plomo* 298
Díes, Juan 74, 80
Diggs, Daveed 408
*Dirty Girls Social Club* 384–385

dislocations 63
displacement, indirect 188–189
*Distancia y destierros* 298
*Divided Borders* 291
*Divine Duty of Servants, The: A Book of Worship* 297
Dixon, Thomas, Jr. 45–46, 50
Dominguez, Richard 389
*Donjuanismo* 150
*Don Juan Tenorio: Drama religioso-fantástico en dos partes* (Don Juan Tenorio: Religious-fantasy drama in two parts) 150
*Don Quixote of La Mancha* 267, 274
Dorson, Richard 66–67
*dos caras del patroncito, Las* 396
*Dos Repúblicas, Las* 27
*Down These Mean Streets* 342
*Dreaming in Cuban* 331
Drehs, Wayne 490
Driever, Steven 65
DuBois, W. E. B. 249, 395
Duigan, John 385
Dumitrescu, Domnita 351
Duncan, Quince 19
Duncan, Robert 298
Dyerson, Mark D. 496
Dylan, Bob 515–516

East, Ed 76, 79
*East Los High* 386
Ebert, Roger 451
*Eccentric Neighborhoods* (*Vecindarios excéntricos*) 287
Echegaray, Luis Miguel 495
*Economical Linguistic System with Maximum Performance, An* 357
Eco, Umberto 511
"Education of Indian Children," 51
*Electric Comedy, The* 297
Eliot, T. S. 267
*Elisa y Los Mutantes* 389–390
Elizondo, Virgilio 220, 227
Elsmore, Maggie 230
Emancipation Proclamation 13
"embodiment" thesis 364
Encinosa, Enrique 495

*EnClave* 293
*End of Watch* 386
"En el nombre de todas las madres que han perdido sus hijos en la guerra," 292
Enghels, Renata xviii
England 41
"En la hora de las semillas," 109
Enriquez, Maria 402
*Enriquillo* 332
EPG 242
*Epoca* (newsletter) 65
Escaja, Tina xvii, 296, 297–298
Escalante, Alicia 143
Escobar, José 27
Escuela de Señoritas o Liceo Fanning, La 158
Espada, Martin 282, 517
Espaillat, Rhina P. 15
*Espaldas mojadas* 441–442
*España* 274
*espanglish* 351
Española, La/Santo Domingo 48–49
Espinal, Isabel 335, 340
Espinosa, Gastón 220, 228
Espinoza, Mauricio 384
Esquival, Rolando 389
Estefan, Gloria 385
*Estéreo, Bomba* 389
Esteves, Sandra Maria xvii, 282, 288–290, 295
Estévez, Rolando 95
Estrade, Paul 416
*Ethiopia* 41
*Ethnic Eye, The: Latino Media Arts* 434
ethnicity 203–212
*ethnurbanisms* 189
Etiemble, René 44
*European Mind, The: The Critical Years—1680-1715* 46
Eustis, Oskar 408
*Eva Luna* 387
Executive Order 9066 31
exile 91

*Facundo o civilización y barbarie* 21
Fairclough, Marta 351
fairs/festivals
    Chamizal Siglo de Oro Festival 398

Festival Internacional de Teatro
    Hispano 394
Festival Latino 394
fairs/festivals/fiestas 65–66
"Fiesta del Sol" and "Fiesta
    Mexicana," 72–73
Faison, Donald 387
Fajardo, Kat 390
*fantasma en el libro, El: La vida en un mundo
    de traducciones* 338–339
farmworkers struggle. *See* Chávez, César
*Fefu and her Friends* 399
feminism. *See also* gender
    Chicana 142–143
    *Feminism, Nation and Myth: La
        Malinche* 155
    third world Latina 160–163
Fernandes, Sujatha 243
Fernández de Castro, Maria Teresa 339
Fernandez de Oviedo, Gonzalo 47
Fernandez, Evelina 403
Fernandez, Kelly 389
Fernández, Laura 388
Fernandez, Lisa 493, 497
Fernandez, Manny 498
Ferré, Luis Alberto 286–287
Ferrera, America 167, 384, 386, 470
Ferré, Rosario 283, 286–287, 290–291, 296
Ferris, Emil 389
"Festival Latino," 73
Fiasco, Lupe 238
Fidler, David P. 487
Fierro, Josefina 137
Fifteenth Amendment to the US
    Constitution 33
Figlerowicz, Matylda xvii–xviii
Figueroa Deck, Allen 227
*filosofía (hispana* or *hispánica,
    hispanoamericana, latinoamericana* or
    *iberoamericana)* 201
Finitzo, Maria 495
Firestone, Shulamith 149
First National Chicano Liberation Youth
    Conference 64
First Seminole War 23
First Spanish Methodist Church (FSMC) 226
*First Time Out* 385

"First Vote, The," 33
*Five Books of Moses, The* 272
Flores, Juan 289, 291, 383
Florez, Tom 490–491
Florida, Richard L. 179
"Flying African"/"Flying Man," 117
Fojas, Camilla 384
Foley, Douglas E. 489
folklore
    as cultural capital 68–69
    defining 63–64
    future directions of Midwest Latinx
        studies 81–83
    wearing 71–72
Fonseca, Roberto 246
Fontenelle, Bernard de 46
*For All of Us, One Today* 97
*Forgetting the Alamo or Blood Memory* 118
Forman, James 225
Fornés, Maria Irene 394, 397, 399–400, 402,
    404–405
Foulis, Elena 69, 73
Four, Los 143
*Four Quartets* 267
France 41
Franco, Alejandro 69
Franco, Roberto 69, 79
Franklin, Benjamin xix–xx, 422–423
Franks, Joel S. 488
freedom of wombs (*libertad de vientre*)
    law 21–22
Fregoso, Rosa Linda 433, 450
"Friends of the Indian," 50
*From Barrio to Burbs* 187
*From Bomba to Hip-Hop* 383
*From Dusk Till Dawn* 386
Frondizi, Risieri 203–205
*Fronteras: A History of the Latin American
    Church in the USA Since 1513* 224, 227
Fructuoso Rivera y Toscana, José 23, 53
*FSG Book of Twentieth-Century Latin
    American Poetry, The* 511
"Fuego, El," 403
Fuentes, Carlos 210, 349
Fugees, The 238
*fundamento* 250
Funky Aztecs 251

*Fury* 386
Fusco, Coco 405
"futuro cercano de EEUU es mestizo y se escribe en Spanglish, El" [The near future of the US is mestizo and will be written in Spanglish] 350

Gacio-Harrolle, Michelle 497
Galasso, Regina xviii
Galeano, Eduardo 23–24, 43
Galindo, Alejandro 441
Ga-li, Raymond Two Crows Wallen 70
*Gallo, El* 136
Galván, Manuel de Jesús 332
Galvez, Francisco 71
Gamboa, Jr., Henry 143, 445, 447
"Game Delay: Latinos Not Yet Scoring with College Athletics," 498
*Game of Their Own: Voices of Contemporary Women in Baseball, A* 489
Gamio, Manuel 221, 227
García Canclini, Néstor 354
Garcia, Cristina xvii, 168, 282, 331, 497, 513
García, Enrique 384
Garcia Espinoza, Julio 446
Garcia, Ignacio 492–493
Garcia, Ivonne M. xix–xx
Garcia, Jorge 200–201, 203–205
García, Mario T. xv, 220, 228, 230
García Márquez, Gabriel xv, 114–116, 277, 299
García, Peter J. 384
Garcia-Romero, Anne 402
Garza, Oscar 389
Gaspar de Alba, Alicia 118, 383
*Gato Negro, El* 389
*Gaucho Martín Fierro, The* 6
gender
    Catholicism and 150–155
    defined 149
    in Latina/Latino culture 148–168
    power relations 149–151
*Gender Trouble* 148
genocide, cultural 51
Gente de Zona 242
Gentes, Eva 338
gentrification 177–179, 183–189
*George Lopez Show, The* 387

Gerbner, George 469
*Geto Boys, The* 238
"Ghetto Gospel," 237
Gilroy, Paul 242
Ginzburg, Ralph 34
*Girlfight* 385, 454, 457
*Glee* 386
Glissant, Édouard xv, 104, 106, 112, 118
*Glosas Emilianenses/Silenses* 272–273
Glück, Louise 298
"Goddess of the Américas in the Decolonial Imaginary: Beyond the Virtuous Virgen/Pagan Puta Dichotomy," 155
Gomes, Jazaline 70–71
Gomes, Miriam 22
Gómez Burns, Manuel 299
Gomez, Marga 405
Gómez Peña, Guillermo 384, 405
Gómez-Quiñones, Juan 219
Gomez, Scott 497
*Gone in 60 Seconds* 386
Góngora, Luis de 274, 319
Gonzáles, Rodolfo "Corky," 136, 445
Gonzáles, Ulises 282, 298
Gonzalez-Barrera, Roberto 352
González, Celina 246
Gonzalez, Christopher 491
Gonzalez, Crystal 389
González de Fanning, Teresa 158
González Echevarría, Roberto 487
González, Eliza 386
González, Erualdo R. xvi
González, Jovita 25–26
Gonzalez, Justo 227
González-Martin, Rachel V. 68
González, Michelle 227
González, Patricia 402
Gonzalez, Rodolfo Corky 53, 138–139
Gonzalez, Sarai 389
Gonzalez, Sergio 230
Goodie Mob 238
Goodson, Christopher 402
Gordan, Maya 468
Gozalez, Justo 220
Gracia, Jorge J. E. 206–207, 209–211
grammars
    *Gramática* 278

*Gramática castellana* 276
*Gramática de la lengua castellana destinada al uso de los americanos, Los* 271, 275
Granados, Roger 225
"Grandes Éxitos en Español, Los," 251
Grandmaster Caz 240
Grandmaster Flash 240
Grant, Ulysses S. 34
Greeley, Andrew 222
Green, Rashaad Ernesto 388
*Greenwood Encyclopedia of American Regional Cultures, The: The Midwest* 67
Grey, Mark A. 489
*Grey's Anatomy* 386, 470
Grito de Lares 159
*Grito del Norte, El* 136
Gross, Larry 469
Grossman, Edith 331, 336
*Growing Up Latino* 509–510
Grupo Atlantico 79
Grupo Cultural Azteca 77
Guadalupe, La 151–153, 249
*Guardians of the Galaxy* 385
Gubern, Jordi 336
*Guernica* 516
Guerra, Gilbert 165
Guerra, Jesús "Chuy," 492
Guerra, Juan Luis 519
Guhl, Mercedes 336
Guillén, Nicolás 243–244
*Gun Hill Road* 388
Gurvich, José xxi
Gutiérrez, Efraín 444
Gutierrez, Félix 468
Gutierrez, Gustavo 220, 223, 256
Gutierrez, Jorge 388
Gutiérrez, José Ángel 139–140, 226, 445, 490
Guzman, Romeo 384

Habell-Pallán, Michelle 383–384
*hacedor, El* 277
Haggis, Paul 386
"Hail Mary," 237
*Hamilton* xix, 394–395, 406, 407–408

Hammurabi 14
*Handbook to Luck, A* 513
Hanisch, Carol 162
Han Kung 223
*Happy Feet* 388
Harris, Amanda Nolacea 155
Harris, James 23
Harris, Roy 341
Hartfield, Charles xx–xxi
Hartman, C. 184
Harvey, David 185
Hatfield, Charles 509–519
"Havana, Haiti: Two Cultures, One Community," 92
Hayek, Salma 167, 384
Hayes, Rutherford B. 34
Hazard, Paul 46
"Hecho in Mexico," 251
Heiskanen, Benita 495
Hemispheric Institute 403
Hendrickson, Brett 221
Henri Betances, María del Carmen 413, 416
*Herencia, Fiestas, Horizontes* 65–66
Hermanos de Causa 242–243, 250
Hernández Cruz, Victor xviii, 309
Hernández, David Manuel 467
Hernández, Elaina 78–79
Hernández, Ester 143
Hernandez, Gilbert 389
Hernandez, Javier 389
Hernandez, Jay 388
Hernández, José 6, 276, 278
Hernández Sacristán, Carlos 359
Herodotus of Halicarnassus 41
*Heroes, Lovers, and Others: The Story of Latinos in Hollywood* 434
Herranz Brooks, Jacqueline 282, 296
Herra-Sobek, Maria 27, 63
Herrera, Brian Eugenio 396, 401, 402, 405
Herrera, Juan Felipe 74
Herrera, Marina 227
Herrera, Patricia 402
Herrera-Sobek, Maria 68
Hidalgo, Bartolomé 276
"Hielo, El," 389
*High Noon* 441
Hightower, Scott 298

"hijos del maíz, Los" (children of
    maize) 252–253
Hijuelos, Óscar 282, 286, 332, 510
Hill, Lauryn 238
Hinojosa, Felipe xvi–xvii
Hinojosa, Rolando 282, 515
hip-hop 236–257, 395
"H is for Box," 297
*Hispania* 272–273
"Hispanic," xi, 11
    versus "Latino," 207–212, 510
*Hispanic Catholic in the United States,
    The* 222–223
*Hispanic Condition: Reflections on Culture
    and Identity in America, The* 340
Hispanidad 4–10
*Hispanoactuante/Angloactuante* 355
*hispanounidenses* 348, 350, 352
histories
    *Histoire des voyages de Escarmentado* 417
    *Historia de la Nueva México* 26
    *Historia de la Revolución Mexicana* 439
    *Histories* 41
    *History of Hispanic Theatre in the USA:
        Origins to 1940, A* 402
    *History of the Spanish Language in Five
        Sentences, A* 271–278
Hitler, Adolf 46
Hoffer, Richard 496
Holland 41
*Holocausto Urbano* (Urban Holocaust) 244
"hombre astral, El," xxi
"Hombre, El," 319
*hombre malo, El* 440
"Hombres necios" ("Foolish Men") 158
*Homenaje a Juan Bautista Alberdi:
    Sesquicentenario de las Bases* 21
Homer 43–44, 272
Homero Villa, Raúl 181–182
Hosmer, Eric 498
*House of Buggin* 385
*House on Mango Street, The* 168
*House on the Lagoon, The (La casa de la
    laguna)* 287
*How the García Girls Lost Their Accent* 336
*How to Get Away with Murder* 470

*How Yiddish Changed America and How
    America Changed Yiddish* 268
*Hoy!* 383–391
Hudes, Quiara Alegria 394–395, 402, 405
Huerta, Dolores 131, 137, 143, 163
Huerta, Joel 490
Huerta, Jorge 401
Hughes, Langston 244
Hurtado, Guillermo 203
Hytner, Nicholas 385

"I Ain't Mad at Cha," 237
*I Am Another You* 75
Ibarra, Armando 190
Iberian Peninsula 12
Iber, Jorge xx, 488–490, 493, 497
iconicity 365
Idar, Jovita and Nicasio 160
identity 164–165, 286, 289, 324
idioma 285–286
*Idler, The* 268
*If the World Were Mine* 299
*I Know Why the Caged Bird Sings* 31–32
*Iliad, The* 43–44, 272
*I Like It Like That* 385
"I Luv U Papi," 389
"Imagine the Angels of Bread," 517
immigration/migration/emigration 8–9,
    19–20, 462. *See also* colonialization/
    conquest
    African, to American Southwest 113
    bilingualism and 316
    Black 45
    Cuban 92–95
    defined 355
    as deterioration of self 8
    as *el retorno* 317
    Hispanic 496
    Immigration Act of 1917 63
    Latin American 229
    Mexican 64–65, 130, 222, 317
    negative perceptions of 465, 469, 474–475
    Pentacostals and 229
    Puerto Rican 222, 288, 396
    shaping cultural forms 63
    social justice and 63

Spanish 277–278, 406
undocumented 475
*Immigration to the United States* 221–222
Immortal Technique 251
*imperio de los sueños, El* 296
"Importance of Building Positive Relationships Between Hispanic Audiences and Major League Soccer Franchises: A Case Study of Public Relations Challenges Facing Houston 1836, The," 495
"*incansable juego, El / The Untiring Game: Dominican Women Writing and Translating Ourselves*," 339–340
Incas 52
income disparities 176–177
*In Darkest Africa* 104
Indelicato, Mark 386
*indios/indigenismo* 129. *See also* colonialization/conquest
  *indianista* 332
  Indian Removal Act 23–24
"individual multilingualism," 365
Infante, Cabrera xviii
Ingenieros, José 22
*ining of Our Souls, The: Excursions into Selected Painting of Edward Hopper* 297
*In My Darkest Hour* 389
Innis-Jimenez, Michael 491–492
Inquisition 336, 421
Institute for Diversity and Ethics in Sport, The (TIDES) 499
insularity 206
International Arts Relations (INTAR) 400
*In the Dark* 389
*In the Game* 495
*In the Heights* 395, 516
*In the White Man's Image* 51
Iowa Latinx Summit 68
Iphegenia, Calliope 386
Irazábal, Clara 189
Irizarry, Ylce 106
Isaac, Oscar 388
Isasí-Diaz, Ada María 220, 227
isolation 73–77
*Itching Parrot, The* 512

*It Concerns the Madness* 299
*It's a Disaster* 386
Iturregui, Félix Córdova 416
"I Wonder if Heaven Got a Ghetto," 237

Jackson, Andrew 23–24, 32, 40
*Jaguar, The* 389
Jakobson, Roman 308
Jaksić, Iván xiii–xiv, 4, 6–7
*Jamás* 449
James the Elder, Saint 249
Jamieson, Katherine M. 493
*Jane the Virgin* 386, 470–471, 475
Japan/Japanese 31–32
Jaramillo, Cleofas M. 160
Jaramillo, Pedrito 68
*jarchas* 516
*Jarchas, Las* 273
*Jardín del Edén, La* 452
Jefferson, Thomas 33
Jelani Cobb, William 238–239
Jenkins, Devin L. 349
Jensen, Ric 495
Jewell, Todd R. 495
Jim Crow Laws (Black Code) 35–36
Jiménez, José "Cha Cha" 163
Johnson, Kevin 469
Johnson, Lyndon 138
Johnson, Samuel 268
Johnson, Sarah E. 414
Jones Act 288
Juan Marcos Presbyterian Church 226
"Juban America," 397
*Julio's Day* 389
Juncos, Manuel Fernández 159
Jurado, Katy 441
justice (social) 234–257
*Justicia* 449

Kadlecik, Sebastian 389
Kahlo, Frida 143, 167
Kammen, Michael 219
Kanellos, Nicolás 66, 159, 330–331, 402
*Kansas Folklore* 66
Kanye 238
Kaplan, Amy 104

Kapp, Joe 491
Kearney, Dennis 30
Kennedy, John F. 138
Kereval, Yann 475
*Keywords For Latina/o Studies* 179
Kid Chocolate 495
Kid Frost 251
*Killer Crónicas* 363, 366
Kinto Sol 251–254
Kipling, Rudyard 40–41
Klee, Paul 6
Kool Herc 240
Kozer, José 95
Krogstad, Jens M. 352
KRS-One 238
Ku Klux Klan (KKK) 33–34
Kumar, Maria Teresa 166
Kurlansky, Mark 487
Kusama, Karyn 385
Kutinski, Vera 114

*Labyrinth of Solitude and Other Writings, The* 8, 150
Lacan, Jacques 309
*La Carreta Made a U-Turn* 293
Lago, Eduardo 333
"Lagrimas Negras," ("Black Tears") 244
Lake Mohonk Conference 50–51
Lakoff, George 360
*Land of the Millrats* 66
Landry, Charles 178–179
Langacker, Ronald 360
language 271–278, 284, 406–407
Lara, Irene 155
Larrea, Pedro 282
Las Casas, Fray Bartolomé de 512–513
Latina/Latinas
  *Latina in the Land of Hollywood, A* 383
  *Latina Lives in Milwaukee* 65
  *Latina/o Midwest Reader* 68
  *Latina/o Stars in U.S. Eyes* 433
  *Latinas* 399
  *Latinas in the United States: A Historical Encyclopedia* 340
Latin America 12, 17, 156–160
*Latin American Theatre Review* 403
Latinidad xiii–xiv, 3, 5–10, 510, 514

*Latin Image in American Films, The* 433
*Latin Looks: Images of Latinas and Latinos in U.S. Media* 434
*Latin Music* 517
*Latin Numbers* 402
Latino/Latinos
  versus "Hispanic," 208, 509–510
  invisibility 469–470
  *Latina/os and the Media* 383–384
  *Latino/a Popular Culture* 383–384
  *Latino/a Theatre in the Time of Neoliberalism* 402
  *Latino City: Urban Planning, Politics, and the Grassroots* 182
  *Latino Gap, The* 472–473
  *Latino Images in Film: Stereotypes, Subversion and Resistance* 434
  *Latino Metropolis* 182
  "Latino Night," 469
  *Latino Pentecostal Identity* 229
  *Latinos and American Popular Culture* 384
  *Latinos and Narrative Media: Participation and Portrayal* 434
  *Latinos Beyond Reel* 462, 464
  *Latinos, Inc.* 383
  *Latinos in the End Zone: Conversations on the Brown Color Line in the NFL* 491
  *Latinos in U.S. Sports: A History of Isolation, Cultural Identity, and Acceptance* 485
  *Latino Urbanism: The Politics of Planning, Policy, and Redevelopment* 182
  *Latino U.S.A: A Cartoon History* 390
  *Latin@ Stories Across Ohio* 69
  media gap 473
  movement 127–144
  population, in the US xi, xix
  "public sphere parado," 463
  studies xi–xiii, 106, 256–257
  the term 200
*latinopia* 403
Latinx 164–165
  defined 391fn1
  history of, in the midwest 64–66
  *Latinx and Chicanx Traditional Culture in the Midwest* 68
  "Latinx Media Now!," 434

"Latinx Performance," 402
Latinx Theatre Commons (LTC) 403
Space for Enrichment & Research
    (LASER) 82
stereotypes 438–440, 457
Latorre, Guisela 384
Lauterbach, Ann 298
Laviera, Tato xvii, 282, 286, 288, 291–294,
    296, 513, 515
*Lawless, The* 441
Lawrence, Jeffrey 298–299
Laws of Burgos/New Laws of Burgos 49
League of United Latin American Citizens
    (LULAC) 66–67, 70
Lea, Leopoldo 203–204
Ledesma, Alberto 390
Lefebvre, Henri 109–110
Leguizamo, John 405
*lengua* 285–286, 294–295
    *Lengua Fresca: Latinos Writing on the
        Edge* 509–510
    *lenguaje* 285–286, 295
    *lenguas del viajero, Las* 298
León, Luis D. 221
*Letterman Show, The* 499
Levin, Jack 469
Levins Morales, Aurora 162–163
Lévi-Strauss, Claude 7
Liberation Theology 223
Liberti, Rita 497
*Liberty: A Daughter of the U.S.A.* 439–440
*Libro de Alexandre* 273
Lida de Malkiel, María Rosa 271
Lida, Raimundo 271
*Life and Adventures of Joaquín Murieta,
    The* 30
*Life of General Villa, The* 439
*Light in the Dark/Luz en lo oscuro* 317, 322
Lima, Alex 296
Limón, José E. 68, 73
Lincoln, Abraham 33
"Linguistic Terrorism," 286
Lipski, John M. 351, 361–362
literature 288–291, 509–519.
    See also bilingualism
*Living in Spanglish* 291
Lizardi, José Joaquín Fernández de 512

*Llámame Brooklyn* 333
Llorente, Renzo 205, 211
Llorona, la 151–152
Lockpez, Inverna 390
*Locos* 332, 335
Lomas, Clara 160
Londoño, J. 185–186
*Lone Star* 452–454, 457
Longoria, Eva 384, 470
Longoria, Mario 485, 489–490
*Looking Out, Looking In: Anthology of
    Latino Poetry* 299
Lopez, Al 487
López García Molins, Ángel 348, 351, 353,
    356, 359
Lopez, Jennifer (J-Lo) 167, 384–385, 389
López, Josefina 167, 405
López Luaces, Marta xvii, 282, 298
López, Manuel Adrián 282
López Morales, Humberto 351
López, Obed 225
López Tijerina, Reies 445
Lorca, Federico García 256, 330–331
Lorde, Audre 64
Lorenzo, Emilio 366
*Lost* 387
Love, Heather 323
"Lower East Side Poem, A," 290
*Lowriders* 386
Lozano Clariond, Jeannette 298
*Lucas Guevara* 331, 335
Lugo, Juan 222
Lugones, Lepoldo 276, 278
Luna, Diego 386
"Luna Llena," 389
*Lunatic Fringe* 389
Lunfardo 278
Lupe 447
Lynch, Benito 276
lynching 34–35
Lynch, Loretta 15

MacDevitt, Jack 469
*Machete* 458
*Machete Kills* 385
machismo 149–151
Machito 239–240, 246

Maciel, David 445
McOndo movement 512
Maduro, Otto 220
*Magical Urbanism: Latinos Reinvent the U.S. Big City* 181
Magnón, Leonor Villegas de 159–160
Magnon, Adolpho 160
Mahootian, Shahrzad 362
*Mainstream Ethics (Ética corriente)* 293
"majority of English-speaking Hispanics in the U.S. are bilingual, A," 352–353
Making Movies 75
*Maldito amor (Sweet Diamond Dust)* 287
Malinche, la 151, 155–156, 251
*Mambo Kings Play Songs of Love, The: A Novel* 332, 510
"Manifiesto Neoyorkino," 333
Manirique, Jaime 331
*Man Who Could Fly, A, and Other Stories* by Rudolfo Anaya xv, 113
*Manual Destructivista/Destructivist Manual* 297–298
maps (cognitive) 3
Maraniss, David 485
Marcano Guevara, Arturo J. 487
Marcos-Marín, Francisco 358
Marcuse, Peter 184–185, 188–189
*Mariachi, El* 385
*María Full of Grace* 455
marianismo 149–156
*Maricones eminentes (Arenas, Lorca, Puig and Me)* 331
Maril, Lee 497
Marín, Cheech 385
Marin, Christine 491–492
Marín, Francisco Gonzalo "Pachín," 340
Marín, Luis Muñoz 290
Markedness model 363
Markusen, Bruce 485
Marqués, René 396
Marrero, Teresa 402
Marsans, Armando 487
Martell, Helvetia 330
Martha and the Vandellas 447
*Martian, The* 386
Martí, José 96, 199, 276, 296, 330, 340, 415–416, 418, 423–424, 512–513

Martinez, Brenda 496
Martínez-Cruz, Paloma 384
Martinez, Daniel 76–77, 79
Martínez, Elizabeth "Betita," 143
Martínez, Jesús 30
Martinez, Richard 229–230
Martin, Ricky 385, 511
Marzán, Julio 318–319, 321
*Mashbone & Grifty* 389
Mastro, Dana 467
Matamoros, Miguel 244
Matovina, Timothy 228–229
Matrix Language 363–364
"Matters of the Sea/Cosas del Mar," 97
Matthews, Austin 497
Matyorga, Liz 389
Mayer, Vicki 467
May, Louis du 46
Mayor Marsán, M. 351
Mbembe, Achille 107–108
McConnell, Ellen 462
McCormick Theological Seminary 225–226
McFarland, Pancho 384
McMillan, Billy 499
McWilliams, Carey 130–131, 135, 222
Mead, Rebecca 408
*Medal for Benny, A* 441
Medina, Cruz 384
Medina, Lara 228–230
Medina, Pablo 283
*Meditaciones del Quijote* xiii, 3
Mediterranean 44
Meillassoux, Quentin 291
*Mein Kampf* 46
Memmi, Albert 324
*Memorias de un vacío* 298
Menchaca, Martha 113
Mendes, Eva 384
Mendieta, Raquel (Kaki) and Ana 94, 206
Mendoza, Alezander 496
Mendoza, Jessica 488–489
Menem, Carlos 22
*Men in Black* 2, 385
Mercado, Nancy 299
Meruane, Lina 282
*Mester of Juglaría* 516
mestizaje 5, 7, 63, 165, 292, 349

Mestizo xi, 510
*Metamorphoses* 44
metaphors 364
Metcalf, John 497
metonymy 308–309
Mexakinz 251
"Mexican American and the Church, The," 223–224
Mexican American Cultural Center 226
Mexican American Generation 137
Mexican-American War 129–130
Mexican American Youth Organization (MAYO) 132, 226
*Mexican Immigrant, The: His Life Story* 221–222
*Miami Sound Machine* 385
Mieder, Wolfgang 23, 50
*Mi Familia* 385
Migrant Ministry 223–224
*milagro de la calle mayor, El* 440
Miranda, Lin Manuel xix, 394–395, 405, 407–408, 516
"Mission Bell," 15
*Mission, La* 388
mission system. *See* Southwest (USA)
Mistral, Gabriela 296
Mitchell, Elmer 486
Mitre, Eduardo 333
*Mi Vida Loca* 385
*Mixturao and Other Poems* 293
Moctezuma, Matos 322
*Modern Family* 386–387
modernismo 22
*Modernista* 276, 288
modernization/modernity 20–21, 52–53
Mohler, Courtney Elkin 404
Mohr, Nicholasa 282, 335
Molina, David 495
Molina-Guzmán, Isabel 464
Molina, Laura 389
Molinar, Maria 269, 277
Molina, Tirso de 150
Molloy, Sylvia 333
Moner, Isabela 386
Monje, Jorge 394, 397
*Monstrous Love Stories* 389
Montaigne, Michel de 44, 199

Montes-Alcalá, Cecilia 365–366
Montesinos, Antón de 48–49, 53
Montez, Mario 447
Montez, Noe 402, 404
Montijo, Rhode 389
Montilla, Patricia M. 384
Moore, Natalie 441
Mora, Delfino 74
Moraga, Cherríe 161–162, 168, 282, 399, 405
Morales, Adam 222
Morales, Ed 289, 291, 351
Morales, Miles 387
Morales, Slyvia 444
morality 9
Moreiras, Alberto 436
Morel, Domingo 177, 184
Morena Villa, José 330–331
Moreno Corona, Amalia and Jorge 77–78
Moreno Corona, Lilly 77–78
Moreno Fernández, Francisco 351, 356
Moreno, Luisa 137
Moreno, Rita 441
Morgan, Michael 469
Mort, Cynthia 386
Morton, Carlos 401, 406
Moschkovich, Judit 64
Mos Def 238
Mother Emmanuel AME Church 15
Movimiento Estudiantil Chicanx de Aztlán/Chicanx Student Movement of Aztlán (MECHA) 66, 133–134
*Mr. Spic Goes to Washington* 389
*Muerto, El* 389
mujerista 227
*Multilingual Anthology [Antología Multilingüe]* 298
Mundo Zurdo, El 164
"Muñoz Dream," 290
Muñoz, José Estéban 404
Muñoz Marín, Luis 288, 515
Muñoz Molina, Antonio 333–334
Muñoz, Rosalio 141
"Muralla," 247
Musa I, 45
music 73–77
Mussolini, Benito 46
Myers-Scotton, Carol 363

*My Family* 451
*My Father was a Toltec and Selected Poems* 118
*My Favorite Thing is Monsters* 389
*My Life on the Frontier: 1864–1884* 27–28
*My Night with / Mi noche con Federico García Lorca* 331

Najo, Leo 487
Narváez, Pánfilo de 25
Nas 237–238
National
    Association of Latino Independent Producers (NALIP) 472
    Chicano Moratorium Committee 141
    Chicano Youth Liberation Conference 138
    Farm Worker Association 223–224
    Folk Festival 73
    Hispanic Media Coalition (NHMC) 472
    Latino Media Coalition 449
nation-building 23–32
"nativos" (New Mexican Hispanos) 27
Nava, Alex xvii
Nava, Gregory 385
Navarro, Rafael 389
Nebrija, Antonio de 273–274, 278
Neciccio, William 384
Negrete, Jesus "Chuy," 74
"Negrita PAN, La," 72
Negrón-Muntaner, Frances 287, 383, 472–473
negrophobia 20, 32–36
Ñengo el Quetzal 251
Neruda, Pablo 277, 515
Newall, Neil 28
"New Latino South," 462–463
*New Latino Studies Reader, The: A Twenty-First Century Perspective* 179
New Mexico 26–27
*Newsletter on Hispanic/Latino Issues in Philosophy* 200
New Urbanism (NU) 178, 181, 185
Nicol, Eduardo 201
Niggli, Josefina 404
nihilism 207–208
*Nina* 386
Noel, Urayoán xviii, 341–342
"Noon-Night," 110

Noriega, Chon 384, 433
Noriega, Jimmy 398, 401, 402, 404
*Norte, El* 385, 450
North Carolina 34
*North From Mexico* 130
*Norton Anthology of Latino Literature, The* 509–517
NOSOTROS 449
"Notes on Chicano Theatre," 401
*Notes on the State of Virginia* 33
"Notes on Writing in Spanish in New York," 330
*Noticiero* 474
"Not Neither," 289
*Novedades, Las* 332
*Novela, Novela* 476
Novello, Antonia 166
Nubiola, Jaime 201
Nuccetelli, Susana xvi, 209
*Nuevo Día, El* 286
Núñez, Abersio 296
Nuñez, Breena 390
Nunez, Oscar 386
"Nuyorican Literature," 288
*Nuyorican Poetry* 357

Obama, Barack 92, 96–97, 99, 144
Obejas, Achy 336
Obsesión 242
Ochoa, Ellen 166
"Odio," 110–130
*Odyssey, The* 272, 297
*Office, The* 386
*ofrenda, La* 452
Ohio
    Arts Council (OAC) 80–81
    Latino Artist Directory 80–81
    Latino Arts Alliance (OLAA) 80
Oiticia, Hélio 447
"Ojalá que llueva café," 519
Ojeda Reyes, Félix 416
*Old Spain in Our Southwest* 160
*Old Tales from Spain* 332
Olivares, Julián 108
Oliva, Tony 487
Olivencia, Tommy 246
Olmos, Edward James 386

Omeyocan Dance Company  69
*On An(archy) and Schizoanalyis*  297
"100 years of Latino Theatre,"  403
"101 Plays by The New Americans, or on Latinidad,"  403
*One Day at a Time*  471
*One Hundred Years of Lynching*  34
*One Hundred Years of Solitude*  271, 274, 515
"One Today,"  97
Onís, Federico de  332
"Only God Can Judge Me,"  237
"On Savages,"  53–54
*On Self-Translation*  268
*On the Move: A History of the Hispanic Church in the United States*  227–228
"Operation Bootstrap,"  288
Orbea, Gilbert  165
Orchard, William  401, 404
Orellana, Marjorie Faulstich  77, 79
Orishas, the  242, 247–248
Orosco, José Antonio  205
Orquesta Alto Maíz (OAM)  76
Orr, Marion  177, 184
Ortega, Gaspar "Indio,"  495
Ortega y Gasset, José  xiii, 3–4, 6, 8
Ortegón, Samuel  222
Ortiz Cofer, Judith  xvii, 285, 286
Ortiz, David  487
Ortiz, Fernando  254, 271, 276, 436
Otero, Loida Martell  227
Otero, Miguel Antonio  27–29
Otero-Warren, Adelina "Nina,"  160
Otheguy, Ricardo  351
otherness  116
Ottoman Empire  13
"Our America,"  415, 418, 424
*Our Sunday Visitor*  222–223
*Outgrowing Plastic Dolls*  389
Ovale, Priscilla  384
"Oval Portrait, the,"  412–413
Ovid  44
*Oxford Book of Jewish Stories, The*  511
Ozomatli  251, 255–256

*Pablo's Inferno*  389
Pachucos  8
Padilla, Eduardo  439
Padilla, Félix  438–439
Padilla, Genero  27
Pagan, Alicia  70–71
"Paisajes del idioma: Spanish in New York: A Moving Landscape,"  333–334
Palmeiro, Rafael  488
Pancho Villa  136
papel picado  71–72
Parada, Daniel  390
*Paradise*  332
Paraguay  22
*Paranoid*  385
Pardue, Derek  244
Paredes, Américo  68, 73, 108, 150–151, 449, 513
Paredez, Deborah  384
Paret, Benny "Kid,"  495
Parra, Violeta  292
Pau-Llosa, Ricardo  282
Paz, Coya  401, 404
Paz, Octavio  8, 150, 199, 277, 332
*péché vraiment capital, Le*  44
*Pedro Páramo*  6
Pemon Indians  54
Peña, Fernando de  389
Peña, Michael  386, 388
Penix-Tadsen, Phillip  384
Pentecostalism  229
*People of Paper*  384–385
Perec, Georges  340
Pereda, Carlos  203–204
Pereira, Gustavo  53–54
Perezagua, Marina  282
Pérez, Emma  118
Pérez Firmat, Gustavo  239, 282, 284, 291–292, 294–295, 307–308
Pérez, Laura  384
Pérez, Loida Maritza  282
Pérez, Rolando  xvii, 296–297
Pérez, Vanessa  334
"Perfection of Perfections,"  110
"Performing Mestizaje,"  388
*periferia*  244
"Perils of Polyglossia, The,"  341
*Periplus of the Erythraean Sea*  43
Peru  52
Pescador, Juan Javier  494

*pharmakos*, levels of 114
philology (Latino) 265–278
  defined 265
philosophy 199–213. *See also* ethnicity; nihilism; reductionism
Picado, Clodomiro 20
Picasso, Pablo 516
Pickett, William P. 45, 50
Pierce, Charles Sanders 294
Pietri, Pedro xvii, 282, 288, 290, 342, 518–519
pigmentocracy 16
Pigna, Felipe 22
Pilsen Neighbors Community Council (PNCC) 72
Piña Rosales, Gerardo 282
Piñero, Miguel xvii, 282, 290, 405, 447
Pitbill 388
"Plan de Santa Barbara, El," 133, 136
"Plan Espiritual de Aztlán, El," 64, 136, 139
Plascencia, Salvador 384–385
Plaschke, Bill 497
*Playing America's Game: Baseball, Latinos, and the Color Line* 487
*Please, Don't Bury Me Alive!* 445–446, 457
Plunkett, Jim 490–491
Poblete, Juan 106
*Pocho in Greater Mexico* 384
Pocho-One 384
Poe, Edgar Allen xix–xx, 412–414
*Poemas del metro de Nueva York* 298
*Poetas y Narradores en Nueva York* 297
*Poet in New York and Other Poems, The* 331
*Poetry for the New Millennium* 298
"Pollito Chicken," 313–316
Polo, Marco 38
Ponce de León, Juan 25
Poplack, Shana 362
population
  Hispanic, in Ohio 81–82
  Latino/a in the US 12, 175–177, 383, 463
*Portable Island, The: Cubans at Home in the World* 95
Portillo, Lourdes 444
Portillo Trampley, Estella 143
Posada, Jorge 488
Pratt, Henry Richard 49–53
Prensa, La 332

*prensa, La* 330–331
*Presencia* 477
Prida, Dolores 405
*Pride of Havana: A History of Cuban Baseball, The* 487
Prieto, Jorge 490–491
Prieto, José Manuel 333
*Primero Sueño* 275
*Problem of Hispanic Philosophy, The (El problema de la filosofía hispánica)* 201
*Professor and the Madman, The* 270
"Progreso Literario de Nuevo México," 27
progress 109
*Promotion and Distribution of U.S. Latino Films, The* 434
"Prop 185," 251–252
*Prophet of Race, The* 7
*Prophets Denied Honor: An Anthology on the Hispano Church in the United States* 228
Public Enemy 239
Puente, Tito 239–240
"Puerto Rican Obituary," 341–342, 518–519

quebradas 244
*Quelle émotion! Quelle émotion?* 311
Quesada, Sarah xv
Quevedo, Francisco de 274
Quijano, Aníbal 109, 283, 414
Quince 389
Quinceañera 454–455, 458
Quine, Willard van Orman 211
Quinones, Sam 494
Quintanales, Mirtha 162
Quinto Imperio 74

Rabassa, Gregory 339
race/racism 12–54, 72, 244. *See also* Christianity
  "cosmic" race 23
  Indians as a "vanishing" race 29
  race as the offspring of racism 13, 36
  racism as a dogma 42–43
  racism as knowledge 36–44
  slavery and 283
  thaumaturgic racism 47

*Raíces de sangre* 449
Rakim 239
*Rambler, The* 268
Ramírez Berg, Charles 384
Ramirez, Daniel 67
Ramírez de Arellano, Lorena 286
Ramírez-Esparza, Nairán 365
Ramirez, Manuel Bernardo 491
Ramirez Rios, Bernardo 492
Ramos-Garcia, Luis A. 401–402
Ramos, Grace (Altagracia) 69–70
Ramos, Jorge 474
Ramos, Silvano 67
Rampersad, Arnold 244
rap 241, 250–256, 408
*raza cósmica, La* 23
*Raza, La* 136
Raza Unida Party, La (RUP) 133, 138–140, 445
*Readings @ Tompkins* 298
Real Academia Española de la Lengua (RAE) 270, 275, 350–351
*Realidades* 449
*Real Women Have Curves* 167, 386, 454, 457–458
*Rebelde, la (The Rebel)* 160
*rebelión pocomía y otros relatos, La* 19
Rechy, John 282
*Reclaiming Poch@ Pop* 384
*Reconquista, La* 273
Reconstruction 34
Recovering the U.S. Hispanic Literary Heritage Project 159
Red Shirts 33
reductionism 206
Reed, Payton 386
Regalado, Samuel O. 485, 488
*reino de este mundo, El/ The Kingdom of this World* 114–115
"Relation," xv, 105–106, 118
religious studies 219–231
  contexts and directions for 230–231
  history and 228–230
  theology and 227–228
"Respuesta a Sor Filotea" ("Reply to Sister Filotea") 158
*Resurrecting Hebrew* 268
*retorno, el* 317–318

Reyes, Alfonso 271
Reyes, Guillermo 405
Reyes, Judy 387
Reyes, Marilyn 62–63
rhetoric 307–324
Richie, Eugene 331
Ridge, John Rollin 30
Ring, Jennifer 489
Rios, Quintiliano "Kin-T," 74–75
Risco, Eliezar 225
*Rita Cetina, La Siempreviva y el Instituto Literario de Niñas: Una cuna del feminismo mexicano 1846–1908* 158
Rivadeneyra, Rocío 468
Rivas, Tlaloc 403
Rivera, Alex 388–389
Rivera, Diego 143, 238–239
Rivera, José 405
Rivera, Mariano 487
Rivera, Naya 386
Rivera-Ramago, Emma 414
Rivera, Raquel 240
Rivera, Ron 490
Rivera, Tomás 104–118, 143, 282
Rizk, Beatriz 402
Road, Christa R 390
Rocha, Gregorio 438–439, 440
*Rocketo* 389
Rodó, José Enrique 7, 22–23
Rodriguez, América 464
Rodríguez de Tío, Lola 159
Rodriguez, Fernando 389
Rodriguez, Graciela 389
Rodriguez, Gregory S. 495, 496
Rodriguez, Michelle 385
Rodriguez, Paul 385
Rodríguez-Peralta, Phyllis 18
Rodriguez, Richard T. 384–385, 513, 515
Rodriguez, Robert 385, 386
Rodríguez-Soltero, Jesús 444
Rodriguez, Tito 239–240
Rodriguez, Vittoria 471–472
Roffé, Mercedes 282, 298
Rogriguez, Amy 495
Roig, Arturo 203–204
Rojas, Vivana 473
*rollos perdidos de Pancho Villa, Los* 438–439

Rolón, Rosalba 394
Romaine, Suzanne 283–284
Roman, Ediberto 467
Romero, Elaine 402, 405
Romero, Mary 383–384
Romero, Tom I. 495
Romo, Rafael E. 489
Rondinone, Troy 495
Rondón, César Miguel 240
Roof, Dylann 15
Roosevelt, Franklin Delano 31, 138
Rosario, Willie 246
Rosenblat, Ángel 271
Ros, Jorge 350
Rossini, Jon D. 396, 401, 402
Rothenberg, Jerome 298
*Routledge Companion to Latino/a Pop Culture, The* 384
Royal Chicano Air Force 143
Roybal, Edward 138
Ruck, Bob 487
Ruffin, Paul 498
Ruiz de Burton, María Amparo 25–26
Ruiz, Vicki L. 332, 340
Rulfo, Juan 6
*Rundown, The* 385
Russell, David O. 386

Salas Hernández, Adalbar 296
Salazar Bondy, Augusto 203
Salazar Jiménez, Claudia 282
Salazar, Rubén 142, 468
Saldaña, Carlos 389
Saldana, Zoe 385, 388
Saldívar, José David 110
Saldívar, Ramón 112–113
salsa 240
Salsipuedes 53
*Salt of the Earth* 441–443, 449, 457
Sánchez, Carlos Alberto 206
Sánchez, George Emilio 403
Sánchez, George I. 222
Sánchez Korrol, Virginia 332, 340
Sánchez Scott, Milcha 397, 399, 405
Sánchez Walsh, Arlene M. 228–229
Sanctuary Movement 230
Sandoval, Moises 224, 227

Sandoval-Sánchez, Alberto 402
Sanguinetti, Julio Maria 53
Sankoff, David 362
San Lázaro (Babalu-Ayé) 96
San Martín, José de 21
Santa Ana, Otto 464, 466
Santana 385
Santana, José 286
Santiago, Esmeralda 168, 283
Santiago, Wilfred 389, 390
Santillan, Richard 488
Santiváñez, Roger 298
Santuario Chimayó 221
Saracho, Tanya 473
Sarduy, Severo 295
Sarmiento, Domingo Faustino 21, 22
Sartre, Jean-Paul 514
satire (trans- and de-colonial) 412–428
*Savage Detectives, The* 299
*Scar Tissue* 295
Schaefer, Richard 496
Scharrón-del Río, Maria R. 165
Schiller, Dan 463
Schlatter, Josiah 490
Schloss, Joseph 240–241
Schroeder Rodríguez, Paul A. xx
Schutte, Ofelia 202–204
*Scott, Ridley* 386
*Scrubs* 387
*Searchers, The* 107
"Searching at Leal Middle School," 107, 112
Secada, Jon 385
*Second Sex* 165
Second Vatican Council 223
*Seguín* 449–450, 457
Selber, Greg 490, 492
Selena 167, 385
*Selena* 385, 451, 457
*Señorita Extraviada* 454
"señor muy viejo con alas enormes, Un"/ "A Very Old Man with Enormous Wings," 114
Sepinosa, Frank 389
Sepúlveda, Juan Ginés de 39, 42, 45–46, 49
Sergeant, John 51–53
Serseción, Serenity 390
sexuality 148–168

*Shadow of a Man* 399
Shango 246–250
Share, Don 298
"Shed So Many Tears," 237
Sherman, William Tecumseh 28, 50
Shklovsky, Victor 324
*Shocken Book of Modern Sephardic Literature, The* 268
*Short Eyes* 447
Siegel, Susanna 206
*Siempreviva, La* 158
*siglo de las luces, El/ Explosion in a Cathedral* 104
Silva-Corvalán, Carmen 358
Silva Gruez, Kristen 412
Simon, Paul 516
Simon, Sherry 334
Simon, Yara 495
*Singer's Typewriter and Mine* 268
*Sin Nombre* 455, 458
Sinophobia 31
Siqueiros 143
slavery. *See also* negrophobia
   historic 13–15
   as "our original sin," 13–14
   *Slavery by Another Name* 36
*Sleep Dealer* 455–456, 458
"Sleeping Giant," 137
Smith, Jack 447
Smith, Neil 184, 186
*Sobrevivendo no Inferno* (Surviving in Hell) 244–245
social theory 17
Sociedad de Socorros Mutuos Nación Lucumí de Santa Barbara 249
*So Far From God* 118
Solalind, Antonio G. 332
*Soldadera* 404
*Soledad* 335
Solis, Javier 447
Solis, Octavio 405
Solomon, Maynard 15
Soltero, José Rodríguez 447
Sommer, Doris xvii–xviii, 296, 307, 334
*Sonambulo* 389
Sones de México Ensemble 74

Sonnenfeld, Barry 385
Sosa, Ernesto 202–205
Sosa, Jason 495
Sotomayor, Sonia 166
Soto, Pauline 78
Southwest (USA) 12, 25
"Soy Yo," 389
Spain/Spanish 41–42, 48
Spanglish 9, 10, 267–268. *See also* bilingualism
   after Treaty of Guadalupe Hidalgo 276
   characteristics of language/ Spanglish 360–361
   defined 267, 291, 351–352, 359
   defining 348–350
   economics of 361–364
   history of 350–352
   integration and 364–366
   issues, perspectives, insights 347–367
   linguistics and 357–360
   as a Rubik's-Cube test 5
   *Spanglish in the Eye of a Linguistic Storm* 357
   *Spanglish: The Making of a New American Language* 267
   today 352–355
   tomorrow 355–357
   uniqueness of 360–361
*Spania* 272
*Spanish American Roots of William Carlos Williams, The* 318
"Spanish Mission Band," 223–224
"Spectacle: Balancing Education, Theory, and Praxis," 404
sports 485–499
   baseball 487–489
   basketball 491–493
   boxing 495–496
   football 489–491
   hockey 496–497
   soccer/*futbal* 494–495
   softball 493–494
   tennis 496–497
*Squatter and the Don, The* 25, 159
Stagira 38
Stanley, Henry M. xv, 104–112
*State Fair* 72

*State of Latino Theater in the USA, The* 401–402
Stavans, Ilan xiii–xiv, xvii, xx–xxi, 211–212, 282, 338, 340–341, 351, 355, 359, 384, 389, 390, 412, 509–519
*Stealing Lives: The Globalization of Baseball and the Tragic Story of Alexis Quiroz* 487
Stein, Karin 76
Sterba, James P. 203
Stevens-Arroyo, Anthony M. 222–223, 227–228
Stone, Oliver 386
*Story of Roberto Clemente, The* 390
storytelling 69–71
*Street and Smith's Sports Business Journal* 496
Stroman, Marcus 486, 498
Suárez Díaz, Ada 414
Suárez, Lucía 95
Subervi-Vélez, Federico 462
Sublette, Ned 240
*Suicide Squad* 388
*Súper, El* 447
Svich, Caridad 397, 405
Sweet, James 117
*Symbol of Heart* 490, 499

Tafolla, Carmen 155
*Tales of the Closet* 389
Tammelleo, Steve 211
Taney, Roger B. 35
Tarsila (de Aguiar) do Amaral 7–8
*Tartamudo* 389
Tate, Julee 476
Tatum, Charles 383, 384
Taylor, Diana 403
Teixador, Felipe 338
*Tejano Religion and Ethnicity* 229
Telemundo 474
telenovelas 475–478
television 462–478. *See also* cinema, mainstream televisual
  representing Latinos on 466–471
  situating the making of 464–466
  Spanish-language 473–475
  streaming 471–473
  telenovelizing 475–477
Telles, Raymond 138

Tellez, Michelle 230
*Telling to Live: Latina Feminist Testimonios* 162
Templete, El 99
Tenayuca, Emma 137
Tenépal, Malintzín 151
"Tengo," 243, 250
"Teoría del Espanglish," 351
Terman, Lewis 486
*Tesoro de la lengua castellana o española* 269, 274
Teteoinnan 152
theater 394–408
  Coatlicue Theater Company xix, 394–395, 406–407
  "Microteatro," 394, 397
  National Memorial Theater 398
  Pregones Theater 394
  Teatro Campesino 140, 394, 396–397, 398–399, 402, 405
  Teatro del Desengaño del Pueblo (People's Enlightenment Theater) 66
  Teatro Nacional de Aztlán/National Theatre of Aztlán (TENAZ) 394
  Teatro Rodante Puertorriqueño [Puerto Rican traveling theater] 394, 396
  Teatrotaller 394
Third Force Act (a.k.a. Ku Klux Act) 34
*This Bridge Called My Back: Writing by Radical Women of Color* 64, 80, 161–162
"This Is Just to Say," 516
"This Solitude," 110
Thomas, Piri 282, 342
*Three Burials of Melquíades Estrada, The* 458
*Through The Eyes of Rebel Women: The Young Lords, 1969–1976* 163
Tibón, Gutierre 271
*Tierra* 110–111
*Tigre, El* 388
Tijerina, Reies López 140
Tió Montes de Oca, Salvador 351, 358
Tlazoltéotl 152–154
"To Live in the Borderlands Means You," 435
Tonantzín 153–154
*Tongue Ties: Logo-Eroticism in Anglo-Hispanic Literature* 284–285, 307–308

topography 3–5, 10
Toro-Morn, Maura 466
Torres García, Joaquin 332
Torres, María de los Angeles 94
Torres, Rodolfo D. 181–182, 190, 351
Torres-Saillant, Silvio xiv, 340
Torrez, John 493–494
Torrez, Mike 488, 493
Torrico, Cesar 489
tortillera 164
*Touchdown: An American Obsession* 489
*Touch of Evil* 441
tourism 8
*Toward a Chican@ Hip Hop* 384
"Traddutora, Traditora: A Paradigmatic Figure of Chicana Feminism," 152
*traductores del viento, Los* 298
transcoloniality 414
transculturation 436–437. *See also* acculturation
*Transformers: The Last Knight* 386
Transit Oriented Development (TOD) 178, 185
*Translated Woman* 397
translation 332–334
*Travels* 38
*Travels of Escaldado, The* xix–xx
Treaty of Guadalupe Hidalgo xii, 25, 210, 275–276, 350, 385, 445
*Tres tristes tigres* 277, 311–313, 317
Trevajo, Malu 389
Treviño, Jesús Salvador 444
Trevino, Lee 497
Treviño, Roberto 228–230
*Tristes tropiques* 7
Tropicalism/Tropicalismo 5, 7–8
*Tropicalizations* 383
"Tropicamp," 447
Tropicana, Carmelita (Alina Troyano) 405
*True Blood* 386
*True Story, A: A Cuban in New York* 336
Trump, Donald 97–99, 352
Tupac 237–238
Tupac Amaru I/II 407–408
Tupac Amaru Shakur 407–408
Turgenev, Ivan 285
"Turning the Times Tables," 294

*2011 Latino Condition, The: A Critical Reader* 179

*Über den Begriff der Geschichte* xiii, 3
*Ugly Betty* 386, 475
Unamuno, Miguel de 199
Underiner, Tamara 402, 406
Underwood, Edna W. 18
United Farm Workers (UFW) union 131
United Mexican American Students (UMAS) 132
*United States of Banana* 296
United We Dream 398
Urban Displacement Project 190
urbanism/urban planning 175–191
defined 180–181
Latino 181–182
Ureña, Pedro Henríquez 271, 511
Urgent Matters: Bodies at Work, Bodies at Risk," 404
Uribe, Guillermo 187–188
Uruguay 23–24, 53
US-Mexican border 5, 9–10, 316, 320, 465

Valdés, Chucho 246
Valdés, Juan de 274, 355
Valdez, Alisa 384–385
Valdez, Luis 66–67, 140, 385, 398–399, 401, 405, 444, 450
Valdez, Mercedes 246
Valdivia, Angharad N. 383–384, 464
Valens, Richie (Ricardo Valenzuela) 399, 450–451
Valenzuela, José Luis 403
Vallejo, Agius Jody 187
Valle, Victor M. 181–182, 190
Van Bolderen, Trish 338
Van Dalen, Raquel Abend 296
Van Van, Los 246
Varderi, Alejandro 282
Vargas, Daisy 230
Vargas Llosa, Marcos 52–53, 206
Vargas, Rodrigo 389
Vasconcelos, José 7, 23
Vasquez, Beatriz 71–72, 79–80
Vega, Ana Lydia xviii, 287–288, 310–311, 313–316, 324

Vega, Lope de 274
Vega-Merino, Alexandra 296
Velázquez, Eugenia Galván 332
Velez, Jr., Ivan 389
Vélez, Lupe (the Mexican Spitfire) 447
*Velvet Barrios* 383
Venezuela/Vanezuelans 19, 53–54
*venganza de Pancho Villa, La* 438–440, 457
Vergara, Sofía 387
*Versos sencillos* 96
*viajes de Escaldado, Los* [*The Travels of Escaldado*] 414, 417–422
Vicko 390
*Vida* 473
Vidal, Juan 498
*vida real, La* 331, 336
Vidorreta Torres, Almudena 282
*viejo y el man, El* 298
"*virgen de Borinquen, La* (*The Virgin of Borinquen*) 412–416, 424–428
Villagrá, Gaspar Pérez de 26–27
villancicos 77
Villanueva Collado, Alfredo 296
Villanueva, Tino xviii, 324
Villegas de Magnón, Leonor 159–160
violence (racist) 16–23
Viramontes, Helena María 168, 282
Virgin
    of Borinquen xix–xx, 425–428
    de Guadalupe 223, 245
    of El Cobre 249
    of Mercy 249
    of Regla 249
Virginia Constitutional Convention 33
*Viva Baseball: Latinos and Their Special Hunger* 485
"voces del olvido, Las," 109
Volpi, Jorge 511–512
Voltaire 417
*Voto Latino* 166
*vuelta de Martín Fierro, La* 276

"Wake Me Up," 389
Walcott, Derek 516
*Walkout* 386
Warao people 54
Ward, Monique 468

Warhol, Andy 447
*War of the Planet of the Apes* 386
Warren, Kenneth 511–512
Waud, Alfred Rudolph 33
"Way Out, A," 51
Weil, Robert 389
Wendel, Tim 485
West-Durán, Alan 243, 250
*West Side Story* 441
"What Did the Chinese Not Invent?," 43
*What Is La Hispanidad?* xiii, 4, 6–7
"What is 'Minor' in Latino Literature," 297
*What Was African American Literature?* 511–512
*When Mexicans Could Play Ball: Basketball, Race, and Identity in San Antonio, 1928–1945* 492
"White Man's Burden, The," 40–41
White Man's League 33
*Who Would Have Thought It?* 159
Williams, Robert Gooding 209
Williams, Robin 388
Williams, William Carlos xviii, 311, 318–323, 511, 516
Willis, Jennifer 469
Wilson, Thomas 142
Winchester, Simon 270
"Witches," 115–116
*With His Pistol in His Hand: A Border Ballad and Its Hero* 108, 449, 513
Wittgenstein, Ludwig 310
wokitokiteki 341–342
Woll, Allen 433, 438
"Woman Who Outshone the Sun, The: The Legend of Lucía Zenteno," 70
"Woman Who Wanted Bridges, The," 94–95
women 148–168. *See also* feminism
Wood, Michael 489
*World Trade Center* 386
writing 330–343
Wu Tang 238

Xicanisma 163

Ybarra, Patricia 402, 407–408
Yehya, Naief 333

*Y no se lo tragó la tierra/ And Earth Did Not Devour Him* 107
*Yo soy chicano* 445, 457
*Yo soy Joaquín* 53, 136, 140, 445, 457
Yosso's Cultural Wealth Model 69
*You Gotta Have Your Tips on Fire* 309–310
Young Lords 163, 224–226
Youth Summit (Iowa) 68–69
*Yo-Yo Boing!* 292, 295–296
*Y soñábamos con pájaros volando: Antología* 298
Yudice, George 289

Zapata, Emiliano 136
Zapata, Miguel Ángel xvii, 282
"Zapatista," 251
Zapatista revolution 7
Zaphaniah 43
Zentella, Ana Celia 351, 352–353, 356–357, 362
Ziyad, Tariq ibn 272
*Zona de carga y descarga* ("Loading and Unloading Zone") 287
*Zoot Suit* 385, 399, 450, 457
Zorrilla, José 150
*zorro de arriba y el zorro de abajo, El* 277
*Zotz: Serpent and Shield* 390